D1732872

AQUILA, SYMMACHUS AND THEODOTION
IN ARMENIA

SOCIETY OF BIBLICAL LITERATURE
SEPTUAGINT AND COGNATE STUDIES SERIES

Series Editor
Bernard A. Taylor

Editorial Advisory Committee

N. Fernández Marcos, Madrid
I. Soisalon - Soininen, Helsinki
E. Tov, Jerusalem

Number 42

AQUILA, SYMMACHUS AND THEODOTION
IN ARMENIA

by
Claude E. Cox

AQUILA, SYMMACHUS AND THEODOTION
IN ARMENIA

by

Claude E. Cox

Scholars Press
Atlanta, Georgia

AQUILA, SYMMACHUS AND THEODOTION IN ARMENIA

by
Claude E. Cox

© 1996
Society of Biblical Literature

Library of Congress Cataloging-in-Publication Data
Cox, Claude E.
    Aquila, Symmachus, and Theodotion in Armenia / by Claude E. Cox.
      p.   cm. — (Septuagint and cognate sutdies series ; no. 42)
    Includes bibliographical references and index.
    ISBN 0-7885-0262-X (alk. paper)
    1. Bible. O.T. Armenian—Versions. 2. Bible. O.T.—Marginal
readings. 3. Bible. O.T. Greek—Versions—Aquila. 4. Bible.
O.T. Greek—Versions—Symmachus. 5. Bible. O.T. Greek—Versions—
Theodotion. 6. Armenia—Church history. I. Title. II. Series.
BS796.C86   1996
221.4'9—dc20   96-7697
                                         CIP

Printed in the United States of America
on acid-free paper

for Elaine
Michael, Jason and Laura

Contents

Contents

Preface

This book had its inception some twenty years ago—though I was not aware of it at the time—when I began work on an edition of the Armenian translation of Deuteronomy, published in the series University of Pennsylvania Armenian Texts and Studies 2 (Scholars 1981). I examined manuscripts in Jerusalem which, I observed, preserve marginal notations attributed to Aquila, Symmachus and Theodotion. There was no occasion then to deal with these notations and, indeed, a volume dealing with the preservation of hexaplaric signs in Armenian manuscripts has intervened between that early research and the volume which appears here. *Hexaplaric Signs Preserved in the Armenian Version* was published in 1986, also by Scholars, in the series Septuagint and Cognate Studies.

Christoph Burchard reviewed *Hexaplaric Signs* for *Theologische Literaturzeitung* (113 [1988] cols. 100–101). In that regard he wrote me to ask whether I had collected the notations of Aquila, Symmachus and Theodotion from Armenian manuscripts, something which he had thought one time of undertaking. I was able to respond that I had collected some materials but had not analyzed them. Given the incentive of his inquiry, I set about analyzing what materials I had and gathering more. I am indebted to the following libraries for copies of manuscripts: the British Library, London; the Armenian Patriarchate, Jerusalem; the Mechitarist library at Venice; the Matenadaran, Yerevan; the Library of Congress, Washington, D.C. Since the largest numbers of manuscripts of the Bible belong to the libraries in Yerevan, Jerusalem and Venice, it is to these three that I am especially indebted. I am also grateful to Bo Johnson of Lund, from whom I was able to borrow microfilm copies of Jerusalem manuscripts 1928 1934.

In Jerusalem I would like to recognize particularly the helpfulness of Archbishop Shahé Ajamian who has helped me on a variety of occasions since we first met at the Patriarchate in 1975. That helpfulness has continued since his establishment of the Mount of Olives Armenian Bible Center. I make mention also of the help of the learned and now very elderly Archbishop Norayr Bogharian, Keeper of Manuscripts at the Armenian Patriarchate.

In 1990 the Association Internationale des Études Arméniennes convened a workshop at Heidelberg on Armenia and the Bible. At that gathering I presented a short study of the Armenian notations, based on my analysis of them up to that time. This was published as "The Translations of Aquila, Symmachus and Theodotion Found in the Margins of Armenian Manuscripts," in *Armenia and the Bible Papers Presented to the International Symposium Held at Heidelberg, July 16–19, 1990* , ed. C. Burchard (University of Pennsylvania Armenian Texts and Studies 12; Atlanta: Scholars 1993) 35–45. I am grateful to the Association, to its President Michael E. Stone, and to the local organizer Christoph Burchard, for the invitation to be part of that useful meeting.

Since the Heidelberg workshop I have been working on a full discussion of all the marginal notations from "the Three" in Armenian biblical manuscripts. When I was well along in doing this the invitation came to participate in the Rich Seminar on the Hexapla. This took place at Yarnton Manor, just outside Oxford, on July 25–August 4, 1994. There I gave a paper entitled "Travelling with Aquila, Symmachus and Theodotion in Armenia," which provided an introduction to and something of a synopsis of the materials extant in the margins of Armenian biblical manuscripts. This paper will appear in due course in the proceedings of the Seminar, which are to be edited by Alison Salvesen. I am grateful to Leonard Greenspoon, Alison Salvesen and Gerard Norton, the organizers of the Seminar, for their kind invitation to be a part of such a stimulating gathering in such a lovely place.

This book is limited to presenting materials preserved in the margins of Armenian biblical manuscripts. I would like to alert the reader to the fact that there are more materials preserved in Armenian biblical commentaries, both those composed in Armenian and those translated from other languages into Armenian. Robert B. ter Haar Romeny is working on Eusebius of Emesa's *Commentary on the Octateuch* at the University of Leiden. (The edition is: Vahan Hovhannesian, ed., *Eusèbe d'Émèse I. Commentaire de l' Octateuque* [Venice: St. Lazar 1980] [in Armenian].)

There is nothing in this commentary relative to the passages discussed in my work here; it has to do mostly with Genesis. John Chrysostom's *Commentary on Isaiah* , in Armenian translation, preserves readings from "the Three." The edition of the Armenian is: Hovhannu Oskeberani (i.e. John Chrysostom), *Meknut'iwn Esayeay Margarēi* [Commentary on Isaiah the Prophet] (*Matenagrut'iwnk' Nakhneats'—Oskeberan* ; Venice: St. Lazar 1880). For a large section of the *Commentary* we have only the Armenian and this evidence was not fully utilized by J. Ziegler, the editor of the Göttingen edition of the Greek text of Isaiah. I am grateful to Geoff Jenkins for bringing this to my attention. There are more readings to be found in (Pseudo-)Ephrem's *Commentary* on Genesis–Chronicles. (The edition is: Ephrem, *Works*, part 1: Commentary on Genesis–Chronicles [Venice: St. Lazar 1836].) There are also notations—at least for Genesis 1—in the medieval Armenian commentator Vartan Arevelts'i's *Commentary on the Octateuch* . Ed Mathews, who is working on these materials, provided me with information in this regard. I am indebted to Michael Stone for bringing Mathew's work to my attention. Finally, Robert W. Thomson has reported to me that there are also notations from Aquila, Symmachus and Theodotion in Vartan Arevelts'i's *Commentary on Psalms* .

In conjunction with presenting the Armenian evidence for 4 Reigns I have added such Georgian evidence as is provided by J. Neville Birdsall in his article "Traces of the Jewish Greek Biblical Version in Georgian Manuscript Sources," *Journal of Semitic Studies* 17 (1972) 83–92. Birdsall, in turn, is dependent upon the work of the Georgian scholar M. Janashvili.

I express thanks to my congregation, which for the past almost ten years has provided me with a place of caring and humour, as well as a place where "the Three"—and I refer here not to that *other* "Three"—have some relevance.

I would like to make mention of Kathy Gibson and the staff at Knox College library, Toronto, for generous borrowing privileges.

Finally it is a pleasure to make mention separately of the help of a number of individuals who have been my teachers, in some cases colleagues, and in all cases friends. I am referring to Albert Pietersma, Michael E. Stone, Robert W. Thomson and J.W. Wevers (my *Doktor Vater*).

The work on this book has brought back again and again memories of a year in Yerevan, at that time—1977–1978—a beautiful, well-treed city where life, if difficult under the Soviet regime, was reasonably secure. During that year I travelled from Yerevan to Baku, a city of similar size, where I visited Armenian churches and came into contact with a large Armenian population, a real community. (The same was true when I travelled to Tbilisi, which at that time had a population that was twenty percent Armenian. I met and spoke with Armenians in various places in the city, from one of the local pastry shops to the Iveria Hotel.) From Baku I travelled to Isfahan to study at the Armenian manuscript library in New Julfa; I visited the university there and met people at a department where Armenian studies were taught. In the intervening years this whole area has undergone a conflagration involving various kinds of turmoil. Political change in the region, the earthquake and the war in Nagorno-Karabagh have brought terrible suffering to the Republic of Armenia and to Armenian communities across the whole region. So it is that, more than would usually be the case, I am aware that this research is indebted completely to the intellectual heritage of the Armenian people.

In Yerevan I recall the kindness of my supervisor Babken Chukaszian, Vice-Director of the Matenadaran, and others there; of Vahé Aftandilian[†] at the Linguistics Institute and his family; of Emma Mkrtchian, my tutor at the university; and of Araxia Ter Manuelian and her family.

This book is dedicated to my wife Elaine and our three children, Michael, Jason and Laura, who make many things possible.

Barrie, Ontario
08/95

Abbreviations

Periodicals, Reference Works, Series, Organizations

AASG	Auctoritate Academiae Scientiarum Gottingensis editum
AAWG	Abhandlungen der Akademie der Wissenschaften in Göttingen
ABD	*Anchor Bible Dictionary* , ed. D.N. Freedman (New York: Doubleday 1992)
AIEA	Association Internationale des Études Arméniennes
BIOSCS	Bulletin of the International Organization for Septuagint and Cognate Studies
CB	Coniectanea Biblica
CGFAL	Calouste Gulbenkian Foundation Armenian Library
CSCO	Corpus Scriptorum Christianorum Orientalium
HAT	Handbuch zum Alten Testament
HATS	Harvard Armenian Texts and Studies
HSM	Harvard Semitic Monographs
IDB	*Interpreter's Dictionary of the Bible*
ICC	International Critical Commentary
IOSOT	International Organization for the Study of the Old Testament
JBS	Jerusalem Biblical Studies
JSS	*Journal of Semitic Studies*
JSSM	Journal of Semitic Studies Monograph
JTS	*Journal of Theological Studies*
MSU	Mitteilungen des Septuaginta-Unternehmens der Akademie der Wissenschaften in Göttingen
NAWG	Nachrichten der Akademie der Wissenschaften in Göttingen

NIV   New International Version

NKGWG Nachrichten von der Königlichen Gesellschaft der Wissenschaften zu
         Göttingen

OTS   Old Testament Series

OTSt   *Oudtestamentische Studiën*

SBLSCS   Society of Biblical Literature Septuagint and Cognate Studies Series

SVTG   Septuaginta Vetus Testamentum Graecum

TU   Texte und Untersuchungen zur Geschichte der altchristlichen Literatur

ThR   *Theologische Rundschau*

UPATS   University of Pennsylvania Armenian Texts and Studies

VTSup   Supplements to *Vetus Testamentum*

ZAW   *Zeitschrift für die alttestamentliche Wissenschaft*

ZDMG   *Zeitschrift der Deutschen Morgenländischen Gesellschaft*

Designations for Armenian Manuscripts[1]

J   Jerusalem, Armenian Patriarchate

LO   London, Bible House Library

LOB   London, British Library

M   Yerevan, Matenadaran

SABE   St. Petersburg, Hermitage

V   Venice, Island of St. Lazarus, Mechitarist Library

W   Vienna, Mechitarist Library

Numbers following these abbreviations usually relate to catalogue numbers
for the respective collections. For example, J1925 identifies a manuscript of the Armenian Patriarchate, Jerusalem, whose catalogue number is 1925; M188 identifies a
manuscript in the Matenadaran, Yerevan, whose catalogue number is 188. Venice
manuscripts are identified by shelf number.

---

[1]Follows Bernard Coulie, "Réportoire des Manuscrits arméniens/Census of Armenian Manuscripts; Liste des sigles utilisés pour désigner les manuscrits (AIEA 1994). Such a system of designation for manusripts was agreed upon by the AIEA at its workshop on "Problems and Tech-
niques of Editions" in Sandbjerg, Denmark, in July, 1989. Cf. AIEA *Newsletter* 14 (January 19-
91) 9.

Abbreviations and Signs Relating to Textual Criticism

*	asterisk: original as opposed to a second copyist's hand
>	is lacking in
∩	indicates parablepsis
→	becomes in/is translated as
←	retroverted from what follows
↑	indicates lines up from the bottom of a page of a manuscript
↓	indicates lines down from the top of a page of a manuscript
⟨ ⟩	indicates what has not been transmitted by the text tradition but, rather, is suggested by the editor
app	apparatus
conj.	conjectura, "conjecture"
c var	cum variis (lectionibus), "with variations"
f	folium, "page"
hab	habe(n)t, "it has" ("they have")
inc	incertus, incerta, incertum, "uncertain"
init	initium "beginning"
ind	index "mark": used to refer to the marks in margin and text which link the marginal reading and the word(s) it refers to in the text
mend	mendose, "by mistake"
mend pro	"by mistake for"
mg	margo, "margin"
MS(S)	manuscriptum (-ta), "manuscript" ("manuscripts")
non hab	non habe(n)t, "does not have"
praep	praepositio "preposition"
r	recto, the front side of a page of a manuscript; in an open codex the page on the right hand side
sed hab	sed habe(n)t, "but it has" ("but they have")
sine	"without"
sine ind	sine indice, "without index (sign)"
sine nom	sine nomine, "without name"
supra	"upon, above"

v   verso, "turned around," i.e. the back side of the page of a manuscript; in
            an open codex the page on the left
var lect   varia lectio, "variant reading"
vid   ut videtur, "as it seems"

In addition to these text critical signs and abbreviations I employ a star (∗) to
indicate that the Armenian—and in 4 Reigns the Georgian tradition as well—is correct at a given passage. This sign follows the chapter and verse numbers. For example, 4 Reigns 2:14 ∗.

Other Abbreviations

A   Codex Alexandrinus (5th century)
Aq   Aquila
Arm   the Armenian translation
B   Codex Vaticanus (4th century)
B-M-Thack^{app} indicates the apparatus to the edition of the Greek text edited
                        by Brooke-McLean-Thackeray
Field^{Arm} the Armenian MS employed by Field
Georg$^{J/B}$ in the Georgian according to Janashvili and Birdsall
inf. cs.   infinitive construct, or bound infinitive
𝔏   symbol for the Old Latin in Brooke-McLean-Thackeray
MT   Masoretic text
Sym   Symmachus
Th   Theodotion
Zoh$^{app(codd)}$ according to manuscripts cited in the apparatus of Zohra-
                        pian's edition
Zoh$^{app(mg)}$ in the margin of Zohrapian's base manuscript for collation,
                        Venice 1508, according to the apparatus of Zohrapian's
                        edition
Zoh^{txt} the text of Zohrapian's edition, as opposed to the apparatus

Abbreviations of Works Frequently Cited

Adjarian

Hr. Adjarian, Հայերեն Արմատական Բառարան [*Hayeren Armatakan Bararan* Armenian Etymological Dictionary] (four volumes; Yerevan: State University 1971–1979).

Arapkerts'i

T'adeos Astuatsaturian Arapkerts'i, Համաբարբառ Հին եւ Նոր Կտակարանաց [*Hamabarbar Hin ew Nor Ktakaranats'* Concordance to the Old and New Testaments] (Jerusalem: St. James 1895).

Barthélemy

Dominique Barthélemy, *Les Devanciers d'Aquila* (VTSup 10; Leiden: Brill 1963).

BDB

Francis Brown, S.R. Driver, Charles A. Briggs, eds., *A Hebrew and English Lexicon of the Old Testament* (Oxford: Clarendon 1907; repr. 1968).

Bedrossian

Matthias Bedrossian, ed., *New Dictionary Armenian–English* (Venice: St. Lazarus Armenian Academy 1875–1879; repr. Beirut: Librairie du Liban 1973).

BH³/⁷

Biblia Hebraica , ed. R. Kittel; Textum Masoreticum curavit P. Kahle; 3rd ed. [1929] newly completed [1937], 7th ed. [1951] extended and corrected by A. Alt and O. Eissfeldt; Stuttgart: Württembergische Bibelanstalt 1962. The books of Samuel were edited by R. Kittel; the books of Kings were also edited by Kittel and, after Kittel's death in 1929, by M. Noth. Following Kittel's death A. Alt was responsible for the editing of the Former Prophets, which includes Samuel–Kings. Samuel appeared in 1933; Kings in 1934.

BHS

Biblia Hebraica Stuttgartensia , ed. K. Elliger and W. Rudolph. Stuttgart: Württembergische Bibelanstalt 1967–1977. A. Jepsen edited the books of Kings (1974).

B-M-Thack

Alan England Brooke, Norman McLean, H.St. J. Thackeray, eds., *The Old Testament in Greek* (Cambridge: University Press 1906–1940). Thackeray joined the project following the publication of Genesis–Ruth. Joshua, Judges and Ruth appeared in 1917; 1–2 Samuel in 1927; 1–2 Kings in 1930. The Cambridge edition is a "diplomatic" edition in that it presents the text of a single witness—Codex Vaticanus (siglum: B)—and collates all the other witnesses against it. On the other hand, the Göttingen edition of the Old Testament in Greek offers an "eclectic" text, i.e. the text has been reconstructed on the basis of all the witnesses employed and is ostensibly as close to the original as one can come.

Field

F. Field, *Origenis Hexaplorum quae supersunt; sive veterum interpretum graecorum in totum vetus testamentum fragmenta* (Oxford: Clarendon 1867, 1874 [two volumes]; repr. Hildesheim: Olms 1964). Field collated one Armenian MS for this project, namely Vatican Armeno 1, copied in Constantinople in 1625.

Freund-Leverett

F.P. Leverett, ed., *Lexicon of the Latin Language: compiled chiefly from the Magnum Totius Latinitatis Lexicon of Facciolati and Forcellini, and the German works of Scheller and Luenemann* ; embracing the classical distinctions of words, and the Etymological Index of Freund's Lexicon; Boston: Bazin & Ellsworth 1850.

H-R

Edwin Hatch and Henry A. Redpath, eds., *A Concordance to the Septuagint and Other Greek Versions of the Old Testament (including the Apocryphal Books)* (Oxford: Clarendon 1897; repr. Graz: Academische Druck-U. Verlagsanstalt 1954).

KBH

William L. Holladay, ed., *A Concise Hebrew and Aramaic Lexicon of the Old Testament*, based on the First, Second, and Third Editions of the Koehler-Baumgartner *Lexicon in Veteris Testamenti Libros* (Grand Rapids: Eerdmans 19-71).

LSJ

Henry George Liddell and Robert Scott, eds., *A Greek-English Lexicon*, revised and augmented by Henry Stuart Jones, with the assistance of Roderick McKenzie; with a Supplement edited by E.A. Barber (Oxford: University Press 1843; 9th ed. 1940; repr. 1968).

Lust

J. Lust, E. Eynikel, K. Hauspie, compilers; with the collaboration of G. Chamberlain, *A Greek-English Lexicon of the Septuagint*, Part I A-I (Stuttgart: Deutsche Bibelgesellschaft 1992).

Miskgian

Ionnes Miskgian, *Manuale Lexicon Armeno-Latinum* (Rome: ex Typographia Polyglotta 1887; repr. Leuven: Institut Orientaliste de l'Université de Louvain 1966).

NIV

The Holy Bible, New International Version, Containing The Old Testament and The New Testament (Grand Rapids: Zondervan 1978).

NRSV

The New Oxford Annotated Bible with the Apocrypha (Oxford: University Press 1991).

Oskan

Ոսկան Երեւանցի, Աստուածաշունչ Հնոց եւ Նորոց Կտա-կարանաց [Oskan Yerevants'i, ed., *Astuatsashunch' Hnots' ew Norots' Ktaka-*

ranats' Bible of the Old and New Testaments] (Amsterdam: Holy Etchmiadzin and Holy Sargis Press 1666).

Payne Smith

　　　J. Payne Smith, ed., *A Compendious Syriac Dictionary* (Oxford: Clarendon 1903; repr. 1976).

Rahlfs

　　　Alfred Rahlfs, *Verzeichnis der griechischen Handschriften des Alten Testaments* (NKGWG; Philologisch-historische Klasse, Beiheft. Berlin: Weidmannsche Buchhandlung 1914).

Reider-Turner

　　　Joseph Reider, *An Index to Aquila* , completed and revised by Nigel Turner (VTSup 12; Leiden: Brill 1966). This is a very useful tool, though there are some problems with it. See Emanuel Tov, "Some Corrections to Reider-Turner's *Index to Aquila* ," *Textus* 8 (1973) 164–174.

Vulgate

　　　Biblia Sacra iuxta Vulgatam Versionem , ed. Bonifatio Fischer, I. Gribomont, H.F.D. Sparks, W. Thiele; revised, with a brief apparatus by R. Weber (Stuttgart: Würtembergische Bibelanstalt 1969; 2nd ed. 1975). Citations from the Latin Vulgate appear in Geneva script.

Zohrapian

　　　Յովհաննու Զոհրապեան, Աստուածաշունչ Մատեան Հին եւ Նոր Կտակարանաց [Hovhann Zohrapian, ed., *Astuastashunch' Matean Hin ew Nor Ktakaranats'* Scriptures of the Old and New Testaments] (Venice 1805; repr. *The Zohrab Bible* , introduction by C. Cox; Delmar, NY: Caravan 1984).

Library of Congress Transliteration System for Armenian

The transliteration system used in this book follows the Library of Congress system. The table reproduced here is taken from the *Journal of Armenian Studies*, which in turn reproduced it from the Library's *Cataloging Service, Bulletin* 121, Spring 1977. It is based on the phonetic values of Classical and East Armenian. Not included here are the phonetic values of West Armenian or references to Reformed orthography.

Ա	ա	A	a	Յ	յ	Y / H	y / h[3]
Բ	բ	B	b	Ն	ն	N	n
Գ	գ	G	g	Շ	շ	Sh	sh[2]
Դ	դ	D	d	Ո	ո	O	o
Ե	ե	E / Y	e / y[1]	Չ	չ	Ch'	ch'
Զ	զ	Z	z	Պ	պ	P	p
Է	է	Ē	ē	Ջ	ջ	J	j
Ը	ը	E	e	Ռ	ռ	Ṛ	ṛ
Թ	թ	T'	t'	Ս	ս	S	s
Ժ	ժ	Zh	zh[2]	Վ	վ	V	v
Ի	ի	I	i	Տ	տ	T	t
Լ	լ	L	l	Ր	ր	R	r
Խ	խ	Kh	kh[2]	Ց	ց	Ts'	ts'
Ծ	ծ	Ts	ts[2]	Ւ	ւ	W	w
Կ	կ	K	k	Ու	ու	U	u
Հ	հ	H	h	Փ	փ	P'	p'
Ձ	ձ	Dz	dz[2]	Ք	ք	K'	k'
Ղ	ղ	Gh	gh[2]	Եւ	եւ	Ew	ew
Ճ	ճ	Ch	ch		or Ու	in Classical orthography	
Մ	մ	M	m	Օ	օ	Ō	ō
				Ֆ	ֆ	F	f

---

[1]This value is used only when the letter is in initial position of a name and followed by a vowel, in Classical orthography.
[2]The acute accent is placed between the two letters representing two different sounds when the combination might otherwise be read as a diagraph (e.g. Դգնունի D´znuni).

---

[3]This value is used when the letter is in initial position of a word or of a stem in a compound, in Classical orthography.

I. Introduction

H.S. Anasean, "Une leçon symmachienne dans les manuscrits arméniens de la Bible (pour l'histoire du texte des Hexaples d'Origène), *Revue des Études Arméniennes*, N.S. 17 (1983): 201–205 (= *Handes Amsorya* 97 [1983], 1–6, cols. 93–100 [in Armenian]). • J.N.Birdsall, "Traces of Jewish Greek Biblical Versions in Georgian Manuscript Sources," *JSS* 17 (1972) 83–92. Birdsall publishes some twenty notations—all from 4 Reigns—drawn from material published in Tbilisi in 1910 by M. Janashvili. • Norayr Bogharian, "Գէորգ Սկեւռացի [George Skewṛatsʻi]," in Հայ Գրողներ [Armenian Writers] (Jerusalem: St. James 1971) 324–329. • idem, ed., Մայր Ցուցակ Ձեռագրաց Սրբոց Յակոբեանց [Grand Catalogue of St. James Manuscripts] (CGFAL; Jerusalem: St. James 1966–1991 [11 vols.]). • B. Botte[†] and P.-M. Bogaert, "Septante et Versions grecques," *Supplément au Dictionnaire de la Bible* , ed. J. Briend and É. Cothenet, Tome 12, Fasc. 68 (Paris: Letouzey & Ané 1993) cols. 536–693. Most of this exhaustive treatment is the work of Bogaert. It is the single best introduction to the LXX: encyclopedic, informative, suggestive, with excellent bibliographies and discussion of the literature. • Sebastian P. Brock, "The Phenomenon of Biblical Translation in Antiquity," *Alta: University of Birmingham Review* 2 (1967) = *Studies in the Septuagint: Origins, Recensions, and Interpretations* , ed. S. Jellicoe (New York: Ktav 1974) 541–571. • Alan England Brooke, Norman McLean, Henry St. John Thackeray, edd., *The Old Testament in Greek* (Cambridge: University Press 1909–1940). • José Ramón Busto Saiz, *La Traduccion de Simaco en el Libro de Los Salmos* (Textos y Estudios "Cardenal Cisneros" 22; Madrid: Instituto "Arias Montano" 1978). • C. Cox, "Concerning a Cilician Revision of the Armenian Bible," in *De Septuaginta: Studies in honour of John William Wevers on his sixty-fifth birth-*

day , ed. A. Pietersma and C. Cox (Toronto: Benben 1984) 209–221. • idem, *Hexaplaric Materials Preserved in the Armenian Version* (SBLSCS 21; Atlanta: Scholars 1986). • idem, "The Translations of Aquila, Symmachus and Theodotion Found in the Margins of Armenian Manuscripts," in *Armenia and the Bible. Papers Presented to the International Symposium Held at Heidelberg, July 16–19, 1990* , ed. Christoph Burchard (UPATS 12; Atlanta: Scholars 1993) 35–45. • Leonard J. Greenspoon, "Aquila's Version," "Symmachus, Symmachus's Version," "Theodotion, Theodotion's Version," *ABD* , 1, 320–321; 6, 251 and 6, 447–448, respectively. • Marguerite Harl, "La « Bible d'Alexandrie» et les Études sur la Septante. Réflexions sur une première expérience," *Vigiliae Christianae* 47 (1993) 313–340. • Kyösti Hyvärinen, *Die Übersetzung von Aquila* (CB OTS 10; Lund: Gleerup, 1977). • Bo Johnson, "Armenian Biblical Tradition in Comparison with the Vulgate and Septuagint," in *Medieval Armenian Culture* , ed. Thomas J. Samuelian and Michael E. Stone (UPATS 6; Chico, CA: Scholars 1984) 357–364. • idem, *Die armenische Bibelübersetzung als hexaplarischer Zeuge im 1. Samuelbuch* (CB OTS 2; Lund: Gleerup 1968). • idem, "Some Remarks on the Marginal Notes in Armenian 1 Samuel," in *Armenian and Biblical Studies* , ed. Michael E. Stone (Supplementary Volume 1 to *Sion* ; Jerusalem: St. James 1976) 18–20. • Koriwn, *Vark' Mashtots'* [Life of Mashtots'], ed. M. Abeghyan (Yerevan: Haypethrat 1941). • R.A. Kraft, "Septuagint," *IDB* Supplementary Volume (Nashville: Abingdon 19-76) 807–815. • Vincent Mistrih, "Trois Biographies de Georges de Skevra," *Studia Orientalia Christiana Armenica* (Extrait de Collectanea 14; Cairo: Editions du Centre Franciscain de l'Etudes Orientales Chrétiennes 1970). • Olivier Munnich, "Origène, éditeur de la *Septante* de *Daniel* ," in *Studien zur Septuaginta—Robert Hanhart zu Ehren* , ed. D. Fraenkel, U. Quast, J.Wm. Wevers (AAWG; MSU 20; Göttingen: Vandenhoeck & Ruprecht 1990) 187–218. • M.K.H. Peters, "Septuagint," *ABD* , 5, 1093–1104. Bibliography: 1102–1104. • Alison Salvesen, *Symmachus in the Pentateuch* (JSSM 15; Manchester: University of Manchester 1991). • Michael E. Stone, "Additional Note on the Marginalia in 4 Kingdoms," in *Armenian and Biblical Studies* , ed. Michael E. Stone (Supplementary Volume 1 to *Sion* ; Jerusalem: St. James 1976) 21–22. • idem, *The Testament of Levi. A First Study of the Armenian MSS of the Testaments of the XII Patriarchs in the Convent of St. James, Jerusalem* (Jerusalem: St. James 1969). • Henry Barclay Swete, *An Intro-*

duction to the Old Testament in Greek ; revised by R.R. Ottley; with an Appendix containing the *Letter of Aristeas* (Cambridge: University Press 1902; repr. New York: Ktav 1968). • Mesrop Ter-Movsessian, *Istoriia Perevoda Biblii na Armianskii Yazyk* [History of the Translation of the Bible into the Armenian Language] (St. Petersburg: Pyshkinskaia Skoropechatnia 1902). • Emanuel Tov, *The Text-Critical Use of the Septuagint in Biblical Research* (JBS 3; Jerusalem: Simor 19-81). • Giuseppe Veltri, "Der griechische Targum Aquilas. Ein Beitrag zum rabbinischen Übersetzungsverständnis," in *Die Septuaginta zwischen Judentum und Christentum* , ed. Martin Hengel and Anna Maria Schwemer (Wissenschaftliche Untersuchungen zum Neuen Testament 72; Tübingen: Mohr [Siebeck] 1994) 92-115. Bibliography: 113-115. • J.W. Wevers, "An Apologia for Septuagint Studies," *BIOSCS* 18 (1985) 16-38. • idem, "Pre-Origen Recensional Activity in the Greek Exodus," in *Studien zur Septuaginta—Robert Hanhart zu Ehren* , ed. D. Fraenkel, U. Quast, J.Wm. Wevers (AAWG; MSU 20; Göttingen: Vandenhoeck & Ruprecht 1990) 121-139. • idem, "Septuaginta Forschungen seit 1954," *ThR* n.F. 33 (1968) 18-76. • idem, "The Lucianic Problem," in *Text History of the Greek Genesis* (AAWG; MSU 11; Göttingen: Vandenhoeck & Ruprecht 1974). • J. Ziegler, ed., *Septuaginta Vetus Testamentum Graecum; Auctoritate Academiae Litterarum Gottingensis editum, XIV Isaias* ; Göttingen: Vandenhoeck & Ruprecht 1939; repr. 1967). • idem, *XVI/1 Ezechiel* (1952). • idem, *XI,4 Iob* (1982).

The Hebrew Pentateuch was translated into Greek in Alexandria in the third century BC. This translation is called "the Septuagint" on the basis of the legend contained in the *Letter of Aristeas* , which explains that the translation was made by seventy translators.[1] The remaining books of the canon were translated into Greek and additional books—such as the books of Maccabees—written in Greek and added to the canon over the next century and a half. Traditionally the entire collection of books that forms this corpus and which then circulated together has been called "the Septuagint." The neutral designation "Old Greek" translation might better be used for books outside the Pentateuch. At least one should be aware of the distinction.

The LXX is not monolithic: the translation was made over a substantial

---

[1] In "An Apologia for Septuagint Studies," *BIOSCS* 18 (1985) 16-38, J.W. Wevers argues that one can accept from the Aristeas legend only that the Septuagint is Alexandrian in origin and that the Pentateuch was translated in the third century BC.

period of time; different books had different translators. It is therefore difficult to
make generalizations that are true of the entire corpus. However, it is possible to
say on the basis of what evidence we have that from a very early period, perhaps
from the outset, there was an ongoing tendency, consciously and deliberately at
times, to bring the Greek translation into greater agreement with the Hebrew text of
the day. More than twenty-five years ago Wevers commented on Baillet's 7Q1
(Exod 28:4–7) LXX of ca. 100 BC: "What the fragments show is an early editing
towards the Hebrew text." (*ThR* 33 [1968] 47). Speaking more generally about the
LXX, Brock has observed that the style of the LXX translation moved from the
more free to the excessively literal and that alongside this there was the continual
desire to "correct" existing translations to bring them into closer line with the Hebrew original." ("The Phenomenon" 351).

The Translations of Aquila, Symmachus and Theodotion

It is in connection with this ongoing process of revision that we can intro-
duce the names of Aquila, Symmachus and Theodotion, and then of Origen and
Lucian.

The first revision which represents what we might call a text type—i.e. it is
extant in a number of witnesses—is connected now with the name of Theodotion
who, in the second century AD placed his name upon, or had his name placed upon
an existing type of text. This type of text Barthélemy identified as the *kaige* text
type on the basis of its characteristic translation of םַגְו by καίγε. (*Devanciers* 31,
81) Tov offers a date of the middle of the first century BC for this revision, which
is probably of Jewish origin. (*Textual Criticism* 144–145) We can speak of this
text type as *kaige* -Theodotion. This type of text was popular in some quarters. Indeed, Theodotion's translation of Daniel virtually displaced the older Old Greek
translation which is extant now in only two MSS! Origen, about whom we shall
speak in a few moments, used Theodotion to bring the Old Greek text to the same
length as the Hebrew and this means that there is a substantial Theodotionic element
in the hexaplaric text. For example, some 800 lines of the translation of Theodotion
under the asterisk bring the Old Greek translation of Job to the same length as the
Hebrew.

In the second century AD two other individuals made translations of the Hebrew Scriptures, apparently based upon *kaige* -Theodotion: Aquila, ca. 125 and Symmachus at the end of the 2nd or beginning of the 3rd century. (Tov, *Textual Criticism* 146–147) These translations are quite different in their character. Geoff Jenkins has expressed the opinion that the versions connected with the names of Aquila, Symmachus and Theodotion emerged apart from the LXX/Old Greek translation. They were not *against* the older translation. They emerged in a stream of things. Philip Alexander has added to this assertion by pointing out that the emergence of translations closer to the Hebrew was bound up with the growing hegemony of rabbinic Judaism which asserted the primacy of the Hebrew text, in a form that would later be identified as the Masoretic Text.[1]

Aquila's translation can only be called woodenly faithful to the Hebrew text. He went so far as to represent אֵת, the Hebrew marker of the accusative, by the preposition σύν and to leave the following word in its normal accusative case. (Cf. Barthélemy, *Devanciers* 15) He used stereotypical renderings of Hebrew words at the expense of context and sense of the original. The translation of the book of Ecclesiastes which circulated in "Septuagint" MSS apparently belongs to Aquila. This book represents an extensive text of his work.

Only fragments of Symmachus' work are extant. His goal seems not to have been so much to produce a Greek text that was necessarily closer to the Hebrew as to produce a translation which had more distinction. To some extent it is a translation for the élite because of the intellectual challenge of its varied vocabulary. Indeed, Salvesen says that the characteristics of his translation "suggest a target audience of middle class, middle-brow Hellenized Jews." By characteristics she means: "He avoids the stereotyping of Aq., while preferring consistency of rendering in similar contexts, and shuns some obvious Hebraistic constructions." (*Symmachus* 263–264) Salvesen believes that Symmachus knew the work of Aquila and that he probably knew the work associated with the name of Theodotion. (262) His translation displays a thorough knowledge of rabbinic exegesis. She locates his work in Caesarea of Palestine ca. 200. (295–297) Finally, Jerome favoured Symmachus' work: he admired its clarity, style and translation approach, which offered

---

[1]In a discussion entitled "The Parting of the Ways: Did the Church Steal the LXX from the Jews?" at the Rich Seminar on the Hexapla, Yarnton Manor, Oxford, July 25–August 4, 1994.

a sense of the original.[1]

In the third century the great text critic and commentator Origen (d. 251) produced a massive work of scholarship which we call the Hexapla, on the basis of its presumed six-column presentation of Hebrew and Greek data. In this work Origen offered a comparison of the Hebrew text with Greek translations of his day. The primary focus of attention was upon the first and fifth columns which presented the accepted Hebrew and traditional LXX texts, word by word or phrase by phrase down the page. The second column offered the Hebrew words in Greek transliteration; the third column Aquila's translation; the fourth Symmachus; the sixth the work of Theodotion. For an example of this arrangement see Swete 62–63. Much is still unknown about the Hexapla, because only fragments remain. Even the six-columned arrangement is questioned.

Origen's contribution to the text history of the Old Greek translation lies in his work on the fifth column, the LXX column. Here he provided signs relating to the quantitative appearance of the Old Greek over against the Hebrew text from which he presumed the Greek had come. Where the Old Greek was shorter than the Hebrew, Origen added what was lacking, from the sixth column it appears, i.e. from Theodotion. What he added he enclosed between an asterisk (※) and a metobelus (✔). Where the Greek text was longer than the Hebrew Origen enclosed the word(s) by which it was longer between an obelus (÷) and metobelus. So it was then that, at a glance, one could see where the LXX of Origen's day was longer or shorter than the received Hebrew text. Whether Origen wanted to bring some illu-mination to the argument between Jews and Christians about who really had the inspired Scripture where Hebrew and LXX differed or whether he intended to provide a means by which Christians could more easily learn Hebrew, or whether it was simply a big academic exercise, this great work of scholarship would have been of unique usefulness to anyone working upon the text of the Old Testament for whatever reason.

The Hexapla was never recopied in its entirety and presumably was destroyed at Caesarea when Muslims overran Palestine in the 730s. Before that happened, however, the fifth column containing Origen's text critical work came to en-

---

[1] Jenny Dines, in "Jerome's View of the Hexapla," a paper given at the Rich Seminar on the Hexapla, Yarnton Manor, Oxford, July 25–August 4, 1994. For these remarks she cites Jerome in De Vir.I11.54 and his commentary on Habakkuk 3:13.

joy immense popularity. Indeed the conflated text of his fifth column corrupted almost the whole text tradition of the LXX translation. The situation became doubly confusing—in hindsight we can observe this—when scribes mixed up the asterisks and obeli or ceased to bother with his text critical signs altogether!

Finally, with the name of Lucian—martyred 311/312—is connected a revision of the Greek Bible made at Antioch. Jerome says that the Lucianic text was well regarded from there to Constantinople. This type of text has been held to have the following distinctions: "substitution of synonyms for the words employed in the LXX"; double renderings; the occurrence of renderings based upon a Hebrew text superior to the extant MT. (Swete, 84–85, citing S.R. Driver.) In the 19th century the Lucianic text was recognized as extant in a handful of Greek MSS (Rahlfs 19-108 82 127 93) for the historical books of the Old Testament. This identification was held to be true for the Pentateuch as well, which is now recognized to have rested on an erroneous assumption. If such a revision ever existed for the Pentateuch, it is not now extant. (Cf. Wevers, "Lucianic Problem," 175.) Further, as is the case with Theodotion, there is a Lucianic type of text extant from before the time of Lucian so that there is some question about what role Lucian played in the formation of the type of text associated with his name.

Origen and the Armenian Translation of the Old Testament

The Armenian translation of the Old Testament in its present form represents a type of text that has been influenced by Origen's work. I say "in its present form" because the original Armenian translation made in the early fifth century on the basis of Greek and Syriac manuscripts of undetermined textual character was revised on the basis of Greek witnesses brought back from Ephesus after the Council of 431, as Koriwn explains in his *Life of Mashtots'* . Those manuscripts were hexaplaric in character. Eusebius of Caesarea (d. ca. 340) explains in the *Life of Constantine* that the Emperor requested fifty copies of the Scriptures be sent from Caesarea to Constantinople. Eusebius fulfilled that request. It is most likely that these fifty copies contained a hexaplaric type of text. After the Council of Ephesus seminarians returned to Armenia with copies of the Scriptures, with which such Armenian Bible translation as existed was revised by Mashtots' and the Patriarch Sahak.

On the basis of the Origenian signs preserved in Armenian manuscripts, Zohrapian rightly connected the Armenian translation of the Old Testament with the work of Origen and surmised that Origen's text had come to Armenia by way of Constantinople and Ephesus. (*Zohrab Bible* xi: see "Zohrapian" under Abbreviations.)

There have been two major editions of the Bible in classical Armenian. The first, that of Oskan Yerevants'i, was published in Amsterdam in 1666–1668. His base manuscript for collation is Matenadaran 180, a Cilician manuscript whose date is 1295. Oskan registered readings from "the Three" in the margin. For bibliographical details see "Oskan" under Abbreviations.

In 1805 the Armenian Bible edited by H. Zohrapian appeared at Venice. For a base manuscript for collation Zohrapian used Venice MS 1508. This manuscript is dated 1319 and is almost certainly Cilician in origin. It contains some Origenian asterisks as well as marginal readings, often signed, that derive from Aquila, Symmachus and Theodotion. This was a fortuitous circumstance because Zohrapian's edition is a full edition of his base manuscript: he places the asterisks in the text and, of more consequence for our interests here, he cites the marginal readings in his textual apparatus below the text of his edition.

In 1875 Field included Armenian materials in his edition of extant fragments of the Hexapla. For the Armenian tradition Field employs a single manuscript, Vatican Armeno 1, copied in Constantinople in 1625. (For a description of this MS see Stone, *Testament of Levi* , 11.) While this manuscript presents the hexaplaric signs tradition, it preserves a marginal notation for only one of the passages collected for this study, 4 Rgn 8:15, at least according to Field. (One can add that Vatican Armeno 1 is mentioned only five times in addition to 4 Rgn 8:15 for the passages analyzed in this book: Judg 15:14; 1 Rgn 10:1; 2 Rgn 15:18; 4 Rgn 17:24; 19:13[1°].) If Field had employed both this manuscript *and* Zohrapian he would have had access to a large part of the notation tradition as well as to important witnesses to the hexaplaric signs in Armenian.

When Brooke, McLean and Thackeray prepared their edition of the Old Greek—published between 1906 and 1940—they depended upon Zohrapian for the Armenian. Because Zohrapian had cited readings from Aquila, Symmachus and Theodotion they were able to cite the Armenian witness in their apparatus. Though Zohrapian's manuscript does not preserve as many such readings as some other manuscripts, and though there are occasional problems with citations of the Armenian in Brooke-McLean-Thackeray, at least biblical scholars became aware that the Armenian Bible preserves such materials.

Like the Cambridge edition, the Göttingen edition of the LXX uses Zohrapian's edition. Since the Göttingen edition does not yet include Joshua, Judges, 1– 4 Reigns, we are concerned only with Job, Isaiah and Ezekiel for which marginal notations are cited in Zohrapian's apparatus. Joseph Ziegler edited all three of these volumes. For Isaiah—first published in 1939—the Armenian was not collated at all. For Ezekiel (1952) and Job (1982) the Armenian was collated but no mention is made of the readings from "the Three" that are found in Zohrapian's apparatus.

The Marginal Notations deriving from Aquila, Symmachus and Theodotion in Armenian: Studies

In 1902 Ter-Movsessian published his important book on the Armenian translation of the Bible. He was of the opinion that the Origenian signs and the citations of the translations of Aquila, Symmachus and Theodotion in Armenian manuscripts go back to the fifth century. Ter-Movsessian had a very low opinion of the Cilician text type, which research has shown to be justified, but his reasoning for such an early date for the Origenian materials is faulty: while Origen's critical signs appear even in Cilician manuscripts, the marginal notations for Aquila, Symmachus and Theodotion do not—at least in the Cilician manuscripts he cites—and therefore, he argues, the notations must be early!! In fact, notations also appear in Cilician manuscripts, indeed in Zohrapian's base MS for collation. Further, it may well be that the asterisks/obeli and notations belong to different stages of the transmission of the text. It seems quite likely to me that the signs do derive from the earliest period but that the notations are much later.[1]

Ter-Movsessian says that he collected notations from Aquila, Symmachus and Theodotion from several Armenian manuscripts and that he intended to publish them. (*Istoriia Perevoda* 222) I do not know that he ever followed through on this

---

[1] Asterisks and metobeli are present in the text of a fragment of the book of Job found at St. Catharine's monastery in the Sinai. Cowe dates the fragment, which consists of Job 37:12–17, 22–38:2, 7–13, 18–23, to the 8th century. S. Peter Cowe, "An Armenian Job Fragment from the Sinai and Its Implications," *Oriens Christianus* 76 (1992) 123–157.

intention. He states that he collected 37 notations from 1 Samuel; 26 from 2 Samuel; 19 from 1 Kings; 107 from 2 Kings. This produces a total of 189 marginal readings. One presumes that these are signed readings. What is not clear is whether two or even three readings found together in the margin for a particular word in the text have been counted separately. He notes that among his list there are some notations already set forth by Zohrapian. Further, a comparison with Field, he says, revealed that a fair number of the notations he had collected are not listed in Field.

Since the marginal notations are most plentiful in the books of Samuel-Kings, it should not be surprising that most of the work on the Aquila, Symmachus and Theodotion readings centres on those books.

In 1928 Zanolli published the readings he had gathered from Venice MS 212 (date: 1327) for the books of Samuel-Kings. He listed and commented upon them in brief fashion. Though his lexical and linguistic observations have not stood the test of time and further research, his list is useful. Unfortunately, the Cambridge edition of Samuel-Kings appeared only in 1927 (1–2 Samuel) and 1930 (1–2 Kings), too late to be of use to him. As a result Zanolli had to rely on the edition of the Greek by H.B. Swete, published in 1895.

Bo Johnson pubished in 1968 a major study of the textual character of the Armenian translation of 1 Samuel. This led him to a further, short study of the marginal readings to be found in Armenian manuscripts of that book. This he published in 1976. It consists of a sort of "bare-bones" list of sixteen marginal readings for which the starting point is the citation of Zanolli's work.

The editor of the book in which Johnson's article appeared, Michael Stone, followed Johnson with a brief note which lists five readings in 2 Kings which a recollation of Venice 212 showed that Zanolli had not dealt with.[1] As well, Stone notes — based upon an article about the Georgian evidence published by Birdsall — that three of the marginal readings in Venice 212 for 2 Kings are also represented in the Georgian version. Indeed, several times Birdsall in that article comments that a particular notation is not otherwise attested than in Georgian. Two of the readings he says cannot be resolved. In the conclusion to the article Birdsall offers his

---

[1] The Venice MSS go by various numbers. What is designated here V212 (catalogue number: 19) bears number 280 in the brief study by Stone. There is no way around this confusing situation and the reader is encouraged to mark this footnote and to keep it in mind since Venice 280 (catalogue number: 10) is also an important witness in this study for the book of Ezekiel.

opinion that the hexaplaric materials "probably came into the Georgian sphere from the Armenian ... but it is not directly related to the Armenian as critically edited hitherto." We can now say that all the Georgian evidence he published is represented in Armenian with five exceptions, two of which—4 Rgn 8:15; 11:15—are inner Georgian glosses. The other three marginalia preserved in Georgian but not in Armenian witnesses are at 14:29—where the proper names *Ozia* (attributed to Aquila) and *Zak'aria* (Symmachus) are found in the margin—and at 18:4 where Georgian MS A646 (15th–16th century) preserves in the margin the name of the brazen serpent as *Nast'an* and attributes it to Symmachus.

In 1983 Anasean wrote about a single Symmachus reading, preserved in Armenian at 2 Rgn 3:33. Unfortunately he did not consult the Cambridge edition of the Greek text and, as a consequence, is unaware that the fragment is not unique to Armenian.

In 1990 I gave a paper at an AIEA symposium in Heidelberg in which I set forth the evidence for Aquila, Symmachus and Theodotion in marginal readings in biblical manuscripts, to the extent that I was familiar with it then. At the time I had not yet correlated my work with that of Zanolli, Johnson, Stone, or Birdsall. Most recently I presented a paper entitled "Travelling with Aquila, Symmachus and Theodotion in Armenia" at the Rich Seminar on the Hexapla, convened at Yarnton Manor, Oxford, July 25–August 4, 1994. That study reflects the near completion of this book.

Finally, one should note that the editors of catalogues of manuscripts have drawn attention to the presence of readings from Aquila, Symmachus and Theodotion when describing the contents of manuscripts. For example, Archbishop Norayr Bogharian has the following note about the books of 1–4 Reigns in Jerusalem 428: "Upon the margins there are noted readings of Symmachus and Aquila. For example, [fol.] 171r. 'and they escaped into the land Արարատայ [of Ararat],' Սիմ. Հայոց [Sym. 'of the Armenians']."

Where did the Notations in Armenian Come From and When?

A major question in the consideration of these marginal notations is that of where they have come from, and when. These readings appear in 13th century manuscripts, which is the earliest we find manuscripts that include not only the Pentateuch but also the historical books. Some "early" manuscripts have no notations at all (e.g. M1500 [date: before 1282]) or few (J1925 [date: 1269] has only three: 3 Rgn 2:1, 4; 4 Rgn 15:5) while others have many (e.g. Zohrapian's base manuscript, V1508 [date: 1319]).

The 13th century was a time of vigorous activity in Armenian scriptoria. It was a time noted for the translation of important works from other languages: for example, the works of Philo.[1] This period was a seminal one for manuscript illumination: Evans calls the era of the Cilician kingdom—between the 12th and 14th centuries—the "golden age of Armenian manuscript illumination." She points out that new political alliances gave artists the opportunity to examine manuscripts from Byzantium and the West and that the inhabitants of Hṛomklay, located west of Edessa on the Euphrates, "included an important community of Syrian Christians whose manuscript tradition influenced Armenian scriptoria." Such contacts had text critical importance too.[2]

The 13th century was a very busy time for the textual criticism of the Armenian biblical text as well as for its adornment with various "helps." In the case of the former, in Cilicia manuscripts appeared which offered in their margins the results of comparison with different text types. This includes so-called "optional readings": see "Concerning a Cilician Revision." The scholar and commentator George Skewṛatsʻi (1246/7–1301) added introductions to the books of the Old Testament as well as tables of chapters and these quickly came to be a part of the manuscript tradition. Mistrih suggests that he appears to have worked on this about 1290–1292. ("Trois Biographies," 21) It was at the end of the 13th century that the division of the biblical text into sections was introduced; eventually chapter divisions were incorporated on the basis of the Latin Vulgate, and finally versification. By the 17th century some Armenian MSS had become virtual repositories of exegetical helps.

Johnson is of the opinion that the marginal notes were taken over from the Greek text during that vigorous period at the end of the 13th century. Further, he

---

[1] See Abraham Terian, "Had the Works of Philo Been Newly Discovered," *Biblical Archeologist* 57:2 (1994) 92.

[2] Helen C. Evans, "Cilician Manuscript Illumination. The Twelfth, Thirteenth, and Fourteenth Centuries," in *Treasures in Heaven. Armenian Illuminated Manuscripts* , ed. Thomas F. Mathews and Roger S. Wieck (New York: Pierpont Morgan Library 1994) 67–68.

suggests that "the uniform character of the notes in the Armenian tradition shows that they emanate from one, at most a few Greek manuscripts." ("Armenian Marginalia," 20) He believes that the Greek witnesses from which these notes were taken may have been related to manuscripts 19-108 (B-M-Thack *b*) which have the same 80-section division of the text of 1 Samuel as is found in Armenian manuscripts.[1]

It is true that the hexaplaric marginal notes in Armenian manuscripts are quite uniform in character, at least in Reigns. I too am of the opinion that they derive from a few sources only, and most likely Greek. Further, if one were to think of the most probable time for the addition of these notes it would be the 13th century. A comparison of the Armenian tradition of preservation with the individual Greek witnesses might produce some further clarification.

The usual order of citation of hexaplaric notes in the margins of Greek manuscripts and the Syro-hexapla is Aquila, Symmachus, Theodotion, which follows the order of their placement left-to-right in the Hexapla. However, in the Armenian tradition the usual order—certainly in 4 Reigns—is Symmachus, Aquila, Theodotion, i.e. Symmachus is placed first. Manuscripts adhering to this order include J428 J1928 J1934 M177 M188 M2628. This might provide a clue to the provenance of the notations in 4 Reigns if this same unusual order can be found among Greek witnesses.

One clue to the dating of the Armenian notations is the use of the word զգզիրսն (the plural of *gzir* , with the direct object marker *z-* and the "farther" demonstrative marker *-n*) "leaders" at 4 Rgn 11:4 in a reading attributed to Aquila. Adjarian I 548 defines the meaning of this word as "the second in charge of a village." He goes on to say that it is a word of the late period and used in modern provincial settings. The authors he cites are of the 17th and 18th centuries. Hübschmann took *gzir* to be a loan-word from Persian but it is also known in Syriac, Arabic, Turkish, as well as other languages. The earliest marginal notations at 4 Rgn 11:4 date from the 13th century but that would still cause us to think "later" (i.e. Middle Ages) rather than earlier for their inclusion.

Finally, it will be noted from the list of manuscripts provided in the

---

[1] Johnson's comment that there are no hexaplaric marginal notes in the old Armenian MSS J1925 and M1500 has to be corrected with regard to the former: as pointed out in the text above, J1925 has a few such marginal notes.

following section that important witnesses for notations derive mostly from the 13th century and the 17th century, with a few witnesses between these extremes. To begin at the end: in the 17th century work on manuscripts was dominated by the Ottoman Turks' capital, Constantinople, and the Safavid Persian capital, Isfahan. To the latter were attracted artisans from Greater Armenia, from Siwnik' and the Lake Van region. On the other hand, in Constantinople Armenian artists and scribes tended to turn to Cilician manuscripts. That was true also of the Crimea, to which Armenians had fled with their manuscripts when the Cilician kingdom fell at the end of the 14th century. In 1639 a peace treaty was made between the Ottomans and Safavids which meant that Armenian books and artists moved freely across the Near East. The result was that "manuscripts in New Julfa [i.e. Isfahan] gradually adopted the fashions of Constantinople."[1] Evans and Merian continue, "The gradual dissemination of the Constantinople style can be traced through the many centers of manuscript production across Anatolia to New Julfa. At the same time such centers were in possession of venerable old Cilician manuscripts to which they could return for inspiration."[2] These remarks concern the illumination of manuscripts but I believe they are relevant to the production of manuscripts more generally; they are relevant to the issue of the origin and spread of the marginal notations. Cilician manuscripts appear to predominate among the earliest and best witnesses to the notations. Excellent 17th century witnesses derive from Constantinople in particular; also from Isfahan, i.e. New Julfa, the Armenian section of the city. The sequence of movement for the tradition of the notations was something like this: the notations appear to originate in work on the Armenian text that was done in Cilicia in the 13th century. Following the fall of the Cilician Kingdom a century later, manuscripts were taken to various other centers. This Cilician tradition of notation was given new life at Constantinople in the 17th century; so too at New Julfa, to which manuscripts had

---

[1] Helen C. Evans and Sylvie L. Merian, "The Final Centuries: Armenian Manuscripts of the Diaspora," *Treasures in Heaven*, 106. I am dependent upon Evans and Merian for the historical data provided earlier in the paragraph. New Julfa was an important economic, cultural and religious centre. The community was established by Shah Abas I in 1605; by 1630 its population may have numbered as many as 30,000 inhabitants, with perhaps another 50,000 settled in two dozen villages nearby. See Vartan Gregorian, "Minorities of Isfahan: The Armenian Community of Isfahan 1587–1722," in *Studies on Isfahan: Proceedings of The Isfahan Colloquium*, Harvard University, Jan. 21–24, 1974, Part II, in *Iranian Studies* 7 (1974) 652–680. The population figures are given on p. 667; a note refers one to works by H.T. Ter Hovnaniants [sic: for Hovhaniants, it seems], L.G. Minasian and L. Lockhart.

[2] "The Final Centuries," 109.

come from the West as well as from Greater Armenia. By this time some manuscripts in Greater Armenia had also incorporated marginal readings that bore the names of Aquila, Symmachus and Theodotion.

An additional piece to this puzzle is provided by manuscripts J297 and V280 in Ezekiel. These two witnesses preserves valuable readings for that book: both were copied at Khlat'—just NW of Lake Van—in the 15th century! It appears that the monastery there had a copy of Ezekiel that was not available in Cilicia in the 13th century.

The Extent of the Armenian Evidence

The Armenian tradition of marginalia which preserves translations of Aquila, Symmachus and Theodotion is limited for the most part to the books of Samuel-Kings, with notes preserved also for Joshua, Judges, Job, Isaiah and Ezekiel.[1] Part of the incentive behind the addition of the notes in Samuel-Kings may lie in the frequent transliterations which one finds in the Armenian text, which was obliged to transmit the transliterations it found in its parent text! Those notes found in Isaiah and Ezekiel, as well as Job, probably represent marginal notes that were widely attested in Greek sources. The total number of referrents in the text is 144, of which the majority involve the book of 2 Kings.

As might be expected, many of the same Armenian manuscripts which preserve Origen's critical signs also preserve the readings from Aquila, Symmachus, and Theodotion to the extent that they are extant in Armenian. In the course of researching the signs material for *Hexaplaric Materials Preserved in the Armenian Version* I made note of which manuscripts preserve readings from "the Three" and in what numbers. For this study I have selected those witnesses which preserve the most readings or which preserve readings where other manuscripts do not. The following manuscripts are employed in this study; they are listed below by library location in alphabetical order, together with their catalogue number (shelf number in

---

[1] It should be noted that the marginalia are a separate source from whatever remnants of the Hexapla the Armenian text might preserve. For example, since the translation of Job is hexaplaric, the Armenian text preserves the 800 lines of Theodotion. This is also true of hexaplaric plusses elsewhere in the Old Testament where Origen used the sixth column, i.e. Theodotion, to bring the fifth column, i.e. the LXX/Old Greek, to the same length as the Hebrew.

the case of Venice manuscripts: catalogue number follows within parentheses), date and provenance. This list does not represent a complete record of all the Armenian MSS which preserve readings from "the Three."

Jerusalem 297	15th century	finished in Khlat'[1]
Jerusalem 428	1620	Constantinople
Jerusalem 501	17th century	unknown
Jerusalem 542	1656	Bethlehem
Jerusalem 1127	1635	Tigranakert[2]
Jerusalem 1925	1269	Erznka[3]
Jerusalem 1927	1653	Constantinople
Jerusalem 1928	1648	unknown
Jerusalem 1934	1643–1646	Isfahan
Jerusalem 2561	1654	Constantinople
London, Bible House Library	before 1667	Cilicia[4]
London, British Library	17th century	unknown
Matenadaran 177	13th century	cavern of Manē[5]
Matenadaran 178	1253–1255	*Yerkaynamōrouk' anapat* [6]
Matenadaran 179	1292	Tarson[7]

---

[1]Town and fortress situated at the northwestern corner of Lake Van. For information about the location of place names in this and the next several notes I am indebted to Avedis K. Sanjian, ed., *Colophons of Armenian Manuscripts 1301–1480. A Source for Middle Eastern History* (Cambridge, MA: Harvard 1969) who, in turn, cites the sources upon which he is dependent. Useful also are the maps by Robert H. Hewsen in *Treasures in Heaven* .

[2]Hamit', or Amid, the capital of Diyarbakir province in Mesopotamia and located about 100 km. northeast of Edessa on the Tigris River.

[3]Town and fortress, now called Erzincan, in eastern Anatolia.

[4]The Cilician provenance is suggested by Errol F. Rhodes, cited in Stone, *Testament of Levi* , 9.

[5]A colophon in the manuscript records that it was copied during the kingship of King Leo, son of Het'um, i.e. King Leo II (1269–1289). This was during the time of the Armenian Kingdom of Cilicia. The Caves of Manè were located about 50 km. northwest of Ani, in the canton of Daranaghik'. See the map in Robert W. Thomson, ed., *Moses Khorenats'i: History of the Armenians* (HATS 4; Cambridge, MA/London: Harvard 1978) 410–411.

[6]"Longbeard plain." Robert W. Thomson informed me that Erkayn Moruk is an unknown site and suggested reference to J. M. Thierry, *Répertoire des monasteres arméniens* (Turnhout: Brepols 19-93)—personal communication 27/03/95.

[7]Or Tarsus, in Cilicia.

Matenadaran 180	1295	Cilicia
Matenadaran 188	1643	Constantinople
Matenadaran 345	1270	Gṛner[1]
Matenadaran 353	1317	Gladzor[2]
Matenadaran 354	14th century	(Aparaner)[3]
Matenadaran 1500	before 1282	Geghard
Matenadaran 2587	1648	Isfahan
Matenadaran 2628	1635	unknown
Matenadaran 3705	17th century	unknown
Matenadaran 4113	1384	unknown
Matenadaran 4905	1649	Shoṛot'[4]
Matenadaran 6569	14th century	Cilicia?
St. Petersburg, Hermitage V-P 1011	14th century	Cilicia
Venice 212 (19)	1327	Ekegheats' region[5]
Venice 229 (4)	1655	likely Lov or Ilvov, Poland
Venice 280 (10)	1418–1422	Khlat'[6]
Venice 623 (3)	1648	Isfahan

---

[1] A monastery near the fortress of Barjr-Berd, in Cilicia Tracheia. See now R.W. Edwards, "Settlements and Toponomy in Armenian Cilicia," *REArm* 24 (1993) 216.

[2] A monastery in Siwnik' province, near Lake Sevan.

[3] The scribe is Grigor of Aparaner (as well as of Gavar). Aparaner was a small place in the region of Ernjak, in the province of Siwnik'. That is, it was located south of Lake Sevan. The location is provided in the index to L. Kh'ach'ikian, A. Mnats'akanian, edd., Ցուցակ Ձեռագրաց Մաշ-տոցի Անվան Մատենադարանի [Ts'uts'ak Dzeṛagrats' Mashtots'i Anvan Matenadarani Catalogue of Manuscripts of the Mashtots' Library] (Yerevan: Academy of Sciences 1965, 1970), vol. 1. On the other hand, Gavar is located south of Lake Van.

[4] Shoṛot' was in the area of Ernjak which, in turn, was located in Siwnik', a province in Armenia Major. This province lay south of Lake Sevan and north of the Araxes River. A colophon in a Miscellany of 1631 (M3138) speaks of the Holy Mother of God hermitage located in the small town of Shoṛot'. See V. Hakobian, A. Hovhannisian, edd., Հայերեն Ձեռագրերի ժէ Դարի Հիշատակարաններ (1621–1640) [Colophons of 17th Century Armenian Manuscripts (1621–1640)] vol. 2 (Սյութեր Հայ Ժողովրդի Պատմության 15 [Resources for the History of the Armenian People 15]; Yerevan: Academy of Sciences 1978) 433, number 626.

[5] Corresponds to the region of Erzincan in Eastern Anatolia. The MS was copied at Erkaini vank', i.e. monastery. Brief description of this MS in Bo Johnson, *Die armenische Bibelübersetzung*, 23.

[6] Description of this manuscript in Stone, *The Testament of Levi*, 7.

Venice 935 (8)	1341–1355	Sultania, Baghdad
Venice 1182 (7)	1656, likely earlier	unknown, possibly Poland[1]
Venice 1270 (9)	14th–15th	unknown
Venice 1507 (13)	1635	unknown
Venice 1508 (1ʹ)	1319	unknown, probably Cilicia
Venice 1634 (2)	1641	unknown[2]
Vienna 11	before 1608	Sĕchʻov[3]

Except for the London manuscripts and Matenadaran 1500—cited for other reasons—these manuscripts preserve readings from "the Three" in differing numbers for various books of the Old Testament. (Listing here does not mean that all notations for any given manuscript have been cited. For example, Jerusalem 297 is employed only for the books of Isaiah and Ezekiel; Jerusalem 428 is used for the books of Samuel and Kings.) An additional witness has been added to the list on the basis of Zohrapian's edition: Venice 1508. Zohrapian used this manuscript as a base manuscript and faithfully reproduced not only the text of the manuscript but also its marginalia for "the Three," the latter being put in an apparatus at the bottom of the page.[4] He also recorded marginal readings from other manuscripts which he had available to him in Venice. In one of those strokes of luck that sometimes falls to a text critic—though unknown to Zohrapian at the time— he happens to have had amongst the manuscripts he employed some of the best Armenian witnesses to readings from Aquila, Symmachus, and Theodotion. This applies especially to the

[1]Michael Stone and Peter Cowe suggest Constantinople: references in *The Zohrab Bible* at xxiii, n. 34.
[2]References to the various catalogues from which information about these manuscripts is drawn can be found in *The Armenian Translation of Deuteronomy* (UPATS 2; Chico, CA: Scholars, 19-81) 16–31. There are descriptions in English of the following manuscripts used here, in Stone, *The Testament of Levi* : J428 J501 J1925 J1927 J1934 V229 V280. Brief descriptions can also be found in Stone, ed., *The Armenian Version of IV Ezra* (UPATS 1; Missoula: Scholars 1979), for the following manuscripts: J1927 J1928 J1934 J2561 M1500 London: Bible House London: British Library.
[3]The same as Sejov and Suchʻava, according to the Matenadaran catalogue index cited above. It is located in Poland. The MS is in the National Library, Vienna.
[4]The reader ought to be made aware that I have not made a recollation of the readings from "the Three" in the manuscript itself; rather, I cite the manuscript on the basis of Zohrapian.

MSS Matenadaran 188 and Venice 1182; but he also had Venice 229, 623 and 1634, aside from his base manuscript. Those manuscripts are all in the list.

The map below records the provenance of the 13th–14th century manuscripts with notations given in the list above—i.e. those witnesses copied during the time of the Armenian Kingdom in Cilicia.[1]

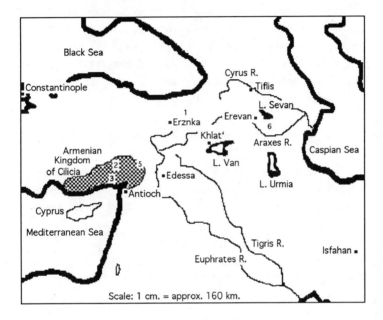

Scale: 1 cm. = approx. 160 km.

Manuscripts of the 13th–14th Centuries and Their Provenance

1.	J1925	1269	Erznka
2.	M345	1270	Gṛner
3.	M179	1292	Tarson
4.	M180	1295	Cilicia
5.	M177	13th	cavern of Manē
6.	M353	1317	Gladzor

[1]This map approximates that by Robert H. Hewsen in *Treasures in Heaven* , 104 and compared with another on p. 66. Hewsen's map is entitled "The Armenian Diaspora (17th Century)." The location of the Caves of Manē is drawn from Thomson, as noted above.

7. V1508	1319	Cilicia (probably)
8. V212	1327	Erznka region, i.e. same as 1.
9. M6569	14th	Cilicia?
10. SABE	14th	Cilicia

Manuscripts whose provenance is simply "Cilicia" are not represented by number on the map. It should be noted that J1925, whose origin is not Cilician, has only three notations from Aquila, Symmachus and Theodotion and none is signed (3 Rgn 2:1, 4 and 4 Rgn 15:5, as noted above). Gladzor is not in Cilcia either but M 353 is a bit later than some of the Cilcian manuscripts. The tradition of the notations had ample time to travel from Cilicia.

Retroverting the Armenian Notations Back into Greek

The translations of Aquila, Symmachus and Theodotion are Greek works and it is a deseridatum to be able to cite the fragments that remain of their work in that language, rather than say, in Latin—like Brooke-McLean-Thackeray did—when the Greek evidence is not extant. Field retroverted Syriac, for example, back into Greek and he used a smaller typeface to indicate such retroversions. His retroversions were well done and have proven useful for subsequent generations of scholars.

In the majority of the cases the Armenian materials deriving from Aquila, Symmachus and Theodotion are also extant in Greek manuscripts and/or in Syriac, i.e. in the Syro-hexapla. While this diminishes somewhat the importance of the Armenian evidence it makes much easier the task of drawing equivalences among Hebrew, Greek and/or Syriac, and Armenian. In those instances where the Armenian witness is until now unique in preserving notations from "the Three" one encounters all the challenges of dealing with this evidence: how can one discover what Greek words underlie the Armenian ones?

The difficulty of making retroversions into Greek from the Armenian notations lies in the following characteristics of the evidence. First, in many cases the vocabulary of the marginalia, as well as that of the related text, involves rare words whose meanings are unclear. After all, that was a primary reason why these translations were offered in the margins. It was not just a matter of an academic enterprise, it seems to me. The Hebrew words are of uncertain meaning, the Greek text may be difficult, and the Armenian words are sometimes rare too. Second, the words in the text and margin in any given instance—of both Greek and Armenian— are often synonymous. They mean very much the same thing: for example, at 4 Rgn 3:4 there are signed readings involving words for "shepherd." The Greek is extant in this case but, even so, sorting out the readings is still difficult.

Third, since the words involved are sometimes (often?) rarely attested, the lexicons leave one short of what one would wish for. This is true of Hebrew, Greek and Armenian dictionaries. While speaking about the tools for such technical work, one might add that the Armenian biblical concordance by Arapkerts'i, though a great help, is not a complete concordance.

Finally, the task of retroversion is made more hazardous because one cannot establish a translation technique: the evidence is simply too fragmentary. An examination of the Greek and Armenian text may reveal a consistency of equivalents that is important for the textual criticism of what is in the text but it cannot be assumed that such equivalences obtain for the marginal notations which were added later and which possibly derive from various scribes, at least from one book to another.

In what follows I have made every attempt to provide suggestions for the Greek which underlies the Armenian when the latter uniquely preserves readings from Aquila, Symmachus and Theodotion. However, in those cases where I am quite uncertain I have resorted, like others before me, to putting the reading into a Latin translation. This is an unsatisfactory solution but not everyone who uses this volume can be expected to know Armenian—citation in Armenian only being the other option. The Armenian is at any rate provided and a Latin translation at least permits someone who does not know Armenian to ascertain the sense of what is preserved in Armenian evidence.

Presentation of the Evidence: Using this Book

The order of presentation follows the order of the biblical books in which the notations appear. Under the title of each book is given a bibliography of relevant books and articles. This list includes most of the works cited in that particular chapter—there are a few footnotes: as a result, in the discussion only an author's name is provided and perhaps a short title. Then there may follow a discussion of the state of the textual criticism of the book in which the notations appear. This is particularly important for the books of Samuel-Kings where such major difficulties confront the textual critic. It is my hope that this information will be sufficiently useful that those outside the field of the textual criticism of the Hebrew and Greek Bibles will be able to put the Armenian marginalia into some sort of context.

Chapter and verse are given in bold type and, if the Armenian evidence is correct—which is usually the case—a star (*) follows. Next is given the Armenian text and notation. The reading of the text is taken from Zohrapian's edition unless otherwise specified; that reading is to the left of the square bracket. To the right of the square bracket is given the marginal notation; if the notation is signed, the signature(s) follow in the order in which they appear in the manuscripts. As I have said, it is usual in 4 Reigns for the order of notation and signature to be Symmachus, Aquila, Theodotion but where there is attestation of the notation in various witnesses it should not be concluded that all witnesses necessarily attest that order. This is especially true of V212 which is cited on the basis of Zanolli.

Below the citation of text, marginal reading and signature there follows the citation of the manuscript(s) which attest the marginal reading(s). Manuscripts are cited according to standard abbreviation: the capital letter identifies the location of the manuscript and the number identifies its shelf (Venice) or catalogue number (Jerusalem; Matenadaran, Yerevan). For example, at 4 Rgn 2:14 the manuscript witnesses include three manuscripts from the Matenadaran (177 188 2628) and one from Venice (212).

Deviations from the evidence cited usually follow in round brackets after the enumeration of the individual witnesses. Also noted in this way is whether a manuscript lacks an index sign or the name of the translator and so on. Many of the notations have been cited in the apparatus to Zohrapian's edition because he found them in the margins of his base manuscript for collation, Venice 1508. Such evidence derived from his apparatus is cited under the siglum Zoh$^{app(mg)}$ which means "cited in Zohrapian's apparatus on the basis of what he found in the margin of Venice 1508." Brooke-McLean-Thackeray cite Armenian evidence on the basis of Zohrapian. The siglum employed to indicate that Brooke-McLean-Thackeray have made

reference to that Armenian evidence is B-M-Thack[app]. In 4 Reigns there is one
more siglum. The witness of Georgian manuscripts is given on the basis of Birdsall's article, which in turn rests on work by Janashvili. The siglum for such citation of Georgian evidence is Georg[B/J], i.e. "Georgian: Birdsall, on the basis of
Janashvili."

The discussion of each notation usually follows a common format. First,
the context is discussed; a translation is provided of the sentence or phrase in which
the word(s) at issue are found, according to the NRSV. The Hebrew word at issue
is located and discussed. Second, the translation of the Old Greek is given and
commented upon. Then the Armenian evidence is analyzed over against the translation of the Old Greek. If the translation(s) of Aquila, Symmachus and/or Theodotion is extant in Greek and/or Syriac, that evidence is brought to bear upon the
elucidation of the Armenian evidence and vice versa. Finally there are given the
equivalents among Hebrew, Greek translations and the Armenian. If the Armenian
uniquely preserves the translation of one (or more) of "the Three" a retroversion
into Greek is usually suggested. Where that is not possible a Latin translation is
provided. The examination of each passage concludes with how the Armenian evidence should now be cited in relevant editions of the Old Greek text. This last part
of the analysis of each notation should be of use even to those who know no Armenian.

As an example of such a discussion we may turn to 4 Reigns 2:14 where
three signed readings are preserved. At the beginning of the books of 1–4 Reigns
there is given a bibliography for and introduction to the textual situation of those
books, which always has to be kept in mind. The entire book of 4 Reigns in many
Greek manuscripts of this book belongs to the so-called *kaige* tradition. That includes manuscript Vaticanus and the minuscule manuscripts—i.e. medieval
manuscripts written in "small" letters as opposed to the those such as Vaticanus,
written in "capital" or uncial letters—like Brooke-McLean-Thackeray's MSS a z
(Rahlfs numbers 707 554). This is important because manuscript B, i.e. Vaticanus,
provides the text printed in the Cambridge edition of 4 Reigns, which I have employed. In 4 Reigns the Old Greek text is to be found in a number of minuscule
manuscripts which have the designation boc_2e_2 in the edition of Brooke-McLean-
Thackeray. The numbers assigned to these manuscripts by Rahlfs in

his *Verzeichnis* and employed in Göttingen editions are 19-108 82 127 93, respectively.

A star (*) follows the textual reference at 4 Reigns 2:14. This indicates that the Armenian evidence is correct. The Armenian evidence is then given. The word ապիփով (*ap'p'ov*) is the word that appears in the text, according to Zohrapian's edition. The marginal readings are եւ արդ (*ev ard* "and now"), which bears the signature of Symmachus—but the եւ "and" is lacking in the marginal reading in manuscripts Matenadaran 177 and Venice 212; նաեւ նա (*naev na* "even he"), a translation signed by Aquila; and եւ նոյնպէս (*ev noynpēs* "and thus"), which has the signature of Theodotion.

The text critical abbreviations such as "sine ind," i.e. "without index (sign)," though in Latin, are standard abbreviations used in the Cambridge and Göttingen editions. I have provided a list of those used in this book; it can be found in the section at the beginning devoted to abbreviations.

These marginal readings are not cited in Zohrapian's apparatus and, presumably, are not to be found in his base manuscript for collation. Otherwise he would have cited them. In that case the sigla Zoh^app(mg) would have been employed, which means "in the margin of Zohrapian's base manuscript, i.e. Venice 1508, according to his apparatus." Because it is not in Zohrapian's apparatus it is not to be found either in Brooke-McLean-Thackeray's apparatus. Were it found in the latter the citation would be B-M-Thack^app, usually the second apparatus, hence B-M-Thack^app2.

Four manuscripts are cited in evidence of these marginal readings: Matenadaran 177 188 2628 and Venice 212. The first, Matenadaran 177 lacks the index sign above the word at issue in the text. The index sign usually appears in text and margin and thus connects marginal note and its referrent. In Armenian manuscripts the index sign looks like a small lightning bolt.

The first line of the discussion of the passage notes that the evidence of Venice MS 212 is given on the basis of Zanolli's article. I have not consulted that manuscript myself to confirm its readings, but Michael Stone has, as he states in his brief article of 1976.

There follow some remarks about the context, which concerns the prophet Elijah and his understudy, Elisha. A translation of the sentence in question is given, according to the NRSV; the Hebrew text is reproduced and the words in question pointed out. Then the Hebrew text is examined and the possibility raised that it is corrupt. Reference is made to the Koehler-Baumgartner-Holladay lexicon and to the note in the apparatus of the Stuttgart edition of the Hebrew text. In connection with this mention of KBH, it should be pointed out that, unless otherwise specified, the meanings of Hebrew words are from that readily available lexicon; meanings of Greek words, unless otherwise stated, are from Liddell-Scott-Jones; meanings of Armenian words are from Bedrossian; for Latin I have used Freund-Leverett and for Syriac Payne Smith.

The Greek text is dealt with next. As is pointed out, the reading of Vaticanus—the manuscript printed in the edition being followed, namely Brooke-McLean-Thackeray—has a transliteration: ἀφφώ. In turn it is noted that the Armenian translation also has a transliteration: ափփով.

The second apparatus of Brooke-McLean-Thackeray presents the evidence for Aquila, Symmachus and Theodotion at the time of the publication of the Cambridge edition. For the text at issue here there are preserved readings for Aquila and Symmachus in Greek manuscripts; no translation is cited for Theodotion. The Greek evidence makes clear what lies behind the Armenian marginal notations, at least for Aquila and Symmachus. A retroversion likely to be correct is suggested for the Theodotion reading preserved in Armenian.

What follows next is a listing of the equivalences among the Hebrew, Greek and Armenian words. On the first line is the Hebrew, its equivalent in Greek manuscript B, then the representation of this in the Armenian text of Zohrapian. On the next line is given Aquila's translation of the Hebrew and how Aquila's translation has been rendered into Armenian; then Symmachus' translation of the Hebrew and how Symmachus' rendering appears in Armenian; finally the translation of Theodotion—conjectural —based upon the retroversion from Armenian.

The analysis of the passage concludes with an assessment of the importance of the Armenian evidence and a presentation of the apparatus of Margolis, or the second apparatus in Brooke-McLean-Thackeray or Ziegler, revised to include the new Armenian evidence.

There are deviations from the format set forth here from time to time because of the nature of the evidence but this brief explanation should prove helpful.

I have tried to make every effort to make the material presented here as accessible as possible to as many people as possible. If it is not, in the words of the anonymous editor of 2 Maccabees "that was all I could manage." (15:37–39)

II. Joshua

Leonard J. Greenspoon, *Textual Studies in the Book of Joshua* (HSM 28; Chico: Scholars 1983).• Max L. Margolis, ed., *The Book of Joshua in Greek according to the Critically Restored Text with an Apparatus containing the Variants of the Principal Recensions and of the Individual Witnesses* (Publications of the Alexander Kohut Memorial Foundation; Paris: Paul Geuthner 1931 [vols. 1–4[1]]). • Alison Salvesen, *Symmachus in the Pentateuch* (JSSM 15; Manchester: University of Manchester 1991).

The Greek text followed is that edited by Margolis. His edition offers a critically established text and the evidence of four "recensions" printed in the apparatus below. These are: the Egyptian "recension" (hence E̲), consisting of Codex Vaticanus, the Coptic and other witnesses; the Syrian (S̲), consisting of the Old Latin and various other witnesses; the Palestinian (P̲), i.e. hexaplaric; the Constantinopolitan (C̲), consisting of Codex Alexandrinus and other witnesses. To these four groups is added a fifth group of manuscripts "which, while not at all (or as the case may be) not necessarily interdependent, rest for the greater part on C̲ but admit readings from the other recensions as well," designated M̲ (i.e. "mixed"). Finally, Margolis provides the witness of several church fathers.

Margolis cites the Armenian version under C̲.

---

[1]On the fifth volume see Emanuel Tov, "The Discovery of the Missing Part of Margolis' Edition of Joshua," *BIOSCS* 14 (1981) 17–21 and Max L. Margolis, *The Book of Joshua in Greek, Part V: Joshua 19:39–24:33* , ed. E. Tov (Monograph Series, Annenberg Research Institute, Philadelphia; Winona Lake, IN: Eisenbrauns 1992).

5:2 *

(ի) զայլախազ (վիմէ)] + յապառաձ Zoh^app(codd); յապառաձ

J428^mg J2561^mg

The context concerns the circumcision of the Israelites after their crossing of the Jordan River. In v 2 the Lord says to Joshua, "Make flint knives (חַרְבוֹת צֻרִים) ..." The Hebrew says literally, "swords of stone." The Old Greek translates μαχαίρας ἐκ πέτρας ἀκροτόμου "knives of sharp stone," according to Margolis' conjecture. He points out that "recensions" ESC read (μαχαίρας) πετρίνας ἐκ πέτρας ἀκροτόμου "stone knives of sharp stone" (= Origen^Greek); and that P has ἐκ πέτρας ἀκροτόμους, with the ἐκ πέτρας under the obelus. It seems clear that Margolis thinks that the word πετρίνας has come from the Hexapla.

Aquila, and Theodotion translate חַרְבוֹת צֻרִים with the words μαχαίρας πετρίνας, according to MS n3 (Rahlfs 344) and this is the reading in the Hexapla-influenced Recension C; hexaplaric witness MS γ (Rahlfs 376) apparently reads μαχαίρας πετρίνας ἐκ πέτρας ἀκροτόμου. (Symmachus' translation for חַרְבוֹת צֻרִים is μαχαίραν ἐξ ἀκροτόμου "a sword out of [something] sharp," according to MS n3. Margolis notes that MS p [Rahlfs 509] has the plural μαχαίρας, "swords.")

The Vulgate reads cultros lapideos "knives of stone."

Zohrapian reads սուր ի զայլախազ վիմէ, "sword out of flint rock" and this is also the reading of the excellent Armenian witness, MS J1925. Zoh^app(codd) reads սուր ի զայլախազ յապառաձ վիմէ "sword out of flint stone rock," i.e. some Armenian MSS have the doublet like Greek MS γ. Since յապառաձ is in the text of some MSS it most likely got there from the margin. The word յապառաձ is redundant because צֻרִים is already represented by ἐκ πέτρας ἀκροτόμου which has become in Armenian ի զայլախազ վիմէ. The question is how the word յապառաձ came to be placed in the margins of Armenian witnesses. It renders the hexaplaric πετρίνας, whose origin lies with Aquila and Theodotion. It would appear therefore that we have here an unsigned reading from those translators.

In this case the Hebrew, Greek and Armenian equivalents are:

צֻרִים → Old Greek ÷ἐκ πέτρας‹ ἀκροτόμου[1] → Zohrapian ի գայլա-

խազ վիմէ

→ Aq Th πετρίνας → sine nom յապառաջ.

The word յապառաջ appears to be an unsigned Aquila and Theodotion reading. Reider-Turner list πέτρα as the translation of Aquila and Symmachus at Judg 7:25 and of Aq Sym Th at Ps 77 (78):15 and Isa 48:21 (twice).

In Margolis' apparatus—or apparatuses!—the witness of the Armenian belongs with the Constantinopolitan recension which, as noted, he records as preserving the longer text with πετρίνας. In fact only some Armenian MSS attest the longer text, either in their text itself or by placing the word յապառաջ (i.e. πετρίνας) in their margin. The hexaplaric plus in some Armenian witnesses could be recorded in Margolis' register for P̲ with MS γ (Rahlfs 376) and the Complutensian Polyglot or as an unsigned reading in the second to last register where we find the readings of Aquila, Symmachus and Theodotion.[2] In the latter case it could be cited as follows:

2/3 μαχαιρας — περιτεμε] α′ μαχαιρας πετρινας και επιστρεψας περιτεμε σ′ μαχαιραν (p. –ρας) εξ αδροτομου και παλιν περιτεμε θ′ μαχαιρας
πετρινας και καθισας περιτεμε n3   μαχαιρας] πετρινας Arm^mss.

It is taken for granted that these various readings are marginalia, so that does not need to be stated. Margolis MS p is Rahlfs 509; n3 is Rahlfs 344.

13:27 *

յեմակն] ձորձոր

J428^mg J1928^mg J1934^mg J2561^mg Zoh^app(mg)

---

[1] The Origenian signs are of course not Old Greek.

[2] It might be suggested that πετρινας is simply a gloss brought from v 3 where we find μαχαίρας πετρίνας ἀκροτόμους "knives of sharp stone." At v 3, however, the Armenian renders
the word πετρίνας with քարեղէն, "stone," not յապառաջ. In a comment about Symmachus' standardization of LXX renderings, Salvesen (246) gives as an example Exod 4:25 where
Symmachus renders צר, the flint with which Zipporah circumcises her son, as ψῆφον πετρίνην,
and goes on to say that πέτρινος is the word used by LXX in translating צרים חרבות, the
"flint knives" with which Joshua circumcised the people at Gibeath-haaraloth. This comment needs
revision in the light of Margolis' reconstruction of the text at Joshua 5:2.

Verse 27 begins, "and in the valley Beth-haram ..." This translates the Hebrew וּבָעֵמֶק בֵּית חָרָם. The Old Greek according to Margolis read καὶ ἐν Αομκ Βαιθαρραν. However, ἐν Αομκ is a conjecture on his part and he also suggests ἐν αεμκ as a possibility. Recension E has ἐν αδωμ; recension S has ἐν αμεκ; recensions PC read ἐν εμεκ. (Note that Margolis does not usually accentuate proper nouns. Therefore these place names are not accentuated here.) The majority Greek text offers some kind of transliteration of בָעֵמֶק.

The Vulgate translates (וּ)בָעֵמֶק in valle.

The Armenian յեմակն in Zoh[txt] represents ἐν εμακ, as Margolis points out; he also notes that in some Armenian witnesses in vallem precedes. Bedrossian gives the meaning "dark or obscure place, valley, side" for եմակ. Does he do this on the basis of this passage where it is however a transliteration?

Zohrapian in his apparatus says that there is in the margin of his base MS the reading ձորձոր "valley" for յեմակն. Some MSS, he says, have taken ձորձոր into the text: so եւ ի ձորձորն յեմակն "And in the valley, in Emak."

Margolis says that בָעֵמֶק was translated ἐν τῇ κοιλάδι by Aquila and Symmachus, citing as evidence Syriac MS L (ܒܥܘܡܩܐ "in the vale") and Eusebius.

According to Reider-Turner κοιλάς is the standard equivalent for עֵמֶק in Aquila, Symmachus and Theodotion. For example, Aquila and Symmachus use it at Jos 7:26; Aq Sym Th at 13:19; Aq Sym at 13:27; Aq Th at 1 Rgn 17:2. Reider-Turner list seven other passages.

The sequence is עֵמֶק → κοιλάς → ձորձոր.

The reading ձորձոր preserves an unsigned reading of Aquila and Symmachus or it has come from the Vulgate. While the latter might be true for MSS J1928 (date: 1648; provenance?) and J1934 (date: 1643–1646; provenance: Isfahan)—they have been extensively compared with the Vulgate—the same is not true for MSS J428 (date: 1620; provenance: Constantinople) and J2561 (date: 1654; provenance: Constantinople). For that reason I am inclined to accept ձորձոր as an unsigned reading which derives from the Hexapla. These MSS from Constantinople are probably dependent upon Cilician witnesses for their marginalia. See the Introduction where the transmission of the marginalia is discussed.

The Hebrew, Greek and Armenian equivalents are:

בָּעֵמֶק → Old Greek ἐν Αομκ (conj.) c var → Zohrapian յԵմակն
→ Aq Sym ἐν τῇ κοιλάδι → sine nom [հ] ձորձորի[ն].

I have added here the preposition հ and the demonstrative/definite marker -ն. Zoh-rapian notes that ձորձորն appears in the text of some MSS and presumably it got there from the margin where it may well have had the demonstrative/definite mark-er, though one might also argue that the -ն was added under the influence of the following յԵմակն, which has such a marker.

On the basis of these marginal readings in a number of Armenian MSS one might revise Margolis' apparatus at 13:27 for the Armenian as follows. The eighth register of the apparatus should indicate that the Armenian attests the translation of Aquila Symmachus:

ενεμεκ] α' σ' εν τη κοιλαδι (ܟܘܡܩܐܒ) Syr^L Arm^mss(sine nom) Eus.

The user of this register of the apparatus will understand that the reading in question is a marginal reading, so that does not need to be indicated.

Margolis has already noted in the seventh register of his apparatus that *in vallem* is attested in the text of some Armenian MSS.

III. Judges

Walter R. Bodine, *The Greek Text of Judges, Recensional Developments* (HSM 23; Chico: Scholars 1980). • Alfred Rahlfs, *Septuaginta. Id est Vetus Testamentum graece iuxta LXX interpretes* (Stuttgart: Württembergische Bibelanstalt 1965 [19-35]).

The textual critical situation of the Old Greek translation of Judges is complex. Witnesses are divided between those which represent a text form like the well-known uncial MS B (Codex Vaticanus) and those which represent a form of text like that found in the similarly well-known uncial MS A (Codex Alexandrinus). Rahlfs printed the two variant texts—one above the other—in his provisional edition of the Old Testament in Greek, published in 1935.

There is only one passage to consider for the book of Judges. In what follows I have used the edition of Brooke-McLean for the Old Greek. Brooke-McLean follow the text of MS B and place all variations from that text in an apparatus.

15:14 *

կարքն] շղթայքն Aq

M4113mg M6569mg Zohapp(mg)(sine nom)

The passage concerns the binding of Samson by the people of Judah who then handed him over to the Philistines. When the Philistines came to get him the spirit of the Lord came upon him "and the ropes that were on his arms became like

flax that has caught fire ..." The word הָעֲבֹתִים "the ropes" is translated τὰ καλώδια "the small cords" in Greek (without variant in Brooke-McLean except that
MS G* lacks the article). This is quite acceptable because the word עֲבֹת means
"cord, rope" (BDB).

Aquila's translation does not appear in the B-M apparatus.

The words τὰ καλώδια are translated by կարքն in Zohrapian's text. կար
means "cord, line, string"; կարքն is the plural, with the definite marker -ն.

Zohrapian notes in his apparatus that his base MS V1508 has շղթայքն in
the margin and that this agrees with what some MSS have as text. (I have not noted
the minor spelling variation in the citation of the evidence which begins the discussion of this passage.) J1928 is such a MS: it has շղթայք in the text and կապքն
in the margin. The word շղթայ means "chain; chain, concatenation, continuity,
series." Zohrapian also points out that some MSS read (եղեւ) կապքն ("the
ropes, cords") instead of կարքն.

The two Armenian MSS cited—M4113 M6569—are both 14th century witnesses. The provenance of the former is unknown; M6569 may have been copied in
Cilicia. Manuscript V1508 is also a 14th century Cilician MS.

The Latin Vulgate reads et sicut solent ad odorem ignis lina consumi ita
vincula quibus ligatus erat dissipata sunt et soluta "and as linen when it is
consumed by fire smells, so the bonds by which he was bound were destroyed and
broken." The critical word—"bonds," i.e. vincula —stands in a different place in
the sentence because the word order has been changed. It seems unlikely that the
reading has come from the Vulgate, especially since it is signed.

In Reider-Turner the equivalences for עֲבֹת are listed as: ἄλυσις "chain,"
βρόχος "noose, slip knot" and πιμελής neut. "fat." One passage is listed for Aquila's translation of עֲבֹת by ἄλυσις: Exod 39:17; two passages are listed where
Aquila used βρόχος for עֲבֹת: Ps 128(129):4 and Isa 5:18. In Isa 5:18 the reading is
Aq Sym Th. The translation of Aquila here was likely ἄλυσις or βρόχος.

There may be a helpful clue for this matter of retroversion at v 13. There we
read that the men of Judah bound Samson "with two new ropes." The word
"ropes" is a translation of עֲבֹתִים, the same word which occurs again at v 14. Field
notes that his MS 85—also number 85 in Rahlfs—has a marginal reading sine nom:
῎Αλλος· βρόχοις. That is, βρόχοις "with ropes" is a reading from "the Three." In

his apparatus he says that he does not know whether this translation might belong to Symmachus and refers the reader to the Hexapla at Isa 5:18; Ezek 3:25. This suggests that οἱ βρόχοι is more likely than αἱ ἁλύσεις at v 14.

The reading provided by Field appears in Brooke-McLean's second apparatus where it is noted as a plus following αὐτόν 2° in v 13. (One should perhaps note that Brooke-McLean's siglum z—which here is Rahlfs 85—is used for Rahlfs 554 in Reigns.)

The Armenian translation at v 13 is կարուկք "with cords." It translates the Old Greek (ἐν δυσὶ) καλωδίοις (καινοῖς) "(with two new) cords."

Field's evidence for v 13 raises the possibility that the Armenian marginal reading at v 14 correctly belongs not there but at v 13. This would require, however, an assumption that the scribe who translated the marginal reading into Armenian applied a marginal reading in the instrumental case at v 13—βρόχοις—to a referent in the nominative case—τὰ καλώδια—at v 14. I am going to accept the correctness of the placement of the marginal reading, though one must recognize the possibility that it derives from the marginal reading known from MS 85 at v 13.

The Hebrew, Greek and Armenian equivalents are:

עֲבֹתִים → Old Greek τὰ καλώδια → Zohrapian կարքն

→ Aq conj. οἱ βρόχοι ← Aq շղթայքն.

The second apparatus in Brooke-McLean at v 14 can be revised as follows: τα καλωδια] α′ lineae Arm.

The readings presented in Brooke-McLean's second apparatus are marginal readings. The editors generally translate Armenian into Latin when the underlying Greek is not extant.

IV. 1 Reigns

Chahé Adjémian [Ajamian], *Grand Catalogue des Manuscrits Armeniens de la Bible* (Bibliothèque Arménienne de la Fondation Calouste Gulbenkian; Lisbon 1992) [in Armenian]. • Anneli Aejmelaeus, "The Septuagint of 1 Samuel," in *On the Trail of the Septuagint Translators* (Kampen: Kok Pharos 1993) 131–149. • Dominique Barthélemy, "Redécouverte d'un chaînon manquant de l'histoire de la LXX," *RB* 60 (1953) 18–29 • idem, *Les Devanciers d'Aquila* (VTSup 10; Leiden: Brill 1963). • B. Botte† and P.-M. Bogaert, "Septante et Versions grecques," *Supplément au Dictionnaire de la Bible*, ed. J. Briend and É. Cothenet, Tome 12, Fasc. 68 (Paris: Letouzey & Ané 1993) cols. 536–693. This excellent work has already been noted in the bibliography to the Introduction. It is likewise helpful for an introduction to the textual complexities of the books of Samuel-Kings. • Sebastian Brock, "Lucian *redivivus* Some Reflections on Barthélemy's *Les Devanciers d'Aquila*," *Studia Evangelica* 4 (1968) = TU 103, 176–181 • C. Cox, "Concerning a Cilician Revision of the Armenian Bible," in *De Septuaginta Studies in honour of John William Wevers on his sixty-fifth birthday*, ed. A. Pietersma and C. Cox (Mississauga, ON: Benben 1984) 209–222. • S.R. Driver, *Notes on the Hebrew Text and the Topography of the Books of Samuel* (2nd ed., revised and enlarged; Oxford: Clarendon 1913.) • N. Fernández Marcos, "La sigla lambda omicron (ʎ) en I-II Reyes-Septuaginta," *Sefarad* 38 (1978) 243–262. • idem, "The Lucianic Text in the Books of Kingdoms: From Lagarde to the Textual Pluralism," in *De Septuaginta: Studies in honour of John William Wevers on his sixty-fifth birthday*, ed. A. Pietersma and C. Cox (Mississauga, ON: Benben 1984) 161–174. • idem, "Some Reflections on the Antiochian Text of the Septuagint," in *Studien zur Septuaginta—Robert Hanhart zu Ehren*, ed. D. Fraenkel, U. Quast,

J.Wm. Wevers (AAWG; MSU 20; Göttingen: Vandenhoeck & Ruprecht 1990) 219–229. • Sidney Jellicoe, *The Septuagint and Modern Study* (Oxford: Clarendon 19-68). • Bo Johnson, *Die armenische Bibelübersetzung als hexaplarischer Zeuge im 1. Samuelbuch* (CB OTS 2; Lund: Gleerup 1968). • idem, "Some Remarks on the Marginal Notes in Armenian 1 Samuel," *Armenian and Biblical Studies* , ed. Michael E. Stone (Supplementary Volume I to *Sion* ; Jerusalem: St. James 1976) 17–20. Lists "the most interesting" of the marginal notes found in Oskan's 1666 edition; the re-edition of Oskan in 1733; Zohrapian; and MSS M179 M180 M345 M353. • J. D. Shenkel, *Chronology and Recensional Development in the Greek Text of Kings* (HSM 1; Cambridge, MA: Harvard 1968). • Bernard A. Taylor, *The Lucianic Manuscripts of 1 Reigns. Volume 1: Majority Text. Volume 2: Analysis* (HSM 50, 51; Atlanta: Scholars 1992, 1993). • Mesrop Ter-Movsessian, *Istoriia Perevoda Biblii na Armianskii Yazyk* [History of the Translation of the Bible into the Armenian Language] (St. Petersburg: Pyshkinskaia Skoropechatnia 1902). • H.St.J. Thackeray, "The Greek Translators of the Four Books of Kings," *JTS* 8 (1906/7) 262–278 • *The Old Testament in Syriac* according to the Peshitta Version, edited on behalf of the IOSOT by the Peshitta Institute, Leiden; Part II, fascicle 2: Judges–Samuel (Leiden: Brill 1978). Samuel prepared by P.A. H. de Boer. • E. Tov, *Textual Criticism of the Hebrew Bible* (Minneapolis/Assen–Maastricht: Fortress/Van Gorcum 1992). • idem, "Transliterations of Hebrew Words in the Greek Versions of the Old Testament: A Further Characteristic of the *kaige* -Th. Revision?" *Textus* 8 (1972) 78–92. • Almo Zanolli, "Lezioni marginali ai quattro libri dei Re. In un codice armeno dell'anno 1328," *Atti del Reale Istituto Veneto di scienze, lettere ed arti* 87 (1927–1928) second part, 1217–1235. Examination of marginal readings from Aquila, Symmachus and Theodotion in Venice MS 212 (catalogue number: 19).

Introductory remarks about the text of Samuel-Kings

The majority of the readings from Aquila, Symmachus and Theodotion preserved in Armenian MSS relate to the text of the books of Samuel and Kings. For that reason it may be helpful to say something about the Hebrew and Greek texts of these books.

No question in LXX studies is more complex than that involving the textual history of the Old Greek translation of Samuel-Kings. The textual criticism of Samuel-Kings has taken two very dramatic steps in this century. The first is associated with Thackeray; the second with Barthélemy.

In 1906/7 Thackeray published his article on the "translators" of Samuel-Kings. His thesis at that time he placed among the "some surprising results" which now and again reward the investigator who approaches the LXX from a linguistic point of view. ("The Greek Translaters," 262) On the basis of linguistic usage Thackeray was able to partition Samuel-Kings into five sections. These are listed below according to the slightly more refined partitioning by Shenkel:

α   1 Sam
ββ   2 Sam 1:1–9:13 (11:1 Thackeray)
βγ   2 Sam 10:1 (11:2 Thackeray)–1 Ki 2:11
γγ   1 Ki 2:12–21:43
γδ   1 Ki 22–2 Ki.

On the basis of some ten shared linguistic peculiarities, Thackeray regarded βγ and γδ as having a common translator, different from that of the other sections and later. He was able to point to affinities of this translator with Aquila and Theodotion; he regarded βγ and γδ as the work of a Palestinian translator of ca. 100 BC.

The second dramatic step in the textual criticism of the Old Greek of Samuel-Kings was taken by Barthélemy. In 1953 he published an article about the Minor Prophets Scroll, dated about the end of the first century AD. ("Redecouverte d'un chaînon.") In this article Barthélemy pointed to agreements between the text of the Scroll and that of Justin Martyr, Aquila, Symmachus and Theodotion, and identified the Scroll's text with a Palestinian recension of the end of the first century AD.

In 1963 Barthélemy published *Dévanciers d'Aquila* . This is one of the most closely argued books I have ever read. I can only point out here some conclusions crucial to the text of Samuel-Kings. Using information derived from the Scroll and building upon Thackeray's observations, Barthélemy completely reversed the order of the textual priority of the Greek MSS of Samuel-Kings. He argued that the supposedly late text type of Lucianic MSS $boc_2 e_2$ (Rahlfs 19-108 82 127 93) offers the original Old Greek translation (hence these MSS are not recensional in the sense previously believed) and identified MS Vaticanus in section βγ—to which he devoted special attention—with *kaige* , a recension previously identified with the name of the second century Theodotion (impossible now because of relative dating) and upon which Aquila based his work. As a consequence, he said, in the Hexapla Origen has in the LXX column not the Old Greek but the recensional text, with the Old Greek text now relegated to the sixth, Theodotion column. In the MS tradition of sections βγ and γδ the following textual development took place:

   1. boc$_2$e$_2$ θ′ = Old Greek

   2. Baz (Rahlfs 707 554) = Palestinian *kaige* pre-hexaplaric text

   3. A(c)x (Rahlfs 376 247) = Palestinian post-hexaplaric text.

Origen caused the *kaige* text-form to supplant the older Old Greek text in parts of Samuel-Kings. He placed in the fifth, LXX column a Palestinian revision and in the sixth another Palestinian revision for sections α, ββ, and γγ and the Old Greek for section βγ. According to Barthélemy Origen put the Old Greek in a seventh column in 2 Kings. (*Devanciers* 143; Bogaert 601)

Manuscript B sometimes preserves the Old Greek—in sections α, ββ, γγ; sometimes the Old Greek text as revised in Palestine (*kaige*)—in sections βγ and γδ.

Only at Antioch, in the form of text we know in MSS boc$_2$e$_2$ (Rahlfs 19-108 82 127 93), did the older text continue in use. In 1–4 Reigns it represents substantially the Old Greek. However—lest this be too simple!—the Antiochian text is not identical with the Old Greek because it too has undergone some revision and been subjected to some stylistic changes, e.g. "improvement" of the Greek in the direction of Attic forms. (Bogaert 593) Such revision in the past has been identified with the work of Lucian—hence we speak of "Lucianic text" with regard to MSS boc$_2$ e$_2$—though we really do not know what role, if any, Lucian had in the transmission of this text type. Finally, the Old Latin sometimes gives us control over the Lucianic text by providing access to a form of text even older.

The implications of Barthélemy's thesis for the critical text of 2 Sam 10:1–1 Ki 2:11 (βγ) and 1 Ki 22–2 Ki (γδ) are clear: we would have to print as "original text" the text of boc$_2$e$_2$, formerly regarded as a later recensional type of text!

The Lucianic text thus appears long before Lucian (3rd cent.). Brock raised the question of whether one might establish that there was a pre-Lucianic and post-

Lucianic Antiochian text, which would allow one to keep the traditional "Lucian." ("Lucian *redivivus* .") In order to avoid the use of such designations as Proto-Lucian and Proto-Theodotion we must simply recognize that the translations/revisions connected with the names Theodotion and Lucian really represent text traditions that are much earlier than these historical figures.

An understanding of the Old Greek text of Samuel-Kings must also take into account the nature of the Hebrew parent text upon which the translation was based. From his early study of Qumran MSS F. M. Cross set forth the hypothesis that "Lucianic readings before Lucian" are due to a revision of the Old Greek towards a Palestinian text form—the original translation being a witness to the "Egyp-

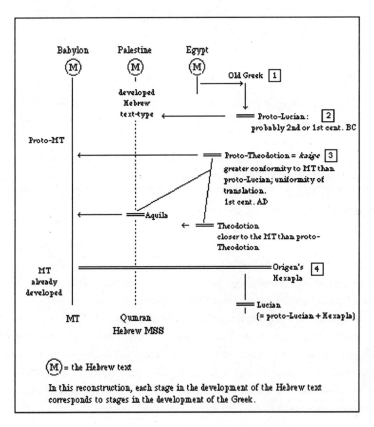

Babylon   Palestine   Egypt
(M)   (M)   (M)

                                             Old Greek [1]

                developed
                Hebrew
                text-type   ←   === Proto-Lucian: [2]
                                                    probably 2nd or 1st cent. BC

Proto-MT

        ←   === Proto-Theodotion = *kaige* [3]
                                             greater conformity to MT than
                                             proto-Lucian; uniformity of
                                             translation.
                                             1st cent. AD

        ←   ===Aquila
                                    ←   === Theodotion
                                             closer to the MT than proto-
                                             Theodotion

MT   === Origen's   [4]
already   Hexapla
developed

                                        === Lucian
        MT   Qumran   (= proto-Lucian + Hexapla)
                     Hebrew MSS

(M) = the Hebrew text

In this reconstruction, each stage in the development of the Hebrew text corresponds to stages in the development of the Greek.

tian" text form. It is helpful to make a diagram of the textual tradition thus conceived. The sketch that is provided relies on Shenkel (*Chronology* 11–12, 18). This
schematization reflects the Cross theory of three local text forms, now largely dis-
counted, and the four stages through which the Old Greek text is conceived to have
passed.

The study of the Dead Sea Scrolls certainly has illuminated the text history
of the Hebrew and Greek Bibles. Most recently Tov (*Textual Tradition* 114–117)
has argued that the Qumran texts belong to five different text groups from the point
of view of their textual status. These are:

1. Texts written in the Qumran practice, which Tov typifies as having a free
approach to the biblical text and reflected "in adaptations of unusual forms to the
context, in frequent errors, in numerous corrections, and sometimes, also in negli-
gent script."

2. Proto-Masoretic Texts. These texts contain the consonantal framework of
MT.

3. Pre-Samaritan Texts. Such texts reflect "the characteristic features of the
Samaritan Pentateuch, with the exception of the latter's ideological readings" and
occasional deviations.

4. Texts close to the presumed Hebrew source of the Old Greek. A few
texts at Qumran are very close to the Old Greek.

5. Non-aligned texts. Many texts are not exclusively close to any of the
texts mentioned in 1–4.

All of these different texts were found in the same Qumran caves. Tov believes this reflects "a certain textual reality in the period between the third century
BCE and the first century CE." This situation is one of "textual plurality and variety." Different kinds of texts were circulating at the same time. This means that the
situation was more complicated than the schema of three local texts reflects.

What about Samuel-Kings? Tov believes that earlier editions of biblical
books such as the Hebrew parent text of the Old Greek "were circulated because at
the time they were considered final." This is true, e.g., of the short texts of 4QJer[b,
d] and Old Greek in Jeremiah. On the other hand, the Hebrew text that lies behind
various sections in the Old Greek of 1 Kings probably reflects a late midrashic development later than MT. (*Textual Tradition* 178–179).

Kaige -Theodotion is reflected in the "LXX" in 2 Sam 11:1[10:1?]–1 Ki 2:11 and 1 Ki 22:1–2 Ki. Following Barthélemy, Tov suggests that in these sections of Samuel-Kings the Lucianic Greek text possibly reflects the original Greek translation. He adds though that the Lucianic text may represent a substratum of the original plus a second layer containing a revision by Lucian (*Textual Tradition* 148).

What all this means for the Armenian text of Samuel-Kings and for the marginal readings from "the Three" is this. The Armenian text of Samuel-Kings represents generally a hexaplaric type of text, the result of Origen's work which, when separated from its context in the Hexapla, became a great revision of the Old Greek towards the Hebrew. The Armenian marginal readings bearing the name of Theodotion in the sections of Samuel-Kings just mentioned represent, oddly enough, access to the original Greek translation!

A large number of the marginal readings in Armenian MSS of 1–4 Reigns involve transliterations. Therefore a word or two should be said about that phenomenon. I follow here the remarks of Tov in "Transliterations." He points out that the historiographies in Judges–Chronicles contain the largest number of transliterations among the Old Greek corpus, "among which 2 Ki presents the largest number, 30 according to our count." (See p. 81 in his article, with literature cited in a footnote.) Indeed, both the Old Greek of 4 Rgn and Theodotion's translation contain a remarkable number of transliterations. The largest number occur in the two revisers Theodotion and the reviser of γδ (*kaige*) in Samuel-Kings, who are probably one and the same, or at least of the same school. Tov suggests that unknown words were left untranslated, which left room for later generations to replace the transliterations with correct renderings.

In 1902 Ter-Movsessian wrote that that marginal notations from Aquila, Symmachus and Theodotion in Armenian MSS are more numerous in the books of Samuel-Kings than elsewhere. He states that he collected them with a view to publication. So far as I know, this intention was never fulfilled.

Ter-Movsessian provides a "for example" list of the MSS from which he drew his materials and we can identify most of them: they are—following his order on p. 222, with their date and place of origin—M2585 (16th cent.; unknown); M2627 (1338; unknown); M2628 (1635; unknown); M206 (1318; Gladzor); M205

(17th cent.; unknown); M354 (14th cent.; Aparaner?[1]); M2587 (1648; Isfahan); M2705 (1368, 1660; Pawlawnia, Kaseria, Kafa); M2706 (1668; Kafa).[2] He goes on to provide the numbers of quotations from Aquila, Symmachus and Theodotion to be found in these MSS for the books of Samuel-Kings: 1 Sam—37; 2 Sam—26; 1 Ki—19; 2 Ki—107. Some of these, he says, have already been noted by Zohrapian; further, he compared his list with Armenian materials cited in Field and found some of what he collected not represented there.

1 Reigns

The Greek text of Brooke-McLean-Thackeray has been used for the discussion of the Old Greek of 1–4 Reigns. It may be helpful to note that the Syro-hexapla version of 1 and 2 Samuel is lost: see Brooke-McLean-Thackeray's "Prefatory Note to the Books of Samuel," viii. This is unfortunate because the Syro-hexapla is such an important witness for the hexaplaric text type and for its witness to the work of Aquila, Symmachus and Theodotion, whose translations it preserves in marginal readings.

In what follows I have incorporated the work of others who have worked on the marginal readings, namely Zanolli and Johnson.

1:13 *

(և շրթունք իւր) ոչ (շարժէին)] մ՚իայն

M180[mg] Oskan[1666mg] Oskan[1733mg]

---

[1]The scribe is Grigor, who was from Aparaner as well as from Gawar. The latter was located in the Kurdish principality of Hakkāri in the province of Van. See the index of geographical terms in A. K. Sanjian, *Colophons of Armenian Manuscripts* .

[2]Provenance and dates of MSS have been corrected to those provided in L. Kh'ach'ikian and A. Mnats'akanian, edd., Ցուցակ Ձեռագրաց Մաշտոցի Անվան Մատենադարանի [Catalogue of Manuscripts of the Mashtots' Library]; introduction by O. Eganian; prepared by O. Eganian, A. Zeyt'unian, P'. Ant'abian; Yerevan: Academy of Sciences of the Armenian SSR, 1965, 1970 (two volumes). The MSS cited here were all previously located at Etchmiadzin and Ter-Movsessian provides Etchmiadzin numbers for them. The Ցուցակ provides a table which lists the Etchmiadzin numbers and their corresponding numbers in the Matenadaran: see vol. 2, cols. 1485–1498.

Cited from Johnson, "Armenian Marginalia," 17.

The context is the birth and consecration of Samuel. In v 13 Hannah is praying. We are informed that she was "praying silently; only her lips moved, but her voice was not heard." The words "only her lips moved" are a translation of רַק שְׂפָתֶיהָ נָּעוֹת. The critical word is רַק "only."

The Old Greek, according to MS B, rendered this phrase with the words καὶ τὰ χείλη αὐτῆς ἐκινεῖτο "and her lips were moving." A few witnesses—cfx (Rahlfs 376 489 247) Arm—negate the verb. Hence in the Armenian we read և շրթունք իւր ոչ շարժէին "and her lips were not moving." This appears to be an exegetically-based alteration, i.e. she was speaking in her heart, her lips were not moving and no one heard her voice: she prayed in complete humility.

B-M-Thack note a marginal reading in MSS b m—i.e. Rahlfs 108 92—with Theodotion's signature for the phrase καὶ τὰ χείλη αὐτῆς ἐκινεῖτο. It is μόνον τῶν χειλέων αὐτῆς σαλευομένωκ(-νη vid b) "only her lips were moving."

The Armenian marginal reading մհայն "only" represents Theodotion's μόνον "only." It is not signed in the Armenian witnesses which include MS M180 (date: 1295; provenance; Cilicia) and two editions of Oskan's Bible, which are based upon MS M180.

The Hebrew, Greek and Armenian equivalents are:

רַק → Old Greek non hab (vid)

→ Greek MSS Acfx (Rahlfs 376 489 247) πλὴν (> 489) ...

οὐκ (> A) → Zohrapian ոչ

→ Th μόνον → sine nom մհայն

The Armenian preserves the translation of Theodotion previously known from Greek witnesses. The second apparatus in B-M-Thack can be revised to include the Armenian witness, as follows:

και 2°—εκινειτο] θ′ μονον των χειλεων αυτης σαλευομενων (-νη vid b) b m| (ουκ)] μονον Arm(sine nom).

2:29 *

որինելով] առնել ոյ mend pro առնլոյ vid

M353 cited from Johnson, "Armenian Marginalia," 18.

The context concerns the condemnation of the house of Eli. In v 29 the subject is sacrifices which Yahweh says Eli and his sons have been abusing. Eli is asked why he would look with greedy eye at the sacrifices offered to Yahweh "and honor your sons more than me by fattening yourselves on the choicest parts of every offering." The words we are interested in are "by fattening yourselves" which are a translation of לְהַבְרִיאֲכֶם.

The word לְהַבְרִיאֲכֶם is the *hifil* inf. cs. of II. בּרא which occurs only here. It means "fatten oneself," according to KBH. Indeed S.R. Driver suggests: "Read probably either the *Nif.* לְהִבָּרַאֲכֶם (Bu [i.e. so K. Budde]) or לְהַבְרִיאָם (Ehrlich [i.e. so A. B. Ehrlich])."

For this unusual word the Old Greek employs the verb ἐνευλογεῖσθαι "to take a blessing to oneself." LSJ cite only four occurrences of εὐλογέομαι, all of them biblical: here, for the middle voice; and Gen 12:3; Acts 3:25; Gal 3:8 for the passive. H-R list nine passages for the verb but in three of these cases the simplex of the verb may be original; a fourth is in Sir 44:21, i.e. without underlying Hebrew; they place a question mark here at 1 Sam 2:29, the only time ἐνευλογεῖσθαι appears to be used for a verb other than בָּרַךְ "bless." It is possible the translator understood בּרך here, especially since the ending כֶם-, i.e. with כ, follows the א.

The Armenian translated ἐνευλογεῖσθαι as if it were the simplex, it would appear. So we read և փառաւորեցեր զորդիսն քո քան զիս, օրհնելով զպտուղ ամենայն զոհիցն Իսրայելի որ է առաջի իմ "and you glorified your sons more than me, with the blessing of the fruit of all the sacrifices of Israel which were before me." The infinitive օրհնել is given an instrumental ending (-ով) which points to the means by which the offense was committed.

The marginal reading in Armenian witnesses is առնելոյ, the infinitive of the verb առնել "to make, do," plus the gen./dat./abl. ending −ոյ. It could be translated, I suppose, with the words "by making." One notes that Bedrossian assigns to առնել ողջակէզ the meaning "to sacrifice." Perhaps առնել զոհ would mean the same thing, in which case the text, with the marginal reading, means "when you sacrificed the fruit of all the sacrifices which were in Israel."

Johnson notes that B-M-Thack give a reading that stands in the margin of
MS z (Rahlfs 554) for ἐνευλογεῖσθαι. The marginal reading is προαπολαβεῖν "to
receive before." LSJ cite only one occurrence of this verb, from the 3rd cent. A.D.
The simplex of the verb is λαμβάνειν "to take." For a "taking" verb we might expect in Armenian a form of առնուլ "to take; to take away." Though the verb προαπολαβεῖν is a complex verb, it is rare and we might well expect a translation of the
simplex λαβεῖν when the verb was rendered into Armenian.

In fact I think that առնելոյ is a corruption of առլոյ "by taking," i.e.
the declined form of the infinitive առնուլ. Arapkertsʻi lists only two occurrences
of the declined form of առնուլ: Որ առերոյ էին դստերս նորա "who
were going to take [i.e. marry] his daughters" (Gen 19:14 where առերոյ ng is the
participium necessitatis [1]); Յաղագս տալոյ եւ Առլոյ "in the matter of giving and receiving" (Phil 4:15).

The marginal reading առլոյ is a suitable Armenian equivalent for προαπολαβεῖν. Unfortunately neither Greek MS 554 nor the Armenian preserves the
signature of the translator of προαπολαβεῖν. Field has this note on προαπολαβεῖν,
which includes a citation from Montfaucon: "Sic Reg. [Cod. 243*, cum προαπο-
λαύειν], tacito interprete."—*Montef.* Scholium esse videtur.

The note in Field means this. He quotes from the older work by de Montfaucon on hexaplaric fragments, where de Montfaucon notes that Codex Regius 24-
33 (Rahlfs 554) attests ῎Αλλος· προαπολαβεῖν.[2] (῎Αλλος means simply "another
[translation]" and is used often in the margins of MSS to indicate readings from "the
Three.") Field has added that his Codex 243* (Rahlfs 731)—the asterisk is part of
the MS designation and distinguishes it from 243—bears witness to the same reading. Finally Field adds that the reading appears to be a scholium, i.e. it belongs to
the tradition of learned comments that typifies catena MSS. Readings from "the
Three" often form part of this tradition of marginalia. There seems to be good rea-

---

[1] This grammatical form is used in classical Armenian to express what will or should happen. See
R.W. Thomson, *An Introduction to Classical Armenian* (Delmar, NY: Caravan 1975) 69. For its
use in biblical materials see "The Use of the *Participium Necessitatis* in the Armenian Translation of the Pentateuch," *International Symposium on Armenian Linguistics (Yerevan, September
21–25, 1982)* , ed. G.B. Djahukian (Yerevan: Academy of Sciences 1984) 337–351.
[2] Bernard de Montfaucon (1655–1741) edited the first collection of extant fragments of the Hexapla.
See Jellicoe, *The Septuagint and Modern Study*, 128.

son to take προαπολαβεῖν and its Armenian translation as deriving from Aquila, Symmachus or Theodotion.

The Hebrew, Greek and Armenian equivalents are:

לְהַבְרִיאֲכֶם ≠ Old Greek ἐνευλογεῖσθαι → Zohrapian օրհնելոյ

→ sine nom προαπολαβεῖν → sine nom առնելոյ.

The Armenian here preserves a reading without signature known previously from Greek witness(es). The second apparatus in B-M-Thack can be revised to include the Armenian evidence as follows:

ενευλογεισθαι] προαπολαβειν z Arm.

2:36 *

դանգի միոց արծաթոյ] pr վասն

M180mg Oskan1666txt Zohapp(Oskan)

M180 and Oskan are cited from Johnson, "Armenian Marginalia," 18. Manuscript M180 was Oskan's base MS for his edition; Zohrapian cites Oskan's edition in his apparatus.

The context is the condemnation of the house of Eli, delivered by a "man of God" (v 27). Eli is told that a faithful priest will replace his family. Any left in his family after God's judgement will come to this faithful priest "to implore him for a piece of silver or a loaf of bread." The words "to implore him for a piece of silver" represent a translation of the Hebrew words לְהִשְׁתַּחֲוֹת לוֹ לַאֲגוֹרַת כֶּסֶף.

The Old Greek renders the Hebrew just cited with the words προσκυνεῖν αὐτῷ ὀβολοῦ ἀργυρίου "to bow down to him for an *obol* of silver." The genitive case of ὀβολοῦ is striking but must be rendered by something like "for." Some witnesses read ἐν ὀβολῷ: see B-M-Thackeray.

The Armenian translation of προσκυνεῖν αὐτῷ ὀβολοῦ ἀργυρίου is երկիր պագանել նմա դանգի միոց արծաթոյ "to bow down to him for one obole/penny of silver." Here too the genitive, i.e. դանգի follows directly upon the verb.

In M180 a marginal reading supplies a preposition for the phrase in question. It is վասն "for, for the sake of": the phrase becomes երկիր պագանել նմա վասն դանգի մի՛ոջ արծաթոյ "to bow down before him for one obole of silver."

As Johnson notes, B-M-Thack present translations of Aquila and Symmachus where the Old Greek reads ὀβολοῦ ἀργυρίου. They are: εἰς συλλογὴν ἀργυρίου "for a collection of silver" (Aquila); ἵνα μησθαρνήσῃ (i.e. μισθαρνήσῃ) "in order that you might work for hire." Both these readings are preserved in Greek MS M; the Symmachus reading is also preserved in MS z (Rahlfs 554).

The Armenian editor used only part of the marginal reading, likely Aquila's which has the preposition εἰς, to clarify the phrase դանգի մ՛ոջ արծաթոյ after the verb երկիր պագանել. It seems to me that the marginal reading does preserve contact with the translation of Aquila. In manuscript M180 we find many marginal readings from "the Three."

The Hebrew, Greek and Armenian equivalents here are:

לְ(אֲגוֹרַת) → Old Greek non hab → Zohrapian non hab

→ Aq εἰς (συλλογήν) → sine nom վասն.

The Armenian marginal reading preserves Aquila's preposition, known already from Greek witnesses. The second apparatus of B-M-Thack can be adjusted as follows to include the Armenian evidence:

οβολου αργυριου] pr εις Arm : α′ εις συλλογην αργυριου σ′ ινα μησθαρνηση M : σ′ ινα μισθαρνηση αργυριου η κολλυρας αρτου z (in textu post αρτον κ̅υ̅).

6:19 [Zohrapian 18]

հածեցան] խնդացին

M179ᵐᵍ M180ᵐᵍ M345ᵐᵍ(ᵛⁱᵈ) M353ᵐᵍ V212ᵐᵍ Zohᵃᵖᵖ(ᵐᵍ)

Cited from Johnson, "Armenian Marginalia," 18; V212 is cited on the basis of Zanolli 1223.

The context concerns the return of the ark of the covenant to Israel. In v 19 we are informed of the punishment which the descendents of Jeconiah brought upon themselves when they did not rejoice with the people of Beth-shemesh at the ark's return. The Hebrew text is corrupt and the NRSV follows the Greek.

At the beginning of v 19 the Hebrew text says, "And he killed some of the people of Beth-shemesh, because they looked into [the ark]" (so NRSV note). The Greek text reads Καὶ οὐκ ἠσμένισαν οἱ υἱοὶ Ἰεχονίου ἐν τοῖς ἀνδράσιν Βαιθ-σάμυς, ὅτι εἶδαν "The descendents of Jeconiah did not rejoice with the people of Beth-shemesh when they greeted [the ark]"

The Hebrew underlying the Greek at the beginning of the verse is suggested by BH³/⁷app: בְנֵי יְכָנְיָה (al הֵרִיעוּ) חָדוּ וְלֹא "and they did not rejoice (or, shout in applause), the sons of Jeconiah." The word in question is חָדוּ—from I חדה "rejoice"—or perhaps, as the editor suggests alternatively הֵרִיעוּ—from רוּע hifil "shout in triumph."

The Greek uses the verb ἀσμενίζειν "to take or receive gladly," as cited above. This verb occurs only here in the Greek Old Testament and H-R rightly mark the citation with a dagger, indicating that the underlying Hebrew is uncertain.

The Armenian translation follows the Greek: ԵԼ ոչ հաՃեցան որդիքն յեքոնեայ ընդ արս բեթսամ'իւսացւոցն "And the sons of Jeconiah did not express their pleasure with the men of Beth-shemesh." The verb հաՃիլ means "be contented, pleased."

We find instead of the verb հաՃեցան in the margin of a number of Ar-menian witnesses the verb խնդացին "they rejoiced." Zohrapian in his apparatus points out that this reading is in fact in the text of some MSS. Johnson, following B-M-Thack, equates խնդացին with ἐχάρησαν "they rejoiced" which is found in the margin of Greek MS p (Rahlfs 106).[1] Indeed that may well be the source of խնդացին, but then where did ἐχάρησαν come from? Is it from "the Three" or is it not simply a gloss brought about by the desire to explain the unusual word ἠσ-μένισαν? I think it more likely to be the latter. B-M-Thack place ἐχάρησαν in their first apparatus which indicates that they do not think it has come from "the Three." A perusal of the second apparatus in B-M-Thack or the Göttingen LXX reveals that the margins of MS 106 are not a repository for readings from Aquila, Symmachus

---

[1]Zanolli suggests that խնդացին derives from εὔφραναν or ἠγαλλιάσαντο but he was unaware of the reading in the margin of MS 106: the edition of 1-2 Samuel by B-M-Thack appeared in 1927, just the year before the publication of his own work. He says that he used the edition of H.B. Swete (1895).

and Theodotion.

Furthermore there have recently come to light the translations of Aquila and Symmachus for the clause in question. Aquila translates καὶ ἐπάταξεν ἐν ἀνδράσι Βεθσάμυς, ὅτι εἶδον ἐν γλωσσοκόμῳ Κυρίου "and he struck the men of Beth-shemesh, because they looked in the chest of the Lord"; Symmachus translates ἐπάταξεν δὲ τῶν ἀνθρώπων τῆς Βεσάμυς, ὅτι κατώπτευσαν τὴν κιβωτὸν Κυρίου "and he struck the men of Beth-shemesh, because they looked [too?] closely at the chest of the Lord." The underlying Hebrew is the common verb רָאָה "see."[1]

It seems likely to me that that Armenian marginal reading derives from a MS like Greek MS 106. The underlying Greek reading ἐχάρησαν may well have been transmitted in the margins of MSS which attested also readings from Aquila, Symmachus and Theodotion. It is certainly well represented in Armenian.

7:12 *

պաղենայ] բեթսանայ հնոյ Aq

M179mg M180mg M345mg M353mg Oskan1666mg(sine nom) V212mg(sine nom) Zohapp(mg)(sine nom)

Cited from Johnson, "Armenian Marginalia," 18; V212 is cited from Zanolli 1223.

The context concerns Samuel's judgeship over all Israel. More immediately it concerns an Israelite defeat of the Philistines at Mizpah. After the victory we are told that "Samuel took a stone and set it up between Mizpah and Jeshanah, and named it Ebenezer." The transliteration of the word "Jeshanah" is based on the Greek and Syriac, as the NRSV margin informs us. The Hebrew is הַשֵּׁן, i.e. שֵׁן with the article ה. The articulated word is joined to the preceding preposition: וּבֵין

---

[1] The signed Aquila reading is found in MS Escorial, Σ.II.19 (Rahlfs 98); the signed Symmachus translation is found in MS Coislinianus 113. The latter MS is described in Rahlfs' *Verzeichnis* 188. For these readings I am indebted to N. Fernández Marcos, "Lucianic Texts and Vetus Latina. The Textual Context of the Hexapla," a paper given at the Rich Seminar on the Hexapla, Yarnton Manor, Oxford, July 25–August 4, 1994. The reference to 1 Samuel 6:19 is precisely half way through the provisional typescript of the paper. The paper will appear in the Proceedings of the Seminar, to be edited by A. Salvesen.

הַשֵּׁן "(between Mizpah) and (between) Shen."

Kittel's BH[3/7app] note on הַשֵּׁן says: "read with Greek (τῆς παλαιᾶς) Syriac (יְשׁ): הַיְשָׁנָה (cf. [S.] Berger's collation of the Old Latin; the margin of [Latin] codex Legionensis, edited by [C.] Vercellone)." That is, the Hebrew text according to MT is corrupt. However, we may note that the word שֵׁן means "tooth"; it can also be used of a tooth, i.e. crag of rock, as at 1 Sam 14:4–5. The word יְשָׁנָה means "old."

(The Old Latin, according to B-M-Thack, has *inter … nouae et veteris* "between … new and old," where ἀνὰ μέσον τῆς παλαιᾶς stands in the Old Greek. The Vulgate translates [inter Masphat et] inter Sen "[between Masphat and] Sen." The Old Latin has a translation, like the Old Greek; the Vulgate follows the Hebrew with a transliterated proper name.)

The Old Greek, according to MS B, for the phrase "between Mizpah and Jeshanah" is ἀνὰ μέσον Μασσηφὰθ καὶ ἀνὰ μέσον τῆς παλαιᾶς, i.e. "between Massephath and the Ancient (Place)." The Hebrew underlying τῆς παλαιᾶς is יְשָׁנָה. Here the Old Greek has translated rather than transliterated.

As we might expect, the Armenian follows the Greek: և կանգնեաց ի մէջ Մասեփայ և ի մէջ պաղեսայ "and he set it up between Masepʻ and Pagheas." The Armenian has taken the Greek παλαιᾶς as a proper name and transliterated it!

The marginal reading in Armenian witnesses offers a transliteration *and* a translation for the word(s) in question: բեթսանայ հնոյ "old Bethsan." The transliteration is dependent on the Hebrew because it is clear that the preposition בֵּין has been read as בֵית. The word שֵׁן has been vocalized differently, as שֵׁן or שָׁן. The place name is then בֵּית־שָׁן, i.e Beth-Shan. With this is offered a translation either of τῆς παλαιᾶς or what underlies it, יְשָׁנָה: hence we have հնոյ "old."

The second apparatus in B-M-Thack cites only the translation of Symmachus among "the Three": where τῆς παλαιᾶς stands in the Old Greek his translation is τοῦ ἀκρωτηρίου "the peak." Symmachus' Hebrew text had שֵׁן which he took in the sense of "crag." His translation is extant in Greek MSS *b* (Rahlfs 108) and z[sine nom] (Rahlfs 554), according to the citation in B-M-Thack.

The Armenian marginal reading is attributed to Aquila.

(Johnson's comment in connection with the marginal reading is misleading. He says, "LXX has της παλαιας which Arm tries to translate in the marginal note. The same translation is found in Vetus Latina." First, the word հին may be an attempt to translate τῆς παλαιᾶς but բեթսանայ is something entirely different: it can only have come from contact with the Hebrew. Second, the same is true of the Old Latin: cf. Kittel's note, cited earlier.)

The marginal reading is anonymous in Zohrapian's MS but he does note that it corresponds to what some Armenian MSS have as their text. It would appear that some witnesses have moved the reading from margin to text.

The Armenian marginal reading is conflated: the word բեթսանայ derives from a transliteration of בֵּירָזְ (Greek Βηθσάν) but the word հին derives from a translation of הַיְשָׁנָ? (Greek τῆς παλαιᾶς). We recall that the Armenian text offers a transliteration of τῆς παλαιᾶς, namely պաղենայ. It is that transliteration that has led to the provision of marginalia.

The word բեթսանայ is explicable only by assuming contact with the Hebrew, either directly or, as is more likely, through a translation. It may well be that it belongs to Aquila. The word հին, however, could come from contact with the Old Greek: it provides a translation of τῆς παλαιᾶς which has been transliterated in the text. Together the two readings form a doublet. Aquila's signature stands with both. Typically Aquila's name would appear above the two readings: that is, Aquila's name, then the word բեթսանայ, then the word հին. It is possible that the word հին does not belong with բեթսանայ.

I am inclined to believe that բեթսանայ represents Aquila's translation and that հին (τῆς παλαιᾶς) was its referrent in the Greek text from which this marginal reading was taken. If հին represents Aquila, then his translation was the same at the Old Greek. In addition we can say that if բեթսանայ belongs to Aquila, the Hebrew parent text was likely different than the parent text of the Old Greek.

In the Greek parent text of the Armenian marginalia τῆς παλαιᾶς stood in the text. Aquila's rendering—Βηθσάν—was in the margin, together with his signature. When the marginal reading was translated into Armenian the scribe noted that its referrent in the Old Greek text was τῆς παλαιᾶς, which should not really have been transliterated պաղենայ but rather translated as հին. If my interpretation of the marginal reading is correct, it should be read something like this: Aquila's

translation where պալեառ j stands is բԹաամաj, whose referent պալեա-
ամj (i.e. τῆς παλαιᾶς) means hևnj. Better than this we cannot do now.

The Hebrew, Greek and Armenian equivalents are as follows. Symmachus' translation has been added for comparative purposes.

בֵּין הַיְשָׁנָה (conj.) ← Old Greek τῆς παλαιᾶς → Zohrapian
                                                 պալեառj

בֵּית שָׁן (conj.) ← Aq conj. Βηθσάν ← Aq բԹաամաj hևnj

בֵּין הַשָׁן → Sym (ἀνὰ μέσον) τοῦ ἀκρωτηρίου.

In this instance the Armenian tradition preserves a reading of Aquila not
otherwise known at present. The second apparatus of B-M-Thack needs to be adjusted to reflect the Armenian evidence. This can be done in the following way:

της παλαιας] α′ Βηθσαν (vid) Arm: σ′ του ακρωτηριου b m(sine nom).

8:3

զoշապալուԹեան] pr վախծանի

M179mg M353mg Zohapp(mg)

Cited from Johnson, "Armenian Marginalia," 18.

The context concerns Samuel's sons, who judged Israel after him. About
them it is said in v 3: "Yet his sons did not follow in his ways, but turned aside
after gain; they took bribes and perverted justice." The words "but turned aside after
gain" are a translation of וַיִּטּוּ אַחֲרֵי הַבָּצַע. The word בֶּצַע means here "(illegal)
profit."

The Old Greek translation of וַיִּטּוּ אַחֲרֵי הַבָּצַע is καὶ ἐξέκλιναν ὀπίσω
τῆς συντελείας. This use of συντέλεια is unusual. LSJ give its occurrence here
separate billing: "IV. *unjust gain* , LXX 1*Ki*. 8.3; = κακία, Hsch.[i.e. the 5th? century lexicographer Hesychius]." The word has a technical meaning in classical
Greek, namely *joint contribution for the public burdens* ; it also is used of *a body of
citizens who contributed jointly* to bear public burdens. Its third well-attested
meaning is of the *consummation* , e.g. of a scheme, a war, of an age (as at Matt 28:
20). The meaning given in LSJ for this passage is derived from the Hebrew. This is

the only time that συντέλεια is used to render בֶּצַע in the LXX/Old Greek corpus
and it has likely come about because the verb בָּצַע and the noun בֶּצַע can have to
do with "ends," in the sense of making a profit (*qal* pattern of the verb), or bringing to an end (*piel* pattern of the verb). Some meaning like "(illicit) ends" suits the
context here.

B-M-Thack cite a reading from Masius' notes on the Syro-hexapla: οπισω
της συντελειας] α' θ' [post] *avaritiam* Syh[m]. (Johnson, citing the evidence of
Syh[m], probably from B-M-Thack, states that the translation *avaritiam* is referred
there to Aquila and Symmachus. This requires correction it would appear.) Fortunately the translation represented by *avaritiam* has been preserved in the text and
margins of Greek MSS: we can cite from B-M-Thackeray's first apparatus: συν-
τελειας] pr πλεονεξιας dp (Rahlfs 107 106); πλεονεξιας b [mg]hoz[mg]c₂e₂Arm-ed
(Rahlfs 108[mg] 55 82 554[mg] 127 93); + πλεονεξιας g (Rahlfs 158) Arm-cod.[1] The
word πλεονεξίας has come from the Hexapla. H-R list it as the translation of Aquila, Symmachus and Theodotion at 1 Rgn 8:3.

The Armenian translation of the clause under examination in Zohrapian is և
թիւրեցան զհետ զoշաքաղութեան "they turned aside after avarice."
Indeed Bedrossian cites this very phrase թիւրիլ զհետ զoշաքաղութեան
"to turn aside after lucre" under զoշաքաղութիւն. The word զoշաքաղութեան is a translation of πλεονεξίας. That means that the translation of one or
more of "the Three" has entered the text of the Armenian version known according
to Zohrapian: it is a hexaplaric reading and the Armenian version was rendered from
a hexaplaric type of Greek text. This reading is attested by J1925 M1500 and I take
it to be original.

Johnson points out that MSS M179 M353 have left a space in the text for the
word noted in their margins, namely վախճանի. That word is a translation of
της συντελείας: վախճան means "end." The marginal reading is intended to be
an "alternate reading"—as indicated by the space left in the text—and is testimony
to a comparison among text types that took place in Cilicia. Manuscript M179,
copied in Tarson in 1292 has, for example, fifteen such readings in Deuteronomy:

---

[1]"Arm-cod" is a bit misleading. B-M-Thack use "Arm-ed" for the text of Zohrapian's edition and
"Arm-cod" for his notes. What Zohrapian's note says here is that in the margin of his MS one
finds Զհետ վախճանի զ oշաքաղութեան at v 3.

see "Concerning a Cilician Revision of the Armenian Bible," especially 219–221 where this MS is dealt with as number 21. Usually such optional readings are derived from differences among the texts of Armenian MSS but in this case the marginal reading appears to derive from a comparison with a Greek text that had τῆς συντελείας. It would be interesting to examine Cilician MSS to see whether the marginal reading appears in the text of any MS.

What may have happened is this. The word πλεονεξίας stood as a reading of one or more of "the Three" in the margin of a MS whose text read συντελείας. Such a MS was the parent text for the Armenian marginalia. The scribe responsible for the marginal readings noted that the marginal reading (i.e. πλεονεξίας) was in fact *in the text* of the Armenian translation. He therefore put a translation of *the text* of the Greek MS (i.e. συντελείας) in the margin of the Armenian.

In conclusion we can say that the marginal reading վախճանի does not belong to "the Three." However, the reading in the text, namely զօրարութիւն is not Old Greek and derives from Aquila, Symmachus and Theodotion. Masius' note from the Syro-hexapla permits us to say that զօրարութիւն represents the translation of Aquila and Theodotion.

The following equivalences obtain:

אַחֲרֵי הַבֶּצַע → Old Greek ὀπίσω τῆς συντελείας → Arm MSS M179ᵐᵍ
M353ᵐᵍ (զհետ) վախճանի

→ Aq Th[1] ὀπίσω τῆς πλεονεξίας → զհետ զօրարութիւն.

This is a fascinating text because it shows that the non-Old Greek translation (ὀπίσω τῆς) πλεονεξίας had entered the text of the parent text of the Armenian. Of course, that this phenomenon had occurred was already clear from the Greek witnesses with which the Armenian is aligned.

9:12 *

բամ] բարունն

---

[1]B-M-Thack: Aq Th; Johnson: Aq Sym; H-R, Reider-Turner: Aq Sym Th. According to Field ὀπίσω τῆς πλεονεξίας is the translation of Aq Th and τῇ πλεονεξίᾳ is the translation of Sym.

M180^{mg} Oskan^{1733mg}

This is cited from Johnson, "Armenian Marginalia," 18. Oskan's base MS is M180.

The context is Saul's search for his father's lost donkeys. He and the boy with him, having no success, look for Samuel the seer. A group of girls on their way to draw water inform them that Samuel is nearby "because the people have a sacrifice today at the shrine." The words "at the shrine" are a translation of בַּבָּמָה. The word בָּמָה means "(cultic) high place."

The Old Greek transliterated בָּמָה: so בַּבָּמָה becomes ἐν Βαμά "at the *Bama* ."

Zohrapian's edition presents the Armenian transliteration of the Old Greek: ἐν Βαμά becomes ի բամա, i.e. "at the *Bama* ." (B-M-Thack use a capital for the Greek but there is no such emphasis in the Hebrew nor the Armenian.)

The marginal reading in Armenian MS 180 is բարձունս "the height." (The word բարձունք is plural in form; the -ս is the indicator of the accusative/ locative.) B-M-Thack cite in their second apparatus the marginal reading ὑψηλή "high" in Greek MS *b* (Rahlfs 108). The reading is unsigned but could be the origin of բարձունս. Unfortunately the Armenian word is also unsigned.

H-R, Reider-Turner cite ὕψωμα "height" as the translation of Aquila here. They are probably dependent upon Field who gives Aquila's translation as ἐν ὑψώματι "at the height" on the basis of Eusebius in his *Onomastico* , p. 98. The noun ὕψωμα could well be rendered by բարձունս in Armenian. H-R cite four occurrences of ὕψωμα in the LXX/Old Greek corpus: Judith 10:8 (Arm: բարութիւն "goodness"); 13:4 (Arm 13:6); 15:9 (15:10); Job 24:24 (24:23) (Arm: բարձրու- թիւն in the last three instances).

The Armenian marginal reading is likely a translation of Aquila.

The Hebrew, Greek and Armenian equivalents are:

בַּבָּמָה → Old Greek ἐν Βαμά → Zohrapian ի բամա

→ Aq ἐν ὑψώματι → sine nom (ի) բարձունս.

In this case the Armenian marginal reading preserves an unsigned reading already known from Eusebius. This item can be added to the second apparatus in B-M-Thack:

εν Βαμα] α' εν (> Arm) υψωματι Arm(sine nom) Euseb^{Onomast}.

9:13 *

հիւրքն Zoh^{app(mg)}] կոչնականքն

M179^{mg} M180^{mg} M353^{mg} V212^{mg} Zoh^{txt}

Cited from Johnson, "Armenian Marginalia," 18; V212 cited from Zanolli 1223. Zohrapian notes in his apparatus that Oskan has կոչնական հիւրքն.

The girls of v 12 continue here their directions to Saul and the boy with him. They explain that the people will not eat at the sacrifice until Samuel comes: he will bless the sacrifice and "afterward those eat who are invited." The words "those who are invited" are a translation of הַקְּרֻאִים. The word הַקְּרֻאִים is just the *qal* passive participle of קָרָא "call; summon; invite" with the article.

The Old Greek rendered הַקְּרֻאִים with οἱ ξένοι "the guests." (The word ξένοι can also mean "stranger, foreigner.")

B-M-Thack offer in their second apparatus two marginal readings for ξένοι in Greek witnesses: κεκλημένοι "those invited" *b* z (Rahlfs 108 554) and κλίτοι "sides, i.e. those who recline?" e₂ (Rahlfs 93).

According to Zohrapian's edition, the text of v 9 reads here և ապա ուտեն կոչնականքն "and then the guests eat." The cognate verb of կոչնական, կոչել "to call," is very close in meaning to the Greek καλεῖν, from which κεκλημένοι has come.

The marginal reading which Zohrapian cites in his apparatus is հիւրքն "the guests."

As is clear from the evidence cited above, there is some question about which reading is original, կոչնականքն which appears in the text of Zohrapian's base MS V1508 (date: 1319; provenance: probably Cilicia) or հիւրքն which stands in the text of MSS M179 (date: 1292; provenance: Tarson) M180 (date: 1295; provenance: Cilicia) M353 (date: 1317; provenance: Gladzor).

Manuscript J1925 (date 1269; provenance: Erznka) has հիւրքն in the text and I take that reading to be original. The reading which should be in the margin is կոչնականըն. Manuscript V1508 represents a type of text which has switched the readings of text and margin.

The conclusion that հիւրքն belongs in the text helps to clarify the relationship of the marginal reading կոչնականըն to the Greek evidence cited by B-M-Thack. In all likelihood կոչնականըն is a translation of κεκλημένοι.

H-R cite Aquila under καλεῖν for 1 Rgn 9:13, i.e. here, probably on the basis of Field. The latter attributes οἱ κεκλημένοι to Aquila and cites Theodoret's *Quaestiones* (XVII in 1 Ki) as evidence. Reider-Turner also record this passage for Aquila (under καλεῖσθαι).

The Hebrew, Greek and Armenian equivalents are:

הַקְּרֻאִים → Old Greek οἱ ξένοι → Zoh^app(mg) հիւրքն

→ Aq κεκλημένοι → sine nom կոչնականըն.

The Armenian marginal reading attests a translation already known from the margins of Greek witnesses. The second apparatus in B-M-Thack can be revised as follows:

ξένοι] κεκλημενοι *b* z Arm : κλιτοι e₂.

10:1

զսրուակն] զկուժն

V212^mg Zoh^app(mg)

V212 is cited from Zanolli 1223.

The context is the anointing of Saul by Samuel. The chapter begins with the words "Samuel took a vial of oil." The word "vial" is a translation of פך.

The Old Greek renders the word פך with τὸν φακόν "flask." The word φακός is usually used of a "lentil" or something "shaped like lentils": so of a *hot-water bottle* in an Oxyrhynchus papyrus of the first century and of the *oil-flask* here and at 1 Rgn 26:11. B-M-Thack cite no variants to the word φακόν in either their first or second apparatus.

Zohrapian's edition has the word զսրուակն where τὸν φακόν stands: սրուակ means "phial, flagon, bottle." However, Zohrapian notes in his apparatus that զկունдն stands in the margin of his MS for զսրուшկն. The word կուժ means "earthen-pitcher, jug, jar." Zohrapian notes further that some MSS have in the text զկունдն սրուшկն, i.e. they have both words in the text! (By the way, at 1 Rgn 26:11, 12 τὸν φακόν is rendered by զկունд. More on this below.)

Manuscript J1925 has զսրուшկ (f.137r, col.2, †12); LOB has զոր-ուшկ (sic). I take զսրուшկ to be original. Those MSS which have զկունдն սրուшկն have taken the marginal reading զկունдն into the text. What we are left with then is: զսրուшկ is original; զկունдն is a marginal reading. The question is where the marginal reading has come from.

Arapkertsʻi lists only four passages for the word սրուшկ, and each involves a flask of oil: 1 Rgn 10:1; 4 Rgn 9:1, 5; Judith 10:5. In the first three instances սրուшկ translates φακός; at Judith 10:5 it translates καψάκης "cruse, flask."

He lists seven passages under կունд: 1 Rgn 26:11, 12, 16; 3 Rgn 19:6; 4 Rgn 2:20; Jer 19:1, 10. In the first four instances կունd is used of a jug of water and translates φακός; at 3 Rgn 19:6 կունd translates καψάκης; in 4 Rgn 2:20 the կունd is the new vessel (ὑδρίσκη "water pot" or just "vessel") into which Elisha put some salt; in Jer we are dealing with an earthenware jug (Greek: βῖκος "jar"). Ostensibly therefore կունd could represent καψάκης, ὑδρίσκη, βῖκος or even some other word. Does it?

At 1 Rgn 16:11, 12 φακός appears in the text and there are extant the translations of Aquila and Symmachus. The translation of the latter is νυκτοπότιον "night-cup," found only here in the biblical corpus. Aquila's translation is ἄγγος "vessel." Is it possible that կունd represents ἄγγος and derives from Aquila?

The word ἄγγος occurs some six times in the LXX/Old Greek corpus, according to H-R. At Deut 23:24 (MT Wevers[1] Zohrapian 25); 3 Rgn 17:10; Jer 19:11; Ezek 4:9 it is rendered by աման "vessel, pot; bag"; at Am 8:1, 2 it is represented by գործի "utensil." In the NT ἄγγος occurs at Matt 13:48 where it is translated by աման. There is no instance in which ἄγγος is translated by կունd.

These are relatively small lists of occurrences. It appears that the words

---

[1]That is, J.W. Wevers, ed., *Septuaginta, Vetus Testamentum Graecum; Auctoritate Academiae Scientarum Gottingensis editum III, 2 Deuteronomium* (Göttingen: Vandenhoeck & Ruprecht 19-77).

upn·ɯɥ and ɥn·d can be used synonymously. It is not possible to determine what Greek word underlies the marginal reading ɥn·d, if indeed it is a translation of a Greek word. I am inclined to think that it is, based on the general reliability of the marginal tradition in 1–4 Reigns. Unfortunately, according to Reider-Turner Aquila's translation of פַךְ is unknown and we have no such index yet for Symmachus and Theodotion.

The Hebrew, Greek and Armenian equivalents are:

פַךְ → Old Greek τὸν φακόν → Zohrapian ɋ upn·ɯɥն

→ sine nom Graeca inc → sine nom ɋ ɥn·dն.

This item can be added to the second apparatus of B-M-Thackeray in the following way:

τον φακον] *hydria* Arm.

The translation *hydria* is taken from Miskgian. The word *hydria* "urn, waterpot" has come into Latin from Greek ὑδρία "water-pot, pitcher; vessel of any kind." The word ὑδρία is used a number of times by Aquila: for כַד "large (pottery) jar; סַף "bowl or shallow cup"; נֵבֶל "(storage-)jar" for wine, wheat, oil, flour. Miskgian provides *urna* "pitcher, waterpot" (Greek: κάλπη) as another translation for ɥn·d; also *lagena* "flagon, flask" from Greek λάγηνος and *ampulla* "jug, flask," used especially for containing oil (Greek: λήκυθος).

H-R cite κάλπη "pitcher" only at 4 Macc 3:12 in the Old Greek among the Greek translations. The word λάγηνος is not listed in H-R. Aquila uses the word ληκύθιον at 3 Rgn 17:12 for צַפַּחַת "jar, jug(let)." Only Aquila among the Greek translators employs ληκύθιον.

It is at least possible to suggest a list of Greek words for what may underlie ɥn·d.

10:14 ∗

ɹնɯɯնɦ] ɦopɏɳ ɓɯɹn

M179ᵐᵍ M180ᵐᵍ M345ᵐᵍ M353ᵐᵍ ᵛⁱᵈ V212ᵐᵍ Zoʰᵃᵖᵖ⁽ᵐᵍ⁾

Cited on the basis of Johnson, "Armenian Marginalia," 18; V212 cited on the basis of Zanolli 1223. This reading is found in the text of MS Vatican Armeno 1, according to Field's apparatus.

When Saul and the boy with him eventually returned home "Saul's uncle said to him and to the boy, 'Where did you go?'" The word "uncle" is a translation of דּוֹד.

The Old Greek translated the word דּוֹד with ὁ οἰκεῖος "one of his kin."

The word οἰκεῖος occurs about twenty times in the LXX corpus. Seven times, six in Lev and once in Num, it renders שְׁאֵר "blood relation." (On Lev 18:17 שַׁאֲרָה cf. KBH: rd. שְׁאֵרָהּ.) Five times it is used to translate דּוֹד: four times in 1 Rgn, all of them in ch 10 (vv 14, 15, 16, 50); once in Amos (6:10).

B-M-Thack cite in their second apparatus a marginal reading in some Greek MSS for ὁ οἰκεῖος: MSS ze₂ (Rahlfs 554 93) have ὁ πατράδελφος "father's brother" in the margin. In z the reading is attributed to Aquila;[1] in e₂ it is sine nom. In MSS b (Rahlfs 19-108) πατράδελφος has been taken into the text after ὁ οἰκεῖος: redundant but very precise!

The Armenian translates ὁ οἰκεῖος with the word ընտանի "a relative." Zohrapian in his apparatus notes that some witnesses have եւ ասեն ըն-տանիքն նորա ցնա "And his family said to him." Cf. B-M-Thack: *dicunt domestici* Arm-codd. This reading is secondary: ընտանի has assimilated to the very commonly used Armenian word ընտանիք, which means "family." In fact the citation in B-M-Thack is misleading: ընտանիք is morphologically plural, singular in meaning. Of course, because it is plural in form, a verb in the plural number is required, hence ասեն. This sort of citation in B-M-Thack points up the difficulty an editor has in representing accurately what a text has without misleading

---

[1] Cf. N. Fernández Marcos, "La sigla lamda omicron (ℷ) en I-II Reyes-Septuaginta," *Sefarad* 38 (1978) 258: "La lectura de I *Reg* 14,50 πατράδελφος probablement haya que restituir la a Áquila. Sóla la atribuye a ℷ el ms m [Rahlfs 92]; jze₂ [Rahlfs 243 554 93] la transmiten *sine nomine*. Pero πατράδελφος para דוד está bien atestiquado en Áquila (cf. I *Reg*. 10,14; Is. 5,1 y dos pasajes del Cantar) por contraposición al uso de la *Septuaginta* que prefiere ἀδελφιδός." Fernández Marcos suggests here that πατράδελφος at 14:50 can probably be restored to Aquila because such a translation for דוד is well attested for him: 10:14 is one of the passages pointed out for comparison. At 14:50 the reading is attributed to λ with the omicron beneath it (so ℷ). Fernández Marcos points out that ℷ is used as a sort of "catch all" for readings from Aquila, Symmachus and Theodotion that were *sine nom*. At least such a symbol provided some indication of their source. (261)

the user.

The marginal reading in Armenian witnesses corresponds precisely to ὁ πατράδελφος. The word հօրեղբայր equally literally means "father's brother." It consists of հայր "father" and եղբայր "brother."

B-M-Thack cite the Armenian marginal reading in their first apparatus: ο οικειος] *avunculus*   Arm-codd. Zohrapian notes that the word հօրեղբայր appears as a marginal reading in V1508; he adds that this agrees with what some other MSS have as their text, i.e. they have հօրեղ բայր in the text rather than ընտանի. The use of "Arm-codd" can be misleading because it makes no mention of the fact that the word in question appears as a marginal reading, which information opens up the way for one to consider whether or not such a marginal reading has entered the text of some MSS. According to the "Prefatory Note to Genesis" in the Cambridge edition of the Old Testament in Greek the following abbreviations obtain with regard to the citation of Armenian evidence: "Arm-ed means Zohrab's text, Arm-cod or Arm-codd [means] variants recorded in his notes." The problem is that such marginal readings as we are dealing with here should not be considered as variant readings, certainly not in the usual sense of that term. But I suppose one can only make these assertions in the light of a study such as is being undertaken here.

H-R cite four occurrences of πατράδελφος in the LXX/Old Greek corpus: Judg 10:1; 2 Rgn 23:9, 24; 1 Ch 27:32. In all four instances it renders דוד.

The Hebrew, Greek and Armenian equivalents at 1 Rgn 10:14 are:

דוד → Old Greek οἱ οἰκεῖος → Zohrapian ընտանի

→ Aq ὁ πατράδελφος → sine nom հօրեղբայր.

The Armenian marginal reading attests the translation of Aquila already known from Greek witnesses. This information can be added to the second apparatus in B-M-Thack as follows:

ο οικειος] α´ ο πατραδελφος ze₂(sine nom) Arm(sine nom).

It must be remembered that all the readings cited for MSS in B-M-Thackeray's second apparatus are marginal readings. That can help the user of their edition to understand the relationship here between the second apparatus and the Armenian variant they cite in the first apparatus, namely ο οικειος] *avunculus* Arm-codd. The word *avunculus* (Armenian հօրեղբայր; Greek πατράδελφος) appears in the text of some Armenian MSS, according to Zohrapian's apparatus. If one remembers that the second apparatus concerns marginalia, one might well be able to conclude—correctly—that the word *avunculus* has come into the text from the margin.

13:3 *

ϑшпшլքն] եբրայեցիքն Aq

M353mg Oskan1666mg(sine nom) Oskan1733mg(sine nom) V212mg Zohapp(mg) (sine nom)

Cited on the basis of Johnson, "Armenian Marginalia," 18–19; V212 cited on the basis of Zanolli 1223.

The context is the beginning of the war with the Philistines during the kingship of Saul. In v 3 we are informed that Jonathan defeated the garrison of the Philistines at Geba. Then "Saul blew the trumpet throughout all the land, saying, 'Let the Hebrews hear!'" The words "the Hebrews" are a translation of הָעִבְרִים.

The Old Greek has οἱ δοῦλοι "servants," which is based upon reading העבדים rather than העברים, i.e. ד has been confused with ר.

For οἱ δοῦλοι B-M-Thack cite a marginal reading in Greek MS *b* (Rahlfs 108) and attested by Theodoret; in the former it is unsigned but in the latter it is attributed to Aquila. The reading is οἱ ἑβραῖοι, "the Hebrews." B-M-Thackeray also cite the Armenian marginal reading (in Latin: *Ebraei*) but in their first apparatus! It clearly belongs in their second apparatus.

The Armenian text reads ϑшпшλքն, "servants," which is a translation of οἱ δοῦλοι. The marginal reading in Armenian witnesses is եբրայեցիքն, "Hebrews," which clearly represents οἱ ἑβραῖοι.

Cf. also 14:21 in B-M-Thack where the same text and marginal reading is extant in a number of witnesses.

The Hebrew, Greek and Armenian equivalents at 13:3 are:

הָעִבְרִים → (העבדים) Old Greek οἱ δοῦλοι → Zohrapian
ϑшпшλքն
→ Aq οἱ ἑβραῖοι → Aq եբրայեցիքն.

The witness of Armenian MSS contributes confirmation for what was already known from Greek MSS. The reading is also signed, confirming Theodoret's identification of the origin of οἱ ἑβραῖοι. (B-M-Thack also cite Aquila from the margins of MSS ze₂ [Rahlfs 554 93]; it is signed in MS z but the part of Aquila's translation that interests us just transmits the Old Greek, i.e. it is preserved in these two MSS as οἱ δοῦλοι.) The second apparatus in B-M-Thackeray can be revised in the following way to reflect the Armenian evidence:

ηθετηκασιν οι δουλοι] α′ ακουσατωσαν (> Arm) οι ἑβραιοι *b* (sine nom)
Arm Thdt: α′ ακουσατωσαν οι δουλοι ze₂(sine nom).

The variant reading citation οι δουλοι] *Ebraei* Arm-mg should be removed from the first apparatus of B-M-Thackeray.

14:23

զրե[թաւանաւ] զ-բամոթաւ

V212ᵐᵍ

Cited according to Zanolli 1223.

The context is the account of the war with the Philistines. In v 23 we read that the Lord gave Israel the victory in a battle in which Jonathan took the lead. The text goes on to say that "The battle passed beyond Beth-aven." The word "Beth-aven" is a transliteration of בֵּ֣ית אָ֑וֶן.

The majority text in the Old Greek tradition has here not "Beth-aven" but τὴν Βαμώθ, i.e. "Bamoth." The Greek MSS dpqtz (Rahlfs 107 106 120 134 554) have βηθαυν (cf. also βηθαυ x [Rahlfs 247], βοθαυ c [Rahlfs 376] and θαυν A[vid]) from which բեթաւան appears to have come.

The Armenian MS V212 has a marginal reading բամոն which is derived from a Greek τὴν Βαμών, it would appear. The latter is a corruption but the marginal reading does indicate contact with another type of Greek text than that upon which the Armenian translation is based.

15:4

(յ)ալիմ] գաղգաղա

V212mg Zohapp(mg)

V212 is cited on the basis of Zanolli 1223.

The context is another story of Saul's rejection. In v 4 we are informed that "Saul summoned the people, and numbered them in Telaim." The word "Telaim" is a translation of בַּטְלָאִים.

In the Old Greek Saul numbers them ἐν Γαλγάλοις, i.e. "in Gilgal," the usual — here declined — Greek translation of בַּגִּלְגָּל. There are virtually no variants to this reading: Or-lat has *Galaad* ; the Sahidic has *Gabaa* . B-M-Thack cite in their second apparatus a marginal reading for ἐν Γαλγάλοις in MS j (Rahlfs 243), namely ἐν ἅρμασιν "in chariots," but it is unsigned.

The Armenian translation records that Saul made his count յալիմ "in Alim." This is cited by B-M-Thack in their first apparatus, though it appears to show contact with the Hebrew. The spelling յալիմ is attested by M1500 (fol. 153r, col. 2, †8) LO; the spelling յելիմ "in Elim" is the text of J1925 (fol. 140r, col.2, †2). Without a larger collation of witnesses it is difficult to say which spelling is original.

Zohrapian notes in his apparatus that his MS has a marginal reading գաղ-գաղ, i.e. "[in] Gilgal," which, he notes, agrees with what some MSS have in their text. In the latter instance I assume that some MSS have taken what was a marginal reading into the text. One may note that M1500 has taken ի գաղգաղա into the text, but placed it after "people," i.e. "Saul summoned the people to Gilgal, and made a count of them at Alim."

The question is where the reading յալիմ came from. The Peshitta Syriac translation for בַּטְלָאִים is ܒܛܠܝܐ, "in T[e]lia."

The Armenian ալիմ "Alim" or ելիմ "Elim" has likely come from a hexaplaric source. That could be the Greek MS from which the Armenian was translated, though in that case it is unusual that no Greek MS cited by B-M-Thack attests it. Still, it is possible and it would have come into that MS when a translation by one or more of "the Three" was used to bring the text into agreement with the Hebrew. In that case the Armenian text attests a reading from "the Three." (Johnson suggests that "perhaps" [veilleicht] the correction stems from "the Three": *1. Samuelbuch* 145.) Of course the Armenian text does include material from "the Three," presumably Theodotion, in hexaplaric plusses but that is quite different. For that reason, աղիմ/եղիմ is an intriguing reading.

The marginal reading գաղգաղա represents comparison with an Old Greek-type of Greek text.

The Hebrew, Greek and Armenian equivalents are:

בַּגִּלְגָּל ≠ Old Greek ἐν Γαλγάλοις → Arm MSS^mg [ի] գաղ-

գաղա

→ "the Three" vid. εν Ταλειμ? ← Arm MSS^txt յաղիմ/

յեղիմ.

The Armenian աղիմ/եղիմ does not attest the *tau* which, however, must have been a part of the original reading. Whether the immediate parent of the reading աղիմ/եղիմ had *tau* is another thing. It is quite possible that the *tau* was lost after *nun* in the course of transmission of the Greek text.

In this case the Armenian preserves in its text an otherwise unattested translation by "the Three." Or so it would appear. In this case it is not in the margin but in the text. For that reason its citation remains in the first apparatus of B-M-Thackeray.

20:19 *

առ երգաբաղ այդորիկ] աս քարիւ

M345^mg V212^mg

M345 is cited from Johnson, "Armenian Marginalia," 19. He cites the marginal reading in the following way: աս(?)քարիւ V212 is cited on the basis of Zanolli 1223.

The larger context is the break in the relationship between Saul and David. More immediately the context concerns a signal which Jonathan arranged to give

David to indicate whether it was safe for him to return to Saul's table. In v 19 Jonathan instructs David to go to a certain hiding place "and remain beside the stone there." A note on the end of v 19 in the NRSV informs the reader: "Meaning of Heb[rew] uncertain."

The words "and remain beside the stone there" are a translation of וְיָשַׁבְתָּ אֵצֶל הָאֶבֶן הָאָזֶל. The verb is simply the *qal* second person singular of יָשַׁב, so "you will stay" or "remain." The word אֵצֶל means "beside." The next word is of course אֶבֶן, the common word for "stone, rock." It is the last word הָאָזֶל which poses the difficulty. KBH have for this word: אָזֶל* :הָאֶבֶן הָאָזֶל IS 20₁₉ rd הַלָּז(א), see אַרְגָּב.† (The symbol † means that the word occurs only here.) At אַרְגָּב we have only this entry: אַרְגָּב: n. terr. Nothing in the latter entry clarifies the meaning of our text. Puzzling. If, however, we look for לָאז in KBH we find: cj. לָאז: IS 20₁₉ cj. הַלָּאז (for הָאָזֶל) = הַלָּז: **yonder, that**.† The word הַלָּז "**this**" occurs at 1 Sam 14:1 in מֵעֵבֶר הַלָּז "over there": see KBH at הַלָּז.

R. Kittel, editor of the Hebrew text here in BH³/⁷, has the following note on the words הָאֶבֶן הָאָזֶל: 1 [i.e. lege(ndum)] הָאַרְגָּב הַלָּאז (𝔊ᴮ εργαβ [Σ Θ λίθον 𝔊ᴸ λίθῳ] ἐκεῖνο). Kittel's note with its citation of the Greek serves to clarify what we find in KBH. The Hebrew text underlying the Greek had not הָאֶבֶן but הָאַרְגָּב; the word הָאָזֶל requires only slight emendation—transposition of the ל— to produce הַלָּאז, from which the word ἐκεῖνο could have come.

The entire last phrase appears in the Old Greek, reproduced in B-M-Thack according to MS B, as καὶ καθήσῃ παρὰ τὸ ἐργὰβ ἐκεῖνο "and you will stay near that *ergab*." That is, the Old Greek transliterated the rare Hebrew word.

B-M-Thackeray's second apparatus presents the translations of Aquila, Symmachus and Theodotion where the words τὸ ἐργὰβ ἐκεῖνο stand in the Old Greek tradition: α′ τῷ λιθῷ ἐκείνῳ, in the margin of MS a (Rahlfs 707); for ἐργάβ: σ′ θ′ λίθον, in the margin of MS j (Rahlfs 243). A glance at B-M-Thackeray's first apparatus reveals that the translation τῷ λίθῳ ἐκείνῳ has entered the textual tradition represented by MSS biᵐᵍo zᵐᵍc₂e₂ (Rahlfs 19-108 56ᵐᵍ 82 554ᵐᵍ 127 93). The question can be raised, of course, whether the Hebrew text from which these later translators worked was not like MT, i.e. read הָאֶבֶן. Perhaps it even read הָאֶבֶן הַלָּאז.

The Armenian text follows a Greek text which had the transliteration: և

Նստցիս առ երգաբաւդ այդորիկ—"and you will sit down beside that *ergab* ." The transliteration երգաբ appears here with the instrumental ending -աւ and the "farther" demonstrative suffix -դ.

The marginal reading in MS M345 is քարիւ "stone," i.e. the word քար with an instrumental ending. Johnson reads two letters before this: he transcribes աս(?). As it turns out the same marginal reading is found in MS M345, which Zanolli transcribes as աս քարիւ. The word աս must be an abbreviation of այս "this."

Unlike Greek—and English—Armenian has three demonstratives, sort of "this," "that," and "that over there." Zohrapian's Armenian text has the middle demonstrative, identifiable by the -դ- in այդորիկ as opposed to -ս- "this" or -ն- "that over there." Perhaps the translator of the marginal reading from Greek took ἐκείνῳ "that" in the sense of "this (stone) over there." I point this out because the use of այս doe not necessarily mean that it represents τούτῳ or τοῦτον "this." (The word այս is undeclined because it stands before the word with which it is used.)

At any rate we can determine that the Armenian քարիւ corresponds to the Greek λίθῳ or λίθον. It would appear then that we have here an unsigned reading from Aquila, Symmachus or Theodotion. Note that neither H-R nor Reider-Turner list this text under λίθος for Aquila. H-R do list this text under λίθος: they cite λίθος as the translation of both Symmachus and Theodotion, on the basis of Field. However, the Armenian marginal reading consists of noun and demonstrative pronoun. That better suits the reading attributed to Aquila in MS a (Rahlfs 707), namely τῷ λίθῳ ἐκείνῳ. That same reading appears in the margins of MSS iz (Rahlfs 56 554). (It should be pointed out that the readings παρὰ τὸν λίθον ἐκείνο and παρά τῷ λίθῳ ἐκείνῳ could easily have been corrupted, from one to the other.)

The Hebrew, Greek and Armenian equivalents are:

MT: [הָאֶבֶן הַלָּאז?] הָאֶבֶן הָאָזֶל

→ Aq τῷ λίθῳ ἐκείνῳ → sine nom աս քարիւ

conj. הָאֶרְגָּב הַלָּאז → Old Greek τὸ ἐργὰβ ἐκεῖνο → Zohrapian երգա-բաւդ այդորիկ.

In this instance the Armenian preserves a reading known previously from Greek witnesses. The Armenian evidence can be added to the second apparatus in

B-M-Thack in the following way:

το εργαβ εκεινο] α΄ τω λιθω εκεινω a Arm(sine nom) Ι εργαβ] σ΄ θ΄ λιθον j.

Finally it is worth noting that M345 and V212 share the unusual word ши. One wonders whether it might be possible to produce a genealogy for the Armenian marginal readings. At any rate, in this case we can say that the hexaplaric marginalia of these two witnesses are related.

21;4 [MT 21:5] *

հաg պիηծ] արծաԿ

V212ᵐᵍ

Cited on the basis of Zanolli 1223–1224.

In the context David escapes to Nob where he asks the priest Ahimelech what he has at hand [to eat]; David asks for five loaves of bread. The priest responds: "I have no ordinary bread at hand, only holy bread." The words "ordinary bread" are a translation of לֶחֶם חֹל.

The word חֹל means "**profane,** approachable & usable w/o ceremony," as opposed to holy.

The Old Greek renders לֶחֶם חֹל with ἄρτοι βέβηλοι, "common loaves of bread." Here βέβηλος means "profane," not holy.

The Armenian translation reads here հաg պիη ծ "profane," that is "ordinary bread." In the margin MS V280 has արծաԿ "free, untied," i.e without restriction. The reading is unsigned.

B-M-Thack in their second apparatus cite the following marginal readings for βέβηλοι: σ΄ θ΄ λαϊκοῖ (-κός j) b jm (Rahlfs 108 243 92): α΄ οὐχὶ βέβηλον ἀλλὰ λαϊκὸν εἶπε l (Rahlfs 370). The adjective λαϊκός means "common," as opposed to consecrated. It is this word which is being rendered by արծաԿ. Zanolli says that, though MS j attributes the word to Sym Th, it certainly belongs to Aquila according to Origen. He cites the reference in Origen's work only by the abbreviation "T. II, 480."[1] The citation in Reider-Turner reads: λαϊκός בֹֿל gen. Regn. I xxi 4 (5) α' σ' θ' FIELD.

The Armenian word ωρδωկ is singular in number but since its referrent in the text—i.e. hωg, the translation for ἄρτοι— is singular it could be a translation of the plural λαϊκοῖ or the singular λαϊκός/λαϊκόν.

The marginal reading in Greek MS 1 (Rahlfs 370) has changed the number of βέβηλοι to the singular so it seems quite likely that this MS does not preserve the correct number for λαϊκός either. Aquila, Symmachus and Theodotion likely all read the plural.

It seems clear enough that ωρδωկ derives from "the Three." The Hebrew, Greek and Armenian equivalents are:

בֹֿל → Old Greek βέβηλοι → Zohrapian ιկηης δ
→ Aq (vid) Sym Th λαϊκοί → sine nom ωρδωκ.

The textual evidence offered in B-M-Thack can be altered to read:

βεβηλοι] σ' θ' λαικοι (-κος j) b jm Arm(sine nom) : α' ουχι βεβηλον αλλα λαικον ειπε l.

This citation of the Armenian evidence does not reflect the fact that the Greek underlying it could either be singular or plural in number.

22:9 *

ωυηηի] ъηηνῦωյъgի Aq

M179mg M353mg(vid) Zohapp(mg) B-M-Thackapp1

Cited on the basis of Johnson, "Armenian Marginalia," 19. Johnson notes that MS M180 has an index sign in the text but no marginal reading.

---

[1]This is taken from Field ad loc where the reference is "Opp. T. II, p. 480." It refers to Mont-faucon's *Origenis Selecta in lib. I Regum* : see Field 485. According to Field's note at 21:4, Montfaucon found a signed note in Codex Regius 2433 (Rahlfs 554) in which λαϊκός is plural— hence λαϊκοί—and attributed to Aquila. B-M-Thackeray cite marginal readings from their z (Rahlfs 554) but do not offer one here so perhaps the reference in Montfaucon (and then Field) is incorrect. Montfaucon's citation from Origen in Opp. T. II, p. 480 reads: Βεβήλους οὐ τοὺς ἀκαθάρτους λέγει, ἀλλὰ τοὺς οὐχ ἁγίους, καὶ ὡς 'Ακύλας ἐξέδωκε, λαϊκούς ... In this instance too the word attributed to Aquila is in the plural.

The context concerns David's flight from Saul. He found help with the priest Ahimelech at Nob. In v 9 we are told that "Doeg the Edomite" reported this fact to Saul. The Hebrew underlying "Doeg the Edomite" is הָאֲדֹמִי דֹּאֵג. A note on v 9 in BH³/⁷ refers us to 21:8 where the "Doeg the Edomite" is also found. There, in turn, a note in the apparatus reads: 𝔊^BA Σύρος (= הארמי). That is, at 21:8 the Greek translation—or rather transliteration—can be explained by the translator's having read a ר instead of a ד. Or perhaps his Hebrew text had a ר.

At 22:9 the Greek reads Δωὴκ ὁ Σύρος "Doeg the Syrian." The explanation for this translation is the same as that for its rendering at 21:8, just referred to. B-M-Thack note in their apparatus: ο συρος] pr o ιδουμαιος g (Rahlfs 158); ο ιδουμαιος boc₂e₂ (Rahlfs 19-108 82 127 93) Arm(mg) Co. This means that ὁ Ἰδουμαῖος "the Edomite" appears instead of ὁ Σύρος in the so-called Lucianic MSS boc₂e₂ and that in MS g there is a doublet, i.e. ὁ Ἰδουμαῖος ὁ Σύρος. The reading ὁ Ἰδουμαῖος represents secondary contact with the Hebrew, likely by way of "the Three." However, B-M-Thack cite no evidence from "the Three" for ὁ Ἰδουμαῖος.

B-M-Thack do cite evidence from "the Three" at 21:7 (MT 21:8): συρος] λ̷ ιδουμαιος jm (Rahlfs 243 92). That is, in the margin of MSS jm we find "the Edomite" and this reading is signed λ with an *omicron* under it, i.e. "the Three." Presumably the same translation stood in Aquila, Symmachus and Theodotion at 22:9.

Zohrapian's text represents a translation based on the Old Greek: Դովեկ ասորի "Doeg the Syrian." In his apparatus he notes that there is a marginal reading in his MS, namely Դովեկ եդովմայեցի "Doeg the Edomite." This marginal reading in Armenian witnesses at 22:9—found in the text of Lucianic Greek MSS— is derived from Aquila, Symmachus and Theodotion.

The Hebrew, Greek and Armenian equivalents are:

הָאֲדֹמִי ≠ Old Greek ὁ Σύρος → Zohrapian ասորի

→ Aq ὁ Ἰδουμαῖος ← Aq եդովմայեցի.

The Armenian evidence should be cited in B-M-Thackeray's second apparatus as follows:

συρος] α' ιδουμαιος Arm.

According to B-M-Thack, the Armenian tradition is unique in preserving the reading as a marginal reading. (A larger collation of Greek MSS might well find some MSS with the translation preserved there too as a marginal reading.) It is preserved in some Greek witnesses where it has been taken into the text itself.

22:18 *

երեքհարիւր] ութսուն

M180^mg Oskan^1666mg Oskan^1733mg

Cited on the basis of Johnson, "Armenian Marginalia," 19. M180 was Oskan's base MS so the three witnesses cited here are in fact a single witness, though an important one for marginal readings from "the Three."

The context is Saul's revenge upon the priests at Nob for helping David. In v 18 we are told that Doeg killed "eighty-five" that day "who wore the linen ephod." The Hebrew for "eighty-five" is שְׁמֹנִים וַחֲמִשָּׁה.

The Old Greek reads here τριακοσίους καὶ πέντε "three hundred and five." (The Hebrew for "three hundred" is שְׁלֹשׁ מֵאוֹת.)

The Armenian version follows the Old Greek and reads երեքհարիւր և հինգ "three hundred and five."

B-M-Thack note in their second apparatus that Greek MS j (Rahlfs 243) has a marginal reading: τριακοσιους] ⅄ ογδοηκοντα j. That is, MS j preserves a reading ὀγδοήκοντα "eighty" and it is signed ⅄ = οἱ λοιποί "the rest," i.e. Aq Sym Th. (See Fernández Marcos, "La sigla lamda omicron" on the ligature ⅄ and/or the note at 1 Rgn 10:14 above.) This is the reading preserved sine nom in the margin of Armenian MS M180.

The Hebrew, Greek and Armenian equivalents are:
שְׁמֹנִים ≠ Old Greek τριακοσίους → Zohrapian երեքհարիւր
→ ⅄ ὀγδοήκοντα → sine nom ութսուն.

The unsigned Armenian marginal reading preserves a translation of "the Three" previously known from a Greek source.

The second apparatus of B-M-Thack should be changed as follows:
τριακοσιους] ⅄ (> Arm) ογδοηκοντα j Arm.

23:7 *

վ ա ծ ա ր ե ա ց] մ ա տ ն ե ա ց

M179mg M345mg M353mg Zohapp(mg) B-M-Thackapp1

Cited on the basis of Johnson, "Armenian Marginalia," 19.

In the context, David relieves the town of Keilah from attack by the Philistines. He then takes refuge there. When Saul finds out he says, "God has given him into my hand." There is a note on "has given" in the NRSV: Gk Tg: Heb *made a stranger of* .

The word meaning "made a stranger of" is נִכַּר, *piel* perfect 3 sg. of נכר. KBH list this passage under *piel* 2. **disfigure, deface** (a place) Je 19₄ ; w. *b^eyad* **deliver over** IS 23₇. On the other hand, BDB cite this passage under † [נכר] vb. denom. **act** or **treat as foreign,** or **strange; disguise, misconstrue**; ... **Pi. Pf.** IS 23⁷, but v. infr.; ... — IS 23⁷ *God hath alienated him into my hand*, but improbable; ⅗ מָכַר (cf. Ju 4⁹) *hath sold him* , so Th[= O. Thenius] Klo[= A. Klostermann] HPS [= H. P. Smith] (cf. We [= J. Wellhausen]). The marginal note in the NRSV can be understood from this entry in BDB.

Kittel's note in BH³/⁷ suggests reading מכר on the basis of the Old Greek and the Targum.

The Old Greek renders the phrase in question Πέπρακεν αὐτὸν ὁ θεὸς εἰς χεῖράς μου "God has sold him into my hand," which rests upon understanding the Hebrew verb as מָכַר which means "sell" but also "hand over, give up, surrender." The NRSV is based upon such an understanding of the text.

B-M-Thack cite here Symmachus' translation of the word in question as ἐξέδωκεν "surrendered" on the basis of signed marginal readings in Greek MSS *b* jmz (Rahlfs 108 243 92 554).

The Armenian translation follows the Old Greek. It translates the clause in question as վածարեաց զնա առաւած ի ձեռս իմ "God sold him into my hand." The marginal reading in the Armenian MSS is մատնեաց "delivered up" or "surrendered," i.e. it reflects ἐξέδωκεν. Johnson notes that the marginal reading corresponds also to the Vulgate's *tradidit* but states that the Armenian reading goes back rather to Symmachus. I concur.

The Hebrew, Greek and Armenian equivalents are:

נָכַר ≠ Old Green πέπρακεν → Zohrapian վածարեաց

→ Sym ἐξέδωκεν → sine nom մատնեաց.

B-M-Thack cite the Armenian reading in their first apparatus, in Latin: *tradidit* Arm(mg). It should be placed in the second apparatus as follows:

πεπρακεν] σ´ εξεδωκεν *b* jmz Arm(sine nom).

23:15 *

նորում] յանտառին

M345mg(vid: ind mend supra յանապատին) V212mg(ind mend supra յանապա-տին) Zohapp(mg vid)(ind mend supra յանապատին)

M345 is cited on the basis of Johnson, "Armenian Marginalia," 19. V212 is cited on the basis of Zanolli 1224. Johnson cites the evidence as follows:

յանապատին] յանտառին Zohrab ի լուս. (?) A345 [i.e. M345] (mg. vid; the variant here refers to the following լեռինն).

Johnson places a question mark following the reference to Zohrapian because Zohrapian failed to indicate that յանտառին is a marginal reading in his base MS. Presumably this is just an oversight.

An examination of the evidence indicates that the Armenian witnesses have the index sign misplaced in the text.

In v 15 we are told that "David was in the Wilderness of Ziph at Horesh when he learned that Saul had come out to seek his life." The words in question are "in the Wilderness, " a translation of (בְּמִדְבַּר־)זִיף.

The entire noun clause is וְדָוִד בְּמִדְבַּר־זִיף בַּחֹרְשָׁה "and David was in the Wilderness of Ziph in Horesh." The Greek translation of this according to the text of B-M-Thack is καὶ Δαυεὶδ ἐν τῷ ὄρει τῷ αὐχμώδει ἐν τῇ καινῇ Ζείφ "and David was in the dry hill country in the new Ziph." There is a widely attested form of the text which reads καὶ Δαυεὶδ ἐν τῇ ἐρήμῳ τῇ αὐχμώδει ἐν τῇ

καινῇ Ζείφ "and David was in the dry desert in the new Ziph." It is this latter text
type that is represented in the Armenian translation.

The Armenian translation of this part of v 15 according to Zohrapian is եւ
դաւիթ նստէր յանապատին ի մւայլ լերինն գիփայի նորում "and David was in the desert in the dark (woody?) hill-country at new Ziph."
Indeed one sees here that the Armenian has a doublet: it attests both ἐν τῇ ἐρήμῳ
"in the desert" and ἐν τῷ ὄρει "in the hill-country." The underlying Greek text
looks like this: καὶ Δαυεὶδ ἐν τῇ ἐρήμῳ ἐν τῷ ὄρει αὐχμώδει ἐν τῇ καινῇ
Ζείφ.

Zohrapian notes that there is a reading յանտառին "in the forest" rather
than յանապատին "in the desert": his note in the apparatus reads (15) եւ
դաւիթ նստէր յանտառին ի մառայլ [sic] լե": That is, he assumes—
presumably following the index signs in his MS—that the word յանտառին is
intended for յանապատին. In fact, this is incorrect.

B-M-Thack cite readings from "the Three" for ἐν τῇ καινῇ] α' ἐν τῇ ὕλῃ
b (sine nom) jm (Rahlfs 108 243 92) | καινῇ] σ' θ' δρυμῷ b (sine nom) j(om θ') m.
The former means "in the forest"; the latter means "[in the] thicket" or, on the basis
of its usage in the LXX/Old Greek corpus, virtually the same as ὕλη, i.e. "forest."
These translators have understood בַּחֹרְשָׁ֫ה to consist of the preposition בְּ plus not
a proper name but חֹרֶשׁ "wood(land)". The entry on (הַ)חֹרְשָׁה in KBH says: n.
loc., = חֹרֶשׁ, frozen loc[ative]. (The Old Greek translator took the word בַּחֹרְשָׁה
as בַּחֹדְשָׁה, i.e. reading the ר as ד and therefore "in the new.")

The word חֹרֶשׁ only occurs twice for certain in the Hebrew Bible. At 2 Chr
27:4 it is rendered by δρυμός, which in Armenian becomes անտառ; at Ezek 31:3
וְחֹרֶשׁ מֵצַל "and forest shade" is not represented in the Old Greek but appears
under the asterisk in the Hexapla as καὶ πυκνός ἐν τῇ σκέπη "and thick (or close)
in its covering." (The hexaplaric text is cited here from the apparatus of Rahlfs'
provisional edition.)

Is it possible to determine whether the Armenian marginal reading reflects
the translation ὕλη (Aq) rather than δρυμῷ (Sym Th)? I do not think so for certain
but it seems to me that the chances are better than even that the Greek underlying
յանտառին is (ἐν τῷ) δρύμῳ.

Arapkertsʻi lists 96 occurrences of the word անտառ in his concordance.

(There are two occurrences at Jos 17:18.) In 51 of these cases անտառ is a translation of δρυμός; in 41 cases it is a translation of ἄλσος "sacred grove," in a negative sense (the two exceptions to this negative sense of the word: 2 Rgn 5:24; Judith 3:11[3:8]); once it is used to translate νάπη "woodland vale, glen" (Num 24:6); once it is used for ῥάδαμνος "bough, branch" (Job 40:17); once it translates ἀγρός "field" (Isa 55:12); once (!) it is used to translate ὕλη (James 3:5). (Recall that Arapkerts'i is not a complete concordance.)

If we look at δρυμός in H-R we find that this word has almost always been rendered by անտառ. First, we can add four occurrences to the equation δρυμός —անտառ drawn on the basis of Arapkerts'i, namely Isa 32:15, 19; Jer 46(26):23; 50(27):32. In only a handful of cases is δρυμός rendered in Armenian by a word other than անտառ: in 55 cases δρυμός is translated by անտառ; in six instances it is rendered by մայրի "wood, forest" (Deut 19:5; Ps 131[132]:6; Eccl 2:6; Mic 3:12; Isa 27:9[Arm 10]; Jer 33[26]:18; in two of the passages, namely those in Mic and Jer ἄλσος δρυμοῦ is rendered by անտառ մայրւոյ); once it is represented by անապատ "desert" (Jer 12:8).

H-R list nine occurrences for the word ὕλη. From that list Ps 68(69):2 (Rahlfs 3) can be removed, since the Armenian follows the reading ἰλύν "dregs; impurity." In two passages the Armenian translation is very free: at Sir 28:10 (Zohrapian 14) κατὰ τὴν ὕλην τοῦ πυρὸς οὕτως ἐκκαυθήσεται "In proportion to the fuel, so will the fire burn" is rendered ԵթԷ փչես ի կայծակն` բորբոքի նա "If you blow upon the embers, it [the fire] will burn"; at 2 Macc 2:24 (Zohrapian 26) διὰ τὸ πλῆθος τῆς ὕλης "because of the mass of material" is translated վասն թանձրութեան հիւթոյ խորութեան բանիցդ "because of the profound depth of those things." In the latter case ὕλη seems to be rendered by բան "thing; matter." At 4 Macc 1:29 ὕλη occurs in the phrase "the jungle of habits and emotions." Ajamian lists no Armenian biblical MSS that contain 4 Macc.

That leaves five passages where ὕλη is used in the LXX/Old Greek corpus: Job 19:29; 38:40; Wisdom 11:17 (Zohrapian 18); 15:13 (14); Isa 10:17. At Job 19:29; Wisdom 11:17; 15:13 ὕλη is translated by նիւթ "matter, substance" because in these passages ὕλη means "the stuff of which something is made." At Job 38:40 ὕλη is rendered by մայրի "wood, forest"; at Isa 10:17 it is translated by the word անտառ. That is, the word ὕλη occurs only four times in the Old Greek with the meaning "forest" or "wood" and in one instance—not counting 4 Macc 1:29—it is rendered by անտառ.

H-R indicate that ὕλη is used only by Aquila among "the Three" and by Aquila only at 3 Rgn 23:15, 16, 19.

As noted above, the word ὕλη occurs once in the NT, at James 3:5, and is there rendered by անտառ.

All that one can conclude from this examination of the use of δρυμός, ὕλη and անտառ is that δρυμός occurs frequently in the LXX/Old Greek collection and is commonly rendered by անտառ and that ὕλη appears rarely with the meaning "forest" but can also be translated անտառ.

The Armenian marginal reading appears in the Gen.-Dat.-Loc. case with the preposition ի and the definite marker -ն, hence յանտառին, and that might be an indication that it represents ἐν τῇ ὕλη since, according to B-M-Thack, the word δρυμῷ, at least in their sources, does not appear with the preposition and article. On the other hand, a translator might well have added the preposition on the basis of the ἐν which stands in the Greek text.

In this connection one might raise the question about the stage at which the word յանտառին became a marginal reading not for նորում but for յանապատին. The Greek phrase ἐν τῷ καινῇ Ζείφ was translated զիփայի նորում and the index should have been placed on նորում. The syntax of this translation is such that յանտառին with its preposition does not easily replace նորում. It seemed much more likely that յանտառին "in the forest" was intended as a marginal reading for յանապատին "in the desert." The index sign was likely put in the wrong place when the marginal reading was added to the Armenian tradition, not subsequently.

In conclusion, the marginal reading in the Armenian witnesses derives from "the Three" but it seems to me impossible to determine for certain whether it has come from ἐν τῇ ὕλη or [ἐν τῷ] δρυμῷ. I think the likelihood that it came from the latter a little stronger than that it came from the former.

The Hebrew, Greek and Armenian equivalents are:

בַּחֹרְשָׁה ≠ Old Greek ἐν τῇ καινῇ → Zohrapian նորում

→ Aq ἐν τῇ ὕλη

→ Sym Th [ἐν τῷ] δρυμῷ

→ sine nom յանտարին

In this case the Armenian witness confirms the translations previously known from Greek sources. In the latter it is signed; in the Armenian translation the reading is not signed.

The apparatus in B-M-Thack should now read:

εν τη καινη] α′ εν τη υλη *b* (sine nom) jm : *in silvam* Arm(sine nom) |
καινη] σ′ θ′ δρυμω *b* (sine nom) j(om θ′) m.

It should be noted here that, among these witnesses at least, the signature of Theodotion is preserved only in MS m.

27:7

չորից] երկուց

V212mg Zohapp(mg)

V212 is cited on the basis of Zanolli 1224.

Here we are informed that David lived amongst the Philistines for יָמִים וְאַרְבָּעָה חֳדָשִׁים "one year and four months."

In the Old Greek the stay is shorter: τέσσαρας μῆνας "four months." The hexaplaric witnesses MS A and Arm represent יָמִים taken literally as "days" and hence attest ἡμέρας τέσσαρες μῆνας "some days, namely four months." B-M-Thack note that in MS j (Rahlfs 243) ἡμέρας καί "days and" stands under the asterisk, i.e. it is a hexaplaric plus. The καί may or may not have been present in the parent text of the Armenian translation.

The Armenian text is hexaplaric and it states that David's stay was աւուրք չորիս ամաց "some days, four months." The marginal reading երկուց changes the length of David's stay to two months. The Greek underlying երկուց is δύο and the Hebrew underlying δύο—were it to go back to a Hebrew text—is שְׁנַיִם (חֳדָשִׁים) "two (months)."

The source of this marginal reading is unknown. It is contrary to the Hebrew text as we know it and lacking in attestation elsewhere. Nevertheless the reading is of interest and might be cited in a critical edition of the Greek text. If so, the citation is, according to the apparatus in B-M-Thackeray:

  τεσσαρας] *duo* Arm(sine nom).

30:8 *

գեդդուրայն] հինին Aq

J428^{mg} M179^{mg} M180^{mg} M345^{mg(mg vid)} M353^{mg} SABE1011^{mg} V212^{mg}
V1507^{mg} Zoh^{app(mg)(sine nom)}

  Manuscripts M179 M180 M345 M353 are cited on the basis of Johnson,
"Armenian Marginalia," 19; V212 is cited on the basis of Zanolli. This is the only
marginal reading from "the Three" in J428 for 1 Rgn.

  In this passage David returns to Ziglag and finds that it has been burned
down by the Amalekites. They have taken prisoners, including his wives. In v 8 he
inquires of the Lord, "Shall I pursue this band (דוּדְגּ)?" In Greek MS B דוּדְגּ is
represented by the transliteration γεδδούρ "Geddur" (reading the final ד as ר). This
transliteration—which, of course, makes no sense—is what appears in the Armenian "translation" գեդդուր.

  The word דוּדְגּ means "marauding band."

  հէն, հինից means "robber, marauder, rover, brigand."

  The second apparatus in B-M-Thack offers us the translations of Aq Sym
Th for γεδδούρ: α′ μονοζώνου "light-armed" az (Rahlfs 707 554); α′ εὐζώνου
"well-equipped" j (Rahlfs 243) Syh ap-Barh[sic]; σ′ λόχου "armed band" j; σ′
ܡܘܢܠܐܪܟ, i.e. ܡܘܢܠܐܪܟ "multitude, crowd, mob" Syh-ap-Barh; θ′ συστρέμ-
ματος "body of men, possibly armed" jz(sine nom).

  How can one determine which of these Greek words հինին represents?
At Gen 49:19(Arm 18) the Armenian has հինի (LXX: πειρατήριον "gang of brig-
ands"); Aquila has εὔζωνος and Symmachus has λόχος. At Job 19:12 Arm has
հէնք (Old Greek: τὰ πειρατήρια); Symmachus: λόχοι; MSS C′ attest μονόζωνοι
for Th—but Syh attests πειραταί for both Aq and Th.

  According to Reider-Turner, Aquila uses εὔζωνος or μονόζωνος to translate דוּדְגּ: the former at Gen 49:19; 1 Rgn 30:8, 15; 2 Rgn 3:22; 4:2; 4 Rgn 6:23;

Ps 17(18):30; Hos 6:9; 7:1; Jer 18:22; the latter at 2 Rgn 3:22. Reider-Turner follow Greek MS j and Syh-ap-Barh at 1 Rgn 30:8. That equation דוזג — εὔξωνος would appear to be confirmed by the evidence at Gen 49:19 and Job 19:12 where the Armenian has հիւի and հէ՛նք, respectively, i.e. հէ՛ն.

The equivalences at 1 Rgn 30:8 are:

דוזג → Old Greek γεδδούρ → Zohrapian զնդդունպայն

     → Aq εὐζώνου → Aq հիւին

The Armenian marginal reading confirms what was already known from Greek sources.

Arm can now be cited with Greek MS j and Syh-ap-Barh:

γεδδουρ] α' ευζωνου j Syh-ap-Barh Arm.

v. 2 Reigns

H.S. Anasean, "Une leçon symmachienne [à 3:33] dans les manuscrits arméniens de la Bible (pour l'histoire du texte des Hexaples d' Origène)," *REArm* N.S. 17 (1983) 201–205. • N. Fernández Marcos and José Ramón Busto Saiz; with the help of María V. Spottorno, Díaz Caro and S. Peter Cowe. *El Texto Antioqueno de la Biblia Griega I: 1-2 Samuel*. Textos y Estudios «Cardenal Cisneros» de la Biblia Políglota Matritense 50; Madrid: Instituto de Filología 1989. "La versión armenia," by Cowe, pp. LXXI–LXXIX. • Hovhannu Oskeberani (i.e. John Chrysostom), *Meknut'iwn Esayeay Margarēi* [Commentary on Isaiah the Prophet] (*Matenagrut'iwnk' Nakhneats'—Oskeberan* ; Venice: St. Lazar 1880). • A. Salvesen, *Symmachus in the Pentateuch* (JSSM 15; Manchester: University of Manchester 1991).

2 Rgn 1:1–9:13 forms section ββ in Thackeray/Shenkel's division of the text of Samuel-Kings; 2 Rgn 10:1–3 Rgn 2:11 forms section βγ. Manuscript Vaticanus—the MS published as text in Brooke-McLean-Thackeray—represents the Old Greek in the former but in the latter it represents a recensional text, the so-called *kaige* text. In section βγ the Old Greek text is represented in MSS boc₂e₂ (Rahlfs 19-108 82 127 93), though the former should not be simply equated with the type of text in these MSS. This complicated situation is discussed in the introduction to 1 Reigns. A bibliography is provided there for the books of 1–4 Reigns.

For the sake of clarity, Codex Vaticanus—MS B—is taken as the point of reference for the Old Greek textual tradition. Up to 10:1 we can speak of MS B as a representative of the Old Greek, but for the following section—2 Rgn 10:1–3 Rgn 2:11—we can do that only when MSS boc₂e₂ and MS B share the same text. Where these textual traditions diverge and the Armenian follows the type of text represent-

ed by MS B—which is generally the case—I cite MS B by itself and do not typify it
as Old Greek.

2:13 *

ի վերայ աղբերն] առ շրբղխին

J428mg(շրբղխին et ind supra աղբերն) V212mg Zohapp(mg)

V212 is cited on the basis of Zanolli 1224.

The context concerns a meeting of the forces of Saul's son Ishbaal and
those of David. In v 13 we read that Joab and the servants of David met the other
side "at the pool of Gibeon." The words within quotation marks are a translation of
עַל־בְּרֵכַת גִּבְעוֹן. As the translation indicates, the word בְּרֵכָה means "pond,
pool."

The Old Greek translated עַל־בְּרֵכַת גִּבְעוֹן with the words ἐπὶ τὴν κρήνην τὴν ἐν Γαβαών "at the well [or spring, fountain] in Gibeon." This is the text
printed in B-M-Thack.

The Armenian translation is ի վերայ աղբերն "above the spring [or
fountain]." Here the preposition ի վերայ translates ἐπί quite literally. Zohrapian
notes in his apparatus that some witnesses attest the preposition առ "beside" rather
than ի վերայ.

Some Armenian witnesses have a marginal reading for the phrase in question. It is առ շրբղխին "beside the fountain [or basin]" which clarifies the literalism of the text.

The Armenian marginal reading is a translation of the translation attributed
to Aq Th in Greek MS j (Rahlfs 243), namely κολυμβήθρας "place for diving,
swimming-bath." The word can also mean "reservoir, cistern" as at 4 Rgn 18:17,
so presumably it could also be translated into English as "pool." B-M-Thack do not
indicate that a preposition is present with the marginal reading κολυμβήθρας in MS
j.[1] Presumably the preposition is still ἐπί, now followed however by the genitive

---

[1]Field cites the reading of 243 (Rahlfs 243) as 'A. Θ. κολυμβήθραν on the basis of Parson's collation (*"teste Parsonsii amanuensi"*). Presumably the citation in B-M-Thack rests on a new collation of MS 243 so we may accept the reading in the genitive case as correct. In the same note Field

case. (Cf. 4:12 where the Old Greek reads ἐπὶ τῆς κρήνης ἐν Χεβρών "at the pool in Hebron," that is the genitive case is employed for κρήνη after ἐπί. In this instance the Armenian preposition for ἐπί is again ի վերայ.)

The Armenian preserves an unsigned reading of Aquila and Theodotion.

The Hebrew, Greek and Armenian equivalents are:

עַל־בְּרֵכַת (גִּבְעוֹן) → Old Greek ἐπὶ τὴν κρήνην → Zohrapian ի

վերայ աղբերն

→ Aq Th [ἐπὶ τῆς] κολυμβήθρας → sine nom առ շրջիկին.

Interestingly the Armenian reading preserves a preposition with the Aquila Theodotion translation. That the marginal reading uses the preposition առ does not mean that a different preposition lies in its parent text than that underlying ի վերայ. The translator of the marginal reading may well have thought that առ was simply a better, less literal rendering.

The second apparatus in B-M-Thack can be revised as follows:

επι την κρηνην 1°] επι (vid) της κολυμβηθρας Arm(sine nom) |κρηνην 1°] α′ θ′ κολυμβηθρας j.

2:29 1°

ընդ արեւելս] ընդ (> J428) արեւմունս

J428mg M188mg

These MSS have this marginal reading and that of the next item together, i.e. ընդ (> J428) արեւմունս յանապատ օգեալ ի գետովն "westwards in the plain which extends by(?) the river" with a single index sign in the text at ընդ արեւելս "eastwards."

Two marginal readings seem to have merged, both of them intended for the same item in the text. This first marginal reading corrects the Armenian to the rest of

---

records that, according to Montfaucon's editing of Codex Reguis 2433 (B-M-Thack j; Rahlfs 554) the translation of Aquila and Theodotion is ἐπὶ τῆς κολυμβήθρας. However, a comparison with the second apparatus in B-M-Thack reveals that this marginal reading in MS 554 belongs to κρήνην 3°!! The phrase ἐπὶ τὴν κρήνην occurs no less than three times in v 13 in the text printed in B-M-Thack. The Armenian marginal reading relates to ἐπὶ τὴν κρήνην 1°.

the Old Greek tradition—and to the Hebrew. That ընդ արեւմուտս յանապատ ծգեալ ի գետովք is indeed two readings seems clear from the fact that the witnesses which Zohrapian cites in his apparatus do not know ընդ արեւմուտս as a marginal reading.

This item might now be cited in the first apparatus of B-M-Thack in the following way:

εις δυσμας] *ad orientem* Arm (sed hab Arm[mss(mg)]).

That MSS J428 M188 share this marginal reading likely says something about the relationship of their marginalia: they share the same tradition.

2:29 2° *

ընդ արեւելս] յանապատան (յանապատ J428 M188) ծգեալ ի գետովք M188[mg(sine ind)] J428[mg(sine ind)] Zoh[app(mss[mg])] et ind supra ընդ ամենայն ծգեալս); անապատան et ind supra ծգեալ ն Zoh[app(mg)] B-M-Thack[app1]

Zohrapian notes in his apparatus that his base MS, V1508, has անապատ ն in the margin with a sign over (ընդ ամենայն) ծգեալ ն in the text; and that where some MSS have ընդ ամենայն ծգեալ ան in the text, in the margin with an index sign we find յանապատան ծգեալ ի գետովք.

The context here is the pursuit of Abner, Saul's military leader, by Joab, his counterpart on David's side. The pursuit ends with words that bring about a disengagement. Then we are told in v 29 that "Abner and his men traveled all that night through the Arabah; they crossed the Jordan, and, marching the whole forenoon, they came to Mahanaim." The words "through the Arabah" are a translation of בָּעֲרָבָה. A note following the word "forenoon" in the NRSV informs us that the meaning of the Hebrew is uncertain.[1] It is כָּל־(הַבִּתְרוֹן)—which is translated here "(the whole) forenoon"—that is uncertain. The index signs in the MSS Zohrapian cites would lead us to believe that the marginal reading relates to כָּל־ הַבִּתְרוֹן.

---

[1]For the translation "forenoon" cf. S.R. Driver, *Notes on the Hebrew Text and Topography of the Books of Samuel* (2nd ed., revised and enlarged; Oxford: Clarendon 1913) 245.

For בְּתְרוֹן, which occurs only here, BDB tell us that it is probably a proper noun referring to a territory, a cleft or ravine, east of the Jordan.

Greek MS B for the phrase that includes בָּעֲרָבָה and כָּל־הַבְּתְרוֹן has καὶ Ἀβεννὴρ καὶ οἱ ἄνδρες αὐτοῦ ἀπῆλθον εἰς δυσμὰς ὅλην τὴν νύκτα ἐκείνην, καὶ διέβαιναν τὸν Ἰορδάνην καὶ ἐπορεύθησαν ὅλην τὴν παρατείνουσαν "and Abner and his men traveled west all that night, and they crossed the Jordan and they traversed the whole expanse."

Aquila transliterates בְּתְרוֹן and gives us βεθωρῶν, according to Greek MS j (Rahlfs 243), as cited in the second apparatus of B-M-Thack. The Latin Vulgate also transliterates: Bethoron.

The Armenian ը”ն, ամ՞ենայ݆ն ծգ՞այ՞ն corresponds to ὅλην τὴν παρατείνουσαν and means the same thing. Where has the marginal reading յա՞նա-պատ՞ն—or, without the definite or demonstrative marker, յա՞նապատ—come from? It means something like εἰς τόν ἔρημον "into the desert," which it represents at Num 23:28.

If we look earlier in v 29, we read that Abner and his men traveled בָּעֲרָבָה "through the Arabah." In the Old Greek, i.e. as preserved in MS B, this becomes εἰς δυσμάς, i.e. "to the west" (!) This is surely very confusing because they had been at Gibeon, west of the Jordan—Gibeon is about 10 km. north of Jerusalem—and were returning home, which lay east of the Jordan.

Aquila and Theodotion translate בָּעֲרָבָה with ἐν ὁμαλῇ "on level ground," according to Greek MSS jz(om θ′) (Rahlfs 243 554). Symmachus translates בָּעֲרָבָה with διὰ τῆς πεδιάδος "through the plain." The Armenian յա՞նապատ՞ն corresponds to Symmachus' translation.[1]

It appears that the index sign—such as it is preserved in MSS which Zohrapian cites—has the wrong word(s) in mind: J1934 which has replaced ծգ՞այ՞ն in the text with ա՞նապատ, placing the former in the margin, is further proof of this.

Zohrapian's text for εἰς δυσμάς has ը”ն, արե՞ել՞ս "to the east" which is correct geographically even if it is not a translation of the Greek.

The word յա՞նապատ՞ն represents Symmachus' translation διὰ τῆς πε-

---

[1]Symmachus has πεδίας for ערבה in various forms elsewhere at 4:7; 15:28; Josh 11:2 (Syh); Jer 39:5; Amos 6:14. He may also have used ἔρημος too, in Jer 39:4, 5; 52:8. See Salvesen 143, n. 3.

διάδος "through the plain." But յաւասպատն is followed by the words ծզեալ ի գետոյ. Together the phrase means "through the plain which stretches out there, because of the river."[1] The word ծզեալ appears in Zohrapian's text—there with the definite marker -ն attached—where it is a translation of the participle τὴν παρατείνουσαν in the clause καὶ ἐπορεύθησαν ὅλην τὴν παρατείνουσαν "and they traversed that whole extended [area]." The underlying Greek for the marginal reading as a whole can probably be recovered, if indeed a Greek parent text underlies the marginal reading as a whole. The Greek may have been διὰ τῆς πεδιάδος τῆς παρατεινούσης [,] ἐπὶ τῷ ποταμῷ. But it seems unlikely that the whole phrase goes back to Symmachus because it does not show contact with the Hebrew. For the moment—or perhaps the century!— it must remain simply intriguing.

Another suggestion is that the Armenian marginal reading is actually two readings: յաւասպատն and ծզեալ ի գետոյ. In this case the word ծզեալ repeats the same word in the text and adds ի գետոյ. If we take it that way then ἐπὶ τῷ ποταμῷ follows καὶ ἐπορεύθησαν ὅλην τὴν παρατείνουσαν: so "and they traversed that whole area, on account of the river." That would make sense.

In summarizing the evidence of this marginal reading, I have divided the reading in two: the first part belongs to Symmachus we know, but the correct placement, meaning and origin of the second part remains an unknown.

The Hebrew, Greek and Armenian equivalents are:

בָּעֲרָבָה → Old Greek εἰς δυσμάς ≠ Zohrapian ընդ արեւելս u

→ Sym διὰ τῆς πεδιάδος → sine nom յաւասպատն.

The second part of the marginal reading can be cited as a plus. In Armenian that citation is: ընդ արեւելս u] + ծզեալ ի գետոյ Arm[mss (mg)].

The marginal reading can be incorporated into B-M-Thackeray's second apparatus in the following way. First, *desertum* Arm(mg) should be removed from the first apparatus: it belongs in the second. The revised second apparatus looks like this:

εις δυσμας] α′ θ′ εν ομαλη jz(om θ′) : σ′ δια της πεδιαδος j Arm(sine

---

[1] The use of the instrumental case with the preposition ի is rare. This example—ի գետոյ —can be added to the two examples offered in the big grammar of A.K. Bagratuni, one of which is repeated by Hans Jensen, *Altarmenische Grammatik* (Indogermanische Bibliothek; Heidelberg: Carl Winter 1959) vol. 1, 132 (§ 351). My translation is probably not the only translation that could be made of this difficult fragment but I have tried to retain the force of the instrumental case which is very unusual and therefore, it could be argued, equally intentional.

nom) : + *extensa ex fluvio* Arm(sine nom).

Further research may provide a clearer picture of how the second part of the marginal reading should be dealt with, i.e. whether or not it relates to τὴν παρατείνουσαν.

3:33 *

եթէ (թէ J1925) րստ մահուանն նաբաղայ (նաբաղա J1925) մեռաւ աբեննէր J1925 Zoh] pr մ՜իթէ որպէս մեռանիցի անզգամ, մեռաւ աբեննէր (աբեննէր V212) J428 M188 V212 Zoh B-M-Thack[appl]; մ՜իթէ որպէս մեռանիցի անզգամ, մեռաւ աբեննէր Sym M177[mg] M178[mg] M345[mg]

M177 M178 M345 are cited on the basis of Anasean; V212 is cited on the basis of Zanolli 1224. I have included the witness of J1925 which has the shorter text and no marginal reading.

This is not a marginal reading but the text in various MSS and in the edition of Zohrapian. Zanolli calls attention to these words and their interest for the textual history of the Armenian translation. It is clear, however, on the basis of the MSS cited by Anasean that we are dealing with a marginal reading that has come into the text of a number of witnesses.

Here David is lamenting the death of Abner. He asks, הַכְּמוֹת נָבָל יָמוּת אַבְנֵר "Should Abner die as a fool dies?"

The Old Greek, as preserved in MS B, translates David's question with the words Εἰ κατὰ τὸν θάνατον Ναβὰλ ἀποθανεῖται ᾿Αβεννήρ; "Should Abner die according to the death of Nabal?"

In the Armenian translation these words are represented by եթէ րստ մահուանն նաբաղայ մեռաւ աբեննէր "Is Abner to die a death like Nabal's?"

B-M-Thack cite a Symmachus reading in the margin of Greek MSS Mj(sine nom) (Rahlfs 243) for the words Εἰ κατὰ τὸν θάνατον Ναβάλ. The reading is μὴ ὡς ἀποθνήσκει ἄφρων "Surely [Abner] will not die as a fool [dies]." The primary difference from the Old Greek translation is the translation of נָבָל (ἄφρων) versus its transliteration (Ναβάλ).

Zanolli is correct in his observation that this Symmachus translation has entered the Armenian text, creating a doublet. The Armenian translation of the Symmachus reading is մխթէ, որպէս մեռանիցի անզգամ "Surely not as a fool dies" to which is added մեռաւ արեննէր "would Abner die?" It is possible that the Symmachus reading from which the Armenian was translated had մեռաւ արեննէր represented; on the other hand, "would Abner die" is required for the Symmachus reading to make a sentence.

What Zanolli does not realize is that the reading in question is not in, for example, J1925 (fol.150v, col.2, †17). It has entered the text from the margin in only some witnesses, including Zohrapian's base MS V1508.

Anasean devoted a brief article to this marginal reading in 1983. Unfortunately he did not consult Field or the edition of B-M-Thack. As a result he treats it as if the Armenian witness is unique, which it is not.

This reading should be cited in the second apparatus in B-M-Thack and removed from the first.

The Hebrew, Greek and Armenian equivalents are:

הַכְּמוֹת נָבָל → Old Greek Εἰ κατὰ θάνατον Ναβάλ → Zohrapian էթէ
            րատ մահուանն նաբաղայ
        → Sym μὴ ὡς ἀποθνήσκει ἄφρων → Sym մխթէ, որպէս
            մեռանիցի անզգամ.

The second apparatus in B-M-Thack should be revised as follows:

ει—ναβαλ] σ′ μη ως αποθνησκει αφρων Mj(sine nom) Arm : + *mortuus est Abenner* Arm.

3:34 *

իբրեւ զնաբաղ առաջի որդւոց (որդւոցն J1925) անիրաւութեան ll անկար J1925 Zoh] + այլ որպէս (> V212) անկանիցին առաջի
    անիրաւաց անկար V212 Zoh B-M-Thack[appl (cum nom)]; այլ որպէս
    անկանիցին առաջի անիրաւաց անկար Sym J428[mg] M188[mg]
    Zoh[app(mss mg)]

V212 is cited on the basis of Zanolli 1224. I have added the witness of J1925, which has the shorter, original text and no marginal reading. The information given above means that the reading in question is a plus in the text of V212 and Zohrapian; it is a signed marginal reading in J428 and M188.

This reading is attested in the margins of other MSS also: J1928 J1934 V1182 V1507. It had a tendency to enter the text as is the case with Zohrapian's base MS V1508 and V212. He has a note about this in his apparatus:

> This section of text այլ որպէս անկանիցին առաջի անիրաւաց անկար is lacking in Oskan [his edition of 1666] in agreement with but one MS, but in the [i.e. our] remaining four MSS in which it is found in the text it is written in the same hand in the margin of two of them signed "Sym," that is "according to Symmachus." But in our [base] MS [i.e. V1508] at this place, beginning at v 33 [init] եւ առ ոդբու until [latter part of v 34] եւ ձողովւացան, the whole verse has been erased and suitably copied again.

What Zohrapian is saying is that in his base MS there has been an erasure, raising the question of what its parent text had. He has followed the MSS which have the marginal reading in the text following the words for which that marginal reading is intended. The result is that Zohrapian, like some MSS, has a doublet in the text.

The context in 2 Samuel concerns the death of Abner, whom Joab, David's military leader, has killed. David laments the murder of Abner. He says of him, "… as one falls before the wicked you have fallen." The Hebrew text is כִּנְפוֹל לִפְנֵי בְנֵי־עַוְלָה נָפָלְתָּ. The critical word here is כִּנְפוֹל.

The Old Greek has taken (כְּ)נְפוֹל as a proper name in consequence of taking נָבָל as a proper name in v 33: thus the translation ὡς Ναβάλ. The translation in v 34—of the whole clause—in Greek MS B is ὡς Ναβάλ, ἐνώπιον υἱῶν ἀδικίας ἔπεσας "(he did not approach) like Nabal, before the unrighteous you fell."

Symmachus understood כִּנְפוֹל as preposition plus infinitive and therefore translated ὥσπερ πίπτουσιν and added the asseverative ἀλλά: ἀλλ᾿ ὥσπερ πίπτουσιν "but as they fell." According to B-M-Thackeray's second apparatus—citing Greek MS j (Rahlfs 243)—Symmachus' equivalent for ὡς Ναβάλ, ἐνώπιον υἱῶν ἀδικίας ἔπεσας is ἀλλ᾿ ὥσπερ πίπτουσιν ἔμπροσθεν ἀδίκων ἔπεσας "but as they fell before the unrighteous, you fell." The marginal reading in the Armenian

MSS is exactly Symmachus: այլ որպէս անկանիցին առաջի անիրաւաց անկար "but as they fell before the unrighteous, you fell."

The equivalences among Hebrew, Greek and Armenian are:

כִּנְפוֹל לִפְנֵי בְנֵי־עַוְלָה נָפָלְתָ → Old Greek ὡς Ναβάλ, ἐνώπιον

υἱῶν ἀδικίας ἔπεσας → Zohrapian իբրեւ զնաբաղ

առաջի որդւոց անիրաւութեան եւ անկար

→ Sym ἀλλ' ὥσπερ πίπτουσιν ἔμπροσθεν ἀδίκων ἔπεσας →

Sym այլ որպէս անկանիցին առաջի անիրաւաց

անկար.

The Armenian reading should be removed from the first apparatus in B-M-Thack and their second apparatus should be altered to include it:

ως—επεσας] σ' αλλ ωσπερ πιπτουσιν εμπροσθεν αδικων επεσας j Arm.

The Armenian MSS preserve a Symmachus reading already known from Greek MS 243.

5:8

ի տունն յեկեղեցի

J428mg M2628mg

M188—which often shares the marginal readings of J428 M2628— does not have this marginal reading.

The context concerns the capture of the "stronghold of Zion." More specifically it concerns a saying that grew out of that victory: "The blind and the lame shall not come into the house (אֶל־הַבָּיִת)."

The Old Greek renders the phrase אֶל־הַבָּיִת "into the house" with the words εἰς οἶκον Κυρίου "into the house of the Lord," making it an explicit reference to the Temple.

Some Greek witnesses, namely MSS dhlp–tz* (Rahlfs 107 55 370 106 120 700 130 134 554*), have instead of οἶκον the word ἐκκλησίαν "assembly." Field includes this reading with the Origenian text: O'. εἰς οἶκον (alia exempl. ἐκκλη-

σίαν) κυρίου. He has a note on the word ἐκκλησίαν in which he states that Montfaucon tacitly edited: Ἄλλος· εἰς ἐκκλησίαν. B-M-Thack do not cite ἐκκλησίαν as
a marginal reading in their second apparatus.

This marginal reading in these Armenian MSS indicates that there has been
secondary contact with Greek texts, that is the marginalia in these excellent sources
of readings from "the Three" includes "non Three" materials. It could be, of course,
that the Greek MSS from which the marginalia were taken already had such marginal readings. One need not think in terms of extensive comparison with Greek MSS.

6:10

գեթացւոյ] ղեւտացւոյ

J428mg J1927mg(sine ind) M188mg Zohapp(mg)

J428 has index signs on գեթացւոյ in both v 10 and v 11. M2628 does
not have this marginal reading now, but it did: it has replaced գեթացւոյ in v 11
with ղեւտացւոյ. M188 has the spellings գեթագnյ and ղեւտագnյ, respectively.

The context concerns David's well-reasoned hesitancy to take the Ark of the
Covenant into his care. Instead he took it "to the house of Obed-edom the Gittite."
The words "the Gittite" are a translation of הַגִּתִּי. This was rendered in the Old
Greek as τοῦ Γεθθαίου, according to MS B. That is, the proper name was translit-
erated.

The Armenian text also has the transliteration: գեթացւոյ.

Some Armenian MSS have the marginal reading ղեւտացւոյ so that
Obed-edom becomes a "Levite!"

We expect Greek *lamed* (λ) to underlie Armenian *ghat* (ղ). B-M-Thack
cite for Γεθθαίου the variant reading χετταίου, which is found in a few Greek
MSS. That spelling likely lies behind the Armenian spelling in the parallel passage in
1 Chron 13:13 where we find քետտացւոյ: Greek *chi* (χ) has become *k'ē* (ք).

This marginal reading is puzzling; it does not represent contact with the
work of "the Three."

6:14 *

(պատմուծան) հանդերձեալ] բեհեզեայ

V212mg Zohapp(mg) B-M-Thackapp1

V212 is cited on the basis of Zanolli 1224.

The context concerns the bringing of the Ark of the Covenant to Jerusalem. In v 14 we are told that when David danced before the LORD he "was girded with a linen ephod." The words in quotation marks are a translation of חָגוּר אֵפוֹד בַּד.

The Old Greek rendering of חָגוּר אֵפוֹד בַּד according to MS B is ἐνδεδυ-κὼς στολὴν ἔξαλλον "wearing a special robe."

The Armenian translation of ἐνδεδυκὼς στολὴν ἔξαλλον is զգեցեալ պատմուծան հանդերձեալ "wearing a special garment." Bedrossian has a translation for պատմուծան հանդերձեալ, namely "coat in reserve, put by or kept for future use," though no text is cited. The word հանդերձեալ can mean "splendid, sumptuous, magnificent" and that appears to be what is intended here in light of the meaning of the Greek.

Some Armenian witnesses have a marginal reading for հանդերձեալ. The word բեհեզեայ means "of byssus," i.e. "of linen." This reading B-M-Thack cite in their first apparatus: εξαλλον] byssinum Arm-codd Syh-ap-Barh.

In the second apparatus in B-M-Thack we find the following translations where στολὴν ἔξαλλον stands in the the Old Greek: α΄ ἐπένδυμα ἐξαίρετον "select upper garment" jz (Rahlfs 243 554): σ΄ ὑποδύτην λινοῦν "undergarment of linen" j. The Armenian բեհեզեայ is a translation of Symmachus' λινοῦν.

The Hebrew, Greek and Armenian equivalents are:

בַּד → Old Greek ἔξαλλον → Zohrapian հանդերձեալ

→ Sym λινοῦν → sine nom բեհեզեայ.

In his apparatus Zohrapian notes that the word բեհեզեայ is in the margin of his base MS but in the text of some others. It came into the text of those MSS from the margin. The reading should be cited in the second apparatus of B-M-Thackeray and removed from the first apparatus. The second apparatus can be revised as follows:

στολην εξαλλον] α′ επενδυμα εξαιρετον jz: σ′ υποδυτην (> Arm) λινουν j Arm(sine nom).

In this case the Armenian preserves a reading already known from Greek sources.

7:1 *

ծառայեցընյց J1925 V212 Zoh^{app(mss)}] հանգոյց; ծառայեցնյց

J428^{mg} M188^{mg} V280^{mg} Zoh^{app(mss mg)} B-M-Thack^{app1(հանգոյց = Arm-ed)}

V212 is cited on the basis of Zanolli 1224–1225. In Zohrapian's base MS (V1508) and M2628 the original text was replaced with the marginal reading հանգոյց. Oskan's text also has հանգոյց, according to Zohrapian. In MS M2628 the text is similarly հանգոյց and ծառայեցընյց and ծառայեցնյց are the marginal readings.

The context is the introduction to the passage dealing with David's desire to build a temple. In v 1 we read "Now when the king was settled in his house, and the LORD had given him rest from all his enemies ..." The words "had given him rest" are a translation of הֵנִיחַ־לֹו. The verb is נוּחַ: in the hifil it means "give rest, quiet," as here.

The Old Greek, according to MS B, translated κατεκληρονόμησεν αὐτόν "[the Lord] gave him an inheritance." It took הֵנִיחַ־לֹו to be the hifil of נָחַל "inherit," with the third person masculine suffix, i.e. as הֵנְחִילֹו "he caused him to inherit."

The Armenian version translated κατεκληρονόμησεν with ծառայեցընյց "[the Lord] caused him to inherit." That is the original reading (so J1925: fol. 152r, col.1, †6) but the textual tradition is complex.

There are two marginal readings. The first is հանգոյց "(he) gave him rest," which represents an unsigned translation derived from "the Three." This marginal reading displaced the original in various witnesses, as noted.

These considerations clarify Zohrapian's text and apparatus. Zohrapian printed հանգոյց, which has entered the text of his base MS from the margin and

replaced the original ծառայեցոյց. In his apparatus he makes the following
remarks: "Oskan [i.e. Oskan's edition: MS M180] has հասոյց սմա; where
some MSS have in the text եւ ընդ ծառայեցոյց նմա, in the margins they
indicate հասոյց and ծառայեցոյց." Zohrapian does not state what readings,
if any, stand in the margin of his base MS, V1508.

In their second apparatus B-M-Thack cite an unsigned marginal reading for
κατεκληρονόμησεν, namely καὶ ἔπαυσεν "and he gave rest," in MS M. This appears to be a corruption of κατέπαυσεν which is found in the text of a number of
hexaplaric and Lucianic MSS: bioz$^{a?}$c$_2$e$_2$ Arm-ed Sa; *tutavit* Lat. (These Greek
MSS are 19-108 56 82 554$^{a?}$ 127 93 according to the Rahlfs numbering.) The
Greek lying behind հասոյց is κατέπαυσεν.

There is a second marginal reading in Armenian witnesses. It is the word
ծառայեցոյց "(he) subdued." Zanolli suggests that this word is a corruption of
ծառայեցոյց: the ծ and ձ were confused. For three reasons this seems
unlikely to me: first, what about the ն in ծառայեցոյց? And second—and
more importantly—why do we not see this corruption in the MSS here: that is,
ծառայեցոյց only appears as a marginal reading. Finally, why does this "corruption" appear together with a reading from "the Three," sharing the same index
sign? It seems to me that ծառայեցոյց might represent a translation from another
of "the Three."

Zanolli offers κατεδούλωσεν as a retroversion for ծառայեցոյց. The
verb καταδουλοῦν is used only a few times in the Old Greek corpus, a few times
for עָבַד and once for רְמָא. Such verbs do not produce a form that looks anything
like הֱנִיחַ־לֹו. The verb τροποῦν is a much more likely candidate as a retroversion. It occurs at 2 Rgn 8:1 in the sentence καὶ ἐπάταξεν Δαυειδ τοὺς ἀλλο-
φύλους καὶ ἐτροπώσατο αὐτούς "and David struck the foreigners and subdued
them." The Hebrew underlying the word ἐτροπώσατο is יַכְנִיעֵם "he humbled
them."

If the Greek underlying ծառայեցոյց at 7:1 is ἐτροπώσατο, then perhaps
the Hebrew was read (heard? interpreted?) as הִכְנִיעַ. That seems plausible. (By
the way, the Armenian at 8:1 is not ծառայեցոյց; it is վանեաց "[he] routed.")

At 8:1 the Hebrew is the *hifil* of כָּנַע: "(he) subdued them." As noted, the
Old Greek is ἐτροπώσατο. Furthermore, the translations of Aquila and Symmachus

are extant. Aquila represents the Hebrew by using the verb ἐκόλασεν "chastised, punished" and Symmachus employs κατήσχυνεν "humiliated."

The order of the marginalia in the Armenian witnesses in Reigns is usually Sym–Aq–Th. In that case the reading հանգոյց (κατέπαυσεν) belongs to Symmachus—which also seems likely because it has been taken up into the Lucianic text—and ծառայեցոյց (ἐκόλασεν?) belongs to Aquila. While the latter retroversion and signature must remain conjectural, the former seems quite certain.

The Hebrew, Greek and Armenian equivalents are:

(הֵנִיחַ)(־לוֹ) ≠ Old Greek κατεκληρονόμησεν (= הֵנְחִילוֹ) → Zohrapian
ծառայեցոյց

→ conj. Aq ἐκόλασεν → sine nom ծառայեցոյց
→ conj. Sym κατέπαυσεν → sine nom հանգոյց.

The second apparatus in B-M-Thack can be revised in the following way:
κατεκληρονομησεν] ⟨α'⟩ punivit Arm : ⟨σ'⟩ κατεπαυσεν (και επαυσεν M) M Arm.

The marginal readings in Armenian witnesses correspond in part to what we knew already from Greek witnesses: the translation "he gave rest" was already known. But the second reading "he subdued, subjected" was not. The Armenian evidence is therefore quite valuable, even if the textual situation is complex.

8:13

զսատրիկ] զիդումա

J428^mg M188^mg M2628^mg

In the context we are informed that David killed "eighteen thousand Edomites." A note in the NRSV explains that its translation has followed the Greek: the Hebrew reads "eighteen thousand Arameans." The word "Arameans" is a translation of אֶת־אֲרָם. The corruption in the Hebrew text has arisen through the confusion of ר and ד, i.e. of אָרם and אָדם.

The "Arameans" become the "Syrians" in the Old Greek text: cf. vv 5–6; in turn these people are սարիք "Syrians" in the Armenian translation of those verses.

In v 13 the Old Greek text reads τὴν᾽Ιδουμαίαν "Idumea," i.e. "Edom," as noted above by the NRSV. The Armenian translation, however, has զասորիս "the Syrians."

The marginal reading in some Armenian MSS likely derives from secondary contact with the Old Greek textual tradition. It is not a marginal reading which would have stood in Greek MSS because the text of such MSS already contained the translation "Edom."

8:18 *

քերեթին եւ ոփելեթին] աղեղնաւորք եւ պարսաւորք

J428mg V212mg Zohapp(mg) B-M-Thackapp2

V212 is cited on the basis of Zanolli 1225.

Cf. 15:18 below.

The context is a list of David's officials. In v 18 we are told that Benaiah son of Jehoiada was over "the Cherethites and the Pelethites." The Hebrew is הַכְּרֵתִי וְהַפְּלֵתִי. In Greek MS B this is transliterated: ὁ Χελεθθεὶ (sic[1]) καὶ ὁ Φελεττεί. So too in the Latin Vulgate: Cherethi et Felethi. It should be noted that Greek MSS boc₂e₂ (Rahlfs 19-108 82 127 93) and the Old Latin have the opposite order of the words, namely "the Pelethites and the Cherethites" (with differences in spelling).

B-M-Thack cite in the second apparatus two unsigned readings. The first is a transliteration. The second is a translation found in the margin of Greek MS M: οἱ σφενδονιταὶ καὶ οἱ τοξόται "the slingers and archers" and with it the Armenian in Latin translation: *sagittarii et funditores* "archers and slingers," i.e. the Armenian has transposed the two words. The presentation of the Armenian evidence in Latin can be eliminated: it is the same reading as in MS M except that the nouns are transposed.

Field cites the reading as follows: Schol. [i.e. scholium "learned note"]

---

[1]Cf. χερεθθεί A Co^W M(cum var) g(Rahlfs 158)(cum var).

Τοὺς σφενδονήτας καὶ τοὺς τοξότας οὕτω καλεῖ "it means this: the slingers and the archers." His footnote states that the note is found in Procopius of Gaza's comments on the books of Kings and Chronicles, as edited by J. Meursius in 1620, p. 126. Field adds: Chaldaeus enarrat [i.e."the Targum says"] עַל־קַשְׁתַיָּא וְעַל־קַלְעַיָּא "over archers and slingers." Note that this is the same order that we find in the Armenian marginal reading. Since the Old Latin and MSS boc₂e₂ attest the same reading, it may be that this was the original order of the Old Greek.

The equivalences in Hebrew, Greek and Armenian are:

הַכְּרֵתִי וְהַפְּלֵתִי → Greek MS B ὁ Χελεθθεί καὶ ὁ Φελεττεί → Zohrapian քերեթին եւ ոփելեթին

→ sine nom οἱ σφενδονιταὶ καὶ οἱ τοξόται → sine nom (transposed) պարասւորք եւ աղեղնաւորք.

The item in B-M-Thackeray's second apparatus can be revised as follows:

ο 1°—φελεττει] οι σφενδονιται και οι τοξοται (tr Arm) M Arm.

Like the Greek witness MS M, the Armenian preserves an unsigned trans-
lation. In light of the translation in the Targum, it is possible that the order of the words has been transposed in MS M rather than the Armenian.

9:7

ափոյ] ինչս

J1928^mg J1934^mg V212^mg(ինչ) Zoh^app(mg)

V212 is cited on the basis of Zanolli 1225.

The context is David's dealings with what is left of the house of Saul. He informs Mephibosheth that, for the sake of his father Jonathan, "I will restore to you all the land of your grandfather Saul." The words "all the land" are a translation of אֶת־כָּל־שְׂדֵה. Two verses later David reports to Saul's servant Ziba, "All that belonged to Saul and to all his house I have given to your master's grandson." The words "All that belonged to Saul" are a translation of כֹּל אֲשֶׁר הָיָה לְשָׁאוּל.

The Old Greek, according to MS B, renders אֶת־כָּל־שְׂדֵה with the words πάντα ἀγρόν, "every field." The use of ἀγρός in the singular is somewhat unexpected and in the Lucianic group of MSS boc₂e₂ (Rahlfs 19-108 82 127 93) we find πάντας τοὺς ἀγρούς "all the fields."

The Armenian translation, զամենայն անդս is plural, "all the fields," but whether one can say that this definitely reflects a parent text that had the plural is another thing.

At any rate there is marginal reading in some Armenian witnesses that replaces անդս "fields" with ինչս "things." Indeed the textual tradition is a bit complicated here because of the parallel text in v 9. The development does not go back to contact with the Hebrew text by way of "the Three" because the marginal reading is against the Hebrew. It appears to be an inner-Armenian development.

M1500 (fol.161r, col.1, ↓14) reads զամենայն անդս "all the fields," like Zohrapian's base MS for collation V1508, and I think that this is probably the original reading. J1925 (fol.153r, col.1, ↑5) reads զամենայն ինչ "everything," but that is at a change of line; perhaps its parent text read ինչս, i.e. the plural. On the other hand, the ինչ in the text of J1925 at v 7 may be a clear indication of corruption that has come from the parallel in v 9. Zohrapian cites in his apparatus the marginal reading զամենայն ինչս, "all the things." Manuscript LO reflects a text conflated with the marginal reading: զամենայն ինչս անդս "all whatever fields." This situation of confusion has arisen because of the similarity of the statement in v 7 to what comes later in v 9 where כֹּל אֲשֶׁר הָיָה לְשָׁאוּל is translated πάντα ὅσα ἐστίν τῷ Σαούλ, which in turn becomes զամենայն ինչ որ է Սաուղայ "all whatever is Saul's."

In conclusion, the marginal reading զամենայն ինչս at v 7 has probably arisen because of the proximity of a parallel passage at v 9.

12:25 *

յեղէղի Zoh; եղղի M188; հեղէղի V212] զգուանս

M188ᵐᵍ V212ᵐᵍ Zohᵃᵖᵖ⁽ᵐᵍ⁾

V212 is cited on the basis of Zanolli 1225. B-M-Thackeray do not cite the reading recorded in Zohrapian's apparatus.

The context concerns the birth of Solomon. "Solomon" is the name given to him by David. But the text says that the Lord loved Solomon and sent a message by the prophet Nathan that he should be called יְדִידְיָה בַּעֲבוּר יְהוָה "Jedidiah, because of the LORD."

The word in question here is יְדִידְיָה which means "beloved of Yah." (BDB 392) The Old Greek transliterated: Ἰεδδειδία (Ἰεδδαιδία o) boc₂e₂; Ἰδεδεί in MS B (the spelling varies among MSS). B-M-Thack inform us in their second apparatus that Aquila and Theodotion also transliterated but Symmachus translated the Hebrew word: ἀγαπητὸς κ̄ῡ "beloved of the Lord." Symmachus' translation is found in the margin of MSS M j (Rahlfs 243).

Zohrapian's note on յեդդեդիհ in his apparatus says: "In the margin [of V1508] on եդդեդիհ there is indicated գեդուաան [vid.] which agrees with what some MSS have in the text; which also some write եդդիհ." The reading գըգ-նուաան means "caresses, endearments" and must be a translation attributable to Symmachus.

Just how complicated the textual situation can become is clear from MSS J1928 J1934. In these witnesses դեդուաան (sic) has moved from margin to text and displaced the transliteration յեդդեդիհ—or some form of the name—and we find in the margin սիրելի "beloved" which has certainly come from the Latin Vulgate's translation Amabilis!

The Hebrew, Greek and Armenian equivalents are:

יְדִידְיָה → Greek MS B et al. Ἰδεδεί c var → Zohrapian յեդդեդիհ
→ Sym ἀγαπητὸς κυρίου → sine nom գգնուաան.

The item in the second apparatus of B-M-Thack can be revised as follows:
ιδεδει] σ' αγαπητος κ̄ῡ (> Arm) M Arm(sine nom).

(Note: B-M-Thackeray's reproduction of Symmachus' translation according to MS j [Rahlfs 243] is given as part of a longer, separate citation.)

In this instance the Armenian preserves an unsigned reading that derives from Symmachus. His translation was already known from a number of Greek witnesses.

15:18

բերեթին և ովելեթին] նետողք և աղեղնաւորք

V212mg

V212 is cited on the basis of Zanolli 1225.

Cf. 8:18 above.

Zanolli's comments here are less than clear: "Cap. XV, 18 բերեթին և
որելեթին *Λ* [= Zohrapian]; cfr. la trascrizione del cod. *Alessandrino:* Χερεθ-
θει και Ωφελεθθει (VIII, 18) in marg. նետողք և աղեղնաւորք ed altrove
(VIII, 18) աղեղնաւորք և պարսաւորք (cioè *τοξόται καὶ σφενδονισταί
[sic]) pure in marg. *E* [= V212]."

In the first place, բերեթին և որել եթին is not the spelling in Zohrapian's edition; perhaps it is the spelling in V212. Second, it would appear that the
first "(VIII, 18)" should be removed. The spelling Ωφελεθθει is not cited by B-M-
Thack at either 8:18 or 15:18—however, Zanolli was using Swete's older edition of
the Greek—but the remarks make sense if one takes it that his reference to MS A is
intended for 15:18. The ed altrove, i.e. "and elsewhere," for աղեղնաւորք և
պարսաւորք must refer to 8:18 in the light of the analysis of that passage provided above in our study.

Unfortunately there is no corroborating evidence for the marginal reading
նետողք և աղեղնաւորք "bowsmen [Bedrossian: Scythians, Sarmatians]
and archers." The words նետողք և աղեղնաւորք occur together at Isa 7:23
(Zohrapian 24) where the Old Greek reads μετὰ βέλους καὶ τοξεύματος "with
darts and arrows." One is inclined to treat the marginal reading at 2 Rgn 15:18 in
V212 as a gloss, loosely drawn from the marginal reading at 8:18, especially since
it is not found in other MSS examined for this study.

One may note that the word order of the marginal reading is the same as at
8:18, i.e. similarly transposed like the Armenian there (if Greek MS M indeed
preserves the correct word order for the marginal reading).

Նատիցի] շրջիցի

V212mg

V212 is cited on the basis of Zanolli 1225.

In the context, David is in flight from Jerusalem after the revolt of Absolom. In v 25 David tells the priest Zadok, "Carry the ark of God back into the city. If I find favor in the eyes of the LORD, he will bring me back."

In the Greek text tradition there is a well-attested hexaplaric plus following the words "in the city." The plus is καὶ καθισάτω εἰς τὸν τόπον αὐτῆς "and let it stay in its place" and it is attested in A (c var: αὐτοῦ) bcoxz(mg)c₂e₂ Arm Sahʲ(ᶜ var) Chr Thdt. (The Rahlfs numbers for these Greek MSS are 19-108 376 82 247 554mg 127 93.) The hexaplaric plus, as just indicated, is part of the Armenian text and has come into Armenian as և նատցի ի տեղւոյ իւրում "and it will stay in its place."

(This passage is cited in Chrysostom's Commentary on Isaiah—in Armenian—but not with the hexaplaric plus: Դարձ զտապանակդ Տեառն ի տեղի իւր. զի թէ գտից շնորհս ... Or maybe the quotation is conflated: instead of "let the ark of the Lord return to the city and let it stay in its place" we have "let the ark of the Lord return to its place that I might find favour ..." At any rate, the crucial element is missing. See the Venice edition, p. 104.)

Presumably a Hebrew text, not now extant otherwise, lies behind the hexaplaric plus. Kittel provides a retroversion into Hebrew from the Greek in his apparatus in BH³/⁷: וְיָשַׁב בִּמְקוֹמוֹ "and it will remain in its place." The hexaplaric plus is not Old Greek but represents an addition made by Origen on the basis of "the Three": Theodotion?

On the face of it, it seems rather unlikely that there should be a marginal reading from one of "the Three" which provides a translation for a reading of another of "the Three." At any rate, there is a marginal reading in Armenian MS V212. It is շրջիցի, perhaps "it will be led around." The verb is շրջիմ "take a walk, go; turn, be changed." The verb is used, e.g., of "walking around" (so of

Abraham in Gen 13:17 [LXX: διόδευσον]) or "changing one's mind" (as of Pharaoh at Exod 14:5 [Arm 6] [LXX: μετεστράφη]). Zanolli offers the retroversion ἐπιστρεψάτω "let it return," which seems to me to be a long reach.

So we are left with this unusual marginal reading. In my opinion the reading is inner-Armenian and probably derives from 7:2 where David says to the prophet Nathan, "See now, I am living in a house of cedar, but the ark of God stays in a tent." The word "stays" is a translation of יֹשֵׁב (qal participle of יָשַׁב); this becomes κάθηται ("sit; stay"; καθίσεται "sit down; stay" boc₂e₂). The Armenian at 7:2 is շրջիցի "go around."

The Armenian translation at 7:2 is interesting exegetically. In the Hebrew the same participle is used of both David and the ark: "I am living in" is a translation of יֹשֵׁב בְּ and "stays in" is a translation of יֹשֵׁב בְּ. The Old Greek rendered the first, of David, as κατοικῶ ἐν "I am living in," and the second, of the ark, as καθίσεται ἐν "stay in." The Armenian translates the first verb and preposition, κατοικῶ ἐν, with բնակեալ եմ ի "I am dwelling in" but the second, καθίσεται ἐν (so MSS boc₂e₂; MS B: κάθηται ἐν) with շրջիցի ի "go about in." The Armenian translation emphasizes the temporary nature of the place where the ark was kept—that is, the ark travelled about in a tent.

To conclude, the marginal reading շրջիցի at 15:25 probably derives from the well-known text at 7:2. Indeed the verb շրջել also occurs at 7:6, 7.

17:19 *

արապուր[թ] նռնն պաղատիս (պաղ ատիս Zoh^app[mg]) Aq

J1928^mg J1934^mg V229^mg V212^mg(sine nom) Zoh^app(mg)(sine nom); բան ջար Zoh^app(mg)(sine nom)

V212 is cited on the basis of Zanolli 1225. The marginal readings recorded in Zohrapian are not cited in B-M-Thack.

Zohrapian, in his apparatus, comments that in the margin of MS V1508 there is a note for արապուր[թ] which indicates that the word means նռնն "pomegranate" and պաղատիս "dried fig, string of dried figs" but that others [i.e. other MSS] indicate it means բանջար "vegetable(s)".

In the MSS where the reading is signed, the name Aquila stands above ՟ւնւnՙն which, in turn, stands above պատ գ տտ խ տ u. That is to say, Zohrapian's comment is correct: ՟ւnւnՙն and պ տ գ տ տ խ տ u should be regarded as separate translations. The attribution to Aquila should be taken to refer to the word immediately under his name—i.e. ՟ւnւnՙն. Therefore the word պ տ գ տ տ խ տ u is without signature. That is useful to bear in mind for the discussion which follows.

The translation բանջար "vegetable(s)" is anonymous and is only found in Zohrapian among the sources cited above.

The context for this verse is the insurrection of Absolom against his father David. David has fled and Hushai's counsel to Absolom has won out over Ahitho-phel's: Absolom will not pursue him immediately. Hushai's servant girl was seen meeting Jonathan and Ahimaaz, who were to take the message to David. So the two fled and came to the house of a man at Bahurim. They hid in a well. Verse 19 tells us that "The man's wife took a covering, stretched it over the well's mouth, and spread out grain (הָרִפוֹת) on it."

For הָרִפוֹת, which occurs only here and at Prov 27:22, BDB point out that the meaning is dubious. They suggest "some grain or fruit." The singular they give as רִיפָה.

Greek MS B—the text in B-M-Thack—gives a transliteration for הָרִפוֹת: ἀραφώθ. There is a translation in boc₂e₂ (Rahlfs 19-108 82 93 127): παλάθας (c var 93).

In the second apparatus B-M-Thack provide the readings of Aquila, Sym-machus and Theodotion. For Aquila Symmachus the translation is πτισάνας "peel-ed barley," according to MSS M (which lacks the name in the case of Aquila) z (Rahlfs 554); for Theodotion the translation is παλάθας "cakes of preserved fruit," according to MS M and Syh-ap-Barh. They provide also an unsigned reading in Greek MS i (Rahlfs 56): παλάθας ητοιμα... σύκων "cakes ... of figs." (I have not placed accents on ητοιμα.) Field cites the reading in MS i as παλάθας ἤτοι μάζας σύκων "cakes or loaves of figs."

The Latin Vulgate translates הָרִפוֹת as quasi siccans ptisanas "concoction of barley."

The Armenian margins offer three translations for הָרִפוֹת — ἀραφώθ —

արաբուկլիթ: նռւռն "pomegranate(s)" attributed to Aquila; պապատիռու "dried figs" and բանջար "vegetable(s)." The last reading, unsigned, we have taken from Zohrapian's apparatus. It has no correspondence among the Greek translations. The reading attributed to Aquila is really two readings, "pomegranate(s)" and "dried figs." Neither of these corresponds to πτισάνη "peeled barley." However, պապատիռու corresponds to παλάθας "cakes of preserved fruit," especially when taken from Greek MS i which adds σύκων "of figs." In fact, պապատիռ would appear to be a loan-word from Greek.

Therefore we may conclude that պապատիռու is the reading of Theodotion and that the attribution to Aquila in the Armenian may be incorrect. Since the order of providing readings in the margins of the Armenian MSS seems to be Sym–Aq–Th, we might expect that, if պապատիռու represents Theodotion's παλάθας, then նռւռն is the reading of Aquila. But նռւռն and πτισάνη are not the same thing. And բանջար has no equivalence. Reider-Turner have πτισάνη as Aquila and Symmachus' translation for רִיפָה but there is only this passage upon which to base that assertion. As noted above, Aquila's name is missing in Greek MS M, so the attribution of πτισάνη to Aquila is based on Greek MS z (Rahlfs 554). Is it possible that նռւռն is in fact Aquila's translation for הָרְפוֹת?

The translation նռւռն, i.e. Greek ῥόας "pomegranates," is based upon reading הָרְמֹן for הָרְפוֹת, as Zanolli points out. If that is so, the translation նռւռն derives from contact with the Hebrew. Whose translation is it then? It may be Aquila. Until there is more evidence for the translations of "the Three" at this passage we cannot be sure. Generally, the Armenian tradition is quite sound so its evidence cannot be easily set aside as inaccurate.

Field attributes πτισάνας to Aquila and Symmachus on the basis of Procopius' comments on the books of Kings and Chronicles, p. 146; however, he adds that MS Coislinianus 1—i.e. MS M—attributes it to Symmachus alone. Manuscript M is a 7th century witness; MS z (Rahlfs 554) is a MS of the 14th century. I am inclined to regard the earlier witness as the more accurate (no surprise!). Further, Field notes that Jerome renders the Hebrew as *ptisanas* and Jerome is often a disciple of Symmachus in his translation. There are good grounds then for concluding that ῥόας is Aquila's translation; πτισάνας is Symmachus'; παλάθας is Theodotion's.

One might take it that the translation բանջար is an inner-Armenian explanatory gloss. The word բանջար translates, e.g., βοτάνη "pasture; herb" (Gen 1:11, 12); χλωρός "green" (Gen 2:5); λαχανεία "herb" (Deut 11:10) or λάχανον—in plural—"garden herbs" (Matt 13:32). However, it is conceivable that some translator used բանջար for πτισάνας. Zohrapian's note indicates that the word բանջար is transmitted in some MSS, while ունունն պաղատիտ(ն) is transmitted in others, like his own base MS. I am inclined to regard բանջար as Symmachus.

The Hebrew, Greek and Armenian equivalents can be represented as follows:

הָרִפוֹת → Greek MS B et al. ἀραφώθ c var → Zohrapian արարոյթ

→ conj. Aq ῥόας ← Aq ունունն

→ Sym πτισάνας → sine nom բանջար

→ Th παλάθας → sine nom պաղ ատիտն.

The second apparatus in B-M-Thack can be revised as follows:

αραφωθ] α΄ ροας Arm : α΄ σ΄ πτισανας M(om α΄) z Arm(sine nom) : θ΄ παλαθας M Syh-ap-Barh Arm(sine nom): παλαθας... συκων i :

The Greek underlying Armenian ունունն is virtually certain, i.e. ῥόας: how many words are there for pomegranate? Nevertheless, it is usually the practice of B-M-Thackeray to translate Armenian into Latin when the Greek is not extant. If one follows that practice, the Armenian for Aquila's translation is represented by the word *granatum* .

The Armenian marginal readings appear to preserve a hitherto unknown translation of Aquila.

19:7

խոսեաց Zoh; խոսեա V212] սփոփեա

M188mg(գփոփեայ vid) J1927(գփոփեայ) V212mg

V212 is cited on the basis of Zanolli 1225.

The context is David's grieving over the death of Absolom. Joab tells David that the day of victory has been turned into one of mourning because of David's behaviour. In v 7 Joab says, "So go out at once and speak kindly to your servants." If he does not, the people will not stay with David, Joab warns. The words "speak kindly" are a translation of וְדַבֵּר עַל־לֵב . The phrase דִּבֶּר עַל־לֵב means "speak pleasantly to s.one": see KBH לֵב 8.

The Old Greek translation of וְדַבֵּר עַל־לֵב is literal: καὶ λάλησον εἰς τὴν καρδίαν "and speak to the heart." No variant readings are cited in B-M-Thack for λάλησον or for the expression as a whole. In some Greek witnesses the word "heart" is in the plural—hence καρδίας—and that may be reflected in the Armenian.

The Armenian translation of καὶ λάλησον εἰς τὴν καρδίαν is և խօ-սեաց ի սիրտս "and speak to the hearts." The only difference from the Greek of MS B is that "heart" is in the plural.

(By the way, խօսեաց is the aorist imperative 2 sg. of խօսիմ "speak," which has a "weak" aorist խօսեցայ. Zanolli has cited Zohrapian as having խօսեաց, i.e. with the short "o" vowel; perhaps his citation of V212 is similarly incorrect. The form խօսեա represents assimilation to the aorist imperative 2 sg. of the strong verb.)

The margin of a number of Armenian witnesses preserves the reading մխիթեա, the aorist imperative 2 sg. of մխիթեմ "console, comfort."

Arapkerts'i lists a few occurrences of մխիթեմ and cognates in the Bible. The noun մխիթուն֊ թիւն occurs at 1 Cor 14:3 as a translation for παραμυθία "comfort, consolation," which occurs only there in the New Testament; for παρα-μύθιον "solace" at Phil 2:1, likewise its only occurrence in the New Testament. The verb մխիթիմ "be consoled" renders παραμυθέομαι "encourage" at 1 Thess 2:12. Finally, two occurrences of մխիթեմ are given. The first is at Sirach 30:24(ET 23) where մխիթեա զանձն քո reflects ἀγάπα τὴν ψυχήν σου "indulge yourself." (Arapkerts'i provides this reference but one will not find it in Zohrapi-an's text of Sirach, which is an abbreviated text. The concordance is based on an 1860 edition of the Bible, published in Venice.) It is the last reference for մխ-իթեմ which is the significant one: at Gen 50:21 καὶ ἐλάλησεν αὐτῶν εἰς τὴν καρδίαν "and he spoke to their heart" is translated և մխիթեաց զսիրտս նոցա "and he consoled their hearts." One cannot help but notice that this text is almost identical to 2 Rgn 19:7.

Zanolli provides the retroversion πράϋνον "soothe, calm" for the marginal reading պիոիփեա. As at 15:25 this retroversion is ill-founded: the verb πραΰνω occurs in the LXX/Old Greek corpus only at Ps 93(94):13; Prov 18:14 and H-R cite no occurrences of it in extant materials for Aquila, Symmachus and Theodotion.

Without corroborating evidence from Greek or Syriac witnesses, it seems possible to me that the marginal reading պիmփեա derives from the parallel in Gen 50:21. On the other hand it is possible that it preserves an as yet unknown translation from one of "the Three."

The Hebrew, Greek and Armenian equivalents are:

דַּבֶּר עַל־לֵב → Old Greek λάλησον εἰς τὴν καρδίαν → Zohrapian և
խоսեաց ի սիրunu
→ inc. *consolare* → sine nom պիոիփեա.

This Armenian reading can be represented in the second apparatus of B-M-Thack as follows:

λαλησον εις την καρδιαν] *consolare* Arm.

One of the shortcomings of representing Armenian by Latin translations is visible here. The Armenian verb is an aorist imperative form but Latin bases its imperative on the present tense. Therefore the translation *consolare* is not morphologically accurate.

19:18 [MT 19]

զուղղութիւն և J1925] զողորմութիւն

V212mg Zohtxt

V212 is cited on the basis of Zanolli 1225.

The reading found to the left of the square bracket is not Zohrapian's text but the text (apparently) of V212. It is also the text of J1925 (fol.159r, col. 2, ↓4).

The context is David's return to Jerusalem after the death of Absolom. In v 18 we learn that Ziba, servant to the house of Saul, and his family and servants, rushed down to the Jordan while David's people were crossing it "to bring over the king's household, and to do his pleasure." The words "and to do his pleasure" translate וְלַעֲשׂוֹת הַטּוֹב בְּעֵינָו. The Hebrew is an idiomatic expression and the English translation reflects that fact.

The Greek according to MS B translates καὶ τοῦ ποιῆσαι τὸ εὐθὲς ἐν ὀφθαλμοῖς αὐτοῦ "and to do what was right in his eyes." The word בְּעֵינָו is rendered literally but הַטּוֹב—the word that interests us here and which literally means "good"—is translated by τὸ εὐθές, i.e. "the right (thing)." It is to be noted that MSS boc₂e₂ (Rahlfs 19-108 82 127 93) represent הַטּוֹב with the words τὸ (> b′ [Rahlfs 19]) ἀρεστόν, i.e. "the pleasing (thing)." (Manuscripts b [Rahlfs 19-108] actually have a doublet: καὶ τοῦ ποιῆσαι τὸ [> b′] εὐθὲς ἐνώπιον αὐτοῦ καὶ τοῦ ποιῆσαι [+ τὸ b] ἀρεστόν "and to do what is right before him and to do what is pleasing.")

The Armenian translation of καὶ τοῦ ποιῆσαι τὸ εὐθὲς ἐν ὀφθαλμοῖς αὐτοῦ is և առնել զուղղութիւն առաջի աչաց նորա "and to do the right thing before his eyes." Here τὸ εὐθές is translated by զուղղութիւն and that is in all likelihood original.

B-M-Thack cite no reading from "the Three" in their second apparatus.

The word զուղղութիւն has been corrupted to the similar looking զողորմութիւն "mercy" in some of the Armenian tradition. Indeed that is the reading in Zohrapian's text. Bedrossian notes in his lexicon that ողորմութիւն առնել and ողորմութիւն տալ mean "to give alms": these combinations occur frequently in the Bible. It is rare that the noun has the object marker զ- but it does occur (2 Ezra 7:28; Ps 65[66]:20). At the same time the word ուղղութիւն "uprightness" is used with առնել about a dozen times in Kings for ποιεῖν τὸ εὐθές (cf. 3 Rgn 11:33, 38). So it was quite possible to confuse the two expressions.

For Armenian equivalents to ἀρεστός one might take, for example, the four cases of its usage in the NT: John 8:29; Acts 6:2; 12:3; 1 John 3:22. In each of these texts the Armenian uses the adjective հաճոյ "pleasing"; in the first and last instances ἀρεστός is used with the verb ποιεῖν "do."

The reading that is the text in Zohrapian's edition, namely զողորմութիւն, is a corruption. This variant reading has been placed in the margins of some witnesses like V212. The issue is an inner-Armenian one and has nothing to do with "the Three."

20:4 *

Ճայնեա առ իս զամենայն այր յուդայ զերիս աւուրս եւ դու
այսր եկեացեալկոչեա դու առ իս զամենայն որդիսն յուդայ
յաւուր երրորդի եւ դու այսր եկեացես Sym

J428mg M188mg M2628mg(non hab եւ դու այսր եկեացես) V1182mg V1507mg
Zohapp(codd[mg]) B-M-Thackapp2(Arm-codd)

Zohrapian has եւ դու այսր եկեացես "and you come here" in his text
which means either that it should not appear in the margin or that the Armenian
translation of the traditional Greek text and the Armenian translation of Symmachus
were the same.

The context here is a revolt against David by Sheba, the son of Bichri.
David in v 4 tells Amasa, his military commander, "Call the men of Judah together
to me within three days, and be here yourself." The Hebrew is הַזְעֶק־לִי אֶת־
אִישׁ־יְהוּדָה שְׁלֹשֶׁת יָמִים וְאַתָּה פֹּה עֲמֹד.

The Greek translation according to B-M-Thack, i.e. MS B, is Βόησόν μοι
τὸν ἄνδρα Ιουδα τρεῖς ἡμέρας, σὺ δὲ αὐτοῦ στῆθι "Call me the men of Judah
in three days, and you appear yourself." Manuscripts boc₂e₂ (Rahlfs 19-108 82
127 93) preserve the Old Greek as Παράγγειλόν μοι τοῖς ἄνδρασιν 'Ιούδα ἐν
τρισὶν ἡμέραις, σὺ δὲ ἐνταῦθα στῆθι "Summon the men of Judah to me in three
days, and you remain here."

The translation for Zohrapian's text is "Summon to me every man of Judah
in three days and you [also] come here." The translation for Symmachus in Armenian is "You call to me all the sons of Judah on the third day and you [also] come
here." B-M-Thack provide the Symmachus reading in Latin in their second apparatus: *voca tu ad me omnes filios Iuda in die tertio et tu huc venies* .

The differences between the two Armenian translations reflect differences in
the Greek translations from which they were made. The differences are three in
number. First, they reflect the fact that the verbs used to translate זָעַק "send out a
call to arms" were different. Greek MS B uses βοάω → ճայնեմ but the translation of Symmachus—կոչեա—reflects, perhaps, κράζω: cf. זָעַק in Reider-

Turner. Second, אֶת־אִישׁ־יְהוּדָה is represented differently in Zohrapian and the translation of Symmachus. In both there is the addition of "every/all" for which B-M-Thack offer no Greek MS evidence. The word "every/all" is an addition easily made: this happens many times in the biblical corpus. Third, Zohrapian reflects a literal translation of a text like Greek MS B τὸν ἄνδρα Ἰούδα; the translation of Symmachus reflects the use of υἱούς. The same obtains for the rendering of שְׁלֹשֶׁת יָמִים "within three days" or "in three days." Zohrapian's text represents a literal translation of a text like Greek MS B τρεῖς ἡμέρας. The Armenian translation of Symmachus reflects a text which had "on the third day," perhaps τῇ τρίτῃ ἡμέρᾳ.

B-M-Thack cite only the Armenian in support of the Symmachus reading in their second apparatus.

The sequence of Hebrew, Greek and Armenian equivalences is as follows:

הַזְעֵק־לִי אֶת־אִישׁ־יְהוּדָה שְׁלֹשֶׁת יָמִים וְאַתָּה פֹּה עֲמֹד → Greek MS

B et al. Βόησόν μοι τὸν ἄνδρα Ἰούδα τρεῖς ἡμέρας, σὺ δὲ αὐτοῦ στῆθι → Zohrapian ձայնեաց առ իս զամենայն այր յուդայ զերիս աւուրս եւ դու այդր եկեսցեն

→ Sym conj. κραύζον σύ μοι [πάντες?] υἱοὺς Ἰούδα τῇ τρίτῃ ἡμέρᾳ, σὺ δὲ αὐτοῦ[? ἐνταῦθα?] στῆθι → Sym կոչեա դու առ իս զամենայն որդիսն յուդայ յաւուր երրորդի եւ դու այդր եկեսցես.

In this instance the Armenian is unique in the preservation of this translation of Symmachus. One might ask why this reading was preserved. It is not a question of the presence of an incomprehensible transliteration in the text, as is often the case. Rather, one must conclude, I think, that sometimes readings from "the Three" were taken over simply for interest's sake, or, to put it more plainly, simply because they were there.

The Armenian has been cited above in Latin translation as it appears in B-M-Thackeray; it need not be reproduced again here.

20:8 *

զհանդերձս J1925] զրահից

J1928 J1934 M2628 Zoh(sed hab mg)

The original text appears to be զհանդերծու (so J1925: f.159v, col.2, †12; զհանդերծոն M1500: f.164v, col.2, †3). Manuscripts J1928 J1934 M2628 V1508(Zoh) have զհանդերծու as a marginal reading and զրահից in the text. It appears that these witnesses have switched what was once a marginal reading (զրահից) with what was in the text (զհանդերծու). In that case the reading we are interested in is զրահից.

Verse 8 describes Joab's apparel when he went to see Amasa. We are told that "Joab was wearing a soldier's garment." This is a translation of יוֹאָב חָגוּר מִדּוֹ לְבֻשׁוֹ. This noun clause can be rendered literally, "Joab had girded himself with his garment for his clothes." The word *מַד is used of "garment" in general. (R. Kittel in BH³/⁷ suggests [מָדּוֹ] מָדּוּ לְבוּשׁ "dressed in a garment [his garment]" for חָגוּר מִדּוֹ לְבֻשׁוֹ. The word *מָדוּ is a very rare word, also meaning "garment," which occurs possibly only at 2 Sam 10:4; 1 Chr 19:4, according to KBH.) The word לְבֻשׁוֹ is just a word for "clothes," with the possessive suffix.

The Old Greek employs the word μανδύα "woollen cloak" (a Persian word?: cf. LSJ) for מַדּוֹ and translates Ἰοάβ περιεζωσμένος μανδύαν τὸ ἔνδυμα αὐτοῦ "Joab was gird with a woollen cloak for his garment." The words τὸ ἔνδυμα αὐτοῦ render לְבֻשׁ; ἔνδυμα means simply "garment."

The Armenian translation of the Greek is յովաբ զգեցեալ էր վարապանակս զհանդերծու իւր "Joab was wearing a cuirass for his clothes." Here the word (զ-)հանդերծու translates ἔνδυμα.

A variant reading in some Armenian MSS—which one surmises has come from the margin—is զրահից "breastplate." It replaces զհանդերծու. Each word begins with զ-: in the case of զհանդերծու it is a marker of the definite object and հանդերծու is in the accusative. As for զրահից, however, զ- is part of the word itself, which stands in the genitive, dative or ablative case, of which the ending -ից is the marker. The translation of the alternate text յովաբ զգեցեալ էր վարապանակս զրահից իւր is "Joab was wearing a cuirass for his breastplate."

Arapkertsʻi lists thirteen occurrences of the word զրահ in his concordance: 1 Rgn 17:5—occurs twice, only the first instance noted by Arapkertsʻi;

17:38; 2 Rgn 20:8; 3 Rgn 22:34; 2 Chr 26:14; 1 Macc 6:2; Wisd 5:19; Isa 59:17; Jer 46:4(Old Greek 26:4); Eph 6:14; 1 Thess 5:8; Rev 9:9, 17. In all these passages except 1 Rgn 17:38—where it is a translation of μανδύαν—the word զրահ renders θώραξ "breastplate." (At 3 Rgn 22:34 the Armenian ընդ զրահսն եւ ընդ թոքսունջսն "between the breastplate and the lungs" represents a transposition of the nouns in ἀνὰ μέσον τοῦ πνεύμονος καὶ ἀνὰ μέσον τοῦ θώρακος "between the lungs and the breastplate." It is not an exception to the equivalence.) This makes it very likely, in my opinion, that the Greek word θώραξ underlies the Armenian marginal reading. The word զրահից is likely to be taken as a dative in case. The Greek equivalent is θώρακι "for a breastplate"; לִבְשׁוֹ "for his garment" was translated θώρακι αὐτοῦ "for his breastplate." The possessive pronoun is not represented in the Armenian marginal reading, nor need it be since the possessive is in the text.

Who among "the Three" employs the word θώραξ? H-R cite only two references: Job 41:18 Sym; Josh 8:18 Aq. The latter can be dismissed: in fact Field cites θώρακι on the basis of a marginal reading in his MS 57 where it is attributed to ᾽Αλλος, i.e. "another." In the former case the word θώραξ is used by Symmachus, apparently as a rendering for the hapax שִׁרְיָה "arrowhead." At least we know that Symmachus used the word θώραξ.

I am inclined to take the word զրահից as a translation of Symmachus because Symmachus readings predominate among the Armenian marginalia.

The variant text makes sense in the Armenian if one understands վարապանակս to be a reference to a particular kind of breastplate, i.e. Joab was wearing a վարապանակ-type of breastplate as his breastplate.

The Hebrew, Greek and Armenian equivalents are:

לִבְשׁוֹ → Old Greek τὸ ἔνδυμα αὐτοῦ → J1925-Zoh[app] զհանդերծն
                                                                                    իւր
                    → conj. Sym θώρακι [αὐτοῦ] → sine nom զրահից [իւր].

In this instance the Armenian preserves a reading from "the Three" not previously known, a reading which may well belong to Symmachus. It can be added to the second apparatus in B-M-Thackeray as follows:

το ενδυμα] ⟨σ'⟩ θωρακι Arm.

21:20 *

մահրնն] ակաj

V212mg(ind supra ռապա j mend pro մահրնն vid)

V212 is cited on the basis of Zanolli 1225. The index sign is on the word ռապա j "Ṛapʻa" at the end of the verse.

Zanolli's citation reads: "Cap. XXI, 20 e 22 ռ ապ ա j, in marg. ակա j *γίγας, cfr. la lezione ἀνὴρ πρόμετρος di SIMM." The citation leads one to believe that the marginal reading occurs at both v 20 and at v 22.

The end of ch 21 relates certain exploits in the war against the Philistines. In v 20 there is described a huge man of Gath who had six fingers on each hand and six toes on each foot. The text says that "he too was descended from the giants." Verse 22 concludes the summary and says of the four large men described: "These four were descended from the giants in Gath." The same word "giants" is used of Ishbi-nebob in v 16: he is said to have been "one of the descendents of the giants"; and of Saph at v 18. In each case the word translated "giants" is הָרָפָה. At v 20 "he too was descended from the giants" translates וְגַם־הוּא יֻלַּד לְהָרָפָה.

For רָפָה in KBH we read: II רָפָה: הָרָפָה: n. pers., presumed ancestor of רְפָאִים 2S 21_{16.18.20.22}; > 1C 20_{6.8}.†

The Greek tradition represented by MS B transliterated the word רָפָה. This occurs consistently at vv 16, 18, 20 and 22. That is the text printed by B-M-Thack. In v 20 the text in B-M-Thack reads καὶ γε αὐτὸς ἐτέχθη τῷ Ῥαφά "and he was born to Rafa."

Manuscripts boc₂e₂ translate רָפָה—as τῶν γιγάντων at vv 16, 18; τίτανος at v 20—except at v 22 where they, too, transliterate. In this last case, however, the word γιγάντων has just preceded: τοὺς τέσσαρας τούτους τοὺς τεχθέντας ἀπογόνους τῶν γιγάντων τῶν ἐν Γὲθ τῷ οἴκῳ Ῥαφὰ κατέβαλε Δαυὶδ καὶ οἱ παῖδες αὐτοῦ "these four descendents of the giants in Gath born to the house of Rafa, David and his servants struck down." (This text is reproduced from Fernández Marcos/Busto Saiz' edition.)

The Armenian follows a Greek text like MS B and we read in v 20, cited above, և ևա ծնաւ ռափայ "and he was descended from Rafa." Manuscript V212 has a marginal reading for Rafa. It is սկայ "giant."

Zanolli suggests that we compare the Armenian marginal reading with Symmachus' translation of מָדֹ֖י, namely πρόμετρος i.e. "(man) of size." According to B-M-Thack, Symmachus' translation is preserved in Greek MSS Mjz (Rahlfs 243 554). Let us look at this.

Verse 20 reads: "There was again war at Gath, where there was a man of great size (מָדֹ֖י), who had six fingers on each hand, and six toes on each foot, twenty-four in number; he too was descended from the giants (הָרָפָֽה)."

First, the text of MT is corrupt: מָדֹ֖י is the Ketib but there is a Qere: מָד֖וֹן "quarrel, dispute," hence אִ֣ישׁ מָד֖וֹן "quarrelsome man." Cf. the translation of Aquila: [ἀνὴρ] ἀντίδικος "adversarial man." (B-M-Thack note that MS z adds to ἀντίδικος the word ἀντιλογίας "of controversy.") Aquila read the Qere. Kittel in his apparatus suggests reading with the parallel passage in 1 Chr (20:6) and the Targum: instead of מָדֹ֖י the word מִדָּ֖ה "of (unusual) size." That reading is reflected in Symmachus' translation πρόμετρος. In MS B we find Μαδών—i.e. a transliteration—so "(there was a man) of Madon."

Manuscripts boc₂e₂ have for מָדֹ֖י ἐκ 'ρααζης which appears to take the מ as a preposition and the following ד as a ר. It is at least recognizable as an attempt at a translation.

The marginal reading in V212 is not upon Մադւոն "Madwon" (spelled thus in Zohrapian's edition) which—following a Greek text like MS B—offers a transliteration. It is upon ռափայ "Rap'a." Could that be correct?

The word սկայք "giants" is used a number of times in the early books of the Bible: for the Nephilim (Gen 6:4; Num 13:33[Arm 34]) and the Rephaim (i.e. רְפָאִים Gen 14:5; Deut 3:11; Jos 12:4; 13:12). Indeed at 2 Rgn 21:11 there is a hexaplaric addition in the Armenian text և ելան: և եհաս ի վերայ նոցա դան որդի յովասայ ի ծննդոց սկայիցն "and they went out; and Dan son of Joas, who was descended from the giants, came upon them." (Here "who was descended from the giants" is a translation of ἐκ τῶν ἀπογόνων τῶν γιγάντων.) The Rephaim (Greek Ραφαείμ; Armenian ռափայյնոցն) are mentioned again in 2 Rgn 23:5.

It would not be surprising to find a marginal note սկայ for ռափայ except that, from the immediate context, it is clear that Rapʿa is one of the giants.

I return to Zanolli's suggestion that maybe the Armenian marginal reading is intended for վահւոն, in which case Symmachus' translation πρόμετρος has been translated ակայ. The index sign could easily become attached to the legendary ancestor of the Rephaim—the giants—whose name was Rapʿa. In favour of this suggestion is the fact that the Armenian marginal readings frequently attest readings also found in B-M-Thackeray's Greek MSS Mjz. Those witnesses attest πρόμετρος here.

The Hebrew, Greek and Armenian equivalents are:

מָדִין → Greek MS B Μαδών → Zohrapian վահւոն

→ Sym πρόμετρος → sine nom ակայ.

The Armenian marginal reading can be represented in the apparatus of B-M-Thack as follows:

μαδων] σ′ προμετρος α′ (>Arm) αντιδικος (> Arm; + η αντιλογιας z) M jz Arm(sine nom et ind mend supra τω Ραφα).

23:10

պարտնեգաւ J1925] վատզեգաւ

J428^mg M188^mg Zoh^(sed hab app)

This item is similar to 20:8 in that Zohrapian's MS has replaced the text with a marginal reading. The word պարտնեգաւ is original here: it has the support, e.g., of J1925 (fol.161v, col.1, ↓5) and M1500 (fol.165v, col.2, ↑30). Manuscript M2628, which is related in its marginalia in Reigns to J428 M188, has պարտնեգաւ as the text and no marginal reading.

The context concerns a battle against the Philistines in which David won a great victory. In v 10 we are told that he struck them down "until his arm grew weary, though his hand clung to the sword." The words in quotation marks are a translation of עַד כִּי־יָגְעָה יָדוֹ וַתִּדְבַּק יָדוֹ אֶל־הַחֶרֶב. The first verb is יגע and means "grow weary"; the second is דָּבַק, which with אֶל means "cling to."

The Old Greek translation of this clause is ἕως οὗ ἐκοπίασεν ἡ χεὶρ αὐτοῦ καὶ προσεκολλήθη (or the simplex ἐκολλήθη, as in MSS bc₂e₂ [Rahlfs 19-108 127 93]) ἡ χεὶρ αὐτοῦ πρὸς τὴν μάχαιραν "until his hand grew weary and his hand stuck to (his) sword."

The Armenian translation derives from a Greek exemplar which was lacking part of this clause. B-M-Thack suggest that it lacks ἐκοπίασεν ἡ χεὶρ αὐτοῦ καί—which would have occurred by parablepsis through homoioteleuton: οὗ to αὐτοῦ. It seems more likely to me however that its parent text lacked καὶ προσεκολλήθη ἡ χεὶρ αὐτοῦ. The cause is the same: the loss occurred by parablepsis: ἡ χεὶρ αὐτοῦ to ἡ χεὶρ αὐτοῦ. As a result the text reads մինչեւ պարտեցաւ ձեռն նորա սրոյն "until his hand was belaboured by the sword." The verb պարտիմ, -եցայ means "be conquered, have the worst of it." The sense is that his hand was worn out because of fighting, which is the sense of the Greek.

Some Armenian MSS have a marginal reading for պարտեցաւ. It is the word մածեցաւ. The verb մածնիմ, -ցեայ means "agglutinor – adhaereo – cohaeresco," i.e. "to glue or stick together," "to adhere to," "to hold fast together." I have taken this from Miskgian: in Bedrossian we are referred to մածանիմ, -ծայ; մածունիմ, -ծեայ which mean the same thing.

The marginal reading represents a translation of either προσεκολλήθη or the simplex ἐκολλήθη. This has one of two explanations. First: the marginal reading may derive from a comparison with an Old Greek type of text which had both ἐκοπίασεν "his hand grew weary" and προσεκολλήθη/ἐκολλήθη "(his hand) stuck to (his sword)." The Armenian translation, as pointed out above, lacks representation for the latter. In this case there has been comparison with the text of a Greek MS and the verb lacking in the Armenian has been added in the margin. If it is such a correction one might expect the word "and (his hand stuck [to his sword])" as well.

Second: the simplex ἐκολλήθη "adhered to" is the reading of the Lucianic MSS bc₂e₂. Is the simplex Old Greek? We recall that in this part of 2 Rgn the Lucianic text offers access to the Old Greek, while MS B represents a developed text type. Josephus also attests the simplex in his use of κολληθῆναι (Jos^ap [= apparatus of the edition of B. Niese] VII 309—so the edition of Fernández Marcos/Busto Saiz *ad loc*.) but it is hazardous to use the evidence of such quotations to establish a text.

Perhaps as elsewhere is often the case, Lucian has taken up a reading from one of "the Three," Symmachus. In that case the Armenian marginal reading derives from a Greek MS which had προσεκολλήθη in the text and ἐκολλήθη in the margin, without signature. The Armenian text lacks the proper referent for ἐκολλήθη, therefore the marginal reading was connected with the verb that was represented there, namely ἐκοπίασεν "(his hand) grew weary," i.e. պարտեցաւ.

This marginal reading is transmitted along with other marginal readings which do derive from "the Three" and I am inclined to regard this one too as deriving from such a source. This might have implications for the establishment of the Greek text: if the marginal reading derives from one of "the Three" then the simplex has been taken up by Lucian, making προσεκολλήθη more likely to be original Old Greek. On the other hand, it is possible that the marginal reading does derive from secondary contact with a Greek MS which did not have the lacuna of the Armenian translation. (See 2:29 1° where, however, the alteration to the Old Greek in the marginalia was made in conjunction with the addition of a reading from "the Three"; 8:13.)

In this instance I am choosing to err on the conservative side and not include this marginal reading among those which more clearly derive from "the Three." A future editor of the Greek text will perhaps be able on the basis of translation technique to establish whether προσεκολλήθη or ἐκολλήθη is original and therefore provide some light for the evaluation of the Armenian evidence. As stated above, the Armenian marginal evidence may be useful for the question of the Greek: it is an issue of where the circle begins!

VI. 3 Reigns

José Ramón Busto Saiz, *La Traduccion de Simaco en el Libro de Los Salmos* (Textos y Estudios "Cardenal Cisneros" 22; Madrid: Instituto "Arias Montano" 19-78). • D.W. Gooding, "Text-Sequence and Translation-Revision in 3 Reigns 9:10–10:33," *VT* 19 (1969) 448–463. • Sidney Jellicoe, *The Septuagint and Modern Study* (Oxford: Clarendon 1968). • A. Jepsen, ed., *Liber Regum* , BHS (1974). • James A. Montgomery, *A Critical and Exegetical Commentary on The Books of Kings* , ed. H.S. Gehman (ICC; Edinburgh: Clark 1951). • For further bibliography: see 1 Reigns.

The Greek text used here is once again that of the Cambridge edition, as prepared by Brooke-McLean-Thackeray. Occasional reference is made to Rahlfs' provisional Greek text of 1935.

The textual situation in Samuel-Kings is complicated. The user is referred to the discussion at the beginning of 1 Reigns. Three of Thackeray's five divisions for Samuel-Kings are present in 1 Kings. They are—with the slight refinement made by Shenkel:

βγ 2 Sam 10:1–1 Ki 2:11
γγ 1 Ki 2:12–21:43
γδ 1 Ki 22–2 Ki.

In sections βγ and γδ the Old Greek text is to be located in the so-called Lucianic group of manuscripts, namely boc₂e₂. The textual tradition represented by MS Vaticanus is a recensional type of text in sections βγ and γδ. It is Codex Vaticanus which forms "the text" in the edition of Brooke-McLean-Thackeray.

So it is that 3 Rgn 1:1–2:11 is part of section βγ; 3 Rgn 2:12–21:43 is part

of section γγ, whose textual situation is like that of earlier sections beginning with
1 Rgn 1:1; the end of 3 Rgn—beginning with 3 Rgn 22:1—belongs to the last section of the books of 1–4 Reigns: the same situation obtains for 4 Rgn as for the
conclusion of 3 Rgn.

1:41

բաց մակա նք] կոչնականք

V212^mg vid Zoh^app(codd)

V212 is cited on the basis of Zanolli 1225. Zohrapian notes in his apparatus
that the reading կոչնականք is found in some MSS; he does not indicate that it is
a marginal reading. Nor in fact does Zanolli, in spite of the fact that the title of his
article would seem to limit his remarks to marginal readings.

1 Ki 1 concerns the difficulties surrounding the succession to David's kingship. Adonijah son of Haggith proclaimed himself king. While he was feasting,
Solomon was anointed king. There was a lot of noisy celebration when Solomon
rode the king's mule in procession. In v 41 we are told: "Adonijah and all the
guests who were with him heard it as they finished feasting." The words "the
guests" are a translation of הַקְּרֻאִים. This word is the *qal* passive participle of
קָרָא and means literally "the invited ones," i.e. "guests."

It appears that the Old Greek may have rendered הַקְּרֻאִים with οἱ ἐσθίον-
τες καὶ πίνοντες μέτ' (αὐτοῦ) "those eating and drinking with (him)." (This is
the reading in MSS oc₂e₂ except that MS e₂ adds "all" before "drinking"; MSS b
[Rahlfs 19-108] attests the same text but has lost καὶ πίνοντες through parablepsis
by homoioteleuton.)

Manuscript B—the text in B-M-Thack—represents הַקְּרֻאִים with οἱ
κλητοί "the invited." The entire phrase is πάντες οἱ κλητοί αὐτοῦ "all his invited
ones," i.e. "all his guests."

Zohrapian's text is translated from a witness like MS B. The words οἱ κλητοί are represented by բաց մակա նք "guests." The question is whether this is
the original translation or whether perhaps կոչ նականք is the original trans-

lation.

The word הַקְּרֻאִים is also used at v 49. In MSS boc₂e₂ הַקְּרֻאִים אֶשׁר
לְ־ is represented by κεκλημένοι ὑπό "those who had been invited by"; in MS B
this expression is represented again by οἱ κλητοί. The Armenian at v 49 is կոչնականքն "the guests" which rests upon a text like MS B.

In J1925 (fol.163r, col.1, ↑16) and M1500 (fol.166v, col.2, ↓20) at v 41
we read կոչնականք (+ն M1500), not բազմականք. The two words are
synonyms but բազմականք, with the meaning "guests," according to Arapkerts'i's—albeit incomplete—concordance, occurs only here and at 3 Macc 5:22
(բազմականքն corresponds to οἱ συνανακείμενοι συγγενεῖς "the kinfolk reclining at table") in the Old Greek. It occurs at least five times in the Gospels, in
those cases always for either οἱ ἀνακείμενοι (Matt 22:10 and 11 "guests"; John
6:11 "those who were seated"; 13:28 "[no one] at the table") or οἱ συνανακείμενοι
(Luke 14:15 "dinner guests"). Amongst texts listed by Arapkerts'i the word բազ
մականք is not used to translate cognates of καλέω "call, invite" such as οἱ
κλητοί.

Arapkerts'i lists a dozen passages for կոչնականք "guests": 1 Rgn 9:13
(οἱ ξένοι "strangers"); 9:22 (τῶν κεκλημένων "of the ones invited"); 3 Rgn 1:49;
six passages in 3 Macc: 4:13(16) (կոչնականս ունիրբել "to invite guests" not
represented in Rahlfs' provisional Greek text); 5:8(14) (τοὺς κλητούς "the ones
invited"), 10(19) (τῶν φίλων "of the friends"), 20(36) (կոչնականացն is not
represented in Rahlfs' text), 24(44) (οἱ φίλοι "the friends"); 6:24(33) (զկոչնա
կանն հրավայէր "was inviting the guests" is not represented in Rahlfs' text);
Zeph 1:7 (τοὺς κλητούς); Mark 6:26 (τοὺς ἀνακειμένους "the guests"; variant
reading: τοὺς συνανακειμένους from the parallel [Matt 14:9]); Luke 14:7 (τοὺς
κεκλημένους "the guests"). In four of these cases կոչնականք is used to
translate cognates of καλέω "call, invite" (1 Rgn 9:22; 3 Macc 5:8[14]; Zeph 1:7;
Luke 14:7).

It would appear then that at 3 Rgn 1:41 կոչնականք is original and that
բազմականք is secondary.

It appears that բազմականք has come into the text of some MSS from
the margin: that is occasionally the case with Zohrapian's base MS for collation,
V1508, which represents on occasion a text where a reading that was in the margin

has been switched with one in the text.

Zanolli suggests that συνανακείμενοι underlies բաց մ ա կա ն ք and this might be correct. In that case the reading may well derive from "the Three." It should probably be cited in the second apparatus of B-M-Thack.

The Hebrew, Greek and Armenian equivalents are:

הַקְּרֻאִ֔ים → Greek MS B-type text οἱ κλητοί → J1925 M1500

Zoh^{app(codd)} կոչ նա կա ն ք

→ conj. συνανακείμενοι ← sine nom բաց մ ա կա ն ք.

In B-M-Thackeray—second apparatus—the entry should appear as follows:

οι κλητοι] *recumbentes* Arm-ed.

2:1 *

պատասխանի] պատուէր

J1925^{mg} V212^{txt}

V212 is cited on the basis of Zanolli 1225.

The words պատասխանի ետ "he gave answer" are the text of Zohrapian; also of M1500 (fol.166v, col.2, ↑1) and J1925 (fol.163r, col.2, ↑18). I take it that this is the original text. J1925 has a marginal reading, using an asterisk (✳ —not ※) as an index sign: ետ պատուէր appears in the margin for ետ պատաս-խանի in the text. V212 has switched the two: it has պատուէր "command" in the text and պատասխանի in the margin, according to Zanolli.

The context is the death of David. Chapter 2 begins: "When David's time to die drew near, he charged Solomon" and then his admonition is given. The words "he charged" are a translation of וַיְצַ֣ו, the preterit of צוה, with ו "and" not represented in the NRSV.

The original Old Greek translation appears to have been ἐνετείλατο "he commanded." This reading is supported by the majority of MSS, which includes boc₂e₂ (Rahlfs 19-108 82 127 93). There is a variant reading that has the support of MSS BAxa₂ (Rahlfs 247 501), namely ἀπεκρίνατο "and he answered." This translation, if it is not simply a mistake, rests upon reading וַיַּ֣עַן "and he answered" instead of וַיְצַו. The Armenian attests that reading too, though B-M-Thack have not cited it.

It appears that the text upon which Origen worked read ἀπεκρίνατο. As a result we have preserved as the translation of Aquila, Symmachus and Theodotion "and he commanded." The citation in B-M-Thack is: και απεκρινατο] α′ σ′ θ′ *et mandavit* Syh. (The word *mandavit* means "he commanded.") Field reproduces the Syriac marginal reading as ܡܦܩܕ, together with the signatures.

It is the word ἐνετείλατο that is represented in the margin of J1925 and formerly in the margin of V212 or its parent text, since the reading was moved at some stage from margin to text.

The Hebrew, Greek and Armenian equivalents are:

וַיְצַו] ≠ Greek MS B et al. καὶ ἀπεκρίνατο → Zohrapian և պատաս-

խանի ետ

→ Aq Sym Th καὶ ἐνετείλατο → sine nom և պատուէր ետ.

The second apparatus in B-M-Thack can be revised as follows:

και απεκρινατο] α′ σ′ θ′ *et mandavit* Arm(sine nom) Syh.

It might be argued that the marginal reading in J1925 has come from comparison with a Greek text that had καὶ ἐνετείλατο—i.e. it does not derive from "the Three"—by way of a marginal reading. That must also remain a possibility because J1925 has so few marginal readings and none of them signed. See the next item and 4 Rgn 15:5.

2:4 *
սպանակենգհ] պակասենգի

J1925mg

The context is once again David's admonition to Solomon. David tells him that if he follows the law of Moses then, just as the LORD promised earlier to David, "there shall not fail you a successor on the throne of Israel." The words "there shall not fail" are a translation of לֹא־יִכָּרֵת.

The Greek translation in B-related MSS—indeed, it is the majority text—is οὐκ ἐξολοθρευθήσεται "there shall not be destroyed utterly." This is an accurate, if literal, translation of the *nifal* of כָּרַת.

B-M-Thack cite a variant reading for ἐξολοθρευθήσεται found in several witnesses, namely boc₂e₂ (Rahlfs 19-108 82 127 93), i.e. the so-called Lucianic MSS, and Old Lat Syh(mg). The reading is ἐξαρθήσεται "there shall be carried away," or "removed," the future middle/passive of ἐξαίρω. It is quite possible that this "variant reading" represents the Old Greek.

Field presents the evidence somewhat differently than B-M-Thack. He sets forth οὐκ ἐξολοθρευθήσεται σοι as the reading Origen had and places ἐξαρθήσεται within parentheses after ἐξολοθρευθήσεται, with the comment "other exemplars." Then he offers a retroversion into Greek of the reading that appears in the margin of the Syro-hexapla. The Syriac reading is ܠܟ ܦܣܘܩ ܠܐ "there will not be cut off for you" or, less literally, "there will not be lacking to you." The verb is the *ethpeʿel* of ܦܣܘܩ . Field retroverts this into Greek as οὐκ ἐκκοπήσεταί σοι "there will not be cut off for you." Field suggests we compare the Hexapla at Ps 36:38 where the Old Greek renders the *nifal* of כָּרַת with the future passive of ἐξολοθρεύω and where Symmachus uses the future passive of ἐκκόπτω. At that same place Field translates the Syriac marginal reading attributed to Aquila—which uses the *ethpeʿel* of ܦܣܘܩ—as ἐκκοπήσεται.

B-M-Thackeray for their part have placed the Syriac reading in the first apparatus at 3 Rgn 2:4. They apparently regard it as a Lucianic reading, not as a reading from "the Three."

The Armenian marginal reading offers a very nice translation of the Syriac, or of the Greek as retroverted by Field. However, it could also be a translation of the Lucianic reading ἐξαρθήσεται. The meaning of պակասեցի, the aorist middle/passive of պակասիմ, is "it will fail, lack, cease." The choice of պակասիմ could be based on taking the verb ἐξαρθήσεται as derived from ἐξαιρέω which also means "remove," but for which LSJ cite a meaning in classical Greek "bring to naught" (see III.2.c). Or it may simply be a very good interpretive translation of ἐξαίρω in the middle/passive.

J1925 has only seven marginal readings in 1–4 Rgn. Four of these are simply corrections (1 Rgn 6:18; 23:10; 3 Rgn 18:4; 19:19); one without doubt preserves a reading derived from "the Three" (4 Rgn 15:5; cf. also 3 Rgn 2:1, cited above); finally the marginal reading here at 3 Rgn 2:4. One takes each one of so few seriously.

That the reading ἐξαρθήσεται appears in the margin of Syh leads one to think that it has come from the Hexapla. The Lucianic witnesses may well have taken it over from there as well. Therefore I am inclined to believe that J1925 preserves at 3 Rgn 2:4 a reading from "the Three." Indeed Reider-Turner have the following entry for ἐξαίρεσθαι: כרת niph. Is. lvi 5 οι λ' Ier. vii 28 ℵ α' θ'. That is, "the Three" do employ ἐξαίρεσθαι for the *nifal* of כָּרַת. In this case, Field's retroversion has proven to be incorrect.

The Hebrew, Greek and Armenian equivalents are:

יִכָּרֵת → Greek MS B ἐξολοθρευθήσεται → Zohrapian uшuшկենցի

→ sine nom ἐξαρθήσεται → sine nom щшկшնեցի.

If this is correct, B-M-Thack could cite ἐξαρθήσεται in their second apparatus as follows:

εξολοθρευθησεται] εξαρθησεται Arm Syh.

The complexity of the textual situation is clearly evident here. The fifth column of the Hexapla contained the word ἐξολοθρευθήσεται; the sixth, so-called Theodotion column contained the word ἐξαρθήσεται. Unknown to Origen, this last column was in fact a representative of the Old Greek text and not really Theodotion!

4:33 [MT 5:13; B-M-Thack 4:29]

յորմն] ի (> J1928 Zoh) щшрիшщ

J428mg(ի щшршщի) J1928mg Zohapp(mg)

M188 has a marginal reading but, on the basis of the microfilm, it is unclear what it is; M2628 has no marginal reading. This reading is not cited in B-M-Thack, though it appears in Zohrapian's notes.

We are told here of Solomon's great wisdom. His knowledge of trees extended "from the cedar that is in the Lebanon to the hyssop that grows in the wall." The words "in the wall" are a translation of בַּקִּיר.

KBH note that קִיר "wall" occurs 74 times in the Hebrew Bible. It is not a rare word or of uncertain meaning.

The Old Greek translation of בַּקִּיר is διὰ τοῦ τοίχου "through the wall." The word τοῖχος can be used of the wall of a house or temple; or of the side of a ship. LSJ note that it later = τεῖχος which also means "wall," but especially "city-wall," that is, a fortified wall. A small number of Greek MSS preserve τεῖχος as variant reading. The entry in B-M-Thack is:

τοιχου] τειχου sxe₂ (Rahlfs 130 247 93) : τειχους d (Rahlfs 107).

It seems quite possible that the variant Greek reading arose out of a simple spelling error. The words look very much alike.

The Armenian translation employs ןɲ౧ʕ౰ "in the wall": the word for "wall" in this phrase is ɲɲ౧ and it has the preposition ɦ joined to it at the beginning of the word and the definite marker -౰ at the end.

There is a marginal reading in some Armenian MSS for ןɲ౧ʕ౰. It is [ɦ] ɥɱɲɦɥɥ in MS V1508(Zoh) or ɦ ɥɱɲɥɥɦ in MS J428. In the former ɥɱ-ɲɦɥɥ is in the accusative case, like the text, hence "in the wall"; in the latter the noun is in the locative case, hence—similarly—"in the wall." This "wall" is the τεῖ-χος: it means "wall, rampart, fortification."

(Field has a note on the Greek translation of בַּקִּיר but it concerns the preposition: some exemplars have ἐκ τοῦ τοίχου "from the wall." B-M-Thack cite MSS Zboc₂e₂ Thdt, i.e. MS Z, the Lucianic MSS (Rahlfs 19-108-82-127-93), and Theodoret as having the preposition ἐκ. That is not the issue with the marginal reading in Armenian MSS: the preposition ἐκ would require ɦ ɥɱɲɥɥɿ "out of the wall." The parent text of ɦ ɥɱɲɥɥɦ or ɦ ɥɱɲɦɥɥ did not have ἐκ.)

H-R provide a list of passages where Aquila, Symmachus and Theodotion use τεῖχος. Reider-Turner do not record Aquila using τεῖχος for קִיר. That leaves the list of passages for Symmachus and Theodotion. In the case of Theodotion: he uses τεῖχος six times for חוֹמָה "wall" (Josh 2:15[twice]; Jer 39[46]:4, 8; Ezek 26:4, 9; 27:11) and once for קִיר (Ezek 4:3). Symmachus uses τεῖχος thirteen times: in ten cases he uses it to translate חוֹמָה (Josh 2:15[twice]; Ps 54[55]:11; Isa 25:12; 60:18; Jer 39[46]:4; 52:7; Lam 2:7; Ezek 26:4; 27:11); twice for קִיר, in what are rendered into English as proper names (Kir-hareseth [Isa 16:7] and Kir-heres [Isa 16:11]); once in reading שׁוּר "wall" for שׁוֹר "ox" (Gen 49:6). For Symmachus we can also add one passage cited in Busto Saiz' index to Pss: at 17:30 he employed τεῖχος to translate שׁוּר (ο′ ε′). We can conclude that "the Three" use τεῖχος mostly for חֹומָה.

If the marginal reading derives from one of "the Three," it is probable that it belongs to Symmachus because his translations predominate in the marginalia. But as we have just seen, Symmachus rarely uses τεῖχος for קִיר. That does not mean however that the reading is not Symmachus.

The most likely answer to the question of the origin of the marginal reading in Armenian MSS is that it represents secondary contact with a Greek MS which had διὰ τοῦ τείχου. It seems less likely to me that it derives from one of "the Three," i.e. most likely Symmachus. Still, it may well have a Greek parent, though undetermined, and it might well be cited in an apparatus to the Greek text. Hence in B-M-Thack it can be put with the witnesses attesting τείχου in the first apparatus:

τοιχου] τειχου sxe₂ Arm-codd : τειχους d (Rahlfs 107).

It is a curious marginal reading.

9:15 *

հանդերձանք աւարիս] սակ հարկին

V212ᵐᵍ Zohᵃᵖᵖ⁽ᵐᵍ⁾

V212 is cited on the basis of Zanolli 1225–1226. This reading is not cited in B-M-Thack, even though it is found in Zohrapian's notes.

The context concerns Solomon's forced levy. Verse 15 begins, 'This is the account of the forced labor that King Solomon conscripted." The words "the account of the forced labor" are a translation of דְּבַר־הַמַּס. The word מַס means "compulsory labor"; דָּבָר, here in the bound form דְּבַר, means of course "word" or "report, explanation."

Verses 15–25 MT have been moved in the Old Greek, though as Jepsen says, "cf. 2,35f–k 2,46d 5,14b 9,9a 10,22a–c." We find much of it in MS B after 10:22: see the text of B-M-Thackeray and the article by Gooding, "Text-Sequence."

Verses 15–25 appear in B-M-Thackeray's first apparatus as a hexaplaric plus. As such דְּבַר־הַמַּס is represented by ἡ πραγματία τῆς προνομῆς "the treatment [i.e. account] of the provision." (LSJ suggest the meaning "store, provision" for 3 Rgn 10:23—i.e. here—but only cite this text for that meaning. Elsewhere it means "foraging," then "plunder, booty.") Does this translation represent Theodotion, upon whom Origen depended heavily to fill out the text of his fifth column?

The long hexaplaric plus is part of the Armenian text after v 14. In Zohrapian the words ἡ πραγματία τῆς προνομῆς are translated հանդերձանք աւարին "arrangement of the booty." The marginal reading in Armenian witnesses is ասկ հարկին "account of the service" or "reckoning of the tribute."

This marginal reading correponds to the translation of Symmachus cited by B-M-Thack in their second apparatus on the basis of Syh: *verbum tributi* . The Armenian witnesses therefore attest Symmachus.

Field reproduces the Syriac as ܟܬܟܒܕܐ ܟܕܠܡ and retroverts it into Greek as ὁ λόγος τοῦ φόρου "the account of tribute."

The Hebrew, Greek and Armenian equivalents are:

דְּבַר־הַמַּס → Origen's hexaplaric plus ἡ πραγματία τῆς προνομῆς →

Zohrapian հանդերձանք աւարին

→ Sym conj. ὁ λόγος τοῦ φόρου → sine nom ասկ հարկին.

Unfortunately Zanolli's article appeared in 1927–1928, just a little too early to take advantage of B-M-Thackeray's edition of Samuel-Kings, which was published in 1927. Zanolli thought that ասկ հարկին was simply a gloss.

The second apparatus of B-M-Thack can be revised as follows:

η—προνομης] σ′ *verbum tributi*   Arm(sine nom) Syh.

9:22 *

հանդերձաւորութիւն] ծառայութիւն

J1928[mg] J1934[mg] V212[mg] Zoh[app(mg)]

V212 is cited on the basis of Zanolli 1226. This reading is not cited in B-M-Thackeray.

As in the preceding item, the context concerns Solomon's use of forced labour. In v 22 we are told מִבְּנֵי יִשְׂרָאֵל לֹא־נָתַן שְׁלֹמֹה עָבֶד "But of the Israelites Solomon made no slaves." At issue is the word "slaves." (Jepsen draws attention in his apparatus to the reading in the parallel passage in 2 Chron 8:9: לַעֲבָדִים "to slaves.") The sense is that he did not "give them over to" (נָתַן לְ) slavery.

Verse 22 is part of the same hexaplaric plus as v 15. There the word הַמַּס was translated ἡ πραγματία. Here לֹא־נָתַן עָבֶד is rendered οὐκ ἔδωκεν εἰς πρᾶγμα "he did not give [the Israelites] over to the task."

B-M-Thack cite marginal readings in the Syro-hexapla for εἰς πρᾶγμα, namely *in servientem* (Aquila) and *servire* (Symmachus). These are more fully dealt with in Field who gives the Syriac for Aquila's translation as ܠܥܒܕ ܟܕ ܡܫܥܒܕ "to the work of slavery" and for Symmachus' as ܠܡܦܠܚ ܒܥܒܕܘܬܐ "to work in slavery" which he, in turn, retroverts into Greek as εἰς δουλεύοντα "to the things of slavery" and δουλεύειν "to act as slaves," respectively.

The words εἰς πρᾶγμα are rendered ի հանդերձանութիւն "to the work" in the Armenian version. The marginal reading for the word հանդերձանութիւն is ծառայութիւն "servitude; slavery." This probably represents the translation of Aquila, though conceivably an Armenian translator might have adapted Symmachus' infinitive to the Armenian context and translated it with a noun.

At v 21 Aquila uses the word δουλεία "slavery" for לְמַס־(עֹבֵד), so perhaps he used it again in v 22 for עָבֶד which is cognate to עֹבֵד. Zanolli retroverts ի ծառայութիւն as εἰς τὴν δουλείαν "into slavery." But see Field's retroversion from the Syriac, just noted.

The Hebrew, Greek and Armenian equivalents are:

עָבֶד → Origen's 5th column πρᾶγμα → Zohrapian հանդերձանութիւն

→ Aq conj. εἰς δουλεύοντα → sine nom [ի] ծառայութիւն.

The second apparatus in B-M-Thack can be revised to include the Armenian as follows:

εις πραγμα] α' *in servientem* Arm(sine nom) Syh.

14:28 *

Zohrapian's text represents a type of text which has taken a marginal reading into it. For that reason the text given to the left of the square bracket in this instance is that of M1500 and J1925. Further, the marginal readings among the various witnesses appear to derive from two traditions. The recording of them is more complex than is usually the case and that is reflected in the way the evidence is cited. It is recorded without any attempt at this stage to correct errors in the signatures.

թեե M1500¹; թեւս J1925] pr տեղի Zoh^txt; աեեեկի Aq; ի թեկուե Sym Zoh^app(mg) B-M-Thack^app²; տեղի; թեկուե; աեեեկի Aq; J1928^mg J1934^mg V1270^mg; ի աեեեկի V212^mg; (ի J428 M188 V1507) աեեեկի Aq; ի թեկուե Sym; յաեկիւե Th J428^mg M188^mg M2628^mg V1507^mg

V212 is cited on the basis of Zanolli 1226. Preservation of the readings in the order Aq–Sym–Th is unusual.

There appear to be two traditions of marginal readings represented among these MSS. The first—which includes J1928 J1934 V212 V1270 and V1508 (Zohrapian's base MS)—preserves the reading տեղի but not the reading յաեկիւե. In MS V1270 (14–15th century) the word տեղի is still in the margin sine nom, but in MS V1508 it has been taken into the text. In the second tradition there are signed readings for each of Aquila, Symmachus and Theodotion. Like the first tradition, it attributes ի աեեեկի to Aquila and ի թեկուե to Symmachus, but its third reading is not տեղ ի but յաեկիւե and this it attributes to "Th," i.e. presumably Theodotion.

The first group of witnesses includes two early 14th century witnesses (V212 V1508), one of which is from Cilicia (V1508), and the other of which is from the region of Erznka (i.e. Ekeghiats‘) in Eastern Anatolia (V212); a MS of the

---

¹In MS M1500 it is often impossible to distinguish ե from է. The spelling in V1270 is թէէ. The reading թեւս in J1925 is corrupt: the original թեե or թէէ has become the plural of the word թեւ "wing"; the reading in the text of Zohrapian, namely թեւէ —hence ի թեւէ "from the wing"—is also corrupt.

14–15th century of unknown provenance (V1270); and two mid-17th century witnesses (J1928 J1934), one of which—J1934—was copied in Isfahan. The second group includes four MSS from the 17th century: J428 and M188, copied in Constantinople in 1620 and 1643, respectively, and M2628 V1507, both copied in 1635 and of unknown provenance.

The context concerns the raid that King Shishak of Egypt made against Jerusalem. It is reported that he took away all the treasures of the temple and the king's house, including the gold shields that Solomon had made. In their place, King Rehoboam had shields made of bronze and gave them to the officers of the guard who kept the door of the king's house. Verse 28 informs us that "As often as the king went into the house of the Lord, the guard carried them and brought them back to the guardroom." At question here is the phrase "to the guardroom": אֶל־תָּא הָרָצִים, i.e. "to the תָּא of the body-guard." What does the word תָּא mean? Holliday says: "guardroom, of palace 1 K 14:28, of temple Ez 40:7–36," its only occurrences.

The B-M-Thack text for this phrase—following MS B—is εἰς τὸ θεὲ τῶν παρατρεχόντων, transliterating תָּא as τὸ θεέ. (This is also used in the Ezekiel passage: meaning?: θέα III.2. auditorium in LSJ 786 [but fem.].) They cite the following Greek witnesses for the variant θεκουέ: bg*i* j(sub o')ozc₂e₂ (Rahlfs 19-108 158 246 243[sub o'] 82 554 127 93) Thdt. What is the meaning of θεκουέ?

Field cites the following notation from Theodoret's *Quaestiones* (number 46 in 3 Reigns, p. 492[1]): ἐν μὲν τῇ τῶν Ἑβραϊκῶν ὀνομάτων ἑρμηνείᾳ τὸ θεκουέ [תָּקוֹן עַ] κρουσμὸς καὶ σαλπισμὸς κείμενον εὗρον "in the interpretation of the Hebrew words they find τὸ θεκουέ means 'music by an instrument' and 'trumpet-call'." The word θεκουέ also represents a transliteration of a Hebrew text.

The second apparatus of B-M-Thack provides us with the Greek translations of תָּא in Aquila and Symmachus. The phrase אֶל־תָּא is rendered by Aquila πρὸς θάλαμον "to the storeroom; chamber" according to MSS jn(sine nom) (Rahlfs 243 119). For אֶל־תָּא Symmachus has εἰς τὸν τόπον "to the place," which is preserved in MS j. The Syro-hexapla preserves for Symmachus' translation of אֶל־תָּא the reading ܡܥܠܬܐ "the presence of [??]." Maybe that is part of a translation of εἰς τὸν τόπον. Field admits that he is at a loss to explain the meaning of the Symmachus' reading in Syriac.

The textual situation of the Armenian witnesses is complex. Let us begin with the text Zohrapian prints, namely ի ստեղի թետ. In his apparatus he points out that some MSS have just ի թետ, i.e.—the spelling is not important—they lack the word ստեղ ի, whose natural Greek equivalent is the (εἰς) τὸν τόπον! Manuscript J1925 attests the shorter text (fol.172v, col.2, ↓11: ի թետս) as does M1500 (fol.172v, col.1, ↓8: ի թեե). Manuscript V1270 also has the shorter text and has readings in both margins: to the left of the column of text, Aquila's signature and the word սենեակի below it, separated by a line; to the right of the column of text, ստեղ ի and, below it, separated by a line, թեկութ, both sine nom. In MSS J1928 J1934 the same situation obtains except that the Aquila signature and reading are set below the other two in the same margin.

The text in Armenian MSS represents a transliteration of θεέ, hence թեե cum var. However, the Armenian witnesses preserve readings for Aquila, Symmachus *and* Theodotion in the margins. For Aquila the word is սենեակ "room," corresponding to θάλαμον; for Symmachus the reading preserved as [ի] ստեղ ի is a translation of εἰς τὸν τόπον. (The reading ի թեկութ is attributed to Symmachus in the second group of witnesses: we will return to that in a moment.) (The transliteration τὸ θεέ occurs a dozen times in the Old Greek text of Ezekiel 40. There it is translated by Symmachus as τὴν παραστάδα "doorpost, pillar, space enclosed between the παραστάδες," hence "vestibule, entrance" in v 7 and as αἱ παραστάδες τῆς θύρας "doorposts, entrance" at v 10. Unfortunately the word παραστάς does not occur in the LXX/Old Greek corpus so we have no access to its translation there into Armenian.[1])

For Theodotion the reading preserved is յանկիւն "in the corner, nook." The word անկիւն is the Armenian translation for γωνία "corner, secluded spot" at Exod 26:13; 3 Rgn 7:34; 4 Rgn 14:13. Could γωνία be the word behind անկիւն here at 3 Rgn 14:28? Possibly.

---

[1] I am indebted here to Johan Lust's remarks about transliterations in the Old Greek of Ezekiel and their counterparts in "the Three," made in his paper "A Lexicon of Ezekiel's Hexaplaric Recensions," presented at the Rich Seminar on the Hexapla, Yarnton Manor, Oxford, July 25–August 4, 1994 and to be published in the Proceedings, edited by Alison Salvesen. He notes that where "the Three" have translations and the Old Greek has transliterations the subject matter is mostly architectural; much of the translation is provided by Symmachus.

That leaves us with the fourth marginal reading ի թեկուէ, transmitted sine nom in the first group of MSS and under the name of Symmachus in the second group. It is this word which B-M-Thack transliterate in Roman characters in their second apparatus: *in Thecue* . The word թեկուէ represents a transliteration of the word θεκουέ, itself a transliteration found in MSS b*gi* j(sub o')ozc₂e₂ Thdt. These Greek MSS include the so-called Lucianic witnesses boc₂e₂ (Rahlfs 19-108 82 127 93), together with *gi jz* (Rahlfs 158 246 243 554). This reading was also transmitted by Theodoret.

The reading ἐν τὸ θεκουέ came into the Armenian MSS from one of three sources: 1) it derives from a marginal reading attributed to Symmachus in a parent manuscript; 2) it comes from a comparison of the Armenian text with the text of a Greek MS like the Lucianic group of MSS; or 3) it has come from Theodoret.

To speak of the third option we must recall that the siglum θ′ was also used for marginalia deriving from Theodoret: see Jellicoe 94, 133. It could be said that it would have been easy for such a reading to become attached to the Aquila and Symmachus readings. It may have been transmitted with the signature originally but the signature got lost, just as the signature of Symmachus got lost in the first group of Armenian MSS. Or, ի թեկուէ may not have had a signature. In the second group of Armenian MSS the Symmachus reading was lost: there were already signed readings for Aquila and Theodotion, so the third reading was erroneously assigned to Symmachus. So it might be argued.

Neither this option nor the second seems as likely to me as the first: ի թեկուէ is a reading attributed to Symmachus and transmitted along with readings from Aquila and Theodotion. Lucian may very well have taken it up into his textual revision from Symmachus. This often happened.

From this long discussion we can come to the conclusion that the Armenian witnesses preserve four readings, those of Aquila, two that have attribution to Symmachus, and Theodotion. Better than this we cannot do at the moment.

In that case the equivalences among Hebrew, Greek and Armenian are as follows:

אֱלִי־לָךְ → Greek MS B εἰς τὸ θεέ → MS M1500 ի թեէ

　　　　　→ Aq πρὸς θάλαμον → Aq ի անենակի

　　　　　→ Sym εἰς τὸν τόπον → sine nom ի տեղի

→ Sym εἰς τὸ θεκουέ → Sym ի թեկուէ

→ Th conj. εἰς τὴν γωνίαν ← Th յանկիւն.

It is also noteworthy that not three—itself uncommon—but four marginal readings are preserved. The textual situation in the Armenian tradition is complicated but probably affords some insight into the transmission history of the marginalia. The later witnesses may divide themselves between Constantinople on the one side and Isfahan on the other.

The second apparatus in B-M-Thackeray can be revised to show the preservation of the translations of each of "the Three," including the two readings that are connected with the name of Symmachus:

εἰς 2°—παρατρεχοντων] α′ προς θαλαμον τον τρεχοντων σ′ εἰς τον τοπον οπου οι παρατρεχοντες j | εἰς το θεε] α′ προς θαλαμον n(sine nom) Arm : σ′ εἰς τον τοπον Arm : σ′ εἰς το θεκουε Arm : θ′ *in angulum* Arm.

21:1 (Old Greek 20:1) *

կալ] pr արքունիիս M2628; + արքունիիս M188 = Zoh^app(ms); յարքունիիս J428^mg

This reading is not cited by B-M-Thackeray.

In this item we see the itinerant movements possible for a marginal reading. Manuscript J428 preserves the original position of the word արքունիիս, namely in the margin. (The preposition ի, now attached to it—hence յարքունիիս—is likely secondary: cf. the other Armenian MSS. The preposition may have its origin in pronunciation. At any rate, it is merely reduplicative after առ.) It is intended to replace the word կալ and MS J428 has an index sign in the text over that word.

Some Armenian scribes moved marginal readings into the text and that is the case with the two other MSS noted above. In this case none replaces the word in the text with the marginal reading. Rather, they add it to the text. In the case of MS M 2628 the word արքունիիս is added before the word for which it is intended: hence մերձ առ արքունիիս կալ "near to the palace the threshing-floor (of the king)"; in the case of MS M188—this MS was used by Zohrapian, so it is the MS referred to in his apparatus as "one exemplar"—the marginal reading has been added after the word for which it was intended: hence սենեճ առ կալ արքունիհս "near to the threshing-floor the palace (of the king)."

This item offers insight into the text history of the marginalia in the following way. Manuscripts J428 M188 M2628 are related in their marginalia in 1–4 Reigns. What we see here is that M188 and M2628, while closely related, are not dependent the one on the other. They may share a common parent, a MS like J428, which here is a step earlier than either of the two other MSS.

The context of 3 Rgn 21:1 is the story of Naboth's vineyard. We are told that "Naboth the Jezreelite had a vineyard in Jezreel, beside the palace of King Ahab of Samaria." The word translated "vineyard" is כֶּרֶם; the words translated "beside the palace" are אֵצֶל הֵיכַל.

The first part of 21:1 according to the Old Greek is Καὶ ἀμπελὼν εἷς ἦν τῷ Ναβουθαὶ τῷ 'Ισραηλείτῃ παρὰ τῷ ἅλῳ 'Αχαάβ "And there was a vineyard which belonged to Naboth the Jezreelite beside the threshing-floor of Ahab." (The spelling 'Ισραηλείτῃ "Israelite" of MS B is corrupt: read rather with MSS like i oc$_2$ [Rahlfs 246 82 127] ιεζραηλίτῃ "Jezreelite.") That is to say, in the Old Greek the words אֵצֶל הֵיכַל "near the palace" are represented by παρὰ τῷ ἅλῳ "near the threshing-floor."

The solution to the problem of how אֵצֶל הֵיכַל became παρὰ τῷ ἅλῳ is provided in Montgomery's commentary: it is the result of the confusion between ΝΑΩ and ΑΛΩ, a suggestion already put forward by O. Thenius in the 19th century. This early corruption means that παρὰ τῷ ναῷ "near the temple" became παρὰ τῷ ἅλῳ "near the threshing-floor." (See Montgomery 333.)

The Lucianic Greek MSS boc$_2$e$_2$ preserve the reading παρὰ τῷ οἴκῳ "near the house" of Ahab. We will return to this translation.

The Armenian version of the selection from v 1 reproduced in Greek above is այգի մի էր Նաբութայ յեզրայելացւոյ, սենեճ առ կալ աքաա-բու "there was a vineyard belonging to Naboth the Jezreelite, near the threshing-floor of Ahab."

The marginal reading in Armenian witnesses—moved from the margin into the text in some—replaces the word կալ "threshing-floor" with արքունիհս "palace." This marginal reading has come from contact with the Hebrew text. In that case, it is most likely that it represents the work of one of "the Three."

Frequently one notices in dealing with the Armenian marginalia in 1–4 Reigns that Symmachus readings have been taken up into the Lucianic text. Further, Symmachus readings predominate among translations from "the Three" preserved in Armenian MSS of 1–4 Reigns. It seems probable to me that արքունիս represents Symmachus and that it is a translation of οἴκῳ. The Armenian translation is not literal — in which case we might expect տուն "house" — but suits well the context. The Armenian translation of οἴκου τοῦ βασιλέως "of the house of the king," i.e. palace is տանն արքունի "of the royal house": see 4 Rgn 11:5 (also vv 11, 19).

The Hebrew, Greek and Armenian equivalents are:

הֵיכָל (אֵצֶל) → Old Greek παρὰ τῷ ἀλῷ [mend pro ναῷ] → Zohrapian

մերծ առ կալ

→ conj. Sym (παρὰ τῷ) οἴκῳ → sine nom (մերծ առ) ար-

քունիս.

This reconstruction means that the Armenian provides the key to understanding the origin of the Lucianic reading οἴκῳ. The Armenian evidence can be placed in the second apparatus in B-M-Thack as follows:

αλω] ⟨σ'?⟩ οικω Arm.

A more conservative citation of the Armenian evidence in terms of B-M-Thackeray's method of citation might simply put the Armenian reading into Latin, without suggesting a signature:

αλω] *palatium* Arm.

21:21 (Old Greek 20:21) 1°

որ միզիցէ զորմով] ի մարդոյ մինչեւ (> M177) գշուն M177mg(ind inc) V212mg Zohapp(mg)

M177 has the marginal reading below 21:21 2°; it has an index sign that looks like a bolt of lightning plus a prime sign—hence ˀ ′ —but this does not appear to be represented in the text. I say "does not appear" because there is a second, smudged mark above զնեղեալն (21:21 2°)—aside from the index sign which belongs there for its correct marginal reading—and perhaps above (v 22) զտունն. In the latter case we would read "And I will make your house like the house [mg: from man to dog] of Jeroboam," which does not seem very likely. There is certainly no index sign over որ մ՛իզիզէ զմարմով. (I might note that the index sign at 21:21 2° is a "lightning bolt"—i.e. ՛—so that the same sign plus the prime sign is intended to indicate "marginal reading number two.")

V212 is cited on the basis of Zanolli 1226.

The context concerns Ahab's "theft" of Naboth's vineyard. In v 20 Elijah begins his announcement of the evil that is going to come upon Ahab and his family. In v 21 he says, "I will bring disaster on you; I will consume you, and will cut off from Ahab every male, bond or free, in Israel." The words "every male" are a translation of מַשְׁתִּין בְּקִיר, literally "one who pees on a wall."

The Old Greek rendering of מַשְׁתִּין בְּקִיר is literal: οὐροῦντα εἰς τοῖχον "one who pees on a wall." B-M-Thack cite no variant readings for this translation.

The Armenian translation is similarly literal, though it uses a clause instead of the participial construction: որ մ՛իզիզէ զորմով "who(ever) pees on a wall." Bedrossian cites ոչ թողուլ յամենայնէ որ զորմով մ՛իզիզէ "not to allow (to live) anyone who pees on a wall" as the expression for "to destroy every male." Cf. 3 Rgn 16:11 ոչ եթող նմա որ մ՛իզիզէ զորմով "and he did not leave him any male."

In some Armenian witnesses there is a marginal reading for the euphemism "who pees on a wall." The reading is ի մարդոյ մինչեւ շգունն "from man to dog." So the sentence, with the substitution, reads "I will destroy of Ahab (everyone) from man to dog, (both) the one who oppresses and the one who is oppressed from Israel." This marginal reading, whose origin I do not know, offers an alternative to the colourful euphemism in the text. I suppose it understands "whoever pees on a wall" to be men (and boys!) and dogs. Or, one might take it as a plus for the euphemism: "whoever pees on a wall, from man to dog!"

It is difficult to determine the origin of the marginal reading. It can be taken as an interpretive rendering of the Hebrew. Because these marginal readings in Armenian witnesses, even when unsigned, often derive from "the Three," this marginal reading cannot be dismissed. It could be just a gloss on the text, i.e. "whoever pees on a wall" means everyone from men to dogs. On the other hand, it rather easily retroverts into Greek, in which case the sentence reads: καὶ ἐξολεθρεύσω τοῦ ᾽Αχαὰβ ἀπὸ ἀνθρώπου (or ἀνδρὸς) ἔως κύνος "and I will destroy what belongs to Ahab, from man to dog!" If the marginal reading is simply a gloss, its easy retroversion into Greek may indicate that it has come from a gloss in the Greek MS from which readings belonging to "the Three" derive. The same holds true if it is just an exegetical plus.

Until further evidence emerges this reading should be put in the second apparatus of B-M-Thack.

The Hebrew, Greek and Armenian equivalents are:

מַשְׁתִּין בְּקִיר → Old Greek οὐροῦντα εἰς τοῖχον → Zohrapian որ

 մի զիցէ զորմով

→ conj. ἀπὸ ἀνθρώπου (or ἀνδρὸς) ἔως κύνος ← sine nom ի

մարդոյ մինչեւ զշուն.

This reading can be placed in the second apparatus of B-M-Thack as follows:

ουρουντα εις τοιχον] *a viris ad canis* Arm.

The marginal reading could be a "plus," in which case the citation is:

ουρουντα εις τοιχον] + *a viris ad canis* Arm.

This marginal reading will await the editor of a critical edition of the Greek text of Reigns. Perhaps it will be found in the margin of some Greek MS.

21:21 (Old Greek 20:21) 2° *

զ ներեալ և զլքեալ] զկապողն (զկապաւտն M177) և զարձակեալն

M177mg V212mg Zohapp(mg)

V212 is cited on the basis of Zanolli 1226. This reading is not cited in B-M-Thackeray.

A translation of v 21 has already been given in 1° above. At issue here are the words עָצוּר וְעָזוּב "bond or free."

The verb עָצַר means "hold back, hinder" and as such can be used of imprisoning or detaining. KBH have a note on the phrase עָצוּר וְעָזוּב, which occurs also at 1 Ki 14:10: "mng. uncert.: slave & free? married man & bachelor? minor & of age? see comm." BDB suggest that the phrase means *shut up and freed* , proverb. phr., = all classes of people Dt 32³⁶ 1 K 14¹⁰ 21²¹ 2 K 9⁸ 14²⁶ (exact meaning dub.; prob. either = bond and free, or [v. (W.) R(obertson) S(mith)(Religion of the) Sem(ites) i. 437, 2nd ed. 456] under taboo and free from it)." See I. עָצַב *qal* 3.

The Old Greek rendered the phrase עָצוּר וְעָזוּב with the words καὶ συνεχόμενον καὶ ἐνκαταλελειμμένον "both the oppressed one and the abandoned one," i.e. "even the oppressed and the abandoned." For συνέχω in the sense of "oppress" cf. Luke 8:45; 19:43: cited by LSJ under συνέχω 5.

The phrase καὶ συνεχόμενον καὶ ἐνκαταλελειμμένον was translated into Armenian as և զնեղեալն և զլքեալն "both the one who is oppressed and the one who is abandoned" or, since these words are both aorist participles and active and passive are not morphologically different, we might translate "both the one who oppresses and the one who is oppressed" which may have been the way it was understood when read in Armenian.

Zohrapian's citation of this marginal reading is as follows: ի վերայ և զնեղեալն, նշանակի , տալ զկապողն և զարձակեալն," i.e. "upon և զնեղեալն there is indicated [in the margin] տալ զկապողն և զարձակեալն "to give (i.e. hand over) the one who binds (or is bound) and the one who is loosed (i.e free)." (Bedrossian cites a phrase կապել և արձակել "to bind & loose": see his entry under կապեմ.) In this reading the word կապող is a present participle, as indicated by the ending -ող. This form, like the aorist in -եալ, can be either active or passive. The phrase զկապողն և զարձակեալն could then mean simply "bound [i.e. slave] and free" but the fact that կապող is a present participle and արձակեալ an aorist participle may be intended to lead the reader to distinguish the first as a still-existing circumstance (i.e. "the one who is still bound") and the second as a past event (i.e. "the one who is— has been—freed"). The plain sense of the passage requires "bound and free."

The phrase զկապողն և զարձակեալն does not occur in the Bible, at least according to the concordance of Arapkerts'i. Zanolli points us in the direction of the Peshitta where he notes the reading ܟܪܝܐ ܘܫܒܝܩܐ, i.e. "both the one who binds and the one who loosens." Whether this could be the origin of the

marginal reading is unclear. It would be very unusual if such a marginal reading in
the Armenian required recourse to the Peshitta as the presumed source.

The marginal reading is synonymous with the reading in the text. Its origin
is unknown. However, it appears to derive from contact with the Hebrew text and
for that reason may be considered to derive from one of "the Three." It should be
cited in the second apparatus of B-M-Thack. Perhaps evidence will be found to
clarify its origin. Because Symmachus readings predominate among the Armenian
marginalia in 1–4 Rgn, one's first inclination is to think it might derive from him.

The Hebrew, Greek and Armenian equivalents are:

עָצוּר וְעָזוּב → Old Greek συνεχόμενον καὶ ἐνκαταλελειμμένον →
Zohrapian զ ևեղեալ և զլքեալ
→ *alligatum et liberum* ← sine nom զկապող ն և զար-
ձակեալ ն.

I have not been able to retrovert the Armenian back into satisfactory Greek
and have therefore resorted to the practice of B-M-Thack. This item, unique to the
Armenian evidence, can be placed in the second apparatus of the Cambridge edition
as follows:

συνεχομενον και ενκαταλελειμμενον] *alligatum et liberum*   Arm.

VII. 4 Reigns

J.N. Birdsall, "Traces of the Jewish Greek Biblical Versions in Georgian Manuscript Sources," *JSS* 17 (1972) 83–92. • José Ramón Busto Saiz, *La Traduccion de Simaco en el Libro de Los Salmos* (Textos y Estudios "Cardenal Cisneros" 22; Madrid: Instituto "Arias Montano" 1978). • John Chrysostom (Hovhannu Oskeberani), *Meknut'iwn Esayeay Margarēi* [Commentary on Isaiah the Prophet] (*Matenagrut'iwnk' Nakhneats'—Oskeberan* ; Venice: St. Lazar 1880). • F.C. Conybeare and St. George Stock, *Grammar of Septuagint Greek, with Selected Readings from the Septuagint* (Boston: Ginn 1905; repr. Peabody: Hendrickson 1988). • Sidney Jellicoe, *The Septuagint and Modern Study* (Oxford: Clarendon 1968). • David M. Lang, *Catalogue of Georgian and Other Caucasian Printed Books in the British Museum* (London 1962). • Ralph Marcus, tr., *Josephus: Jewish Antiquities* , vol. VI (Loeb Classical Library; London: Heinemann; Cambridge, MA: Harvard University 1937; repr. 1966). • J. Molitor, *Glossarium Ibericum in quattuor Evangelia et Actus Apostolorum antiquioris versionis etiam textus Chanmeti et Haemeti complectens* (CSCO 228, 237; Subsidia 20, 21; Louvain 1962). • James A. Montgomery, *A Critical and Exegetical Commentary on The Books of Kings* , ed. H.S. Gehman (ICC; Edinburgh: Clark 1951). • W.F. Moulton and A.S. Geden, *A Concordance to the Greek Testament* , 4th ed. rev'd by H.K. Moulton (Edinburgh: Clark 1963; repr. 1967). • Alison Salvesen, *Symmachus in the Pentateuch* (JSSM 15; Manchester: University of Manchester 1991). • Michael E. Stone, "Additional Note on the Marginalia in 4 Kingdoms," in *Biblical and Armenian Studies* , ed. M.E. Stone (Supplementary Volume I to *Sion* ; Jerusalem: St. James 1976) 21–22. [Provides a list of readings in margins at 8:8; 17:1; 19:13, 37; 23:35: based upon a recollation of MS V212—his V280—which revealed that

Zanolli had failed to record five readings. Also cites Georgian for 10:13; 11:12; 14:7 on the basis of Birdsall.] • H.B. Swete, *An Introduction to the Old Testament in Greek* , revised by R.R. Ottley (Cambridge: Cambridge University 1902; repr. New York: Ktav 1968). •Emanuel Tov, *Textual Criticism of the Hebrew Bible* (Minneapolis: Fortress/Assen-Maastricht: Van Gorcum 1992). • Julio C. Trebolle-Barrera, *Jehú y Joás. Texto y composición literaria de 2 Reyes 9–11* (Universidad Pontificia de Salamanca; Valencia: Artes Gráficas Soler 1984). • J.J.S. Weitenberg and A. de Leeuw van Weenen. *Lemmatized Index of the Armenian Version of Deuteronomy* (Leiden Armenological Publications 1; SBLSCS 32; Atlanta: Scholars 1990). • John William Wevers, *Septuaginta, Vetus Testamentum graecum auctoritate academiae scientarum gottingensis editum, I Genesis* (Göttingen: Vandenhoeck & Ruprecht 1974); *II, 2 Leviticus* (1986). • Zanolli: see 1 Rgn. • Joseph Ziegler, *Septuaginta Vetus Testamentum graecum auctoritate academiae scientarum gottingensis editum, XV Ieremias, Baruch, Threni, Epistula Ieremiae* (1957).

The Greek text used is again that of Brooke-McLean-Thackeray.

The entire book of 4 Reigns belongs to the section γδ. Indeed, that section extends from 3 Rgn 22 to the end of 4 Rgn. Here the so-called Lucianic MSS boc_2 e_2 may offer our best access to the Old Greek translation; Codex Vaticanus—MS B—is a revised form of text. It is the latter which serves as the base manuscript for collation in B-M-Thackeray.

Georgian evidence is provided on the basis of Birdsall's article and is cited as $Georg^{J/B}$, i.e. the Georgian according to material collected and published by Janashvili and Birdsall. In his article Birdsall transliterates the Georgian, on the basis of Lang's system he says on p. 85, n. 1. However, in Lang's system the following equivalences obtain: თ *t‘* ; ფ *p‘* ; ქ *k‘* , but in the article by Birdsall we find: თ *t’* ; ფ *p’* ; ქ *k’* . I follow the former and include the Georgian in its original script, as well as the transliteration. The "original script" is given on the basis of Birdsall's transliteration: I have not made a new examination of the evidence.

For further information on the textual history of 1–4 Reigns see the introduction to 1 Rgn.

1:1 *

Ա2կահենագ] անգունենագ; ապատամ՚բեագ (> M177)

M177mg M188mg(sine ind) M2628mg

Manuscript J428 lacks marginal readings for its first page having text, which involves vv 1–13a. This is really just one column—on the recto of a folio—because the first page that has text includes one column of chapter summaries. The lack of marginal readings for this one column—there is a marginal reading for the second line of the following page (for v 13b)—is probably the result of an oversight by the scribe who placed the marginal readings. At the same time it shows that the marginal readings in MSS M188 M2628 do not derive from MS J428, though J428 (date: 1620) is fifteen (in the case of M2628) and twenty-three (in the case of M188) years younger than those MSS. Both MSS J428 and M188 were copied in Constantinople; M188 is of unknown origin. Since it seems likely that these three MSS are indebted to the same exemplar for their marginalia in 4 Rgn, the marginalia may offer a clue to the provenance of M188.

4 Rgn 1:1 says "After the death of Ahab, Moab rebelled against Israel." The important word is "rebelled," יִּפְשַׁע. Greek MS B has for this ἠθέτησεν "deal treacherously with, break faith with." LSJ cite this passage for that meaning. Interestingly, Reider-Turner list ἀθετεῖν pass. as Aquila's translation for יִּפְשַׁע. That is the only equivalence given. They list ἀθεσία and ἁμαρτία as the two words used for the noun cognate to יִּפְשַׁע, namely פֶּשַׁע.

Zohrapian's text represents ἠθέτησεν with the word ա2կահենագ "revolt; reject." The same reading is attested by M1500 (f.175v, col.1, ↑24: Ա2գահե[ш]g) so I take it to be original.

Armenian witnesses cite two marginal readings: անգունենագ "he despised, slighted" and ապատամ՚բեագ "he rebelled." In M2628 the order of the marginal readings is usually Symmachus, then Aquila and that is probably true here as well.

For ἠθέτησεν there is an unsigned reading in the second apparatus of B-M-Thack: ἀπέστη "revolted" is preserved in Greek MS j (Rahlfs 243). Field suggests this belongs to Symmachus: it is his translation of שֶׁפַע at 8:20. That may be so or not be so because Symmachus is not so stereotypical in his translations as Aquila.

The Armenian MSS usually place the readings from "the Three" in the order Sym–Aq–Th. We would expect then that ապստամբրեաց "revolt, rebel" is the translation of Aquila. Indeed, ապստամբրիմ translates ἀφίστημι, for example, at Gen 14:4; Deut 32:15; 2 Chron 13:6, 21. It would appear therefore that ἀπέστη–ապստամբրեաց could preserve the translation of Aquila.

The word անգոսնեաց likely belongs to Symmachus. What is the Greek word underlying it? Arapkerts'i lists 31 occurrences of անգոսնեաց: five times it translates ἀθετέω (1 Rgn 13:3; 2 Chr 10:19; Wisd 5:1; Jer 3:20 [twice]); eighteen times its translates ἐξουδενέω "set at naught, disdain, scorn" (so Lust) or its neologisms ἐξουδενόω and ἐξουθενόω (2 Rgn 6:16; 1 Chr 15:29; 2 Chr 36:16; Prov 1:7; Cant 8:1, 7 [twice]; Wisd 4:18; Sir 34:26 [Rahlfs 31:22], 41 [Rahlfs 31:31]; Amos 6:1; Zech 4:10; Rom 14:3, 10; 1 Cor 16:11; Gal 4:14) or its cognate noun (1 Macc 1:41; Ps 30:19); five times it translates μυκτηρίζω "turn up the nose, sneer at" (4 Rgn 19:21 [‖ ἐξουδενέω, rendered by արհամարհեմ "despise"[1]]; Prov 15:5; 23:9; Lk 16:14; 23:35); twice it translates φαυλίζω "hold cheap" (Prov 22:12; Isa 37:22 [‖ μυκτηρίζω, rendered by արհամարհեմ]); once it is used to translate οὐ προσποιέομαι "pretend the contrary" (Job 19:14).

This examination of the words which անգոսնեմ renders in the biblical corpus makes it likely that it is used here at 4 Rgn 1:1 for the verb ἐξουδενέω or μυκτηρίζω — both are used by Symmachus, though neither is used for שֶׁפַע. The former of these two verbs is more likely than the latter. We might expect the underlying form to be ἐξουδένησεν "he despised."

The equivalences among Hebrew, Greek and Armenian are:

שֶׁפַע? → Old Greek ἠθέτησεν → Zohrapian ուշկահեաց

→ sine nom (conj. Aq) ἀπέστη → sine nom ապստամբրեաց

→ conj. Sym ἐξουδένησεν ← sine nom անգոսնեաց.

The Armenian evidence probably makes the identification of ἀπέστη with Aquila possible and likely preserves the translation of Symmachus, not otherwise attested.

---

[1]The verb μυκτηρίζω also appears parallel to ἐξουδενέω at 2 Chr 36:16, cited just four lines above: the former is rendered by արհամարհեմ.

The second apparatus in B-M-Thack can be revised to include the Armenian:
και—ισραηλ] και απεστη μωαβ του ιηλ j |αθετησεν] ⟨α'⟩ απεστη Arm :
⟨σ'⟩ *despexit* Arm.

A new edition of the Greek text could indicate the conjectures that ἀπέστη is likely the translation of Aquila and that *despexit* is probably the translation of Symmachus; further that ἐξουδένησεν may underlie the Armenian ական գ nu u ն ա g.

1:2 *

pահալ q ծ ա ն ծ ի կ] pալ q ur nn Aq

M188^mg M2628^mg

Ahaziah has fallen through the lattice in his upper chamber in Samaria. Injured, he sends messengers to "inquire of Baal-zebub, the god of Ekron." The word in question is the proper name בַּעַל זְבוּב "Baal-zebub." The name of this deity also occurs in the New Testament at Mark 3:22 and parallels as Βεελζεβούλ "Beel-zebul," a slightly different spelling: there appears to be some contamination backwards in the tradition, as one sees below.

In Greek MS B the messengers are told to inquire ἐν τῷ Βάαλ μυῖαν θεὸν ᾿Ακκαρών "by Baal, fly god of Ekron."

B-M Thack give the translations of Aquila, Symmachus and ῾Εβραῖος in their second apparatus. According to Greek MS j (Rahlfs 243), Aquila translated בַּעַל זְבוּב as βεελ ζεβούβ;[1] according to Greek MSS jz (Rahlfs 243 554) and Syh, Symmachus rendered the name as βεελ ζεβούλ; according to MSS jz, εβρ. reproduced the name as βαβαλ ζεβούβ(-βουλ z). One can probably see here in the spelling with -εε- and -λ contamination that comes from the text in the New Testament.

The Armenian text offers a translation of a MS like Greek MS B: "Baal, fly [god]." The marginal reading attributed to Aquila appears to have been contaminated with the -λ spelling: hence "Baal-zabul." And the vowel -ε- in ζεβουβ has become -α-. The Armenian thus reflects βααλ ζαβούλ.

The equivalences among Hebrew, Greek and Armenian can be represented

---

[1] This corrects Field who followed the transcription of Holmes and Parsons, namely Βααλζεβούβ.

thus:

בַּ֣עַל זְב֔וּב → Greek MS B Βάαλ μυῖαν [θεόν] → Zohrapian բահալ
q ծառ ծիկ

→ Aq βάαλ ζεβούβ → Aq բաալ q արուղ.

The transliteration preserved in the Armenian MSS appears to have assimilated to a slightly different spelling. The Armenian marginal reading can be recorded
in B-M-Thackeray's second apparatus as follows:

δευτε—ακκαρων] α′ πορευθεντες εκζητησατε εν βααλ ζεβουβ θεω
ακκαρων j : σ′ απελθοντες πυθεσθε παρα του βεελ ζεβουλ θεου εκρων jz Syh
| εν 3°—ακκαρων] εβρ. βαβαλ ζεβουβ(-βουλ z) ελων εκρων jz : βααλ μυιαν] α′
baal zebul Arm.

1:13 *

պատուեսցի] երեւեսցի Aq

J428mg J1928mg(sine nom) J1934mg(sine nom) M188mg M2628mg

In this passage king Ahaziah sends messengers to find Elijah. In v 13 a
captain and fifty men approach him. The captain falls on his knees and entreats
Elijah: "O man of God, please let my life ... be precious in your sight." At issue is
תִּיקַר־נָא, translated "please let be precious." According to Holladay יקר means
here "be precious, rare."

In all the Old Greek tradition—aside from two or three mistakes—
תִּיקַר־נָא is represented by ἐντιμωθήτω "be held in honour," or ἐντιμωθήτω δή
"may ... be held in honour." (LSJ cite this passage for that meaning.)

Պատուեսցի is a good translation of ἐντιμωθήτω and means "be honoured, respected." The marginal reading երեւեսցի is the subjunctive of երեւիլ "to
appear, to show one's self, to offer one's self." The sentence would then say "May
my life and the lives of these your fifty servants appear [i.e. find recognition?] before your eyes."

Reider-Turner give τιμᾶν pass. as a translation for יקַר in Aquila. Under
τιμᾶσθαι pass. "to be honoured" only two passages are given: Ps 71(72):14 and

Zech 11:13. If one looks at the cognates of יָקָר it would appear, based on the limited evidence, that יָקָר and cognates are rendered by τιμᾶν and cognates in Aquila.

The question is whether τιμᾶν lies behind երևիլ here. If not, where did the reading come from? Not from the Latin Vulgate—a source of marginal readings in J1928 J1934—which has noli despicare.

The cognate adjective for երևիլ is երևելի h which means "visible, evident" but also "eminent, important, noble." It is a bit of a stretch but, in the light of the adjective, perhaps երևեցուgh could represent τιμωθήτω. If not, it is unclear what Greek word lies behind երևեցուgh.

I am inclined to accept that this is a genuine Aquila reading, though there is no corroborating evidence. The Armenian tradition is generally reliable in the preservation of these materials.

The Hebrew, Greek and Armenian equivalents are:

אַל־יְקַר־נָא → Old Greek ἐντιμωθήτω → Zohrapian պատուեցուgh
→ Aq conj. τιμωθήτω ← Aq երևեցուgh.

This reading can be added to the second apparatus in B-M-Thack:
εντιμωθητω] α′ *appareat* Arm.

2:1 *

շարժմամբ] մրգով Sym; մրրկաւ Aq

J428^mg M188^mg M2628^mg

The passage concerns Elijah's ascent to heaven. 2:1 says "Now when the LORD was about to take Elijah up to heaven by a whirlwind, Elijah and Elisha were on their way from Gilgal." The word in question is סְעָרָה "gale, heavy windstorm"; in the NRSV "whirlwind."

The Old Greek tradition translates בַּסְעָרָה with ἐν συνσεισμῷ "in a hurricane." The word συσσεισμός LSJ define as "commotion of earth or air, earthquake or hurricane." The word շարժումն "movement; earthquake" is quite adequate for συσσεισμός.

B-M-Thack in their second apparatus cite a reading for Aquila. They offer: ἐν συνσεισμῷ] α′ *in procella* ["tempest, hurricane"] Syh(sine nom) Syh-ap-Barh. So Aquila's translation is preserved in Syriac. Field uses the words *in turbine* to translate the Syriac ܚܒܠܐ which, he says, occurs at a *membrana abscissa* "cut or tear in the parchment." The underlying Greek word is uncertain, Field adds.

The margins of MSS J428 M188 M2628 give us signed readings from Aquila and Symmachus. The reading for Aquila is մրրիկ "tempest, storm," put, of course, into the instrumental case; that for Symmachus is մէգ "fog, mist," also in the instrumental case.

What Greek words lie behind the Armenian ones? Reider-Turner provide three words that Aquila uses to translate סְעָרָה: λαῖλαψ "furious storm, hurricane, whirlwind sweeping upwards"; καταιγίς "squall, descending from above, hurricane"; πρηστήρ "hurricane or waterspout attended with lightning." Reider-Turner do not list this passage. A random check of passages where մրրիկ occurs makes it most likely that καταιγίς is the word translated մրրիկ at 4 Rgn 2:1: καταιγίς is translated մրրիկ at Ps 10:7; 49:3; 80:8; Prov 1:27; Isa 21:1; 28:15, 17, 18; ἀτμίς "moist steam, vapour" is rendered մրրիկ at Gen 19:28; συστρόφη (πνεύματος) "*whirl* wind" becomes մրրիկ at Hos 4:19; λαῖλαψ is translated մրրիկ at Mk 4:37.

What Greek word stands behind the Armenian translation of Symmachus? An examination of passages where մէգ occurs reveals that it often translates γνόφος "darkness." LSJ do cite a passage in Aristotle where γνόφος in the plural means "storm-clouds" so the aspect of "storm" might be present if one took the darkness to indicate a storm.

The equivalences among the Hebrew and the Greek and Armenian translations can be set forth as follows:

בַּסְעָרָה → Old Greek ἐν συνσεισμῷ→ Zohrapian զարդմամբ

     → Aq conj. ἐν τῇ καταιγίδι → Aq մրրկաւ

     → Sym conj. ἐν γνόφῳ ← Sym մհգնվ.

The Armenian adds further attestation for Aquila's translation—previously known only in Syriac—and provides a translation for Symmachus, not known before.

The Armenian evidence can be added to the second apparatus in B-M-Thack as follows:

εν συνσεισμω] α' *in procella* Arm Syh(sine nom) Syh-ap-Barh : σ' *in nebula* Arm.

2:4 *

կենդանի է անձն քո] կենաւք անձին քոյ (քn M188; իմnյ M2628)
    Sym

J428mg(sine ind) M188mg M2628mg

Elijah tells Elisha to stay at Bethel because the LORD has sent him to Jericho. Elisha refuses to be separated from Elijah. Elisha says "As the LORD lives, and as you yourself live, I will not leave you." The words in question are חֵי־נַפְשְׁךָ translated in the NRSV "as you yourself live."

The Old Greek translates חֵי־נַפְשְׁךָ with ζῇ ἡ ψυχή σου "as your soul lives," i.e. "as you live."

The text of Zohrapian gives us a translation of a MS like Greek MS B, which is representative of the Old Greek: կենդանի է անձն քո "as your [sg.] soul is alive."

No reading from "the Three" is cited for this passage in B-M-Thack.

The Armenian preserves the translation of Symmachus in a marginal reading. The words կենաւք անձին քոյ mean "by the life of your [sg.] soul," or less literally "by your very life." (The pronoun իմnյ—1 sg.—in M2628 is secondary.) The Greek from which this was translated might have been τῷ ζῆν τῆς ψυχῆς σου.

The equivalences among Hebrew, Greek translations and Armenian are:
    חֵי־נַפְשְׁךָ → Old Greek ζῇ ἡ ψυχή σου → Zohrapian կենդանի է
        անձն քո
    → Sym conj. τῷ ζῆν τῆς ψυχῆς σου ← Sym կենաւք
        անձին քո.

This reading can be added to the second apparatus in B-M-Thackeray:

ζῇ ἡ ψυχή σου] σ′ *vita animae tuae* [1] Arm.

2:8 *

զմաշկեակն] զաղարդոնն Sym; զնամփորտն (զնափորտն M188)
Aq

J428[mg] M188[mg] M2628[mg]

This verse concerns the crossing of the Jordan on dry ground, thanks to Elijah's trusty mantle. The text says that "Elijah took his mantle (אֶת־אַדַּרְתּוֹ) and rolled it up, and struck the water ..." The word in question here is אַדֶּרֶת "robe, garment."

The Old Greek translation of אֶת־אַדַּרְתּוֹ is τὴν μηλωτὴν αὐτοῦ. The word μηλωτή means "sheepskin, any rough woolly skin." There are no variants to τὴν μηλωτήν in B-M-Thack.

Zohrapian's text offers the translation մաշկեակ "sheepskin coat" for μηλωτή.

B-M-Thack in their second apparatus have a Symmachus reading from Syriac which includes a pronoun: την μηλωτην αυτου] σ′ *vestem suam* Syh Syh-ap-Barh (α′ pro σ′).

To this evidence we can add the Armenian translation for Symmachus and a reading for Aquila. For Aquila the Armenian is նամփորտ "cloak." Since this word is not in Arapkerts'i's concordance it is difficult to know what Greek word lies behind it. Help comes from Reider-Turner who note for אַדֶּרֶת the translation στολή "garment, robe" at Josh 7:21. Perhaps that was his translation at 4 Rgn 2:8 also.

For Symmachus also it is difficult to determine what Greek word lies behind the Armenian աղարդոն "cloak, mantle." This word is not in Arapkerts'i's

---

[1]The variant reading իմոյ "my" may indicate that the word քո "your [sg.]" was understood to be a possessive adjective rather than a personal pronoun. Thomson gives քոյոյ or քոյ as the form of the possessive adjective in the genitive case; քո is the form of the second person singular of the personal pronoun in the genitive case. See *An Introduction to Classical Armenian* , 52, 76. The Latin *tuae* represents the possessive adjectival form.

concordance either. It is not in Miskgian—an Armenian-Latin dictionary—but a
Latin equivalent can be drawn from B-M-Thack who provide us with the Syriac,
put into Latin, *vestem* , i.e. *vestis* "garment, robe." Freund-Leverett give us the
Greek equivalents of *vestis* : ἐσθής, from which it is a loan-word; ἔσθημα; and ἱμά-
τιον. The word ἐσθής "clothing, raiment" is used by Symmachus at Lam 4:14 for
לְבוּשׁ "garment; coll. clothes," according to H-R. Symmachus uses ἱμάτιον at 4
Rgn 9:13 for בֶּגֶד "clothes, garment" where it is also the translation in Greek MS
B.

Field retroverts the Syriac ᴍᴅᴀᴌᴌ for Symmachus into Greek as τὸ
περιβόλαιον αὐτοῦ "his cloak" and suggests comparing the Hexapla at 3 Rgn
19:13 where he notes that the word ᴋᴅᴀᴌᴌ stands for περιβόλαιον at Isa 59:17
and for διπλοῖς at 1 Rgn 15:27 in the text of Masius. Finally Field comments that
his retroversion seems more probable than that of [P.J.] Bruns, which is τὸν
χιτῶνα αὐτοῦ.

The equivalences among Hebrew, Greek translations and Armenian can be
summarized as follows:

(י)אֶת־אַדַּרְתּוֹ → Old Greek τὴν μηλωτήν → Zohrapian զմաշկեակն

                → Aq conj. τὴν στολήν → զնամափնրան

                → Sym conj.[Field] τὸ περιβόλαιον→ զպարպրդ ն ն ն.

The Armenian evidence adds confirmation to the evidence in Syriac for the
translation of Symmachus and preserves a translation for Aquila as well. Unfortunately the original Greek translations are not preserved so we are not certain what
Greek words underlie the translations.

The Armenian evidence can be added to the second apparatus in B-M-Thack
as follows:

την μηλωτην αυτου] σ′ *vestem suam* (> Arm) Syh Syh-ap-Barh (α′ pro
σ′) Arm | την μηλωτην] α′ *pallium* Arm.

2:9 *

ոգիդ] ոգւոյդ Sym; ոգւոյդ (ոգւովդ M188) քող sine nom

J428ᵐᵍ M188ᵐᵍ M2628ᵐᵍ

Before Elijah is "taken up" he asks Elisha what he may do for him. Elisha replies, "Please let me inherit a double share of your spirit." The request in Hebrew is : וִיהִי־נָא פִּי־שְׁנַיִם בְּרוּחֲךָ אֵלָי In this sentence פִּי־שְׁנַיִם means "double portion" (BDB 805, 5b) or "2/3" (KBH 289). The difficulty is בְּרוּחֲךָ and in particular how to take the preposition בְּ prefixed to רוּחַ "spirit." The NRSV nicely gets the sense of the statement by using the word "inherit" for וִיהִי־נָא, literally "(And) pray, let there be ...," so that בְּרוּחֲךָ becomes "of your spirit."

Greek MS B has for this statement Γενηθήτω δὴ διπλᾶ ἐν πνεύματί σου ἐπ' ἐμέ "Let there be double in your spirit upon me." The issue is again how to render the preposition in בְּרוּחֲךָ. The ἐν is "wooden."

The translation of the Greek in Zohrapian's text is եղիցի կրկին զդ֊ հո քո ի վերայ իմ "May there be double your spirit upon me." Here նգ "spirit" is in the nominative case and նգհո զո "your spirit"—ն is a demonstrative marker: "that spirit of yours"—may go back to a Greek text that had τὸ πνεῦμα τὸ ἐπί σοι δισσῶς "the spirit which is upon you double," attested in Greek MSS bforu z(mg)c₂e₂ (Rahlfs 19-108 489 82 700 372 554ᵐᵍ 127 93). (This Greek text with τὸ πνεῦμα τὸ ἐπί σοι δισσῶς may be the Old Greek. 3 Rgn 22–4 Rgn is Thackeray's section γδ where the Lucianic MSS boc₂e₂ offer access to the Old Greek and where MS B is revisional.)

There are no notes on this verse for "the Three" in Field or in B-M-Thack.

The reading *sine nom* is probably that of Aquila since in these Armenian MSS the order of citation is Sym–Aq–Th and here we have two readings with Symmachus cited first. The reading նգւնյն զոյ in MS M2628 gives us the gen./dat./abl. of նգ "spirit" + 'further,' i.e. "that over there" demonstrative suffix ն, followed by the second sg. possessive pronoun in the instrumental case, զոյ. The translation is something like "of your spirit," though noun and pronoun might be expected to share the same case: so, in MS M188 both noun and pronoun are in the same case նգւնվն զոյ "by your spirit," which could follow from the Greek preposition ἐν.

The marginal readings are in the Armenian MSS to clarify what is meant by կրկին նգ: it means "double *of* your spirit" (Sym) or "double *by* your spirit" (Aq). The Greek text behind the Armenian may be the same as that represented by Greek MS B: ἐν πνεύματί σου.

The equivalences among Hebrew, Greek translations and Armenian can be set out as follows:

בְּרוּחֲךָ → Greek MS B ἐν πνεύματί σου → Zohrapian ոգիդ քո

      → conj. Aq ἐν πνεύματί σου ← sine nom ոգւոյդ քով

      → Sym conj. πνεύματός σου ← Sym ոգւոյդ.

The Armenian witnesses preserve readings not otherwise known. They can be added to the second apparatus in B-M-Thack:

ἐν πνευματι σου] ⟨α′⟩ *spirito tuo* σ′ *spiriti tui* Arm.

2:10 *

 զդիւարինս] բագումս Aq

J428mg M188mg M2628mg

Elijah responded to Elisha's request noted above in v 9 by saying, "You have asked a hard thing." This is a translation of הִקְשִׁיתָ לִשְׁאוֹל which consists of the *hifil* of קשה "make hard" with לְ plus the infinitive of שאל "ask," hence "ask something difficult."

The Old Greek translation of this sentence—reflected in MS B—is Ἐσκλή- ρυνας τοῦ αἰτήσασθαι, a literal translation consisting again of a verb "harden"— σκληρύνω—and an infinitive of a verb "to ask." The meaning is something like "What you have asked is hard."

The Armenian translation represented in Zohrapian's text turns the Greek around somewhat: the verb "to ask" is now a finite verb խնդրեցեր "you have asked" and "what is difficult" is represented by an adjective in the plural զդ- ւարինս "difficult things": "You have asked difficult things."

For the statement ἐσκλήρυνας τοῦ αἰτήσασθαι there is a reading, sine nom, from "the Three" cited in the second apparatus of B-M-Thack: δύσκολον ᾐτήσω "you have asked [something] difficult" found in Greek MS j (Rahlfs 243). This translation turns the Hebrew around too: the verb "ask" is now finite rather than infinitive and what is difficult is an adjective. The word δύσκολος is not cited in Reider-Turner. Is it a word Aquila would have used? In Reider-Turner's

Hebrew-Greek index the root קָשָׁה is represented in Aquila by σκληρός and cognates. The Old Greek translation has already used σκληρύνω.

The Armenian marginal reading provides the name of the translator: Aquila. However, բազնիւն—plural of բազնիւ—"too much," is not a literal translation of δύσκολον. There are a number of possibilities here and they include: 1) δύσκολον is Aquila but բազնիւն is just not a literal translation of it; 2) բազնիւն is not Aquila, but Symmachus; 3) բազնիւն is just an interpretive reading, inner-Armenian, for դժուարին and does not come from "the Three."

I think we may disregard 3) because the Armenian tradition of the marginal readings is quite accurate; 2) is possible; 1) is also possible since the Armenian translation of the text has already used an adjective which is a good equivalent of δύσκολος, namely դժուար "difficult": a translator had to choose some other equivalent and perhaps chose a non-literal one.

The reading in B-M-Thackeray's second apparatus does not appear sufficiently literal for Aquila. Perhaps it belongs to Symmachus in which case the Armenian marginal reading—if derived from that Greek reading—preserves the incorrect signature and is such a free translation that it makes the connection with δύσκολον impossible to demonstrate.

We can only cite the Armenian reading for now, without being sure either of its signature or the Greek from which it has come.

הִקְשִׁיתָ לִשְׁאוֹל → Greek MS B ἐσκλήρυνας τοῦ αἰτήσασθαι → Zohra-
                pian դժուարին խնդրեցեր
        → sine nom δύσκολον ᾐτήσω → Aq բազնիւն [խնդրեցեր].

One cannot help noting that the translation of Zohrapian's text would make a literal translation of δύσκολον ᾐτήσω.

This reading can be added to the second apparatus in B-M-Thackeray as follows:

εσκληρυνας του αιτησασθαι] δυσκολον ητησω j | εσκληρυνας] a' nimis
Arm.

2:14 *

ափփուլ] եւ (> J428 M177 V212) արդ (յարդ J428) Sym; նաեւ նա Aq; եւ

(> J428 M188 V212) նոյնպէս Th

J428mg M177mg(sine ind) M188mg M2628mg V212mg

V212 is cited on the basis of Zanolli 1226. In MS J428 the Theodotion reading is run together with that of Aquila. That is, there is a line separating the Symmachus reading from the Aquila reading, as is customary, but the Aquila reading includes that of Theodotion: under the name Aquila we read նաՆեւ նա թէ նոյնպէս.

Elisha picked up the mantle of Elijah, now departed, and took it to the bank of the Jordan. He struck the water and said, "Where is the LORD, the God of Elijah?" That is אַיֵּה יְהוָה אֱלֹהֵי אֵלִיָּהוּ אַף־הוּא in Hebrew. The words in question are אַף־הוּא, literally "even he," perhaps.

The suspicion is that the Hebrew text here is corrupt, that we should read אֵפוֹא "then, so" which, following the interrogative particle אַיֵּה "where," would mean "Where then ..." Cf. KBH under אַיֵּה. BH³/⁷ suggest אֵפוֹא [הוּא] on the basis of Greek MSS B and A, which have ἀφφώ.

As just noted, Greek MS B has ἀφφώ. The transliteration is Old Greek. The Armenian text also transliterated, so we find ափփով in Zohrapian. What did not make sense in Greek makes no more sense when transliterated into Armenian! Marginal readings offering the translations of Aquila, Symmachus and Theodotion made a real contribution to understanding the text in instances such as this.

In B-M-Thack the second apparatus presents the readings of Aquila and Symmachus. According to Greek MS j (Rahlfs 243) the translation of Aquila for אַף־הוּא was καίπερ αὐτός "even he" and that for Symmachus καὶ νῦν "and now." Greek MS r (Rahlfs 700) preserves νῦν: part of the Symmachus reading? The Syro-hexapla preserves the translation of ἑβρ., namely ܐܦܘ. The translation of Theodotion is not preserved, at least not according to Field or B-M-Thack.

The Armenian witnesses preserve readings for Aquila, Symmachus *and* Theodotion. For Aquila: նաեւ նա "even he"; for Symmachus: եւ արդ "and now"; for Theodotion: եւ նոյնպէս "and thus, so." In Greek Theodotion's translation is probably καὶ οὕτως.

The equivalences among Hebrew, Greek translations and Armenian are:

[? אָן־דִּא] אָן־דֵּיה־הָו → Greek MS B ἀφφώ → Zohrapian ապփոպ

    → Aq καίπερ αὐτός → Aq նաև նա

    → Sym καὶ νῦν → Sym եւ արդ

    → Th conj. καὶ οὕτως ← Th եւ նոյնպէս.

For this passage the Armenian preserves Theodotion, which we did not have before.

The second apparatus in B-M-Thack can be revised as follows:

που—αφφω] α′ που $\overline{κ\varsigma}$ ο $\overline{θ\varsigma}$ ηλια καιπερ αυτος σ′ που $\overline{κ\varsigma}$ ο $\overline{θ\varsigma}$ ηλιου και νυν j | αφφω] α′ καιπερ αυτος Arm : σ′ και (> r) νυν r (sine nom) Arm : θ′ et sic Arm.

3:4 *

ներկայ Zoh^{txt}; ներկէք Zoh^{app}] խաշնատես Sym; հաւատարջծ շպես Aq

J428^{mg}(հաւատարջծ sub nom Aq et շպես sub nom Aq) J1927^{mg}(hab solum շպես sine nom) J1928^{mg}(non hab շպես) J1934^{mg} (non hab շպես et sine ind) M177^{mg} M188^{mg} M2628^{mg}(հաւատարջծան) V212^{mg} Zoh^{app(mg)}(hab solum շպես sine nom)

V212 is cited on the basis of Zanolli 1226-1227. Zohrapian notes that his MS has in the margin the word շպես and that some other witnesses have in the margin the words խաշնատես and հովատրջծ. This gives some weight to the suggestion, made below, that խաշնատես and հովատրջծ circulated apart from շպես but that the two streams came together, resulting in two readings attributed to Aquila.

The reading cited in Zohrapian's apparatus is not recorded in B-M-Thackeray.

The transmission of these marginal readings is quite confused. In Zohrapian's base MS only շպես appears in the margin, without signature. He notes that some other MSS have խաշնատեu and հովատրջծ. Because շպես was written on a line separate from հովատրջծ they became separated from one another. For example in MS J428 (fol. 163r) the readings are located between the columns and look like this:

Here հաւտաբոյծ is separated from չպես and each is given the signature "ակ," i.e. Aquila.

The context is Israel's war with Moab. We are introduced to the king of Moab in v 4 as follows: "Now King Mesha of Moab was a sheep breeder." "Sheep breeder" is a translation of the word נֹקֵד.

B-M-Thack have νωκήθ in their text on the basis of MSS A B(c var) h (Rahlfs 55); the spelling νωκήδ is well attested in their apparatus. The transliteration is Old Greek. It is the phenomenon of the transliteration which has summoned the readings of Aquila, Symmachus and Theodotion into the margins of various witnesses.

The Armenian text is a transliteration too, of the Greek. Hence, նեկաթ or ներեթ. Bedrossian does have an entry for նեկաթ, in which he says "s[ubstantive] Hebrew w[ord] sheep-master or -owner." That item is probably based on this passage.

B-M-Thack provide in their second apparatus readings for Aquila and Symmachus. For Aquila the translation of נֹקֵד is ποιμνιοτρόφος "shepherd," according to Greek MS j (Rahlfs 243) Syh(vid) Syh-ap-Barh-ed; for Symmachus the translation is τρέφων βοσκήματα "one who feeds animals," i.e. "one who feeds sheep," according to Greek MS j. B-M-Thack offer *caput pastorum* "chief of shepherds" for Symmachus' translation of נֹקֵד, according to Syh(vid) Syh-ap-Barh (α' pro σ' codd). In Greek MS z (Rahlfs 554) there is a marginal reading offering ἀρχιποίμενα as an explanation for νωκήθ but this is attributed simply to οἱ ἄλλοι ἑρμηνευταί. *Caput pastorum* and ἀρχιποιμήν appear to be the same thing; the latter reading—as ἀρχοποιμήν (sic)—has found its way into Greek MS r (Rahlfs 700), according to B-M-Thackeray's first apparatus.

The three Armenian words խաշնածու (խաշն "sheep" + ածու "see, tend"), հովուապնջ (հով "flock" + պնջ "nourishment") and չպան (a loanword from Middle Persian: Ajarian III 542), all mean "shepherd." The fact that հովուապնջ and չպան appear together but are synonyms contributed to their being separated from one another. Indeed one might wonder whether չպան does not represent a third translation. This is a complicated question, however, because in 4 Rgn the text of the Greek as printed in B-M-Thack represents the third member of "the Three," namely (*kaige* -) Theodotion (Tov 145). Transliterations are part of Theodotion's style and here we have the transliteration νωκήθ (the spelling according to MS B). It is clear that the Old Greek used transliterations too: MSS boc₂e₂ also have a transliteration for נֹקֵד.

The word խաշնածու is attributed to Symmachus. Zanolli thinks that it corresponds not to τρέφων βοσκήματα (MS j) but to ἀρχιποιμήν, confirmed by *caput pastorum* in the Syriac witnesses. The translation ἀρχιποίμενα is preserved in MS z. H-R cite ἀρχιποιμήν as occurring only here, in Symmachus. However, in my opinion there is nothing about the word խաշնածու which would allow one to say that it is a translation of ἀρχιποίμενα rather than τρέφων βοσκήματα. It simply means "one who watches over sheep"; there is no "head" element to the word.

The word խաշնածու is not listed in Arapkerts'i. Moulton-Geden cite one occurrence of the word ἀρχιποιμήν in the NT: it is at 1 Pet 5:4 where it is translated հովուապետ "chief shepherd" (Zoh[txt]) or հովուապան "chief of a flock, pastor" (Zoh[app]). The element -պան clearly represents the element ἀρχι-. It seems more likely to me therefore that the word խաշնածու represents τρέφων βοσκήματα than ἀρχιποίμενα. It is admittedly a difficult problem to resolve.

Zanolli suggests that հովուապնջ չպան corresponds to ἀρχιποιμνιο-τρόφων, i.e. "chief shepherd." No such reading is preserved. The reading preserved for Aquila is ποιμνιοτρόφος. The translation հաւանապնջ is a precise translation: հաւանա- corresponds to ποιμνιο- and -պնջ corresponds to -τρόφος. Reider-Turner cite ποιμνιοτρόφος as a word unique to Aquila and occurring only here and at Amos 1:1. How the word ջպէա is necessary with հովարոյծ is not clear to me. There are two explanations possible: the word ջպէա represents a second translation of the Aquila translation—so that the witnesses with both հովա-րոյծ and ջպէա represent the confluence to two traditions—or ջպէա represents a third translation. In the former case the Armenian witnesses preserve two translations into Armenian of the Aquila translation; in the latter an anonymous translation has become attached to the Aquila translation and been given his signature. Some credence to the latter suggestion may lie in the fact that MSS J1927 V1508 have only ջպէա and that sine nom.

The Hebrew, Greek and Armenian at 4 Rgn 3:4 can be set forth as follows:

נֹקֵד → Greek MSS νωκήθ c var → Zohrapian[txt] անկաթ

     → Aq ποιμνιοτρόφος → Aq հովարոյծ ջպէա

     → Sym τρέφων βοσκήματα → Sym խաշնատես.

In this instance the Armenian gives us the Armenian equivalents for the readings of Aquila and Symmachus.

The second apparatus in B-M-Thack can be revised as follows:

ην νωκηθ] α′ ην ποιμνιοτροφος j Syh(vid) Syh-ap-Barh-ed : σ′ τρεφων βοσκηματα j Arm | νωκηθ] αρχιποιμενα οι αλλοι ερμηνευται ειπον τον νωκηδ z : α′ ποιμνιοτροφος Arm Syh(sine nom) : σ′ caput pastorum Syh(vid) Syh-ap-Barh(α′ pro σ′ codd).

This citation of the Armenian evidence does not cite separately the reading ջպէա which is given a separate signature in MS J428. If indeed this represents a separate tradition for the translation of Aquila, it should be cited as well: α′ pastor Arm.

3:21 *

առ սահմանաւն] լերամբն Sym; ի հանդիպոց Aq

J428[mg] M188[mg] M2628[mg]

The context is once again the war with Moab. The kings of Judah, Israel and Edom went out against Moab. Verse 21 says that when the Moabites heard that the kings had come out against them everyone who could put on armor did so and "were drawn up at the frontier." The words translated "at the frontier" are עַל־גְּבוּל. The word גְּבוּל means "mountain; boundary; territory." BDB list the passage under "border, boundary."

The Old Greek translation of עַל־גְּבוּל is ἐπὶ τοῦ ὁρίου "upon the boundary." The Armenian translation in Zohrapian is առ սահմանաւն "beside the border," a perfectly acceptable equivalent. Nevertheless some Armenian witnesses provide the translations of Aquila and Symmachus. These readings are not otherwise extant: at least these translators are not cited in Field or B-M-Thack.

The Armenian reading for Aquila consists of a double preposition: ի "to" + հանդէպ "before, in front." This combination results in an adverb meaning "before, in front," with հանդէպ in the locative case. According to Reider-Turner the equivalent to גְּבוּל for Aquila is ὅριον, which the Old Greek has here. What translation of Aquila would result in the Armenian ի հանդիպյունջ? One is tempted to see a text behind Aquila involving מוּל "in front" which can be used with the preposition אֶל. That is doubly conjectural, however. Arapkerts'i cites no instance of ի հանդիպյունջ under his entry for հանդէպ.

How Symmachus understood the word in question is much clearer. The Armenian [առ] լերամբն "beside the mountain" has come from a Greek text that understood גְּבוּל as τὸ ὅρος "mountain." It is not clear that the preposition առ should be read with լերամբն because the person who translated the Symmachus reading may well have adjusted the case of լեառն "mountain" to agree with the case required in the text. The preposition առ with լեառն in the instrumental case is rare in the Bible: at Num 20:19 առ լերամբրդ translates παρὰ τὸ ὅρος; at Mk 5:11 առ լերամբն translates πρὸς τῷ ὅρει; cf. also Josh 15:11 where անցանէն առ լերամբ translates παρελεύσεται ὅρος "it passes along to the mount." A possible Greek text underlying the Armenian here at 4 Rgn 3:21 might be ἐπὶ τὸ ὅρος.

The equivalences among Hebrew, Greek translations and Armenian can be represented as follows:

עַל־גְּבוּל → Old Greek ἐπὶ τοῦ ὁρίου → Zohrapian առ սահմանաւն
→ Aq *ante* ← Aq ի հանդիպյունջ

→ Sym conj. ἐπὶ τὸ ὄρος ← Sym [առ] լերասրն.

The Armenian witnesses uniquely preserve the translations of Aquila and Symmachus. This evidence can be added to the second apparatus in B-M-Thack:

επι του οριου] α' *ante* σ' *in montem* Arm.

3:27 *

զիղջ] աարկութիւն Aq

J428mg M2628mg V212mg(sine nom) Zohapp(mg)(sine nom)

V212 is cited on the basis of Zanolli 1227.

The context is the war conducted against Moab by Israel, Judah and Edom. When the battle was going against him, v 27 says that the king of Moab sacrificed his son. Then the text says that "great wrath came upon Israel" so they withdrew. "Great wrath" is a translation of קֶצֶף־גָּדוֹל. The word קֶצֶף means "anger, rage" and is used mostly of God in the Hebrew Bible (so KBH). Montgomery suggests that here the Old English word "dread" might well translate קֶצֶף and that more objectively "panic" would best express it.

The Greek translation for קֶצֶף, as represented in B-M-Thack, is μετάμελος "repentance, regret" so that the clause reads "and great regret came upon Israel." B-M-Thack cite two variant readings to μετάμελος μέγας: they are λύπη μεγάλη, cited from Holmes and Parsons[1]—their MS 71 (also Rahlfs 71)—and *tristitia magna* from the Old Latin.

The Armenian version renders μετάμελος with the word զիղջ (Zohtxt) or զեղջ (Zohapp) "regret, grief."

The citation of another translation in the margin arose out of the perplexing statement about "regret" which led to the coalition army's departure from Moab. B-M-Thack cite a marginal reading in Syriac sources: μετάμελος] α' *irritatio* Syh Syh-ap-Barh. Reider-Turner provide Aquila's Greek equivalent for קֶצֶף, namely παροξυσμός "irritation, exasperation," in their Hebrew-Greek index but the entry

---

[1] R. Holmes and J. Parsons, *Vetus Testamentum Graecum cum variis lectionibus* (Oxford: 1798–1827).

παροξυσμός is missing from the Greek-Hebrew index! H-R cite Jer 10:10 for Aquila under παροξυσμός.

In Armenian witnesses we find the marginal reading ԱՀապկութիւն "terror, dismay, affright." This translation is derived from contact with the Hebrew. It is not the translation of παροξυσμός we might expect since the latter has the sense of provocation, irritation, exasperation that may lead to conflict. H-R cite only two occurrences of παροξυσμός: Deut 29:28(27) (Zoh 28) and Jer 39(32):37 (Zoh 32:37) where the same expression occurs, namely, ἐν θυμῷ καὶ ὀργῇ καὶ παροξυσμῷ μεγάλῳ σφόδρα, except that in the latter the personal pronoun μου follows the first two nouns and σφόδρα is lacking. In Deut 29:28 the Armenian reads բարկութեամբ եւ սրտմտութեամբ եւ զայրացմամբ մեծաւ յոյժ "with anger and with wrath and with very great indignation." (The word զայրացութիւն means "anger, indignation; passion." The cognate verb means "to irritate, to put in a passion, to enrage.") In the Jeremiah passage a different word is used to render παροξυσμός: բարկութեամբ եւ սրտմտութեամբ իմով, եւ գաամամբ մեծաւ "with anger and with my wrath, and with great indignation." (The noun գաունմն means "anger, indignation, passion, wrath, ire, rage, fury.") Either of these words—զայրացութիւն or գաունմն would have been good translations for παροξυσμός in the marginal reading at 4 Rgn 3:27.

The Armenian marginal reading bears the signature of Aquila. The translation ԱՀապկութիւն *can* represent παροξυσμός if one considers the semantic range of both words. Indeed, Field independently makes the same suggestion: he retroverts the Syriac ܪܘܓܙܐ ܚܪܝܦܐ "sharp anger" as παροξυσμός (μέγας).

The Armenian reading attests the translation of Aquila, already known in Syriac.

The Hebrew, Greek and Armenian equivalents are:

נִחָם → Old Greek μετάμελος → Zohrapian զղջ
        → Aq conj. παροξυσμός → Aq ԱՀապկութիւն.

The second apparatus in B-M-Thack can be revised as follows:

μεταμελος] αʹ *irritatio* Arm Syh Syh-ap-Barh.

4:8

իշանէր] խոտորէր

M188ᵐᵍ M2628ᵐᵍ Zohᵃᵖᵖ⁽ᵐˢˢ ᵗˣᵗ⁾

Zohrapian notes in his apparatus that some MSS have this marginal reading in their text: անդ խոտորէր իջանէր ուտէլ եւ րմ՛ "there he used to turn aside [,] he used to go down to eat and drink." That is, some witnesses have moved the reading into the text so that now there is a doublet.

The context concerns Elisha's visits to the house of a woman who lived at Shunem. We are told that "whenever he passed that way, he would stop there for a meal." The words "would stop" are a translation of יָסֻר, "turn aside," the *qal* impf. aspect of סוּר.

The Old Greek rendered יָסֻר with the word ἐξέκλινεν "he turned aside." It will be helpful to cite the complete clause: ἐξέκλινεν τοῦ ἐκεῖ φαγεῖν "he turned aside there to eat."

In Armenian this clause became անդ իջանէր ուտէլ և րմպէլ "(when he went) there he used to go down to eat and drink." (The Greek aorist was translated with the imperfect tense, an improvement since it's a question of habitual behaviour.)

There is a marginal reading in some Armenian MSS for the word իջանէր "he used to go down." It is the word խոտորէր "he used to turn aside," the same as the Old Greek—though not in terms of tense—and the Hebrew. The word խոտորել commonly renders ἐκκλίνω, its equivalent: cf., e.g. in Deut: in six (2:27; 5:32; 17:11; 24:17; 29:18; 31:29) of nine occurrences (exceptions: 17:17 με-θίστημι "turn away"; 27:17 μετατίθημι "change (the position of)"; 32:5 διαστρέφω "mislead" i.e. "pervert"[1]).

This marginal reading derives from contact with the Hebrew or Old Greek texts. The Armenian translation in the text is free; that in the marginal reading follows the Greek literally. Because the Armenian MSS cited here so often convey readings from "the Three" it is possible that this reading too derives from that source. If so it is difficult to retrovert from the Armenian to what the underlying Greek might be, since the underlying Greek is most naturally what one finds in the Old Greek text. As a consequence we must consider the option that the marginal

---

[1]Meanings of the verbs are from F.W. Gingrich, *Shorter Lexicon of the Greek New Testament* (Chicago: University of Chicago 1965). The list of occurrences is from Weitenberg/de Leeuw van Weenen.

reading represents secondary contact with the Old Greek tradition.

See also 4:10.

4:10

մացէ] խոտորեսցի

J428mg M188mg M2628mg(խոտորիցէ)

Manuscript M2628 has the present subjunctive rather than the aorist subjunctive. They are frequently confused in the manuscript tradition but the meaning is the same.

The story continues. The woman suggests preparing a room for the prophet "so that he can stay there whenever he comes to us." The words "he can stay" represent יָסֻר, the same verb that was used in v 8. A more literal translation of the Hebrew וְהָיָה בְּבֹאוֹ אֵלֵינוּ יָסוּר שָׁמָּה is "and whenever he comes to us, he can turn aside there."

The Old Greek again uses the verb ἐκκλίνω: so καὶ ἐκκλινεῖ ἐκεῖ "and he will turn aside there." This is quite adequate.

In Armenian the clause in question is again given a free rendering: մացէ անդր "he can go in there."

This time MS J428 has the marginal reading as well: խոտորեսցի "he will turn aside." This is the verb we might have expected in a literal rendering of the Old Greek.

The issue is the same as at v 8. The marginal reading corrects the text to the Old Greek and to the Hebrew. The Old Greek is already a literal rendering of the Hebrew so it is hard to see why a translation from one of "the Three" would be placed in the margin. No, I think this marginal reading again represents secondary contact with an Old Greek text. It makes this popular story a little closer to the original and gave some learned preacher a little antiquarian help.

It is noteworthy that the Old Greek text again uses ἐξέκλινεν at v 11: "he turned aside (to the upper room)." The Armenian translation is again free: եմուտ "he went in"—same verb as in v 10 but there is no marginal correction.

4:39 *

արիով[թ] բանջար վայրենի (վարի M177; վայրի V212 Zoh) Sym;
կտատեակ (M188vid; տատեակ J428) Aq

J428mg(ind supra արիովթ et supra ազոխ) M177mg(hab solum բանջար վայրենի sine
nom) M188mg(ind supra արիովթ et supra ազոխ) M2628mg V212mg(hab solum բանջար վայրենի sine nom) Zohapp(mg)(hab solum բանջար վայրենի sine nom)

V212 is cited on the basis of Zanolli 1227. He does not actually say there is
an index sign on արիովթ but says that the marginal reading is in the margin at
արիովթ. He adds that the marginal reading can only correspond to the "other"
Greek interpreters, i.e. Aquila, Symmachus or Theodotion. Zohrapian's base MS
has only the Symmachus reading, *sine nom* , and that is not recorded in B-M-
Thackeray.

The clarification of the relationship of the marginal readings to items in the
text and then to what Greek words underlie them is complicated. Manuscripts J428
M188 M2628 record two marginal readings, both signed, in the typical order Sym–
Aq; two of these three witnesses—J428 M188—have an index sign on *both*
արիովթ, a transliteration of ἀριωθ, and upon ազոխ "sour grapes," used to
translate the word τολύπην "gourd." In MS J428 the first index sign is the typical
"lightning bolt" shape; the second is made up of the same sign with a prime sign,
hence ⁷′ , which clearly means "index number two." It seems to me that this might
be important for the solution to the problems raised by the evidence here. (M188
has the same index sign over both արիովթ and ազոխ, which appear on the
same line of text.) Let us take up the marginal readings in connection with արիովթ first because all the witnesses record an index sign upon that word.

The context is one of the miracles stories about Elisha; this one concerns a
spoiled pot of stew. Though there was a famine Elisha told his servant to make a
pot of stew for the company of prophets. One of them "went out into the field to
gather herbs." The word translated "herbs" here is אֹרֹת. The entry in KBH reads:
II *אֹרְדָה: I אֹורָה: pl. אֹרֹת: mallow (Malva rotundifolia), 'light-plant', very sensi-
tive to light 2 K 4₃₉.†

Greek MS B offers a transliteration of אֹרֹת, namely ἀριώθ. The only variant cited by B-M-Thack is ἄγρια "wild (plants)" in the Greek witness y[b] (Rahlfs 121), also attested in the Old Latin[(l)]. The reading in Greek MS y[b] probably comes from "the Three."

In the second apparatus of B-M-Thack we find the following citation: ἀριώθ] ἀριόθ Syh; οἱ λοιποί ἄγρια λάχανα (ἀγριολάχανα z) z (Rahlfs 554) Thdt. (I have added the accents to their citiation.) The identification οἱ λοιποί likely means Aquila, Symmachus and Theodotion, or one of them plus perhaps others. Reider-Turner offer ἄγρια λάχανα "field herbs" as Aquila's translation for אֹרֹת.

The Armenian text also offers a transliteration of the Greek ἀριώθ, i.e. արիովթ. The marginal readings are intended to offer a translation for the transliteration. The word attributed to Aquila, կատամնեակ, means "marsh-mallow." The Latin equivalent to կատամնեակ is *malva* "mallow."[1] This corresponds to the meaning of the Hebrew suggested in KBH so that we have no difficulty connecting կատամնեակ with արիովթ and, in turn, with ἀριώθ and then אֹרֹת.

Symmachus' բանջար վայրենիի means "herbage of the field": բանջար means "herbage, vegetables" and վայրենիի is an adjective which means "wild" (cf. the cognate noun վայր "field, country"). It is an good translation of ἄγρια λάχανα, attributed to οἱ λοιποί in Greek MS z Thdt. It is also an exact translation—even following the word order—of the signed Symmachus reading βοτάνην ἀγρίαν which B-M-Thack cite for τολύπην ἀγρίαν "wild gourds."

Let us look at the latter. Recall the two index signs in MSS J428 and M188.

Later in v 39 we read that "he [i.e., one of the prophets] found a wild vine and gathered from it a lapful of wild gourds." The words "wild gourds" are a translation of פַּקֻּעֹת שָׂדֶה. Under פַּקֻּעֹת (sic) in KBH we read: (wild) gourd, *Colocynthis vulgaris* 2K 4₃₉.† The word occurs only here (undisputedly) in the Hebrew canon.

The words פַּקֻּעֹת שָׂדֶה are translated τολύπην ἀγρίαν "wild gourds" in the Old Greek.[2] The word τολύπην means "a kind of a *gourd , pumpkin* ."

---

[1] The equivalent Greek word—according to Freund-Leverett—is μαλάχη. However, LSJ point out that the relation of μαλάχη to Latin *malva* and English "mallow" is uncertain.

[2] MS B reads τολύπην ἀγρίαν "wild gourds" but, as mentioned in the discussion of this passage, the word ἀγρίαν is lacking in quite a number of witnesses: Adefmnp–uw (Rahlfs A 107 52 489 92 119 106 120 700 130 134 372 314) Arm Old Latin[(2)]. B-M-Thack for τολύπην cite ⅹ *olera*

Perhaps it would be useful to cite the Armenian to this point in the verse. It is: եւ ել յանդն քաղել արիովթ. և եգիտ որթ յանդինն, և քաղեաց 'ի նմանէ ազոխ լի շալակաւ իւրով "and he went into the field to gather *ariōt*' ; and he found a vine in the field, and he gathered from it sour grapes, so that he had a full load." In the Armenian translation the word τολύπην is represented by ազոխ "sour grapes." (The word [τολύπην] ἀγρίαν is not represented and is also lacking in a number of Greek witnesses: see B-M-Thack.)

The word τολύπην occurs only here in the LXX/Old Greek corpus, according to H-R. Its meaning was apparently not known to the Armenian translator.

For the words τολύπην ἀγρίαν B-M-Thack provide the following entry in their second apparatus: τολύπην ἀγρίαν] σ' βοτάνην ἀγρίαν *b* (sine nom) j. This is followed by an entry for τολύπην alone: τολύπην] λυπιν[1] Syh : α' σ' *cucurbitas* Syh Syh-ap-Barh (om σ'). (I have added the accents to the citations here from B-M-Thack.)

The signed Symmachus reading in Armenian witnesses corresponds to the signed Symmachus reading in MS j (Rahlfs 243), βοτάνην ἀγρίαν "wild herbage." It appears that the Greek parent text of the Armenian marginalia had a marginal notation for both ἀριωθ and for τολύπην ἀγρίαν, namely ἄγρια λάχανα and βοτάνην ἀγρίαν, respectively. For each the Armenian translation is quite adequately բան շար վայրենի. Rather than repeat the marginal reading the scribe simply placed an index sign upon ազոխ as well as upon արիովթ.

There is no signed Aquila reading for ἀριώθ. However, for τολύπην there is the reading preserved in Syriac sources, cited by B-M-Thack in their second apparatus. The Latin *cucurbitas* means "gourds." Field cites the marginal reading ܩܪܐ "gourds"—the *cucurbitas* —from the margin of the Syro-hexapla—with the signatures of Aquila and Symmachus—and retroverts it into Greek as κολοκυνθίδας, "gourds." In fact the word is to be found in the first apparatus in B-M-Thack: κολοκυνθίδα is preserved in the margin of MS j and as a correction in MS z (Rahlfs 554); κολοκυνθίδας in MS y[b] (Rahlfs 121) and Old Latin[(2)]. Indeed, H-R

"pot herbs" in Syh. Field suggests that this is an error: it is ἀγρίαν, lacking in various witnesses, which should stand under the asterisk. There is then some question whether the Old Greek rendered שָׂדֶה.

[1]Sic: this appears to be part of the word τολύπην, with an itacism. The scholium follows. See Field.

cite it as Aquila's translation in this verse. It seems to me that the marginal reading in MS j should have been put in the second apparatus.

My conclusion is this. The Armenian marginal readings relate to the transliteration արիովթ. The reading ἄγρια λάχανα can now be provided with a signature, namely Symmachus, beyond the generic οἱ λοιποί of Greek MS z Thdt. Further, we now have Aquila's translation for אֹרֹת as well: in Armenian it is the word կոատեակ in Greek likely μαλάχη, which in the context perhaps has the form τὰς μαλάχας. As well it may be that the Armenian marginal reading is intended to represent βοτάνην ἀγρίαν, a Symmachus translation for פַּקֻּעֹת שָׂדֶה a few words later in the same verse and represented by the words τολύπην ἀγρίαν in the Old Greek. This latter suggestion is conjectural, of course.

The Hebrew, Greek and Armenian equivalents are:

אֹרֹת → Old Greek ἀριώθ → Zohrapian արիովթ

    → Aq conj. τὰς μαλάχας ← Aq կոատեակ

    → Sym ἀγρία λάχανα → Sym բանջար վայրենի.

The second apparatus in B-M-Thack can be revised as follows:

αριωθ] αριοθ Syh : οι λοιποι αγρια λαχανα (αγριολαχανα z) Thdt : α′ *malva* σ′ αγρια λαχανα Arm.

4:42 *

պաղատիոս բակեղաթաւ[1] մուրկ շալակաւ Sym; փափուկս շալակաւ Aq; կտունեալս եւ փափուկս բակեղաթաւ Th; մուրկ
պասատաւկալաւ Aq

M188^mg M2628^mg

J428^mg J1928^mg J1934^mg have only the reading of Symmachus, as it is cited above.

There is something quite puzzling about these marginal readings. First, there are two readings attributed to Aquila. The order of citation given above is that

---

[1]Zohrapian notes in his apparatus that some MSS have the spelling բակեղ եթաւ, which is presumably the original spelling.

found in M2628, which begins with the common order of signature, namely Sym–
Aq–Th. Then it gives a second translation for Aquila. Second, this is not the order
in M188. There the four readings follow immediately upon the marginal readings
for 4:39; they are in the order Aq–Th–Aq–Sym; the index sign is with the Symmachus reading. Perhaps the scribe overlooked the Symmachus reading—the last
reading at 4:39 has Aquila's signature—and then added it at the end. It appears that
at some stage in the transmission of the marginalia either there was access to
another (Armenian) translation of Aquila's rendering or the translator of the marginalia added another translation of Aquila after he had finished the three renderings into Armenian. In the latter case we might expect the second rendering of Aquila's
translation to be more accurate, perhaps more literal. The solution to the problem of
the two Aquila readings may be as simple as that.

Several witnesses communicate only the Symmachus translation. In that
case we must imagine a sort of "simplified" marginalia, whereby only the first of
the translations in the margin was preserved. That is, the translation of Symmachus
stood first and was followed by those of Aquila and Theodotion, as in M2628, but
the last two translations were not recopied. After all, why does one need more than
one?

The context here is another of the miracle stories about Elisha. This one is
the miracle of the twenty loaves. In v 42 we are told "And a man came from Baal-
shalishah, bringing food from the first fruits to the man of God: twenty loaves of
barley and fresh ears of grain in his sack." At issue is כַּרְמֶל בְּצִקְלֹנוֹ "fresh ears
of grain in his sack." The NIV renders this "along with some heads of new grain,"
with which it appears to forego translating בְּצִקְלֹנוֹ.

The Hebrew for the whole clause and a word-for-word translation are:
וַיָּבֵא לְאִישׁ אֱלֹהִים לֶחֶם בִּכּוּרִים עֶשְׂרִים־לֶחֶם שְׂעֹרִים וְכַרְמֶל בְּצִקְלֹנוֹ
"and he brought to the man of God bread of the first fruits: twenty loaves [made
from] barley [flour] and fresh grain in his צִקְלֹן."

For בְּצִקְלֹנוֹ cf. KBH: *צִקְלֹון: צִקְלֹנוֹ 2 K 4₄₂: txt. corr., rd. קְלָעַת.†
BDB state similarly that this is a doubtful word; the Syriac and Targum render "garment"; BDB also cite the reading in Greek MS A and the Armenian, on the basis of
which Lagarde proposed בְּקַלְעָתוֹ "in his wallet."

Tov, in *Textual Criticism*, 367, makes some comments about the word

בְּצִקְלֹנוֹ. He points out that, on the basis of some Ugaritic texts, "it is generally accepted that the *bet* in fact belongs to the root of a word בְּצִקְלֹן, "ripening stalk" or "(green) wheat." The Masoretic text should not then be emended.

The Old Greek apparently did not translate בְּצִקְלֹנוֹ: Greek MS B has simply—for כַּרְמֶל—παλάθας "cakes of preserved fruit"; the Syro-hexapla after παλάθας adds ⸔ θ′ ܟܡܠܐ ⸔ "in a large basket" which indicates that בְּצִקְלֹנוֹ was not represented in the text upon which Origen worked.[1] Greek MSS Ax (Rahlfs 376) have the transliteration βακελλέθ (κακελέθ x), which is the transliteration underlying the translation in the Syro-hexapla! From the Greek the word returned to another Semitic language—i.e. Syriac—where the word ܒܩܠܬܐ was seen to consist of the preposition ܒ "in" plus the word ܩܠܬܐ "large basket." This represents an amazing turn of events. Further, the word ܩܠܬܐ is the Greek word κάλαθος. It is just possible that the reader of the word βακελλέθ might have related it to κάλαθος and thus made some sort of sense out of it!

The Armenian պաղատիտա բակեղաթաւ "dried figs in a *bakeghat'* " contains a transliteration of the hexaplaric plus βακελλέθ, namely բակեղաթ, with the instrumental case ending -աւ. This of course is meaningless in both Greek and Armenian; that incomprehensibility is the reason why translations were added in the margins. The dictionary entry in Bedrossian: "բակեղաթ, *h s[ubstantive]*. wallet, bag" is not helpful because the word in question is not Armenian. Cf. the entry բակեղեթ in Ajarian I 391 who correctly points out that բակեղեթ or բակեղաթ is a transliteration of a Greek transliteration of Hebrew.

The marginal readings in Armenian witnesses reflect an interest in providing a translation or translations for the transliteration բակեղաթ.

Manuscripts J1928 J1934—besides offering the translation of Symmachus—give a reading derived from comparison with the Latin Vulgate: մուրկ մախաղով "roasted wheat *in a bag* "; cf. Latin *pera* "bag, pouch to carry victuals in" (Greek: πῆρα). These two MSS give the symbol Ֆ, i.e. "Frankish," i.e. "Latin" with that reading. This rendering we can, of course, dismiss but it is interesting that it carries the identification of its source.

Perhaps it would be helpful to set out the translations of כַּרְמֶל(וְ) בְּצִקְלֹנוֹ

---

[1] B-M-Thack cite the Syriac in Latin translation as *in canistro* "in a basket."

attributed to "the Three" in the Armenian witnesses:

      Մուրկ շալակաւ "roasted wheat in a load" Sym

      փափուկս շալակաւ "soft things in a load" Aq

      կտուեալ ս եւ փափուկս բակեղաթաւ "fresh and soft things (or

            "cut delicacies") in a *bakeghat'* " Th

      Մուրկ պաստառակալաւ "roasted wheat in a piece of fine

            linen-cover" Aq.

The word כַּרְמֶל is translated Մուրկ "roasted wheat" by Aquila and Symmachus, փափուկս "soft" by Aquila, and կտուեալս եւ փափուկս "fresh
and soft things" or "cut delicacies" by Theodotion.[1] In the latter two cases, the
translations are linked morpholgically, it seems, with the barley loaves, the
Նկանակս գարեղէնս: note the accusative plural marker -ս on each of the
words. This may well have occurred at the point of the translation into Armenian
and was facilitated by the fact that the *waw* (i.e. וְ) attached to כַּרְמֶל was not represented in the marginal readings from which the Armenian was translated.

The difficult word בְּצִקְלֹנוֹ is translated by շալակաւ "with a load"—
շալակ "back, shoulder, load; hand-barrow" + աւ instr. ending—by Aquila and
Symmachus and պաստառակալաւ "in a piece of fine linen"—պաստա-
ռակալ + աւ instr. ending—by Aquila. Theodotion has the transliteration բակեղաթ, Greek βακελλέθ, which Origen put under the asterisk in his fifth column;
from there it has come into MSS Ax.

The two Aquila translations represent a conflation in the tradition—one of
them may be secondary: the second translation attributed to Aquila could belong to a
fourth translator; or it could represent a second attempt at translation of the Aquila
translation *or* it could have been added to the other three translations after separate
translation elsewhere into Armenian. It is unclear what has happened.

The marginal reading for Theodotion may represent more than an equivalent
for παλάθας βακελλέθ. That is, the presence of the եւ, i.e. καί, may indicate that
the word կտուեալս "[freshly] cut" relates to the word κριθίνους (καὶ παλάθας
βακελλέθ). In that case—presuming that Theodotion used κριθίνους—his translation read "bread [made from] freshly cut barley and tender in a *kelleth* ." This

---

[1] I am indebted to Archbishop Shahé Ajamian for the translation "fresh and soft"—in a personal
communication, dated 22/11/94.

suggestion has some merit, though the fact that the other three translations relate strictly to כַּרְמֶל בְּצִקְלֹנוֹ may stand against it.

It is also possible that the marginal reading attributed to Theodotion represents a conflation. Perhaps Theodotion's translation was կոտւեալ u "fresh," and that it has been corrupted by the addition of փափուկ "soft" from Aquila.[1]

It is difficult to determine what Greek text lies behind the Armenian translations of Aquila, Symmachus and Theodotion, not otherwise extant for this passage.

The word մուրկ "roasted wheat" (cf. մրկել "to roast") has only two entries in Arapkertsʻi: Lev 2:14 and 23:14, in both of which it translates χῖδρα "unripe wheaten-groats." (The usual Armenian word for wheat is ցորեան, Greek σῖτος. Adjarian III 363 defines մուրկ as ցորենի հատիկ, աղացած, i.e. "small grains of wheat, roasted.") Miskgian offers for մուրկ the meanings *arista, far, spica* ("ear of corn"; Greek: στάχυς), each of which refers to some form of *frumentum* "corn."

In Lev 2:14 instruction is given for an offering of the first fruits. It is to consist of אָבִיב קָלוּי בָּאֵשׁ גֶּרֶשׂ כַּרְמֶל "ears of grain, parched with fire, grits newly ripe." The LXX translation of this is νέα πεφρυγμένα χῖδρα ἐρεικτά "fresh parched wheaten-groats, pounded." (The word ἐρεικτά "pounded" translates כַּרְמֶל "newly ripe." Aquila and Symmachus rendered כַּרְמֶל with ἁπαλά "tender": see Wevers' edition ad loc.[2] As we will see, Aquila probably used ἁπαλά for כַּרְמֶל in 4 Rgn 4:42.) The Armenian translation of the Greek is մուրկ նոր փխրեալ և մաքրեալ "roasted wheat, fresh, roasted and cleaned." The word մուրկ represents χῖδρα. One notes also that the Greek word χῖδρα is closely connected in the translation of the passage with the Hebrew כַּרְמֶל. It seems quite likely that the word χῖδρα underlies մուրկ at 4 Rgn 4:42 in the translation of Symmachus, and in the second translation attributed to Aquila.

Two passages are listed in Arapkertsʻi for շալակ "back, shoulder, load; hand-barrow": 4 Rgn 4:39 and 2 Macc 9:8, in the first of which it translates ἱμάτιον "an outer garment"; in the latter case շալակաւ translates ἐν φορείῳ "[car-

---

[1] I am indebted to A. Pietersma for the suggestion that the Theodotion reading may be corrupt—personal communication, dated 01/11/94.

[2] H-R, it appears, took χίδρα ἐρεικτά to be the translation for גֶּרֶשׂ because they cite גֶּרֶשׂ for both χίδρα and ἐρεικτά at Lev 2:14: see the entries ἐρικτός and χίδρον. The word ἐρεικτός occurs only here in the biblical corpus.

ried] in a litter." Aquila uses the word ἱμάτιον for the common word בֶּגֶד "clothes, garment," as does the Old Greek and the other two translators, Symmachus and Theodotion. The word φορεῖον is not listed in Reider-Turner.

It is of note that the word շալակ occurs a few verses earlier at v 39. There we read that one of the prophets gathered a "lapful" of gourds from a wild vine. The word "lapful" is a translation of מְלֹא בִגְדוֹ, i.e he filled "his garment." Both the Old Greek and Aquila rendered בִּגְדוֹ with the words τὸ ἱμάτιον αὐτοῦ "his garment." (In both the Hebrew and the Greek the sense is "the fold[s] of his garment.") The Greek πλῆρες τὸ ἱμάτιον αὐτοῦ was translated into Armenian as ի շալակաւ իւրով "his whole garment full." This shows that շալակ can render ἱμάτιον and does so in the very context. I think we can reconstruct the Greek underlying շալակաւ as ἐν τῷ ἱματίῳ.

The word փափուկ means "soft, delicate; delicious, tender." It is the translation of ἁπαλός at Gen 27:9 where it refers to "choice" goats. But ἁπαλός can also be used of tender fruit, as at Mk 13:28 where, however, the Armenian translation employs a construction involving the verb կակղանամ "become tender." Reider-Turner cite ἁπαλός as a word which Aquila uses, indeed in the neuter pl. for כַּרְמֶל at Lev 2:14 (α′ σ′)—noted above—and at Lev 23:14 (οἱ λ′: ἁπαλά [Field pro ἄναλα: sec. Rab. כַּרְמֶל = מַל זַרְךְ]). So it seems quite possible that Aquila's translation of כַּרְמֶל at 4 Rgn 4:42 was ἁπαλά. In that case ἁπαλὰ ἐν τῷ ἱματίῳ "choice things in a garment" likely underlies փափուկս շալակաւ.

The Symmachus' translation մուրկ շալակաւ can be retroverted to χίδρα ἐν τῷ ἱματίῳ with some confidence on the basis of the information provided above.

The marginal reading attributed to Theodotion is կոռւեայս եւ փափուկս բակեղաթաւ "(bread) [made from] freshly cut barley and soft in a *bakeghat'*." It can certainly be read that way in Armenian: this translation understands the word կոռւեայս to relate to գարեղէնս "barley." Perhaps it would be helpful to see the whole sentence in Armenian: և երեր առ այն աստուծոյ նկանակս յառաջնոց արմտեաց նկանակս գարեղէնս, և պաղատիտս բակեղաթաւ "and he brought to the man of God loaves [made from] the first fruits, loaves of barley and dried figs in a *bakeghat'*." If we replace the end of the sentence with Theodotion's translation we read նկանակս գարեղէնս

կտուեալ ու եւ փափուկս բակեղ աթա, i.e. "loaves of barley, freshly cut
and tender in a *bakeghat'*." Because the Armenian does not represent gender, both
adjectives—կտուեալ ու եւ փափուկս—can be construed as modifying "loaves
of barley." In reconstructing the Greek underlying the Armenian we should almost
certainly construe at least փափուկս as a substantive. If both կտուեալ ու եւ
փափուկս are intended for պաղատիոս then they could both be substantives,
in which case we might translate "loaves of barley and [freshly] cut things and tender things," or, putting կտուեալ ու եւ փափուկս together "freshly cut delicacies." On the whole, it seems likely to me that կտուեալ ու relates to գարեղէնս (Greek: κριθίνους) and that եւ փափուկս alone should stand where καὶ
παλάθας stands in the Old Greek. The translation that follows from construing the
sentence that way is "loaves of [i.e. made from, freshly] cut barley and delicacies in
a *bakeghat'*." But we noted above that the Theodotion reading is probably corrupt
and that only կտուեալ ու "fresh" should be attributed to him. In that case we must
read նկանակս գարեղէնս կտուեալ ու բակեղ աթա "loaves of barley,
fresh, in a *bakeghat'*.

Կտուել "cut, trim"—which appears in the plural participle, accusative
case կտուեալ ու—is not listed in Arapkertsʻi. Adjarian II 676 has an entry for the
noun կտեւ "the outside of a walnut or pomegranate" and, with it, the following
meaning for the verb կտուել, derived from M. Awgerean's grammar of 1865: "to
clean, to shell walnuts." He also adds for կտուել a quotation from Nerses Shnor-
hali (12th century): "to clean raisins, apples and similar fruits of their seeds; to remove lentils, chick-peas, beans from their outsides." The participial substantive
կտուեալ ու must mean something like "things that have had their seeds removed"
or "shelled things." If the word կտուեալ ու is taken to refer to the barley it must
mean "threshed," and then "fresh."

Words for "threshing" are quite specialized. In classical Hebrew—at least in
the Bible—there are only a few words for "thresh": in the main, the verb דֹּוּשׁ
which means "trample; trample out (grain), i.e. thresh" (e.g., Deut 25:4; 2 Ki 13:7;
1 Chr 21:20; Isa 21:10; 28:27 [of dill], 28; 41:15; Am 1:3; Mic 4:13); its cognate
דַּיִשׁ "threshing(-time) (Lev 26:5†); and perhaps חָבַט "beat out (grain, accom-
plishing what threshing does)" (Judg 6:11; Isa 28:27 [of cummin]). The usual
Greek equivalent for דֹּוּשׁ is ἀλοάω "thresh" and ἀλοάω is rendered in turn usually

by կասեմ/-իմ/-ում "thrash": that sequence of equivalences is followed at 1 Chr 21:20; Isa 41:15; Mic 4:13; 1 Cor 9:10. The participial form ἀλοῶντα "threshing [ox]" at Deut 25:4 (for בְּדִישׁוֹ) is rendered by կալնուլոյ "thresher" (cf. կալ "threshing floor": Lev 26:5; 1 Chr 21:20). *If* the word կտուեալս relates to the barley then the underlying Greek word is probably a form of ἀλοάω, maybe the passive participle of this verb: ἀλοηθέντας—masculine plural to agree with κριθίνους. The result would be ἄρτους κριθίνους ἀλοηθέντας καὶ ἀπαλὰ βακελλέθ "loaves of threshed barley and choice things [in a?] *bakelleth* ."

However, there may be two reasons why this reconstruction—in which կտուեալս is construed as modifying "barley"—is probably incorrect. First, as has been noted earlier, the readings attributed to Aquila and Symmachus relate only to כַּרְמֶל בְּצִקְלֹנוֹ, of which the Old Greek has translated just the first word, i.e. כַּרְמֶל, as παλάθας "cakes of preserved fruit." Second, the verb կտուեմ is not used of threshing in the biblical corpus: it refers instead to removing the outer shell of some kinds of fruit or vegetables, or to removing the seeds of various kinds of fruit. The substantive կտուեալս must then mean something like "shelled things." If the marginal reading attributed to Theodotion is *not* corrupt, he must have employed two words for כַּרְמֶל. On the other hand, the argument from silence is not always completely convincing: the corpus of materials concerning threshing in the biblical corpus is not large; further, the marginalia belong to the Middle Ages.

A. Pietersma has suggested to me that Theodotion may have used the word ἄλφιτα "barley-groats" for כַּרְמֶל. At Lev 2:14 ἄλφιτα appears to have been Theodotion's translation for גֶּרֶשׂ כַּרְמֶל "coarse new grain." The ἄλφιτα, Pietersma says, are "ears of grain roasted and then the kernels are rubbed out. If כַּרְמֶל is new/fresh grain, ἄλφιτα would be a pretty decent rendering. Furthermore, ἄλφιτον is not only LXX (for קָלִי) but also Theodotion for the same Hebrew."[1] (The word ἄλφιτον occurs only four times in the LXX/Old Greek corpus; each time it is rendered փոխինձ "flour of parched corn" in Armenian: Ruth 2:14; 1 Rgn 25:18; 2 Rgn 17:28; Judith 10:5.) It may well be that ἄλφιτα is Theodotion's translation of כַּרְמֶל at 4 Rgn 4:42.

The second reading attributed to Aquila is մուրկ պատատուակալայաւ "roasted wheat in a piece of linen." The word մուրկ is likely a translation of

---

[1] Personal communication, dated 01/11/94.

χῖδρα, as noted above in connection with Symmachus' translation. But what underlies պատատակալ ալ ւ?

Arapkerts'i lists three passages for պատատակալ "fine linen-cover,
bed-sheet, drapery, tapestry": at Judg 14:12AB and Luke 23:53 it translates σινδών
"fine cloth, linen"; at Judg 14:33A it translates ὀθόνιον "fine linen, cloth."

H-R cite only four occurrences of σινδών: Judg 14:12, 13A (ὀθονία MS B);
Prov 31:24; 1 Macc 10:64A (πορφύραν MSS SR)—in the first three cases, where it
is a question of a translation, the underlying Hebrew is סָדִין "undergarment, ?
shirt" (Judg 14:12f.; Isa 3:23; Prov 31:24†); and only three occurrences of ὀθόνιον: Judg 14:13B (σινδόνας MS A); Hos 2:5 (MT 7), 9(11)—in the first case the
Hebrew is סָדִין and in Hosea the Hebrew is פֵּשֶׁת "flax, linen." Aquila, Symmachus and Theodotion are not cited in H-R or in Reider-Turner as employing either
Greek word. That does not mean they did not, it only means that in extant fragments they have not used these words.

Miskgian offers as the meaning of պատատակալ the words *sindon*
[i.e. σινδών] and *linteum* "a linen cloth." The word סָדִין is not cited in the
Hebrew index in Reider-Turner, but the word פֵּשֶׁת is. There we find that λινοῦς
gen. is used for פֵּשֶׁת by Aquila. Under the entry for the word λινοῦς we read:
פֵּשֶׁת gen. Ez. xliv 18[α'] σ'. The word λίνον means "linen, linen-cloth." In the
singular it can refer to a linen garment (so Rev 15:6). Reider-Turner also have an
entry for λίνος which cites only one passage, namely Isa 42:3 where λίνος is used
to represent קָנֶה "stalk."[1] There is another entry for λίνον where, again, one passage is cited: it is Hos 2:5(MT 7) where λίνον translates פֵּשֶׁת. It would appear that
one of these words could lie behind պատատակալ ալ ւ. "In a piece of linen"
could be represented in Greek as ἐν τοῖς λινοῖς. The difficulty is that בְּפִשְׁתִּים
"in linen" does not look very much like בְּצִקְלֹנוֹ.

The usual Armenian word for "linen" is կտաւ. It is this word that the
translators used at Hos 2:5, 9 (in both cases for ὀθόνιον); Ezek 44:18 (twice for
Old Greek λινοῦς). At Isa 42:3 the Armenian employs the word պատրոյկ
"wick" for λίνον, true to the sense of the passage. I make mention of the translation
in these texts because they have been referred to in the previous two paragraphs. If

---

[1] The Old Greek uses λίνον for פִּשְׁתָּה "wick of flax" (so KBH) which occurs in the second part
of the same line.

the word underlying պատատակալ ալ were the ordinary Greek word for linen, we might well have expected an Armenian translation that used կտաւ. Therefore we return to the possibility that the underlying Greek word was σινδών or ὀθόνιον. The former Miskgian offers as a translation of պատատնակալ so perhaps we may think of it first, rather than its synonym ὀθόνιον. In that case the underlying Greek may have been ἐν σινδόνι "in a linen garment" or "in a piece of linen." On the other hand the somewhat unusual word պատատնակալ may have been the choice of the Armenian translator, who used it—rather than կտաւ— for ἐν τοῖς λινοῖς.

I am suspicious about the second reading attributed to Aquila. It may not, in fact, go back to Aquila, may not have a Greek parent reading, and may thus not indicate contact with the Hebrew. Still, one must investigate the various possibilities.

In the following equivalences, the Armenian translations of Aquila, Symmachus and Theodotion appear with conjectural Greek retroversions. The Hebrew, Greek and Armenian are as follows:

כַּרְמֶל בְּצִקְלֹנוֹ → Old Greek παλάθας

→ hexaplaric Greek text παλάθας βακελλέθ → Zohrapian պաղատիտա բակեղափա

→ Aq conj. ἁπαλὰ ἐν τῷ ἱματίῳ ← Aq փափուկս շալակաւ

→ Sym conj. χῖδρα ἐν τῷ ἱματίῳ ← Sym մուրդ շալակաւ

→ Th conj. ἄλφιτα καὶ ἁπαλά ἐν βακελλέθ ← Th կրտո-
ւեալս եւ փափուկս բակեղափա

→ Aq conj. χῖδρα ἐν τοῖς λινοῖς ← Aq մուրդ պատատակալ ալ.

The Armenian MSS give us here readings for Aquila, Symmachus and Theodotion not otherwise extant. The rare word כַּרְמֶל was rendered by Aquila as "choice things," by Symmachus as "roasted wheat," and by Theodotion as "fresh and choice (things)." The hapax legomenon בְּצִקְלֹנוֹ is taken by Aquila and Symmachus as "(the folds) in a garment"; Theodotion simply transliterates, producing the word βακελλέθ *bakelleth* .

A second translation is attributed to Aquila. In it the כַּרְמֶל is once again "roasted wheat" and בְּצִקְלֹנוֹ is taken to mean something like "in a piece of linen."

These significant readings can be added to the second apparatus of B-M-Thack as follows:

παλαθας] α′ *delicata in veste* σ′ *tritica in veste* θ′ *secta et delicata bakelate* α′ *tritica linteo* Arm.

The editor of a new critical edition of 1–4 Reigns will make the decision to use Latin like B-M-Thack or, where possible, to employ conjectural Greek renderings. It seems to me that the latter are far more useful, so long as the reader is aware that translations are conjectural.

This treatment of 4 Rgn 4:42 may well be more extensive than the reader had hoped. Thanks for bearing with me.

5:3 *

ưưưﬔ] քջկեր Aq

J428ᵐᵍ M188ᵐᵍ

M2628 has քջկեր "cure" in the text and ưưưﬔ "cure, deliver from sickness" in the margin, attributed to Aquila. That is, in M2628 the readings have been switched. Manuscripts M177 V1508—Zohrapian's base MS—have here ưրբեր as an unsigned marginal reading. I am inclined to think that this is an inner-Armenian development, based upon the occurrence of ưրբեմ "cleanse" several times in the passage.

The context is Elisha's healing of Naaman the Syrian. A young Israelite captive who served the leprous Naaman's wife said to her, "If only my lord were with the prophet who is in Samaria! He would cure him …" The words "would cure" are a translation of יֶאֱסֹף.

אָסַף means "gather, remove" and here with מִצָּרַעַת "from leprosy" means "remove (set free) a man from leprosy" (BDB 62).

The Old Greek renders יֶאֱסֹף with ἀποσυνάξει "he will [would] make him recover" from ἀποσυνάγω "recover a man from," according to LSJ who, however, cite only this passage for that meaning. Indeed this is an unusual translation: ἀποσυνάγειν occurs only in this passage in the LXX/Old Greek corpus, at vv 3, 6,

7, 11. It is this unusual word that has brought forth the marginal readings.

The Latin Vulgate translates יֶאֱסֹף with curasset "would cure."

(The other "healing" word used in the passage is טָהֵר "be clean, pure." It is used in vv 10, 12, 13, 14. In each case the Old Greek employs the verb καθαρίζω "purify" for the translation of טָהֵר. In the Armenian translation of the passage ἀποσυνάγω is translated by ատամբել "cure" and καθαρίζω is rendered by սրբել "cleanse.")

The Armenian text in Zohrapian has ատամբէր "he would cure, deliver from sickness" for ἀποσυνάξει. Ատամբել is the verb employed also at vv 6, 7, 11 to translate ἀποσυνάγω. It is a good translation. Nevertheless the synonym բժշկէր "he would cure" has been added in the margin of a number of Armenian MSS. The Greek underlying բժշկէր we would expect to be either the verb ἰάομαι or θεραπεύω. The Reider-Turner index does not list θεραπεύειν among Aquila's extant vocabulary so it is likely that Aquila's translation at 4 Rgn 5:3 involved the verb ἰάομαι "heal, cure."

The Hebrew, Greek and Armenian equivalents are as follows:

יֶאֱסֹף → Old Greek ἀποσυνάξει → Zohrapian ատամբէր

→ Aq conj. ἰάσεται ← Aq բժշկէր.

The Armenian witnesses provide an Aquila reading not previously known. It can be added to the second apparatus of B-M-Thack:

αποσυναξει] α′ currasset Arm.

6:8 *

յեղմունի] յայս նիշ

J428mg M177mg M188mg J1934mg V212mg Zohapp(mg)

M2628 has յայս նիշ in the text and յեղմունի in the margin. That is, in that MS the reading in the text has been exchanged for the marginal reading. V212 is cited on the basis of Zanolli 1227.

This reading is not cited in B-M-Thackeray.

Chapter 6 continues with stories about Elisha. Vv 8–23 concerns the

blinding of the Aramaean army. V 8 introduces this story: "Once when the king of
Aram was at war with Israel, he took counsel with his officers. He said, 'At such
and such a place shall be my camp.'" At question is this directive which reads in
Hebrew אֶל־מְקוֹם פְּלֹנִי אַלְמֹנִי תַּחֲנֹתִי and in particular the words פְּלֹנִי
אַלְמֹנִי.

KBH offer for פְּלֹנִי here the meaning "**a certain one**." Under אַלְמֹנִי
KBH offer: *pᵉlōnî 'almōnî* , a **certain** place 2 K 6₈, man Rt 4₁. The entry for
אַלְמֹנִי in BDB is as follows: † [= 'All passages cited'] אַלְמֹנִי adj. **some one, a
certain** (name *unspoken*); 'א פְּלֹנִי מְקוֹם I S 21³ 2 K 6⁸; 'א 'פ alone, of
person, = *such-an-one, so-and-so* Ru 4¹.

The words אֶל־מְקוֹם פְּלֹנִי אַלְמֹנִי at 1 Sam 21:3 (English: 21:2) are
translated "for such and such a place" in the NRSV; "at a certain place" in the NIV.
At Ruth 4:1 the NRSV translates פְּלֹנִי אַלְמֹנִי as "friend" in Boaz' remark to the
next-of-kin "Come over, friend; sit down here." The NIV translates the statement in
2 Ki 6:8 "I will set up my camp in such and such a place." The NIV is similar to the
NRSV also at Ruth 4:1: "Come over here, my friend, and sit down."

A look at the apparatus in B-M-Thack reveals that the Old Greek translators
had difficulty with the expression פְּלֹנִי אַלְמֹנִי; that is true also for the Syriac.
The translators resort to transliteration. In Greek MSS bc₂e₂(Rahlfs 19-108 127 93)
⟨246⟩ the translation of אֶל־מְקוֹם פְּלֹנִי אַלְמֹנִי תַּחֲנֹתִי is εἰς τὸν τόπον τοῦ
φελμουνεὶ ποιήσωμεν ἔνεδρον "in the place of *phelmunei* we will make an ambush." This translation appears to represent a case of parablepsis in which the translator's eye skipped from the ל of פְּלֹנִי to the ל of the next word, אַלְמֹנִי. In
Greek MS B the translation is Εἰς τὸν τόπον τόνδε τινὰ ἐλιμωνὶ παρεμβαλῶ
"In such and such a place *elimōni* I will encamp." The word אַלְמֹנִי has been
transliterated. (In the majority Greek text the spelling is ἐλμωνί.) The Old Latin,
such an important witness, also attests a transliteration—*phalmunum* —according
to the Leon MS edited by C. Vercellone (B-M-Thack siglum: £ᵛ). (The Old Latin
MS edited by J. Belsheim—£ᵇ in B-M-Thack—has, instead of the transliteration,
the words *pertramus vim* "we are going to conduct a force.")

The transliteration has passed into the Armenian translation of the king of
Aram's directive: ի տեղւոյ մի յեղմոնի բանակեցայց ի դարանի,
i.e. "In a place *eghmoni* I will set up camp for an ambush." It is the transliteration

which has led to the translation being cited in the margin.

The marginal reading for *eghmoni* in Armenian MSS is յայս նիշ "in such and such."

B-M-Thack cite the readings for o′ α′ σ′ from the margin of Greek MS j (Rahlfs 243) for εἰς — ἐλιμωνί as follows:

o′ εἰς τὸν τόπον τόνδε τινὰ ἐλμουνί

α′ πρὸς τὸν τόπον τὸν δεῖνα τόνδε τινά

σ′ κατὰ τόπον τόνδε.

The fullest of these translations is that of Aquila: פְּלֹנִי is represented by τὸν δεῖνα "such a one; so and so" and אַלְמֹנִי is represented by τόνδε τινά "such and such." Symmachus is the shortest: פְּלֹנִי אַלְמֹנִי is represented by τόν- δε. In the case of o′ פְּלֹנִי is represented by τόνδε τινά and the transliteration ἐλμουνί follows.

The Armenian preposition ի — յ before a vowel — with the accusative means "to," with the locative case "in," but the preposition may have been added to the marginal reading to agree with what is in the text, i.e. յեղմունի which carries the preposition, repeated in order to tie եղմունի to ի տեղւոյց մի. The best we can probably conclude is that the Armenian reading is an Aquila Symmachus reading, more likely the latter than the former because of its brevity.

The Hebrew, Greek and Armenian equivalents here are:

פְּלֹנִי אַלְמֹנִי → majority Greek text τοῦ ἐλμωνί → Zohrapian յեղ-

մունի

→ Sym τόνδε → sine nom յայս նիշ.

The Armenian can be cited with those witnesses which preserve a Symma- chus reading. The second apparatus of B-M-Thack can be adjusted as follows to include the Armenian evidence:

εἰς — ελιμωνι] o′ εἰς τον τοπον τονδε τινα ελμουνι   α′ προς τον τοπον τον δεινα τονδε   σ′ κατα τοπον τονδε   j : εν ετεροις βιβλιοις ΓΡ εις τον τοπον φελμουνι z | ελιμωνι] ⟨σ′⟩ *in sic* Arm.

6:25 *

ꟼիստւն 1°] ութստւն Aq Sym

M188mg J1928mg(Sys pro Sym) J1934mg(Sys pro Sym)

The order of citation is Aq–Sym, not Sym–Aq, which is of some interest. Both names appear on the same line, with their reading beneath. One wonders whether these readings where Aquila's name appears first do not derive from a different source than those where Symmachus' name stands first. If not, how is that in some cases Aquila's name stands first, rather than Symmachus'? It appears to be a question of those instances where Aquila and Symmachus share the same reading that we find Aq–Sym.

In MS M188 the marginal reading is the abbreviation ά "eighty." In the other two witnesses—J1928 J1934—the word "eighty" is spelled out in full. The mutually shared spelling error in J1928 J1934 shows that these MSS are closely related in the matter of the marginalia.

Manuscript J428 has here վաթսուն "sixty," attributed to Symmachus; M2628 lacks the marginal reading entirely.

In this story about Elisha, King Ben-hadad of Aram's seige of Samaria is repulsed by divine intervention. In v 25 we are told that the seige produced a famine which was so great that "a donkey's head was sold for eighty shekels of silver." The words "for eighty shekels of silver" are a translation of בְּשְׁמֹנִים כֶּסֶף. The word שְׁמֹנִים means "eighty."

In the Old Greek translation we find not "eighty" but "fifty": πεντήκοντα ἀργυρίου "fifty [pieces] of silver." (The number "fifty" in Hebrew is חֲמִשִׁים.) According to B-M-Thack only one Greek witness has "eighty," i.e. ὀγδοήκοντα, namely Josephus. That "eighty" is attested in Josephus indicates that it is an "old" reading.

The Armenian translation of 6:25 follows the Old Greek tradition in reading յիսուն "fifty." The marginal readings provide the translation of Aquila and Symmachus which is ութսուն "eighty." That means that those Greek translators/revisers were working with a Hebrew text that read like the MT.

The Hebrew, Greek and Armenian equivalents here are:

שְׁמֹנִים ≠ Old Greek πεντήκοντα → Zohrapian յիսուն

→ Aq Sym ὀγδοήκοντα ← Aq Sym ութսուն.

Armenian alone preserves here the reading of Aquila and Symmachus. This can be added to the second apparatus in B-M-Thack:

πεντηκοντα] α′ σ′ *octoginta* Arm.

The Armenian marginal reading gives some added weight to the witness of Josephus.

7:4 *

դիմեացուք] անկցուք Aq; անծամատուրք լիցուք Sym

J428mg (անկցուք est sine nom) M188mg(vid) M2628mg; J1928mg et J1934mg hab անկց sine nom et non hab Sym

The context is the same as for 6:25. The seige of Samaria is going badly for those inside the city. Four leprous men outside the city gate decide that they would be better off to desert to the enemy. They say, "Let us desert to the Aramean camp; if they spare our lives we shall live." The crucial words are "Let us desert," Hebrew נִפְּלָה.

The meaning of נָפַל here is "surrender" (KBH) or "desert, fall away to, go over to" (BDB). However the Old Greek translator has chosen to use the verb ἐμπίπτω, which like נָפַל means "fall" and various other related things. With εἰς it can mean, for example, to "fall into" a camp: cf. the reference to Xenophon in LSJ, ἐμπίπτω 4.b. LSJ do offer the meaning — their 10. — "desert" but the only reference they provide is to 4 Rgn 25:11, i.e. to translation Greek.

It may be the unusual meaning required of ἐμπίπτω that has called forth the readings of Aquila and Symmachus in the margins. The whole statement in Greek MS B is καὶ νῦν δεῦτε καὶ ἐμπέσωμεν εἰς τὴν παρεμβολὴν Συρίας "come now and let us fall into the camp of the Syrians."

The Armenian translation conveys the sense of escape. It employs the verb դիմեմ "run, have recourse" in the form դիմեացուք "let's run."

A number of Armenian witnesses have marginal readings from Aquila and Symmachus. The Aquila reading is անկցուք, from անկանիմ "fall, escape," hence "let's escape." In the Reider-Turner index we are informed that נָפַל is translated by Aquila using the Greek verbs πίπτω, ἐμπίπτω, ἐπιπίπτω, ἐκπίπτω. Amongst these perhaps ἐκπίπτω, which can mean "escape," is the likeliest to lie behind աւնկցուք. In the Armenian Bible, աննակիմ translates καταφεύγω "flee for refuge" at Deut 4:42; 19:5 but καταφεύγω is not in the Reider-Turner list of Aquila's renderings of נָבֵל. If Aquila used a form of ἐκπίπτω, that form was likely ἐκπέσωμεν "let's escape." This suggestion remains conjectural.

For Symmachus the Armenian witnesses have աննձնատուրք լիցուք "let us surrender." This agrees with the Symmachus reading preserved in the Syro-hexapla and cited in Latin in the second apparatus of B-M-Thack, namely *tradamus nos* "let us surrender ourselves." At Josh 10:1, 4; 4 Rgn 3:8; 10:19 աննձնա-տուր լինեմ "surrender, capitulate" translates αὐτομολέω "change sides, desert." The only exception to the equation αὐτομολεῖν = աննձնատուր լինել in the five occurrences of αὐτομολεῖν in the LXX/Old Greek corpus which rest on a Hebrew text is 1 Rgn 20:30 where the participle of the verb is translated աննձնա-մատն (adj.) "that betrays himself." According to H-R, Symmachus employs the verb αὐτομολεῖν four times in his translation of Jeremiah: 37(44):13; 38(45):19; 39 (46):9(twice). In all four cases Symmachus uses αὐτομολεῖν to translate נָבֵל used in the sense of "desert." It may very well be that Symmachus also employed this verb at 4 Rgn 7:4. Indeed, independently the same retroversion is suggested by Field, namely αὐτομολήσωμεν "let us desert" on the basis of ܠ ܝܘ ܢܫܠܡܝܘ "and we will give ourselves up" in the Syro-hexapla.

The Hebrew, Greek and Armenian equivalents in this citation are:

נִפְּלָה → Old Greek ἐμπέσωμεν → Zohrapian դիմեսցուք

→ Aq conj. ἐκπέσωμεν ← Aq աննկցուք

→ Sym conj. αὐτομολήσωμεν ← Sym աննձնատուրք

լիցուք.

The Armenian provides here another source for Symmachus— aside from the Syro-hexapla—and is unique in preserving the translation of Aquila. The Armenian evidence can be added to the second apparatus in B-M-Thackeray:

και 5°—εμπεσωμεν] σ' *eamus igitur et tradamus nos* Syh | εμπεσωμεν] α' *effugiamus* σ' *tradamus nos* Arm.

8:8 *

մաննա] պատարագ

M177mg(vid) V212mg

V212 is cited on the basis of Stone 20. The reading of M177 is difficult to ascertain without recourse to the MS itself.

When Elisha went to Damascus, King Ben-hadad sent his officer Hazael to meet him. The King told Hazael, "Take a present with you and go to meet the man of God." The word "present" is a translation of מִנְחָה.

The Greek tradition represented by MS B rendered מִנְחָה with a transliteration, which is variously spelled among the MSS belonging to that form of text. It appears as μααná in MS B; as μαναá in many other witnesses; as μαννá in MS vᵇ (Rahlfs 245) and the Ethiopic. In Armenian the spelling represented is μαννá.

(The Old Greek may have had a translation, δῶρα "gifts": that is the text of MSS bgoy(mg)c₂e₂ [Rahlfs 19-108 158 82 121ᵐᵍ 127 93]—Lucianic witnesses—and Josephus.)

The Armenian marginal reading is պատարագ "gift." In their second apparatus B-M-Thack cite Symmachus' translation on the basis of the Syro-hexapla: *munera* "gifts." The Greek underlying the Syriac marginal reading ܩܘܪ̈ܒܢܐ "presents, offerings" is δῶρα "gifts" which appears in the Lucianic MSS noted in the previous paragraph. That its translation into Armenian has resulted in a morphologically singular noun is not significant: the noun can be understood as a collective singular.

The Hebrew, Greek and Armenian equivalents are:

מִנְחָה → Greek MS 245ᵇ Aeth μαννá → Zohrapian մաննա
→ Sym δῶρα → sine nom պատարագ.

The Armenian corroborates the evidence of the Syro-hexapla. It can be added to B-M-Thackeray's second apparatus as follows:

μααná] σ′ *munera* Arm(sine nom) Syh.

The hexaplaric evidence might indicate that Lucian took the Symmachus translation into his text.

8:15 *

մաքման] ընկողին Aq Sym

J428mg(րնկողի) J1927mg(անկողին sine nom) J1928mg(անկողին) J1934mg (ան -
կողին) M177mg M188mg(hab րնտիր vid) M2628mg(յրնկողինն) V212mg (րն-
գողին) Zohapp(mg) FieldArm B-M-Thackapp2; Ⴕძოφo ძοφე GeorgJ/B(sine nom)

V212 is cited on the basis of Zanolli 1227. The Georgian is cited on the basis of Birdsall 91. This is the first time the Georgian evidence appears in this study;
it extends through ch 18.

(The citation of MS witnesses above records only variations from the main
citation: J428 preserves the signatures and differs from the main citation only in the
lack of the definite/demonstrative marker -ն. Manuscript J428 also, e.g., records
the signatures as ակ lι սիմ "Aq and Sym." I have not noted the presence of the
"and" in recording the signatures. Manuscript M177 preserves the order Sym–Aq
for the signatures.)

In this story about Elisha, the prophet goes to Damascus while King Ben-
hadad was ill. Elisha informs Hazael that he is to be king. We are told in v 15 that
Hazael "took the bed-cover and dipped it in water and spread it over the king's face,
until he died." The word translated "bed-cover" here is מַכְבֵּר. The word occurs
only in this verse and KBH say of it: "s.thg twisted or interlaced: **blanket** or **mat**
(oth: netting)."

The Old Greek rendered this word with στρῶμα "mattress, bed" according
to MSS bhioza?(txt)c₂e₂ (Rahlfs 19-108 55 56 82 554a?[txt] 127 93).

The majority of MSS of the Greek tradition, however, give a transliteration
for מַכְבֵּר: in MS B it is τὸν χαββά but in other MSS we find, e.g., μαχβάρ (in j
z(mg) [Rahlfs 243 554mg]), μακβάρ (MS u [Rahlfs 372]), μαχμά (Nz*(txt) and
others).

The Armenian word մաքման is a transliteration of the Greek. Bedrossian offers the meaning "handkerchief; thick cloth" but that is based upon the context
in this passage. The word մաքման is not an Armenian word. The same transliteration passed into the Georgian version: see Adjarian III 291f.

In their second apparatus B-M-Thack provide the translations of Aquila and
Symmachus. According to Greek MS j (Rahlfs 243) the translation of Aquila and
Symmachus is τὸ στρῶμα "mattress, bed." They cite Arm—from Zohapp(mg)—
with Syh-ap-Barh for Aq Sym: *stragulum* , i.e. the equivalent in Latin of τὸ στρῶ-

μα. There is a note in the Syro-hexapla that Severianus found *Machbar* in the Hexapla in the Hebrew tradition and that this was translated by Aquila, Symmachus and Theodotion as *stragulum* . The translation στρῶμα is also found in Greek witnesses of the Lucianic tradition, which happens to be representative of the Old Greek.

The Armenian translation ընկողին or անկողին means "bed; mattress." It is still the word for "bed" in modern Armenian.

Georgian MS 646 has a marginal reading here sine nom. It is წმიდა ბადე *çmida bade* "sacred net." (Birdsall's *cmida* must surely intend *çmida* .) Underlying this, he suggests, is the construing of מַכְבֵּר as מִכְבָּר "grating," a word which occurs a few times in the Hebrew Bible, all of them in Exodus: 27:4; 35:16; 38:4f, 30; 39:39. He notes—as does Montgomery—that Josephus also has the translation δίκτυον "net" (at *Antiquities* IX 92). Birdsall adds, "The cognate δικτυωτόν ["latticed"] appears in the rendering of מִכְבָּר in Exod. xxvii. 4, with which the "sacred" of the Georgian may suggest a link."

Marcus' comment about Josephus' translation is as follows: "Josephus's rendering, δίκτυον "mesh," would seem to fit better Heb. *mikmar* or *mikmereth* , less probably (as Weill[1] suggests) Heb. *mikbar*   "network" (of metal, wood, etc.; cf. LXX Ex. xxvii. 4)."

The Georgian marginal reading is certainly odd with its addition of the word "holy." It does not represent a reading from "the Three" and Birdsall notes that "On paleographical grounds it is clear that this is not an ancient gloss but a relatively recent note by some reader."

The Hebrew, Greek and Armenian equivalents are:

מַכְבֵּר → Greek τὸν μαχβάρ c var → Zohrapian մաքրան

→ Aq Sym τὸ στρῶμα → Aq Sym ընկողին.

The Armenian translation supports the Greek and Syriac witness to this reading.

The second apparatus of B-M-Thackeray already notes the Armenian reading:

τον χαββα] α′ σ′ *stragulum* Arm Syh-ap-Barh.

---

[1]J. Weill, translator of *Ant. i.–x. in Oeuvres Complètes etc* ., vol. i. 1900, vol. ii., 1926—so Marcus' list of abbreviations.

A critical edition of 4 Rgn will likely take into account Josephus' citation, in which case the Georgian might also be cited. Did the reader with the antiquarian interests who added the marginal note in MS 646 know the reading from Josephus?

8:17 *

քաառասուն Zoh[app]] ութ Aq; իբր ութ Sym

J428[mg] M188[mg] M2628[mg]

M188 uses the abbreviation for ութ in the Symmachus reading, namely, ը with a line above it: ը̄. The order of citation is Aquila, then Symmachus.

Zoh[txt] reads ութ: this represents the switching of readings in text and margin. The resulting marginal reading—now քաառասուն—has not been preserved in Zohrapian's base MS V1508. Zohrapian does note in his apparatus that the majority of MSS he used for his edition have քաառասուն rather than ութ as their text.

Chapter 8, v 17 tells us that Jehoram was thirty-two years old when he became king of Judah and that "he reigned eight years in Jerusalem." At issue is the number. The Hebrew has שְׁמֹנֶה "eight."

The relevent citation in B-M-Thack, who print τεσσεράκοντα "forty" on the basis of Greek MS B is as follows: τεσσεράκοντα BAd₂ Arm-codd] δεκα oc₂e₂; οκτω N rell Arm-ed Aeth Syh. Manuscript d₂ is a one-leaf, 11th century fragment;[1] oc₂e₂ are Rahlfs 82 127 93. To judge from this citation, the other Lucianic MSS— 19-108—apparently have ὀκτώ.

Ութ "eight" is the reading in the text of Zohrapian.

The marginal reading arose because the text read "forty": the readings in the margin were intended to correct the text toward the Hebrew.

The Armenian witnesses preserve uniquely the readings of Aquila and Symmachus who offer the translations "eight" and "about eight," respectively. The Hebrew, Greek and Armenian equivalents are:

---

[1] Rahlfs (1915): Oxford, Bodl.[eian] Libr., Laud. gr. 36 (Lect.); B-M-Thackeray (1930): "probably came from the Sinai monastery, and is now the property of Göttingen University Library—so "Prefatory Note to the Books of Kings."

שְׁמֹנֶה → Greek MSS ὀκτώ → Zohrapian^{txt} ունթ

    ≠ Greek MSS τεσσαράκοντα → Zoh^{app} քառասուն

    → Aq conj. ὀκτώ ← Aq ունթ

    → Sym conj. ὡς ὀκτώ ← Sym իբր ունթ.

The Armenian tradition alone preserves the readings of Aquila and Symmachus. Their translations can be represented in the second apparatus of B-M-Thackeray as follows:

    τεσσαρακοντα] α′ *octo* σ′ *ad octo* Arm.

9:11 1° *

մոլիկ]պատանին Sym; բախածն Aq

J428mg(ատանին et non hab բախածն ; ind mend supra անհրաւութիւն) M188mg
(ատանին [vid] Sym; պախածն [vid] Aq) M2628mg

Manuscripts M188 M2628 are "two peas in a pod" when it comes to marginalia for Aquila, Symmachus and Theodotion. For vv 11–12 the marginalia are somewhat confusing. In MS M188 there are three readings, with signatures, separated by lines thus:

    սիմ

    ատանսիմ (vid)

    ակ

    պախածն (vid)

    խալն

    ն տեա

The first two readings are difficult to read, at least from the microfilm. What is intended is clear from M2628. It appears almost as if the readings in M188 were copied from a MS lacking the first letters of the first two readings; the result does not make sense. There are two indexes in the text: the first is upon մոլիկ and the second is upon (v 12) անհրաւութիւն.

In MS M2628 there are three readings, like M188:

    սիմ

պատան
ին
ակ
բախածն
խաւլն
ատես

In this MS there is an index sign only upon մղ_հն in the text.

In MS J428 also the Symmachus reading is corrupt: it has become the word ատանիհն, a word not in the dictionaries but which, by relating it to ունւն "false, untrue, lying," one might make sense of over against its referent in the text անիրաունւթիւն "injustice." The reading for Aquila in the parent text may also have been corrupt. That would explain why the MS preserves only the signature of Aquila, but no reading: that is, J428 has the signature of Symmachus, Symmachus' translation, and below that the signature of Aquila, but no Aquila reading.

I take it that the first two readings in MSS M188 M2628 are intended for մղ_հն and that the third, unsigned, reading is intended for զբա_շաղանս. On the latter, see the next item.

The context concerns Elisha's meeting with Jehu. When Jehu returned to his officers they asked, "Why did that madman come to you." "Madman" is the translation for עֲשֻׁגָּע.

The Old Greek translation of עֲשֻׁגָּע employs the adj. ἐπίλημπτος. So: τί ὅτι εἰσῆλθεν ὁ ἐπίλημπτος οὗτος πρὸς σέ; "Why did this epileptic come to you?" The word ἐπίλημπτος means "caught or detected in anything; II. suffering from epilepsy.

The Armenian word մղ_հ means "mad." (All three of the Armenian words—մղ_հ and the two marginal readings—carry the definite/demonstrative marker -ն.)

B-M-Thack give a translation of Aquila in their second apparatus, on the basis of the Syro-hexapla: α' demens (ܫܢܐ ["insane, mad"]) Syh. Demens means "mad."

The Armenian translations of Aquila and Symmachus are բախած and պատանի, respectively. The word բախած means "foolish, wanton, mad," i.e. demens. It is not in Arapkerts'i. The cognate verb բախեմ "strike, beat" translates either ἐγκρούω "knock, hammer in" (Greek MS B) or πήγνυμι "stick, fix in" (Greek MS A) at Judg 4:21; բախիւ "be beaten; attack" translates συντρίβω "shatter, crush" at 1 Macc 7:42 and συνάπτω at 1 Macc 10:49 (συνῆψαν πόλεμον "they met in battle"). The basic idea behind բախած seems to be that of having suffered a blow and being rendered senseless or mad. Cf. Adjarian I 389.

Reider-Turner offer ἀγνόημα "ignorance" as Aquila's equivalent for מְשׁוּגָה but the Greek-Hebrew index provides only Job 19:4 for such a translation. At any rate ἀγνόημα seems unsuitable here. The word μαίνεσθαι or μανία come to mind—cf. Acts 26:24—but H-R do not indicate that these words occur among fragments of Aquila that are extant. Another possibility is παράφρων "senseless" which, according to H-R, Symmachus employs at 1 Rgn 21:14(15).

1 Rgn 21:14–15 is quite relevant because forms of the verb שׁגע occur three times in vv 14–15 (MT 15–16). David feigns madness, leading King Achish of Gath in v 14 to ask his servants, "Look, you see the man is mad (מִשְׁתַּגֵּעַ)." The Old Greek translation for מִשְׁתַּגֵּעַ is ἐπίλημπτον but B-M-Thack in their second apparatus give us both Symmachus and Aquila: for Symmachus the equivalent is παράφρονα "senseless; deranged" in Greek MSS b jm (Rahlfs 108 243 92); for Aquila the translation is παραπληκτευόμενον "mad"; there is also the marginal reading ἔκφρονα "demented" in MS b (sine nom).

The King continues in v 15, "Do I lack madmen (מְשֻׁגָּעִים) that you have brought this fellow to play the madman (לְהִשְׁתַּגֵּעַ) in my presence?" The word מְשֻׁגָּעִים is translated ἐπιλήμπτων in the Old Greek and μαινομένων "those driven mad" by Symmachus, according to Greek MS j; Aquila is not extant. The infinitive לְהִשְׁתַּגֵּעַ is translated ἐπιλημπτεύεσθαι in the Old Greek; μαίνεσθαι by Symmachus and παραπληκτεύεσθαι by Aquila, according to Greek MS j. Reider-Turner, in their Greek-Hebrew index, indicate that this verb παραπληκτεύεσθαι is unique to Aquila and cite this passage, 1 Rgn 21:14, 15. It would appear likely that Aquila used it also at 4 Rgn 9:11 and that παραπληκτευόμενον lies behind the word բախած. Field arrived at virtually the same conclusion: he retroverts from the Syriac to παράπληκτος "mad" in the sense of παραπληκτευόμενος.

More problematic still is the Armenian word given for Symmachus' translation, պատանի. It has nothing to do with mental status but means "youth; domestic, servant." It is the translation of παῖς "I./II. child; III. servant" at Gen 18:7; of παιδάριον "little boy" at 2 Rgn 1:5; of νεανίσκος "youth, young man" at Lk 7:14. With the reading պատանի, the sentence reads "Why did that child come to you?" At 1 Rgn 21:14, 15, dealt with just above, Symmachus' translations of מִתְהֹלֵל (v 14), מְשֻׁגָּעִים and לְהִשְׁתַּגֵּעַ (v 15) are παράφρονα, μαινομένων and μαίνεσθαι respectively.

The Hebrew, Greek and Armenian equivalents at 4 Rgn 9:11 are:

מְשֻׁגָּע → Old Greek ὁ ἐπίλημπτος → Zohrapian մոլին

　　　　→ Aq conj. ὁ παράπληκτος → Aq բախածն

　　　　→ Sym conj. ὁ παῖς[1] ← Sym պատանին.

The Armenian readings confirm the evidence of the Syro-hexapla for Aquila; unfortunately the Symmachus reading appears to be corrupt. The Armenian evidence can be added to the second apparatus of B-M-Thack in the following way:

　　　ο επιλημπτος] α′ demens　Arm Syh : σ′ puer　Arm.

9:11 2° *

զբա շաղակնu] խաւլնu տեu

M188mg(ind mend supra [12] անհրաւթուիթիւն) M2628mg(sine ind)

Jehu responds to the question of his servants with the statement, "You know that sort and how they babble." The words "how they babble" are a translation of וְאֶת־שִׂיחוֹ, literally "and his babble."

The Old Greek translated וְאֶת־שִׂיחוֹ with the words καὶ τὴν ἀδολεσχίαν αὐτοῦ "and his prating."

The word ἀδολεσχίαν was rendered as զբա շաղակнu "idle talk" in Armenian. (The word բա շաղակնp is morphologically plural.)

Armenian witnesses have a marginal reading, apparently for զ բա շաղակնu, namely խաւլնu "foolish" or "senseless things." In the context խաւլնpu could mean "foolish talk." The word տեu means "see" and probably means

---

[1] This conjecture represents a retroversion from the Armenian but the transmission of the Symmachus reading appears to have been corrupted. In that event the corruption may have taken place during the transmission of the Symmachus reading in Greek, at the point of its rendering into Armenian, or conceivably during its transmission in Armenian.

here "[instead of] qɸɯ ̨ɕɯ ̨ɯ ̨ɯ ̨ɯ [in the text] read ̨ɯ ̨ɯ ̨ ̨ɯ ̨ɯ."

The word ̨ɯ ̨ɯ ̨ or—in its later spelling—̨ɯ ̨ɥ has no entry in Arapkerts'i so it is difficult to determine Greek equivalents easily. Miskgian provides the following relevant Latin equivalents: *insanus, insipiens* . For *insanus* Freund-Leverett offer the Greek equivalents μανικός, παράφρων; for *insipiens* "foolish, silly" Greek ἀνόητος.

B-M-Thack record a marginal reading in the Syro-hexapla for καὶ τὴν ἀδολεσχίαν αὐτοῦ, namely *et colloquium eius* "and his conversation" attributed to Aquila and Symmachus. Field retroverts the Syriac words ܡܠ ܪ ܟܘܠܠ ܢ "and his converse" as καὶ τὴν ὁμιλίαν αὐτοῦ "and his company" but possibly "and his talk" (cf. ὁμιλέω III. 3. "speak to, address, harangue"; generally "talk to, converse").

The fact that the Syriac preserves the translation of Aquila and Symmachus means that the Armenian reading is likely authentic, though unsigned.

The Hebrew, Greek and Armenian equivalents are:

וְאֶת־שִׂיחוֹ → Old Greek καὶ τὴν ἀδολεσχίαν αὐτοῦ → Zohrapian ̈

         qɸɯ ̨ɕɯ ̨ɯ ̨ɯ ̨ɯ ̨ɯ

  → Aq Sym conj. [so Field] καὶ τὴν ὁμιλίαν αὐτοῦ → sine nom

    [̈] qɯ ̨ɯ ̨ɯ ̨ɯ ̨ɯ [̨ɯ ̨ɯ ̨ɯ].

The Armenian evidence can be added to the citation in B-M-Thack in the following way:

και 4°—αυτου 2°] α′ σ′ *et colloquium eius* Syh | την αδολεσχιαν] *colloquium* Arm.

9:20 *

ɯ ̨ ̨ɯ ̨ɯ ̨ɯ ̨ɯ ̨ ̨ɯ ̨ɯ ̨ɯ ̨ɯ ̨ɯ ̨ɯ ̨ɯ ̨ɯ ̨ɯ ̨ɯ ̨ɯ ̨ɯ ̨ɯ ̨ɯ ̨ɯ ̨ɯ ̨ɯ ̨ɯ ̨ɯ
(ɯ ̨ɯ ̨ɯ Zoh[app]) Sym

J428[mg] M177[mg] M188[mg(vid)] Zoh[app(mg)] B-M-Thack[app2]

After Jehu told his officers the message sent to him by Elisha, they proclaimed him to be king. He set off for Jezreel where King Joram was recovering from battle with the King of Aram. The sentry at Jezreel saw a company approaching. In v 20 he describes their approach: "It looks like the driving of Jehu son of Nimshi; for he drives like a maniac." The words in question are וְהַמִּנְהָג כְּמִנְהַג יֵהוּא "It looks like the driving of Jehu." The Hebrew literally says "and the one who leads (does so) like Jehu leads."

The text printed in B-M-Thack—based on MS y (Rahlfs 121)—translates the Hebrew as καὶ ὁ ἄγων ἦγεν τὸν Εἰού "and the one who was leading lead Jehu." For ὁ ἄγων ἦγεν witnesses bzc₂e₂ (Rahlfs 19-108 554 127 93) Thdt have ἡ ἀγωγή ἀγωγή "the leading (as) leading," i.e. "the movement (is) the movement of Jehu." This translation may represent the Old Greek.

The Armenian text renders the phrase եւ որ ածէրն ած զյէու "and the one who was leading led Jehu."

Symmachus' translation for וְהַמִּנְהָג כְּמִנְהַג יֵהוּא, according to Greek MS j (Rahlfs 121), is ἡ δὲ ἀγωγὴ ὡς ἀγωγὴ ἰηού.

The Armenian translation of Symmachus is եւ վարելն իբրեւ զվարելն յէուայ "and the driving [is] like the driving of Jehu." It corresponds precisely to the Greek.

The Hebrew, Greek and Armenian equivalents here are:

וְהַמִּנְהָג כְּמִנְהַג יֵהוּא → Greek MS y καὶ ὁ ἄγων ἦγεν τὸν Εἰού →

Zohrapian եւ որ ածէրն ած զյէու

→ Sym ἡ δὲ ἀγωγὴ ὡς ἀγωγὴ ἰηού → Sym եւ վարելն

իբրեւ զվարելն յէուայ.

The Armenian evidence is already cited in the second apparatus of B-M-Thack, as follows:

καὶ 2° — ειου] σ′ et vectio tanquam vectio Ieu   Arm.

One might miss in this method of citation the fact that the Armenian evidence is precisely the same as that preserved for Symmachus in Greek MS j (Rahlfs 243), except that its evidence is not as extensive.

10:7

ի կողովս] ի քթոցս

M177ᵐᵍ

The context concerns the capitulation of the leaders of the city of Samaria to the demands of Jehu. They killed Ahab's sons and "put their heads in baskets and sent them to him at Jezreel." The word translated "in baskets" is בַּדּוּדִים. The noun in the singular, without the preposition, is דּוּד.

The translation of בַּדּוּדִים in the Lucianic group of MSS boc₂e₂ (Rahlfs 19-108 82 127 93) along with MS r (700) is εἰς καρτάλλους "in baskets with a pointed bottom." The reading of the majority text—including MS B and thus the text in B-M-Thack—differs only in the matter of the preposition, namely ἐν instead of εἰς, which produces ἐν καρτάλλοις.

The Armenian rendered the Greek with ի կողովս "in baskets."

Armenian MS M177 has a marginal reading sine nom which offers a synonyn for կողովս. The reading is ի քթողս "in baskets." Bedrossian's entry for քթող is: "S[ee]. կողով."

There is nothing in Field or B-M-Thack for εἰς καρτάλλους which would help in determining the authenticity of this marginal reading as a remnant of the work of "the Three."

The margins of MS M177 are a repository for various kinds of readings, including the translations of Aquila, Symmachus and Theodotion. One does not dismiss its evidence hastily, though in the absence of confirmation among other witnesses, it is most likely that this is an inner-Armenian gloss.

10:8 *

զրահանս Zoh M2628^mg] կոյանս

M2628^txt

Manuscript M2628 has switched a marginal reading and the reading in the text. M188 has զրահանս in the text and no marginal reading.

Jehu laid the heads of the Ahab's sons "in two heaps at the entrance of the gate." The words "in two heaps" are a translation of שְׁנֵי צִבֻּרִים. KBH offer the rendering "heap, pile" for *צָבֻר which occurs only here in the Hebrew Bible. It is that kind of rarity of appearance which led to the citation of alternatives in Greek translation.

The Old Greek translation of צְבָרִים is βουνούς "heaps." The word βουνός occurs not infrequently in the LXX/Old Greek corpus—more than a column in
H-R—where it usually renders גִּבְעָה.

The Armenian translation of βουνούς is գրահաևս "heap, mass, pile." It
is a word which is morphologically plural but has a singular meaning according to
Bedrossian. However, Adjarian II 111 cites the lexical entry as գրահաև "hill,
heap, heap of stones." He notes that it occurs only in the accusative plural form, at
4 Rgn 10:8, and once in the form գրահեաևսև in ՄԶբ. 242 (i.e. Գիրք որ
կոչի Ձգոև, արարեալ Մ. Յակոբայ երիցս երաևեալ հայրապե-
տին ՄԶբին քաղաքի [Մոլիս 1824 (Ե դար)], i.e. "The book which is
called *Wise* , completed by the Blessed Patriarch Hakob the Elder at the city of
Mtsb, p. 242"). It is therefore a rare word.

It is possible that the marginal reading կոյսս "heaps, piles" may be an inner-Armenian gloss occasioned by the use of the rare word գրահաևս in the text.
The alternate reading may already have been in the margin of the parent manuscript
of M2628 in which case the scribe switched the marginal reading with the rare word
in the text. On the other hand, M2628 may preserve a genuine reading from "the
Three." Since it is synonymous with the reading in the text, it is difficult to determine what Greek word may underlie it. Miskgian gives as one of the Latin equivalents of կոյս the word *cumulus* "a heap or pile." Freund-Leverett.offer θίς "heap"
as an equivalent for *cumulus* .

The word θίς is used a few times in the LXX/Old Greek corpus, four according to H-R: on the three occasions when there is a Hebrew parent text, it is used for גִּבְעָה (Gen 49:26; Deut 12:2; Job 15:7; fourth occurrence: Bar 5:7). H-R
cite a handful of times when θίς is used by Aquila, and from Reider-Turner we can
determine that he used it for גָּלִיל "Galilee" (Isa 9:1[8:23]; Ezek 47:8), גְּלִילָה
"district" (Joel 3[4]:4; Jer 4:4[?]) and גַּל "heap" (Jer 9:11[10]). H-R do not indicate
that θίς is a word employed by Symmachus.

Miskgian offers several other Latin equivalents for կոյս: *acervus* "heap,
hoard, or pile" (Freund-Leverett Greek equivalents are: σωρός "heap, especially of
corn"; ὄγκος "bulk, size, mass of a body"; θήμων "heap"); *congeries* "mass, heap,
pile, hoard" (συμφόρημα "that which is brought together, compound"; συναθροισ-

μός "collection, union"); *caterva* "multitude of men who belong together, as a troop of soldiers"); *moles* "a mass, heap, lump of huge bulk or weight" (ὄγκος; μέγεθος "magnitude"); *frequentia* "frequency." This round-about exercise produces only the word θήμων as a word likely to underlie կոյտ, aside from θίς.

The word θήμων does not occur in the LXX/Old Greek corpus but θημωνία—which means the same thing—does. It occurs four times where there is a Hebrew parent text and where that is not in question: in Exod 8:14(10) it is used of heaps of dead frogs ([twice] for חֹמֶר); at Job 5:26 θημωνία ἅλωνος "threshing-floor heap" translates גָּדִישׁ "stack of grain"); at Cant 7:2(3) it is used of "heap (of wheat)" to render עֲרֵמָה "heap"). This does not take us anywhere either.

It may be that the Greek underlying կոյտ identified צְבָרִים with the word צָרִים "stones." Two of the better known stories about heaps of stones are in Gen 31 and Josh 7. In the former Jacob sets up a גַל "heap" in making a covenant with Laban; the LXX renders this with the word βουνός (v 46), but one notes that the hexaplaric plus in v 46 uses the words σώρευμα "heap, pile" and σωρός: see Wevers' critical apparatus. In the latter instance Joshua makes a גַל־אֲבָנִים "heap of stones" over Achan (7:26); this is rendered in the Old Greek by σωρὸν λίθων.

Perhaps the best conjecture one can make is that the word underlying կոյտ is σωρούς "heaps." Further, we can add that the nameless translator is likely Symmachus because Symmachus readings predominate in the marginalia in these Armenian witnesses.

H-R note that Symmachus uses σωρός twice in extant fragments of his work: at Cant 7:2(3) for עֲרֵמָה "heap" (Old Greek: θημωνία, as noted above); at Jer 50(27):26 ὡς σωρός for כְּמוֹ־עֲרֵמִים "like heaps of grain," according to MS 86. (The Syro-hexapla preserves ὡς γλωσσόκομον "like a coffin" for Symmachus at Jer 27:26 and ὡς σωρεύοντες "like piling up stones" for Aquila.) See Ziegler's critical apparatus.

The Hebrew, Greek and Armenian equivalents are:

צְבָרִים → Old Greek βουνούς → Zohrapian զրահանս

→ conj. Sym σωρούς ← sine nom կոյտ.

This reading can be cited in the second apparatus of B-M-Thackeray as follows:

βουνους] ⟨σ′⟩ *cumulos* Arm.

The limitations of citing such readings in Latin are apparent here: the reader knows only that there is a synonym in the margin of the Armenian witness. Citation of a conjectural Greek retroversion also has its drawbacks.

10:10 (Zoh 10:9) *

ապփով] արդ (> J1927 Zohᵃᵖᵖ B-M-Thackᵃᵖᵖ) այժմ Sym

J428ᵐᵍ J1927ᵐᵍ(sine nom) M177ᵐᵍ M188ᵐᵍ M2628ᵐᵍ V212ᵐᵍ Zohᵃᵖᵖ (mg)(sine nom) B-M-Thackᵃᵖᵖ1(sine nom)

V212 is cited on the basis of Zanolli 1227.
Cf. 2:14.

In the context Jehu has arranged for the deaths of Ahab's seventy sons. In v 9 he admits responsibility for killing King Joram but disclaims responsibility for the deaths of Ahab's sons. He asks, "who struck down all these?" Verse 10 continues, "Know then that there shall fall to the earth nothing of the word of the LORD." At question is the word אֵפוֹא, translated here as "then." That is the translation given in KBH for אֵפוֹא in this passage.

In much of the Greek text tradition אֵפוֹא is represented by a transliteration: e.g. in MS B it is ἀφφώ. Cf. B-M-Thackeray's first apparatus: αφφω] αφφο Syh(mg): απφω efmnsw (Rahlfs 52 489 92 119 130 314): αμφω hv (55 245): om b oc₂e₂ (19-108 82 127 93): + ※ σ' *igitur nunc* ◄ Syh. Field cites the Syriac for Symmachus as ܟܐܡ ܠܗܘܢ "therefore now."

Symmachus' translation is preserved in Greek in the margin of MS j (Rahlfs 243). His translation of the beginning of v 10 is ἴδετε οὖν νῦν, in which אֵפוֹא is represented by οὖν νῦν. See B-M-Thackeray, second apparatus.

The Armenian text preserves the transliteration: ապփով. The marginal reading is the equivalent of Symmachus' translation: արդ այժմ "now therefore."

The equivalents among Hebrew, Greek and Armenian are as follows:
אֵפוֹא → Greek MS B et al. ἀφφώ → Zohrapian ապփով
     → Sym οὖν νῦν → Sym արդ այժմ.

The Armenian witness corroborates the evidence of Greek MS j (Rahlfs

243) Syh. The second apparatus in B-M-Thack can be adjusted in the following way:

ιδετε—πεσειται] σ′ ιδετε ουν νυν οτι ου πεσειται α′ γνωτε καιπερ οτι ου πεσειται j | αφφω] *ergo* p (int lin) : σ′ *ergo nunc* Arm.

10:13 *

զ որացել նյու] աշխարհատիկունզ ̣u Aq

J428ᵐᵍ M177ᵐᵍ⁽ˢᵘᵇ ⁿᵒᵐ ˢʸᵐ ᵖʳᵒ ᴬ𐞥⁾ M188ᵐᵍ M2628ᵐᵍ V212ᵐᵍ⁽ˢᵘᵇ ⁿᵒᵐ ˢʸᵐ ᵖʳᵒ Aq) Zohᵃᵖᵖ⁽ᵐᵍ⁾ B-M-Thackᵃᵖᵖ² Georgᴮ/ᴶ

V212 is cited on the basis of Zanolli 1227–1228; Stone 22: V280—our V212—attributes the reading to Symmachus; Birdsall (cited by Stone) notes that the Georgian version attributes the marginal reading to Aquila. The Georgian is cited on the basis of Birdsall 85.

Jehu set out for Samaria after killing all Ahab's family in Jezreel. On the way he met relatives of King Ahaziah of Judah. When he asked who they were, they responded, "We are kin of Ahaziah; we have come down to visit the royal princes and the sons of the queen mother." הַגְּבִירָה is the word translated "queen mother." The entry in KBH for גְּבִירָה includes: 2. 'lady,' title of **queen mother** 2K 10₁₃.

The Old Greek translation of גְּבִירָה is—in the genitive case—τῆς δυναστευούσης "of the one (fem.) who is ruling." The Armenian translation is literal: զ որացել նյու "of the one who is ruling." Both δυναστεύω and զ որաւաւմ are verbs connoting "power."

The margin of the Armenian MSS offers Aquila's translation for גְּבִירָה. It is, when put in the genitive case, աշխարհատիկունզ. The word աշխար-հատիկիու—literally "lady of the land"—means "queen." Like զ որացել նյու in the text, the marginal reading has suffixed the nearer definite marker -u, hence աշ-խարհատիկունզ ̣u "of this here queen," to put it colliquially.

B-M-Thack cite the Armenian as the sole evidence for Aquila in their second apparatus: της δυναστευουσης] α′ *reginae* Arm.

The marginal reading in Georgian MSS is დიდებულისათა *didebulisat'a* "(the ones) of the glorified one," which Birdsall—surely correctly— takes to be a corruption of დედოფალისათა *dedop'alisat'a* "(the ones) of the queen," i.e. the word დედოფალი with the singular genitive ending -ისა and the plural mark-er -თა. It appears that the Georgian translator has taken the -u at the end of աշխարհատիկնոⳉu as a plural marker—it is also this in Armenian, but not following a genitive ending—which requires reading the word under the star of Georgian morphology. This would at least account for the plural marker -თა at the end of the Georgian word დედოფალისათა, or at the end of its corrupted form დიდებულისათა. In the Georgian the reading is also attributed to Aquila.

Reider-Turner provide two equivalents for גְּבִירָה in the work of Aquila: δυναστευούσα and βασίλισσα, the latter on the basis of the Syriac at Jer 36(29):2. It is virtually certain that our passage can be added to those where Aquila employed βασίλισσα "queen" for גְּבִירָה.

The Hebrew, Greek, Armenian and Georgian equivalents are:

הַגְּבִירָה → Old Greek τῆς δυναστευούσης → Zohrapian զ օրագեԼnյu

→ Aq conj. βασιλίσσης ← Aq աշխարհատիկնոⳉu

→ Aq დიდებულისათა mend pro დედოფალისათა.

The Armenian marginal reading preserves the translation of Aquila; the Georgian witness is dependent upon the Armenian.

The second apparatus in B-M-Thack already cites the Armenian evidence, as noted above. The Georgian can be added to the citation thus:

της δυναστευουσης] α' *reginae* Arm; α' *eos gloriosae* mend pro *eos reginae* Georg.

10:18

ժηηnվ եաց] նախաննձեցnյց

J428^mg M188^mg M2628^mg

After Jehu killed all the royal house in Samaria, we are told that he "assembled all the people." The word "assembled" is a translation of יִּקְבֹּץ. The verb קָבַץ means here "gather, assemble."

The Old Greek translation for יִּקְבֹּץ is συνήθροισεν "he gathered." That reading is attested by MSS boc₂e₂ (Rahlfs 19-108 82 127 93); it also represents the majority text.

The text printed in B-M-Thack is ἐζήλωσεν, perhaps "he was zealous toward." This reading is preserved in Greek MSS ABvx (Rahlfs 245 247), the Ethiopic and the text of the Syro-hexapla. If this reading represented a Hebrew text, the underlying Hebrew word would be יְקַנֵּא "he was zealous." It is unlikely that it does, however. The reading ἐζήλωσεν is more likely to be a corruption dependent upon the use of the aorist infinitive of ζηλόω in v 16: Δεῦρο μετ᾽ ἐμοῦ καὶ ἴδε ἐν τῷ ζηλῶσαί με τῷ κυρίῳ "Come with me and see how I am zealous for the Lord." This is an early corruption because ἐζήλωσεν stood in the fifth column of the Hexapla. For that reason, we have preserved Symmachus' translation, likely συνήθροισεν, which happens as well to be the rendering of the Old Greek. (In Field the attribution on the basis of the Syro-hexapla is to Aquila.)

The Armenian text preserves ժողովեաց "he gathered together." This reading in Zohrapian's base MS is that also of J1925 (p.350, col.2, ↑5) and M1500 (f.178v, col.2, ↓7). I take it to be original. It is important to establish that because, if marginal reading and reading in the text had been switched at some point in the Armenian tradition, as one sees sometimes in some MSS which have been utilized in this study—and thus նախանձեցուցանէգոյց was the reading in the text and ժողով-եաց was the marginal reading—this analysis would have a far different conclusion.

The text and margin of Armenian MSS attests the divided Greek tradition: MS B et al. have ἐζήλωσεν, rendered into Armenian նախանձեցուգոյց, perhaps "he caused to be zealous"; Greek MS N et al. have συνήθροισεν (יִּקְבֹּץ) rendered ժողովեաց "he gathered."

The marginal reading in Armenian MSS represents secondary contact with a Greek text like MS B or, possibly, contact with a Greek witness which preserved readings from "the Three" in the margin. The scribe who copied the marginalia noted that the reading in the margin of his parent Greek text ("he gathered") was, in fact, in the text of his Armenian translation so he added in the margin of his Armenian MS what was *in the text* ("he was zealous") of that parent Greek text. If this reconstruction of events is correct, the marginal reading in Armenian MSS indirectly confirms the translation preserved in the margin of the Syro-hexapla.

B-M-Thack give Symmachus' translation, based on the Syro-hexapla, in their second apparatus: καὶ ἐζήλωσεν] σ′ *et congregavit* Syh.

10:19 *

խարանաւք] հնարիւք Sym; խելաւք Aq

J428mg M188mg M2628mg

Jehu asked that everyone connected with the worship of Baal should be summoned to him. We are then told that "Jehu was acting with cunning in order to destroy the worshipers of Baal." The word in question is בְּעָקְבָּה, translated in the NRSV "with cunning." The entry in KBH is: עָקְבָּה: **cunning, craftiness** 2K 10₁₉.† That is, the word occurs only here in the Hebrew Bible.

The Old Greek translation for בְּעָקְבָּה is ἐν πτερνισμῷ "with subtlety." LSJ offer for πτερνισμός the meaning "craft, subtlety" but the only texts cited are both in the Old Testament, namely, the text here and Ps 40(41):10.

The Armenian translation of ἐν πτερνισμῷ is խարանաւք "with deceit," i.e. the word խարանք in the instrumental case. That is certainly an adequate translation. Nevertheless we are offered in the margin the translations of Aquila and Symmachus.

Aquila's translation of בְּעָקְבָּה, when translated from Greek into Armenian, is խելաւք, instrumental case of խելք, which has an adverbial meaning "skilfully, cleverly," hence perhaps "cunningly." Only three references are provided for խելք in Arapkertsi's concordance: 3 Macc 4:15; Mark 4:38; 2 Cor 12:16. Only the last is relevant. There խելաւք translates δόλῳ "by deceit." However, there is only one text cited for Aquila under δόλος in Reider-Turner, Job 15:35 where Aquila uses it for מִרְמָה "fraud, deceit." The Latin equivalent of խելաւք is *astute* "craftily, cunningly" (Freund-Leverett's Greek equivalent is πανούργως), *dolose* "craftily, cunningly, deceitfully" (Freund-Leverett's Greek equivalent for *dolus* is δόλος)."

Symmachus' translation of בְּעָקְבָּה, when translated from Greek into Armenian, is հնարիւք, instrumental case of հնարք "means; fraud, trick." Arapkerts'i has thirteen references to հնար or հնարք but only one is relevant: Eph 6:11 where readers are admonished to "Put on the whole armor of God, so that you may be able to stand against the wiles (πρὸς τὰς μεθοδείας) of the devil." The word μεθοδεία does not occur in the LXX/Old Greek corpus or in what is extant of Symmachus' work, according to H-R. A Latin equivalent of հնարք is *insidiae* "treachery, artifice"; then of հնարիւք "treacherously" *insidiis* or *per insidias*.

Freund-Leverett suggest no Greek equivalent for *insidiae* or its use adverbially but they do suggest a Greek equivalent for the cognate adverb *insidiose*. That equivalent is ἐπιβούλως "treacherously." The adverb ἐπιβούλως is not cited in H-R but its cognate noun is: ἐπιβουλή "plot, scheme." This noun is used by Symmachus at 1 Rgn 22:4 and 4 Rgn 17:4. Its use in the former passage is unusual because the Hebrew is II. מְצוּדָה "stronghold." Symmachus seems to have taken the Hebrew as I. מְצוּדָה "hunting-net"—a usage found only three times and only in Ezekiel—i.e. as "trap."

In 4 Rgn 17:4 Symmachus employs ἐπιβουλή for שֶׁקֶר "lie, deception." This passage offers usage similar to 4 Rgn 10:19 and, based upon it, one might at least suggest the possibility that Symmachus' Greek translation of בְּעָקְבָּה was ἐν ἐπιβουλῇ "with treachery."

Since the translations of Aquila and Symmachus appear to be preserved uniquely by the Armenian, no help is found in Field or B-M-Thack.

The Hebrew, Greek and Armenian equivalents are:

בְּעָקְבָּה → Old Greek ἐν πτερνισμῷ → Zohrapian խարանաւք

→ Aq conj. ἐν δολῷ ← Aq խեղառք

→ Sym conj. ἐν ἐπιβουλῇ ← Sym հնարիւք.

The Armenian marginal readings can be added to the second apparatus of B-M-Thack as follows:

εν πτερνισμω] α′ *astute* σ′ *insidiis* Arm.

10:21 *

ծայր ի ծայր] ամենայն ամենեւին Sym; բերան ի բերան sine nom

J428mg J1928mg(non hab բերան ի բերան) J1934mg (non hab բերան ի բերան) M188mg M2628mg

Manuscript J428 has the marginal reading beside (25) զողջակէզն; the marginal reading which "correctly"—see 10:24—belongs there is beside (10:21) ծայր ի ծայր. The scribe corrected this error by connecting the marginal reading beside v 21 with its intended referrent by use of an asterisk. One might also note that in this MS the reading without signature precedes the signed Symmachus reading.

In response to Jehu's summons, all the worshipers of Baal assembled. Verse 21 concludes by informing us that they entered the temple of Baal "until the temple of Baal was filled from wall to wall." The phrase "from wall to wall" is a translation of פֶּה לָפֶה.

פֶּה לָפֶה means "from end to end," according to BDB who cite this passage: see פֶּה "mouth" 5.a.

The Old Greek translation of the phrase פֶּה לָפֶה is στόμα ἐπὶ (εἰς MS B and the majority of witnesses) στόμα "entrance to entrance." The text with ἐπί is supported by MSS borc₂e₂ (Rahlfs 19-108 82 700 127 93), so-called Lucianic witnesses.

The Armenian translation of στόμα εἰς/ἐπί στόμα is ծայր ի ծայր "from one end to the other." The translation is not literal but certainly conveys the sense of the Greek.

The marginal readings offer the translations of Aquila and Symmachus. (There is little question but that բերան ի բերան, sine nom, belongs to Aquila.) In the case of Aquila, բերան ի բերան, literally "mouth to mouth," represents precisely στόμα εἰς στόμα. However, in Armenian the phrase բերան ի բերան more naturally means "face to face," according to Bedrossian. (The Greek idiom for "face to face" is κατὰ στόμα or στόμα κατὰ στόμα [cf. Num 12:8] or στόμα πρὸς στόμα [2 Jn 12]: cf. LSJ στόμα I.3.g.) According to Reider-Turner,

Aquila's equivalent for פֶּה is στόμα. This is arrived at by retroversion from Syriac (Exod 16:21), Armenian (Isa 52:15) and Latin (*os* : Ezek 16:56). (Such retranslations in Reider-Turner are usually based on Field: see pp. IX, 324.) On the basis of the Armenian marginal reading and Reider-Turner one is led to the conclusion that Aquila's translation for פֶּה לְפֶה was στόμα εἰς στόμα which, however, is the reading of the majority Greek text in B-M-Thack.

The citation of a translation by Aquila in a margin was likely sometimes occasioned simply by a learned interest in such citation. That appears to be the case here. Both the Old Greek στόμα ἐπὶ στόμα and the reading στόμα εἰς στόμα are quite comprehensible in the context yet Aquila's rendering was still cited. Further, his translation appears to have been the same as that of the majority text.

The translation of Sym in Armenian is ամենայն ամենեւին "entirely, wholly." That is, the house of Baal was "completely" filled. It is a translation that conveys well the sense of the Hebrew phrase פֶּה לְפֶה. The Latin equivalent of the Armenian is perhaps *omnis omnino* "fully entirely." Symmachus' Greek translation was something like πάνυ παντελῶς "very completely."

The Hebrew, Greek and Armenian equivalents are:

פֶּה לְפֶה → Greek στόμα εἰς στόμα → Zohrapian ծայր ի ծայր
 → conj. Aq στόμα εἰς στόμα ← sine nom բերան ի բերան
 → Sym conj. πάνυ παντελῶς ← Sym ամենայն
 ամենեւին.

Aquila and Symmachus are not otherwise extant for the translation of פֶּה לְפֶה so there is no other evidence with which to compare the Armenian translation of their work. Their translations can be cited in the second apparatus of B-M-Thack as follows:

στομα εις στομα] ⟨α' ⟩ *os ad os* σ' *omnis omnino* Arm.

10:24 *

խուն ն կու] պատրուծական Aq Sym

J428^mg M188^mg M2628^mg

In all three witnesses the order of citation is Aq Sym; more precisely it is ակ եւ սիմ "Aq and Sym."

On MS J428 see 10:21: this MS has պատրուծակակա beside (21) ծայր ի ծայր; the reading which correctly belongs at v 21 is at 10:25. The scribe has corrected this error by placing as asterisk over signature and marginal reading at v 21 and its intended referrent at v 25 (mend pro 24).

In all three cases the MS has the index sign on (25) զողջակէզուն "sacrifices" (Greek τὴν ὁλοκαύτωσιν). However, the Syro-hexapla preserves readings for α′ σ′ θ′ ε′ on τὰ θύματα in v 24 and it is most likely that the Armenian reading derives from the same tradition.

First, the context. Jehu has gathered all the worshipers of Baal in Baal's temple. Verse 24 informs us that "Then they proceeded to offer sacrifices and burnt offerings." The word זֶבַח is translated here "sacrifices." It is that word which is in question.

The words τὰ θύματα "sacrifices" appear in the text of B-M-Thack on the basis of MSS Bgin (Rahlfs 158 56 119) and the Old Latin. (The presence of the Old Latin in support of τὰ θύματα may indicate that this reading represents Old Greek.) The majority text however—which includes witnesses boc_2e_2 (Rahlfs 19-108 82 127 93)—is θυμιάματα "fragrant stuffs, i.e. incenses" and it is that kind of text upon which the Armenian translation of the verse has been based: խունկ means "incense." The provision of a translation of Aquila and Symmachus in the margins offered a correction for Greek MSS which had θυμιάματα in the text. The same holds true for the Armenian witnesses.

B-M-Thack offer the translation of Aquila and Symmachus in their second apparatus on the basis of the marginal reading in the Syro-hexapla: ܕܕܒ̈ܚܐ "sacrifices."

According to Reider-Turner, Aquila used θυσία "I. burnt offering, sacrifice; II. victim, offering" and θυσίασμα "victim, offering" to translate זֶבַח. Field retroverts the reading of the Syro-hexapla to τὰς θυσίας.

The Armenian translators used a Greek text that read θυμιάματα "incenses"; their translation is խունկս "incenses." The reading in the margins of the Armenian MSS is պատրուծական. The word պատրուծակ means "beast for sacrifice." At 1 Rgn 25:11 and 2 Rgn 17:29 պատրուծակ in the plural translates τὰ πρόβατα "sheep." In 4 Rgn 10:24 it could render either θυσίας or θυσιάσματα.

The Hebrew, Greek and Armenian equivalents are:

ПЗƷ → Greek majority text τὰ θυμιάματα → Zohrapian խունկս

      → Aq Sym conj. (Field) τὰς θυσίας → Aq Sym պատրու-
           ճականս.

The Armenian evidence corroborates that of the Syro-hexapla for the work
of Aquila and Symmachus. It can be cited in the second apparatus of B-M-Thack as
follows:

    τα θυματα] α′ σ′ ܟܬܕ̈ܐ θ′ ε′ ܒ̈ܕܐ Syh : α′ σ′ *sacrificia* Arm.

10:27 *

լուալխ] ապարահանգու Sym; տրտնգու Aq; յաղբնգու Th

J428mg(ևստտնգու Aq vid; աղբնգու Th) M177mg(solum Th hab) M188mg (տստսգու Aq;
աղբnգու Th) M2628mg(ևստտնգու Aq) V212mg(solum Th hab) Zohapp(sine nom) Georg
J/B(hab Sym et vel Aq)

V212 is cited on the basis of Zanolli 1228. The readings noted without signature by Zohrapian are not cited in B-M-Thackeray. Only the reading յաղբնգու
is preserved in the margin of Zohrapian's base MS—V1508—but he notes that
some other witnesses add also in the margin the other two readings, which he cites
as ապարահանգու and տրտնգու. He records no signatures for any of the
three.

Birdsall discusses what appear to be two readings in Georgian witnesses,
though there is only one signature—that of Symmachus. It appears that the Aquila
reading stands first: the two readings are "for going out" and "for making dung."
(86) On the other hand, perhaps the Georgian is simply expansive here in its reproduction of the Symmachus reading.

Witnesses listed have the marginal readings and signatures as they are cited
above, except for the minor variations noted. It appears that the initial ա of
ապարահանգու has been changed to q - in MS J428: a photocopy made from a
microfilm—for which I am indebted to Archbishop Shahé Ajamian—is difficult to

read at this point; the Aquila and Theodotion readings are also not perfectly clear.

All the worshipers of Baal were put to death; the sacred pillar was burned. In v 27 we are told, "Then they demolished the pillar of Baal, and destroyed the temple of Baal, and made it a latrine to this day." The words "and made it a latrine" are a translation of וַיְשִׂמֻהוּ לְמֹחֲרָאוֹת.

As BHS points out in the apparatus, the word לְמֹחֲרָאוֹת "to a latrine"— from * מַחֲרָאָה, only here indisputably in the Hebrew Bible—is the Ketib. The Qere is לְמוֹצָאוֹת "latrine." The word * מוֹצָאָה occurs only here and at Mic 5:1— where it means "origin"—in the Hebrew Bible. The entry in BDB for מַחֲרָאָה is: [מַחֲרָאָה] †n.f. only pl. **cloaca, cesspool**; — מחראות 2 K 10²⁷ Kt (Qr מוֹצָאוֹת). One can conclude that these are both rare words: מַחֲרָאָה occurs only here; מוֹצָאָה occurs only here with the meaning "latrine" and only elsewhere once.

The Old Greek text tradition is divided on the translation of לְמֹחֲרָאוֹת or לְמוֹצָאוֹת. Following MS B and other witnesses, B-M-Thack read εἰς λυτρῶνας (v.l. λουτρῶνας) "(struck it down) into bath-houses." Other witnesses, borz(mg)c₂ e₂ (Rahlfs 19-108 82 700 554ᵐᵍ 127 93), with some variation in spelling, attest κοπρῶνα "place for dung, privy." In 4 Rgn the reading of the so-called Lucianic MSS boc₂e₂ should usually be taken to represent the Old Greek. That appears to be the case here because the translation "latrine" is supported by 𝔏ᵇ.

The Armenian translation follows those Greek witnesses which read "into bath-houses": ի լուանիս means "into a wash-house, bath," or "into wash-houses, baths." (The word լուանիք and its morphologically plural form լուանիքս both mean "bath.") In the margin of the Armenian MSS cited above we are provided with the translations of Aquila, Symmachus and Theodotion.

Aquila's translation of the Hebrew, now rendered into Armenian, is առունգ "draught-houses," i.e. a place to void excrement. (The form առունգու has the plural marker -ու suffixed.) In Latin the equivalent is *forica*, i.e. "privy." See under "draught" in Freund-Leverett who, in turn, give the Greek equivalent of *forica* as ἀφοδευτήριον (LSJ: "night-stool"). Greek MS yᵇ (Rahlfs 121ᵇ: the ᵇ indicates a correction by a later hand), according to B-M-Thackeray's first apparatus, has the translation ἀφοδευτήρια in v 27. It seems possible therefore that this could be Aquila's translation.

Some Armenian MSS have աստունգու "seats" rather than առունգու. On the basis of the other two translations, this appears to be a secondary development.

B-M-Thack cite Symmachus' translation of לְמוֹצָאוֹת/לְמֹחֲראוֹת from the Syro-hexapla. This they render into Latin as *in sterculinium* , i.e. "into a dunghill." The Greek equivalent is κοπρών, according to Freund-Leverett's lexicon. That translation is represented in various Greek witnesses, as noted above. It would be useful in the margin of MSS which read like Greek MS B.

Field retroverts the Symmachus marginal reading in the Syro-hexapla as εἰς ἀφοδευτήριον and suggests comparing the Hexapla at Isa 36:12 where the Hebrew—Ketib!—has אֶת־חַרְאֵיהֶם "their dung." That translation is attributed to *both* Aquila and Symmachus in Greek MSS 86 88, the witnesses in which it is found.

The translation of Theodotion in Armenian is յաղբրոց "into privies": cf. աղբ "excrement." Miskgian defines աղբրանոց as *cloaca* , which, in turn, Freund-Leverett provide with the following meaning: "*a subterranean canal by which the filth was carried off from the city with the rains; a common sewer, sink, drain,* whether public or private, ἀφεδρών." The word ἀφεδρών "privy" does not occur in the Septuagint/Old Greek corpus, according to H-R. It does occur in the NT at Mk 7:19 (par. Matt 15:17) with the preposition εἰς, which is then rendered "into the sewer" by the NRSV. The Armenian translation in Mk and Matt employs the more general word արտաքս "out." If Theodotion used ἀφεδρών it would appear as [εἰς] ἀφεδρώνας. However, the so-called Lucianic MSS boc₂e₂ attest κοπρῶνα and that may in fact underlie աղբրոց since in 4 Rgn these witnesses attest the *kaige* -Th text tradition. That is to say, the text represented by boc₂e₂ stood in the sixth column and should be cited under the name of Theodotion.

If the translation κοπρῶνα belongs to Theodotion, then possibly its synonym ἀφεδρώνας is the translation of Symmachus. This remains hypothetical, of course. It does appear certain that we are dealing with three different translations, since the Armenian attests three different words for the three signatures.

The Georgian marginal reading is სასავლად და საskoრედ *sasavlad da saskored* "for going out and for making dung." It is attributed to Symmachus. Birdsall considers that the "for going out" may have a connection to Aquila. If the Georgian is dependent upon the Armenian, the rendering is euphemistic. That is likewise true if the Georgian is dependent upon a Greek source. In all the Armenian witnesses, the Symmachus reading is cited first. It would be unusual for the order to be reversed by the Georgian scribe.

The Hebrew, Greek and Armenian equivalents at 10:27 are:

לְמֹוצָאֹות/לְמְֹחֲרָאֹות → MS B et al. εἰς λυτρῶνας → Zohrapian ի

լուալ իս

→ Aq conj. [εἰς] ἀφοδευτήρια ← [ի] ատոngu

→ Sym conj. [εἰς] ἀφεδρῶνας ← Sym [ի] ապարահանgu

→ Sym ბაბაჯრომ ჲა ბაბჯმჩჯომ

→ Th conj. εἰς κοπρῶνα ← Th juηբngu.

The task of determining the Greek words underlying the Armenian translations of Aquila, Symmachus and Theodotion here is certainly complex. Nevertheless, there are not that many words for "privy" in Greek and Armenian, or Latin,
and the suggestions above hold merit.

The Armenian witnesses preserve translations by Aquila and Theodotion
and corroborate the Syro-hexapla for Symmachus. The marginalia have passed into
the Georgian tradition, which preserves the Symmachus reading and probably the
Aquila reading. The second apparatus in B-M-Thack can be revised in the following
way to reflect the Armenian and Georgian evidence:

εἰς λυτρωνας] ※ (> Arm) σ' in (> Arm) sterculinium (sterculinia Arm)
Arm Syh : σ' exire et excrementum facere   Georg : θ' in cloacas Arm | λυτ-
ρωνας] α' foricas Arm.

Following the convention of B-M-Thack the preceding does not offer the
retroversions back into Greek that are offered above.

11:4 *

գբորին եւ գրասիմ] գաւ ժանդական Sym; գզգ իրան Aq

J428mg M177mg(ind supra գրասիմ) M188mg(գգդիրան vid) M2628mg (գjաւ -
ժանդական; ind supra գբորին) V212mg(գաւ ժանդականան) Zohapp (mg) B-M-
Thackapp2 (գդգիրան) GeorgJ/B

Manuscript V212 is cited on the basis of Zanolli 1228.

The Georgian is cited on the basis of Birdsall 86–87. He comments that the

Armenian marginalia "probably represents the source of the Georgian, which uses the Armenian calque *gzir* ." (86)

The context concerns the priest Jehoida's arrangements for the coronation of Joash in the time of the evil Athaliah. Verse 4 tells us that Jehoida summoned "the captains of the Carites and of the guards and had them come to him in the house of the LORD." The phrases "of the Carites and of the guards" are under discussion. They are a translation of לַכָּרִי וְלָרָצִים.

The entry for כָּרִי in KBH reads: n. peop. הַכָּרִי, coll. **Carites** 2S 20₃₃ 2K11₄.₁₉.† As for רָצִים, the entry under רוּץ includes: 2. pt. רָץ **runner** (of the king) 1K1₅. The notes to 2 Ki 11:4 in *The New Oxford Annotated Bible* NRSV— contributed by William F. Stinespring and Burke O. Long, edited by Bruce M. Metzger and Roland E. Murphy—suggest that the word "Carites" may only be an error for Cherethites (1 Sam 30:14; 2 Sam 8:16–18).[1]

The MS B-related Greek tradition offers transliterations of the two words: hence we read in MS B τὸν Χορρεὶ καὶ τὸν 'Ρασείν. (The spelling of 'Ρασείν in the majority text is 'Ρασείμ and that is the spelling represented in the Armenian version.) According to B-M-Thack, in their second apparatus, ο' θ' εβρ. also used transliterations. It is the use of these transliterations that has led to the inclusion of translations by Aquila, Symmachus and others in the margins of various textual witnesses, including the Armenian.

Greek MSS boc₂e₂ (Rahlfs 19-108 82 127 93) also attest the transliteration, like MS B, so we can take the transliterations to be Old Greek. B-M-Thack indicate that in the Lucianic MSS the transliterations are preceded by the words τῶν παρα-τρεχόντων καί "of the runners and." This is a later textual development.

It appears that Aquila and Symmachus took the לַכָּרִי וְלָרָצִים as referring to one group. Greek MS j (Rahlfs 243) in its margin preserves what appears to be Aquila—B-M-Thack place the signature in square brackets: hence [α']—for these words: τοὺς τρέχοντας "the runners." (The square brackets mean that the signature cannot be read clearly.) Greek MS j also preserves the translation of Symmachus for לַכָּרִי וְלָרָצִים, namely τοὺς παρατρέχοντας "the runners" (of a king's bodyguard).

The Syro-hexapla preserves a reading in the margin for καὶ τὸν 'Ρασείν

---

[1](New York: Oxford 1991) ad loc.

which B-M-Thack record in Latin as *et currentes* "and runners." Field cites the Syriac marginal reading as ܘܠܐܡܨ̈ܐ ܘܪܗܛܐ "and the runners" and retroverts it to καὶ τοὺς τρέχοντας (or παρατρέχοντας).

The Armenian text also transliterates לַכָּרִי וְלָרָצִים, following the Greek tradition: զքորին եւ զռասիմ "the *k'orin* and the *ṛasim*."

The Armenian marginal evidence should simply corroborate the evidence already known for Aquila and Symmachus from Greek and Syriac witnesses. In the case of Symmachus, it does. The word աւժանդակ means "runner; auxiliary." However, the index signs are unstable here in the Armenian tradition: the signs appear above one or the other word or in such a way that it would appear that both զքորին եւ զռասիմ are involved. That latter appears to be correct, to judge from the Greek tradition.

In the case of the word in Armenian bearing Aquila's name the situation is more difficult. It appears that a corruption has taken place. B-M-Thack have ըզդդգիրսն which, when one removes the direct object marker զ-, the "far" demonstrative marker -ն and the plural direct object marker -ս, gives us the lexical form դգիր. No such word can be found in the dictionaries, though one may find դգի, a synonym for ձի "horse." (Adjarian I 658) B-M-Thack of course follow Zohrapian's apparatus where it is often difficult to distinguish դ from զ, though the word given by Zohrapian appears to me more like զզզիրսն—with a զ— than զդդգիրսն.

The word զզզիրսն does not mean "runners." Զզիր appears in Bedrossian with the meaning "rush," i.e. bulrush. Adjarian I 548 is more to the point: he offers զզիր «գիւղի տանունտերի երկրորդը» "the second in charge of a village." He goes on to say that it is a word of the late period, used in modern provincial settings. The authors he cites are of the late 17th and 18th centuries. In Zachariah Sarkavagi's *History* (1699) the word is already interpreted as «քիզիր. աւանապետ ["head of a region"].» Adjarian cites Hübschmann, *ZDMG* 35 (1881), 657 who takes the word to be a loan-word from Persian. Indeed the word is widely distributed in the Near East and is found in Persian (*gizer* "head of a village"), Syriac, Arabic, Turkish and other languages. It seems a long way removed from Aquila's τοὺς τρέχοντας. I do not know how the latter has become զզզիրսն "village leaders."

The Georgian preserves for Symmachus ᶚინამცორვალნი *çinamcorvalni* "forerunners" or "running footmen"—Birdsall's translation; the reading for Aquila is ზგირნი *gzirni* "scouts." These translations coincide with the Armenian.

The Hebrew, Greek, Armenian and Georgian equivalents for 4 Rgn 11:4 are:

לַכָּרִי וְלָרָצִים → Old Greek τὸν Χορρεὶ καὶ τὸν Ῥασείμ → Zohrapian զքոռիս եւ զռասիմ

→ conj. Aq τοὺς τρέχοντας ≠ Aq զզգիրսն

→ Aq զգիրնո

→ Sym τοὺς παρατρέχοντας → Sym զաւժանդակսն

→ Sym ᶚինამცორვალნი.

We can conclude that the Armenian corroborates other witnesses to Symmachus' translation of לַכָּרִי וְלָרָצִים. The word attributed to Aquila in Armenian remains something of an enigma, though Birdsall's translation of the Georgian as "scouts" may resolve the difficulty.

The second apparatus in B-M-Thack cites the Armenian evidence in Armenian characters (under τον 1°—ρασειν). Why that should be done here and not elsewhere is not clear. The Armenian—and Georgian—can be cited as follows if we follow their normal practice:

τον 1°—ρασειν] εβρ. ܪܨܝܡ, ܪܟܒ̈ܐ Syh-ap-Barh : α′ *duces vici* σ′ *currentes* Arm Georg.

Cf. also 11:19.

11:8 *

ի uաղերուվթեն]ի փողոցան Aq

J428mg M177mg(ի ժողովին vid) M188mg M2628mg(փողոցան) V212mg(ի ժողով ն) Zohapp(mg)(փողոցան) B-M-Thackapp2(փողոցան) GeorgJ/B

The Georgian is cited on the basis of Birdsall 87.

According to Zanolli 1228, V212 has in the margin ի ժողովն "into the assembly," attributed to Aquila. I am inclined to take that as a corruption, which it shares with MS M177. (These two MSS agree in their marginal readings at times, against other witnesses: cf. 11:4.) The word ժողովք translates a number of Greek words in the Bible: e.g., συναγωγή "assembly" (Gen 1:9; 28:3); σύστημα "accumulation" (Gen 1:10); σύστρεμμα "band, company" (2 Rgn 15:12); σύνοδος "assembly, meeting" (3 Rgn 15:13). It fits nicely in the context and one could suggest Greek equivalents which work equally well: indeed, σύστημα and σύστρεμμα can be used of a corps of soldiers, which is the meaning that the NRSV ("ranks") gives to the Hebrew. Still, to be a genuine reading of one of "the Three," it would have to be a Symmachus reading with the incorrect signature—since Aquila and Theodotion shared the same translation, according to Greek witnesses—and preserve it uniquely over against other reliable Armenian MSS. The Georgian witness may give some control here since its witness is apparently dependent upon the Armenian but preserves only ի ժողովրդսն and the signature of Aquila, in Georgian of course.

Jehoiada made arrangements for the protection of the young Joash. He told the temple soldiers that were to come on duty on the Sabbath to surround the king; that וְהַבָּא אֶל־הַשְּׂדֵרוֹת יוּמָת "whoever approaches the ranks is to be killed." At issue is the meaning of the word הַשְּׂדֵרֹת, here translated "ranks." The NIV[txt] also has "ranks"; NIV[mg] has "precincts."

The entry concerning הַשְּׂדֵרוֹת in KBH is as follows: *שְׂדֵרָה: pl. שְׂדֵרֹ(וֹ)ת: unexpl. archit. term; perh. = s ⁱderôt **aligned beams** 1K 6₉ 2K 11₈.₁₅ 2C 23₁₄.† The entry in BDB is more explanatory: †[שְׂדֵרָה] **n.f. 1. row, rank** of soldiers in line. **2.** architectural term. (prob. for סְדֵרָה, v. supr. ...);— only pl. abs. 2 K 11⁸ 2 Ch 23¹⁴, רֹת- 1 K 6⁹ 2 K 11¹⁵;— **1.** *rows, ranks,* 2 K 11⁸, and v¹⁵ = 2 Ch 23¹⁴ (where thought to be a gloss by Benz, on account of מִבַּיִת, *within*). **2.** term. techn. of building, גֵּבִים וּשְׂדֵרֹת בָּאֲרָזִים 1 K 6⁹, meaning unknown.

Greek manuscript B has for the clause cited above καὶ ὁ εἰσπορευόμενος εἰς ἀηδὼθ ἀποθανεῖται "and the one who goes into *aēdoth* will die." However, ἀηδώθ is corrupt: the original reading is likely τὰ σαδηρώθ, represented in MSS N*b* ijnxy(txt)z*c₂ (Rahlfs 108 56 243 119 247 121[txt] 554* 93) Thdt and, with minor variation, by MSS A*g* (Rahlfs 158); b'z[a?] (Rahlfs 19 554[a?]).

The reading τὰ σαδηρώθ is of course a transliteration. The Armenian translation simply transliterates the Greek: hence Zohrapian has սադերովթն. Bedrossian explains with his entry: *H[ebrew].w[ord].* sateroth, ranges of the Temple.

The marginal reading of Aquila comes as a welcome clarification. According to B-M-Thack, the translations of Aquila and Theodotion are extant: both translated the phrase אֶל־הַשְּׂדֵרוֹת into Greek as πρὸς τοὺς περιβόλους "to the precincts." (see LSJ περίβολος: 2. *area enclosed, enclosure* ; of a temple, *precinct* .) That is, πρὸς τοὺς περιβόλους is attributed to Aquila in MS j (Rahlfs 243) and to Theodotion in MS z (Rahlfs 554). The Syro-hexapla also preserves Aquila's translation in its margin, namely as ܟܝܠ ܐܢܠ "toward the enclosured areas" which, put into Latin in B-M-Thack, becomes *ad saepta* "toward the palisades" (Freund-Leverett: Greek φράγμα).

The phrase πρὸς τοὺς περιβόλους becomes in Armenian ի փողոցսն. The word փողոց means "street" but also, according to Miskgian, *platea* "street; a broad place in the house, area, court"; and *forum* "street; Forum, i.e. marketplace." It can mean then much the same as περίβολος and as the Latin *saeptum* . (Unfortunately περίβολος does not occur in the LXX/Old Greek corpus or in the NT, precluding any easy search for Armenian equivalents.) The translation of the Armenian clause with the reading of Aquila inserted, i.e. եւ որ մտանիցէ ի փողոցսն մեռցի, might then be "and whoever enters the courtyards shall die."

The Georgian is similar to the Armenian, namely გოლოცთა *p'oloct'a* "to the walls," which could refer to the courtyards so enclosed.

The Hebrew, Greek, Armenian and Georgian equivalents are:

אֶל־הַשְּׂדֵרוֹת → Old Greek εἰς τὰ σαδηρώθ → Zohrapian ի սա-

դերովթն

→ Aq Th πρὸς τοὺς περιβόλους → Aq ի փողոցսն

→ Aq გოლოცთა.

The second apparatus in B-M-Thack can be revised. It is not clear to me why the Armenian should be cited in this instance in Armenian script, i.e. as փողոցսն, the reading in Zohrapian's apparatus. Why not cite it in Latin translation, as elsewhere? The reading they cite differs only in number from that of the Syro-hexapla, which they cite in Latin translation. At any rate, the word should be cited in its plural form, based upon its citation in a number of MSS. The Armenian and Georgian can be cited with the Syro-hexapla, as follows:

και 3°—αηδωθ] α' και ο εισερχομενος προς τους περιβολους j | εις

αηδωθ] θ′ προς τους περιβολους z : α′ *ad saepta* Arm Georg Syh | αηδωθ]
σαδι Syh.

The second citation from the Syro-hexapla is a bit confusing here. Field
explains that the Syro-hexapla has in the text ܟܐܟܡܠ, with the Greek letters ΣΑΔΙ
added.

11:9 ∗

ի՛մասւոուն] քահանայ Aq

J428mg M188mg M2628mg GeorgB/J(*sacerdos* in txt et *sapiens* in mg)

The Georgian is cited on the basis of Birdsall 90; the citation of the Georgian evidence above represents the readings of MS 646. More will be said about the
Georgian evidence in a moment.

In v 9 we are informed that "The captains did according to all that the priest
Jehoida commanded." In this sentence "the priest" translates what is the usual word
for priest in Hebrew plus the article, namely הַכֹּהֵן.

The translation of הַכֹּהֵן is represented in the B-related text by, oddly
enough, ὁ συνετός, "the intelligent, sagacious, wise." H-R cite 4 Rgn 11:9 under
συνετός but place a dagger (†) after the passage, indicating that the identification of
the Greek and Hebrew is doubtful. One would have expected for הַכֹּהֵן the translation ὁ ἱερεύς. In fact, ἱερεύς appears after συνετός in MS z (Rahlfs 554) and as
the first word of a longer "plus" in MSS b orc₂e₂, i.e. the so-called Lucianic MSS bo
c₂e₂ (Rahlfs 19-108 82 127 93) plus r (Rahlfs 700). The reading ὁ συνετὸς
ἱερεύς "the wise priest" looks like a conflated text.[1]

The Hebrew text which Origen worked with and the Greek text he had must
have had the readings הַכֹּהֵן and ὁ συνετός, respectively, since the differing translation of Aquila has been preserved.

The Armenian text follows a B-related type of text that had ὁ συνετός: the
Armenian reads ի՛մասւոուն "wise," without the word "priest." The margin of

---

[1]Cf. Birdsall's comment (p. 90) "The Greek tradition however knows nothing of "the priest" as a
Septuagintal reading, ..."

the MSS cited above preserves the translation of Aquila: քահանայ i.e. [ὁ]
ἱερεύς. The second apparatus of B-M-Thack records that the Syro-hexapla preserves *sacerdos* "priest" as the translation of both Aquila and Symmachus. The
Syriac marginal reading is ܟܗܢܐ ܗܘ "the priest," according to Field.

The Georgian situation is complex. The text of MS 570 reads simply "Judah"; the text of MS 646 reads "Judah the Priest"; the text of MS 51 has "Judah the
wise priest." The word for "priest" here is მღდელმან *mġdelman* and that for
"wise" is ბრძენმან *brdzenman*. In the margins of MSS 570 646 we find the reading
ბრძენმან *brdzenman* "wise," attributed to Aquila. It appears that the Georgian evidence represents an instance of where the reading of text and margin have been in-
terchanged at some stage. That is true of MS 646 and it also explains that marginal
reading in MS 570, even though the latter lacks the word "priest" in the text.

The Hebrew, Greek, Armenian and Georgian equivalents are:

הַכֹּהֵן → B-type text ὁ συνετός → Zohrapian իմաստուն

      → Aq Sym ὁ ἱερεύς → Aq քահանայ

           → MS 646 Aq ბრძენმან in mg et მღდელმან

           in txt.

The Greek underlying the Armenian and Syriac is not in question: the plus
in MS z (Rahlfs 554)—so indicated in the first apparatus of B-M-Thack—is in all
likelihood hexaplaric. The Armenian corroborates the witness of the Syro-hexapla
for the translation of Aquila.

The second apparatus in B-M-Thack can be revised as follows:

o συνετος] α' σ'(> Arm) *sacerdos*   Arm Syh : α' *sapiens*   in mg
Georg[570 646] et *sacerdos* in txt Georg[646].

11:12 *

զյեզերն] զարբութիւնն Sym; զզատուցեալն Aq

J428[mg] J1927[mg](hab solum արբութիւն sine nom) M177[mg](hab solum արբութիւն)
M188[mg] M2628[mg](զարբութիւն) V212[mg](hab solum արբութիւնք) Zoh[app(mg)](hab
solum զարբութիւն sine nom) B-M-Thack[app2] (*sanctitatem* sine nom) Georg[B/J]

Citation in: Trebolle-Barrera 65; Stone (citing Birdsall).

V212 is cited on the basis of Zanolli 1229.

The Georgian is cited on the basis of Birdsall 87, 92. His conclusion based upon this passage—"… the readings at xi. 12 indicate that it [i.e. the readings from "the Three" in Georgian 4 Rgn] is not directly related to the Armenian as critically edited hitherto" (92)—can now be withdrawn. Birdsall's point rests upon the fact that Georgian witnesses preserve a reading for Aquila at 11:12, while B-M-Thack (i.e. Zohrapian) does not indicate that such is preserved in the Armenian. The collation of the Armenian evidence cited above shows that it preserves both readings and signatures for Aquila and Symmachus. The source of the Georgian readings is clear here, as elsewhere. The Georgian readings derive from the Armenian.[1]

When all the guards were in place Jehoida brought out the king's son, "put the crown on him, and gave him the covenant; they proclaimed him king." The words "the crown" are a translation of אֶת־הַנֵּזֶר, i.e. the word נֵזֶר with the definite marker הַ and the direct object marker אֶת.

The meaning of נֵזֶר is straightforward: cf. KBH: 2. a kind of crown, **diadem, headband** (of silver or gold w[ith]. lacing-holes, as mark of being consecrated): of king 2K 11₁₂, …

Greek MS B and the majority of Greek MSS reflect a corruption in which נ and ר were confused in the process of transliteration. Hence the text printed in B-M-Thack reads καὶ ἔδωκεν ἐπ' αὐτὸν ἰέζερ καὶ τὸ μαρτύριον "and he put upon him the *iezer* and the testimony." (The word ἰέζερ has the definite article τόν in the majority of witnesses, correctly. It has been lost by parablepsis through homoioteleuton in MSS Bj [Rahlfs 143]: [ἐπ' αὐ]τὸν ∩ τὸν ἰέζερ.)

In Lucianic MSS boc₂e₂ (Rahlfs 19-108 82 127 93) and Theodoret we find the reading τὸ ἀγίασμα "consecration, sanctification" (Lust). H-R list two passages where ἀγίασμα is used to render נֵזֶר: Ps 88(89):39; 131(132):18; and one where it renders the cognate verb נֵזֶר in the *nifal* : Ps 131(132):8. Lust cites *Am 2:11 εἰς ἀγιασμόν -נזר/ל? *for consecration* for MT נזרים/ל *for nazirites* ; neol[ogism]. This points toward some connection between the Hebrew and Greek

---

[1]It might be useful to offer Birdsall's comment in its entirety. He states: "It [i.e. the hexaplaric material in Georgian] probably came into the Georgian sphere from the Armenian, as so much else in general has done, and as certain specific loan-words and shared interpretations show; but the readings at xi. 12 indicate that it is not directly related to the Armenian as critically edited hitherto."

roots. Is the reading τὸ ἁγίασμα Old Greek or has it come from the Hexapla?

The transliteration ἱέζεϼ is responsible for the citation of translations from Aquila, Symmachus and Theodotion in the margins of various witnesses. Some Armenian MSS attest the translations of Aquila and Symmachus in the margin. Fortunately their translations are also extant in Greek so that we know whence the Armenian words have come.

The Armenian text follows the transliterated Greek with a transliteration into Armenian: hence զյեզերն in Zoh[txt] or զյազերն in Zoh[app].

The Armenian translation of Aquila's translation of the Hebrew is զզատուցեալն "the consecrated things." The word is the participle of զատուցանեմ, with the plural marker -ս, the farther demonstrative marker -ն, and the prefixed marker of the direct object զ-. The Greek word from which it has come is τὸ ἀφωρισμένον "what has been ordained," a participle in the singular number. According to B-M-Thack, τὸ ἀφωρισμένον is preserved in Greek MS j (Rahlfs 243); they also offer Aquila's translation on the basis of the Syro-hexapla, translated into Latin as *separatum* "separate," i.e. consecrated. The Armenian appears to be in error in respect of number.

Symmachus' translation of אֶת־הַקֹּדֶשׁ is τὸ ἅγιον "what is holy," according to Greek MS j; *sancta* "sacred" according to the Syro-hexapla. (Not too much should be made of the plural number attested by the Syro-hexapla [Field: ܩܘܕ̈ܫܐ] because the s[e]yāmē —i.e. the plural marker—is not stable in Syriac.) In Armenian this becomes զսրբութիւնն "what is holy," with the farther demonstrative -ն (Greek τό) at the end and the direct object marker զ- prefixed. B-M-Thack cite the Armenian in their second apparatus as *sanctitatem* "sacredness" but without the name of the translator because the name of the translator is not in Zoh[app], upon which they are dependent. It is clear from the Armenian MSS cited above that the translator is Symmachus.

The Georgian evidence is like the Armenian. For Symmachus the marginal reading is სიწმიდე *sicmide* "holy"; for Aquila the reading is განკუთვნებული *gankut'vnebuli* "reserved, set apart." (The transliteration of the Symmachus reading in Birdsall's article is *siccmide* , which requires the spelling სიწწმიდე. The spelling given above is the lexical form.)

The Hebrew, Greek, Armenian and Georgian equivalents are:

אֶת־הַנֵּזֶר → Greek MS B et al. [τὸν] ιἐζερ → Zohrapian զյեզեր̅ն

    → Aq τὸ ἀφωρισμένον → Aq զզատուցեալն

        → Aq განკვეთებულო

    → Sym τὸ ἅγιον → Sym զսրբութիւնն

        → Sym სოჶმოჩ.

Here the Armenian and Georgian readings corroborate the evidence in the margins of Greek MSS and the Syro-hexapla.

The second apparatus in B-M-Thack can be revised as follows:

ιεζερ—μαρτυριον] α′ το αφωρισμενον και την μαρτυριαν σ′ το αγιον και τα μαρτυρια j | ιεζερ] α′ separatum (separata Arm) σ′ sancta (sanctum Arm Georg) Arm Georg Syh : θ′ ε′ secundum σ′ ܗܪܟܠ Syh.

11:14 1° *

(ի վերայ) սեանն ըստ օրինի իւրում, եւ երգիչք]սեդքանն ըստ սովորութեանն եւ իշխանք Aq

M177mg V212mg(սովորութեան)

V212 is cited on the basis of Zanolli 1229. Zanolli relates a marginal reading կազմաձ attributed to Symmachus to this verse but it belongs with 12:5 (2°). Without examining the MS one might suppose that the reading stands between columns, with 11:14 on the one side and 12:5 on the other.

The noise of the coronation of Joash alerted the wicked Athaliah. She went into the temple and "when she looked, there was the king standing by the pillar, according to custom, with the captains and the trumpeters beside the king." The words עַל־הָעַמּוּד כַּמִּשְׁפָּט וְהַשָּׂרִים are translated in the NRSV "by the pillar, according to custom, with the captains." In the NIV the translation is as follows: "by the pillar, as the custom was. The officers ... "

What has occasioned the marginal reading is the rendering of הַשָּׂרִים, translated "the captains" in the NRSV. The word שַׂר means "offical, leader." The B-related Greek text has for the words cited in Hebrew above ἐπὶ τοῦ στύλου κατὰ τὸ κρίμα, καὶ οἱ ᾠδοί "at the pillar according to custom, and the singers."

Instead of הַשָּׂרִים the Greek has read הַשָּׁרִים, i.e. "singers." The difference involves only שׂ and שׁ. It is, however, the reason that Aquila's translation has been cited in the margin of the Armenian witnesses.

The Armenian text follows a Greek text like that printed in B-M-Thack. It has (ի վերայ) սեանն ըստ օրինի իւրում, եւ երգիչք "(upon, i.e. at) the pillar according to his custom, and (the) singers."

Aquila's translation is preserved in MSS M177 V212. There is a spelling error in the citation: սեանն "the pillar," gen./dat./loc. form of սիւն with the demonstrative -ն, has become սեղանն "the table." The reading is, with the correction: սեղանն (mend pro սեանն) ըստ սովորութեանն եւ իշխանք "[at] the pillar according to the custom and the commanders."

In retroverting ըստ սովորութեանն "according to the custom" back into Greek we are faced with two possibilities: either Aquila's rendering of כְּמִשְׁפָּט was not literal here or, perhaps more likely, the Armenian rendering of Aquila is not precisely literal. (And, yes, I suppose there is a third possibility: the non-literal rendering indicates that the reading really belongs to Symmachus.) The Hebrew is כְּמִשְׁפָּט, whose translation by Aquila—to judge from Reider-Turner—should involve κρίμα "decision, judgement," κρίσις (same meaning), or δικαίωσις "making or accounting righteous." The Greek already has κατὰ τὸ κρίμα "according to judgement," literally. The word սովորութիւն means consuetudo , i.e. "custom, habit"; for the latter Freund-Leverett give as the Greek equivalent ἔθος "custom, habit." However, ἔθος is not listed in Reider-Turner as a word that Aquila uses. Perhaps therefore the Armenian rendering of Aquila's translation is not literal, which would somewhat defeat the purpose of having it! Since Aquila is literal in his translations, we will assume that the freer rendering սովորութիւն belongs to the Armenian translator.

The word իշխան means "prince, chief, ruler, commander."[1] What Greek word does իշխանք, the plural, translate? Reider-Turner give as Aquila's equivalents for שַׂר the words ἄρχων "ruler, commander" and δεσπότης "master, ruler." In the Armenian Bible իշխան is commonly used for ἄρχων; տէր "lord" is commonly used for δεσπότης, though the latter is rendered by իշխան at Job 5:8.

---

[1] Lake Sevan in Armenia is famous for a type of fish that goes by the name իշխան. Relating this fact provides nothing useful for textual criticism but it might lighten up the discussion a bit.

More than likely Aquila used ἄρχων here at 11:14.

The Hebrew, Greek and Armenian equivalents are:

עַל־)הָעַמּוּד כַּמִּשְׁפָּט וְהַשָּׂרִים → (ἐπὶ) τοῦ στύλου κατὰ τὸ κρίμα,

καὶ οἱ ᾠδοί → Zohrapian (ի վերայ) սեանն ըստ

օրինի իւրում, եւ երգիչք

→ Aq conj. (ἐπὶ) τοῦ στύλου κατὰ τὸ κρίμα [ἔθος?], καὶ οἱ

ἄρχοντες ← Aq սեղանն (mend pro սեանն) ըստ

սովորութեանն եւ իշխանք.

The Armenian witness is unique in preserving the translation of Aquila. Though the text behind սովորութեանն may be questionable, that behind իշխանք is virtually certain, i.e. ἄρχοντες. This item can be added to the second apparatus in B-M-Thack in the following way:

του— ωδοι] α' *mensam* (mend pro *columnam*)   *iuxta morem et duces*
Arm.

11:14 2° *

դաւ է, դաւ է] հակառակ յարոյց Sym; ապստամբութիւն Aq

J428mg(sine ind) M188mg(sine nom; ապստամբութիւն; ind supra [15] ապստուեր mend)
M2628mg(ind supra [15] ապստուեր mend); *rebellio rebellio* Sym GeorgJ/B(hab solum Sym)

The Georgian is cited on the basis of Birdsall 88.

When Athaliah realized what was happening she "tore her clothes and cried, קֶשֶׁר קָשֶׁר "Treason! Treason!"

The word קֶשֶׁר means "alliance, **conspiracy**"—KBH cite this very passage.

The Old Greek translated קֶשֶׁר קֶשֶׁר with the words Σύνδεσμος, σύνδεσμος "Conspiracy, conspiracy!" This meaning is found under σύνδεσμος IV. in LSJ but only this passage is cited with the word *al[ibi]*. = "elsewhere in the same author." The word usually means "that which binds together." It is the unusual use of σύνδεσμος which has led to the addition of the translations of Aquila and Symmachus.

The Armenian text translates the exclamation with the words դաւ է, դաւ է "It's a trick, it's a trick!"

B-M-Thack have signed and unsigned readings cited in their lower apparatus. Their citations read: συνδεσμος συνδεσμος] σ' *Rebellio rebellio* Syh | συνδεσμος 1°] ανταρσια επιβουλια h: ... σις y. (MS h is Rahlfs 55; y is 121.) In their first apparatus B-M-Thack cite the variant ανταρσις ανταρσις "insurrection, insurrection" found in Greek MSS j(mg)z[a]? (Rahlfs 243[mg] 554[a]?), witnesses often cited in the lower apparatus because of readings from Aquila, Symmachus and Theodotion found in their margins. The variant reading ἄνταρσις ἄνταρσις derives from "the Three." LSJ cite this passage under ἄνταρσις and indicate that the word belongs to Symmachus.

The word attributed to Aquila in Armenian is ապստամբութիւն "rebellion." In the Armenian Bible ապստամբութիւն translates ἀποστασία/ἀπόστασις "defection, revolt" (Josh 22:22; 3 Rgn 21(Gk 20):13; 2 Chr 28:19; 29:19; 33:19; 1 Macc 2:15; Jer 2:19; Acts 21:21; 2 Thess 2:3); ἀποστροφή "turning back; II. turning away from" (Jer 3:11(ℵ); 5:6; 6:19; 18:12); ἀπείθεια "disobedience" (Rom 11:30; Eph 2:2); ἀπέχθεια? "hatred" (3 Macc 3:4). Ἀποστασία and ἀπόστασις are both used by Aquila but not for קֶשֶׁר in what is extant of his work. Reider-Turner give σύστρεμμα "band, company"—but perhaps also "conspiracy"[1]—as Aquila's equivalent for קֶשֶׁר at Ezek 22:25. It is very difficult to determine, therefore, what Aquila used for קֶשֶׁר קֶשֶׁר. Perhaps it was ἀποστασία. Perhaps it was ἐπιβουλία "treachery" since Reider-Turner list the cognates ἐπιβουλεύειν, ἐπιβουλή and ἐπίβουλος for Aquila. Note however that Aquila employs this group of words for * הות "attack" (Ps 62[61]:4 †), הַוּוֹת "ruin" (e.g. Ps 5:10). Of these various possibilities, σύστρεμμα seems the most likely because we know that Aquila used it for קֶשֶׁר.

For Symmachus the Armenian is հակառակ յարույց "He has risen up in opposition!" or "He has rebelled!" (The word յարույց is the aorist 3 sg. of յարուցանեմ "raise opposition, withstand, resist.") It is obvious that this is not a literal translation of Symmachus, at least according to what we know of Symma-

---

[1] Cf. cognate συστρέφω III.—Pass. "club together, conspire." LSJ cite 4 Rgn 10:9 and, in the active mode, 3 Rgn 16:9.

chus' translation from the Syro-hexapla. There is another possibility: the attribution of ἄνταρσις ἄνταρσις to Symmachus rests upon the signature in the Syro-hexapla: the marginal reading is sine nom in MS j. Perhaps the signature is inaccurate and ἄνταρσις ἄνταρσις really belongs to Aquila. Not so: the Georgian evidence makes it likely that the first suggestion is correct: the Armenian marginal reading is not a literal translation of Symmachus.

The Syriac marginal reading is ܟ݁ܬܢܝܢܚܕ ܟ݁ܬܢܝܢܚܕ "rebellion, rebellion," according to Field. It bears Symmachus' signature. Field asks us to compare the Hexapla at Isa 8:12; Amos 7:10. In the former case the word ἄνταρσις is attested by both Procopius and Jerome as Symmachus' translation for קֶשֶׁר; in the latter case, however, the Symmachus' reading is corrupt and Field suggests that the simplest conjecture is ἄνταρσις, on the basis of 4 Rgn 11:14 and Isa 8:12, a line of reasoning which could be taken to be somewhat circular. On the basis of the Isaiah passage, it seems clear that Symmachus employed ἄνταρσις for the word קֶשֶׁר.

Georgian witnesses preserve a Symmachus reading: ჰდომა ჰდომა, *hdoma hdoma* "revolt, revolt." See Birdsall 88. This reading could be important as a control for the non-literal rendering of the Symmachus reading in the Armenian witnesses. However, Birdsall points out that in the text of the Georgian one finds განგდა განგდა *gandga gandga* "he is in revolt, he is in revolt"—the tense of the verb is actually aorist—which he believes must equally be derived from the version of Symmachus! This raises the possibility that the readings of text and margin have been switched. Such a phenomenon is also found in Georgian MSS: Mzekale Shanidze informed me that this occurs in Georgian MSS during a visit to the Institute of Manuscripts in Tbilisi in June 1978. "He is in revolt" coincides with the Symmachus translation, as known in Armenian, though in Georgian this is repeated, so "he is in revolt, he is in revolt." Since the marginal reading is signed, it seems that less likely to have been moved from the text. The one word "revolt"— also repeated—which one finds in the margin coincides with the translation of Aquila as it is known in Armenian.

(Molitor cites στάσις "revolt, rebellion"[1] as the word which underlies ჰდომა at Acts 15:2.)

Finally, there is a marginal reading in Greek MS h (Rahlfs 55): ἀνταροία

---

[1] Gingrich, *Shorter Lexicon* .

ἐπιβουλία "insurrection, treachery." Where does that translation derive from?

The equivalents are not clear in this passage. The best we can suggest is as follows:

קֶשֶׁר קֶשֶׁר קֶשֶׁר → Old Greek σύνδεσμος σύνδεσμος → Zohrapian դաւ է,

դաւ է

→ Aq conj. σύστρεμμα [σύστρεμμα] ← Aq ապստամբութիւն

[ապստամբութիւն]

→ Sym ἄνταρσις ἄνταρσις → Sym հակառակ յարոյց

→ Sym ჯთმა ჯთმა.

I have added in square brackets what was likely true of Aquila's translation, namely that the word used for קֶשֶׁר was repeated to represent the second קֶשֶׁר.

What does the Armenian evidence contribute here? It provides a signed reading for Aquila and a non-literal translation of Symmachus into Armenian. The Aquila reading appears to be unique.

The Armenian and Georgian evidence can be added to the second apparatus of B-M-Thack as follows:

σύνδεσμος σύνδεσμος] α′ *rebellio*   σ′ *surrexit contra* Arm : σ′ *Rebellio rebellio* Georg Syh | σύνδεσμος 1°] ανταρσια επιβουλια h : ...σις y.

11:15

(განყოვებით) ეჯე (სადგრმნით)] ეჯე განდგომილი Aq

Georg^{J/B}

This is one of four readings set out by Birdsall which is not attested in Armenian witnesses. The others are at 8:15; 14:29; 18:4; 8:15 and 11:15 appear to be inner-Georgian glosses. The following is based upon Birdsall 90.

Athaliah was in the temple when she cried out, "Treason! Treason!" Then Jehoida the priest commanded the captains who were over the army, "Bring her out between the ranks, and kill with the sword anyone who follows her." The words "Bring her out between the ranks" are a translation of הוֹצִיאוּ אֹתָהּ אֶל־מִבֵּית לַשְּׂדֵרֹת.

The Old Greek renders this clause Ἐξαγάγετε (ἐξάγαγε B*) αὐτὴν (αὐτοὺς B*) ἔσωθεν τὸν σαδηρώθ (ἀσηρώθ B*) "Take her out from within the *sadērōth* ."

The Armenian follows the Old Greek text: հանէք զդա ի ներքուստ սադերովթայդ "take her from within the *saderōth* ."

According to Birdsall the Georgian text reads განიყვანეთ ეგე საჳერონით *ganiqvanet' ege saderonit'* "lead her from the *saderon* ." There is a variant attributed to Aquila, namely ეგე განჳტემული "her, the apostate" or "that apostate." (The word განჳტემული is the participial form of the verb გან-ჳტემჳა "to commit apostasy.") This reading is not attested anywhere else, so Birdsall says. His remark remains accurate, even with the additional Armenian readings presented in this volume. The comment "that apostate" appears to be an inner-Georgian gloss.

11:18 *

զմաթան] զերկերիր Aq

J428mg M177mg(sine nom) M188mg M2628mg V212mg Zohapp(mg) B-M-Thackapp2
GeorgJ/B(+ *sacerdotes*)

V212 is cited on the basis of Zanolli 1229. Manuscripts J1928 J1934 have the reading sine nom at the parallel text, 2 Chr 23:17. The Georgian is cited on the basis of Birdsall 88.

Athaliah was put to death. Then the priest Jehoiada made a covenant between the people and the Lord. In v 18 we read that the people tore down the temple of Baal "and they killed Mattan, the priest of Baal." The name "Mattan" is a transliteration of מַתָּן.

The Old Greek transliterates the Hebrew: the majority text is τὸν ματθάν. B-M-Thack cite Arm in support of μαθάν. The reading printed in B-M-Thack, following Greek MS B, is τὸν Μαγθάν.

The Armenian text follows the Greek with a transliteration: զմաթան, i.e. մաթան with the direct object marker զ-.

Armenian MSS preserve the translation of Aquila: զերկերիր, i.e.

accusative marker զ + երկերիւր "200." B-M-Thack cite Aquila in Latin, based
on the Armenian, as *ducentos* "two hundred." The Greek underlying զերկերիւր
is τοὺς διακοσίους; the Hebrew underlying the Greek is מָאתַיִם "two hundred" in
the construct state, defectively written: מֹתֵי is easily confused with מֹתֵן (so Zanolli
1229).

Aquila understood the Hebrew to be saying "They killed two hundred
priests of Baal." Or perhaps he had a text which read מָאתָיִם.

The Georgian has the same reading as the Armenian, except that it adds the
word "priests," hence ორასი ქურუმი *orasi k'urumi* , i.e. "two hundred priests."

(Tchoubinof comments on the Georgian word ქურუმ: "arm[enian].
քուրմ."[1] The latter means "heathen or pagan priest." The Georgian appears to be
a loan-word from Armenian; or perhaps more correctly both languages have bor-
rowed from Syriac: cf. ܟܘܡܪܐ "priest" and Adjarian IV 596.)

The Hebrew, Greek, Armenian and Georgian equivalents are:

מֹתֵן → Greek τὸν μαθάν → Zohrapian զմաթան

→ Aq conj. τοὺς διακοσίους ← Aq զերկերիւր

→ Aq ორასი ქურუმ.

The Armenian and Georgian uniquely preserve the translation of Aquila.
The second apparatus in B-M-Thack already cites the Armenian evidence; the Georgian can be added as follows:

τον μαγθαν] α' *ducentos* (+ *sacerdotes* Georg) Arm Georg.

By the way, Birdsall comments that "The Latin rendering of the margin of
the Armenian as *ducentos* in the apparatus of Brooke-Maclean [sic] is another rendering which has slipped through the net of Reider-Turner."

11:19 *

զքութին եւ զռասիմ] զդասան եւ զաւրհանդական Sym

J428ᵐᵍ M188ᵐᵍ M2628ᵐᵍ(զաւրհա նդակս) Georgᴶ/ᴮ(sub nom Aq)

---

[1]David Tchoubinof, *Dictionnaire Géorgien–Russe–Français* (St. Petersburg: Imperial Academy of
Science 1840).

Cf. v 4.

The Georgian is *dasni igi da çinamcorvalni aẖlad* "those bands and the forerunners again." Birdsall notes that *dasni* uses a Georgian loan-word from Armenian and suggests that it "appears to be a rendering based upon an orthography χοροι (cf. χορι in *v.* 4) understood as the plural of χορός ["choir, troop (of dancers and/or singers)"] (in Hellenistic and Byzantine pronunciation). This might represent an early interpretation of כרי, but this would be difficult to prove, and we have no other evidence of Aquila's alleged understanding of the term." (87) It should perhaps be noted that the Georgian evidence is that of a single MS here: Birdsall employs the evidence of two MSS in his study—namely A 570 (15th century) and A 646 (15th–16th century)—but the first is not legible at this point in its margin and in A 646 the word *aẖlad* "again" "is not part of this note, but stands several verses later." (87, n.1)

In v 19 we are told that Jehoiada took "the captains, the Carites, the guards, and all the people of the land" and brought the king down from the temple to the king's residence. The words וְאֶת־הַכָּרִי וְאֶת־הָרָצִים are translated here "the Carites, the guards." For the meaning of these words see the discussion of v 4 above.

As at v 4 the Old Greek provides a transliteration of the Hebrew: in MS B we read καὶ τὸν Χορρεὶ καὶ τὸν Ῥασσείμ. It takes these words as proper nouns. According to the first apparatus in B-M-Thack, the Syro-hexapla after Ῥασσειμ adds ※ α′ *cursores* ⸜ "runners." Field reproduces the Syriac—its text— as ⸜ ܪ̈ܗܛܐ ܀ ※ ܘܪܣܝܡ. That is, the Syriac has the transliteration *Rsim* followed by Aquila's translation, the latter and its signature enclosed within asterisk and metobelus. The translation is "the runners." Field retroverts the Aquila reading as τοὺς τρέχοντας.

Once again the Armenian translation follows the Greek, with the transliteration զքորին եւ զռասիմ "the *K'oṛin* and the *Ṛasim* ."

Symmachus' translation of the Hebrew, now in Armenian, is զդասս եւ զսուրհանդակն "the divisions and the runners." At v 4 the translation of Symmachus for הָרָצִים is τούς παρατρέχοντας "the runners." The word employed in Armenian for that is different at v 4 but the possibility, even likelihood remains that Symmachus used the same Greek word in each case.

For הַכָּרִי the Armenian version of Symmachus is դասանն, i.e. դաս "order, rank, division" with the accusative plural marker -ն and the "far" demonstrative marker -ն. The corresponding Greek word is διαίρεσις "division of troops."

The Georgian is დასნი იგი წინამცორვალნი dasni igi çinamcorvalni and is attributed to Aquila.

With some degree of likelihood Symmachus' Greek translation can be determined on the basis of the Armenian. Birdsall notes that the word used in the rendering of Aquila in Georgian is that which at v 4 translates the rendering of Symmachus: it would appear that the signature in the Georgian is incorrect.

The Hebrew, Greek, Armenian and Georgian equivalences are:

וְאֶת־הַכָּרִי וְאֶת־הָרָצִים → καὶ τὸν Χορρεὶ καὶ τὸν ʿΡασσείμ → Zohrapian եւ զքրոին եւ զռասիմ

→ Sym conj. καὶ τοὺς διαιρέσεις καὶ τοὺς παρατρέχοντας ←
Sym [եւ] զդասանն եւ զունւրհանդական

→ Aq (mend pro Sym) დასნი იგი წინამცორვალნი.

Armenian and Georgian alone preserve these readings. It is likely, on the basis of the Syro-hexapla text, that Aquila's translation of וְאֶת־הָרָצִים was καὶ τοὺς τρεχόντας: cf. v 4. The Symmachus evidence can be added to the second apparatus of B-M-Thack as follows:

τον Χορρει και τον Ρασσειμ] σʹ (αʹ mend pro σʹ Georg) *ordones et cursores* Arm Georg.

12:4 (MT 12:5)

արծաթ 2°] զնng

J428mg(ad [5] ի վածունէ) M177mg(ad [5] ի վածունէ) M188mg M2628mg(ad [5] ի վածունէ) V212mg(ad [5] ի վածունէ); + զնng et etiam hab ad (5) ի վածունէ Zohapp(mg)

V212 is cited on the basis of Zanolli 1230. This reading is not cited in B-M-

Thackeray.

Jehoash gave instructions concerning donations for the repair of the temple. His rather convoluted remarks are, "All the money offered as sacred donations that is brought into the house of the LORD, the money for which each person is assessed—the money from the assessment of persons—and the money from the voluntary offerings brought into the house of the LORD, (next verse) let the priests receive …" The words כֶּסֶף עוֹבֵר אִישׁ are rendered in the NRSV "the money for which each person is assessed." At issue is the word עוֹבֵר.

KBH does not cite this passage under עָבַר but does offer the translation "silver (at the) current (rate)" for כֶּסֶף עוֹבֵר at Gen 23:16. Indeed, the apparatus in BHS suggests reading עֵרֶךְ instead of עוֹבֵר. The former means "estimate, valuation" and BDB provide the translation "money of a man's valuation" when that emendation is made.

The Old Greek translation for כֶּסֶף עוֹבֵר is ἀργύριον συντιμήσεως "money of valuation."

The word շրջափ 2° "silver; money" corresponds to ἀργύριον 2° "money." However, the Armenian version did not render (ἀργύριον 2°) συντιμή-σεως: the MS Zohrapian follows (V1508) does not represent it, nor does J1925 (f.184v, col.2, ↓21) or M1500 (f.179r, col.2, ↓6). I take it that this shorter text is original.

For v 4 Zohrapian states in his apparatus that the marginal reading գնոյ agrees with what some other MSS have in the text. That is, some MSS read շրջափ գնոյ which corresponds to ἀργύριον (2°) συντιμήσεως. The Armenian means the same as the Greek: "money of valuation."

Գին, գնոյ "price, value" corresponds to the Greek συντιμήσεως 1° "valuation" and is intended not as a replacement for the word շրջափ in the text but as an addition to it. It is an inner-Armenian reading There is confusion in the tradition about where it belongs: at v 4 շրջափ 2°, at v 4 շրջափ 3°, at v 5 ի վաճունէ, or at both verses (see Zoh^app). In MS M2628 at v 5 it appears with the Symmachus reading on ի վաճունէ and in MS M177 at the same place. This makes the situation rather confusing.

Zanolli cites this marginal reading—from his MS V212—at v 5 for ի վա-ճունէ.

12:5 (MT 12:6) 1° *

ի վաճառք] ի (> J428 M188) գործոյ Sym

J428mg M188mg M2628mg J1934mg(hab solum nom Sym sine verbis)

The context concerns repairs to be made to the temple. Jehoiada in v 4
speaks of various assessments of money and donations. In v 5 he says, "let the
priests receive from each of the donors." The words "from each of the donors" are
a translation of אִישׁ מֵאֵת מַכָּרוֹ. The word in question here is מַכָּרוֹ. The entry in
KBH concerning it is: מַכָּר*: sf. מַכָּרוֹ; pl. sf. מַכָּרֵיכֶם: **trader** (perh. business
assessor &c.) 2K 12₆.₈.† The word therefore occurs only twice without dispute in
the Hebrew Bible. In BDB the suggested meaning is "acquaintance, friend" (dub[i-
ous].).

The Old Greek translation of the first part of v 5 is λαβέτωσαν ἑαυτοῖς οἱ
ἱερεῖς ἀνηρ ἀπὸ τῆς πράσεως αὐτοῦ (v.l. αὐτῶν) "let the priests receive for
themselves, each (literally "a man") from his sale." The translation πρᾶσις "sale"
for מַכָּר* connects the latter with the root מכר which has to do with selling. It is
an educated guess at a translation.

The Armenian text in Zohrapian has for the first part of v 5 առցեն
յիւրեանս քահանայքն, այր իւրաքանչիւր ի վաճառք իւրեանց
"let the priests receive for themselves, each man from their business." The word
վաճառ means "sale, purchase; business, trade, commerce, dealings." But vv 4–
5 are difficult and that has led to the inclusion of the marginal readings.

The Armenian preserves a marginal reading for ի վաճառք "from business, sale." It is ի գործոյ "from work, deed; business; commission" and is attributed to Symmachus. The Greek equivalent to գործ is ἔργον "work, deed" or ἐρ-
γασία "work, business," both of which, of course, Symmachus uses. B-M-Thack
do not indicate that a reading from Aquila, Symmachus or Theodotion is preserved
anywhere else and do not have the Symmachus reading in Armenian because it is
not in Zohrapian.

The Hebrew, Greek and Armenian equivalences are:

מֵאֵת מַכָּרוֹ → Old Greek ἀπὸ τῆς πράσεως (αὐτοῦ [v.l. αὐτῶν]) →

Zohrapian ի վ ա ծ ա ն է (ո ւ ր ե ա ն ց)

→ Sym conj. ἀπὸ τῆς ἐργασίας [αὐτοῦ] ← Sym ի գ ո ր ծ ո յ
[ո ւ ր ո ւ է].

The translation using ἔργον is ἀπὸ τοῦ ἔργου [αὐτοῦ].

This reading can be added to the second apparatus in B-M-Thack as
follows:

απο της πρασεως] σ' *ex labore* Arm.

12:5 (MT 12:6) 2° *

գ ր ե ղ ե կ] պ ի տ ո յ ի կ ա գ վ ա ծ Sym

J428mg M177mg(non hab պ ի տ ո յ ի) M188mg Zohapp(mg)(sine nom) B-M-Thackapp
1(sine nom); *necessitati* Aq *necessitatis vas* Sym in GeorgJ/B

The Georgian is cited on the basis of Birdsall 88–89.

V212 has the reading կ ա գ վ ա ծ, attributed to Symmachus. Zanolli has
discussed it with the wrong passage, namely 11:14. See Zanolli 1229 and 11:14
above. Manuscript M2628—which is so closely allied with J428 M188 in the
matter of marginal readings—lacks this one. Zohrapian cites the reading as պ ի-
տ ո յ ի կ ա գ վ ա ծ, but MS J428 quite clearly separates the ի from the preceding
word.

Zohrapian cites the marginal reading պ ի տ ո յ ի կ ա գ վ ա ծ but its second
word is not represented in the τα δεοντα cited in B-M-Thackeray's first apparatus.
Indeed the marginal reading τὰ δέοντα should, it seems to me, be placed in the
second apparatus because it is clearly hexaplaric (on the basis of the second apparatus where it is cited as a marginal reading in MS j [Rahlfs 243]).

Verse 5 continues: "and let them repair the house wherever any need of
repairs is discovered." This is a translation for וְהֵם יְחַזְּקוּ אֶת־בֶּדֶק הַבַּיִת לְ-
כֹל אֲשֶׁר־יִמָּצֵא שָׁם בָּדֶק: . The Greek translation for these words is καὶ αὐτοὶ
κρατήσουσιν τὸ βέδεκ τοῦ οἴκου εἰς πάντα οὗ ἐὰν εὑρεθῇ ἐκεῖ βέδεκ "and
they will repair the *bedek* of the house in all whatever *bedek* should be found
there." That is, the Old Greek simply transliterated the word in question, בֶּדֶק. (We

may note in passing that the translation "repair, make good"—based on the Hebrew—has only this passage for support in the range of meanings listed in LSJ: see their VI. under κρατέω. The meaning "repair" is however attested a number of times in the book of Nehemiah: cf. 3:3, 13, 14 of "repairing," i.e. strengthening gates.)

KBH assign the meaning "chink, crack" to בֶּדֶק here in 2 Ki 12: 6ff.; leak (in ship) at Ezek 27:9. BDB offer the meaning "fissure, rent, breach" and note that the word occurs only in 2 Ki 12 and Ezek 27:9, 27.

The Armenian translation follows the Greek—was there a choice? —with a transliteration: բեդեկ. Bedrossian offers the meaning "repair" without indicating that the word is not Armenian, but Hebrew.

B-M-Thack indicate in their first apparatus that Greek MS h (a 10th century miniscule, Rahlfs 55) and the Armenian in their margins attest the reading τὰ δέοντα, "that which is binding, needful, right." The origin of these readings can be determined by checking with the second apparatus in B-M-Thack. Greek MS j (Rahlfs 243) has two marginal readings, both attributed to Symmachus: 1) καὶ αὐτοὶ ἐπισκευασάτωσαν τὰ δέοντα τοῦ οἴκου ὅπου ἂν εὑρέθη δεόμενον ἐπισκευῆς "and let them repair what is needful of the house wherever there is found need of repair"; 2) καὶ αὐτοὶ ἐνισχύσουσιν τὴν ἐπισκευὴν τοῦ οἴκου εἰς πᾶν εὑρεθήσεται ἐκεῖ ἐπισκευασθῆναι "and they will strengthen the repair of the house everywhere it will be found to have to be repaired." Field says this second reading is to be assigned to Aquila.

(Reider-Turner suggest that Aquila's equivalents for בֶּדֶק are ἐπισκευή, ἐπισκευάζειν pass. inf. When one looks then under ἐπισκευασθῆναι one finds: בֶּדֶק Regn. IV xii 5 [6] α′ σ′; under ἐπισκευή: בֶּדֶק Regn. IV xii 5 [6] α′ σ′ Ez. xxvii 27. It would appear therefore that Reider-Turner consider Aquila's equivalent to בֶּדֶק to be ἐπισκευή, ἐπισκευάζειν. The second reading in Greek MS j attributed to Symmachus is mend pro Aquila.)

The Armenian translation of τὰ δέοντα is պիտոյ կազմած, according to B-M-Thack. The word պիտոյ means "necessary, suitable"; կազմած means "goods, furniture; preparation," possibly also "construction." If one takes the reading as պիտոյ ի կազմած, it could mean "what is necessary for (re-)construction." In fact, կազմած is cognate to the verb in the same sentence: եւ նոքա կազմեսցեն ... "and they will put in repair" so that կազմած could

have something to do with "repairing." Zohrapian notes that some MSS have կաq-
վեսgեն կաqված եկ տանն տեառն "they will repair the repairs (i.e.
make repairs) outside the house of the Lord." In this latter case կաqված has
entered the text.

We note above that MS M177 lacks պիտոյի. As we have just seen, Zohrapian cites witnesses which also attest simply կաqված, without պիտոյի. One
might wonder therefore whether պիտոյի կաqված is not a conflated reading:
պիտոյ is the equivalent of τὰ δέοντα; կաqված— which has to do with "preparing, building"—is the equivalent of ἐπισκευή. This seems possible. On the other
hand, perhaps պիտոյ ի կաqված is Symmachus' translation for אֶת־בֶּ֫דֶק
הַבַּ֫יִת, equivalent to τὸ βέδεκ τοῦ οἴκου.

Enter now the Georgian evidence! One always welcomes more evidence but
the Georgian witness to the marginalia here clarifies little because it appears to be
itself confused. According to Birdsall, MSS 570 and 646 preserve readings for both
Aquila and Symmachus. These appear to be related to the Armenian readings: that
is, there is the single word საჭმრაჯ[1] *sak'mrad* "for necessity"—which corresponds to the word պիտոյ, or better, պիտոյի, attributed to Aquila; and there are
the words საჭმის ჭურჭერი *saḥ mris č̣urč̣ eri* "a vessel of necessity"—which corresponds to պիտոյի կաqված, at least in its first element, attributed to Symmachus.

The Armenian word կաqված can be used of utensils, but the translation
ჭურჭერი seems somewhat far-fetched. (The Georgian word is used for σκεῦος
"vessel" at Mk 11:16 in the Opiza Four Gospels MS [date: 913] and Luke 8:16 in
the Tbethi Four Gospels [date: 995]; in the latter for ἀγγεῖον "vessel, flask" at Matt
25:4. It is also used, like its variant spelling ჭურჭელი [Mk 3:27], for τὰ σκεύη
"things, objects"[2] [Matt 12:29].[3])

In fact, Birdsall's comment relative to the Georgian is also helpful for the
Armenian:

    … it is clear that the Georgian is the result of a translation based on rather

---

[1]Read as საჭმრაჯ *sah mrad* , i.e. with ჭ rather than ჯ: according to the transliteration in Birdsall's
article the spelling is საჭმრაჯ. Is that the spelling in the MSS? This question does not arise in
connection with the Symmachus reading.

[2]Gingrich, *Shorter Lexicon* .

[3]These references are drawn from Molitor, *Glossarium Ibericum* .

inadequate understanding (which in its turn may go back to the Armenian).
The Symmachan reading in [B-M-Thack] j ends with the words δεόμενον
ἐπισκευῆς; the Georgian attributed to Symmachus, "a vessel of necessity",
appears to be related to this by the root meanings of the Greek.
It seems to me that this explanation may well serve the Armenian as well: the words
պիտոյի կագմած "goods? of necessity."

The Hebrew, Greek, Armenian and Georgian equivalents are:

פֶּדֶק → Old Greek τὸ βέδεκ → Zohrapian զբեդեկ

→ Sym δεόμενον ἐπισκευῆς → Sym պիտոյի կագմած

→ Sym საჭმოს ჭურჭელი.

The Armenian confirms the Greek tradition and it preserves for us the name
of Symmachus. We can also add the witness of the Georgian for the translation of
Aquila, though its relation to the Armenian and Greek is not clear. Perhaps it represents τὰ δέοντα, also attributed to Symmachus in Greek MS j.

The second apparatus in B-M-Thack can be revised as follows:

βεδεκ] δεον i : α' *necessitati*   Georg : σ' *necessarium ad constructionem*
Arm Georg.

As noted above, these readings are also preserved in Greek.

14:7 *

ի մայիլալի ծորն աղտից Sym

J428mg J1927mg(sine nom) J1928mg J1934mg M177mg M188mg V212mg Zohapp
(mg)(sine nom) B-M-Thackapp2(sine nom) GeorgJ/B

V212 is cited on the basis of Zanolli 1230. The Georgian evidence is cited
on the basis of Birdsall 89.

The Armenian reading is noted in Stone 22, who cites Birdsall on the Georgian.

The context concerns the activities of the reign of King Joash of Israel. In v
7 we are told: "He killed ten thousand Edomites in the Valley of Salt ..." In
question are the words "in the Valley of Salt" which translate the Hebrew

בְּגֵיא־הַמֶּלַח. The Qere for הַמֶּלַח (sic) is מֶלַח.

The majority Greek text has for גֵּיא־הַמֶּלַח a transliteration, like γαιμέλα in MSS AN; B-M-Thackeray's "rell[iqui, i.e. the rest]" reading is γεμάλα. (Greek MS B, followed by B-M-Thack, has the corrupt Ῥεμέλε.) The Lucianic MSS also have a transliteration, but add the words ἐν πολέμῳ (so MSS orc₂e₂ [Rahlfs 82 700 127 93]) except in the case of MSS b (Rahlfs 19-108) which apparently have just the transliteration. (The words ἐν πολέμῳ could be a corruption that has come from later in the verse: ἐν τῷ πολέμῳ occurs a few words after the reading in question.)

It is this transliteration that has led to the citation of Symmachus' translation in the margins of some witnesses, including the Armenian. B-M-Thack[app2] cite the Armenian marginal reading in Latin as *in valle salum* , i.e. reproducing the genitive plural աղուհց in *salum* but there is no need for this: cf. Bedrossian's example ձով աղուհց "salt-marsh." The citation with the plural might mislead the reader to think that something different underlies the Armenian than underlies the Latin they offer for the marginal reading in the Syh, which they cite as *in valle salis* . The Syriac marginal reading is ܕܡܠܚܐ ܚܠܬܐ "in the valley of salt," according to Field. The translation bears Symmachus' signature in the Syro-hexapla.

The Armenian Մաշիլա attests the transliteration, though the γαι-/γη-/γε- of the Greek witnesses is not represented.

The Armenian MSS offer us a signed reading in the margin: Symmachus, they point out, had the translation ի ձորն աղուհց, i.e. "in the valley of salt." B-M-Thack note the Armenian reading but, since they are dependent upon Zohrapian, must record it as unsigned. The Syro-hexapla has it too, signed, as stated earlier. Finally, B-M-Thack record that in Eusebius' Onomasticon the words φάραγγα ἁλῶν "valley of salt" are attributed to Aquila Symmachus.

Zanolli retroverts the Armenian reading back into Greek as ἐν τῇ φάραγγι τῶν ἁλῶν—following Field, one presumes—but the Eusebius reading makes it possible that the Armenian was translated from εἰς φάραγγα τῶν ἁλῶν.

The Georgian marginal reading is ჰევსა მას მარილოვანთასა *hevsa mas marilovant'asa* "in the valley of the salts (or salteds)." It carries the signature of Symmachus and is identical to the Armenian reading.

The Hebrew, Greek, Armenian and Georgian equivalents are:

בְּגֵיא־הַמֶּלַח → majority reading ἐν γεμέλα → Zohrapian ի մայրւ
    → Sym conj. ἐν τῇ φάραγγι τῶν ἁλῶν → Sym ի ծորն
           աղտից
                → Sym ვეჴსა მას მარილოვანსა.

The signed marginal reading in the Armenian witnesses confirms the reading preserved in Eusebius, the Syro-hexapla and the Georgian version. The second apparatus in B-M-Thack can be revised as follows:

    εν ρεμελε] σ′ *in valle salis* Arm Georg Syh.

14:14 *

խառնակութեանցն] պատանդացն Sym (mend pro Aq); գարշելեացն Th

J428mg M177mg(hab solum Th) M188mg V212mg(hab solum գարշելեաց Th) Zohapp (mg)(hab solum Th) B-M-Thackapp2(hab solum Th)

V212 is cited on the basis of Zanolli 1230.

The context concerns the defeat of King Amaziah of Judah by King Jehoash of Israel at Beth-shemesh. Verse 14 describes the booty which King Jehoash took from Jerusalem after that battle. We are told that he took all the gold and silver, and all the vessels in the temple and in the treasuries of the king's house, "as well as hostages." The word "hostages" is a translation of the word בְּנֵי הַתַּעֲרֻבוֹת. NIV also renders these words "hostages."

KBH have this entry under תַּעֲרֻבוֹת: coll. pl. **pledge**; *bᵉnê taʻ ᵃrûbôt* **hostages** 2K 14₁₄ 2C 25₂₄.† The word is therefore extremely rare. It occurs only here and in its parallel text in Chronicles.

The words בְּנֵי הַתַּעֲרֻבוֹת are translated τοὺς υἱοὺς τῶν συμμίξεων "sons of commingling, commixture" according to MS B, the text followed in B-M-Thack. LSJ have the following note on this (mis-)translation under υἱός: III. οἱ υἱοὶ τῶν σ. mistranslation of Hebr. *bᵉnê hatta'arûbôth* 'sons of pledges', i.e. 'hostages', through confusion of root with *'êreb* 'mixed hord', LXX 4*Ki.* 14.14. Cf. KBH II עֶרֶב, עֵרֶב : **mixed people** or **race**. The explanation in LSJ is doubtless correct.

The inadequacy of the Old Greek translation led to the citation of other translations in the margins of various witnesses.

(The Lucianic text is extant as a longer text in some Greek MSS [bgorc₂e₂ (Rahlfs 19-108 158 82 700 127 93)] and Thdt: see the first apparatus in B-M-Thack. The translation of בְּנֵי הַתַּעֲרֻבוֹת as τοὺς υἱοὺς τῶν συμμίξεων is followed in Lucian by τῶν βδελυγμάτων "of the abominations." This is also a mistranslation. This latter translation connects the word הַתַּעֲרֻבוֹת with the root תעב: cf. תוֹעֵבָה "something abominable." This translation appears also to be preserved in the Armenian marginal reading գարշելեացն "of the abominable things." [The adjective գարշելի means "abominable, detestable."] More on that in a moment.)

The Armenian translation represented by Zohrapian's text follows the B-related text, what is Old Greek and, indeed, the majority text: զորդիս խառնակութեանցն, literally "sons of confusion, disorder."

The second apparatus in B-M-Thack presents the following information about the translations of Aquila, Symmachus and Theodotion for the phrase in question: και 5°—συμμίξεων] καὶ τοὺς υἱοὺς τῶν ὁμήρων j | τῶν συμμίξεων] τῶν ὁμήρων y: θ [sic: lacks 'prime' sign, i.e. '] *immundorum* Arm: α´ *obsidum* σ´ *immundorum* SS-ap-Barh. (MS j is Rahlfs 243; MS y is Rahlfs 121; S is the siglum for the Syro-hexapla; S-ap-Barh represents the Syro-hexapla as cited by Barhebraeus, according to the 1897 edition of Schlesinger. All readings are found in margins.)

The word ὅμηρος "pledge, surety, hostage" is cited as the translation of Aquila here in Reider-Turner. Its Latin equivalent is *obses, idis* . So that much is clear: τῶν ὁμήρων is Aquila.

Symmachus' translation is apparently not preserved in Greek. Symmachus' translation is preserved in the Syro-hexapla and Syro-hexapla excerpted by Barhebraeus: B-M-Thack give as Symmachus (in Latin equivalent) the translation *immundorum* "of the unclean, dirty, filthy, nasty, foul, impure." (The Greek equivalent of *immundus* is ἀκάθαρτος, according to Freund-Leverett's lexicon). The Syriac is ܕܡܣܝܒܐ "of the defiled, abominable," the *Pael* passive participle of

ᴐɑɑ.[1] Zanolli cites Field's suggestion that Symmachus' Greek was τῶν μεμιασ-
μένων or μεμολυσμένων "of the defiled." This retroversion is likely wrong: τῶν
βδελυγμάτων in the Lucianic MSS is probably Symmachus.[2]

We also have in the Armenian witnesses a reading attributed to Symmachus: it is պատանդացն, i.e. the genitive plural of պատանդ "hostage,"
whose Greek equivalent would be ὅμηρος. The solution to this impass is this: the
marginal reading attributed to Symmachus is really that of Aquila. The signature is
incorrectly preserved.

B-M-Thack also use the word *immundorum* to convey "Theodotion" in Armenian. For գարշելի Miskgian gives the Latin equivalents "detestabilis, de-
testandus, exsecrandus, odibilis, miserrimus, abominabilis, foedus, turpis." The
word գարշելեացն could translate τῶν βδελυγμάτων; hence *abominabilis* for
գարշելի is a better choice than *immundus* .

As noted in Jellicoe (94, 133), θ can sometimes refer not to Theodotion but
to Theodoret in the margins of Greek MSS. That could be true here. Zanolli notes
that in his 14th century MS, Venice 212, the signature with the reading գարշելեացն is Թդդ; Zohrapian cites the signature in the MS(S) he is following as
Թդն. The usual abbreviation of Theodotion's name is Թդ. Perhaps Թդդ and
Թդն are clues: we are intended to understand that գարշելեացն is the translation found in Theodoret, which is in fact the case. However, it would be most unusual to find a reading from Theodoret with Aquila, Symmachus and Theodotion
readings in these Armenian MSS. The readings from "the Three" travel in a kind of
"package deal" sort of way.

It is possible that the Theodotion reading carries the wrong signature also.
That is, գարշելեացն should be attributed to Symmachus. In that case we might
conclude that the signatures belonging to the two readings in the Armenian wit-

---

[1] A note from J.W. Wevers, 09/09/93, informed me that B-M-Thack are wrong in their citation of
Syh. The word is *dmsyb'* , i.e. without the *sᵉyāmē* , and therefore singular. Field edited the word,
because it appears as a plural in his citation.

[2] I have discussed this passage with J.W. Wevers. He wrote: "I suspect that *bdelugmatwn* is Symmachus. What happened in Lucian is the following. His OG text had as you surmised *twn*
summixewn . Since the real Lucian revised his text according to Sym he, in his usual fashion,
added the Sym reading. From this comes the doublet in boc₂e₂." Wevers goes on to add, "As far as
I am concerned, Field's guess about *immundorum* is simply wrong. It should have been the same
as the Luc. doublet." 07/12/94

nesses have simply been mixed up: Aquila has been given the signature of Symmachus; Symmachus has been given the signature of Theodotion.

With regard to the Armenian marginal readings we can draw the following two conclusions: 1) the reading attributed to Symmachus is really that of Aquila; 2) the reading attributed to Theodotion may well belong to Symmachus. This remains a difficulty. B-M-Thackeray's citation of θ in Armenian as *immundorum* is not a helpful translation of զարշելիի! It may, however, call the reader's attention to the same reading attributed to σ′ in the Syro-hexapla and Syh-ap-Barh.

The Hebrew, Greek and Armenian can be represented as follows.

הַתַּעֲרֻבוֹת → Old Greek τῶν συμμίξεων → խառնակութեանցն

→ Aq τῶν ὁμήρων → Sym պատանդացն

→ Sym τῶν βδελυγμάτων → Th զարշելեացն.

The Armenian marginal readings add one more witness to those attesting Aquila's translation.

The second apparatus in B-M-Thack can be revised as follows:

και 5°— συμμιξεων] και τους υιους των ομηρων j |των συμμιξεων] των ομηρων y : α′ *obsidum* σ′ *immundorum* Arm(σ′ mend pro α′; θ′ mend pro σ′) Syh Syh-ap-Barh.

I have retained the Latin *immundorum* for զարշելեացն for the sake of consistency in B-M-Thackeray's citation. The word *abominabilium* is a better choice.

14:29 *

'Αζαρίας] ზაქარია Sym; ოზია Aq

GeorgJ/B

The Georgian evidence is cited on the basis of Birdsall 90. He does not give the reading in the text, so I have given the Old Greek to the left of the square bracket.

In 14:29 we are told that Jeroboam died and that "his son Zechariah" succeeded him. The word "Zechariah" is in Hebrew זְכַרְיָה.

The Old Greek form of the proper name is ʼΑζαρίας.

Zohrapian's edition has զաքարիա *Zakʻaria* but in his apparatus he notes that some MSS have ազարիա *Azaria* . The latter is the spelling in both J1925 (f.186r, col.2, ↓3) and M1500 (f.180r, col.1, ↓13). The form in V1508—Zohrapian's base MS—could well be a corruption occasioned by the *-tsʻ* sound at the end of the preceding word: i.e. Թագաւորեաց ազարիա "Azaria ruled" became Թագաւորեաց զաքարիա "Zakaria ruled" or simply by the occurrence of both names in the context (cf. 15:8).

The Georgian preserves two marginal readings and if they appear in the order Birdsall cites them then the order is Symmachus Aquila, just like is usually the case in Armenian witnesses in 4 Rgn.

Symmachus' rendering of the proper name is ზაქარია *Zakʻaria* . In B-M-Thack the spelling Ζαχαρίας is supported by MSS bpᵃ?c₂(ζ ex χ)e₂ Arm-ed Jos Anon[1]. These witnesses include the Lucianic MSS bc₂e₂ which sometimes attest Symmachus readings in their text, and that is possible in this case too. Manuscript p is Rahlfs 106.

More problematic is the Aquila reading. According to the Georgian marginal reading Aquila represented the proper name as ოზია *Ozia* . Molitor 443 notes that ოზია = Armenian and that it represents ʼΟζίας at Matt 1:8 in the Adysh (date: 897) and Urbnisi Four Gospels (10th century). The Greek ʼΟζίας probably represents עֻזִּיָּה: cf. H-R, "Supplement," 123. It seems unlikely that Aquila used ʼΟζίας to render זְכַרְיָה.

There is confusion amongst the three names Ζαχαρίας, ʼΑζαρίας and ʼΟζίας in chh. 14 and 15: note the apparatus in B-M-Thack at 14:21; 15:1, 7, 8, 11, 13, 17, 27, 30, 32, 34. It appears that there is confusion between the first two names, then between the last two. So ʼΟζίας could be a variant reading upon ʼΑζαρίας. Note also in B-M-Thackeray's second apparatus the marginal reading upon ʼΑζαρίου at 15:6 in the Syro-hexapla: it is ܐܝܙܥܘ, i.e. "of ʼwzia ." (The Hebrew at 15:6 is עֲזַרְיָהוּ, so the marginal reading in the Syro-hexapla does not agree with the MT.)

It might be possible to argue that the Aquila reading belongs somewhere else in the context, rather than at 14:29.

The Hebrew, Greek and Georgian equivalents are:

זְכַרְיָה → Old Greek 'Αζαρίας

→ Sym Ζαχαρίας ← Sym ზაქარია

→ Aq 'Οζίας ← Aq ოზია.

We can add the Georgian evidence to the second apparatus in B-M-Thackeray as follows:

αζαριας] α' ozia   σ' zak'aria   Georg.

15:5 *

(ի տանն) ապիփուունքի] ի ձաձուկ Sym

J428mg J1925mg (ձաձուկ sine nom) M177mg(ձաձուկ sub nom Aq) M188mg
M2628mg V212mg(ձաձուկ sub nom Aq) Zohapp(mg)(ձաձուկ sub nom Aq) B-M-
Thackapp2(sub nom Aq) GeorgJ/B(sub nom Aq)

V212 is cited on the basis of Zanolli 1230–1231. Zanolli cites the same marginal reading at 4:5: see p. 1227. This must be erroneous because ապիփուունքի does not occur in the text there.

The Georgian is cited on the basis of Birdsall 89.

The context concerns King Azariah of Judah. In v 4 we are told that, in spite of doing what was right in the sight of the Lord (v 3), he did not remove the high places. Consequently, the Lord struck the king, "so that he was leprous to the day of his death, and lived in a separate house." The words "separate house" in the NRSV are a translation of the words בְּבֵית הַחָפְשִׁית. The NIVtxt has similarly "in a separate house" but the NIVmg has "in a house where he was relieved of responsibility." No explanation is offered for the alternate translation but BHSapp has a note: nonn Mss et 2 Ch 26,21 K[etib] הַשׁוּ–; G[reek, i.e. all or the most important witnesses in Rahlfs' edition of the LXX] αφφουσωθ vel sim.

The entry for חָפְשִׁית in KBH reads: (בְּ)בֵית הַחָפְשִׁית 2K 155 2C 2621 Q[e]r[e]: domicile of leprous King Azariah; ? house of separation, exemption fm. state affairs. The entry for חָפְשׁוּת is brief: 2C 2621 K[e]t[ib]: see Qr חָפְשִׁית.† At issue then is the meaning of a rare word.

The Old Greek resorts to a transliteration: in MS B we read ἐν οἴκῳ ἀφφουσώθ, according to the text of B-M-Thack. Other Greek MSS offer variations in the spelling of the transliteration. According to B-M-Thackeray's first apparatus the Syro-hexapla[txt] reads ܐܟܒܣܡܕ ※ σ *inclusus* ◄ . That is, the Syriac also has a transliteration but the Syro-hexapla provides the translation from Symmachus following that: *inclusus* "shut up, confined."

The Armenian translation of (ἐν οἴκῳ) ἀφφουσώθ, like the Old Greek before it, is a transliteration: ապիփուսով̔թ. That has led to the citation of a translation in the margins of various Armenian MSS. One notes that even J1925 has the marginal reading here. The Armenian witnesses are divided in their attestation: some attribute it to Aquila, others to Symmachus. B-M-Thack in their second apparatus cite the Armenian according to Zohrapian's apparatus: α′ *secreto* "separate, apart; in solitude." The Armenian is ի ծածուկ "in secret, privately." Cf. ծածկել "to cover; to hide, to conceal."

Aquila's (signed) translation of בְּבֵית הַחָפְשִׁית is preserved in Greek MS j (Rahlfs 243) and the Syro-hexapla. It is ἐν οἴκῳ τῆς ἐλευθερίας, literally "in a house of freedom." The reading preserved in Armenian MSS is not Aquila.

Symmachus' translation of the words יֵשֶׁב בְּבֵית הַחָפְשִׁית is ᾤκει ἐγκεκλεισμένος "he was living shut up, confined." This is preserved in Greek MSS j and z (Rahlfs 243 and 554). As noted above the Syro-hexapla has the same translation under the asterisk in its text, also attributed to Symmachus. The meaning of the Armenian marginal reading is closer to Symmachus than to Aquila. But there is a third possibility.

B-M-Thack cite a marginal reading for the words ἐν οἴκῳ ἀφφουσώθ in Greek MS z and attributed to οἱ λοιποί, i.e. "the Three." The reading is κρυφαίως "secretly." The Armenian ի ծածուկ corresponds precisely to κρυφαίως. Zanolli suggests that κρυφαίως may be Theodotion's translation.

The Georgian marginal reading is ფარულად *p'arulad* "in secret" and carries the signature of Aquila. Birdsall connects this reading with κρυφαίως and suggests that the attribution to Aquila stems from a misreading of Α′ for Λ′, the latter being an abbreviation for οἱ λοιποί.

The Hebrew, Greek, Armenian and Georgian readings can be compared as follows.

(בְּבֵית) הַחָפְשִׁית → Old Greek (ἐν οἴκῳ) ἀφφουσώθ → Zohrapian (ի ոաև) ափփունունվ|թ

→ οἱ λ. κρυφαίως → Sym or Aq ի ծածուկ

→ Aq գօհշշոց.

The Armenian marginal readings attest the work of "the Three" in their translation ի ծածուկ "secretly." However the attribution is confused: the names of both Aquila and Symmachus are given among the witnesses but the reading, while closer to Symmachus, does not appear to belong to either. The Greek underlying ի ծածուկ is in all likelihood κρυφαίως, attributed to "the Three," but quite possibly belonging to Theodotion.[1]

The second apparatus in B-M-Thack can be changed as follows:

εν οικω αφφουσωθ] κρυφαιως z(sub οι λ.) Arm(sub α′ vel σ′) Georg(sub α′).

15:25 *

ի շորեքարիւրոցև] ի գաղաադէ Aq

J428mg M177mg M188mg(vid) M2628mg V212mg Zohapp(mg) B-M-Thackapp2

V212 is cited on the basis of Zanolli 1231.

The context concerns a revolt by Pekah son of Remeliah against King Pekahiah of Israel. We are told that Pekah conspired against Pekahiah "with fifty of the Gileadites" and attacked him in Samaria. At issue is the translation of the words מִבְּנֵי גִלְעָדִים rendered in the NRSV "of the Gileadites."

The MS B-type MSS have for מִבְּנֵי גִלְעָדִים the words ἀπὸ τῶν τετρακοσίων, i.e. "of the four hundred." The Hebrew (מִ)בְּנֵי גִלְעָדִים) does not look very much like אַרְבַּע מֵאוֹת "four hundred." Where does such a rendering come from? There is no reference to any "four hundred" in the context.

The Armenian translation follows the Vaticanus-type tradition: it has ի

---

[1]Barthélemy has pointed out that at a certain point ὁ λ, instead of meaning α′ σ′ θ′, began to be taken as a reference to "λουκιανος" and from this time on Antiochian readings were added to that siglum. See "A Reexamination of the Textual Problems in 2 Sam 11:2–1 Kings 2:11 in the Light of Certain Criticisms of *Les Devanciers d'Aquila*," in *1972 Proceedings IOSCS*, 88. He refers to Ziegler, ed. 12 prophets, 32 (or 72?).

ξπ եքարիւրոգն "of the four hundred." There are many Greek MSS which attest γαλααδιτῶν "of the Gileadites": MSS Ndefmpstw (Rahlfs N 107 52 489 92 106 130 134 314); the Lucianic witnesses have "sons of the Gileadites" (c var MSS borc₂e₂ [Rahlfs 19-108 82 700 127 93]). Fernández Marcos–Busto Saiz print ἀπὸ τῶν υἱῶν τῶν γαλααδιτῶν as the Antiochene text.

The reading in the margins of the Armenian MSS is a signed Aquila reading: ի գալաատէ "of Gilead." According to B-M-Thack^app2, the Armenian is the only hexaplaric witness to this reading.

The Hebrew, Greek and Armenian readings can be set out as follows:

מִבְּנֵי גִלְעָדִים ≠ B-related MSS ἀπὸ τῶν τετρακοσίων → Zohrapian ի ξπ եքարիւրոգն
→ Aq conj. ἀπὸ Γαλαάδ → ի գալաատէ

The Armenian is a unique witness to Aquila's translation here. The citation in B-M-Thack is:

απο των τετρακοσιων] α′ ex Galaad Arm.

16:6 *

եդոմայեցիք] ասորիք

J428^mg(ասորի) M177^mg M188^mg V212^mg Zoh^app(mg) B-M-Thack^app1; M2628 hab ասորիք in txt et եդոմայեցիք in mg

V212 is cited on the basis of Zanolli 1231.

The context concerns the siege of King Ahaz in Jerusalem by King Rezin of Aram and King Pekah of Israel. In v 6 we are told: "At that time the king of Edom [footnote: C(o)n(jecture): Heb *King Rezin of Aram*] recovered Elath for Edom [footnote: Cn: Heb *Aram*], and drove the Judeans from Elath; and the Edomites came to Elath, where they live to this day." At issue for us here is the word "Edomites": the BHS text reads (וַ)אֲרֹמִים "Aramaeans [?]" which is a corruption of the Qere וְאֲדֹמִים.

The Greek tradition follows the Qere "and the Edomites." The BHS apparatus points out that many MSS, i.e. more than 20, plus the Syriac, Targum MSS and

Vulgate MSS attest ‏וארמים‎.

The Armenian text follows the Greek: "Edomites." The marginal reading ասորիք "Syrians," i.e. Aramaeans, follows the Ketib. The reading is unsigned in the Armenian MSS.

B-M-Thack point out in their second apparatus that the Syro-hexapla preserves a reading from ϵβρ., namely ‏ܐܪ̈ܡܝܐ‎ "Aramaeans." The Hexapla is the source of the Armenian marginal reading. (In the Armenian Bible the Aramaeans are Syrians: cf. Gen 22:21.)

The Hebrew, Greek and Armenian witnesses can be compared as follows.

Qere ‏אדמים‎ → Old Greek 'Ιδουμαῖοι → Zohrapian Եդովմայեցիք

Ketib ‏וארמים‎/‏ארמים‎ → ϵβρ. conj. Σύροι → sine nom ասորիք

The Armenian can be added to the Syro-hexapla as a witness to the reading found in ϵβρ. The second apparatus in B-M-Thack can be revised in the following way:

ιδουμαιοι] ϵβρ. ‏ܐܪ̈ܡܝܐ‎ Syh : *Syri* Arm(sine nom).

16:9 *

(ի) կիւրէն] երկիր Aq

J428mg M188mg M2628mg

The context concerns deportations which King Tiglath-pileser made. We are told that he took Damascus and carried its people captive ‏קִירָה‎ "to Kir."

The notes in the BHS apparatus inform us that ‏קִירָה‎ is not attested in the original Greek text; the Lucianic witnesses (i.e. borc₂e₂ [Rahlfs 19-108 82 700 127 93]) have τὴν πόλιν (so, "he took into captivity the city"); it is suggested we compare the Vulgate and Eusebius at Isa 17:1. It is also pointed out that Aquila has Κυρήνηνδε.

Κυρήνηνδε is a plus attested, according to B-M-Thack, in Alexandrinus, the Armenian and the Syro-hexapla. In the Syro-hexapla it is under the asterisk and signed with Aquila's name. This reading is cited in Swete 41, where Κυρήνηνδε is offered as an example of one characteristic of Aquila's translation, namely the representation of the "directive ה" by the enclitic δε.

The Armenian text has Aquila's translation but in the margin the MSS like those listed above we find the word երկիր "land; country" with Aquila's name. Is this an interpretive comment, intended to explain what կիւրէն is? Possibly so. That is to say, the Armenian text already contains the marginal reading so the translator of these notations was left with the option of omitting the note or—and perhaps he had already copied the signature—of turning the notation κυρήνηνδε into the interpretive note that he did. The marginal note in the Armenian MSS indirectly attests the translation of Aquila.

One should cite the Armenian evidence, whose importance is clear if the reading is explained.

The Hebrew, Greek and Armenian evidence is as follows:

קִירָה → v.l. κυρήνηνδε → Zohrapian ի կիւրէն

            → Aq κυρήνηνδε → Aq երկիր.

The Armenian marginal reading can be cited as follows in the second apparatus of B-M-Thack:

(κυρηνηνδε)] ܠܡܐ̈ . ܠܡܐ̈ Syh : α′ terra Arm.

17:1

երկոտասաներորդի] երկրորդ

V212ᵐᵍ

V212 is cited on the basis of Stone 21.

"In the twelfth year of King Ahaz of Judah, Hoshea son of Elah began to reign in Samaria." So begins ch 17. The words "In the twelfth year" are a translation of בִּשְׁנַת שְׁתֵּים עֶשְׂרֵה.

According to the text printed in B-M-Thack this has become in the Old Greek Ἐν ἔτει δωδεκάτῳ "in the twelfth year." There are a few variant readings among Greek MSS which place the accession in the 10th, 11th and 14th year; none places it in the second year.

Zohrapian's text reads Յամի երկոտասաներորդի "In the twelfth

year." The marginal reading in V212 is երկրորդ "second," i.e. "(In the) second (year)."

17:3 *

մաննայ] յայտնի ինչ Sym

J428^mg M177^mg M188^mg M2628^mg V212^mg Zoh^app(mg)

V212 is cited on the basis of Zanolli 1231. This reading is not cited in B-M-Thackeray, even though it has the signature in Zohrapian's apparatus. Perhaps Thackeray—who collated the Armenian—could not make any sense of it.

The context concerns the reign of King Hoshea of Israel. We are told that King Shalmaneser of Assyria came up against him and that Hoshea paid him מִנְחָה, i.e. "tribute."

Much of the Greek tradition offers for מִנְחָה a transliteration: μανάχ B; μααυα is*(vid)u (Rahlfs 56 130*[vid] 372); μαναα̣μ x; μαναα ANp*s^a (Rahlfs 106* 130^a) and other witnesses. The translation δῶρα is attested by MSS bgop^a?rc_2 e_2 (Rahlfs 19-108 158 82 106^a? 700 127 93), that is the Lucianic witnesses.

The Armenian text attests the transliteration: մաննայ. Bedrossian offers us for this word the meaning "offering, gift" without indication however that it is a loanword from Hebrew by way of the Greek Bible.

For the Greek transliteration there is a signed Symmachus translation in MSS jz (i.e. Rahlfs 243 554) and the Syro-hexapla. It is φόρον "tribute."

The signed Symmachus reading in the margins of the Armenian MSS is յայտնի ինչ "something clear, evident or notable." How did φόρον become յայտնի ինչ? B-M-Thack may have regarded the Armenian as a mistake since they do not cite it in their apparatus. Zanolli is probably on the right track when he begins with a retroversion from the Armenian into Greek. He suggests that φανερόν τι is the Greek underlying յայտնի ինչ: the Armenian scholar who translated φόρον misread it. Zanolli thinks φανερόν τι was misread for φόρον τι and that suggestion seems to me to offer a plausible explanation for an otherwise nonsensical reading in the Armenian.

In that case the Hebrew, Greek and Armenian can be represented as follows.

מִנְחָה → Greek conj. v.l. μάννα → Zohrapian մաննայ
→ Sym φόρον τι → Sym յայտնի ինչ.

As a consequence of the preceding explanation one can say that the Armenian confirms the witness of the Greek MSS and the Syro-hexapla to Symmachus' translation φόρον. The second apparatus in B-M-Thack can be revised in the following way:

μαναχ] α' δωρον jz : σ' φορον jz Arm(clara res mend pro *munera*) Syh : ※ *munera* Syh.

17:9 1° *

բարձունս] բագինս Sym

J428mg J1928mg J1934mg(ind supra յաշտարակ) M177mg(sine nom) M188mg Zohapp(mg)(sine nom) GeorgJ/B; hab բագինս in txt et բարձունս in mg M2628

The Georgian is cited on the basis of Birdsall 89–90.

Zanolli cites V212 as having this marginal reading (sine nom) at v 11 where բարձունս occurs in the text again. It belongs here.

This reading is not cited in B-M-Thackeray.

The context explains the reason why the Assyrian king was able to capture Samaria. In v 9 we are told that the people committed offenses against their God. They built בָּמוֹת "high places" everywhere, among other misdemeanours.

The Old Greek tradition translates בָּמוֹת with the word ὑψηλά "high things." This becomes in the Armenian translation բարձունս "heights."

B-M-Thack in their second apparatus cite for ὑψηλά a marginal reading, *sine nomine* , from the Syro-hexapla: *altaria* "altars." (The Syriac, according to Field, is ܥܠܘܬܐ "high places, altars.") They do not cite Zohrapian in support of this reading though they might have because the Armenian is a witness to that translation: բագինս means "altars." As a consequence, we can identify the reading as that of Symmachus. Further, we can suggest that Symmachus' Greek translation

was τοὺς βωμούς since βωμός—բագին seems to be a standard equivalence.
Field retroverts the Syriac ܟ݂ܢܘܫ݂ܬ݂ܐ to βωμούς and suggests that it belongs to Symmachus. He was right, though B-M-Thack did not follow his suggestion.

The Georgian marginal reading is ბაგინნი *baginni* "altars" and it is attributed to Symmachus. Cf. Armenian բագին "altar of an idol."

The Hebrew, Greek, Armenian and Georgian equivalents are here:

בָּמוֹת → Old Greek ὑψηλά → Zohrapian բարձունս

   → Sym conj. τοὺς βωμούς → Sym բագին

         → Sym ბაგინნი.

The Armenian tradition provides us with the signature for a reading already
known from the Syro-hexapla. The second apparatus in B-M-Thack can be revised
to include Armenian and Georgian evidence:

υψηλα] σ′ *altaria* Arm Georg Syh(sine nom).

17:9 2° *

ամուր] պարապատր Sym

J428mg M188mg M2628mg(sine nom) GeorgJ/B(sub nom Aq et ind mend supra բաղաքս
իրեանց)

The Georgian is cited on the basis of Birdsall 90–91.

Verse 9 continues by informing the reader that the high places were built "at
all their towns, from watchtower to fortified city." The words "to fortified city" are
a translation of עַד־עִיר מִבְצָר.

The Old Greek renders this phrase with the words ἕως πόλεως ὀχυρᾶς.
This is an adequate translation because ὀχυρός "strong" can be used of strongholds
and cities. Cf. πόλεις ὀχυράς at 4 Rgn 19:25.

The Armenian translates the Greek ἕως πόλεως ὀχυρᾶς with the words ի
քաղաքն ամուր "to strong city." In fact, as a noun the word ամուր can
mean "fortification." The Armenian translation is quite adequate.

Nevertheless we have preserved in the margins of Armenian witnesses the
word պարապատր, attributed to Symmachus in MSS J428 M 188. Underlying

the Armenian word is likely the adjective τειχήρης "within walls" (cf., e.g. Josh 19:35) or the passive participle of its cognate verb (cf. ἐν πόλει τετειχισμένῃ at Lev 25:29). Πόλεις τειχήρεις "fortified cities" occurs several times in 2 Chronicles (11:5, 10; 14:5; 32:1; 33:14) where the adjective τειχήρης is translated պարսպաւոր. The passive participle of τειχίζω underlies պարսպաւոր at 2 Chron 21:3.

If the attribution to Symmachus is correct, the Armenian and Georgian uniquely preserve his translation for מִבְצָר in 17:9. The other possibility is that some Armenian scribe added for ամուր its synonym պարսպաւոր in the margin, with the signature of Symmachus. (In the latter case the synonym did not come from a parallel passage in 2 Chr because the Kings passage is not reproduced in Chronicles.) I am of the opinion that this is a genuine Symmachus reading.

The Georgian preserves the reading მოზღუდვილთა *mozgudvilt'a* "having a wall around," "fortified": cf. მო-ზღუდვა "⟨ob⟩saepire," i.e "enclose" in Molitor. It attributes this reading to Aquila and refers it to "their cities" in the text. Birdsall states that he thinks it unlikely that the marginal reading has been misplaced from ἕως πόλεως ὀχυρᾶς later in the verse, but that is in fact what has happened.

We can suggest the following equivalences:

מִבְצָר → Old Greek ὀχυρᾶς → Zohrapian ամուր

→Sym conj. τειχήρους/τετειχισμένης ← Sym պարսպաւոր

→ Aq მოზღუდვილთა.

This item can be added to the second apparatus in B-M-Thack:

οχυρας] σ′ *munitae* Arm Georg(sub α′ ind mend supra ταῖς πόλεσιν αὐτῶν).

17:11 1°

բարձունս] բագինս

V212mg(mend pro 9 vid)

See v 9.

17:11 2° ∗

զովովւ] բանս չարս Sym

J428mg M177mg(sine nom) M188mg(sine ind) V212mg; J1928 et J1934 hab ind in txt
et mg sed non hab verba in mg; M2628 hab բանս չարս in txt et զաւզաւղս
Sym in mg

V212 is cited on the basis of Zanolli 1231.

The explanation for Israel's woes adds in v 11 that the people did דְּבָרִים
רָעִים "wicked things."

The Old Greek translated these words with κοινωνούς. LSJ offer the
translation "familiar spirit" for κοινωνός in this verse, but cite only this passage for
such a meaning. The Greek translator has read רָעִים as רֵעִים "companions." Perhaps the parent Hebrew text lacked דְּבָרִים, lost through parablepsis by homoioteleuton. At any rate, the Greek translation makes little sense unless one takes it in
the sense of "(bad) alliances" or something like that.

The Armenian text follows the Greek with its translation զովւղս "ac-
complices." See զովղղ in Bedrossian.

In this situation it is easy to see why an alternative to κοινωνούς appears in
the margin of various witnesses. According to B-M-Thackeray's second apparatus
there is an unsigned marginal reading in MS j (Rahlfs 243): λόγους πονηρούς
"evil words, matters" which in Armenian would be բանս չարս, just as we indeed find in Armenian witnesses. B-M-Thack also cite the Syro-hexapla where, in
the place where κοινωνούς is represented, we find the marginal reading α' σ' ε'
(sic) *verba mala* . The original Syriac is ܒܝܫܬܐ ܡܠܐ "evil things," according to
Field.

The Hebrew, Greek and Armenian equivalents are as follows.

דְּבָרִים רָעִים ≠ Old Greek κοινωνούς → Zohrapian զովւղս

→ Sym λόγους πονηρούς → Sym բանս չարս.

The Armenian tradition provides a signature for the reading found in Greek
MS j and confirms the attestation for Symmachus in the Syro-hexapla. The second
apparatus in B-M-Thack can be revised as follows:

και 2°—εχαραξαν] και εποιησαν λογους πονηρους j | κοινωνους] α'(>
Arm) σ' ε'(> Arm) *verba mala* Arm Syh.

17:24 *

քու[թայ]] մովքուվ[թայ

J428ᵐᵍ M188ᵐᵍ M2628ᵐᵍ Georgᴶ/ᴮ

Georgian evidence is cited on the basis of Birdsall 91–92.

"The king of Assyria brought people from Babylon, Cuthah" and other
places and settled them in the cities of Samaria. The word "Cuthah" is a translation
of the Hebrew כּוּתָה, which appears here with the preposition מִן and *waw* .
Hence we have וּמִכּוּתָה, literally "and from Cuthah."

The proper name and the preposition are rendered into Greek as ἐκ Χουνθά
in MS B. This spelling with -ν- is corrupt. The entry in B-M-Thack is: χουνθα]
⟨χουνθαι 74⟩ : χουνθαν v (Rahlfs 245) : χουθα uxy (Rahlfs 372 247 121) Arm
Jos : χωθα boc₂e₂ (Rahlfs 19-108 82 127 93) On : χουα Ag (Rahlfs 158).

The Lucianic MSS boc₂e₂—which often in 4 Rgn preserve the Old Greek—
attest the spelling Χωθά. This represents a different vocalization of the Hebrew
כּוּתָה.

The spelling Χουθά is represented in the Armenian text, as B-M-Thack indicate.

Manuscripts M188 M2628 are an excellent source of marginal reading from
"the Three" so their witness must be taken seriously. Moreover, the marginal reading մովքուվ[թայ attests contact with the Hebrew text. In this transliteration the
preposition מִן has been taken to be part of the place name. The Greek spelling underlying the Armenian is Μωχωθά.

Where does this reading come from? There is no marginal reading in the Syro-hexapla or Greek witnesses that can help us. The reading Μωχωθά does appear
to be related to that in boc₂e₂. One might surmise that there is some relationship between the two.

In my opinion the reading Μωχωθά derives from one of "the Three," likely either Aquila or Symmachus because Theodotion readings in these marginalia are rare; and more likely Symmachus than Aquila because readings from the former predominate. For the time being the reading must be cited as *sine nom*.

The marginal reading in Georgian is მოქოთოთ *mokʿotʿitʿ* ; like the Armenian evidence it is sine nom. Birdsall has this reading from Janashvili; no MS(S) are cited by number. Janashvili gives one word only from 17:24, namely ქუთით *kʿutʿitʿ*, which corresponds to Greek ἐκ Χουθά. Birdsall offers the opinion that the marginal reading მოქოთოთ *mokʿotʿitʿ* is to be taken "as a variant form of the proper name with the adverb *mo* [i.e. მო] ("away, thence", often like German "hin") prefixed: but it is hard to find a parallel." Then "the marginal variant would render καὶ ἐκ Χωθα understood as an adverbial phrase after the verb ἤγαγεν."

The Armenian evidence makes it likely however that მო- *mo-* is part of the proper name itself, not an adverb. The marginal reading in Georgian reflects the same spelling as the Armenian; it adds the sense "from" by the addition of the ablative ending -ოთ -*itʿ*.

The Hebrew, Greek, Armenian and Georgian equivalents are:

מִכּוּתָה → Old Greek vid ἐκ Χουθά → Zohrapian ի Քութայ

→ conj. Sym Μωχωθά → sine nom մոկոթուայ

→ sine nom მოქოთოთ.

An entry for the second apparatus of B-M-Thack can be written as follows: εκ χουνθα] *moꞩkʿoꞩtʿa* Arm : *ex mokʿotʿa* Georg.

The transliteration of the Armenian offered here adheres to the Library of Congress system. B-M-Thack would likely have represented the Armenian as simply *mokotha*.

17:34

իրաւանց] պատուիրանաց

M2628^{mg} Zoh^{app(codd)}

The context concerns the worship which resulted from the settlement of foreigners in Samaria by the king of Assyria. These people worshiped the LORD but

also their own gods. It is explained in v 34 that "They do not worship the LORD
and they do not follow the statutes or the ordinances or the law or the commandments that the LORD commanded the children of Jacob, whom he named Israel."
The textual issue here relates to the deuteronomic phrase "statutes ... ordinances ...
law ... commandments," more particularly the word וּכְמִשְׁפָּטָם, rendered here "or
the ordinances." The marginal reading in the Armenian witnesses offers the word
"commands" for "ordinances."

For וּכְמִשְׁפָּטָם the Vaticanus-related Greek text has καὶ κατὰ τὴν κρίσιν
αὐτῶν "and according to their judgement."

The Lucianic MSS have καὶ τὰς ἐντολάς "and the commands" for
וּכְמִשְׁפָּטָם.

Manuscript M188 has իրաւանց "(according the their) law" in the text;
M2628 has պատուիրանաց "(according to their) commands" in the text and
իրաւանց in the margin. The word պատուիրանաց coincides with the one of
the elements—τὰς ἐντολάς—in the Lucianic MSS. Zohrapian notes that պատուիրանաց appears in the text of some witnesses where իրաւանց appears in
his base MS.

M2628 has likely switched the text and marginal readings but has kept the
older reading in the margin. Cf. 17:11 where M2628 switches the text and marginal
readings.

The question is whether M2628 preserves a reading from "the Three" in the
margin. The alternative is that this is an inner-Armenian development in which MSS
with different readings have influenced each other.

It might be helpful for comparative purposes to set out the various texts,
Hebrew, Greek and Armenian:

	B-related MSS	Zohrapian	Lucianic	M2628mg
כְּחֻקֹּתָם	δικαιώματα	կրоնիg	δικαιώματα	
וּכְמִשְׁפָּטָם	κρίσιν	իրաւանg	κρίματα	պատուիրանաg
וְכַתּוֹרָה	νόμον	օրինաg	ἐντολάς	
וְכַמִּצְוָה	ἐντολήν	պատուիրանին	νόμον.	

The Armenian text follows a B-related type of Greek text, not the Lucianic type of text.

I take it that the text represented in Zohrapian's base MS is the original. That said, the textual situation among Armenian witnesses is complex because of the repetition of deuteronomic phraseology. Manuscript M1500 (fol.181r, col.1, ↓9) has omitted the second element—i.e. եւ ըստ իրաւանց նոցա— by parablepsis: եւ մինչեւ գայժաւր առնեն նոքա ըստ կրաւնից նոցա. եւ ըստ աւրինաց. եւ ըստ պատուիրանին զոր պատուիրեաց նոցա տէր "and until today they act according to their religion, and according to their laws, and according to the command which the Lord commanded them."

In J1925 (p.359, col.1, ↑22) the singular number of the fourth element has been attracted to the plural of the first three: եւ առնեն ըստ կրաւնից նոցա եւ ըստ իրաւանց նոցա եւ ըստ աւրինաց, եւ ըստ պատուիրանաց, զոր պատուիրեաց տէր "and they act according to their religion and according to their laws and according to their judgements, and according to the commands, which the Lord commanded."

From this brief analysis we can see that the Armenian text tradition is unstable in this verse. We can make some observations from which we can suggest the most likely solution to this textual puzzle. First, the equivalent of պատուիրանաց in the comparison made above is ἐντολάς: both mean "commands." The Hebrew equivalent is מִצְוֹת, i.e. מִצְוָה in the plural.

H-R offer only two instances where ἐντολή is used for מִשְׁפָּט in the Old Testament in Greek: Deut 11:1; 3 Rgn 9:4. It seems unlikely therefore that պատուիրանաց derives from contact with the Hebrew.

A suggestion can be made for how the marginal reading came about. Perhaps most importantly, there is the influence of parallel passages of a deuteronomic character where such lists are given: that would account for the occurrence of պատուիրանաց in the text of MSS like Zohrapian cites in his apparatus. The word պատուիրանաց as the second element in this list began with a copyist who remembered too well its occurrence in other such lists. From there it may have gone to the margin when MSS were compared, only to return to the text again in MS M2628 when marginal reading and reading in the text were switched.

This suggestion raises its own questions. What we can conclude is that պատուիրանաց does not appear to represent a reading from "the Three."

18:4 *

ეესთან] ნასთან Sym

Georg$^{J/B}$

The Georgian evidence is cited on the basis of Birdsall 91.

Birdsall's comments about this item are brief and can be cited in their entirety:

> The text of [MS] 646 gives the name of the brazen serpent as *Eestan* with boc$_2$e$_2$: its margin ascribes to Symmachus the version *Nast'an*. This runs contrary to the evidence of [Greek MS] j in which Ναασθαμ is ascribed to Aquila, Νεεσθαμ to Symmachus.

The context in ch. 18 records the various righteous acts carried out by good king Hezekiah. We are told that "He broke in pieces the bronze serpent that Moses had made, for until those days the people of Israel had made offerings to it; it was called Nehushtan." The word "Nehushtan" is a transliteration of נְחֻשְׁתָּן.

Greek MS B is corrupt here: it reads Νεσθαλεί, which B-M-Thack print as their text. Indeed, corruption of the spelling of the word is well represented in the tradition. It might be useful to reproduce the first apparatus of B-M-Thack on this point:

νεσθαλει B] νεσθαν Ajn : εσθαν z(txt) : εεσθαν boc$_2$e$_2$: νεσθαμ v: νεεθαν fm : νεεσθαμ eq*(vid)x : νεεσθαν Ng(vid)p(χαρκομα vid suprascr)q$^{a?}$z(mg) rell Arm Thdt : ⟨νεεσθμαν 236.242⟩ :

(The Rahlfs numbers for these MSS are, in the order they occur in this citation: j 243; n 119; z 554; boc$_2$e$_2$ 19-108 82 127 93; v 245; f 489; m 92; e 52; q 120; x 247; g 158; p 106; q 120; z 554. The numbers 236 and 242 are Holmes and Parsons numbers which Rahlfs also uses.)

It appears that the majority text preserves the Old Greek, in which case the spelling is Νεεσθάν. The Lucianic witnesses boc$_2$e$_2$ attest that spelling, though they have lost the initial ν-.

The Armenian spelling is that of the majority text, i.e. ὺ&&u|θuὺ according to Zohrapian's edition.

The translations of "the Three" for the word in question are preserved in MS j and are cited as follows—along with part of Aquila's spelling in MS c_2 (sine nom)—in the second apparatus in B-M-Thack:

νεοθαλει] α′ ναασθαμ σ′ νεεσθαμ θ′ νεεσθεν εβρ. νοοσθαμ j : ναας c_2.

Georgian MS 646 (15–16th century) provides a marginal reading attributed to Symmachus, with the spelling ნასთან *Nast'an* . This represents a corruption of the spelling of Aquila or Symmachus' renderings. The "a" vowel in the first consonant makes it closer to Aquila's spelling but the signature is that of Symmachus. In Armenian witnesses to the marginalia in 4 Rgn the order of citation is Symmachus–Aquila–Theodotion and if only one source is cited it is usually Symmachus. For that reason one is inclined to take the attribution seriously, especially if it is to be considered dependent upon an Armenian source.

(It is also possible that the reading in the text and the reading in the margin have been switched: note the reading εεσθαν in the Lucianic MSS bo c_2e_2. Lucian frequently took up Symmachus readings into his text. If that is so here it might show that the final consonant -μ in Greek MS j is corrupt.)

We can do little more than cite the Georgian evidence, without note that it may be mend pro Aquila.

The Hebrew, Greek and Georgian equivalents are:

‏נְחֻשְׁתָּן‎ → Old Greek νεεσθάν → Zohrapian ὺ&&u|θuὺ

→ Sym νεεσθαμ → Sym ნასთან.

The Georgian evidence can be added to that of the Greek witnesses as follows in B-M-Thackeray's second apparatus:

νεοθαλει] α′ ναασθαμ σ′ νεεσθαμ θ′ νεεσθεν εβρ. νοοσθαμ j : ναας c_2 : σ′ *nast'an* Georg.

This is the second case where the Georgian evidence preserves what appear to be authentic readings not extant in Armenian witnesses used in this study. The other instance is at 14:29.

18:20 *

Աշկահեցեր զիս] հակառակ յերեար ինձ Sym

J428mg M188mg M2628mg Georg J/B(sine nom)

The Georgian evidence is cited on the basis of Birdsall 91.

The context concerns the king of Assyria's appearance in Judah in the days of Hezekiah. His officer, the Rabshakeh, on behalf of the Assyrian king Sennacherib, posed the question to Hezekiah "On what do you base this confidence of yours? (v 19) In 18:20 Hezekiah is asked, "On whom do you now rely, that you have rebelled against me?" The last clause, "that you have rebelled against me" is a translation of the words כִּי מָרַדְתָּ בִּי. The verb מָרַד means "revolt, rebel" and with the preposition בְּ means "revolt, rebel against." It occurs also in v 7.

The Old Greek tradition translates these words with ἠθέτησας ἐν ἐμοί "(since) you have dealt treacherously with me."

The Armenian translation employs the verb Աշկահեմ "revolt, rise against," and so Աշկահեցեր զիս means "you revolted against me." This is a good translation.

Nevertheless we are offered in the margins of some Armenian MSS an alternative, namely the translation of Symmachus. In Armenian that translation is հակառակ յերեար ինձ "you joined (together?) against me." The verb used is յարիմ "to be joined, united, attached to; fig. to adhere, to be attached to; — յոտ "to take the part of, to follow, to keep company with, to stand by the flag of." The form is the aorist middle-passive, second person singular.

Reider-Turner have for Aquila's translation of מָרַד בּ the Greek word ἀφιστᾶν "revolt," which can be used with a number of prepositions including ἀπό. They cite it as the translation of Aquila, Symmachus and Theodotion for סוּר at Prov 30:11; Job 9:34; Isa 5:23; Jer 39(32):31; for מָרַד בּ at Isa 36:5. To this list of passages H-R add the following for Symmachus' use of ἀφιστᾶν/ἀφιστάναι/ ἀφιστάνειν: Josh 10:19; Ps 21(22):2; 43(44):19; 77(78):30; Prov 7:11; Isa 7:17; 8:11; 30:11; 36:5. A check of מָרַד with בְּ in the Hebrew Bible and its translation into Greek indicates that the preposition of choice is ἀπό. However the Armenian preposition հակառակ would lead one to think that the underlying preposition is κατά or πρός.

Arapkerts'i gives thirty-two references for the verb յարիլ, extending from Leviticus through Colossians. In the majority of cases this verb is used either for κολλάω pass. "join together" or for the compound προσκολλάω pass. The precise reckoning of equivalents is: κολλάω pass. (ten times: Deut 6:13; Ruth 2:8; 3 Rgn 11:2; 4 Rgn 1:17[B-M-Thack 18c]; 5:27; 18:6; Sir 2:3; Luke 15:15; Acts 8:29; 9: 26); προσκολλάω pass. (seven times: Lev 19:31; Num 36:7; Ruth 2:21, 23; Sir 6:35 [Rahlfs 34]; 13:20[16]; Dan 2:43[Theodotion]); πρόσκειμαι "be involved in" or "be bound up with" (five times: Lev 22:18; Num 15:15; Deut 1:36; 4:4; Josh 22:5); προσέρχομαι "come *or* go to" (three times: Lev 19:33; Num 9:14; Acts 18:2; LSJ cite a reference in Xenophon where the verb is used in a hostile sense "attack," with πρός); ἀνίστημι, i.e. ἀνίσταμαι "rise up" (twice: Neh 2:18[2 Esd 12:18]; 1 Macc 9:44—in both cases 'Αναστῶμεν is represented by ելցուք յարեցուք "Join together"); προσγίνομαι "attach oneself to, especially as an ally" (Num 15:13[LXX 14]); προσπορεύομαι "attach oneself to" (Lev 19:34); προστίθημι (middle voice) "side with" (Deut 13:4); συνεγείρω pass. "rise together" (Col 2:12); once an underlying Greek is not represented in Rahlfs' provisional edition (3 Macc 6:1).

This brief survey indicates that, from the references cited by Arapkerts'i at least, the verb յարիմ is used most frequently for κολλάω and προσκαλλάω in the passive. Their uses in the texts cited are not, however, in the sense of "joining together against." The verb that suits the context of 4 Rgn 18:20 best is ἀνίστημι: Lust cites Hos 14:1 where ἀνίστημι is used as "to stand up against, to resist [πρός τινα]." That would fit very nicely here and ἀνίστημι is a verb used by Symmachus. Perhaps we could offer it as a conjecture, in which case the Greek is ἀνέστησας πρός με "you rose up against me." This verb lacks the sense of "together."

The Georgian preserves the marginal reading აჯომდოღ ომდოღჯ მე *mhdomad agmideg me* "you have risen against me in hostile fashion." In his article, Birdsall suggests that აჯომდოღ *mhdomad* "in hostile fashion" has been added to make the rendering of ἀφιστάναι as accurate as possible.

The Hebrew, Greek, Armenian and Georgian equivalents here are:

מָרַדְתָּ בִּי → Old Greek ἠθέτησας ἐν ἐμοί → Zohrapian ապշտանեցէր

զիս

→ Sym conj. ἀνέστησας πρός με ← Sym հակառակ յերեւար
իՆծ

→ sine nom ᲛᲣᲚᲛᲝᲓ ᲝᲚᲛᲝᲚᲔᲒ Ა Ა.

This translation of Symmachus is not otherwise extant so it is of considerable interest. This item can be added to the second apparatus in B-M-Thack as follows:

ηθετησας εν εμοι] σʹ *conjunxisti contra me* Arm Georg(sine nom).

Freund-Leverett offer συζεύγνυμι "join together"—and συνάπτω—as a Greek equivalent for *conjungo* .

We might add that part of this verse—4 Rgn 18:20—is cited by Chrysostom in his *Commentary on Isaiah the Prophet* , preserved in Armenian, but not the part of the verse which might be of use here.

19:13 1° *

արքայն 1°] աստուածն Sym

J428ᵐᵍ M188ᵐᵍ M2628ᵐᵍ

The context is Sennacherib's seige of Jerusalem in 701 BCE. Verses 10–13 contain the Rabshakeh's words to Hezekiah, warning him about expecting deliverance. In v 13 he says, "Where is the king of Hamath, the king of Arpad, the king of the city of Sepharvaim, the king of Hena, or the king of Ivvah?" At question is the word מֶלֶךְ, i.e. "king" (of Hamath).

The Old Greek translates מֶלֶךְ with—as one might expect—ὁ βασιλεύς "the king." The Armenian equivalent is արքայն "the king" and that is what we find in the Armenian translation.

Where does this reading come from? One notes that the parallel passage 18: 34 speaks of "the god of Hamath" et al.: the marginal reading in these Armenian MSS could be ex par. Indeed, in MS J428 18:34 stands in the adjoining column, directly across from 19:13: աստուածն եմաթայ "the god of *Emat'* " (18:34) stands two lines above արքայն եմաթայ "king of *Emat'* " (19:13), the former in the column on the left hand side of the page, the latter in the column on the right hand side of the page.

However, the reading is signed and the witness of these Armenian MSS is generally reliable. For those reasons I think we must consider the possibility that we have here a genuine Symmachus reading. In that case it is intended in a sarcastic sort of way: "where is the god, i.e. the king who thinks he is a god...?"

The Hebrew, Greek and Armenian equivalents are:

מֶלֶךְ → Old Greek ὁ βασιλεύς → Zohrapian արքայն

→ Sym conj. ὁ θεός ← Sym աստուածն.

Symmachus translation can be represented in the second apparatus of B-M-Thack as follows:

ο βασιλευς] σ' *deus* Arm.

19:13 2°

գաւայ V212txt Zohmg (աւաj)] այհաj

V212mg Zohtxt

Cited from Stone, *Biblical and Armenian Studies* , 20–21.

For the context see the preceding item. At issue here is וְעִוָּה "or (the king) of Ivvah." The Hebrew וֹ might be vocalized -wᵉ- in which case the transliteration is "Iwwah": the Greek seems to understand it thus.

Greek MS B, which B-M-Thack follow, has καὶ Οὐδού. The word Οὐδού is certainly a secondary spelling; it is attested only by MS B. In their apparatus B-M-Thack provide for Οὐδού the following: ουδου B] αυτα A: αβα deᵃ?pz; αυανα g*: ανα ij: այհաj Arm-ed: *Agugaue* Eth: αυε Ne* (vid)gᵃ? rell Arm-codd. (The Rahlfs numbers for these MSS are as follows: d is 107; e 52; p 106 z 554; g 158; i 56; j 243.) The reading of the majority text has a great deal better claim to originality than the reading of MS Vaticanus.

One has to consider with this passage 18:34 where the list of place names also occurs: "Where are the gods of Sepharvaim, Hena, and Ivvah?" Here the majority Greek text is σεπφαρουάιμ ἀνὰ [or ἀνὰ] καὶ αὐά, i.e. עִוָּה is represented by αὐά.[1] The Armenian renders this last word զաւայ according to Zohrapian's edition. This then seems to be the origin of the marginal reading at 19:13, if indeed it is not original there.

In fact, we should consider that. At 19:13 J1925 (p.360, col.2, †4) reads անա եւ աւայ; at 18:34 it reads անա եւ եւայ; M1500 (fol.181v, col.1, ↓3) has եննա եւ աւա (19:13) and անա եւ աւա, respectively. The reading այհայ is in all likelihood secondary, quite possibly a corruption of աւայ. If we had a full collation of Armenian MSS we could say more. The marginal reading in V212 indicates comparison with the inferior text-type represented by V1508, Zohrapian's base MS. Though I have not made an extensive comparison, I note that այհայ also appears in the text of M2628 J428 and V841 (այհա) at 19:13. The well-corrected, or rather, well-corrupted MS M177 demonstrates here the process by which the earlier reading gave way to the later: originally it read աւայ; this was corrected to զաւայ by the addition of զ above the line; this was then further corrected by the addition of the word այհայ in the margin!

Arapkerts'i has five references under Այհա in his concordance: 2 Rgn 21: 8, 10, 11; 1 Chr 1:40; Neh 10:27. In 2 Rgn 21 we learn that Aiah was the father of Rizpah, one of Saul's concubines. (See also 3:7 where, however, Old Greek [and Armenian] differ from the Hebrew in the matter of the name of Rizpah's father.) In Hebrew the name is spelled אַיָּה. That in turn becomes Αἰά in Greek. (At Neh 10:27 [Greek 2 Esdras 20:27] the Hebrew is אַחְיָה which becomes Αἰα in Greek, according to Rahlfs' edition. That as well then becomes in Armenian Այհա.) I provide these references to show that այհայ is a word known elsewhere in the Old Testament corpus.

In my opinion the word այհայ is probably a corruption at 19:13.

19:28 1° *

խայտալդ] հպարտութիւն Sym

J428mg(sine ind vid) J1928mg(ind supra կարթ) J1934mg(ind supra կարթ) M188mg

---

[1] Accentuation of αυα can differ: H-R, Supplement 26, give four possibilities: Αὐά, Αὐά, Αὐα, Αὐα.

M2628ᵐᵍ

The context is the prophet Isaiah's words about King Sennacherib. In v 28 we read,

> "Because you have raged against me
>> and your arrogance has come to my ears,
> I will put my hook in your nose
>> and my bit in your mouth;
> I will turn you back on the way
>> by which you came."

The word in question is שַׁאֲנַנְךָ, translated "your arrogance." KBH offer the meanings "at ease, untroubled" for שַׁאֲנָן. According to BDB, when it is used as a substantive שַׁאֲנָן means "arrogance."

The Old Greek rendering of the first two lines above is:

διὰ τὸ ὀργισθῆναί σε ἐπ' ἐμέ,

καὶ τὸ στρῆνός σου ἀνέβη ἐν τοῖς ὠσίν μου·

The word שַׁאֲנָן is translated by τὸ στρῆνος, an uncommon word meaning "insolence, arrogance." Indeed, LSJ cite this passage amongst only a handful of occurrences. According to H-R the word στρῆνος occurs only here in the various Greek translations of the Old Testament.

It is the rarity of the word στρῆνος that has elicited the provision of an alternate translation. B-M-Thack offer the translation of Symmachus on the basis of a marginal reading in the Syro-hexapla: *iactatio* "boasting, vain-glory, ostentation, empty display, vanity." The Syriac is ܘܫܘܒܗܪܟ "and your boastfulness, vainglory," according to Field, who also provides the translation of Jerome: *et superbia tua* "and your arrogance."

The Armenian translation of τὸ στρῆνός σου is խայտալդ քո. The verb խայտալ means "to leap for joy, to be in extasy [sic], to frolic, to sport about"; plus գլխի it means "to become insolent, to rebel." It is obviously the latter meaning which it has here.

The marginal reading in the Armenian MSS is հպարտութիւն "arrogance, pride, vain-glory." It bears the signature of Symmachus. The word հպարտութիւն translates ὕβρις at Lev 26:19 and Jer 13:9, for example, and ὑπερηφανία at Exod 18:21; Num 15:30; 1 Rgn 17:28; 1 Macc 2:47; 2 Macc 9:4. Additional examples of Symmachus' use of ὑπερηφανία can be found listed in H-R. It seems possible to me that ὑπερηφανία underlies հպարտութիւն here at 4 Rgn 19:28. Field, however, retroverts the Syriac to καὶ ἡ ἀλαζονεία σου "and your boastfulness" (Lust) on the basis of Isa 37:29.

If that is so, the following equivalences obtain.

שְׁאַנַנְךָ‎ → Old Greek τὸ στρῆνός σου → Zohrapian խայտալիդ քո

→ Sym conj. (Field) καὶ ἡ ἀλαζονεία σου → Sym հպարտութիւն [քո]

In this instance the Armenian offers evidence in addition to the Syro-hexapla for the translation of Symmachus.

The Armenian evidence can be added to the second apparatus in B-M-Thack:

καὶ 1°—σου 1°] σ′ et (> Arm) *iactatio tua* (> Arm) Arm Syh.

19:28 2° *

կարթ] շրուշակ

J428mg M177mg(շաւրուշակ) M188mg M2628mg V212mg(շաւրաշակ) Zohapp (mg)(շրաւշակ)

V212 is cited on the basis of Zanolli 1231–1232.

This reading is not cited in B-M-Thackeray.

The context has been discussed above at 19:28 1°. Sennacherib is told, "I will put my hook in your nose." The words "hook in your nose" are a translation of חַחִי בְּאַפֶּךָ‎. The word in question, חַח, means "**thorn, hook** through the nose or cheek to lead animals & prisoners 2 K 19₂₈."

The word חַח occurs only a few times in the Hebrew Bible, three times in the singular: Exod 35:22 ("brooches"); 2 Ki 19:28 // Isa 37:29; six times in the plural: 2 Chr 33:11; Ezek 19:4, 9; 29:4; 38:4.

The Old Greek employs for חַח the word ἄγκιστρον "hook, fish-hook." The latter is used by both Aquila and Symmachus for *עִי? (or *עָרֶה? ?) "(fire-)

shovel (for cleaning the altar) at 1 Ki 7:40(26). (Reider-Turner add Symmachus to Aquila as attesting ἄγκιστρον at 4 Rgn 25:14 also, contra B-M-Thack.)

The unsigned marginal reading in some Armenian witnesses is զրունչակ "nose-band; twitch; bridle." This word is not to be found in Miskgian's lexicon or in Arapkertsʻi's concordance. The Latin word for "bridle" is *frenum* , whose Greek equivalent is χαλινός "bit, bridle, curb, rein," according to Freund-Leverett.

The word χαλινός occurs later in the Old Greek translation of v 28: καὶ θήσω τὰ ἄγκιστρά μου ἐν τοῖς μυκτῆρσίν σου καὶ χαλινὸν ἐν τοῖς χείλεσίν σου—this from B-M-Thackeray's text—"and I will put my hooks in your nostrils and a bit in your lips." (The whole line of the Armenian equivalent is և արկից կարթ ի քիթս քո, և դանդանաւանդ ի կզակս քո "and I will put a hook in your nose, and a bit in your snout.")

Instead of կարթ "hook" the Armenian marginal reading offers զրունչակ "bridle."

If the retroversion to χαλινός is correct, we have something to work with. H-R list six occurrences of the word χαλινός in the Old Greek corpus, where it is used for מֶתֶג "bridle" (here at 4 Rgn 19:28; Ps 31[32]:9; Isa 37:29) and רֶסֶן "bridle" (Job 30:11); twice there is no Hebrew equivalent (Hab 3:14; Zech 14:20). H-R also cite the use of χαλινός by Aquila, Symmachus and Theodotion. One of the two passages cited for Symmachus is Ezek 29:4; two of the passages cited for Theodotion are Ezek 29:4; 38: 4(*Qere*)—passages noted above where חחי appears. In both passages we read, "I will put hooks (חחים) in your jaws." This is very close to 4 Rgn 19:28.

Because Symmachus and Theodotion employ χαλινός for חחי in the Ezekiel passage(s), there is the likelihood that the same equivalent was employed in the passage under discussion. Symmachus' translations predominate over those of Theodotion among Armenian marginal readings, so it is likely that this marginal reading belongs to Symmachus. That is the suggestion I am putting forward.

The Hebrew, Greek and Armenian equivalents are:

חחי → Old Greek τὰ ἀγκιστρὰ μου → Zohrapian կարթ

         → conj. Sym τὸν χαλινόν [μου] ← sine nom զրունչակ.

In this instance the Armenian uniquely preserves the translation, at least possibly! This can be added to the second apparatus in B-M-Thack as follows:

τα αγκιστρα] ⟨σ'⟩ *frenum*   Arm.

19:37 *

ապարապայ] հայոց Sym

J428ᵐᵍ M177ᵐᵍ M188ᵐᵍ M2628ᵐᵍ V212ᵐᵍ Zohᵃᵖᵖ⁽ᵐᵍ⁾ B-M-Thackᵃᵖᵖ²

Stone, *Biblical and Armenian Studies* , 22 notes that this reading with signature is in the margin of V212 but was overlooked by Zanolli.

The context concerns the death of Sennacherib. We are told that his sons
killed him and fled into the land of אֲרָרָט "Ararat."

The Greek tradition has various spellings for Ararat: B-M-Thack print that
of MS B, namely 'Αραράθ. However, in their first apparatus B-M-Thack cite the
marginal reading ἀρμενίαν "Armenia" found in Greek MS j (Rahlfs 243) and the
Syro-hexapla. In B-M-Thackeray's second apparatus they cite the marginal reading,
with signature, found in Armenian witnesses: αραραθ] σ' *Armeniorum* . This reading they derived from Zohrapian.

The precise equivalent of ἀρμενίαν is հայաստան but the Greek phrase
"to the land of Ararat" or, according to MS j and Syh "to the land of Armenia" easily
becomes in Armenian "to the land of (the) Armenians." The word հայոց "of (the)
Armenians" derives from 'Αρμενίαν. Cf. the parallel in Isa 37:38: εἰς 'Αρμενίαν.
(Cited in Conybeare/Stock 308.) The Old Greek εἰς 'Αρμενίαν is rendered հ
հայս "to Armenia" or "to the Armenians."

The Hebrew, Greek and Armenian equivalents are:

אֲרָרָט → Greek 'Αραράτ → Zohrapian ապարապայ
      → Sym 'Αρμενίαν → Sym հայոց.

Armenian witnesses supply the signature for the reading known also in
Greek MS(S) and Syh. On the basis of the Armenian evidence the marginal readings
of MSS j (Rahlfs 243) and Syh should be placed in the second apparatus in B-M-
Thack, not the first.

The Armenian evidence is already cited by B-M-Thack:

αραραθ] σ' *Armeniorum*   Arm.

If the marginal readings in MS j and Syh are placed in the second apparatus we are able to cite the Greek underlying the Armenian:

αραραθ] σ′ (> j Syh) αρμενιαν j Arm Syh.

22:5 *

զօրացուցանել զբեդեկ] զի կազմեսցեն զկազմած Sym

J428mg(զի կազմիցեն կազմած) M177(solum կազմած cum nom) M188mg (զի կազմիցեն կազմած) M2628mg V212mg(solum զկազմած sine nom) Zohapp(mg) (solum զկազմածս cum nom) B-M-Thackapp2(*apparatum* cum nom)

V212 is cited on the basis of Zanolli 1232.

Cf. the discussion of בֶּדֶק, զբեդեկ and կազմած at 12:5.

The context concerns repairs to be made to the temple. Josiah orders that money that has come into the temple be given to those who have over-sight of the temple and that they, in turn, should give it to the workers לְחַזֵּק בֶּדֶק הַבָּיִת for "repairing the house." The word in question is בֶּדֶק "**chink, crack** (in temple) 2 K 12₆ff, **leak** (in ship) Ez 27₉." (KBH) NRSV does not translate בֶּדֶק; nor does NIV.

The Old Greek transliterates: τοῦ κατισχῦσαι τὸ βέδεκ τοῦ οἴκου "to strengthen the *bedek* of the house."

The Armenian translation of the Greek transliterates in turn: զօրացուցանել զբեդեկ "to strengthen the *bedek* ."

The transliteration has led to the marginal reading which offers a translation of the word in question. Armenian witnesses preserve the translation of Symmachus. Zohrapian in his apparatus notes the marginal reading զկազմածս with its signature. The word կազմած means "apparatus; preparation; furniture; equipage" but possibly also "construction." Cf. the cognates կազմ "construction; preparation, furniture, ornament" and the verb կազմել "to construct, erect, build; to arrange; to put in repair." Indeed MSS J428 M188 M2628 offer Symmachus' translation not just for בֶּדֶק but for לְחַזֵּק as well. Hence we read զի կազմեսցեն (or կազմիցեն, the present versus aorist subjective of կազմել: the meaning is the same) զկազմուած "in order that they might put in order the construction."

The particle զի likely stands for ἵνα. The verb կազմեցի is used in connection with the *bedek* six times in the Armenian translation of 4 Rgn 12: once it translates κρατεῖν (v 5[1] [MT 6]); three times it renders κραταιοῦν "to make fast?" (vv 6, 7, 14 [MT 7, 8, 15]); once it is used for ἐνισχῦσαι "to strengthen" (v 8 [MT 9]); once it translates κατέχειν "to secure?" (v 12 [MT 13]).

It is very difficult to know what Symmachus' translation was here. The verb used to render לְחַזֵּק was not κατισχύειν: otherwise the Armenian would not cite a different verb in the margin than it has in its text. It would appear that ἵνα plus a finite verb was used. Further, since the Armenian verb կազմեսցեն and the following noun զկազմուած are cognates, perhaps Symmachus' choices of verb and noun were also cognates. But one cannot be sure. Symmachus does employ κρατεῖν for the *hifil* of חזק (Jer 8:21; 28[51]:12). The sequence of cognates might then be κρατεῖν κράτος or κραταιοῦν κραταίωμα. The words κράτος and κραταίωμα are both used by Symmachus. One might then suggest the following retroversion into Greek from Armenian for Symmachus: ἵνα κρατήσωσιν τὸ κράτος "in order that they might strengthen the strength (of the house)" This however would not readily lead to the Armenian, which has the sense of forming or building, so one is reluctant to put it forward. One can likely say for sure that Symmachus used a purpose clause to translate the Hebrew infinitive.

The Hebrew, Greek and Armenian equivalents are:

לְחַזֵּק בֶּדֶק → Old Greek τοῦ κατισχῦσαι τὸ βέδεκ → Zohrapian զ որագուցանել զբեդեկ

→ Sym conj. ἵνα κρατήσωσιν τὸ κράτος ← Sym զի կազմեսցեն զկազմուած.

The Armenian is unique here in its preservation of the translation of Symmachus. The witnesses cited above add to the information already provided by Zohrapian and, in turn, B-M-Thack by preserving the particle, finite verb and noun object rather than just the object. The second apparatus in B-M-Thack can be revised

---

[1]LSJ cite only this passage for the meaning "repair, make good": "VI. *repair, make good,* τὸ βεδὲκ (Hebr.) τοῦ οἴκου LXX 4 Ki 12:5." Note that at 4 Rgn 12:5 κρατέω is the reading of MS B; there is a variant reading in B-M-Thack: κραταιόω is attested in MSS br vzc₂e₂ (Rahlfs 19-108 700 245 554 127 93) and Thdt. In 4 Rgn the Lucianic MSS boc₂e₂ generally offer access to the Old Greek text.

as follows:

το βεδεκ] σ' *ut parent apparatum* Arm.

22:13 1° *

խնդրեցէ՛ք] հարցէ՛ք Sym

J428mg M177mg M188mg M2628mg V212mg Zohapp(mg)(sine nom)

V212 is cited on the basis of Zanolli 1232.

This reading—which lacks a signature in Zohrapian's base MS—is not cited in B-M-Thackeray.

After Josiah heard the words of the book of the law found in the Temple, he told a number of people, "Go, inquire of the LORD for me." The word "inquire" is a translation of דִּרְשׁוּ, the imperative of the verb דָּרַשׁ.

The Old Greek translated the word דִּרְשׁוּ with ἐκζητήσατε "seek out." The simplex ζητεῖν "seek, inquire" is used some fifty times in 1–4 Rgn, always, it would appear, for בִּקֵּשׁ: cf. H-R. The compound ἐκζητεῖν occurs a handful of times in 1–4 Rgn: H-R cite it without variant among the uncials as the translation for בִּקֵּשׁ at 1 Rgn 20:16; 2 Rgn 4:11; 3 Rgn 3:1(2: 40). H-R cite four passages for ἐκζητεῖν in 1–4 Rgn where the Hebrew is דָּרַשׁ: at 3 Rgn 14:5 it is the reading in MS Alexandrinus; at 4 Rgn 1:16 it is the reading in MS R (MS B has the simplex; MS A has ἐπιζητεῖν) and, later in the same verse, it is the reading in MS A; finally there is the passage under consideration here. That is to say, 4 Rgn 22:13 is the only passage in 1–4 Rgn where there is not confusion over the use of ἐκζητεῖν for דָּרַשׁ. (Generally speaking, however, in the Greek Old Testament ἐκζητεῖν is used for דָּרַשׁ.)

The Armenian translation uses խնդրեմ "ask" as a translation for ἐκζητεῖν here at 4 Rgn 22:13.

The marginal reading in the Armenian MSS is հարցէ՛ք, the aorist imperative of the verb հարցանեմ "ask, inquire." This verb is used, for example, as the translation for ἐρωτᾶν "ask; entreat" in the Armenian translation of Deut 6:20; 13:14; and for the compound ἐπερωτᾶν at Deut 4:32. H-R offer only one passage extant for Symmachus where he uses ἐρωτᾶν, namely Jer 15:5. Nevertheless ἐρωτᾶν would appear to be the most likely verb to underlie հարցանել here. It was already suggested independently by Zanolli.

The Hebrew, Greek and Armenian equivalents are:

דִּרְשׁוּ → Old Greek ἐκζητήσατε → Zohrapian խնդրեցէք

→ Sym conj. ἐρωτήσατε ← Sym հարցէք.

The Armenian uniquely preserves the translation of Symmachus. This item can be added to the second apparatus in B-M-Thack:

ἐκζητησατε] σ΄ rogate Arm.

22:13 2° *

բորբոքեալ] հանդերձեալ Sym

J428mg J1928mg J1934mg M188mg M2628mg

Josiah says that they should inquire of the Lord because "great is the wrath of the LORD that is kindled against us." The words "that is kindled" are a translation of אֲשֶׁר־הִיא נִצְּתָה. The nifal נִצְּתָה is from יצת and is used metaphorically of God's anger: so **become inflamed, break out**. KBH list this passage and v 17 in their lexicon for this meaning .

The Armenian բորբոքեալ, aorist participle of բորբոքել "inflame, kindle," is a translation of ἐκκεκαυμένη, perfect participle passive of ἐκκαίεσθαι "light up, kindle," which is Old Greek and the majority text. (B-M-Thack follow MSS Bg (Rahlfs 158) and print ἐκκεχυμένη, the perfect participle passive of ἐκχεῖν "pour out,"—which is a corruption.)

The Armenian translation of Symmachus is հանդերձեալ "prepared; that is to be."

All the possible difficulties of dealing with the Armenian evidence are present here: Symmachus is only extant in Armenian; the Armenian has a variety of meanings, making it hard to determine what Greek underlies it; one has to retrovert twice (from Armenian to Greek, from Greek to Hebrew) and try to make logical connections among the three languages.

If one begins with the Hebrew, one has a rather rare word in נִצָּתָה: since the Greek—which one might presume lies under the Armenian—does not mean the same thing as the Hebrew, one must try to ascertain whether Symmachus read נִצָּתָה as some other word, from some other root. So, can the difference between the presumed Greek and the Hebrew be attributable to Symmachus' seeing some other Hebrew root here? Or, could it be that this is a translation that cannot be "retroverted" because it is so free? If that is not so, could it be that the Armenian translator is responsible for the fact that one cannot work back to a Greek that would connect with the Hebrew? As J.W. Wevers used to say, "In that way madness lies!" One must begin with the assumption that one can make sense of the relationships between the Armenian, a reconstructed Greek and the Hebrew.

If one begins with the Armenian participle հաևդերձեալ, in the concordance we can find a number of passages where the sense seems like that here at 4 Rgn 22:13: at Gen 49:10 մինչեւ եկեսցէ նա որոյ իւրն է հաևդերձեալքն [Arapkerts'i: հաևդերձեալ քն] "until it will come for whom those things are prepared for him" where the word ἀποκείμενα from ἀπόκεισθαι "II. be laid up in store" underlies հաևդերձեալքն; at Prov 23:5 հաևդերձեալ է նորա իւր թեւս "at the ready for him are his wings" where κατεσκεύασται "equipped, furnished; prepared" underlies հաևդերձեալ է; at Prov 15:18 and several places in the NT (Heb 13:14; Rev 2:10; 3:16; 6:11; 12:5; 17:8) forms of the verb μέλλειν "to be destined or likely to; II. to be about to" underlie հաևդերձեալ. All three Greek words are used by Symmachus, according to H-R.

The problem is that none of these Greek words can readily be connected with the root יצת. In relevant passages where יצת occurs in the *nifal*, it is rendered in Greek by the verbs ἀνάπτειν "II. light up, kindle" in the passive (Jer 9:12 [11]); ἐμπιπράναι "kindle, set on fire" in the passive (Neh 1:3). The verb יצר "form, fashion" is translated by κατασκευάζειν at Isa 45:7 and perhaps 45:9 but the confusion of יצת and יצר seems unlikely. Therefore one is not sure how Symmachus translated the Hebrew. It appears that he has offered a non-literal translation.

The Hebrew, Greek and Armenian equivalents can be set out as fol-lows.

נִצָּתָה → Old Greek ἡ ἐκκεκαυμένη → Zohrapian բռրբռքեալ է

→ Sym conj. ἡ κατεσκευασμένη ← Sym հաևդերձեալ [է].

The Armenian MSS preserve a reading of Symmachus not otherwise extant.

The Greek underlying the Armenian, however, can only be conjectured.

This item can be added to the second apparatus of B-M-Thackeray in the following way:

η εκκεχυμενη] σ′ *praeparata [est]* Arm.

23:4 1° *

պահապանաց] դռնապանաց Sym

J428ᵐᵍ M177ᵐᵍ(դռնպահաց) M188ᵐᵍ M2628ᵐᵍ V212ᵐᵍ(դռնապահաց)

V212 is cited on the basis of Zanolli 1232. Դռնապահաց is an alternate spelling.

Chapter 23 deals with the reforms and death of Josiah. Verse 4 concerns commands which Josiah gave to priests and to "the guardians of the threshold." "The guardians" is a translation of (הַסַּף) אֶת־שֹׁמְרֵי.

The Old Greek translates שֹׁמְרֵי with τοῖς φυλάσσουσιν "to those who guard."

The Armenian translation պահապանաց means the same as the Greek, though it employs the noun պահապան rather than a participial construction.

Armenian witnesses preserve a translation of Symmachus in the margin, namely դռնապանաց "to the door-keepers," from դռնապան. The Latin equivalent is *ianitoribus* . Freund-Leverett offers the word θυρωρός as the Greek equivalent of *ianitor* . We might conjecture therefore that Symmachus' translation of שֹׁמְרֵי was θυρωροῖς. (Independently Zanolli suggests *θυρωρῶν for դռնապահաց, as the latter is spelled in his MS.) The problem with this retroversion is that we do not know that Symmachus uses the word θυρωρός. H-R cite only three occurrences of θυρωρός in the Old Greek corpus where there is a Hebrew parent text (2 Rgn 4:6 [but H-R indicate this is problematic]; 4 Rgn 7:11; Ezek 44:11) and no instances of its use by any of "the Three."

The Hebrew, Greek and Armenian equivalents are as follows.

אֶת־שֹׁמְרֵי → Old Greek τοῖς φυλάσσουσιν → Zohrapian պահապանաց

→ Sym conj. τοῖς θυρωροῖς ← Sym ηⲛⳑⲙⲙⳟⲙⳑⲙⲙⳟ.

Armenian is unique in preserving Symmachus' translation. It can be added to the second apparatus in B-M-Thack:

τοις φυλασσουσιν] σ′ *ianitoribus* Arm.

23:4 2° ⋆

ի ⲙⲙⲣⲧⳑⲩⳟⲛⳡⲫ] ի ծⲣⳡⲛ Sym

J428mg J1928mg(sine nom) M177mg M188mg M2628mg V212mg(solum ծⲣⲙⳑ cum nom)

V212 is cited on the basis of Zanolli 1232. He introduces the item with *Ibid.* ⲙⲙⲣⲧⳑⲩⳟⲛⳡⲫ which precedes, whereas it should follow, 23:4 [1°].

Verse 4 continues. We are told that Josiah had all the vessels dedicated to idols brought out of the temple. These he burned "outside Jerusalem in the fields of the Kidron." The words "in the fields of" are a translation of בְּשַׁדְמוֹת.

The majority Greek text in B-M-Thack has ἐν σαδημώθ, a transliteration. (Manuscript B, which B-M-Thack follow, has the corrupt ἐν σαλημώθ.) This in turn is followed by the Armenian text: ի ⲙⲙⲣⲧⳑⲩⳟⲛⳡⲫ. The Lucianic Greek text— attested by MSS boc₂e₂ (Rahlfs 19-108 82 127 93) and generally a good witness to the Old Greek text in 4 Rgn—reads ἐν τῷ ἐμπυρισμῷ τοῦ χειμάρρου "in the burning (place) of the ravine."

The translation of Symmachus and Theodotion is preserved in the margins of Greek MSS jz (i.e. Rahlfs 243 554). It is ἐν τῇ φάραγγι "in the valley." (Syh and Syh-ap-Barh attest a reading *in incendio rivi* "in the burning [place] of the stream" that is similar to the Lucianic text. It is attributed to ε′, i.e. likely ἕτερος "other." Maybe this is the source of the reading in the Lucianic MSS.)

Symmachus' ἐν τῇ φάραγγι becomes in Armenian ի ծⲣⳡⲛ "in the valley."

The Hebrew, Greek and Armenian equivalents are:

בְּשַׁדְמוֹת → Greek MSS ἐν σαδημώθ → Zohrapian ի ⲙⲙⲣⲧⳑⲩⳟⲛⳡⲫ
→ Sym ἐν τῇ φάραγγι → Sym ի ծⲣⳡⲛ.

The Armenian marginal reading confirms Symmachus' translation, already known from Greek witnesses. The second apparatus in B-M-Thack can be adjusted accordingly:

εν σαλημωθ κεδρων] σ' θ'(> Arm) εν τη φαραγγι κεδρων(> Arm) jz Arm.

23:5 1° *

զքոյվմարիմ'ուն] զմեհեանան Aq

J428mg(զմեհեանան) M177mg(ad v 4 cum ձոր̈ն) M188mg M2628mg(sine ind in mg)
V212mg(զմեհեանու sub nom Sym) Zohapp(mg) B-M-Thackapp2

> V212 is cited on the basis of Zanolli 1232.
>
> Josiah deposed אֶת־הַכְּמָרִים "the idolatrous priests."
>
> The word כֹּמֶר "(idol-)priest" is a rare word in the Hebrew Bible. At most it occurs four times: 2 Kings 23:5; Hos 10:5; Zeph 1:4; at Hos 4:4, conjectured. Except for Lucianic MSS boc₂e₂ (Rahlfs 19-108 82 127 93)—in which we find the translation ἱερεῖς "priests"—the Old Greek tradition has a transliteration. (The translation ἱερεῖς is also found in the margin of MS i [Rahlfs 56] and the Syro-hexapla: its appearance in the latter place leads one to suspect it belongs to one of "the Three." Perhaps it is a Symmachus reading.) B-M-Thack print the transliteration as it is found in MS B, i.e. χωμαρείμ.
>
> The Armenian text follows the type of text which has a transliteration. It too has a transliteration: զքոյվմարիմ'ուն. This word, though it has the Armenian accusative marker զ-, plural marker -ս and demonstrative or definite marker -ն, is no more Armenian than it is Greek! The transliteration into Latin characters is k'ōmarim.
>
> The transliteration has led to the addition of translations in the margins of a number of witnesses. B-M-Thack cite the Latin translation of a reading attributed to Aquila in the Syro-hexapla: sacerdotalia "priestly things." (Freund-Leverett give ἱερατικός as the Greek equivalent for sacerdotalis.) The Syriac is ܟܗ̈ܢܘܬܐ "[belonging to] the priests," according to Field. Zanolli suggests—following Field— that the underlying Greek is τὰ ἱερά "sacred objects." He also points out that the

Armenian զմեհեանս probably does not presuppose a Greek text different than that underlying the Syriac ܒܝܬ̈ܐ because մեհեանք can mean not only "temples (of pagan gods)" but also the sacred items contained in them. (In the Armenian MS employed by Zanolli the reading is attributed to Symmachus. This is a mistake. Readings from Symmachus occur more often than those from Aquila and the Symmachus reading precedes that of Aquila in the Armenian marginal tradition in 4 Rgn, where both are given.) In that case the Latin translation assigned by B-M-Thack to the marginal reading in Armenian witnesses is misleading: *delubra* —their word—means "shrine, temple."

The Hebrew, Greek and Armenian equivalents are:

הַכְּמָרִים → Old Greek τοὺς χωραμείμ → Zohrapian զքովմա-
            րիմ ն

→ Aq conj. τὰ ἱερά → Aq զմեհեանսն.

The Armenian witness confirms the testimony of the Syro-hexapla concerning Aquila's translation. The second apparatus in B-M-Thack can be changed as follows:

τους χωμαρειμ] α′ *sacerdotalia* Arm Syh.

The reading α′ *delubra* Arm should be removed.

23:5 2° *

զաստեղաց] զարդուն Sym

J428mg (ind supra զաւրութեան) M177mg(զզարդ et ind supra զլուսնի) M188mg(ind supra զաւրութեան) M2628mg(ind supra զաւրութեան) V212mg(զզարդ et ind supra զլուսնի)

V212 is cited on the basis of Zanolli 1232.

Josiah deposed the idolatrous priests and "those who made offerings to Baal, to the sun, the moon, the constellations, and all the host of the heavens." The words "(to) the constellations" are a translation of לַמַּזָּלֹות.

מַזָּלֹות is a *hapax legomenon* in the Hebrew Bible: it occurs only here. KBH offer as the root *מַזָּל and for the plural give the meaning "**zodiacal**

signs. "

The Old Greek transliterates: τοῖς μαζουρώθ. The Armenian text has a translation, զաստեղաց "that to the stars." (The զ- is a marker of the accusative, which is then followed by the dative case.) This translation for the transliteration probably came about because of the sense of the passage: sun and moon precede—"stars" naturally follows.

The marginal reading in Armenian MSS came from the marginal reading offered to clarify the meaning of τοῖς μαζουρώθ. However, (զդ-)զպրդունն "(that) to the stars" is just a synonym for զաստեղ աց. It was that fact which may have led to the confusion about where the index sign should be put. In three of the five Armenian MSS cited above the index sign in the text is upon զաւրուն-թեանն (Greek: τῇ δυνάμει "to the power"); in the other two it is upon զլունանի "that to the moon."

B-M-Thack in their second apparatus give an unsigned marginal reading in Greek MS i (Rahlfs 56) for μαζουρώθ. It is ἄστροις "to the stars." It seems to me that this ἄστροις is the origin of զպրդունն. Since the latter is signed in Armenian witnesses, we can say that Symmachus' translation for לַמַּזָּלוֹת was τοῖς ἄστροις. That is, we can now identify the origin of the marginal reading in the Greek MS.

(Field cites MS 243^mg [B-M-Thack j] for a reading τῶν ἀστέρων "of the stars" as part of a scholium: Μαζουρὼθ τὰ συστήματα λέγει τῶν ἀστέρων, ἃ ἐν τῇ συνθείᾳ ζώδια καλοῦνται. "Mazuroth refers to the constellations of the stars, which are called in combination signs of the zodiac.")

The Hebrew, Greek and Armenian equivalents can be set out as follows.

לַמַּזָּלוֹת → Old Greek τοῖς μαζουρώθ → Zohrapian զաստեղաց

→ Sym τοῖς ἄστροις → Sym (զ)զպրդունն.

The Armenian provides the signature for the reading τοῖς ἄστροις. The second apparatus in B-M-Thackeray can be adjusted accordingly:

μαζουρωθ] σ'(> i) αστροις i Arm.

23:6 *

զանտառն] շրջանակաւ զբագինն Sym

J428mg(2ր2ωնωնկωι գբωգինն) M177mg(2ր2ωնωնկωιք բωգինն vid et ind supra [5]
գորուբեωն) M188mg M2628mg (2ր2ωնωնկωι գբωգիննն) V212mg(2ր2ωնω-
նկωιք բωգինն et ind supra [5] գորուբեωնց)

V212 is cited on the basis of Zanolli 1232.

In J428 the last two letters of 2ր2ωնωնկωι are uncertain: the last letter
looks like a "ն" that has filled with ink; this letter then has a stroke above it (').

Josiah then "brought out the image of [NRSV margin: Heb lacks 'image
of'] Asherah from the house of the LORD." The Hebrew for "the Asherah" is אֶת־
הָאֲשֵׁרָה.

The B-related Greek tradition renders אֶת־הָאֲשֵׁרָה with the words τὸ ἄλσος "sacred grove." Lucianic MSS boc₂e₂ (Rahlfs 19-108 82 127 93) add cum var
τῆς ἀσηρώθ, i.e. a transliteration.

The Armenian translation for τὸ ἄλσος is straightforward: գωնտωռն
"the wood, grove."

Armenian witnesses have for գωնտωռն a marginal reading. In manuscript M177 the index sign in the text is misplaced; the same is true of the MS which
Zanolli used, though he has not recognized that fact.

The marginal reading 2ր2ωնωնկωι գբωգինն means "around the idol,
altar." The underlying Greek may have been κύκλῳ τοῦ εἰδώλου or, better, Zanolli's suggestion τὸ περιβώμιον "round the altar." The latter is a word used by
Symmachus: 4 Rgn 17:16; 21:7; 23:4, 7.

The Hebrew, Greek and Armenian equivalents are:

אֶת־הָאֲשֵׁרָה → Old Greek τὸ ἄλσος → Zohrapian գωնտωռն
→ Sym conj. τὸ περιβώμιον ← Sym 2ր2ωνωնկωι գբωգինն.

The Armenian provides here a reading of Symmachus not otherwise attested. It can be added to the second apparatus in B-M-Thack as follows:

το αλσος] σ′ circa altarium Arm.

23:7 ∗

կωդ եսիմωցն] նուիրωցն Sym

J428mg(ունիրաց) M177mg(ունիրունացն vid) M188mg M2628mg(ունիրնաց)
V212mg

V212 is cited on the basis of Zanolli 1233.

Josiah, we are told, "broke down the houses of the male temple prostitutes." The words "of the male temple prostitutes" are a translation of the word הַקְּדֵשִׁים. The entry for קָדֵשׁ in KBH gives the meaning "**consecrated person, cult prostitute.**"

The Old Greek tradition gives for the word הַקְּדֵשִׁים a transliteration: τῶν καδησείμ, with slight variations in spelling. Καδησείμ is the spelling in MS B, reproduced in B-M-Thack.

The Armenian translation follows the Old Greek: it too has a transliteration, i.e. կադեխիմացն, which consists of կադեխիմ + the genitive plural marker -աց plus the demonstrative/definite marker -ն.

B-M-Thack, in their second apparatus, reproduce a signed Symmachus translation for הַקְּדֵשִׁים found in Greek MS j (Rahlfs 243): τῶν τελετῶν "of the religious rites." (Cf. LSJ τελετή III. a *priesthood* or *sacred office* , Decretum quoted in Demosthenes [384–322 BCE] 59.104.) Their Latin translation for the Symmachus reading in the margin of the Syro-hexapla is *completionis* "completion, finishing," which appears to be related to the Greek τῶν τελετῶν (cf. τέλος "conclusion") except that the former is singular in number instead of plural. The Syriac is ܪ (sic: so Field) "of the completion, consecration," according to Field.

The Armenian translation of Symmachus' rendering is նուիրացն, literally "of the offerings, sacrifices." The word նուէր means "offering" and the verb նուիրեմ means "to offer," but note that the participial form of the verb—նրնուիրող—means "priest," i.e. "one who makes an offering." Zanolli states that the Armenian նուիրացն is not independent of τῶν τελετῶν and I think he is right. One can see, however, that in using the translation of Symmachus, translators used some imagination. The Armenian is hardly literal and the rendering into Latin, if B-M-Thack are to be followed, is not helpful at all.

The Hebrew, Greek and Armenian equivalents are:

הַקְּדֵשִׁים → Old Greek τῶν καδησείμ → Zohrapian կադեխիմացն
→ Sym τῶν τελετῶν → Sym նուիրացն.

The Armenian confirms the translation already known from Greek witness(es). It is fortunate that the Greek is extant here because one would be hard pressed to retrovert precisely from either the Armenian or the Syriac back into Greek.

The second apparatus in B-M-Thack can be revised as follows:

τον—αλσει] σ' τον οικον των τελετων των εν τω οικω κ̅υ̅ οπου αι γυναικες υφαινον των περιβωμιων j |των καδησειμ] ο εβρ. ακκοδασιμ j : σ' *donorum* Arm : α' *scortatorum* σ' *completionis* Syh.

The Armenian evidence might rather be cited as attesting the reading τῶν τελετῶν of MS j which provides the Greek parent reading. The citation in Latin, while an accurate representation of the Armenian, is misleading unless some sort of explanation is given—for which there is no space in the apparatus of a text. The Armenian should not be thought either to preserve a reading different from that found in the Syro-hexapla, though the Latin equivalents of the two readings are not the same.

23:9 ∗

բարձանցն] բագնացն Sym

J428^mg M177^mg(բագնաց) M188^mg M2628^mg(բագնաց) V212^mg(բագնաց)

V212 is cited on the basis of Zanolli 1233.

The text goes on to say that Josiah brought the priests out of all the towns of Judah (v 8) but that כֹּהֲנֵי הַבָּמוֹת "the priests of the high places" did not come up to the altar in Jerusalem. The word whose translation is in question here is בָּמֹה.

בָּמָה means in about 80 of its about 100 occurrences in the Hebrew Bible "(cultic) **high place**." These 80 occurrences are found especially in 1 and 2 Ki and 2 Chr. The standard equivalent for בָּמָה in these three books is ὁ ὑψηλός and of the plural בָּמוֹת, which predominates, it is οἱ ὑψηλοί "the high things." Thus we read in the Old Greek at 23:9 for הַבָּמוֹת כֹּהֲנֵי οἱ ἱερεῖς τῶν ὑψηλῶν "the priests of the high things."

The Armenian translation բարձանցն "of the high things" is a literal rendering of the Greek.

Symmachus' translation rendered into Armenian is բագնացն "of the altars." The word բագին means "altar."

We may note 4 Rgn 17:9 where the Old Greek has ὑψηλά "high things" and the Syro-hexapla has a marginal reading cited in B-M-Thack as *altaria* , i.e. "altars." The Syriac is ܐܬܠܒܐ, according to Field.

What word underlies բագնացն at 23:9? A check in the concordance—Arapkerts'i—indicates that τῶν βωμῶν mostly likely underlies the Armenian.

The equivalents are:

הַבָּמֹ֑ת → Old Greek τῶν ὑψηλῶν → Zohrapian բարձանցն

→ Sym conj. τῶν βωμῶν ← բագնացն.

The Armenian marginal reading uniquely preserves Symmachus' translation. This item can be added to the second apparatus in B-M-Thack as follows:

των υψηλων] σ′ *altariorum*   Arm.

23:10 *

զԹոփէոթ] զտափետէն Sym

J428^mg M177^mg(զարէթն) M188^mg(զտափետէն) M2628^mg(զտափէթ) V212^mg (զափետն)

V212 is cited on the basis of Zanolli 1233.

In v 10 we are told that Josiah "defiled Topheth." The English is a transliteration of תֹּפֶת. The word appears with the article and the direct object marker, hence אֶת־הַתֹּפֶת.

The Greek translations offer a variety of spellings for their transliteration of תֹּפֶת. B-M-Thack print Ταφεθ, the spelling in MS B; the Lucianic MSS boc₂e₂ (Rahlfs 19-108 82 127 93) preserve θάφφεθ.There was some exegetical interest in the place name, demonstrated by the preservation of a comment by Victor of Antioch (d. 450?) in catena MSS. The following comment appears in MS Paris Nat. Bibl. Coisl. 8 (B-M-Thack j; Rahlfs 243): Τὸ «Ταφὲθ» τόπος ἦν οὕτω λεγόμενος. Λέγει δὲ τὸν ἐλάσσονα, ἔνθα εἰδωλολάτρει ὁ Ἰσραὴλ ἐν προαστείοις τῆς Ἰερουσαλήμ. Ταύτης τῆς φάραγγος καὶ ὁ Ἡσαΐας μέμνηται εἰπών· «ἐν φάραγγι Σιὼν πλανῶται ἀπὸ μικροῦ ἕως μεγαλοῦ» (XXII, 5).[1] The translation is: "The place was thus called 'Tapheth'. It means 'inferior,' where Israel was idolatrous in the environs of Jerusalem. Of this valley Isaiah also makes mention: 'In the valley of Zion it went astray, from the smallest to the greatest' (22:5)." The Armenian text has a transliteration based upon the exemplar from which it has come. It has ｐｎ[ｈｎ]ｐ with the object marker ｑ -. That is, the Armenian text has a spelling with two short "o" vowels. The Greek spelling underlying the Armenian is θόφοθ.

The marginal reading from Symmachus simply offers another spelling, this time with the "a" and "e" vowels, like Greek MS B. In their second apparatus B-M-Thack present readings for Symmachus from Greek and Syriac witnesses: according to Greek MS j (Rahlfs 243) Symmachus' rendering of תֹּפֶת־אֶת is τὸν τά-φοθ;[2] according to the Syro-hexapla both Symmachus and Theodotion, in Syriac, have ܕܦܕ(Θαφέθ?: so Field). The latter is not really much help without vowels.

At least it indicates that Symmachus and Theodotion had a spelling different from the text of MS B. The spelling of the first reading following Symmachus' name in MS j does not coincide with the spelling of Symmachus' reading known from Armenian, though maybe the "o" vowel of τάφοθ might reduce to "e" with loss of stress, depending upon pronunciation. The second spelling in the MS j marginal reading for Symmachus is θαφεθ.

Zanolli's MS has the spelling of MS M177 cited above. Such a reading he derives from an original Greek πυρητόκος, ἔναυσμα, ἔκκαυμα, or πυρίαμα. Unfortunately the spelling ｗｐｔ[ｐ is a corruption!

The Hebrew, Greek and Armenian are as follows:

תֹּפֶת־אֶת → Greek MS conj. τὸν θόφοθ → ｑ[ｐｎｈｎ]ｐ
→ Sym τὸν θάφεθ/τὸν θάφεθ → Sym ｑｗｗｗｈｔ[ｐｌ

In this instance the Armenian attests a reading for Symmachus; its spelling of the proper name involved seems to be a mixture of the two spellings of the name

---

[1]Cited in R. Devreesse, ed. *Les anciens commentateurs grecs de l'Octateuque et des Rois (fragments tirés des chaînes)* (Studi e Testi/Bibliotheca apostolica vaticana 201; Vatican City: Bibliotheca vaticana 1959) 181.

[2]Note that in B-M-Thack there is a second translation given in MS j for the Hebrew sentence in question. Both translations follow Symmachus' signature. In the second translation the spelling of Topheth is τὸν θάφεθ.

with Symmachus' signature in Greek MS j.

The second apparatus in B-M-Thack can be revised as follows:
τον ταφεθ] σ' *tapheth* Arm : σ' θ' ձ֋ձ Syh.

The transliteration of the name in Armenian according to the Library of Congress system is *tap'et'* .

23:11 *

ի գանձանակի] առ պատշկամբին Sym

J428mg(ind supra ի մունու) M177mg(առ պաշտկամբի et ind supra ի մունու) M188 mg(առ պատշկամբն vid et ind supra ի մունու) M2628mg(առ պատրգքամբն et ind supra ի մունու) V212mg(կաշտկամբի) Zohapp(mg) B-M-Thack app2

V212 is cited on the basis of Zanolli 1233.

The context is once again Josiah's iconoclastic actions at the Temple. We are told in v 11 that he removed the carved horses which stood "at the entrance to the house of the LORD, by the chamber of the eunuch Nathan-melech." The word in question is לִשְׁכָּה "room, chamber," which appears here in the bound form with the preposition אֶל. So we read אֶל־לִשְׁכַּת נְתַן־מֶלֶךְ "toward (NRSV "by") the chamber of Nathan-melech."

The Old Greek translation for אֶל־לִשְׁכַּת is εἰς τὸ γαζοφυλάκιον "in the treasury." Actually the Lucianic MSS boc₂e₂ (Rahlfs 19-108 82 127 93) preserve the preposition πρός so the Old Greek translation may have been πρός τὸ γαζοφυλάκιον "near the treasury."

The Armenian translation follows the Greek: ի գանձանակի means "in the treasury."

The marginal reading from Symmachus offers a different translation: առ պատշկամբին means "at the side-chamber." B-M-Thack cite the reading but have it misspelled: առ պաշտկամբին! It is correct in Zohrapian's apparatus so the error is theirs. Armenian alone preserves the reading.

Arapkerts'i lists a number of passages where the word պատշկամբ is found. They are, with the underlying Greek: Judg 3:23 (MS A text: προστάδα "vestibule"; MS B text: διατεταγμένους); Ezek 42:4, 6 (ἐξεδρῶν), 7 (ἐξωτέρας), 8 (ἐξεδρῶν), 13 (αἱ ἐξέδραι). Zanolli says that պատուշկամբ at 23:11 doubtless presupposes ἐξέδρα "hall, arcade" as in Ezek 40; 44–46. (Zanolli's MS reads կաշոկամբի which he takes to be a dialectical variant of պատուշկամբի.)

The Hebrew, Greek and Armenian equivalents are:

אֶל־לִשְׁכַּת → Old Greek var lect εἰς τὸ γαζοφυλάκιον → ի գանձա-

նակի

→ Sym conj. πρὸς τῇ ἐξέδρῃ ← առ պատուշկամբին.

The Greek is a retroversion from Armenian. It is unclear what preposition Symmachus used with ἐξέδρα. That the Armenian translation of Symmachus does not use ի makes it uncertain that the underlying Greek preposition was εἰς.

In this instance Armenian uniquely preserves Symmachus. The second apparatus in B-M-Thack should be changed to:

εἰς το γαζοφυλακιον] σ' *apud vestibulum*   Arm.

It is unclear to me why B-M-Thack should have cited the Armenian in Armenian characters here when that is not usually their practice. Latin is more useful than Armenian misspelled.

23:12 *

ի հեղեղատն] ի ձորն Sym

J428^mg M177^mg M188^mg M2628^mg V212^mg(sine nom)

V212 is cited on the basis of Zanolli 1233.

In v 12 we are told that Josiah broke down various altars and threw the rubble אֶל־נַחַל קִדְרוֹן "into the Wadi Kidron." The word in question is נַחַל, a word which occurs quite frequently in the Hebrew Bible—140 times—and means "stream-bed, wadi."

The Old Greek translated אֶל־נַחַל with the words εἰς τὸν χειμάρρουν "into the valley." This is reflected in the Armenian rendering ի հեղեղատն "into the ravine."

The Symmachus reading in the margins of Armenian MSS is ի ձորն "into the valley." The underlying Greek word is in all likelihood φάραγξ "ravine, valley," a word that Symmachus uses at 23:4, 10. (Cf. also 14:7 in B-M-Thack.) It is, of course, a synonym of χείμαρρος and is commonly used in the LXX/Old Greek as a translation for נַחַל.

In this instance the citing of Symmachus amounts to no more than the providing of a synonym for the translation in the text. Zanolli says that ի ծորն is confirmed by Greek MS 243, which reads εἰς τὴν φάραγγα, but no such MS is cited either by Field or B-M-Thack so we must regard his citation as erroneous.

The Hebrew, Greek and Armenian equivalents are:

אֶל־נַחַל → Old Greek εἰς τὸν χειμάρρουν → Zohrapian ի հեղեղատն
→ Sym conj. εἰς τὴν φάραγγα ← Sym ի ծորն.

The Armenian is unique in preserving the Symmachus reading, along with its signature. This item can be added to the second apparatus in B-M-Thack:

εἰς τον χειμαρρουν] σ′ in valle Arm.

23:13 *

մՕսափթայ] ապականչին ապականութեան Sym

J428mg M177mg M188mg vid M2628mg(ապակ",ան չին արկ²նութեան) V212mg
Zohapp(mg)(ապակ'ան չին ապականութեան9) B-M-Thackapp2

V212 is cited on the basis of Zanolli 1233–1234.

We are told that King Josiah defiled the high places that were east of Jerusalem מִימִין לְהַר־הַמַּשְׁחִית "to the south of the Mount of Destruction." The Hebrew represents a play on the word הַמִּשְׁחָה "(Mount of) Olives": see Montgomery 540.

The Old Greek employs a transliteration in its rendering of מַשְׁחִית in the phrase just cited: ἐκ δεξιῶν τοῦ ὄρους τοῦ Μοσοάθ "on the right side of Mt. Mosoath." (The spelling of the transliteration here is that of MS B, which B-M-Thack follow.)

The Armenian follows the Greek transliteration with one of its own: hence we read ընդ աջմէ լերինն Մոսաթայ, literally "to the right of Mt. Mosat'."

Citing Symmachus provides a translation to replace the transliterations. B-M-Thackeray's citation of the Armenian evidence reflects a plural noun since they follow Zohrapian. As a result, their translation from Armenian into Latin is *corruptoris corruptionum* . The Latin translation of ապականչին ապականու-թեան—where the noun is in the singular number—is *corruptae corruptionis* "of Corrupting Corruption," i.e. "of Utter Corruption."

Is it possible to provide a retroversion from Armenian into Greek? At Jer 51:25 (Old Greek 28:25) we read מַשְׁחִית, which is translated into Greek as τὸ ὄρος τὸ διεφθαρμένον τὸ διαφθεῖρον "the corrupting mountain which corrupts." It is clear that at 4 Rgn 23:13 Symmachus has taken the word מַשְׁחִית as the *hifil* participle of שָׁחַת "spoil, ruin." While διαφθείρειν is a verb that Symmachus uses, it remains of course hypothetical that he used it here. If he did, the Greek might have been τῆς διαφθειρούσης τῆς διαφθορᾶς "of Corrupting Corruption."

Field cites a reading for Aquila here based on the Syro-hexapla. The reading attributed to Aquila is ܕܐܒ݂ܕܢ "of destruction," which he retroverts to φθορᾶς or διαφθορᾶς. He suggests comparing Ezek 25:15. B-M-Thack cite this Syriac reading in Latin as *perniciei* .

The Hebrew, Greek and Armenian equivalents are as follows.

מַשְׁחִית → Old Greek c var τοῦ Μοσοάθ → Zohrapian Մոսաթայ

  → Sym conj. τῆς διαφθειρούσης τῆς διαφθορᾶς ← Sym ապա-

կանչին ապականութեան.

In this instance the Armenian witnesses are unique in preserving a signed translation of Symmachus. The second apparatus in B-M-Thack can be changed to:

μοσοαθ] σ′ *corruptae corruptionis* Arm.

23:15 *

գբարծր] գբլուրն Sym

J428^mg M177^mg M188^mg M2628^mg V212^mg(բլուրն)

V212 is cited on the basis of Zanolli 1234.

Josiah's destruction of altars and images continues. In v 15 we are told that he pulled down הַבָּמָה "the high place" erected by Jeroboam at Bethel.

The Old Greek translates הַבָּמָה quite literally: τὸ ὑψηλόν "the high (thing)." Armenian զբարծր "the high (thing)"—with the direct object marker -զ—follows the Greek precisely.

The word בָּמָה does of course mean "mountain ridge, **height**, a) of land" and Symmachus translates it as such: բլուր means "hill."

The word բլուր translates θίς "heap," at Deut 12:2 but θίς only occurs four times in the Old Greek corpus and is not extant as a word which Symmachus used. It is much more likely that the word βουνόν "hill" underlies բլուր: the latter often translates the former. Zanolli independently suggests the same.

The equivalents among Hebrew, Greek and Armenian are:

הַבָּמָה → Old Greek τὸ ὑψηλόν → Zohrapian զբարծր

→ Sym conj. τὸν βουνόν ← Sym զբլուն.

The Armenian uniquely preserves Symmachus here. This item can be added to the second apparatus in B-M-Thack:

το υψηλον] σ' *collem* Arm.

23:16 *

ի քաղաքին] ի լերինն Sym

J428mg M177mg M188mg M2628mg V212mg Zohapp(mg) B-M-Thackapp2

V212 is cited on the basis of Zanolli 1234.

We are told in v 16 that when Josiah visited the high place at Bethel he saw "the tombs there on the mount." The words "on the mount" are a translation of בָּהָר.

The B-related—and majority—Greek text has for בָּהָר the words ἐν τῇ πόλει "in the city." The Hebrew equivalent of ἐν τῇ πόλει is בָּעִיר.

One notes that Greek MSS (Lucianic) boc₂e₂ (Rahlfs 19-108 82 127 93) have ἐν τῷ ὄρει "on the mountain."

The Armenian translation follows the majority Greek text: ի քաղաքին "in the city."

It is not surprising that we find a marginal reading to correct the reading in the text. B-M-Thack cite both the Armenian and the Syro-hexapla for the signed Symmachus reading which they offer in Latin, i.e. *in monte* "on the mount." The Syriac is ܟ݂ܛܘܠ݂ܐ "on the mountain," according to Field.

The Armenian marginal reading is ի լեռինն "on the mountain," which in all likelihood derives from ἐν τῷ ὄρει. This has also been suggested independently by Zanolli. The marginal reading bears the signature of Symmachus, as in the Syro-hexapla. It may be that Lucian got the translation ἐν τῷ ὄρει from Symmachus.

The Hebrew, Greek and Armenian equivalents are:

בָעִיר ≠ ἐν τῇ πόλει → Zohrapian ի քաղաքին

→ Sym ἐν τῷ ὄρει → Sym ի լեռինն.

In this instance the Armenian confirms the witness of the Syro-hexapla for the Symmachus reading. The B-M-Thack citation can remain as it is:

ἐν τη πολει] σ′ *in monte*   Arm Syh.

23:21 *

զզատիկ Zoh^txt; զատիկ Zoh^app] պասէք Sym

M2628^mg

This marginal reading is not preserved in either J428 or M188.

After King Josiah had reformed worship in the land he commanded the people, "Keep the passover." The word "passover" is a translation of פֶּסַח.

The Old Greek has here the word πάσχα, a transliteration of the Aramaic form of the word.

In Armenian the word πάσχα became զատիկ "Easter." According to Bedrossian զատիկ Հրէից, literally "Easter of the Jews" is the Armenian for Passover.

The word պասէք means "Passover" and it too is a transliteration: cf. φασέκ, φασέχ in H-R. It bears here the signature of Symmachus, whom we know tends to transliterate Hebrew words of cultic significance. (Salvesen 194) H-R cite φασέκ, φασέχ as Symmachus' translation of חֶסֶפ at Exod 12:11; Num 9:2; Josh 5: 10.[1]

We have here Symmachus' transliteration of חֶסֶפ. The Hebrew, Greek and Armenian equivalents are:

חֶסֶפ → Old Greek πάσχα → Zohrapian զատիկ

→ Sym conj. φασέχ ← Sym պասեք.

This item can be added to the second apparatus in B-M-Thack:

πασχα] σ′ *pasek* Arm.

The Library of Congress transliteration is *pasek'*.

23:24 *

զթերափիմ] տաւնահմայս

J428mg M177(զտաւնակմ այն) M188mg M2628mg V212mg(զտաւնակմայս) Zohapp(mg) B-M-Thackapp2

Note: see below for a corrected citation of the MS evidence.

V212 is cited on the basis of Zanolli, who discusses this passage on pp. 1222, 1234.

We are told in v 24 that "Josiah put away the mediums, wizards, teraphim, idols [mg: 'Or *household gods* '], and all the abominations that were seen in the land of Judah and in Jerusalem." The Hebrew for "mediums, wizards, teraphim, idols" is אֹבוֹת, יִדְּעֹנִים, תְּרָפִים, גִּלֻּלִים. The word in question appears with the article and direct object marker, hence אֶת־הַתְּרָפִים "teraphim."

The Old Greek transliterated תְּרָפִים: so we read in B-M-Thack— who print MS B—τὰ θεραφείν. (Note the spelling in MSS jnp(vid)vyc₂ [Rahlfs 243 119 106 245 121 93], namely θεραφείμ; MS e [Rahlfs 52] reads θραφίμ: these preserve the consonant מ at the end of the word.)

The Armenian translation follows the Greek by offering a transliteration: թերափիմ. (Զ- is the direct object marker; -ս is the indicator of the plural.) The marginal reading is տաւնահմայս "sacred diviners," a word which combines

---

[1] See Salvesen's discussion of Symmachus at Exod 12:11 at pp. 83–85 of her book.

the word տաւ ն, later spelled տoն, "feast, festival" and հմ ա յք "diviners, sorcerers." Perhaps we could translate it "sacred diviners."

Zanolli's MS has a corruption similar to M177. His comments are on the word զտաւնականհմայս. The first part of the word is clear enough but his derivation of the second part from նամակ goes nowhere, as one might expect.

The marginal reading is unsigned. Aquila's translation for תְּרָפִים is μορφώματα, literally "forms, shapes": see Reider-Turner.[1] B-M-Thack cite Aquila on the basis of the Syro-hexapla: *similitudines* , i.e. μορφώματα. (The Syriac is ܟܕܡܘܬܐ "images," according to Field.) The Armenian is not that.

B-M-Thack cite for Symmachus *idola* . Symmachus is not above using a transliteration for תְּרָפִים: note Gen 31:19 where he has θεραφείν (var lect θεραφείμ) in place of LXX εἴδωλα. The Armenian word here at 4 Rgn 23:24 seems a bit complex to have come from *idola* . Field cites the Syriac as ܘܨܠܡܐ "and the idols" which he then retroverts as καὶ τὰ εἴδωλα.

Perhaps տաւնահմայս is not intended for τὰ θεραφείν, i.e. perhaps the index sign is incorrectly placed in the Armenian tradition. B-M-Thack present Aquila's and Symmachus' translations of אֹבוֹת "mediums" as follows: (Old Greek) τους θελητας "wizards"] α' *magos* σ' *ventriloquos* . The Armenian word տաւնահմայս is the equivalent of *ventriloquos* and refers to holy diviners. The Greek word is ἐγγαστριμύθους "ventriloquists," i.e. "those who deliver oracles." (H-R cite Symmachus for 4 Rgn 23:24 under ἐγγαστρίμυθος.) It seems to me therefore that տաւնահմայս is Symmachus. The index sign has been misplaced in Armenian witnesses, possibly because so often marginal readings are there to help with transliterations of words like תְּרָפִים.

We may note in passing that Symmachus' translation of אֹבוֹת, i.e. ἐγγαστριμύθους has come into the Lucianic MSS boc₂e₂ (Rahlfs 19-108 82 127 93).

The Hebrew, Greek and Armenian equivalents are:

אֶת־הָאֹבוֹת → τοὺς θελητάς → Zohrapian զկհուկս "conjurers"

→ Sym τοὺς ἐγγαστριμύθους → sine nom տաւնահմայս.

In this instance Armenian can be added to the evidence of the Syro-hexapla which attests τοὺς ἐγγαστριμύθους (B-M-Thack *ventriloquos*) as Symmachus'

---

[1]Cf. Swete, *Introduction* , 40: Aquila's use of μορφώματα is cited as an example of his use of vocabulary of a classical or literary type.

translation of אֶת־הָאֹבֹות. B-M-Thackeray's apparatus must be corrected at this point as follows:

τοὺς θελητας] α' *magos* (> Arm) σ' *ventriloquos* Arm(sine nom et ind mend supra τα θεραφειν) Syh.

The citation of the Armenian evidence that I have provided at the beginning of this item also needs correction to:

զվհուկս] նասնահմ̌այս

J428mg M177mg(զնասնակմ̌ այս) M188mg M2628mg V212mg(զնասնակմ̌այս) Zohapp(mg) B-M Thack app2: in omnes ind mend supra զթերապհիմ̌ս.

The word վհուկ means "wizard, sorcerer." It turns out then that, in this instance, the Symmachus reading offers a synonym for the reading in the text for which it was originally intended. As it stands now in the Armenian margin—because the index sign is misplaced—the *teraphim* have become synonymous with the first two words in the four-part list. We now do not have "mediums, wizards, *teraphim* , idols" (Hebrew) or "wizards, diviners (τοὺς γνωριστάς MSS BA ghin [Rahlfs 158 55 56 119]; γνώστας N rell), *teraphim* , idols" (Greek B-related text) or "wizards, sorcerers, *teraphim* , idols (Armenian text) but "wizards, sorcerers, sacred diviners, and idols" (Armenian, when նասնահմ̌այս replaces զթերա-պհիմ̌ս). This is of some interest exegetically.

23:29 *

ներաւով] կալ Aq

J428mg M177mg M188mg V212mg Zohapp(mg)(sine nom) B-M-Thackapp2(sine nom)

V212 is cited on the basis of Zanolli 1234.

The writer is concluding his remarks about Josiah. He now tells us how Josiah died. It happened, he says, when "Pharaoh Neco king of Egypt went up to the king of Assyria." The word in question here is Neco, i.e. נְכֹה, the name of the

Pharaoh.

The Old Greek transliterates his name as Νεχαώ [1°].

The Armenian follows the Greek with a transliteration: Նեքաուով.

In some Armenian MSS we find a marginal reading attributed to Aquila.
(The reading is unsigned in the MS[S] employed by Zohrapian and is therefore cited
without signature in B-M-Thack.) The word in the margin of these MSS is կաղ
"lame, halt, crippled." B-M-Thack offer a Latin translation for կաղ, namely
claudus . The Greek equivalent is χωλός.

Aquila took the word נְכֹה to be a cognate of the common verb נכה which
occurs most frequently in the *hifil* where it means "strike, hit, beat." Cf. *נָכֶה or
*נֵכֶה — whose bound or construct form is נְכֵה: "struck, hit, beaten." The phrase
נְכֵה רַגְלַיִם means "crippled" (2 Sam 4:4; 9:3).

Zanolli says the Aquila reading is confirmed by the Syriac ܟܝܫܠܐ , i.e.
claudus and by the Jonathan targum which has חגירה. He too suggests χωλός for
Aquila.

The Hebrew, Greek and Armenian equivalents are:

נְכֹה → Old Greek Νεχαώ → Zohrapian նեքաուով

→ Aq conj. χωλός ← Aq կաղ.

The Armenian witnesses uniquely preserve Aquila's translation of Pharaoh's name. The second apparatus in B-M-Thack can be adjusted to include Aquila's signature:

νεχαω 1°] α′ *claudus* Arm.

23:35 *

ասկի Zoh^app(mg)] կարի

M177^mg V212^mg Zoh^txt

V212 is cited on the basis of Stone, "Additional Note on the Marginalia in 4
Kingdoms," 22. Zohrapian notes that the marginal reading in his MS for collation
agrees with what some other MSS have as their text. Indeed J428 has կարի
"ability" in its text, without any marginal reading. The original Armenian text is

 սալի "reckoning": it is the text of J1925 (f.191, col.2, ↑15) and M1500 (f.183, col.1, ↓7).

Pharaoh Neco deposed the Judean king, Jehoahaz, and installed in place of him Jehoiakim. In order to satisfy the Pharaoh's demands for tribute, we are told, he exacted gold and silver from the people of the land, "from all according to their assessment." The words "according to their assessment" are a translation of כְּעֶרְכֹּו.

The B-M-Thack text for כְּעֶרְכֹּו is κατὰ τὴν συντίμησιν αὐτοῦ "according to his valuation." This Greek translation is represented in the text of Armenian MSS J1925 M177 M1500 V280 and Zoh^{app}: սալի "reckoning."

The Armenian translation represented by Zohrapian's text has ըստ կարի իւրում "according to his ability." It is also represented in M177^{mg} V280^{mg}. This is a translation of κατὰ τὴν δύναμιν αὐτοῦ which is the Greek text of MSS boc$_2$e$_2$ (Rahlfs 19-108 82 127 93), the so-called Lucianic group of MSS.

B-M-Thack note that the hexaplaric-derived witnesses οἱ λ'—i.e. οἱ λοιποί, literally "the remainder"—are cited in the Syro-hexapla as translating כְּעֶרְכֹּו with *secundum potentiam suam* "according to his ability," i.e. δύναμιν. The Syriac is ܐܝܟ ܚܝܠܗ "as his ability," according to Field. Is it possible that the marginal note in M177 V280 is derived from such a marginal reading? Yes, it is. The Armenian marginal reading is the same as that found in the Syro-hexapla.

What was a marginal reading—կարի—has entered the text of various Armenian witnesses, including Zohrapian's base MS V1508.

The Hebrew, Greek and Armenian equivalents are:

כְּעֶרְכֹּו → Old Greek κατὰ τὴν συντίμησιν αὐτοῦ → ըստ սալի
     իւրում
  → οἱ λ' κατὰ τὴν δύναμιν αὐτοῦ → sine nom [ըստ] կարի
     [իւրում].

In this instance the Armenian witnesses corroborate the evidence of the Syro-hexapla. Their evidence can be added to the second apparatus of B-M-Thackeray:

κατα—αυτου] λ' *secundum potentiam suam* Syh | συντιμησιν] *potentiam*
Arm.

It appears that this reading has come into Lucian from one of "the Three."

24:14 *

զդաhիծս] սուրhանդակս Aq (mend pro Sym vid)

J428mg M188mg M2628mg

Cf. 11:19 where Symmachus' translation of וְאֶת־הָרָצִים "and the guards"
is rendered into Armenian as եւ զսուրhանդակսն "and the runners." The underlying Greek is likely καὶ τοὺς παρατρεχόντας "and the runners." Such a translation is attested for Symmachus at 11:4.

Jerusalem has fallen to the Babylonians. Verse 13 tells of the treasures of
the temple that King Nebuchadnezzar carried off; verse 14 lists categories of profes-
sional people that he took away. Among the latter are "all the artisans" and הַמַּסְגֵּר
"the smiths."

In KBH II.מַסְגֵּר is assigned the meaning "metal-worker, fitter." It appears
as a collective here and in v 16 and is only elsewhere clearly attested in the Hebrew
Bible at Jer 24:1; 29:2. BDB offer for its collective sense the meaning "smiths."

The Old Greek translated הַמַּסְגֵּר with the words τὸν συνκλείοντα. LSJ
give the meaning "smith" for ὁ συγκλείων, citing this passage: see συγκλείω 4.
The only other passage cited under 4. is 3 Rgn 6:20 where the passive of this verb
is used of gold overlay (i.e. "closed up" with gold). It would appear that the meaning here has been assigned on the basis of the Hebrew, not the Greek.

The Greek translator may have related the Hebrew word in question to I.
הַמַּסְגֵּר "dungeon" (only certainly occurs at Isa 24:22; 42:7; Ps 142:8) or, in greater likelihood, to סָגַר "shut, close" in which case the Greek might mean something
like "gate-keepers." Would one arrive at the meaning "smith" for τὸν συνκλείοντα
without consulting the Hebrew? It is true that it follows the words πᾶν τέκτονα
"every craftsman," so that the context might dictate a meaning like "one who closes
up," i.e. with overlay. One can use the meaning "gate-keeper" for the Greek—the
word συγκλείω is used of closing gates—before and after consulting the Hebrew,
though it might not go as well as "overlayer," perhaps "smith" in the context.

The Armenian translation for τὸν συνκλείοντα is զդաhիծս, here with
the direct object marker զ- and the marker of the plural -ս. The word դաhիծ

means "hangman, executioner; attendant; torturer." Its use here is derived from interpreting the Greek as referring to someone who locks up people. The Armenian translator understood τὸν συνκλείοντα as some sort of gate-keeper.

Symmachus' translation for מַסְגֵּר is extant for Ps 141(142):8: it is συγκλεισμός "a being shut up, confinement." Cf. Busto Saiz 678. It is also his translation at Isa 24:22. Aquila, however, preferred a different prefixed preposition: for מַסְגֵּר at Ps 141(142):8 he has ἀποκλεισμός "exclusion" (here "prison," according to LSJ, without further reference); for the verb סָגַר the word ἀποκλείειν; for סָגוּר the word ἀπόκλειστος. For references see Reider-Turner. We might therefore expect some cognate of ἀποκλείειν at 4 Rgn 24:14.

The Armenian translation of Aquila's Greek—whatever that was—for מַסְגֵּר is [զ]ունրհաւնղակս, at least according to the MSS cited above. The word ունրհաւնղակ means "courier, express, messenger, estafet," according to Bedrossian. Arapkert'si lists fourteen passages in which it occurs in the Bible, all of them in the Old Testament. Except for two passages in Proverbs where it is used for δρομεύς "runner" (6:11; 24:34), all instances involve the verb τρέχειν "to run," and predominantly participles of the compound παρατρέχειν: 1 Rgn 8:11 προτρέχοντας; 22:17 τοῖς παρατρέχουσιν; 2 Rgn 15:1 and 3 Rgn 1:5 παρατρέχειν; 3 Rgn 14:27//2 Chr 12:10 τῶν παρατρεχόντων; 3 Rgn 14:28//2 Chr 12:11 οἱ παρατρέχοντες and τῶν παρατρεχόντων;[1] 4 Rgn 10:25 τοῖς παρατρέχουσιν; 11:19 τῶν παρατρεχόντων; 2 Chr 30:6, 10 οἱ τρέχοντες. In these various texts οἱ παρατρέχοντες "the runners" refers to a group of the king's bodyguards. Especially noteworthy in connection with 4 Rgn 24:14 is 3 Rgn 14:27-28.

In 3 Rgn 14:27 we read of the "leaders of the runners (οἱ ἡγούμενοι τῶν παρατρεχόντων) who guard (οἱ φυλάσσοντες) the gate of the King's house." This text offers a point of contact between the ունրհաւնղակք "couriers, i.e. runners" and those who shut gates or confine people within them (οἱ συγκλείοντες), and more especially an elite group of the latter.

The usual equivalent of οἱ παρατρέχοντες for the Armenian translator of 1-4 Rgn is ունրհաւնղակք. That equivalent need not hold for the translator of the marginalia. Indeed, if τοὺς παρατρεχόντας is the Greek underlying զունրհաւնղակս it is unlikely that the marginal reading belongs to Aquila: παρατρέχειν

---

[1] Aquila has at v 27 the simplex τρέχοντων: cf. B-M-Thack[app].

is not a verb that we know Aquila used and neither it nor the simplex τρέχειν could represent a translation that is literal enough for Aquila. It might be possible to argue that the signature is wrong: perhaps զսուրհանդակս—as a translation for τοὺς παρατρεχόντας—belongs to Symmachus.

The choice is this: if παρατρέχειν in participial form underlies the Armenian, the Greek was not a literal translation of the Hebrew and therefore does not likely belong to Aquila; on the other hand, perhaps the Armenian զսուրհանդակս is not a literal translation of the Greek from which it came and in this case the reading may belong to Aquila but cannot be determined precisely. (There is, of course, a third option: the marginal reading may be completely erroneous. I am disinclined to accept that possibility because the Armenian marginalia in 4 Rgn are generally accurate.)

Is the reading that of Aquila (consequence of choosing the second possibility above) or of Symmachus (first possibility)? Because readings from Symmachus predominate among these marginal readings it seems more likely that the direction of error would be toward signing Symmachus' name upon those not belonging to Symmachus rather than signing Aquila's erroneously. Of course, an error in the signature could also belong to the source from which these readings were taken, not to their transmission in Armenian.

It seems to me likely that Aquila's translation of מַסְגֵּר was τὸν ἀποκλείοντα, which utilizes the verb he connects elsewhere with the root סגר. Because there was a relationship established in 3 Rgn 14 between the սուրհանդակք and the keeping of gates, it is possible I suppose that an Armenian translator employed սուրհանդակ for Aquila's "gate-keeper." Would an Armenian translator, in rendering a single word here, remember the reference in 3 Ki 14? Possibly, since there are not that many marginal readings—a translator might refer back.

If one does not follow the suggestion outlined, it seems to me that one must say that զսուրհանդակս is really Symmachus'. The Greek literally underlying it, probably τοὺς παρατρεχόντας, would have to be his translation of מַסְגֵּר.

Generally the marginalia in the Armenian witnesses in 4 Rgn are accurate. So for the time being I assume that the reading is accurate. I am doubtful about the signature.

The Hebrew, Greek and Armenian equivalents are:

הַמַּסְגֵּר → Old Greek τὸν συνκλείοντα → Zohrapian զդպհիծu

→ conj. Sym τοὺς παρατρεχόντας ← Aq զուդրհանդալդ.

The Armenian is unique in preserving this reading. It can be cited in the second apparatus of B-M-Thack as follows:

τον συνκλειοντα] α′ (mend pro σ′) *cursores* Arm.

It is possible that Aquila's translation of הַמַּסְגֵּר was τὸν ἀποκλείοντα.

25:5 *

յարարpnվ[թ] յաճ zինիճ Sym

J428mg M177mg M188mg M2628mg V212mg Zohapp(mg) B-M-Thackapp2

V212 is cited on the basis of Zanolli 1234–1235.

The context concerns the fall of Jerusalem. In v 5 we are told that the Babylonian army pursued King Zedekiah and overtook him בְּעַרְבֹת "in the plains" of Jericho. The word in question is עֲרָבָה "desert," here in the plural with the preposition בְ "in."

The Greek, represented by MS B, has a transliteration: ἐν ἀραβώθ. The Armenian translation follows, in turn, with the transliteration յարարpnվ[թ. (The յ- is the form the preposition ի "in" takes before a vowel.) We may note that the Lucianic MSS preserve the translation κατὰ δυσμάς "to the west," which appears to be a reading derived from Theodotion: see the readings preserved in MS z (Rahlfs 554) and compare them with those preserved in the margins of the Armenian and the Syrohexapla, as cited in the second apparatus of B-M-Thack.

The Armenian witnesses noted above preserve Symmachus' translation for בְּעַרְבֹת. It is յաճ zինիճ "in the uninhabited (area)": preposition ի + աճ zէն (literally) "where there are no buildings" in the locative case + demonstrative marker -ճ. Symmachus is also preserved in a marginal reading in the Syro-hexapla. B-M-Thackeray's rendering of the Armenian and Syriac evidence is *in inhabitabili* "in an uninhabited (area)." The Syriac is ܒܠܐ ܥܡܝܪܬܐ, according to Field. The underlying Greek is probably ἐν τῇ ἀοικήτῳ, again according to Field. For Symmachus' use of ἀοίκητος "uninhabited" see Salvesen 143, n. 5: she gives a list of passages in the course of commenting upon Deut 34:8.

It appears that the translations of "the Three" are preserved in the text of Greek MS z (Rahlfs 554). See B-M-Thackeray's first apparatus where we find: εν αραβωθ] pr εν ομαλεσιν εν τη αοικητω κατα δυσμας z. The middle reading, i.e. ἐν τῇ ἀοικήτῳ, is that of Symmachus.

The Hebrew, Greek and Armenian equivalents are:

בָּעֲרָבֹת → B-related Greek MSS ἐν ἀραβώθ → Zohrapian յարաբովթ

→ Sym ἐν τῇ ἀοικήτῳ → Sym յանշինին.

In this instance the Armenian is not unique in preserving the translation of Symmachus. It confirms the witness of the Syro-hexapla. Both explicate the readings in Greek MS z which, in turn, provides Symmachus' original Greek translation. The citation of the Symmachus' evidence in the second apparatus in B-M-Thack can be revised as follows:

εν αραβωθ] σ' εν τη αοικητω z(in txt sine nom) Arm Syh.

25:13

զմնքենովթուն Zoh^app (զմնեք. Zoh^txt)] զխարիսխն   Sym

M2628^mg

Ex v 16, which see.

There is confusion in the tradition of marginalia among vv 13, 14 and 16. This arose because the words אֶת־(הַ)מְּכֹנוֹת) "(the) stands" in v 13 and אֶת־(הַ)יָּעִים) "(the) shovels" in v 14 were both transliterated into Greek but in the Armenian text there is a *translation* for the transliteration (καὶ τὰ) ιαμείν in v 14. This meant that the Symmachus marginal reading intended for ιαμείν (զկատ-ուսյան in Armenian) became attached to what remained in transliteration, namely զմնքենովթուն (μεχωνώθ). Since there was already a reading for զմնքե-նովթուն with a Symmachus signature, the other reading had its signature changed to Aquila. Finally, the fact that the transliteration զմնքենովթուն occurs at both v 13 and v 16 was a factor in the confusion.

25:14 *

զկատսաjան] զթակnjկան Aq mend pro Sym et ind mend supra (13)
զմեքենnվթան

J428ᵐᵍ M177ᵐᵍ M188ᵐᵍ M2628ᵐᵍ Zohᵃᵖᵖ⁽ᵐᵍ⁾ B-M-Thackᵃᵖᵖ²

The context is the pillaging of the Temple by the invading Babylonians. Beginning in v 13 a list is provided of the things they took away. The list includes the bronze pillars, the stands (אֶת־הַמְּכֹנוֹת), and the bronze sea. In vv 14–15 the list continues: they took "the pots, the shovels (אֶת־הַיָּעִים), the snuffers, the dishes for incense, and all the bronze vessels used in the temple service, (15) as well as the firepans and the basins." In v 16 it is noted that the weight of "the two pillars, the one sea, and the stands (אֶת־הַמְּכֹנוֹת)" and "the bronze of all these vessels was beyond weighing."

The Hebrew words given in the reproduction of this list were transliterated in the Old Greek translation. The translation of "the stands" (אֶת־הַמְּכֹנוֹת) will be examined in the next item, at v 16.

In v 14 the (וְאֶת־הַ)יָּעִים) "(the) shovels" was transliterated in the Old Greek: hence we read (καὶ τὰ) ιαμείν "(and the) *iamein* .

In the Armenian translation of v 14 we are surprised to find that the (καὶ τὰ) ιαμείν is not transliterated—as is common practice in such cases—but, rather, has been given a translation, namely զկատսաjան. The word կատսաj—see under կաթսաj in Bedrossian—means "copper, caldron, kettle, pot": so զկատսաjան (զ- is the definite object marker; -ս is the marker of the plural; -ն is the marker of the definite/demonstrative) means "the kettles." The translator probably guessed at the meaning of τὰ ιαμείν, based upon the context.

B-M-Thack cite marginal readings for Aquila and Symmachus that offer translations where τὰ ιαμείν stands in the Old Greek text:

και τα ιαμειν] α′ *et uncos* Syh | ιαμειν] α′ αγκιστρα σ′ αναληπτηρας j.

The Aquila translation is "hooks," in MS j (Rahlfs 243) and the Syrohexapla (ܟܠܘܒ̈ܐܕ , according to Field). The Symmachus translation is ἀναληπτῆρας "ladles" or "bowls."

The Armenian marginal reading is զԹակnյկան "pitchers, vessels; bowls." Zanolli suggests that the Greek underlying this is τὰς ὑδρίας: see his remarks about the reading զԹակnյկան at v 16. It is much more likely that the Armenian is a translation of Symmachus' ἀναληπτῆρας. The attribution to Aquila is erroneous.

The Hebrew, Greek and Armenian equivalents are:

אֶת־הַיָּעִים → Old Greek τὰ ἰαμείν → Zohrapian զկատաման

→ Sym (τὰς) ἀναληπτῆρας → Aq զԹակnյկան.

The Armenian reading attests the translation previously known from Greek MS j (Rahlfs 243). The second apparatus in B-M-Thack can be revised accordingly:

ιαμειν] α' αγκιστρα (> Arm) σ' (α' mend pro σ' Arm) αναληπτηρας j Arm.

B-M-Thack cite this reading at v 13 where it appears as μεχωνωθ] α' vasa Arm. That must be removed.

25:16 1°

զմեքենովԹան] զԹակnյկան Aq

J428^mg M188^mg M2628^mg V212^mg

> V212 is cited on the basis of Zanolli 1235.
> See vv 13, 14: the translation and attribution to Aquila belong at v 14.

25:16 2° *

զմեքենովԹան] զխարիխան Sym

J428^mg M188^mg

> Cf. v 13. Manuscript M2628—which is closely related to MSS J428 M188 in its marginalia—has the reading at v 13.

> Verse 16 provides further information about items already listed as booty

taken by the Babylonians from the Temple. It says that the weight of the bronze—
of which the things were made—was beyond weighing. The items are listed again
and included are הַמְּכֹנוֹת "the stands."

The Old Greek once again transliterates: τὰ μεχωνώθ.

The Armenian translation follows the Greek and transliterates: զմեքե-
նովթան. The transliteration is responsible for the desire for the translations
which the margins of some Armenian MSS supply.

The Symmachus reading reflects τὰς βάσεις, as at v 13. The Syriac is
ܘܬܚܒܠܢ "and the bases," according to Field.

The Hebrew, Greek and Armenian equivalents are:

> אֶת־הַמְּכֹנוֹת → Old Greek τοὺς μεχωνώθ → Zohrapian զմեքե-
> նովթան
>
> → Sym τὰς βάσεις → Sym զխարիսխն.

See the Lucianic MSS by(mg)c₂e₂ (Rahlfs 19-108 121mg 127 93) at v 13 for
the underlying Greek, τὰς βάσεις.

The Armenian զխարիսխն "the base(s)" confirms the reading for Symmachus, as known from the Syro-hexapla. The second apparatus in B-M-Thack can
be revised as follows:

> και τα μεχωνωθ] σ′ ε′(> Arm) et (> Arm) bases Arm Syh.

25:17 1° *

քովթար] ծայր սեանն Sym; կողակ Aq

The evidence is complicated to cite because the Aquila reading has been connected either with the word սարակ (MSS J428 M177 M2628) or with քովթարայն (MS M188). For that reason I will now cite the Symmachus and Aquila
readings separately, beginning with Symmachus, together with the MS evidence belonging to each.

քովթար] ծայր սեանն Sym

J428mg M177mg M188mg M2628mg(ծայր սեղանն) V212mg(ծայր սեան) Zohapp

V212 is cited on the basis of Zanolli 1235.

քովթար] կզակ Aq

J428^{mg} M177^{mg} M2628^{mg} hab ind mend supra սարակ; M188^{mg} hab ind mend supra քովթարայն

In v 17 the pillars of v 16 are described: we are told that "the height of the one pillar was eighteen cubits, and on it was a bronze capital." The word translated "capital" is כֹּתֶרֶת.

The Old Greek rendered the Hebrew word with a transliteration which, with the article, appears as τὸ χωθάρ.

The Armenian translation, in turn, has the transliteration քովթար. The marginal readings are a response to these transliterations which are incomprehensible to anyone who does not know Hebrew.

The difficulties of this item and their solution are linked to those of the next item and are discussed there in detail. Both Aquila's and Symmachus' translations of כֹּתֶרֶת are preserved in Armenian, though the marginal reading preserving Aquila's rendering—i.e. կզակ "capital"—became attached to the wrong word in the text, namely սարակ (σαβαχά, i.e. שְׂבָכָה "lattice").

The word կզակ means "architrave; lateral construction; wood-work," according to Bedrossian. It is used several times in Ezekiel 40 for τὸ θέα "place for seeing from," "auditorium." That is little help. Adjarian, however, defines կզակ as "buttress, lashing of a building, the capital of door-posts, … " (II 613) In a second entry for the word կզակ he refers us to խզակ which means "the fruit of the cypress, plane-tree and similar trees." (II 383) In that case the reference could be to fruit-shaped decorations on the capitals of the pillars: "and cypress fruit and pomegranate shapes upon it." The second usage works nicely alongside the pomegranates but is too far removed from the original.

The Greek underlying կզակ is κεφαλίς "capital," preserved in MS j (Rahlfs 243).

Symmachus' translation of כֹּתֶרֶת is also preserved in MS j. It is ἀκρογωνιαῖον "at the extreme angle." That is represented in Armenian by the words ծայր
սեանն "the extremity of the pillar."

The Hebrew, Greek and Armenian equivalents are:

כֹּתֶרֶת → Old Greek τὸ χωθάρ → Zohrapian քովթար

      → Aq κεφαλίς → Aq կոզակ

      → Sym ἀγρογωνιαῖον → Sym ծայր սեանն.

Greek and Armenian witnesses preserve Symmachus. The Armenian is already cited in B-M-Thack in support of the Symmachus reading; the Armenian witness can now be added for the Aquila translation as well:

χωθαρ 1°] α′ κεφαλις σ′ ακρογωνιαιον j Arm : χοθραθ Syh.

25:17 2° *

սարակ] վանդակս Sym (ind mend supra քովթարայն)

J428ᵐᵍ M177ᵐᵍ(վանդակ) M188ᵐᵍ(ind supra սարակին) M2628ᵐᵍ

The tradition of the marginal readings is doubly corrupted in this verse. The
Aquila reading which belongs with քովթար has become connected to սարակ or
քովթարայն and the Symmachus reading վանդակս "lattices" has become
connected to քովթարայն or to սարակին.

The textual situation is complex in v 17, rendered so because of the repetition of transliterations in the Old Greek text. In order to clarify the relationships
among Hebrew, Greek and Armenian it is useful to offer the text in its various
forms in parallel columns. The Hebrew, the text of MS B—printed in B-M-Thack,
the Armenian and the Lucianic texts are presented below. Two corruptions have
been replaced in MS B: σακαχαρθαί has been replaced by σαβαχά καὶ ροαί and
γαβαχά has been replaced by σαβαχά. These changes I have enclosed in square
brackets. The relevant marginal readings provided by B-M-Thack are found in an
additional column. Finally, I have underlined the transliterations.

MT	MS B	Arm	Lucianic	Mg. readings
שְׁמֹנֶה	ὀκτὼ καὶ	յութ-	ὀκτωκαί	
עֶשְׂרֵה	δέκα	տասն	δεκα	
אַמָּה	πήχεων	կանգուն	πήχεων	
קוֹמַת	ὕψος	բարձրու-	τὸ ὕψος	
		թիւն		
הָעַמּוּד	τοῦ στύλου	սիւնջ	τοῦ στύλου	
הָאֶחָד	τοῦ ἑνός,	անանն.	τοῦ ἑνός,	
וְכֹתֶרֶת	καὶ τὸ χωθὰρ	եւ բնկ-	καὶ τὰ ἐπι-	α΄ κεφαλίς
		թար	θέματα	σ΄ ἀγρογωνιαῖον
עָלָיו	ἐπ᾽ αὐτοῦ	զղնօի	τὰ χαλκᾶ	
נְחֹשֶׁת	τὸ χαλκοῦν,	ի վերայ	τῶν στύλων,	
		սրա.		
וְקוֹמַת	καὶ τὸ ὕψος	եւ բարձ-	τριῶν	
		րութիւն	πήχεων	
		սիւնջ	τὸ ὕψος	
הַכֹּתֶרֶת	τοῦ χωθὰρ	բնկթարաj	τοῦ ἐπιθέματος	
שָׁלֹשׁ	τριῶν	յերից		
אַמָּה	πήχεων	կանգունց:	τοῦ ἑνός,	
וּשְׂבָכָה	[σαβαχὰ	եւ սաբակ,	καὶ δίκτυον	σ΄ ἐπίθεμα
				rete sine nom[1]
וְרִמֹּנִים	καὶ ῥοαὶ]	եւ նռնա-	καὶ ῥοαὶ	
		ձեւք		
עַל־	ἐπὶ	ի վերայ	κύκλῳ	
הַכֹּתֶרֶת	τοῦ χωθὰρ	բնկթար-	τοῦ ἐπιθέματος,	
		այն		
סָבִיב	κύκλῳ,	շուրջա-		
		նակի		
הַכֹּל	τὰ πάντα	ամենայն	τὰ πάντα	

---

[1]Note that in B-M-Thack the referrent for these marginal readings is placed within round brackets, i.e. there is doubt about whether the marginal readings should be connected with σαβαχά. This is important in the case of ἐπίθεμα "capital," which would more appropriately belong as an explication for χωθάρ.

נְחֹשֶׁת	χαλκᾶ·	պղնձի:	χαλκᾶ·	
וְכָאֵלֶּה	καὶ κατὰ τὰ	րստ նմին	καὶ κατὰ τα	
	αὐτὰ	օրինակի	αὐτὰ	
		եւ		
לָעַמּוּד	τῷ στύλῳ	սեանն	τῷ στύλῳ	
הַשֵּׁנִי	τῷ δευτέρῳ	երկրորդի	τῷ δευτέρῳ	
עַל־	ἐπὶ	ի վերայ	ἐπίθεμα	
הַשְּׂבָכָה	τῷ [σαβαχά.]	սարսակին:	καὶ δίκτυον	
			καὶ ῥοαὶ	
			ἑκατόν.	

The translation of these various texts is as follows. The (literal) translation of the Hebrew is my own.

MT: "Eighteen cubits was the height of the one pillar and the capital upon it was made of bronze. The height of the capital was three cubits and there were lattice-work and pomegranates upon the capital, around it. The whole was bronze and as these so also the second pillar, upon the lattice-work."

Old Greek (MS B): "Eighteen cubits was the height of the one pillar and the chōthar upon it was made of bronze. The height of the chōthar was three cubits; there were sabacha and pomegranates upon the chōthar around, all of bronze. Like these was the second pillar, upon the sabacha ."

Armenian (Zohrapian): "Eighteen cubits was the height of the one pillar and the k'ovt'ar was bronze upon it. The height of the one k'ovt'ar was three cubits. There were sabak and pomegranate shapes upon the k'ovt'ar round about, all of bronze. In the same way also the second pillar, upon the sabak ."

Lucianic text: "Eighteeen cubits was the height of the one pillar and the capitals of the pillars were made of bronze. Three cubits was the height of the one capital and there were lattice-work and pomegranates around the capital, all of bronze. Like these was the capital of the second pillar and there were lattice-work and one hundred pomegranates."

Marginal readings cited in B-M-Thackeray's second apparatus for v 17 are as follows:

χωθαρ 1°] α′ κεφαλις σ′ ακρογωνιαιον j Arm : χοθραθ Syh | (σαβαχα)] σ′ επιθεμα j : *rete* Syh.

Aquila translated כֹּתֶרֶת(?) with the word κεφαλίς "capital"; Symmachus represented it with ἀκρογωνιαῖον "at the extreme angle," maybe then "at the extremity (of the pillar)." There is also a transliteration in the margin of the Syrohexapla, namely χοθραθ (ܚܘܬܪܬ, ΧΟΘΡΑΘ [sic: correct to ΧΟΘΑΡΘ?]), according to Field).

In the second citation of marginal readings in B-M-Thack for v 17, the referent in the text is σαβαχα [1°], which of course does not appear or, rather, is misspelled in MS B and therefore is enclosed in parentheses in the citation. Manuscript j (Rahlfs 243) has a marginal reading attributed to Symmachus, ἐπίθεμα "capital," and the Syro-hexapla has an unsigned reading which B-M-Thack cite in Latin: *rete* "lattice-work." There is a problem with this citation, which becomes acute with the addition of the Armenian evidence: the σαβαχά is "lattice-work" and the word ἐπίθεμα could hardly stand in its place as a translation for שְׂבָכָה. One might suggest that this marginal reading stands better in place of σαβαχα [2°]: indeed the Lucianic MSS have such a text and it makes sense at the end of the verse. Lucian may have taken the reading over from Symmachus, whose signature it bears in MS j.

The transliterations in the Armenian version and the marginal readings as they appear in the various MSS are as follows:

քով[թար] ձայր սեանն Sym J428 M177 M188 M2628 V212
                                Zoh^app(mg)

քով[թարայ

սաբակ] կոգակ Aq J428 M177 M2628
քով[թարայն] կոգակ Aq M188
                      վանդակ Sym M177
                      վանդակս Sym J428 M2628
սաբակին] վանդակս Sym M188.

I suggest the following solutions to the problems here. First, կոզակ "capital" is unlikely to have stood in Aquila's text where the transliteration սաբակ (i.e. σαβαχά) stands. Rather, I think that կոզակ belongs as Aquila's translation where քովթար stands. That is, կոզակ is a translation of κεφαλίς "capital."

In the Armenian witnesses the Symmachus reading in 4 Rgn usually stands before, literally above, the Aquila reading. In MS J428 there are five marginal readings in a column in the margin beside vv 16–17:

ակ

գթակ

ոյկան

սիմ

գխարիս

խն

սիմ

ծայրւսեանն

ակ

կոզակ

սիմ

վանդակս

It seems to me that the readings սիմ ծայր սեանն and ակ΄ կոզակ belong together: the translation of Aquila typically follows that of Symmachus. Each is a translation for the transliteration քովթար. Aquila's translation mistakenly became attached to the next word in transliteration, namely սաբակ (σαβαχά).

In turn the Symmachus translation became attached to the wrong referent. The word վանդակս "lattice-work" should be the marginal reading for սաբակ (σαβαχά, i.e. שְׂבָכָה "lattice"). This is the equivalent of the unsigned reading in the Syro-hexapla, Latin *rete* "lattice." Field gives the Syriac as ܪܡܝܬܐ, to which he adds "sic," presumably because of the two dots above the ܡ. The word ܪܡܝܬܐ means "net, snare," but can be used in an expression for lattice windows.

It appears then that the Armenian provides a signature for the translation "lattice-work," B-M-Thackeray's *rete* in the Syro-hexapla.

Reider-Turner note *rete* as the Latin equivalent for δίκτυον "lattice-work" in the Latin translation of α' σ' at Jer 5:26. The Greek is also extant for that passage. Reider-Turner's citation for δίκτυον is as follows (their underlining indicates retroversion):

δίκτυον רֶשֶׁת ["net; network"] Ps 30(31):5; שְׁכִי [NRSV "trap": meaning uncertain] Jer 5:26 [α'] σ' θ' ✗.

δίκτυον שְׁכִי Jer 5:26 α' σ' lat. (*rete*).

Zanolli already suggested that it is the Symmachus reading in Armenian which reflects the word δίκτυον "lattice-work," found in some Greek MSS, specifically the Lucianic MSS boc₂e₂ (Rahlfs 19-108 82 127 93). He was correct in this supposition, in my opinion.

It is puzzling why δίκτυον is represented by the plural վանդակս. If the plural is the result of attraction to the plural նռնաձևք "pomegranate shapes," we would expect վանդակք. (I tend to dismiss the singular վանդակ, preserved in M177: the scribe of the marginalia of that MS seems to have been rather careless.)

The Hebrew, Greek and Armenian equivalents are:

שְׂבָכָה → Old Greek σαβαχά → Zohrapian սաբակ

→ conj. Sym δίκτυον → Sym վանդակս.

In this instance the Armenian provides the signature for a translation already known from the margin of the Syro-hexapla. The Greek underlying both the Syriac and Armenian is known from Lucianic MSS. The second apparatus in B-M-Thack can be revised as follows to reflect the contribution which the Armenian evidence makes:

(σαβαχα)] σ' δίκτυον Arm Syh(sine nom).

As suggested above, it seems likely that σ' επιθεμα j—which B-M-Thack place with this item—belongs with γαβαχά, i.e. MS Vaticanus' corruption of σαβαχά [2°]. (The word σαβαχά [1°] is also corrupt in MS B, as noted.)

25:19 *

եւթն] վաթսուն

J428mg M188mg(Ꝗ) M2628mg(Ꝗ) Zohapp(mg); cf. B-M-Thackappl

Manuscripts M188 M2628 have the abbreviation Ꝗ, i.e. Ꝗ with a line above.
In vv 18–19 there is a list of various people whom the Babylonian captain
of the guard took from Jerusalem. Included among these are "sixty men of the people of the land." The word "sixty" is a translation of םִשִּׁשׁ.

The Old Greek represents םִשִּׁשׁ with the word ἑξήκοντα "sixty," according to MS B. There is some variation in the textual tradition and that is reflected
in B-M-Thackeray's first apparatus:

ἑξήκοντα] ἑξι g : ἑξ Ndeᵃ? p–vz Syh : επτα A Arm-ed.

That is to say, various witnesses attest "six" rather than sixty; MS A and the Armenian version attest "seven." (MS g is Rahlfs 158; d 107; e 52; p 106; q 120; r 700; s
130; t 134; u 372; v 245; z 554.) The Syro-hexapla is among those witnesses which
has "six" in the text. It has a marginal reading "sixty" which B-M-Thack cite in their
second apparatus:

ἑξήκοντα] σ′ (?) sexaginta Syh.

Field cites the Syriac marginal reading as follows: ܫܬܝܢ . ܣ . The signature is ε′ (Quinta) which B-M-Thack suggest might rather be σ′. (Presumably, B-
M-Thackeray's citation of the evidence represents a re-checking of whatever is
found in Field and thus should be more reliable.) It is unfortunate that the Armenian
preserves no signature.

The marginal reading reflects contact with the Hebrew or with a Greek text
that read "sixty." The latter includes much of the Old Greek text tradition; indeed it
appears likely that Origen's fifth column read ἑξήκοντα. A marginal reading from
"the Three" only makes sense if the text for which it is intended did not read ἑξήκοντα. At the same time, one must add a qualification: sometimes it is not clear why
a reading from "the Three" is provided in the margin.

It seems to me that there is some question about whether the marginal
reading here is a genuine translation of one of "the Three," or Quinta for that matter.
It could have been derived from comparison among Greek MSS.

The Hebrew, Greek and Armenian equivalents are as follows:

םִשִּׁשׁ → Old Greek ἑξήκοντα

→ MS A type text ἑπτά → Zohrapian եւթն

→ σ′ (?) ἑξήκοντα → sine nom վաթսունն.

The Armenian evidence can be added to that of the Syro-hexapla in B-M-Thackeray's second apparatus:

ἑξήκοντα] σ′ (?) *sexaginta* Arm(sine nom) Syh.

25:27 *

(յամ՝ի) թագաւորութեան իւրոյ Zoh^app] յորում թագաւորեաց Sym

J428^mg M2628^mg Zoh^txt

The context concerns the release from prison of King Jehoakin of Judah. We are told that King Evil-merodach of Babylon did this בִּשְׁנַת מָלְכוֹ אֶת־רֹאשׁ "in the year that he began to reign."

The Old Greek translation for this is ἐν τῷ ἐνιαυτῷ τῆς βασιλείας αὐτοῦ τὴν κεφαλήν, "in the year of his kingship, the first" according to MS Vaticanus. B-M-Thack cite no variants to that text.

The reading Zohrapian cites in his apparatus corresponds to this rendering: յամ՝ի թագաւորութեան իւրոյ զգլուխ. This text is in fact original: it is the text of J1925 (f.192v, col.2, ↓20) and M1500 (f.183v, col.1, ↓4). Zohrapian's base MS—Venice 1508—represents a text which has switched original text and marginal reading. Somewhat similarly, in MS M177 the text has simply been corrected in a very obvious sort of way to what was a marginal reading, i.e. to յամին յորում թագաւորեաց.

Zohrapian's text has now յամին յորում թագաւորեաց զգլուխ "in the year in which he ruled, the first" which is identical to the parallel passage in Jer 52:31. The underlying Greek at Jer 52:31 is ἐν τῷ ἐνιαυτῷ ᾧ ἐβασίλευσε τὴν κεφαλήν.

What is now the text in Zohrapian was once a marginal reading which, in MSS J428 M2628, is identified as the translation of Symmachus. The words which appear in the margin are յորում թագաւորեաց "in which he ruled."

Zohrapian's base MS, dated 1319, already has the marginal reading but it is without signature. Though MSS J428 and M2628 are both 17th century witnesses their marginalia are of a piece with those of the earlier MSS which are part of this study. I am more inclined to accept the genuineness of the marginal reading here than to regard it simply as ex par.

The Greek underlying the Armenian marginal reading may well be the same as the Old Greek in Jer 52:31. In that case the following equivalents among Hebrew, Greek and Armenian can be set out:

מָלְכֹו → Old Greek τῆς βασιλείας αὐτοῦ → Armenian (Zohrapian apparatus) Թագաւորութեան իւրոյ

→ Sym conj. ᾧ ἐβασίλευσε ← Sym յորում Թագաւորեաց.

The difference between the Old Greek and the translation of Symmachus lies in the way the bound phrase is treated. The Old Greek translates literally "(the year) of his kingship"; Symmachus translates מָלְכֹו with a clause ᾧ ἐβασίλευσε "when he ruled."

This Symmachus reading can be represented in the second apparatus of B-M-Thackeray as follows:

της βασιλειας αυτου] σ' *quo regnavit* Arm.

VIII. 2 Chronicles

There are only two marginal readings for 2 Chronicles and both are taken from the parallel texts in 4 Rgn.

23:17

զմաթան] զերկերիւր

J1928 J1934

This marginal reading is drawn from the parallel passage in 4 Rgn 11:18 where զերկերիւր is Aquila's translation—which see. Manuscripts J1928 J1934 often have marginal readings whose origin is the Latin Vulgate, but that is not the case here: the Vulgate reads Matthan.

36:3

Ներաւով] կաղ   Sym

M3705ᵐᵍ

The MS uses ※ for an index sign. This marginal reading appears to have been taken from the parallel passage in 4 Rgn 23:29, which see.

IX. Job

Working with the marginal readings in Armenian Job is rendered complex because the Hebrew text is difficult and the Old Greek translation is so free; further, the Armenian notes seem to be free renderings.

Usually Aquila is abbreviated to ակ in MSS but V623 has ակիւ at Job 2:7 and ակիւլ at 3:23.

Greek text: J. Ziegler, ed., *Septuaginta, Vetus Testamentum Graecum; Auctoritate Academiae Scientiarum Gottingensis editum, XI,4 Iob* ; Göttingen: Vandenhoeck & Ruprecht 1982. Ziegler does not cite Armenian evidence for readings from "the Three," even though he collates the Armenian on the basis of Zohrapian who has this evidence in his apparatus.

J. R. Busto Saiz, *La Traduccion de Simaco en el Libro de Los Salmos* (Textos y Estudios "Cardenal Cisneros" 22; Madrid: Instituto "Arias Montano" 1978). • S. Peter Cowe, "An Armenian Job Fragment from Sinai and its Implications," *Oriens Christianus* 76 (1992) 123–157. • C. Cox, *Hexaplaric Materials Preserved in the Armenian Version* (SBLSCS 21; Atlanta: Scholars 1986).• Édouard Dhorme, *A Commentary on the Book of Job* , tr. Harold Knight (Nashville: Thomas Nelson 1984 [1967; French 1926]). • Peter J. Gentry, *The Askerisked Materials in the Greek Job* (SBLSCS 38; Atlanta: Scholars 1995). • G.W.H. Lampe, ed., *A Patristic Greek Lexicon* (Oxford: Clarendon 1968 [1961]). • Solomon Mandelkern, *Veteris Testamenti Concordantiae Hebraicae atque Chaldaicae* (Schocken 1937; repr. Graz: Academische Druck-U. Verlagsanstalt 1955). • Natalio Fernández Marcos, "Some Reflections on the Antiochian Text of the Septuagint," in *Studien zur*

318   Job

Septuaginta — Robert Hanhart zu Ehren , ed. Detlef Fraenkel, Udo Quast, John
Wm. Wevers (AAWG; MSU XX; Göttingen: Vandenhoeck & Ruprecht 1990)
219–229. • Ursula and Dieter Hagedorn, *Nachlese zu den Fragmenten der jüngeren
griechischen Übersetzer des Buches Hiob* (NAWG; I. Philologisch-Historische
Klasse 10; Göttingen: Vandenhoeck & Ruprecht 1991). I am grateful to Peter Gen-
try for bringing this work to my attention. • J.W. Wevers, ed., *Septuaginta, Vetus
Testamentum Graecum; Auctoritate Academiae Scientarum Gottingensis editum,
III, 2 Deuteronomium* (Göttingen: Vandenhoeck & Ruprecht 1977).

2:1 *

կալ 2°] արձակագետալ Aq

J1928mg J1934mg(ind supra կալ 1°) M177mg(sine nom) M354mg(sine nom) M2587mg
(sine ind in txt) V623mg V935mg V1270mg V1507mg(sine ind in txt) V1634mg W11mg
(sine nom) Zohapp(mg)(ind supra կալ 1°)

In this verse we read, according to the Hebrew text: "One day the heavenly
beings came to present themselves before the LORD, and Satan also came among
them to present himself before the LORD." The words "to present himself" are a
translation of לְהִתְיַצֵּב. The Hebrew is the *hitpael* infinitive of the root יצב, a
verb which occurs only in the *hitpael* in the Hebrew Bible. It means "take one's
position."

The Old Greek translation alters the last clause:

It took place when this day came
and the angels of God came to stand (παραστῆναι) before the Lord,
and the devil came in their midst.

According to Zeigler's second apparatus, the catena group of MSS —i.e. *C*
—preserve in their margins a signed hexaplaric reading for the end of the verse.
The citation in Zeigler is as follows: **1c** fin] α' θ' + ※ παραστῆναι ἐναντίον
τοῦ κυρίου *C* . (Note: this is Gentry's 2:1d—see *Asterisked Materials* , 31–32.)

That is, the hexaplaric plus which has come from Aquila and Theodotion adds "to stand before the Lord." By the way, Ziegler notes that this is the first stichos with an asterisk in Job: see p. 134 of his edition.

The Armenian translation of v 1, cited according to Zohrapian's edition, is as follows:

Եւ եղեւ իբրեւ զօրս զայս.
և եկին հրեշտակք աստուծոյ կալ առաջի աստուծոյ.
եկն և սատանայ ի մէջ նոցա ✳ ընդ նոսա կալ ✳ առաջի
տեառն:

And it took place in these days
and the angels of God came to stand before God;
Satan also came in the midst of them ✳ with them to stand ✳ before the
Lord.

As one can see, the Armenian text already has hexaplaric additions. The last line reads "Satan also came in their midst, ✳ with them to stand ✳ before the Lord." Properly marked the hexaplaric plus is ✳ կալ առաջի տեառն [◄], i.e. ✳ παραστῆναι ἐναντίον τοῦ κυρίου ◄. (Not all Armenian witnesses attest ընդ նոսա "with them": cf. Zohrapian's apparatus. It is secondary.)

Since the hexaplaric plus is represented in the Armenian text itself, what are we to make of the marginal reading? The verb կալ corresponds to παραστῆναι: that is clear from the second line.

The verb արձանանալ means "to become like a statue, to be firm, fixed; to stop; to stand, to stand upright." Its meaning in this context is simply "to stand" which makes it a synonym for կալ. It appears here in its past participial form արձանացեալ "standing." The lexical form of the marginal reading does not therefore coincide with the form of the Hebrew from whence it has ostensibly come. Aquila's translation, namely παραστῆναι, does agree with the Hebrew infinitival form.

In Armenian the Aquila reading in the past participial form makes sense after "Satan also came ..." Arapkerts'i has a few references for the verb արձանանալ in his concordance: it translates στηλόω "*set up as a* στήλη or *monument* ; pass. *to*

be so set up, stand firm " (Judg 18:16[Alexandrinus text], 17 [no Vaticanus text]; 1
Rgn 17:16 [o´]; 2 Rgn 1:19; 18:30; 23:12) except at Judg 18:16 (Vaticanus text: ἵσ-
τημι, i.e. ἐστῶντες).

What has happened here? The Armenian marginal reading attributed to
Aquila may be an inner-Armenian exegetical gloss of some kind. On the other hand,
the following is possible. The Armenian marginal reading may derive from a (presumably Greek) manuscript which had the hexaplaric reading in the margin. That
marginal note was παραστῆναι ἐναντίον τοῦ κυρίου. The translator of the note
saw that this was already represented in the Armenian text and therefore offered an
alternative to կալ which stands in the text. The alternative he chose was արձանացալ, a synonym which as a participle could modify կալ, hence "stood upright." That seems to me to be a possible explanation. It means that the signed hexaplaric reading is genuine but has been altered because of the circumstances of the
text.

The Hebrew, Greek and Armenian equivalents are:

לְהִתְיַצֵּב → Aq Th παραστῆναι → Zohrapian կալ

→ Aq Th παραστῆναι → Aq արձանացալ.

Ziegler does not cite the Armenian marginal evidence, probably because it is
confusing. It should be cited in the second apparatus, perhaps as follows:

1c fin] α´ θ´ + ✳ παραστῆναι (sub nom α´ Arm) ἐναντίον τοῦ κυρίου *C*.

3:23 *

փակեաց գնովաւ] ոչ իմացյոց նմա Aq

J1928mg J1934mg J2561mg M177mg M354mg M2587mg V623mg V1270mg
V1507mg Zohapp(mg)

In ch 3 Job curses the day of his birth. In v 23 he laments:

Why is light given to one who cannot see the way,
whom God has fenced in?

The second line is a translation of וַיָּסֶךְ אֱלוֹהַּ בַּעֲדוֹ. The verb סכךְ means in the *hifil* —though KBH indicate the form here at 3:23 may be *qal* also— "block off, cover, make unapproachable." The *hifil* form suggested only occurs at Exod 40:21; Ps 5:12; 91:4; and here. The preposition בַּעַד is used idiomatically with verbs of shutting or closing the door behind oneself, or upon oneself, therefore of shutting oneself off. Literally the Hebrew here says "and God shut him in." The Old Greek translation of v 23—typically free—is:

θάνατος ἀνδρὶ ἀνάπαυμα,
συνέκλεισεν γὰρ ὁ θεὸς κατ' αὐτοῦ·
Death is peace for a man,
For God has shut [the door] against him.

The Armenian translation of v 23 is:

Մահ մարդոյ հանգիստ է [×] յորմէ ծանապարհն
թաքեաւ ի մՖանէ [ˇ].
զի փակեաց զնոյան աստուած:

The Armenian translation contains the hexaplaric plus at the end of the first line. Ziegler identifies the plus as Theodotion's translation and provides the Greek in his apparatus: οὗ ἡ ὁδὸς ἀπεκρύβη ἀπ' αὐτοῦ. With that plus the English translation of the Armenian is:

Death for a man is rest [×] from the one whose way is hidden from
    him [ˇ];
because God has closed it up around him.

According to Ziegler, Symmachus' translation of 23b is extant. It is:

ἀπέφραξεν ὁ θεὸς κατ' αὐτοῦ
God shut [it?] against him.

This is like the Old Greek but uses the synonym ἀποφράσσειν rather than συγκλείειν. The only citation for Aquila in v 23 comes at the end where Ziegler cites Aquila as having κατ᾽ αὐτόν instead of κατ᾽ αὐτοῦ.

The marginal reading attributed to Aquila in the Armenian witnesses is ոչ իմացոյց նմա "he [i.e. God] did not let him understand." It is intended for the words փակեաց զնովաւ "he [God] enclosed him." The full line would then read "because God has not let him gain understanding." That is not a literal rendering of the Hebrew: see the Hebrew text given above. How does one get from "block off" to "not let understand?" The answer is to be found in BDB.

BDB derive the word יָסֶךְ from †II.[סוּךְ, סׂיךְ] "hedge, or fence about, shut in," parallel form of שׂוּךְ which occurs at 1:10. They suggest comparing Syriac ܣܟ "finish," Pa'el ܣܟ [sayek] "finish, conclude, comprehend." It would appear therefore that there are grounds for concluding that Aquila saw in this rare Hebrew root the meaning "comprehend." It remains impossible to determine what Greek word Aquila used. The best one can do is to cite the Armenian in "kitchen Latin."[1]

The Hebrew, Greek and Armenian can be cited as follows:

בַּעֲדוֹ ... יָסֶךְ (וַ) → Old Greek συνέκλεισεν ... κατ᾽ αὐτοῦ → Zohrapian փակեաց զնովաւ

→ Aq *non instruxit eum* ← Aq ոչ իմացոյց նմա.

The Armenian is unique in preserving this reading of Aquila. It can be cited in Ziegler's second apparatus for 23b as follows:

23b] σ᾽ ἀπέφραξεν ὁ θεὸς κατ᾽ αὐτοῦ C′ (Olymp) | συνέκλεισεν ... κατ᾽ αὐτοῦ] α᾽ *non instruxit eum* Arm | κατ᾽ αὐτοῦ] α᾽ κατ᾽ αὐτόν 252.

4:6

կաակաձր] յոյս Aq

J1928mg J1934mg J2561(mg)(sine nom) M177mg(յոյս ֊ֆn sine nom) M354mg(sine nom) Zohapp(mg)(sine nom)

---

[1]"Kitchen Latin" is J.W. Wevers' description of the somewhat wanting Latin employed in retroversions that one finds, e.g. in B-M-Thackeray: it gets the point across though it lacks good style.

Chapter 4 is the first discourse of Eliphaz. In v 6 he poses a question:

Is not your fear of God your confidence,
and the integrity of your ways your hope?

The word underlying "your hope" is תִּקְוָתֶךָ.

The Old Greek renders these two lines:

πότερον οὐχ ὁ φόβος σού ἐστιν ἐν ἀφροσύνῃ
καὶ ἡ ἐλπίς σου καὶ ἡ ἀκακία τῆς ὁδοῦ σου;
Is not your former fear a matter of foolishness
and your hope the blamelessness of your way?

The words ἡ ἐλπίς σου translate תִּקְוָתֶךָ.

The Armenian translation of these two lines of Greek is:

Ո՛չ ապաքէն երկեւղդ քո անգգաւութիւն է.
Եւ կասկածդ քո, եւ անչարութիւն ճանապարհի քո:
Your fear is not then foolishness;
nor your doubt; nor the blamelessness of your way.

The Armenian translation uses not "hope" to translate ἡ ἐλπίς but the word կասկած "doubt," an unusual choice to be sure. It is probably the result of the translator taking καὶ ἡ ἐλπίς σου with ἀφροσύνῃ. There are other instances in the Armenian Bible where կասկած is used for ἐλπίς where the context indicates that the "hope" is more a "forboding"—a meaning which ἐλπίς can also have in classical Greek: see Isa 28:10, 13, 19; 32:9, 10.

The word equivalent which we might expect for ἐλπίς in v 6 is յոյս, i.e. "hope." Arapkerts'i cites eleven occurrences of յոյս in Job and in each of these յոյս represents ἐλπίς: 2:9; 5:16; 6:8; 8:13; 11:17 (Ziegler: 18), 20; 14:7; 17:15; 19:10; 27:8; 30:15.

That brings us to the marginal reading in the Armenian MSS. It is signed "Aquila." Fortunately Aquila's translation of the second line of v 6 is extant in

Greek catena MSS. Ziegler cites it in his second apparatus: ἡ ὑπομονή σου καὶ ἡ ἁπλότης τῶν ὁδῶν σου "your patience and the integrity of your ways." Aquila's equivalent for תִּקְוָה "hope" is therefore the word ὑπομονή "patience; endurance." The Armenian equivalent for ὑπομονή is a word like համբերութիւն "patience" (which is used to translate ὑπομονή at Ps 38[39]:7; 61[62]:5; 70[71]:5; throughout the New Testament) or ակնկալութիւն "expectation, hope" (used for ὑπομονή at Jer 14:8; 17:13).

It is unlikely that a translator would have used յոյս to render the word ὑπομονή.

One can conclude that the word յոյս in the margins of these Armenian MSS only with unlikelihood can take us back to Aquila's ὑπομονή. What is more likely is that the marginal reading represents a comparison with the text of Greek MSS: it serves to correct the (mis-?)translation կասկած. Aquila's name was attached sometime later in some manuscripts. Indeed, that among the witnesses cited above only J1928 J1934 carry Aquila's signature makes one suspicious at the outset. These two 17th century MSS are virtually sister witnesses so that the evidence is further reduced.

6:27 *

խաղացեալ էք] ոտն հարկանէք

J1928mg J1934mg J2561mg M177mg M354mg M2587mg W11mg(pr և) Zohapp(mg)

Manuscript W11 has և with the marginal reading rather than in the text before խաղացեալ էք.

Job responds to this accusers in the Hebrew text:

You would even cast lots over the orphan,
and bargain over your friend.

The word translated "bargain" is תִכְרוּ, from II. כרה which means 1. "purchase, buy," or, as here, 2. "haggle, bargain (over s.thg. עַל) Jb 6:27; 40:30. †

The word—at least with this meaning—is rather rare.

The Old Greek translates this verse:

πλὴν ὅτι ἐπ' ὀρφανῷ ἐπιπίπτετε,
ἐνάλλεσθε δὲ ἐπὶ φίλῳ ὑμῶν.
Except that you fall upon an orphan,
and leap upon your friend.

Here the word וְתִכְרוּ is translated by ἐνάλλεσθε, rendered here as "leap (upon)." Dhorme suggests that the Old Greek seems to connect וְתִכְרוּ with the root כרר "dance, jump." (93)

The Armenian translation of the verse reads:

Բայց զի իբրեւ ի վերայ որբոյ յարուցեալ էք ի վերայ իմ·
և խաղացեալ էք ի վերայ բարեկամի ծերոյ:
But as upon an orphan you have risen up upon me;
and you have leaped upon your friend.

The Armenian uses the words խաղացեալ էք—the participle is from խաղամ "to jump, leap; *fig.* ridicule, mock"—to render the Greek ἐνάλλεσθε. Both words have a literal and figurative meaning; therefore the Armenian translation is quite adequate.

The Armenian marginal reading for խաղացեալ էք is ոտն հարկանէք "you trod under foot," or "despised." The two are synonymous. It is difficult to see what has been contributed by providing the marginal reading, except perhaps a more striking expression.

Ziegler cites a marginal reading in Greek MS 406 but it has ἐνάλλεσθε, just like the Old Greek, and is unsigned. If this is a reading from "the Three" one might think it unlikely to be the source of the Armenian marginal reading since the translation is the same, at least for the first part of the line concerned. That need not be the case, however.

The Vulgate translates this verse: super pupillum inruitis et subvertere nitimini amicum vestrum. Translated this is "upon an orphan you rush and you are exerting yourselves to overturn (i.e. destroy) your friend." In this case ἐνάλλεσθε is translated by *subvertere nitimini*: it is most unlikely that the Armenian marginal reading has come from this periphrastic rendering in the Vulgate.

So where has the marginal reading come from?

In his second apparatus Ziegler provides for v 27b the hexaplaric reading of MS 406: ἐνάλλεσθε κα⟨ὶ⟩ ⟨φι⟩λίαν σχηματίζ⟨ετε⟩ (σχειμ. cod) "you leap upon and you fashion friendship." (This appears to represent two different renderings of תִּכְרוּ.) It is just possible that this reading appeared in the margin of some MS to which Armenian scribes had access, in which case it afforded an opportunity for them to give another translation for the word ἐνάλλεσθε. That other translation is ոտն հարկանէք which indicates secondary contact with Greek ἐνάλλεσθε.

It is difficult to be sure that the retranslation of ἐνάλλεσθε represents contact with "the Three" rather than simply secondary contact with the Old Greek tradition.

This reading might be cited in Ziegler's second apparatus as follows:

27b] ἐνάλλεσθε κα⟨ὶ⟩ ⟨φι⟩λίαν σχηματίζ⟨ετε⟩ (σχειμ. cod) 406 | ἐνάλλεσθε Arm.

7:1

զփորձութիւն] հիւանդն

J1925mg(sine ind) M177mg(inc)

In MS W11 the word հիւանդն is in the text, following զփորձու֊թիւն.

The English of the first line of v 1 is "Do not human beings have a hard service on earth, …?" The words "Do not human beings have a hard service" are a translation of הֲלֹא־צָבָא לֶאֱנוֹשׁ. Literally this says, "Is it not hard service for people?" The word צָבָא is used frequently in the Hebrew Bible for military service.

The Old Greek renders this line πότερον οὐχὶ πειρατήριόν ἐστιν ὁ βίος ἀνθρώπου ἐπὶ τῆς γῆς "Is not it a trial, the life of a person on earth?" The word in question is πειρατήριον which means "trial."

The Armenian text printed by Zohrapian reads for this line Ո՞չ ապաքէն իրրեւ զփորձունիւն՞ են վարք մարդոյ ի վերայ երկրի, i.e. "Is it not then as a trial the life of a person upon earth?" The word փորձունիւն is a good translation for πειρατήριον.

The marginal reading in the Armenian witness(es) is հիւանդն, which means "sick." The adjective հիւանդ has the demonstrative/definite suffix -ն. Surely this is an interpretive comment: it explains what kind of trial Job's life has become.

Ziegler cites Aquila's translation of this line on the basis of Greek catena MSS. Aquila uses the word στρατεία, "expedition, campaign" for צָבָא.

It seems quite a reach to take հիւանդ as a translation of στρατεία. I conclude therefore that հիւանդ is probably an inner-Armenian reading.

7:21

կանխեալ] քանզի առաւատ է

J1928mg J1934mg M177mg M2587mg W11mg Zohapp(mg)

Manuscript M354 has index signs above կանխեալ in the text but no marginal reading.

Job says to the Almighty:

> Why do you not pardon my transgression
> and take away my iniquity?
> For now I shall lie in the earth;
> you will seek me, but I shall not be.

The last two lines form a conclusion to a series of rhetorical questions. Job threatens God with the consequences of God's non-intervention, namely his death. The words "For now I shall lie in the earth; you will seek me, but I shall not be" are the NRSV's translation of אֶשְׁכַּב וְשִׁחֲרְתַּנִי וְאֵינֶנִּי כִּי־עַתָּה לֶעָפָר.

The Old Greek translates the last two lines in the following way:

νυνὶ δὲ εἰς γῆν ἀπελεύσομαι,
ὀρθρίζων δὲ οὐκέτι εἰμι.

but now I will go away to the earth,
no longer rising early in the morning.

Dhorme explains ὀρθρίζων for שֲׁחַרְתָּנִי as follows: "In the light of שַׁחַר
'dawn', וְשִׁחַרְתַּנִי is rendered ὀρθρίζων in G, …" (111)

The Armenian translation of these two lines is:

Արդ աւա յերկիր դառնայցեմ կանխեալ,
և այլ ոչ եւս իցեմ։

Now indeed to the earth I will return early,
and I will be no more.

The Armenian has taken ὀρθρίζων with the previous line. The verb կանխել
means "rise, get up early," i.e. it is a good equivalent for ὀρθρίζων. Standing as it
does with the verb դառնայցեմ, "I will return," it is best rendered by the adverb "early."

The marginal reading քանզի առաւաւտ է means "because it is morning." It is cited here on the basis of the 13th century Cilician MS M177 and four
17th century witnesses. (A [the original?] copyist has placed "lightning-bolt"
signs—somewhat like the Hebrew yod , i.e. י—above կանխեալ as well as
above the index sign. This sign is used for an index sign in Armenian MSS; it is also used for corrections. Perhaps it means in MS M177 that the marginal reading is
to be disregarded, though one cannot be sure.)

The marginal reading is connected with կանխեալ, i.e. ὀρθρίζων, which
can be used of getting up early (in the morning).

Ziegler cites the Symmachus translation κἂν ζητήσῃς με, οὐχ ὑπάρξω
"and if you seek me, I will not be" which is preserved in catena MSS, the Syro-
hexapla, and Pitra's collection Analecta sacra spicilegio Solesmensi parata .

This marginal reading does appear not to come from "the Three" since it
does not relate to the Hebrew וְשִׁחַרְתַּנִי. It is a very unusual reading and one is
puzzled to make sense of it. It appears to be related to a secondary contact with the

word ὀρθρίζων, which is used of getting up early *in the morning* . The confusion has arisen because the old Armenian translation took this word ὀρθρίζων with the first stich, rather than the second. When the marginal reading was added, the scribe was constrained to attach it to կանխեալ which stands with the first stich.

8:21 *

գոհութեամբ] ապապական Sym (ind supra 21a ծառ ու)

V935mg

Chapter 8 is Bildad's first speech at the end of which he says that God will not reject a blameless person (v 20); further that (v 21):

He will yet fill your mouth with laughter,
and your lips with shouts of joy.

The word "laughter" is a translation of שְׂחֹוק; "with shouts of joy" represents תְּרוּעָה. The former means 1. **laughter** Ps 126₂; — 2. **fun, sport** Pr 10₂₃; — 3. **mockery, laughingstock** Je 20₇. Brown-Driver-Briggs cite Job 8:21 under the meaning "laughter."

The word תְּרוּעָה has the following meanings: 1. (**signal of**) **alarm**: *hêrî a' t ᵉrû'â* Jos 6₅; — 2. **shout (of joy)** 1S 45ᵣ; — 3. (any) **signal** (given w. wind instrument) Lv 25₉. BDB offer the same meanings as KBH generally speaking (1. *alarm* of war; 2. *blast* for march; 3. *shout of joy* with religious impulse) but place Job 8:21 in a separate category, namely *shout of joy* , in gen[eral].

The Old Greek rendered the verse as follows:

ἀληθινῶν δὲ στόμα ἐμπλήσει γέλωτος,
τὰ δὲ χείλη αὐτῶν ἐξομολογήσεως·
He will fill the mouth of the true with laughter,
and their lips with thanksgiving.

(Lust assigns the meanings "confession of gratitude, thanksgiving" to the word ἐξομολόγησις. In LSJ we find "admission, confession"; "confession of gratitude.") That is to say, the word שׂיׂחׂוׂק is rendered by γέλως "laughter"; תׂרׂוׂעׂה is represented by ἐξομολόγησις.

The Armenian translation of v 21 is:

Բերանք ճշմարտից լցցին ծաղու,
և շրթունք նոցա գոհութեամբ:
The mouths of the true will be filled with laughter,
and their lips with thanksgiving.

In the Armenian translation the word γέλωτος "with laughter" is translated by ծաղու "with laughter"; the rendering of ἐξομολογήσεως by գոհութեամբ is similarly satisfactory.

Nonetheless in the margin of MS V935 we find cited the translation of Symmachus, namely աղաղակաւ "with a cry, shout." The index sign is upon ծաղու but this is almost certainly mistaken.

Ziegler cites no readings from "the Three" extant for 21a but has the following for 21b: ἐξομολογ.] α′ θ′ ἀλαλαγμοῦ 252 (sub α′) C ; σ′ σημασίας 252.

The word σημασία means "the giving of a shout or command," among other things. The word աղաղակ means "cry, alarm, shout." That is, աղաղակ means, or can mean, the same as σημασία.

Further indication that աղաղակաւ is intended for the word գոհութեամբ lies in their case designation: these two words are both in the instrumental case. On the other hand, the word ծաղու—from ծաղր—is in the genitive case.

Symmachus understood תׂרׂוׂעׂה in the sense of raising a cry of command, which only the healthy can do. The Armenian marginal reading preserves that understanding of the Hebrew.

The Hebrew, Greek and Armenian equivalents are:
תׂרׂוׂעׂה → Old Greek ἐξομολογήσεως → Zohrapian գոհութեամբ
          → Sym σημασίας → Sym աղաղակաւ.
The Armenian reading can be added to the second apparatus in Ziegler:

21b ἐξομολογ.] α′ θ′ ἀλαλαγμοῦ 252 (sub α′) C ; σ′ σημασίας 252 Arm(ind supra 21a γέλωτος).

It is extraordinary that this Symmachus reading is preserved only in V935 among MSS which I have examined. This mid-14th century MS is an excellent resource for the study of the hexaplaric signs tradition, indeed it "should be regarded as the single most important Armenian witness to Hexaplaric materials in those two books [i.e. Gen Exod]." (*Hexaplaric Materials* 8) This MS appears to stand apart from what is a quite unified tradition of preservation of hexaplaric readings in Job.

9:11 *

եթէ անցցէ առ ինեւ] յորժամ այց առնիցէ Aq (mend pro Sym)

V935mg

In ch 9 Job responds to Bildad. He says he can recognize God's greatness and power, but in v 11 complains:

> Look, he passes me by, and I do not see him;
> he moves on, but I do not perceive him.

We are interested in the words "he moves on," which are a translation of the Hebrew וַֽיַחֲלֹף. (In the English translation the *waw* is not represented.) In KBH this very passage is cited for the meaning "**pass by**, of God."

The Old Greek translation of v 11 is:

ἐὰν ὑπερβῇ με, οὐ μὴ ἴδω·
καὶ ἐὰν παρέλθῃ με, οὐδ᾿ ὡς ἔγνων.
If he went over me, I would not notice;
and if he passed by me, I would not even know.

In the Old Greek translation the verb παρέρχομαι is used to render יַחֲלֹף.

The Armenian translation of v 11 is:

Եթէ վերասցի քան զիս՝ ոչ տեսից.
և եթէ անցցէ առ ինեւ՝ և ոչ այնպէս գիտացից:
If he soared beyond me, I would not see;
and if he passed by me, in the same way I would not know.

In this translation the word παρέλθῃ (i.e. παρέρχομαι in the aorist subjunctive) is rendered by անցցէ (i.e. aorist subjunctive of անցանեմ "pass; flow; run; pass away, end, cease; pass over, omit"). This represents a good match of equivalents.

The Armenian marginal reading for v11b եթէ անցցէ առ ինեւ "if he passed by me" is յորժամ այց առնիցէ "when he should make a visit." There are two index signs in the text, one after անցցէ and the other above ինեւ but it seems likely that եթէ "if"—and perhaps also և "and"—is also to be replaced. The line then reads: "and whenever he should make a visit, in the same way I would not know."

Attempts to retrovert the marginal reading into Greek can have two starting points. First we might begin with the marginal reading. Arapkertsʻi lists some 46 occurrences of the expression այց առնեմ "make a visit" in the Bible. An examination of all of these makes the equation of this expression with the verb ἐπισκέπτομαι "visit; to look upon or at" (Lust) virtually complete. (The only exceptions are Judith 13:7[Rahlfs 5] where այց առնեմ renders ἀντιλαμβάνομαι "help"; 2 Macc 8:2 where it translates ἐπεῖδον "look upon" [NRSV]; and Ezek 36:37 where it renders ζητηθήσομαι "be sought after.") In that case, the marginal reading might be retroverted as ὅταν ἐπισκέψηται "whenever he should visit."

The problem with this retroversion is that Aquila—and Symmachus—use the verb ἐπισκέπτομαι almost exclusively to render פָּקַד "make a search, have a look." Cf. Reider-Turner under ἐπισκέπτεσθαι and the references for Symmachus in H-R under the same verb.

There is another direction to try. We can begin with the signature on the marginal reading and the Hebrew text. The reading is attributed to Aquila and the Hebrew verb is חָלַף. According to Reider-Turner this verb is rendered in Aquila by οἴχεσθαι, which means "I. rarely in a general sense, *go* or *come* , without the idea of departure, and without a perfect sense." There is record of Aquila using this verb three times for חָלַף, indeed once in Job: the three occurrences are at Job 4:15;

Isa 8:8; 21:1 (retroverted by Turner from the Armenian of Chrysostom's commentary). This verb is not used in the LXX or the Old Greek translations, or in the NT; nor does it have an entry in Lampe. The verb οἴχομαι is apparently used only by Aquila among the Greek translators.

At Job 4:15 Aquila uses the imperfect tense of οἴχομαι, namely the third person sg. ᾤχετο "used to come." It is not clear what form he would have used at 9:11,which requires a subjunctive mood. In LSJ there is no instance cited of the use of οἴχομαι in the subjunctive; no aorist form of the verb is cited. One might posit the present subjunctive, οἴχηται "he would come" following the word ὅταν, which յոդժամ likely represents. That is a possibility.

The use of ὅταν poses a problem for an identification of the marginal reading with Aquila because it represents some freedom of translation. Perhaps the signature on the reading is incorrect—perhaps this reading really belongs to Symmachus. This suggestion gains weight when one notices that all the signed marginal readings in Armenian Job carry Aquila's signature. At 37:18 and 39:1 the marginal readings really belong to Symmachus; at 28:10 1° there is a correction is attributed to Aquila.

That takes us back to the verb חָלַף. The verb I. חָלַף occurs some 28 times in the Hebrew Bible, of which 14 occurrences are in the qal . The Old Greek translators used a variety of words to render I. חָלַף, most commonly compounds of ἔρχομαι (in seven cases). The verbs used for I. חָלַף are, beginning with the ἔρχομαι compounds: ἀπέρχομαι "depart from" (1 Rgn 10:3; Cant 2:11); διέρχομαι "pass through" (Isa 21:1); ἐπέρχομαι "come upon" (Job 4:15); παρέρχομαι (Ps 89[90]:5, 6; Job 9:11); ἀλλάσσομαι "change" (Ps 101[102]:27); ἀφαιρέω "take away" (Isa 8:8); κατακρύπτω "hide" (Isa 2:18); καταστρέφω "upset, overturn" (Job 11:10); μεταβάλλω "turn about" (Hab 1:11); πενθέω "mourn" (Isa 24:5); at Job 9: 26 the Hebrew verb is not represented in the Old Greek translation. It seems clear that the Old Greek translators treated I. חָלַף with a fair degree of latitude: they suited the translation to the context. In none of these cases do we have the meaning "visit" but we do see how the freedom of a translator like Symmachus might have permitted his use of ἐπισκέπτομαι in Job 9:11.

(Busto Saiz offers Symmachus' equivalents for I. חָלַף in the three Psalms passages: 101:27 ἀλλάσσομαι—so the same as Old Greek; 89:5 ἀνατέλλω "rise up"; 89:6 παρέρχομαι—again identical to Old Greek. In the last two of the three cases the Greek represents retroversions drawn from Field.)

Therefore I return to the suggestion made earlier. It may be conjectured that the Greek underlying the Armenian is ὅταν ἐπισκέψηται "whenever he visits." In that case the attribution to Aquila is likely incorrect; the marginal reading probably belongs to Symmachus.

Interestingly Symmachus' translation for the second part of 11b is extant in catena MSS. Rather than οὐδ' ὡς ἔγνων, Symmachus has οὐδὲ ἐννοήσω "I wouldn't take note of it." His translation of the entire second line of v 11 can be reconstructed as:

καὶ ὅταν ἐπισκέψηται με, οὐδὲ ἐννοήσω.
And whenever he might visit me, I wouldn't even take notice.

The Hebrew, Greek and Armenian equivalents are:

ฦֲלֹף(וּ) → Old Greek (καὶ) ἐὰν παρέλθῃ → Zohrapian եթէ անցցէ
      → conj. Sym ὅταν ἐπισκέψηται ← Aq յորժամ այց
   առնիցէ.

This reading can be added to the second apparatus in Ziegler as follows:

11b ἐὰν παρέλθῃ] α′ (mend pro σ′) ὅταν ἐπισκέψηται Arm | οὐδ' ὡς ἔγνων] σ′ οὐδὲ ἐννοήσω *C* .

28:10 1°

զպողոտ Zoh^txt; զպողոտս J1127^txt; զպտտոյտս M354 W11 Zoh^app] պտտոյս
      Aq

J1127^mg

The first line of v 10 says that בַּצּוּרוֹת יְאֹרִים בִּקֵּעַ "They [miners: cf. v 3] cut out channels in the rocks." The words "in the rocks" are a translation of the Hebrew בַּצּוּרוֹת.

The Old Greek renders this line δίνας δὲ ποταμῶν ἔρρηξεν "the whirlpools of rivers he broke asunder." The word δίνας "whirlpools" renders בְּצוּרוֹת. As Dhorme comments: "G δίνας, Aq. and Symm. ῥεῖθρα ["streams"] seem to see streams in בצורות, from the root בצר 'to cut' whence 'fissures', 'gorges', 'torrents'." Theodotion has related בַּצוּרוֹת to בצור "strengthened" and so translates τὰ ὀχυρώματα. (405)

Zohrapian's text reads Չպոյն զետաց պատառեաց "He broke the pot of [i.e. which holds? the] rivers." The word զպոյն is a corruption of pq-պտտյոյու "whirlpools." In the latter case the translation is "Whirlpools of rivers he broke."

Manuscript J1127 has զ պոյոու in the text. In the margin it has [pq-] պտտյու which is attributed to Aquila. Both readings are corrupt: in the text J1127 has the same corruption found in the text of Zohrapian, except that the word is now in the plural, "pots." The marginal reading is intended to be պտտյոյու, i.e. "whirlpools," but lacks the second -ո-! This marginal reading has come from a comparison among Armenian MSS: it is unlikely that it has come from Aquila since other MSS which commonly have readings drawn from "the Three" are not represented here. Rather, it is most likely that the reading is intended to be a correction. Aquila's name has become attached to it.

It seems to me that this marginal reading is inner-Armenian: one need not assume secondary contact with a Greek text.

28:10 2° *

ակն իմ] ակն նորա Aq

V1270^mg V1508^mg Zoh^app(mg)

The verse reads:

They [i.e. miners (cf. v 3)] cut out channels in the rocks,
and their eyes see every precious thing.

We are interested in the second line, the Hebrew for which is:

וְכָל־יְקָר רָאֲתָה עֵינוֹ.

The subject in these verses is not made definite. No subject is identified in v 3: the NIV says "Man ..." while the NRSV changes the number and suggests, based on the context, "Miners ..." It follows that, while in v 10 the subject is singular, the NRSV makes it plural. More literal is the NIV which translates:

> He tunnels through the rock;
> his eyes see all its treasures.

At any rate, the reading of Aquila relates to the pronominal modifier for עֵינוֹ: it is third person singular, hence "his eyes."

The Old Greek translates the verse:

> δίνας δὲ ποταμῶν ἔρρηξεν,
> πᾶν δὲ ἔτιμον εἶδέν μου ὁ ὀφθαλμός·
> The whirlpools of rivers he broke asunder,
> every precious thing my eye saw.

Here the possessive pronoun used with "eye" is first person singular, not as in the Hebrew—third person singular.

A few Greek witnesses have the third person singular pronoun, namely, according to Ziegler, A-S^c-Iul and La^μ (*oculus eius*). As Ziegler points out, this equals the MT and he refers us to his second apparatus wherein is collected the hexaplaric materials. There we find: **10b** μου ὁ ὀφθ.] λ′ ⟨ὁ ὀφθαλμὸς⟩ αὐτοῦ C [i.e. catena MSS]. The abbreviation λ′, i.e. οἱ λοιποί, is a generalization for citing Aquila, Symmachus and Theodotion.

The Armenian witness identifies the reading at 10b as that of Aquila. It seems to me that this marginal reading might have arisen as a correction based upon the "person" of 10a, but one cannot disregard the signature.

The Hebrew, Greek and Armenian equivalents can be set out as follows:

עֵינוֹ → Old Greek μου ὁ ὀφθαλμός → Zohrapian ակն իմ
            → Aq ⟨ὁ ὀφθαλμὸς⟩ αὐτοῦ → Aq ակն նորա.

The Armenian marginal reading gives us the signature for the marginal reading otherwise known only as a reading of "the Three." It can be added to the second apparatus in Ziegler as follows:

10b μου ὁ ὀφθ.] λ′ ⟨ὁ ὀφθαλμὸς⟩ αὐτοῦ *C* | μου] α′ αὐτοῦ Arm.

37:18 *

հնւթիւնu] հասատուthիւն Aq (mend pro Sym)

J1127mg J1928mg J1934mg J2561mg(հnւu.) LOBmg(հասատուthեաu ad 21 sine nom) M177mg M354mg(sine nom) M2587mg V623mg(sine ind in txt) V1270mg V1634 mg(հաu qաu ad 21) W11mg(sine nom)

Manuscript M354 has simply հասատ in the margin with dots over the հ and u; in the text it has matching dots over the հu of հնւթիւնu. Presumably the marginal reading was read as a plural. Manuscript M2587 has հասատաu in the margin and must have been read the same way. Some MSS have the reading at v 21, where the word հնւթիւնu also occurs: LOB V1634, the former without signature.

Chapter 37 continues Elihu's fourth speech. In. vv 14ff. Elihu asks a series of questions of Job. Included among these is v 18:

> Can you, like him, spread out the skies,
> hard as a molten mirror?

The first line here is a translation of:

.תַּרְקִיעַ עִמּוֹ לִשְׁחָקִים

The word in question is שְׁחָקִים, sg. שַׁחַק, which in the plural means "clouds."

The Old Greek did not translate v 18. This however has been supplied by Origen under the asterisk from Theodotion and has entered the Armenian text. So v 18 in Ziegler's text is not Old Greek but Theodotion. Theodotion's translation of verse 18a is:

στερεώσεις μετ' αὐτοῦ εἰς παλαιώματα.

The translation of this is something like "Will you with him give strength to the things of old?" In this translation לְשָׁחָקִים is represented by εἰς παλαιώματα. Aquila's translation of 18a is:

αὐτὸς ἐστερέωσε τὸν οὐρανὸν εἰς [τ]ροπάς.

He made the heaven strong in (its) solstices.

In Aquila לְשָׁחָקִים is rendered by εἰς τροπάς. His reading is preserved in catena MSS and fragments of Olympiodor.

Symmachus' translation of 18a is:

ἐξ ὕψους συνέσει αὐτοῦ ἐν τῷ στερεώματι εἰς αἰθέρα.

Symmachus is preserved in Greek MS 252 and Syh. The ἐξ ὕψους comes from the end of v 17, where Symmachus read ממרום for מֵרֹדד: see Dhorme 569. (Ziegler notes that Syh has συνέσῃ αὐτῷ [sic].) Here לְשָׁחָקִים has become εἰς αἰθέρα "in ether," or "in the heavens": so Dhorme. But Symmachus has also employed the prepositional phrase ἐν τῷ στερεώματι "in the firmament" in his translation of לְשָׁחָקִים. The English translation of the entire line is something like:

> From the heights, by his understanding in the firmament toward the
> ethereal regions.

The critical element for our purposes is the use of the word στερέωμα. The prepositional phrase ἐν τῷ στερεώματι is part of Symmachus' rendering of לְשָׁחָקִים.

The Armenian translation of v 18a is:

հաստատեցես ըն ի նմա ի հնութիւն.

Will you give strength with him to the things of old?

This is a literal translation of the Greek of Theodotion, cited above.

The marginal reading in the Armenian witnesses is հաստատութիւն "firmness," which when used with երկնից means "firmament." That is what it means here. If we replace հնութեանն with հաստատութիւն we read:

հաստատեսցես ընդ նմա ի հաստատութիւն.
Will you make (things) firm with him in the firmament?

(I have rendered "firm" and "firmament" to indicate that the verb հաստատել and հաստատութիւն are cognates.)

The marginal reading is not the translation of Aquila but clearly that of Symmachus: στερέωμα is the same as հաստատութիւն. The word հաստատութիւն replaces the word հնութիւնն (i.e. παλαιώματα) where we might have expected an Armenian equivalent for αἰθέρα to do so. Nothing needed to be done about the Armenian preposition ի because it can represent either ἐν or εἰς.

The Hebrew, Greek and Armenian equivalents are:
לַשְׁחָקִים → Theodotion εἰς παλαιώματα → Zohrapian ի հնութիւնն
→ Sym ἐν τῷ στερεώματα (εἰς αἰθέρα) → Aq (mend pro Sym)
ի հաստատութիւն.

The Armenian MSS show us that Symmachus' translation made its way into the Armenian tradition and they also indicate that not just εἰς αἰθέρα but also (ἐν τῷ) στερεώματα was cited as his translation for לַשְׁחָקִים. This is an interesting exegetical development.

The Armenian witness can be represented in Ziegler's second apparatus as follows:

18a] α' (σ' sec C) αὐτὸς ἐστερέωσε τὸν οὐρανὸν εἰς [τ]ροπάς C' (Olymp); σ' ἐξ ὕψους (= *mimarom* pro *midarom* 𝔐 **17b**) συνέσῃ αὐτῷ (sic Syh; συνεσει αυτου 252) ἐν τῷ στερεώματι εἰς αἰθέρα 252 Syh |εἰς παλαιώματα] α' εἰς ῥοπάς 252 C (250-680-740 mend εις τροπας; 138-255-612 mend εκροπας); α' (mend pro σ') ἐν τῷ στερεώματα Arm; σ' εἰς αἰθέρα C .

38:32 ∗

բանայցես գմազգարով[թն] ելանիցէ սայլն Aq (mend pro Sym)

M177mg(solum ելանիցէ) M354mg(sine nom) M2587mg(solum ելանիցէ sine nom)
J1127mg J1928mg(sine nom) J1934mg(sine nom et ind supra կամ բանայցես) J2561mg
V1507mg V1634mg (ելանիցէ սայլ) Zohapp(mg)

Unless indicated otherwise the index sign in the text is upon the word զգ-մազգարով[թն]. It would appear that the marginal reading refers to the two words բանայցես գմազգարով[թն] since the marginal reading consists of a verb and a noun.

Chapter 38:1–40:2 contains Yahweh's first speech to Job. In 38:31–33 Job is questioned about his knowledge of astronomy. In v 32 he is asked:

> Can you lead forth the Mazzaroth in their season,
> or can you guide the Bear with its children?

A note on v 32 by Samuel Terrien/Roland E. Murphy in the NRSV *New Oxford Annotated Bible* says that "The determination of these stars is uncertain."

We are interested in the first line:

הֲתֹצִיא מַזָּרוֹת בְּעִתּוֹ.

The marginal reading concerns the word מַזָּרוֹת. The entry in KBH for this word is: "**constellations**; sugg. Venus as evening & morning star; Hyades (in Taurus); boat of Arcturus; southern constellations of zodiac.†" (The dagger following the entry means that this word occurs only here for certain in the Hebrew Bible.)

The NRSV employs a transliteration: Mazzaroth; the NIV translates: "the constellations."

The Old Greek does not translate v 32. It was added to the text by Origen and therefore appears under the asterisk. The translation is that of Theodotion. He too employed a transliteration:

ἢ διανοίξεις Μαζουρωθ ἐν καιρῷ αὐτοῦ.
Or will you reveal Mazuroth in his proper time?

Ziegler cites Symmachus' translation for 32a, with its evidence, as follows:
σ′ ἢ ἀναφύσεις τὰ σκορπισθέντα κατὰ καιρὸν αὐτοῦ (αυτων C ; + ἕν 252)
ἕκαστον 248 252 C Syh (mend sub α′). The translation is:

Or will you bring back again the scattered elements according to its time,
each one?

Here מַזָּרוֹת is translated by τὰ σκορπισθέντα "the scattered elements." While the
translation "the scattered elements" might seem far removed from מַזָּרוֹת, a glance
at the entry in LSJ under which the verb σκορπίζω is found reveals its connection to
σκορπιανός "born under or belonging to Scorpio." So τὰ σκορπισθέντα has an
astrological connection.

The Armenian translation also transliterates:

Կամ բանայցես զմազարովթն ի ժամանակի իւրում.
Or will you spread the Mazarot in his time?

In the margin of various Armenian MSS one finds a translation for Mazarot,
namely եւանիցէ սայլն "he will bring out Arcturus." Literally սայլ means
"wagon, chariot"; astrologically it refers to "arcturus; boötes." "Arcturus" is Ἀρκτοῦρος, i.e. "the principal star in the constellation of Bootes" (Cicero) or "the constellation itself" (Virgil). Boötes is Βοώτης, i.e. "the constellation called also Arctophylax" (Cicero). And Arctophylax? The Ἀρκτοφύλαξ is "a constellation near the
Greater Bear, Bootes" (Cicero). So Boötes = Arctophylax. For the sake of comments about to be made, let us consider Arctos or Arctus (Ἄρκτος): "the constellation of the Bear (properly, two, the Greater and the Lesser, the former of which is
likewise called Charles's Wain." (These citations from Freund-Leverett's lexicon.)
Dhorme notes that the Syriac has for מַזָּרוֹת the word ܥܓܠܬܐ which
literally means "cart, wain, wagon" but which astrologically refers to "the constellation Charles' Wain, the Waggoner." (Payne Smith)

When we insert the marginal reading եւանիցէ սայլն into the Armenian text we read:

Կամ եւանիցէ սայլն ի ժամանակի իւրում.
Or will Arcturus come out in its time?

(Bedrossian cites եւանէ արեգակն as "the sun rises or begins to appear on the horizon" so perhaps v 32a with the marginal reading could be translated "Or will Arcturus rise in its time?" See Bedrossian under եւանեմ.)

Does the reading եւանիցէ սայլն come from Aquila? If not, where could it have come from?

First we note that Ziegler cites Olympiodor—deacon in Alexandria in the first half of the 6th century—who has the third person διανοίξει rather than the second person διανοίξεις, either in his commentary or as known in catena notations, or both. (Cf. Ziegler, 21 on the meaning of Ziegler's "Ol.") Olympiodor is the only source cited that has the verb in the third person. Some Greek catena MSS contain hundreds of notations from his commentary, which is a rich source of readings from "the Three": see Ziegler, 157–158. Unfortunately often Olympiodor employs the generalization οἱ λοιποί = λ' or οἱ ἄλλοι rather than the individual names of Aquila, Symmachus and Theodotion so that the importance of his witness to their work is of little value. Ziegler says that he does not cite Olympiodor in such cases where the names of individual translators are not given.

Is it possible that the reading with the verb in the third person belongs to Aquila? That seems unlikely to me, considering Aquila's faithfulness to a principle of literal translation.

On that other hand, there is the matter of սայլն, under which lies the Greek Ἄρκτος or Ἀρκτοῦρος. Is it possible that Aquila equated מַזָּרוֹת with one of these? The Syriac does with its translation ܥܓܠܬܐ. At least one can conclude that there was an exegetical tradition which equated the Mazzaroth with Ἄρκτος. The Armenian marginal reading reflects that exegetical tradition.

Perhaps 37:9 is relevant to the discussion because there Aquila uses a transliteration for מְזָרִים, "north winds," a word which occurs only here in the Hebrew Bible. His transliteration is Μαζουρίμ (so Syh) or Μαζούρ (so Greek MS 248) and is based on the assumption that the Hebrew word refers to an astrological pheno-menon. Cf. the Latin Vulgate for מַזָּרוֹת‎: ab Arcturo. Theodotion shares Aquila's transliteration, according to the Syro-hexapla. In the light of how Aquila dealt with 37:9 it seems likely that he employed a transliteration also at 38:32.

I conclude therefore that the very interesting note at 38:32 does not derive from Aquila.

We may note that the Symmachus translation preserved in 248 252 *C* Syh is, in the Syro-hexapla, preserved under the name of Aquila. It seems likely to me that the marginal reading in the Armenian MSS is in fact that of Symmachus. The person is now third instead of second and the puzzling "scattered elements" has be-come Arcturus. The former change could have occurred when ἀναφύσεις τὰ σκορπισθέντα was translated into Armenian: the neuter plural could have been taken as the subject, the second person verb in that case regarded as a mistake. As we note generally in the book of Job, the Armenian marginal readings are almost all at-tributed to Aquila, by mistake in some cases.

The Hebrew, Greek and Armenian equivalents are:

הֲתֹצִיא מַזָּרוֹת → Theodotion διανοίξεις Μαζουρώθ → Zohrapian

ⲣⲁⲛⲁⲩⲅⲉⲛ ⳪ ⳑⲙⲁⳉⲁⲣⲟⲩⳏⳁⲛ

→ Sym ἀναφύσεις τὰ σκορπισθέντα → Aq (mend pro Sym)

ⲉⳑⲙⲁⲛⲓⲅⴇ ⲙⲁⳑⲛ.

(The parent text of the Armenian marginal reading may already have had the wrong signature. This corruption did not necessarily happen at the hands of Armenian scribes.)

It is difficult to represent the Armenian reading in the second apparatus of Ziegler. On the one hand, we may simply cite it with other witnesses to the Sym-machus reading—so:

32a] σ′ ἢ ἀναφύσεις τὰ σκορπισθέντα κατὰ καιρὸν αὐτοῦ (αυτων *C* ; + ἕν 252) ἕκαστον 248 252 *C* Syh (mend sub α′) | διανοίξεις Μαζουρώθ] α′ (mend pro σ′) ἀναφύσεις τὰ σκορπισθέντα Arm.

This citation of the Armenian leaves something to be desired: while it seems probable that the Armenian marginal reading derives from the Symmachus trans-lation, it has the verb in the third person singular and "the scattered elements" have become Arcturus. In this instance a citation in Latin might even be appropriate! In that case the Armenian could be cited as follows:

διανοίξεις Μαζουρώθ] α΄ (mend pro σ΄) *exebit Arcturus* Arm.

39:1 *

յամոուրաց] յայ ĵ ձ բաղ ա ց Aq (mend pro Sym)

J1127ᵐᵍ J1928ᵐᵍ(ա ĵ ձ բաղ ա ց) J1934ᵐᵍ(ա ĵ ձ բաղ ա ց) J2561ᵐᵍ LOBᵐᵍ
(ա ĵ ձ բաղ ա ց sine nom) M177ᵐᵍ(vid) M354ᵐᵍ(ա ĵ ձ բաղ ա ց sine nom) M2587ᵐᵍ(sine ind
in txt) V229ᵐᵍ(ա ĵ ց բաղ ա ց) V623ᵐᵍ(ա ĵ ձ բաղ ա ց) V1270ᵐᵍ(ա ĵ ձ բաղ ա ց) V1507ᵐᵍ
V1634ᵐᵍ Zohᵃᵖᵖ(ᵐᵍ)(ա ĵ ձ բաղ ա ց)

Unless otherwise noted the MSS cited have the signature. (One might note that MSS V229 V623 V1634 were employed by Zohrapian, apart from V1508.)

The voice from the whirlwind continues with the devasting series of questions addressed to Job. In 39:1 he is asked:

Do you know when the mountain goats give birth?
Do you observe the calving of the deer?

The first line is a translation of הֲיָדַעְתָּ עֵת לֶדֶת יַעֲלֵי סָלַע. The word in question is יַעֲלֵי which, bound to סָלַע "rock(s)," is rendered "(mountain) goats."

The word יָעֵל in KBH has the following entry: **ibex**, *Capra nubiana* , or **mountain goat**, *Capra sinaitica* . The word only occurs, according to Mandelkern, at 1 Sam 24:3, where it is part of a proper name; Ps 104:18; Job 39:1; Prov 5:19 in the feminine bound form. It is therefore a rare word.

The Old Greek translator did not translate the first line of 39:1. Rather, what we have there now in Ziegler's edition is from Theodotion, placed under the asterisk by Origen. Theodotion's translation of the first line of 39:1 is:

εἰ ἔγνως καιρὸν τοκετοῦ τραγελάφων πέτρας.
Do you know the time of the delivery of the wild goats of the rock?

Theodotion has used the word τραγέλαφος to render יָעֵל. The entry in LSJ indicates that the precise meaning of τραγέλαφος is not clear. On the one hand, in classical sources it is a "*goat-stag* , a fantastic animal, represented on Eastern carpet and the like"; on the other, later a real animal of Arabia, or on the Phasis, prob. a kind of *wild goat* or *antelope* ." The only other occurrence among the Greek translators of the Hebrew Bible cited in H-R is at Deut. 14:5. There it renders אַקּוֹ, a word which occurs only there, and means according to KBH "(edible) **wild goat**, *Capra aegagrus* . At Deut 14:5 the Armenian translation of τραγέλαφος is խարբուզ "roe-buck."

The text at Deut 14:5 is interesting because it contains a list of such animal vocabulary as we are dealing with at Job 39:1. The list is as follows. I have underlined such words as are important for the passage at hand.

Hebrew	ET	LXX	ET	Armenian	ET
אַיָּל	deer	ἔλαφος	deer	եղ ջերու	stag; hart
צְבִי	gazelle	δορκάς	gazelle [in Syria and Africa]	այծեամն	wild goat; deer: cf. այծ = goat
יַחְמוּר	roebuck	βούβαλος	antelope	գոմէշ	buffalo
אַקּוֹ	wild goat	<u>τραγέλαφος</u>	wild goat; antelope [prob.]	<u>խարբուզ</u>	roe-buck
דִּישֹׁן	ibex	πύγαργος[1]	white-rump (name of an antelope)	այծքաղ	chamois; wild goat
תְאוֹ	antelope	ὄρυξ	kind of gazelle or antelope	<u>յամոյր</u>	wild goat; antelope
זָמֶר	mountain-sheep	καμηλο-πάρδαλις	camelo-pard, i.e. giraffe	անապուռ	giraffe

[1]Wevers notes in his second apparatus that MS M^mg has αἴγαγρον, i.e. "wild goat."

It should probably be noted that in the lexicography of some of these rare words there may be some circuitous elucidation of meanings through the kind of comparisons that are made above. Therefore the quest for meanings of words can become rather frustrating.

At any rate, from the comparison we can see that at Deut 14:5 τραγέλαφος is translated by խարբուզ; յամ'njր is a translation of ὄρυξ; այծքաղ is a translation of πύγαργος. It also appears clear that in some of these cases the Armenian translator was not very sure about the meaning of these animal names which occur rarely in the Greek Bible.

The Armenian translation of Theodotion at Job 39:1a is:

Եթէ գիտիցես զ ժամանակ ծննդեան յամուրաց քարան-ծաւաց:

Would you know the time of the birth of the wild goats who live in the rocks?

The translator used the word յամ'njր to translate τραγέλαφον.

Since Theodotion is the text, the marginal reading in Armenian MSS at 39:1 must come from Aquila, Symmachus or neither. It carries the signature of Aquila.

The word יָעֵל occurs only four times in the Hebrew Bible, as noted above: at 1 Sam 24:3 it is part of a proper name הַיְּעֵלִים (צוּרֵי), transliterated in the kind of text which MS B attests, but translated τῶν ἐλάφων in hexaplaric witnesses. In Armenian that becomes եղ ջերուաց. At Ps 104:18 לַיְּעֵלִים has been translated in the Old Greek ταῖς ἐλάφοις which then becomes in Armenian եղ ջերուաց. In its fourth occurrence—our text is the third—at Prov 5:19 יַעֲלַת־חֵן the Greek translation, according to MS B, is ἔλαφος φιλίας, which in turn becomes in Armenian եղ ն սիրոյ. The word եղ ն means "hind, roe," and is related to եղ-ջերու. Thus in its three occurrences outside Job 39:1 the word יָעֵל is rendered by a form of ἔλαφος which becomes in Armenian եղ ջերու or եղ ն.

(It should perhaps be noted that the second line of 39:1 is:

הֹלֵל אַיָּלוֹת תִּשְׁמֹר:

Do you observe the calving of the deer?

The Old Greek for this is:

ἐφύλαξας δὲ ὠδῖνας ἐλάφων·
Have you kept watch over the birth-pangs of deer?

We take note of this because the Armenian translation of this second line is:

զգուշանայցես երկանց եղանց:
Will you watch over the birth-pangs of deer?

The word אַיָּלָה "doe of a fallow deer" is rendered by ἔλαφος which, in turn, is translated by եղն. It would appear that Theodotion has identified יָעֵל with אַיָּלָה since ἔλαφος is part of his translation of the former.)

What I am getting at by this tying together of יָעֵל–ἔλαφος–եղ ջերու/ եղն is this: Reider-Turner give ἐλαφίνης "fawn" as Aquila's equivalent for יָעֵל at 1 Sam 24:3 and indicate that this word is used only by Aquila. It seems to me that if at Job 39:1 Aquila had employed a form of ἔλαφος, we might expect the Armenian translation of that to use եղ ջերու/եղն. But that is not what we find at 39:1: the marginal reading is այծքաղաց, i.e. the word այծքաղ. (The word այծ-քաղ is made up of two words: այծ "goat" and քաղ "he-goat, goat.")

For a moment let us consider the possibility that the marginal reading in the Armenian witnesses is not Aquila but Symmachus. Ziegler cites no translation extant for Aquila at 39:1a but he does cite one for Symmachus. For יָעֵלִי Symmachus has νεβρῶν, "of fawns." (The reading νεβρῶν is preserved in Catena MSS where it is often erroneously attributed to Theodotion. Manuscript 3005 [Genuensis Durazzo-Giustiniani A I 10 (9th-10th cent.)] has the correct signature, i.e. Symmachus: see Hagedorn 408.)

The word νεβρός "fawn" occurs five times in the Greek Old Testament. All occurrences are in Canticles. Three times νεβρῷ ἐλάφων "(to a) fawn of deer" becomes in Armenian որդենի եղանց "young of deer" (2:9, 17; 8:14); twice νεβ-ροί becomes ուլս "kids, fawns" (4:5; 7:3[4]). Bedrossian also gives the word եղ ունոր$ for fawn. H-R cite Symmachus' use of νεβρός at 3 Rgn 10:3—apparently in error—and Job 39:1. There are only these seven references for νεβρός in H-R.

If the marginal reading from which the Armenian marginalium was translated involved νεβρός I think we might have expected a word like որթ (եղ ասց) or ուլ or եղ ունորթ which more clearly indicates "fawn." The Armenian word այծ-քաղ refers to a "goat" or "antelope" type of animal. (I am aware that there is an overlapping in the terminology for these species. One need only consult an English dictionary to determine this. Thus one learns that our word "antelope" comes from a Medieval Greek word *antholops* "deer" and that the "goat antelope" refers to "any of several bovid ruminants intermediate in their characteristics between goats and antelopes, as the serow, goral, and chamois."[1])

All these observations bring us to a conclusion. We do not have a sufficiently large basis of comparison to determine what the Armenian word այծքաղ may or may not have been translated from. We cannot establish a translation technique based upon one occurrence in Deuteronomy and the marginal reading here at Job 39:1. The two occurrences at any rate belong to different translators. The word այծքաղ can refer to a deer-like animal, namely the chamois; further, at Deut 14:5 it is used to translate the name of a type of antelope. It is possible that, because of the context— which speaks of animals which live among the rocks—the translator of the marginal reading chose the word այծքաղ rather than a word that would reproduce the Greek word for "fawn," namely νεβρός. That is, I think it more likely that here we have the Symmachus reading than an unknown reading of Aquila.

The Hebrew, Greek and Armenian equivalents are:

יַעֲלֵי (סָלַע) → Theodotion τραγελάφων → Zohrapian յասՐուրաց

→ Sym νεβρῶν → Aq (mend pro Sym) այծքաղաց

In this instance the Armenian preserves a Symmachus reading known already from Greek sources. The Armenian evidence can be added to the second apparatus in Ziegler:

τραγ. πέτρας] α' (leg σ' Arm) θ' (leg σ' C) νεβρῶν ἐν πέτρᾳ C Arm.

---

[1] *Webster's New World Dictionary of American English* , ed. V. Neufeldt (3rd College ed.; New York: Simon & Schuster 1988).

X. Isaiah

One may note that LOB MS 8833 has an interesting series of marginal readings in Isaiah that point to secondary contact with Greek MSS, as well as comparison with other Armenian MSS and possibly the Latin Vulgate. Perhaps someone will pursue this sometime.

Joseph Ziegler, ed., *Septuaginta, Vetus Testamentum Graecum; Auctoritate Academiae Litterarum Gottingensis editum, XIV Isaias* ; Göttingen: Vandenhoeck & Ruprecht 1939; repr. 1967. • idem, "Text-kritische Notizen zu den jüngeren griechischen Übersetzungen des Buches Isaias," in *Sylloge* (MSU 10; Göttingen: Vandenhoeck & Ruprecht 1971) 43–70 = Nachrichten d. Akademie d. Wissenschaften zu Göttingen, Philolog.-Hist. Klasse 1939, 75–102 (= Septuaginta-Arbeiten Nr. 1). • idem, *Untersuchungen zur Septuaginta des Buches Isaias* (Alttestamentliche Abhandlungen XII, 3; Münster i. W.: Verlag der Aschendorffschen Verlagsbuchhandlung 1934).

29:7 *

երուսաղեմիյ արիելի Sym

J297mg(արիել sine ind) J501mg(արիել) J1934mg(արիել) M2587mg V229mg
V1507mg(արիել) V1634mg Zohapp(mg)

Isa 29:1–8 deals with Judah's eventual restoration. The word "Ariel" occurs a number of times in the passage: for example, v 1 begins:

> Ah, Ariel, Ariel,
> the city where David encamped!

The NRSV has the following note on the word Ariel: "Probable meaning, *altar hearth* ; compare Ezek 43:15."

In v 7 we read:

> And the multitude of all the nations that fight against Ariel,
> all that fight against her and her stronghold, and who distress her,
> shall be like a dream, a vision of the night.

"Ariel" is a transliteration of the word אֲרִיאֵל. KBH suggest the meaning "altar hearth" for the references in Ezek 43:15, 16. A second entry follows the first: II. אֲרִיאֵל: n. loc.: ? = I, Jerusalem or part of it, Is 29₁f.₇.†

The Old Greek translation of v 7, according to Ziegler, is as follows:

καὶ ἔσται ὡς ὁ ἐνυπνιαζόμενος ἐν ὕπνῳ ὁ πλοῦτος τῶν ἐθνῶν πάντων, ὅσοι ἐπεστράτευσαν ἐπὶ Αριηλ, καὶ πάντες οἱ στρατευσά- μενοι ἐπὶ Ιερουσαλημ καὶ πάντες οἱ συνηγμένοι ἐπ' αὐτὴν καὶ θλί- βοντες αὐτήν.

And the abundance of all the nations will be as what one sees in a dream, such a number as came upon Ariel, and all who fight against Jerusalem and all those who gather upon her and oppress her.

As one can see from the translation, אֲרִיאֵל has been transliterated by the Greek translator.

In Ziegler's edition we find a note in his second apparatus concerning the word Ariel: Αριηλ] οι γ' αριηλ Q Syh (adn. יאמר?: inc.). The reading Αριηλ in the text is supported by his group *oI* Hi (i.e. Jerome). The "translations" ισραηλ and ιερουσαλημ are widely attested variants.

Ziegler's comments in "Textkritische Notizen" on 29:7 are helpful. He suggests there that the Syriac יאמר? should likely be taken as a bowdlerized transcription of the abbreviation ιλημ, i.e. ιερουσαλημ "Jerusalem." This suggestion he be-

lieves has high likelihood of correctness because at the same place in Greek MS Q
we find the marginal note ιλημ οι γ΄ αριηλ. The Syriac translator could not manage the abbreviation which the copyist of Q transmitted correctly.

The Armenian translation of the rather free Old Greek rendering is:

Եւ եղիցի որպէս ոք զի տեսանիցէ երազ ի տեսլեան գի-
շերոյ, մեծութիւն ամենայն հեթանոսաց յարձակելոց ի
վերայ երուսաղեմի. եւ ամենայն ժողովելոցն ի վերայ
նորա, եւ որ նեղեցինն զնա:

And it will be as one who sees a dream in a night vision, a greatness of all
the heathen coming upon Jerusalem; and of all the ones gathering upon it
and who will oppress it.

As is clear from the translation, the Armenian has "Jerusalem" rather than "Ariel."
The Armenian belongs among the witnesses cited by Ziegler as follows: 86 *O* '-
Q^mg *L* '^-233 Wirc.

In the margin Armenian witnesses have the reading արիէլի (i.e. արիէլ,
with ի ending), "Ariel," attributed to Symmachus. Indeed, according to Greek MS
Q and Syh, "Ariel" is the reading of "the Three"—Aquila, Symmachus and Theodotion. What kind of clarification this could have offered a reader is not immediately clear!

The Hebrew, Greek and Armenian equivalents are:

אֲרִיאֵל → Old Greek, according to Ziegler: Αριηλ

    → var lect ιερουσαλημ → Zohrapian երուսաղեմի

    → Aq Sym Th αριηλ → Sym արիէլի.

The Armenian witnesses here provide the reading of Symmachus. According to the Greek and Syriac hexaplaric evidence, Aquila and Theodotion also had
this reading.

The Armenian evidence can be added to the second apparatus in Ziegler, as
follows:

Αριηλ (ιερουσαλημ Arm)] οι γ΄ (σ΄ Arm) Q Syh (adn. יאמר: inc.) Arm.

32:6 *

(q)հայհոյութիւն] մոլորութիւն

J501mg Zohapp(mg)

Note: the evidence is restated below.

Zohrapian comments in his apparatus that the marginal reading agrees with what some other MSS have as their text. Indeed both J1925 (f.287r, col.2, ↑17) and M1500 (f.305r, col.2, ↓28) have մոլորութիւն as their text. It seems very likely therefore that J501 and V1508 represent a form of text in which the reading in the margin and the reading in the text have been switched. A full collation of Isaiah MSS might well produce a witness that has հայհոյութիւն in the margin. We must a least conjecture that such is part of the textual history of this marginal reading.

Isaiah 32:1–8 speaks of a coming age in which fools will be recognized for what they are (vv 5–6). The first part of v 6 states:

כִּי נָבָל נְבָלָה יְדַבֵּר
וְלִבּוֹ יַעֲשֶׂה־אָוֶן
לַעֲשׂוֹת חֹנֶף
וּלְדַבֵּר אֶל־יְהוָה תּוֹעָה

For fools speak folly,
  and their minds plot iniquity:
to practice ungodliness,
  to utter error concerning the LORD, ...

The words "to practice ungodliness" represent לַעֲשׂוֹת חֹנֶף. According to KBH, the word חֹנֶף occurs only here in the Hebrew Bible. However, a cognate verb, noun and adjective add another nine instances of the appearance of this root with the sense either of "godlessness" or defilement. The root חנף in the *qal* and with the meaning **be defiled** (of land) is found at Isa 24:5; the adjective חָנֵף "godless" is used at Isa 10:6. Still, it is a rare word.

The Old Greek translation of the four lines above is:

ὁ γὰρ μωρὸς μωρὰ λαλήσει,
καὶ ἡ καρδία αὐτοῦ μάταια νοήσει
τοῦ συντελεῖν ἄνομα
καὶ λαλεῖν πρὸς κύριον πλάνησιν, ...
For the fool will speak foolish things,
and his heart will conceive worthless things
to carry out lawless things
and to speak to the Lord deception ...

Ziegler in his second apparatus sets out readings from "the Three" for the second and third lines. They are: μάταια νοήσει] α' θ' ποιησει αδικιαν 86 | τοῦ συντελεῖν ἄνομα] α' σ' θ' του ποιησαι υποκρισιν 86. That is to say, instead of "conceive worthless things," Aquila and Theodotion translate ποιήσει ἀδικίαν "will do wrongdoing"; instead of "to carry out lawless things," "the Three" translate τοῦ ποιῆσαι ὑπόκρισιν "in order to commit hypocrisy."

All that has been said so far really is necessary to determine what is happening in the Armenian translation. It will be helpful to set it out in verse like the Hebrew and Greek. Note that I have restored զմոլորութիւն to its rightful position in the text.

Քանզի յիմարն յիմարութիւն խօսեսցի,
և սիրտ նորա զանարութիւն խորհեսցի.
կատարել զանորէնութիւն,
և խօսել առ աստուած զմոլորութիւն.
Because the fool will speak foolishness,
and his heart will think upon inanity;
to accomplish wrongdoing,
and to speak to God folly.

What we note here is that the word մոլորութիւն is the translation of the Old Greek πλάνησιν. In fact, մոլորութիւն can mean "straying," like the Greek

Old Greek πλάνησιν. In fact, մոլորութիւն can mean "straying," like the Greek word and its cognates.[1]

All of this brings us to the Armenian marginal reading հայհոյութիին "blasphemy; slander."

The word հայհոյութիւն is likely a rendering of ὑπόκρισιν, attributed to "the Three" in Greek MS 86 as their translation of חֶנֶף.

The word ὑπόκρισις occurs only once in the LXX/Old Greek corpus, namely at 2 Macc 6:25, where it is rendered by (վասն իմ) կեղծաւորեալ "(on account of my) being hypocritical." In the New Testament ὑπόκρισις is rendered similarly by կեղծաւորութիւն in its few occurrences (Matt 23:28; Mk 12:15; Luke 12:1; Gal 2:13; 1 Tim 4:2; 1 Pet 2:1). On the other hand the Greek underlying the word հայհոյութիւն in the New Testament is βλασφημία "slander, blasphemy."

The Armenian word for hypocrisy is կեղծաւորութիւն and the word for slander is հայհոյութիւն. The former is something that one practices; the latter is something that one speaks. Here in Isa 32:6 we expect the word կեղծաւորութիւն for ὑπόκρισιν. However, in the Armenian MSS the referrent for ὑπόκρισιν is not now ἄνομα "lawless things" but the word (λαλεῖν) ... πλάνησιν, that is "(to speak) ... deception." That is, now it is a question of *speaking* and the word կեղծաւորութիւն is not suitable because one does not *speak* hypocrisy—hypocritically yes, but hypocrisy no. The idiom requires a word that connects with speaking, like the word հայհոյութիւն "slander."

This difficult and somewhat conjectural explanation has been required because the translation ὑπόκρισιν in the Armenian tradition—or perhaps in the parent text of the Armenian marginal reading—was understood in error to refer not to ἄνομα but to πλάνησιν. When this occurred a different word than the usual word for hypocrisy—կեղծաւորութիւն—was required because now the noun followed a word for "speaking."

---

[1] "The usual translation of πλάνη ("wandering" from the path of truth, "error, delusion, deception") and its cognates πλανός and πλανόω in the New Testament is մոլորութիւն ("wandering, straying") and its cognates." See "The Vocabulary for Good and Evil in the Armenian Translation of the New Testament," in the proceedings of the Symposium on the Armenian New Testament, St. John's Armenian Church, Southfield, Michigan, May 22–24, 1992, published as *Text and Context: Studies in the Armenian New Testament* , ed. Shahé Ajamian and Michael E. Stone (UPATS 13; Atlanta: Scholars 1995) 49–57.

follows:

(զ)ամորէնութիւն] հայհոյութիւն in mg (conj.) et ind mend supra զմՈլ որուԹիւն.

In that case the following equivalents obtain:

դןֆ → Old Greek ἄνομα → Zohrapian զ ամորէ նութիւն

　　　　　　　→ Aq Sym Th ὑπόκρισιν → sine nom հայհոյnւԹիւն.

The Armenian evidence can be added to Ziegler's second apparatus in the following way:

τοῦ συντελεῖν ἄνομα] α′σ′θ′ του ποιησαι (> Arm) υποκρισιν 86 Arm (sine nom. et ind. mend. sup. πλάνησιν).

It is difficult to set forth the complex state of affairs in the Armenian evidence. Another way it might be presented is:

τοῦ συντελεῖν ἄνομα] α′ σ′ θ′ (sine nom. Arm) του ποιησαι (> Arm) υποκρισιν 86 Arm(υποκρισιν in txt. mend. et πλάνησιν in mg).

This will probably not satisfy some future editor. Perhaps by then the word հայհոյnւԹիւն will be found in the margin of some MS and the matter of citation will be simple.

37:30 *

զմնագործուն] ինքնեակ Sym

J501mg J1928mg J1934mg LOBmg M2587mg V229mg V1270mg V1507mg V1634mg Zohapp(mg)

Isaiah 36–39 is also preserved in 2 Kings 18–20.

In 37:22–29 we read Isaiah's taunt of the Assyrian king Sennacherib who attacked Judah in 701 B.C. Following that, in 39:30–32, an assurance is made to the Judean king, Hezekiah. In v 30 we read:

> And this shall be the sign for you: This year eat what grows of itself, and in the second year what springs from that; then in the third year sow, reap, plant vineyards, and eat their fruit.

The words "and in the second year what springs from that" are a translation of ‏וּבַשָּׁנָה הַשֵּׁנִית שָׁחִיס‎. Within that section of text the word ‏שָׁחִיס‎ has been translated "what springs from that." It is this word ‏שָׁחִיס‎ that is in question.

The word ‏שָׁחִיס‎ receives the following entry in KBH: ‏שָׁחִיס‎ Is 37₃₀: < refer to ‏סָחִישׁ‎.† When we look up the latter we find: ‏סָחִישׁ‎: **what grows of its own accord** (after the 2nd year harvest of grain) 2K 19₂₉.† That is, these words occur only in these parallel passages and the meaning has been determined by the context.

The Old Greek rendered ‏וּבַשָּׁנָה הַשֵּׁנִית שָׁחִיס‎ with the words τῷ δὲ ἐνιαυτῷ τῷ δευτέρῳ τὸ κατάλειμμα "and in the second year the remnant." The words τὸ κατάλειμμα "the remnant" represent ‏שָׁחִיס‎.

Ziegler's second apparatus provides us with the translations of Aquila, Symmachus and Theodotion for ‏שָׁחִיס‎. Unfortunately there is some disparity among the sources concerning the translation by Symmachus. According to Greek MS 86 and Theodoret the three translators used the same word for ‏שָׁחִיס‎, namely αὐτοφυῆ "what is self-grown"; according to Eusebius and Jerome, Aquila and Theodotion employed αὐτοφυῆ but Symmachus used ἀπό δένδρων (Jerome: *pomis vescere* "by eating tree-fruit").

The Armenian translation of the words τῷ δὲ ἐνιαυτῷ τῷ δευτέρῳ τὸ κατάλειμμα is և յամէ երա կերիցեն զմնացորդսն "and the next year you will eat those things that are left over." In the margin there is a reading for զմնացորդսն which is attributed to Symmachus: ինքնեակ "that comes of its own; self-produced." The word ինքնեակ is clearly a translation of αὐτοφυῆ.

The difficulty lies with the attribution to Symmachus. We can only note here that there is some question about this. The reading is certainly that of Aquila and Theodotion.

The Hebrew, Greek and Armenian equivalents are:

‏שָׁחִיס‎ → Old Greek τὸ κατάλειμμα → Zohrapian զմնացորդսն
→ Aq Sym Th αὐτοφυῆ → Sym ինքնեակ.

We can now add the Armenian to the Greek and Latin witnesses which we knew had readings from "the Three."

The Armenian evidence can be added to the second apparatus in Ziegler:
φάγε—ἀμήσατε] οι γ´ φαγετε επ ετος αυτοματα (α´ σ´ θ´ αυτομ. 86;

οι λ′ π′ αυτομ. Eus.) και τω δευτερω αυτοφυη (α′ σ′ θ′ αυτοφ. 86) εν δε τω
ετει τω ⟨τριτω⟩ σπειρατε και θερισατε Tht.; α′ και τω ετει τω δευτερω
αυτοφυη σ′ και τω ετει τω δευτερω απο δενδρων (σ′ *pomis vescere* Hi.)
θ′ και τω ετει τω δευτερω αυτοφυη Eus. | τὸ κατάλειμμα] σ′ αυτοφυη
Arm.

39:2

quüónιg] üωpnψβωg

LOB^mg J1928^mg J1934^mg M2587^mg Zoh^app(codd)

Zohrapian notes in his apparatus that some MSS have as their text üωpnψβωg quüónιg, i.e. the marginal reading has been brought into the text. He
does not cite üωpnψβωg as a marginal reading in his base MS.

Isaiah 39:1–8 describes Merodach-baladan's embassy to Jerusalem. We are
told that Hezekiah welcomed them and showed them, among other things, "his
treasure house." This is a translation of אֶת־בֵּית נְכֹתֹה.

The word *נְכֹת occurs only here and in the parallel passage at 2 Ki 20:13
in the Hebrew Bible.

The Old Greek transliterated the troublesome word. Hence we read that
Hezekiah showed them τὸν οἶκον τοῦ νεχωθα "the house of *nechōtha* ."

Ziegler notes that various MSS have a marginal reading for the word νεχωθα, namely των αρωματων "house of spices." This reading is found in the margins
of MSS 311 309-564 538; it appears as a correction in MS 36; it is the text of the Syro-hexapla. Finally the first apparatus in Ziegler notes that τον οικον των αρωματων is in the text, following νεχωθα, in MS 91.

An arrow in the first apparatus directs one to the second, hexaplaric apparatus. There we find that a variety of witnesses identify the translation τὸν οἶκον
τῶν ἀρωμάτων as that of Aquila and Symmachus. These witnesses include cum
var Q 86 566 Eus. Chr. Tht. Hi^lat. Ziegler also cites a reading in Chrysostom with
the signature of Symmachus—retroverted from the Latin as τὸν οἶκον τῶν
ὅπλων "the house of weapons."

The Armenian translation records that Hezekiah showed the embassy ꜱɢ-ᴜᴏᴜᴜ ɋᴜᴜᴏᴜ ɢ, literally "the houses of treasures," i.e. "treasure houses." This is a good contextual translation, especially since the parent text of the Armenian almost certainly had the transliteration. One feels some regret that the Armenian version was not collated for the Göttingen edition of Isaiah because here, e.g., it is of considerable exegetical interest.

In the margin of some Armenian witnesses we find the transliteration ᴜᴜ-ꜱᴜ ɥ[ᴩᴜɢ, i.e. ναχωθα. This spelling is attested in MSS 239′ (-δα 239). Conceivably the marginal reading could have come from secondary contact with such a Greek MS. Another suggestion also has plausibility, in my opinion.

The parallel passage to Isa 39:2 is 4 Rgn 20:13. There too the Old Greek employs a transliteration, νεχωθά according to MS B. The spelling ναχωθά is not attested there except in the Armenian version. It seems most likely to me that the marginal reading at Isa 39:2 is ex par., i.e. some scribe has added it on the basis of the parallel in 4 Rgn 20:13.

49:23

ʞᴜᴜᴜꞁꝑ] һ²ᴣᴜᴜꝑ

J501mg Zohapp(mg)

Zohrapian notes in his apparatus that һ²ᴣᴜᴜꝑ is in the margin of his base MS for collation and that it appears in the text of some other witnesses.

The context is Isaiah's words about return and restoration. In v 22 we are told that a signal fire will announce the beginning of Judah's restoration. Then comes v 23:

> Kings shall be your foster fathers,
> and their queens your nursing mothers.

The words "and their queens" are a translation of וְשָׂרוֹתֵיהֶם. The word I. שָׂרָה occurs only a handful of times in the Hebrew Bible—Judg 5:29; 1 Ki 11:3; Isa

49:23; Lam 1:1; Est 1:18— and means "**lady, gentlewoman.**"

The Old Greek rendered וְשָׂרוֹתֵיהֶם with the words αἱ δὲ ἄρχουσαι "and female rulers." We read:

καὶ ἔσονται βασιλεῖς τιθηνοί σου,
αἱ δὲ ἄρχουσαι τροφοί σου·
and kings will be your guardians,
and female rulers your nurses;

(The words αἱ ἄρχουσαι should probably be understood here as "queens," though perhaps as "princesses"—cf. Lust under ἄρχω. I have used the "wooden" translation "female rulers" in order to indicate that the Old Greek does not employ the common word for "queen.")

The Vulgate translates וְשָׂרוֹתֵיהֶם(ְ) with the word reginae "queens."

In Armenian αἱ δὲ ἄρχουσαι is rendered և կանայք նոցա "and their wives." (The Armenian attests the hexaplaric plus αὐτῶν "their.") It reads:

Եւ եղիցին թագաւորք դայեակք քո,
և կանայք նոցա մանկակալք քո.
And kings will be your caregivers,
and their wives your nurses;

This is a good translation since in the context—and certainly with the hexaplaric plus "their"—the nurses might well be the wives of the kings just mentioned.

In the margin of MSS J501 V1508 we find for կանայք the reading իշ-խանք "rulers, princes." (As noted already, Zohrapian indicates that some MSS have իշխանք as their text. Manuscript J1925 [f.293v, col.2, ↓2] reads the same as Zohrapian.) If this represents secondary contact with the Old Greek text—as seems likely—we might expect իշխանակին "princess, sovereign's wife," or թագուհի "queen." The same holds true if the marginal reading represents contact with Symmachus' translation.

According to Field, Symmachus translated וְשָׂרוֹתֵיהֶם with the words καὶ ἄρχουσαι αὐτῶν "and their queens." That is, the Symmachus translation is almost ἄρχουσαι αὐτῶν "and their queens." That is, the Symmachus translation is almost identical to the Old Greek. According to Ziegler it is only preserved in Eusebius. Since it is the same as the Old Greek one can understand why it is not also extant in the margins of MSS of the text of Isaiah.

It seems to me that the Armenian marginal reading most likely represents secondary contact with the Old Greek text. It represents a correction, or perhaps a "mis-correction," since the word ḥʒʰwuⁿᵖ "rulers" (masculine) is not the equivalent of αἱ ἄρχουσαι "rulers" (feminine). The reading ḥʒʰwuⁿᵖ does have some interesting exegetical consequences: male nurses?

51:1

hwⱡwⱶᵻpⱶ qḥⱷwⱷnⱷuⱷw] qhⱶⱷ ⱶⱷⱷwⱷⱷ ḥⱷwⱷwⱷg

J501ᵐᵍ LOBᵐᵍ Zohᵃᵖᵖ⁽ᵐᵍ⁾

Zohrapian notes that the marginal reading in his MS agrees with what is in the text of some other MSS.

The first half of ch 51 announces salvation for Abraham's children. The prophet summons his listeners in v 1 with the words:

שִׁמְעוּ אֵלַי רֹדְפֵי צֶדֶק.

Listen to me, you that pursue righteousness.

This is rendered in the Old Greek with:

Ἀκούσατέ μου, οἱ διώκοντες τὸ δίκαιον.

The sense of this translation is the same as that of the Hebrew.

The Latin Vulgate renders:

audite me qui sequimini quod iustum est .
Hear me, (you) who follow what is just.

Here רֹדְפֵי צֶדֶק is rendered "(you) who pursue what is just."

In Armenian the Old Greek is translated in Zohrapian as:

Լուարուք ինձ որ հայածէք զիրաւունս.

Listen to me, (you) who pursue righteousness.

The verb հայածեմ "pursue" has the "farther" demonstrative/definite marker -դ attached to the second plural form. In MSS J1925 (f.294r, col.1, ↓7) M1500 (f. 389v, col.1, ↑29) հայածէք appears without the -դ, so perhaps that is a secondary development.

In some Armenian MSS there is a marginal reading for հայածէք զիրաւունս. It is (որ) զհետ երթայք իրաւանց "you (who) go after righteousness." This is synonymous with what is in the text.

The expression զհետ երթամ "follow" occurs fairly frequently in the Armenian Bible. For example, there are the admonitions not to go after other gods: Deut 6:14; 8:19; 28:14; Judg 2:19; 3 Rgn 11:10; Jer 7:9; 11:10; 13:10; 42(35):15. In all these instances զհետ երթամ translates πορεύομαι ὀπίσω, except at Jer 11:10 where it renders βαδίζω ὀπίσω "go after."

"To *pursue* righteousness" is quite different than going after other gods and it should not surprise us that πορεύομαι ὀπίσω is never used as a translation of רדף in the Old Greek complex, according to H-R.

The expression զհետ երթամ is, however, used in a number of contexts like that in Isa 51:1. For example: at 1 Macc 6:23 κατακολουθεῖν τοῖς προστάγμασιν αὐτοῦ "to live by what he said" is rendered by երթալ զհետ հրամանաց նորա "to follow his commands"; at Prov 15:9 διώκοντας δὲ δικαιοσύνην ἀγαπᾷ "he loves those who pursue righteousness" is translated իսկ որ երթայ զհետ արդարութեան սիրէ զնա "but the one who pursues justice he loves him"; 1 Tim 6:11 and 2 Tim 2:22 are almost identical to Prov 15:9; at Rom 14:19 Ἄρα οὖν τὰ τῆς εἰρήνης διώκωμεν "Let us then pursue what makes for peace" is rendered Արդ այսուհետեւ զհետ երթիցուք խաղաղութեան "Therefore, let us pursue peace"; and finally at 1 Cor 14:1 διώκετε τὴν ἀγάπην "Pursue love" is translated Զհետ երթայք սիրոյ "Pursue love."

that this verb is used for pursuing enemies, or of pursing with an ill intent. Jeremiah 36(29):18 may serve as an example, chosen at random: հալածեցից զնոսա սրով և սովով "I pursue them with sword and famine." (The underlying Greek is part of a hexaplaric plus, the relevant part of which reads ἐκδιώξω κατόπισθεν [διώξω ὀπίσω in MSS O -233] αὐτῶν "I will pursue after them." This plus bears the name of Theodotion in MSS Q 86.) However, this is not exclusively true because it is the verb հալածեմ which is used in Matt 5:10: Երանի որ հալածեալ իցեն վասն արդարութեան "Blessed are those who should pursue righteousness."

The marginal reading might attest the preposition ὀπίσω "after"—or κατόπισθεν—following the verb διώκω or a compound of διώκω: Reider-Turner give διώκω and its compounds καταδιώκω, περιδιώκω as Aquila's renderings of רדף.

It might be argued that the rarity of usage of հալածեմ for the pursuit of the good has led to the marginal reading: the scribe who added it was providing a more suitable translation, namely զհետ երթամ, or perhaps simply a more familiar phrase. In that case the marginal reading represents a learned note.

The MSS which preserve the reading—particularly J501 V1508—are excellent witnesses for the preservation of readings from "the Three." For that reason, it cannot simply be dismissed. Nevertheless, on balance it seems to me that the marginal reading is an inner-Armenian development.

The Hebrew, Greek and Armenian equivalents are:

רֹדְפֵי צֶדֶק → Old Greek οἱ διώκοντες τὸ δίκαιον → Zohrapian որ հալածէք զհրաւունս

→ conj. οἱ [κατα?]διώκοντες ὀπίσω τῆς δικαιοσύνης → որ զհետ երհայք իրաւանց.

In this instance "equivalents" is used with the caution that the Armenian reading in all likelihood does not rest upon an underlying Greek.

The Armenian tradition preserves for certain only three readings in Isaiah which derive from "the Three"; none is preserved uniquely. This makes its preservation of such a reading at 51:1 somewhat unlikely.

XI. Ezekiel

Norayr Bogharian, *Grand Catalogue of St. James Manuscripts* , vol. 2 [MSS 241–600] (CGFAL; Jerusalem: Armenian Convent 1967). • Georg Fohrer, *Ezechiel* (HAT, First series 13; Tübingen: Mohr [Siebeck] 1955). • John L. McGregor, *The Greek Text of Ezekiel. An Examination of Its Homogeneity* (SBLSCS 18; Atlanta: Scholars Press 1985). • Joseph Ziegler, ed., *Septuaginta, Vetus Testamentum Graecum; Auctoritate Academiae Litterarum Gottingensis editum, XIV Isaias* ; Göttingen: Vandenhoeck & Ruprecht 1939; repr. 1967). • idem, *XVI/1 Ezechiel* (19-52).

The Greek text employed is that of Ziegler.

The marginal readings in J297 are particularly important in Ezekiel. The scribe explains apologetically in a colophon that the MS was copied from several exemplars. Ezekiel was apparently copied from a MS that included Job, the writings of Solomon and the prophets. It must be about this exemplar that the scribe complains in a note following Baruch: «Ով եղբարք, գրի սխալանացս անմեղադիր լերուք, զի օրինակ հին է եւ խառնակ, եւ գիրն վատ» "O brothers, please excuse this writing of its mistakes because the parent text is old, mixed up, and badly written." (Bogharian 129) Manuscript J297 belongs to the 15th century and was copied in Khlat', northwest of Lake Van.

The same can be said of marginal readings preserved in V280. This MS too is especially important. It also belongs to the 15th century—the date is 1418–1422—and, like J297, it was copied in Khlat'! It might very well be that they derive their readings from the same exemplar.

Noteworthy also is the preservation of the marginal reading at 17:22 in

V935. This MS dates from the mid-14th century and was copied in Sultania, Baghdad.

One might also mention the reading preserved in LOB and V1182 at 16:33.

It appears that for Ezekiel a handful of readings are well attested in Armenian while others are preserved only in a few witnesses and perhaps only a single witness. This indicates that in the case of this book the tradition of "the Three" is really quite scattered in its preservation.

3:13 *

 չարժման] թէ մի մեծ Aq mend pro մի մեծ Aq Th

V280mg(sine ind)

In the context Ezekiel is describing the sights and sounds that accompanied his ascent in the spirit. He says that "it was the sound of the wings of the living creatures brushing against one another, and the sound of the wheels beside them, that sounded like a loud rumbling." The words "that sounded like a loud rumbling" are a translation of וְקוֹל רַעַשׁ גָּדוֹל.

The Old Greek translation does not represent the word גָּדוֹל "great, i.e. loud." It says Ezekiel heard φωνὴ τοῦ σεισμοῦ "a sound of an earthquake."

Ziegler has the following in his first apparatus: τοῦ σεισμοῦ] + (※ O) μεγαλου (του μεγ. 88 46) O -62 46 = 𝔐 ↓; + μεγαλη 538-V-449 Tht.; σεισμου μεγαλου L -311-Z^V (μεγαλη). The arrow points us to the second apparatus for the source of this hexaplaric plus. In that second apparatus we find this citation: σεισμοῦ] α' θ' + ※ μεγαλου Q^{txt}; α' σ' + του μεγαλου 86. That is to say, the word μεγάλου—which represents גָּדוֹל—has the signatures of Aquila and Theodotion in the margin of MS Q and the signatures of Aquila and Symmachus in MS 86.

The Armenian marginal reading corresponds to the reading in MS Q and carries the same signatures. The words մի մեծ mean "a big."

The Hebrew, Greek and Armenian equivalents are:
גָּדוֹל → Old Greek non hab → Zohrapian non hab
    → Aq Th (MS Q) μεγάλου → Aq Th մի մեծ.

The Armenian evidence can be added to the second apparatus in Ziegler as follows:

σεισμοῦ] α′ θ′ + ※ (> Arm) μεγαλου Q^{txt} Arm; α′ σ′ + του μεγαλου 86.

Ziegler states in his introduction to the edition of Isaiah that the hexaplaric readings cited in the second apparatus are marginal notations almost exclusively in MSS Q Syh 86 and 710: therefore the exponent ^{mg} is not used. (See *Isaias* 114.) The same can be understood to be true of the Armenian readings cited in the second apparatus, as above.

It is also probably clear that the Armenian marginal reading represents a plus after σεισμοῦ, so that in the citation of the Armenian a plus sign can be used, as in the citation of the evidence in Q and 86.

5:2 *

զ ξηրրնրդ 1° 2° 3°] երրնրդ Aq Sym

J297mg(hab mend ad 4:12–14 sine ind)

Three times MS J297 has the marginal reading, one below the other, but these readings have been misplaced to 4:12–14. This is about three-quarters of a column from their proper location. In v 11 the prophet is told to drink water by measure—"one sixth of a hin." Perhaps that has attracted the marginal reading "one third," but its three-fold repetition must have been confusing.

At the beginning of ch 5 the prophet is told to take a razor and cut his hair and beard, then weigh it. Verse 2 continues: "One third of the hair you shall burn in the fire inside the city, when the days of the siege are completed; one third you shall take and strike with the sword all around the city; and one third you shall scatter to the wind, …" In each case the words "one third" translate שְׁלִשִׁית or, with the article, הַשְּׁלִשִׁית.

The Old Greek translation has an additional clause after the statement about the first third, i.e. after the word "completed." That is to say, Ezekiel in the Greek text divides his hair into *four* parts. The additional clause in the Old Greek reads: καὶ λήμψῃ τὸ τέταρτον καὶ κατακαύσεις ἀπὸ ἐν μέσῳ αὐτῆς "and you will take the quarter and burn it in its midst," i.e. in the midst of the city. This seems to be a repetition of the first clause, so that we see Ezekiel burning two-quarters of the cut hair in the city! At any rate, the Old Greek reads τὸ τέταρτον "the quarter" four times.

Ziegler cites three witnesses as lacking that second clause: 46 Sah Arm. It has likely been lost by parablepsis. As a consequence the Armenian translation uses "quarters" of hair—the Armenian for τὸ τέταρτον is զ չորրորդ մասն(ն) "the quarter part"—but accounts for only three "quarters." That must have raised an eyebrow for the thoughtful exegete.

The Armenian marginal reading solves the dilemma by providing the translation of Aquila and Symmachus, both of whom read τὸ τρίτον "the third." The entry in Ziegler's second apparatus is as follows:

τὸ τέταρτον 1° 2° 4°] α′ σ′ θ′ (α′ θ′ sec. 87) το τριτον 86 87.

There are marginal readings for only the first, second and fourth occurrence of τὸ τέταρτον because the third is not in the Hebrew text. Since the third clause is also lacking in the Armenian, 1° 2° 4° of the Greek apparatus become 1° 2° 3° in the citation of the marginal reading on the basis of the Armenian edition.

The Hebrew, Greek and Armenian equivalents are:

שְׁלִשִׁית 1° 2° 3° → Old Greek τὸ τέταρτον 1° 2° 3° 4° → Zohrapian 1° 2° 4° զ չորրորդ մասն

→ Aq Sym Th τὸ τρίτον 1° 2° 3° → Aq Sym [զ]երրորդ մասն(ն).

The Armenian evidence can be added to the second apparatus of the edition of Ziegler:

τὸ τέταρτον 1° 2° 4°] α′ σ′ θ′ (α′ θ′ sec. 87; α′ σ′ Arm) το τριτον 86 87 Arm.

16:4 *

ոչ որք եհար զպորտ քո] ոչ հատաւ պորտ քո Aq

J297mg J1927mg (զ պորտ) J1928mg J1934mg M177mg M2587mg V229mg(հատապորտ) V623 mg V1270mg Zohapp(mss mg)

Ezekiel 16 contains the allegory of the two sisters. In v 4 we read:

> As for your birth, on the day you were born your navel cord was not cut, nor were you washed with water to cleanse you, nor rubbed with salt, nor wrapped in cloths.

The words "your navel cord was not cut" are a translation of לֹא־כָרַּת שָׁרֵּךְ. The word *שֹׁר occurs only here and at Canticles 7:3, where it means "navel."

The Old Greek "translation" of the clause in question is οὐκ ἔδησαν τοὺς μαστούς σου "they did not bind your breasts." Ziegler notes in his first apparatus that a hexaplaric based translation has come into various witnesses, namely οὐκ ἐτμήθη ὁ ὀμφαλός σου "your umbilical cord was not cut."

The Armenian translation as reproduced by Zohrapian has a doublet here. The text includes "and they did not bind your breasts" preceded by "your umbilical cord no one struck." So we read: ոչ ոք եհար զպորտ քո, և ոչ պնդեցին զստինս քո. In his apparatus Zohrapian notes a number of textual matters concerning this part of v 4. In several MSS, he says, the words ոչ ոք եհար ըզպորտ քո "no one struck your umbilical cord" are missing whereas in another MS we find ոչ ոք եհատ զպորտ "no one cut the umbilical cord." Zohrapian goes on to comment that two other MSS have the words ոչ հատաւ պորտ քո "your umbilical cord was not cut" in the margin and attribute them to Aquila. The text has become corrupt: եհար "struck" and եհատ "cut" have become confused.

The Armenian MSS cited above have the marginal reading about which Zohrapian speaks. The words ոչ հատաւ պորտ քո mean "your umbilical cord was not cut" and are a translation of the hexaplaric οὐκ ἐτμήθη ὁ ὀμφαλός σου. In the Armenian witnesses the translation is attributed to Aquila.

In his second apparatus Ziegler notes the hexaplaric reading οὐκ ἐτμήθη ὁ ὀμφαλός σου which is attributed to δ' in MS Q^mg and in Or.VIII 381 to εβρ' (*non est excisus umbilicus tuus*). Ziegler does not have δ' in his list of hexaplaric sigla (cf. pp. 81–82) but, according to Field, δ' = α' σ' ο' θ'. See Field *ad loc* . Therefore, the translation is attributed to "the Three" in MS Q and to the mysterious εβρ' in Origen's *Homilies and Selections to Ezekiel* (See Ziegler's Introduction, pp. 64–65. These works of Origen transmit eleven hexaplaric readings.)

The Armenian marginal reading therefore represents the translation not only of Aquila but also of Symmachus, Theodotion and perhaps ϵβρ′ as well.

The Hebrew, Greek and Armenian equivalents are:

לֹא־כָרַּת שָׁרֵּךְ → Old Greek οὐκ ἔδησαν τοὺς μαστούς σου → Zohrapian nչ պևդեցին զատիևս քո
→ Aq Sym Th ϵβρ′ οὐκ ἐτμήθη ὁ ὀμφαλός σου → Aq nչ
հատատ պորտ քո.

In this instance the Armenian MSS preserve a reading also known from Greek sources. The Armenian evidence can be added to the second apparatus in Ziegler as follows:

οὐκ ἔδ. τοὺς μ. σου] δ′ (α′ Arm) ουκ ετμηθη ο ομφαλος σου Q Arm; ϵβρ′ *non est excisus umbilicus tuus* Or.VIII381.

16:33 *

ուղ երծէ իր Zoh[app]; աւղ երծէիր Zoh[txt]] պարգեւեիր; չնորհեիր;
ծգեիր

LOB[mg] V1182[mg]

These readings are not cited by Zohrapian even though V1182 is one of the MSS he uses.

The prophet continues here with his allegory of the unfaithful wife. In vv 35–43 Ezekiel tells the wife, Jerusalem, that her lovers will turn against her; further that God himself will divorce her.

In v 33 we read:

Gifts are given to all whores; but you gave your gifts to all your lovers, bribing them to come to you from all around for your whorings.

The word that concerns us is "bribing," which is a translation of the finite verb תְּשַׁחֲדִי. The verb שׁחד occurs only twice in the Hebrew Bible, here and at Job 6: 22. KBH assign the meaning "**give a gift**." The cognate noun שֹׁחַד "gift, present; bribe" occurs more frequently, some 23 times.

The Old Greek renders this verse in the following way:

πᾶσι τοῖς ἐκπορνεύσασιν αὐτὴν προσεδίδου μισθώματα, καὶ σὺ δέδω-
κας μισθώματα πᾶσι τοῖς ἐρασταῖς σου καὶ ἐφόρτιζες αὐτοὺς τοῦ
ἔρχεσθαι πρὸς σέ κυκλόθεν ἐν τῇ πορνείᾳ σου.

to all who made use of her for fornication she used to give rental money,
and you have given rental money to all your lovers and you used to load
them down (with presents) so that they would come to you from all around
in your immorality.

The Old Greek differs here substantially from the Hebrew. In fact, the Old Greek
goes its own way from v 32 where we read that "The adulterous wife such as you
takes rental money even from her own husband" (whereas) (v 33) "to all who ..."
In the Hebrew v 33 begins with a statement that—translating literally—says "To all
whores they give gifts but you ..."

The Old Greek translates יִתְּנוּ־נֵדֶה with the word ἐφόρτιζες "you used to
load them down."

The Armenian translation of v 33 is:

Ամենայն պոռնիկք կաւզէնս առնուն անձանց իրեանց,
և դու սայիր վարձու սիզեւաց քոց, և ատերօձէիր [ուղ եր-
օձէիր Zohᵃᵖᵖ] զնոսա զալ առ քեզ յամենայն կողմանց ի
պոռնկութիւն քո:

All whores receive monetary reward for themselves, and you used to give
gifts to your whore-keepers, and you used to make them presents to come
to you from every side for your fornications.

In the Armenian translation the word ատերօձէիր is used to represent ἐφόρτιζες.
The verb ատերօձել means "to make a present; to win with gifts, to seduce." It is
for the word ատերօձէիր (ἐφόρτιζες) that we have the marginal readings in the
Armenian MSS.

There are three unsigned readings. If we were to presume that these readings might be the translations of Aquila, Symmachus and Theodotion, we would be correct. In his second apparatus Ziegler provides the relevant translations of Aquila and Symmachus:

33 καὶ ἐφόρτιζες αὐτούς] α΄ και εδωροδοτεις αυτους Q 87(-δοτη)-91 (uterque sine και); σ΄ ⟨και⟩ εδοματιζες ⟨αυτους⟩ 87-91.

Aquila's translation of ‏וַתְּשַׁחֲדִי‎ was therefore ἐδωροδότεις "you used to give presents"; Symmachus' translation was ἐδομάτιζες "you used to bestow presents on." According to H-R, these two verbs occur only here among the Greek translations of the Hebrew Bible.

The three unsigned Armenian readings belong to "the Three." Theodotion's translation follows those of Aquila and Symmachus when his translation is cited at all in Armenian MSS. Therefore we may set aside ձգէիր for the moment. That leaves the first two readings, պարգեւեթիր (i.e. պարգեւէթիր) "you used to give, distribute generously" and շնորհէթիր (i.e. շնորհէթիր) "you used to give as a present or favour." Which of these represents ἐδωροδότεις as opposed to ἐδομάτιζες?

In 4 Rgn where we have Aquila–Symmachus and Aquila–Symmachus–Theodotion readings, the order is usually Symmachus–Aquila–Theodotion, i.e. Symmachus precedes Aquila. But that need not be so here; at any rate, we have only one case among the readings extant in Armenian for Ezekiel, or Isaiah, where we have both Aquila's and Symmachus' names: that is in MS J297 at Ezek 4:12–14.

One clue we may have lies in the fact that Aquila's translation uses a cognate of the common word δῶρον "gift": the Armenian word պարգեւէթիր contains the common cognate պարգեւ "gift." I think therefore that պարգեւէթիր represents Aquila; in that case շնորհէթիր represents the translation of Symmachus.

Ziegler cites no evidence for Theodotion. The third reading in the Armenian witnesses is most likely to be attributed to him. The word ձգէիր (i.e. ձգէիր) is the imperfect, second person singular of ձգեմ "to drag; allure, entice."

A check of all the citations for ձգեմ in Arapkerts'i produces only a few instances of its use in contexts like that here: Eccl 2:3; Cant 1:3 (Old Greek 1:4); Jer 38:3 (MT 31:3); John 6:44; 12:32. In all these cases ձգեմ translates ἑλκύω "draw; attract." It seems probable that ձգէիր is a translation of εἷλκες "you used to attract."

The Hebrew, Greek and Armenian equivalents can be set out as follows.

יַּחֲשֹׁךְ → Old Greek ἐφόρτιζες → Zohrapian ոιη երծէիր

→ Aq ἐδωροδότεις → sine nom պարգեւէիր

→ Sym ἐδομάτιζες → sine nom շնորհէիր

→ Th εἱλκες → sine nom ծգէիր.

In this instance the Armenian witnesses preserve the translations of Aquila, Symmachus and Theodotion. The translations of Aquila and Symmachus are known also in Greek witnesses; not so the translation of Theodotion, so the Armenian evidence is significant in that respect. We can add the Armenian evidence to the second apparatus of Ziegler as follows:

καὶ ἐφόρτιζες αὐτούς] α′ και (> Arm) εδωροδοτεις αυτους (> Arm) Q 87(-δοτη)-91 Arm(anon.); σ′ ⟨και⟩ εδοματιζες ⟨αυτους⟩ 87-91 Arm(anon.); ⟨θ′ ⟩ ⟨και⟩ ειλκες ⟨αυτους⟩ Arm.

It should be noted that the Theodotion reading is a conjectural retroversion.

17:22 *

թշնեցից եւ անկեցից] ի սրտէ, ի զլխոյ կտրեցից Sym

V935mg

Ezekiel 17:22–24 contains the allegory of the cedar. In v 22 the Lord says that he will take a sprig:

Thus says the Lord GOD:
I myself will take a sprig
    from the lofty top of a cedar;
    I will set it out.
I will break off a tender one
    from the topmost of its
            young twigs;
I myself will plant it
    on a high and lofty mountain.

This is a translation of the Hebrew which, set out according to the English translation, reads:

כֹּה אָמַר אֲדֹנָי יְהוִה
וְלָקַחְתִּי אָנִי
מִצַּמֶּרֶת הָאֶרֶז הָרָמָה
וְנָתָתִּי
מֵרֹאשׁ יֹנְקוֹתָיו רַךְ אֶקְטֹף
וְשָׁתַלְתִּי אָנִי
עַל־הַר־גָּבֹהַּ וְתָלוּל:

There are a few difficulties here, as one can judge from a comparison of the Hebrew with the English translation. The words "take a sprig" are understood on the basis of the context. Next, one might wonder whether וְנָתָתִּי "I will set it out" should be read with what follows, leaving אֶקְטֹף "I will break off" to stand by itself or be read with what follows it. Finally, the word תָלוּל "towering" occurs only here in the Hebrew Bible.

Fohrer pares away various accretions in the Hebrew text: הָרָמָה ;אֲדֹנָי ("specifying gloss"); וְנָתָתִּי ("a gloss at the formation of a new sentence"); יֹנְקוֹתָיו with the Greek ("specifying gloss"); וְתָלוּל with the Greek ("explanatory gloss")! (*Ezechiel* ad loc)

The Old Greek translation is as follows:

διότι τάδε λέγει κύριος
Καὶ λήμψομαι ἐγὼ
ἐκ τῶν ἐπιλέκτων τῆς κέδρου,
ἐκ κορυφῆς καρδίας αὐτῶν ἀποκνιῶ
καὶ καταφυτεύσω ἐγὼ ἐπ' ὄρος ὑψηλόν·
Therefore thus says the Lord:
"And I will take [it]
from the choice ones [i.e. branches] of the cedar,
from the summit of their heart I will snip [it]
and I will plant [it] upon a high mountain;"

Rahlfs points out in his apparatus that the majority text reads καὶ δώσω ἀπὸ κεφαλῆς παραφυάδων αὐτῆς "and I will give (appoint?) from the top of its off-
shoots"—which stands under the asterisk in Origenian witnesses—before καρδίας
αὐτῶν. That majority text includes the Armenian.

The Armenian translation of the verse is:

Վասն այնորիկ այսպէս ասէ ադոնկայի տէր,
և առից ես յրնտիր րնտիր մայրից բարձուանդակին.
և տաց ես ի գլխոյ շառաւիղացն նորա ի սիրտս նոցա.
քշտեցից և տնկեցից ի վերայ լերինն բարձու.

For this reason, thus says Adonai Lord:
"And I will take from the choicest of the cedars of the highest hill;
and I will take from the top of its shoots, from their hearts;
I will prune [it] and plant [it] upon a high mountain;"

The Armenian has a hexaplaric plus, namely τῆς ὑψηλῆς, following the word κέδρου, along with L'' Tht.: it appears as բարձուանդակին "of the highest hill."
The longer hexaplaric plus—καὶ δώσω ἀπὸ κεφαλῆς παραφυάδων αὐτῆς—is
rendered as "and I will take from the top of its shoots." This creates a doublet,
namely ի (գլխոյ) շառաւիղացն նորա "from (the top of) its shoots" and ի
սիրտս նոցա "from their hearts."

Manuscript V935 has a marginal reading with the index sign upon քշտեցից "I will prune" (Greek ἀποκνιῶ "I will snip"). The marginal reading is ի
սրտէ, ի գլխոյ կտրեցից "from the heart, from the top I will cut." The words
ի սրտէ "from the heart" and ի գլխոյ "from the top" also represent a doublet, it
appears. Since ἐκ ... καρδίας is represented in the Old Greek text, perhaps the
marginal reading is saying "in place of ի սրտէ—which stands in the text from
which this marginal reading was taken—read ի գլխոյ—which of course already
stands in the Armenian translation, having come there from the Hexapla!

To repeat: the textual situation has been rendered more complicated by the
fact that the Armenian translation is already a hexaplaric text and contains καὶ δώσω
ἀπὸ κεφαλῆς παραφυάδων αὐτῆς, which Ziegler correctly places in his second
apparatus. When the marginal readings were placed in the Armenian MS, hexaplaric

readings were being cited for a hexaplaric text!

The verb կտրեցից "I will cut" is, of course, intended for բշտեցից "I will prune." It appears to me that this may well be a second reading, i.e. ի զլխոյ should be separated from կտրեցից. Support for this suggestion comes from Ziegler's second apparatus where we note that MS 86 preserves Aquila's translation for אֶקְטֹף (Old Greek ἀποκνιῶ): he used the word περικλάσω "I will break off."

The Hebrew for which the translation(s) in the margin stand(s) is ... מֵרֹאשׁ אֶקְטֹף "from the topmost ... I will break off."

There are twenty passages cited under կտրեմ "cut" in Arapkerts'i. An examination of these reveals that the verb is used to translate a variety of Greek verbs in the Bible: ἀποκόπτω "cut off" (Judg 1:6 AB [of fingers and toes]; 2 Rgn 10:4 [of garments]) and ἐκκόπτω "cut" (Luke 13:7 [of cutting down a fig tree]); αἴρω "remove" (John 15:2 [of removing dead wood]); ἀφαιρέω "remove; cut off" (Isa 18:5 [cut off shoots]; Ezek 23:25 [cut off nose and ears]); γλωσσοτομέω "cut out the tongue" (2 Macc 7:4); διαιρέω "divide" (3 Rgn 3:25, 26 [of cutting a child in two]; Jer 41(34):18, in the hexaplaric plus [of cutting an animal in two]); διχοτομέω "cut in two" (Matt 24:51 // Luke 12:46 [as punishment]); ἐκτίλλω "strip the leaves off" (Dan 4:23[Zohrapian 20]); κείρω "shear; cut hair" (Gen 38:13; Deut 15:19 [of shearing]; Job 1:20; Mic 1:16; Jer 7:29 [of cutting hair]); κολοβόω "mutilate" (2 Rgn 4:12); πρίζω "saw" (Am 1:3).

It seems likely that we can now add the verb περικλάω "break off" to this list. It is rendered quite suitably for the context by the word կտրեմ "cut off."

Fortunately we have Symmachus' translation for מֵרֹאשׁ יְנִקוֹתָיו. It is ἀπὸ τοῦ ἄκρου (τῶν) θαλλῶν "from the top of the young branches," according to MS 86: see Field. The Armenian preserves only ἀπὸ τοῦ ἄκρου. It is similarly fortunate that we have Aquila's translation of אֶקְטֹף.

If the analysis above is correct we have preserved here two marginal readings, one with signature and one without.

The Hebrew, Greek and Armenian equivalents for the first are:

מֵרֹאשׁ → Old Greek ἐκ κορυφῆς → Zohrapian ի զլխոյ

→ Sym ἀπὸ τοῦ ἄκρου → Sym ի զլխոյ.

The Hebrew, Greek and Armenian equivalents for the second are:

אֶקְטֹף → Old Greek ἀποκνιῶ → Zohrapian բշտեցից

→ Aq περικλάσω → sine nom կտրե ցհց·

The Armenian evidence can now be added to the second apparatus in Ziegler's edition as follows:

ἐκ κορυφῆς] σ′ [θ′] + ⟨και δωσω απο⟩ του ακρου των θαλλων 86; σ′ του ακρου Arm; θ′ + ⁜ και δωσω απο κεφαλης παραφυαδων αυτης Q[txt] 86 (anon.) Hi.[lat] | ἀποκνιῶ] α′ περικλασω 86 Arm(anon.).

20:43 *

կոծես ցիք] դժկամակ լինիցիք Aq; ամդ ապարտես ցիք Sym; տապտկացէք Th

V280mg(sine ind)

Chapter 20 concerns the fall and rise of Israel. In vv 40–44 we learn that after the new Exodus God will restore his people to Zion and their sacrifices will again be acceptable—so reads the summative note in the Oxford Annotated Bible.

In v 43 the text says, "There [i.e. in Israel] you shall remember your ways and all the deeds by which you have polluted yourselves; and you shall loathe yourselves for all the evils that you have committed." The words whose translation is at issue are וּנְקֹטֹתֶם בִּפְנֵיכֶם, rendered in the NRSV as "and you shall loathe yourselves."

The verb קוט in the *nifal* with בְּ means "feel a disgust for"; the *nifal* occurs a handful of times in the Hebrew Bible, mostly in Ezekiel: Ezek 6:9; 20:43; 36: 41; Job 10:1; cj. Ps 95:10. In our text the word פָּנִים "face" is used in the sense of "self," hence the translation "you shall feel a disgust for yourselves," or, as in the NRSV "you shall loathe yourselves."

The Old Greek translation of וּנְקֹטֹתֶם בִּפְנֵיכֶם is καὶ κόψεσθε τὰ πρόσωπα ὑμῶν "and you will beat your faces"—a striking (!) expression, but one in keeping with one of the uses of κόπτω: see II. Middle: *beat* or *strike oneself, beat one's breast* or *head* through grief. (LSJ) The same verb is used at 6:9 where we read: καὶ κόψονται πρόσωπα αὐτῶν "and they will beat their faces."

Ziegler's second apparatus provides the translations of Aquila, Symmachus and Theodotion for בְּפָנֵיכֶם קוֹטָם. They are:

α′ δυσαρεστηθήσεσθε (-θαι cod.) ... "you will be displeased ..."
σ′ μικροὶ φανήσεσθε ἐν αὐτοῖς "you will appear little because of them"
θ′ προσοχθιεῖτε (-ται codd.) κατέναντι αὐτῶν "you will be weary before them."

These readings are preserved in MSS 86 87-91. (Manuscripts 87-91 lack both ἐν αὐτοῖς and κατέναντι αὐτῶν.)

The Armenian translation of καὶ κόψεσθε τὰ πρόσωπα ὑμῶν is եւ կոծ-ծեաջիք զերեսս ձեր "and you will beat your faces," according to Zohrapian's edition. This represents a literal translation of the Old Greek.

Was this literalism responsible for the inclusion of the marginalia? In MS V280 there are alternate translations drawn from "the Three"; they are provided in the order Aquila, Symmachus and Theodotion. The three translations are:

Aq դժկամակ լինիցիք "you will be displeased"
Sym անդ ապարտեաջիք "there you will be brought to ill repute"
Th տաղտկայցէք "you will be disgusted."

Aquila's rendering in Greek is translated into Armenian as դժկամակ լի-նիցիք "you will be displeased." That is, the translation consists of the adjective դժկամակ "angry, displeased" and the verb լինիմ "be, become." The verb is in the present subjunctive mood.

The Symmachus translation is անդ ապարտեաջիք "there you will be brought to ill repute." The verb ապարտեմ means "to besprinkle with salt [cf. աղ "salt"]: to spoil, to desolate: to cast a stain upon, to wound the reputation of, to slander, to calumniate." The sense of the Greek and the Armenian is that these people are going to be brought down.

Arapkerts'i cites just one reference for ապարտել: Judges 9:38. There the Hebrew אֲשֶׁר מָאַסְתָּה בּוֹ "you made light of" is translated by the Old Greek as ὃν ἐξουδένωσας "whom you disdained." (The Vaticanus and Alexandrinus MS traditions have the same reading.) In turn the Armenian translation is զոր դուն ազարտեիր "whom you used to disparage."

Theodotion's Greek translation is rendered into Armenian as տաղտկայցէք. The verb տաղտկամ means "be disgusted, wearied, sick or tired of;
to loathe, nauseate." It appears here in the present subjunctive mood, so "you will
be weary of"—to follow the sense of the Greek.

The Hebrew, Greek and Armenian equivalents are:

םֶכיֵ֖נְפִּ֑ב → Old Greek κόψεσθε → Zohrapian կոծեսջիք

→ Aq δυσαρεστηθήσεσθε → Aq դժկամակ լինիցիք

→ Sym μικροὶ φανήσεσθε → Sym անդ աղարտեսջիք

→ Th προσοχθιεῖτε → Th տաղտկայցէք.

This evidence can be added to the second apparatus in Ziegler in the follow-
in way. I have made "bold" the parentheses enclosing the relevant section.

43 init.—ὄνομά μου (v. 44)] σ′ και οτε μηνσθησεσθε εκει τας οδους
⟨υμων⟩ και ⟨πασας⟩ (α′ θ′ και παντα 86) τας εννοιας υμων εν αις εμιαν-
θητε ⟨και⟩ μικροι φανησεσθε εν αυτοις (α′ δυσαρεστηθησεσθε (-θαι cod.) σ′
μικροι φανησεσθε εν αυτοις θ′ προσοχθιειτε (-ται codd.) κατεναντι αυτων
86 87-91 Arm (87-91 Arm om. εν αυτοις et κατεν. αυτων)) δια πασας τας
κακιας υμων ας εποιησατε (α′ θ′ ※ αις εποιησατε Q^txt 91 (sine ※).

21:7 (21:12 MT Rahlfs) *

ամենայն երանք ապականեցջին գիջութեամբ] յամենայն (inc
M177) ձնգաց իջջէ ջուր Sym

J1927^mg(sine nom) J1934^mg(sine ind in txt) M177^mg(ind supra ամենայն 5°)
M2587^mg(sine ind in txt) V229^mg(sine ind in txt) V623^mg(sine ind in txt) Zoh^app(mg)(sine
nom)

Zohrapian notes in his apparatus that his base MS has the marginal reading
which some other witnesses preserve under the name of Symmachus.

Chapter 21 contains "Oracles on the sword." In vv 1–7 God draws his
sword: because of its heterodoxy Judah will be cut down. In v 7 we read:

And when they say to you, "Why do you moan?" you shall say, "Because
of the news that has come. Every heart will melt and all hands will be
feeble, every spirit will faint and all knees will turn to water. See it comes
and it will be fulfilled," says the Lord.

The words "all knees will turn to water" are a translation of the Hebrew
כָּל־בִּרְכַּיִם תֵּלַכְנָה מָּיִם. This clause contains a euphemistic use of the verb
הָלַךְ: cf. KBH 8b: בִּרְכַּיִם תֵּלַכְנָה מַּיִם (KBH use transliteration of these words)
= urinate. Passages given for this sense are Ezek 7:17; 21:12, i.e. here. For the
translation "turn to water" see BDB under הָלַךְ, no. 3: "*all knees shall flow down
in water*, i.e. be as weak as water."

The Old Greek translated the clause with the words πάντες μηροὶ μολυνθήσονται ὑγρασίᾳ "all thighs will be defiled with moisture." This is quite literally
reproduced in the Armenian translation found in Zohrapian's text: ամենայն
երանքապականեցին զիշութեամբ "all knees will be defiled with
moisture."

Ziegler cites Symmachus' translation of the clause in the second apparatus
of his edition: σ' και δια παντων γονατων ρευσει υδατα (σ' ρευσει υδατα 86)
Syh. That is, the Symmachus reading is extant in the margins of Greek MS 86 and
Syh. (He does not cite the Armenian evidence even though the Symmachus translation is cited in Zohrapian's apparatus, which he collated.) This translation means
"and through all knees waters will flow."

The Symmachus translation is reproduced in Armenian as յամենայն
ծնգաց իջցէ ջուր "water will descend on all knees." This accurately represents both the Greek and the Hebrew, the sense of which appears to be "they will
pee their pants" (with fear).

The Armenian marginal reading reproduces the entire clause from Symmachus' translation, which is more than Greek MS 86mg: the latter has only the words
ῥεύσει ὕδατα "waters will flow."

The Hebrew, Greek and Armenian equivalents can be set out as follows:
כָּל־בִּרְכַּיִם תֵּלַכְנָה מָּיִם → Old Greek πάντες μηροὶ μολυνθήσονται
ὑγρασίᾳ → Zohrapian ամենայն երանք ապականեցին
զիշութեամբ

→ Sym διὰ πάντων γονάτων ρεύσει ὕδατα → Sym յամենայն ծնգաց իրգէ ջուր.

In this case the Armenian preserves a complete clause. This is a refreshing
change from individual words. The Armenian witness should be added to the Syro-
hexapla in Ziegler's apparatus: it preserves more than the Greek evidence he cites.
The Armenian evidence can be added as follows:

καὶ π. μηροὶ μολ. ὑγρ.] σ′ και (> Arm) δια παντων γονατων ρευσει
υδατα (σ′ ρευσει υδατα 86) Arm Syh.

23:3 *

(ի) կուսութենէ իրեանց] կուսութեանց իրեանց Sym

J297mg

Ch. 23 contains the allegory of the two sisters, Oholah and Oholibah. In v 3
we read that:

> they played the whore in Egypt; they played the whore in their youth; their
> breasts were caressed there, and their virgin bosoms were fondled.

The words "and their virgin bosoms were fondled" are a translation of וְשָׁם
עִשּׂוּ דַּדֵּי בְּתוּלֵיהֶן. The verb here is the *piel* perfect of עָשָׂה. That is a rare form
for עָשָׂה and KBH confine its usage to this chapter: vv 3, 8, conj. 21. It means
"press, squeeze." Literally the clause just cited means "and there the breasts of their
virginity were squeezed." The Hebrew word for "virginity" is a noun that is plural
morphologically: בְּתוּלִים.

The Old Greek translation of the clause in question is ἐκεῖ διεπαρθενεύθησαν "there they were deflowered." This is, of course, not a literal translation. Origen brought it into line with the Hebrew; Ziegler's presentation of the hexaplaric
addition is as follows: διεπαρθενεύθησαν] + (✳ O - Syh) τιτθοι (τιθοι Q*) παρ-
θεν(ε)ιων αυτων O = 𝔐 ↓. The hexaplaric text therefore reads: ἐκεῖ διεπαρθενεύθησαν τιτθοὶ παρθενείων αὐτῶν "there the breasts of their virginal state were de-

flowered."

Ziegler provides the translation of Symmachus for the clause in question in his second apparatus: ἐκεῖ διεπαρθενεύθησαν] σ′ ⟨καὶ ἐκεῖ⟩ ηκμασαν (σ′ και εκει ηκμασαν Syh) τιτθοι (τιθθοι cod.) παρθενειων αυτης 86. The English translation of Symmachus, according to MS 86 (and the Syro-hexapla) is "and there the breasts of her virginity were ripe." The possessive αὐτῆς "her" does not agree with the Hebrew, which has the plural possessive "their," i.e. יְהֵן֒: the latter in Greek is represented by αὐτῶν in Origen's text.

The word παρθενείων is plural. Indeed παρθένειος or παρθένιος occurs only in the neuter plural in the LXX/Old Greek corpus, i.e. τὰ παρθένεια/παρθένια, always as a translation for the morphologically plural בְּתוּלִים: Deut 22:14, 15, 17 (twice), 20; Judg 11:37, 38. H-R also cite Symmachus here at Ezek 23:3.

All of this brings us to the marginal reading in the Armenian witness.

The Armenian translation of the last clause of v 3 in Zohrapian's edition is անդ անկան ի կուսութենէ իրեանց "there they fell from their virginity." This is a translation of a text like the Old Greek and not the hexaplaric text, as can be seen from a comparison with those texts. In his apparatus Zohrapian notes that some MSS, instead of the words just quoted, have եւ անդ անկան ի կուսութենէ "And there they fell from virginity," i.e. lack the possessive իրեանց "their."

It might be useful now to quote the entire verse in Armenian:

Եւ պոռնկեցան յեգիպտոս ի մանկութեան իրեանց. անդ անկան ստինք իրեանց. անդ անկան ի կուսութեանէ իրեանգ:

and they committed fornication in Egypt in their youth. There their breasts fell; there they fell from their virginity."

One notes here that the possessive իրեանց "their" occurs in both of the first two clauses in v 3; therefore the shorter Armenian text which lacks the possessive in the third clause is likely original. This conclusion is born out by checking the verse in MSS J1925 (f.424v, col.2, ↑4) and M1500 (f.337v, col.1, ↑25): both attest the shorter text.

At any rate the text of J297 reads եւ անդ անկան ի կուսութենէ "and there they fell from virginity." Only then does the marginal reading become significant: it provides the plural of the noun and the possessive pronoun, i.e. կուսութեանց իրեանց. The number of the pronoun has been adjusted in the light of the plurals elsewhere in the verse, it would seem. The singular αὐτῆς has become the plural իրեանց. One notes, however, that the Origenian text has the plural αὐτῶν.

The Hebrew, Greek and Armenian equivalents are:

עָשׂוּ דַּדֵּי בְּתוּלֵיהֶן → Old Greek διεπαρθενεύθησαν → Zohrapian ան-

կան ի կուսութենէ

→ Sym (ἤκμασαν τιτθοὶ) παρθενείων αὐτῆς (αὐτῶν *O*) →

Sym կուսութեանց իրեանց.

In this case the Armenian preserves part of Symmachus' translation of the last clause of v 3. It corroborates the witness of Greek MS 86, though it has the plural of the possessive pronoun like *O* .

The Armenian evidence can be added to the second apparatus in Ziegler:

ἐκεῖ διεπαρθενεύθησαν] σ′ ⟨και εκει⟩ ηκμασαν (σ′ και εκει ηκμασαν Syh) τιτθοι (τιθθοι cod.) παρθενειων αυτης (σ′ παρθενειων αυτων Arm) 86.

23:4 *

ողա et ողիրայ] խորան և սեա et խորան ի նմա Sym(vid)

J297mg(sine ind)

The names of the two sisters are given in v 4. Marginal readings in the margin of MS J297 provide translations for the two names. These are provided below the marginal reading for v 3, examined above, and do not have an independent signature. Presumably it is intended that these readings be attributed to Symmachus as well. The text and marginal readings in MS J297 appear as follows.

Margin	Text
սիմ	Անդ անկան ստիք իրրգ: եւ անդ
կուս	անկան ի կուսութենէ: [4] Անուն դր
ութg	ստերն երիցու որդա, և քեռ
իւրg	ն͞, ո͞ ողիբայ: եւ եղեն ինձ, եւ ծր
խորւն	նան ուստերս, եւ դստերս: եւ անու
եւ եա	անք ն͞ջ՝ անուն շամրնի, ո ողա՝ եւ
խորւ	ե͞մի, ո͞ ողիբայ: [5]
ն ի նմ	

The relationship of the lines of the marginal reading to those of the text is not represented precisely in the facsimile given here. In the MS խորւան է սեա and խոր-
րան ի նմա stand opposite the limits of v 4.

The translation of the Armenian of v 4 in MS J297 is:

> The name of the daughters—of the elder O Ogha, and of her sister O Oghi-
> ba. And they were mine and they gave birth to sons and daughters. And
> their names: the name of Samaria [is] O Ogha and of Jerusalem O Oghiba."

The English translation of v 4—NRSV—is as follows:

> Oholah was the name of the elder and Oholibah the name of her sister. They
> became mine, and they bore sons and daughters. As for their names, Oho-
> lah is Samaria, and Oholibah is Jerusalem.

All we are interested in here is the names of the two sisters. "Oholah" is a
translation of אָהֳלָה; "Oholibah" is a translation of אָהֳלִיבָה.

Under אָהֳלָה in BDB we find, following the transliteration, in parentheses: "for אָהֳלָה *she who has a tent, tent-women* , i.e. worshipper at tent-shrine, v.
Sm [i.e. Smend]." Likewise under אָהֳלִיבָה, following a transliteration: "=
אָהֳלִיבָה *tent in her* = (in meaning) אָהֳלָה cf. Sm [i.e. Smend]." Cf. אֹהֶל "tent."
These names occur only in Ezek 23.

The Old Greek simply transliterated the proper names: hence we read Οολα and Οολιβα, respectively. These were then transliterated in the Armenian translation as ո ողա "O Ogha" and ո ողիբայ "O Oghiba."

There is no note in Ziegler at any of the occurrences of these names in ch 23 indicating that a translation from "the Three" is extant for them. As a result the Armenian marginal readings are of considerable interest.

The marginal reading for ո ողա is խորան է սեա "a tent is to her" (i.e. "she has a tent") and for ո ողիբայ it is խորան ի նմա "a tent (is) in her." These are exactly the meanings assigned to the names by Smend. It's unlikely the Armenian got these meanings from him! The Armenian marginal readings could only have come from contact with the Hebrew.

The Greek underlying խորան է սեա is σκηνὴ ἔστιν αὐτῇ "a tent is to her" (i.e. "she has a tent"); that underlying խորան ի նմա is probably σκηνὴ ἐν αὐτῇ "a tent (is) in her." At least we may suggest these as retroversions.

These translations of the Hebrew either belong to Symmachus or another of "the Three" or they are an exegetical note of undetermined origin, though based upon the Hebrew text. The Armenian witnesses are rather reliable, so it seems likely to me that the readings are genuinely Symmachus.

The Hebrew, Greek and Armenian equivalents are:

אָהֳלָה → Old Greek ἡ Οολα → Zohrapian ողա

→ Sym conj. σκηνὴ ἔστιν αὐτῇ ← Sym խորան է սեա;

אָהֳלִיבָה → Old Greek ἡ Οολιβα → Zohrapian ողիբայ

→ Sym conj. σκηνὴ ἐν αὐτῇ ← Sym խորան ի նմա.

In this instance the Armenian preserves readings not otherwise extant. They can be added to the second apparatus in Ziegler as follows:

4 Οολα] σ´ σκηνὴ ἔστιν αὐτῇ Arm |Οολιβα] σ´ σκηνὴ ἐν αὐτῇ Arm.

23:23 *

զփակուդ եւ զսուէ եւ զկուէ] զհանդիսաւորն (հանդերհաւորս J542; զհդուաւորն V280) [et] զբունաւորն (զ զլխաւորին J542; զբունաւորն V280) եւ (> J542 V280) զզլխաւորն (զբունաւորն J542; զզլխաւորն V280) Aq

J297mg(sine nom) J542mg V280mg

In MS V280 the marginal readings appear in the order 1-3-2. This order is then corrected by the use of differing index signs, which enables the user to put them in the right order. This phenomenon in V280 explains what has happened in J542 which, similarly, has three index signs but now connects the second and third word in the margin with the wrong referrent in the text.

The whole of ch 23 is devoted to the oracle of the two sisters, Oholah and Oholibah. In vv 22–35 we are told that their faithlessness, religious and political, will be punished. In v 23 is given a list of the adversaries who will come upon Judah:

> the Babylonians and all the Chaldeans, Pekod and Shoa and Koa, and all the Assyrians with them ...

The words that we are interested in are "Pekod and Shoa and Koa." These three proper names, with their conjunctions, are a translation of פְּקוֹד וְשׁוֹעַ וְקוֹעַ.

KBH in their citations of these three words define them simply "n. terr." (for פְּקוֹד) and "n. peop." Fohrer is more helpful in his textual notes on v 23:

> J. v[an]. d[er]. Ploeg, according to *OTSt* 5 (1948), p. 142–150, wants here to read פָּקוּד and to derive קוֹעַ from Arabic "crippled": all Babylonians, from great noble to the cripple. It is however a matter of names of peoples: פְּקוֹד (elsewhere Jer 50:21) is an Aramaean nomadic tribe in Babylonia; קוֹעַ (perhaps also at Isa 22:5 by altering the text) and שׁוֹעַ (elsewhere Isa 22:5) are peoples on the Dyala, a tributary of the Tigris.[1]

The Old Greek simply transliterated the three words: Φακουδ καὶ Σουε καὶ Κουε.

Ziegler provides a note in his second apparatus concerning the translation Φακουδ—Κουε: ⟨α΄⟩ επισκεπτην και τυραννον και κορυφαιον 86; σ΄ θ΄ et LXX

---

[1]*Ezechiel* 133. The word פָּקוּד—participle of פָּקַד—refers to "one entrusted w. a task, commissioned" (e.g. 2 Ki 11:15): so KBH.

phacud et sue et cue Hi. This note informs us that, according to Jerome, Symmachus and Theodotion followed the practice of the Old Greek and offered only a transliteration of the Hebrew words. However there is a marginal note in Greek MS 86 which Ziegler takes to be the translation of Aquila. With the accents added it reads: ἐπισκέπτην καὶ τύραννον καὶ κορυφαῖον "inspector and tyrant and chief." The sign ⟨α′ ⟩ means that Ziegler has added the attribution α′, i.e. Aquila.

Aquila took the word פְקוּד as the participle of פקד, i.e. as referring to someone who takes care of things. The word שׁוֹעַ means "noble" at Isa 22:5; Job 34:19 [†]. With what did Aquila associate קוֹעַ?

The Armenian translation of v 23 follows the Old Greek in giving a transliteration of the words in question: զփակուդ եւ զսուէ եւ զկուէ, i.e. "Pʻakud and Suē and Kuē ."

The Armenian marginal reading is that of Aquila. The words զհանդիսաւորն [et] զբռնաւորն եւ զգլխաւորն mean "the champion (or: important person) and tyrant and prince." (That the word τύραννος at Job 2:11 is translated by բռնաւոր makes this order most likely; further, զգլխաւոր is a good literal translation for κορυφαῖον.) Manuscript J542 reverses the order of the last two words, offers a different word for the first one (read զհանդերծաւորս, i.e. "clothiers"), and makes all three plural; yet it has the signature lacking in MS J297. Manuscript V280 has the same order of words in the margin as J542 but corrects the order with its index signs. It too makes all three words in the margin plural.

The Hebrew, Greek and Armenian equivalents are:

וְקוֹעַ וְשׁוֹעַ פְּקוֹד → Old Greek Φακουδ καὶ Σουε καὶ Κουε → Zohra-
    pian զփակուդ եւ զսուէ եւ զկուէ

    → Aq ἐπισκέπτην καὶ τύραννον καὶ κορυφαῖον → Aq զհան-
        դիսաւորն [et] զբռնաւորն եւ զգլխաւորն.

In this instance the Armenian provides the signature for Aquila's reading, lacking in other sources. The second apparatus in Ziegler can be altered to reflect the addition of the Armenian evidence:

Φακουδ — Κουε: α′ (sine nom 86) επισκεπτην και τυραννον και κορυφαιον 86 Arm; σ′ θ′ et LXX *phacud et sue et cue* Hi.

28:21

սիդովնի] ծայդոնու Sym

M3705^{mg} Zoh^{app(mg)(sine nom)}

Zohrapian notes in his apparatus that the spelling ծայդոնու is found in
the text of some MSS; J1934 is one such MS.

Ezekiel 28:20–23 contains an oracle against Sidon. It begins with Yahweh's
command to the prophet: "Mortal, set your face toward Sidon." The word "Sidon"
is simply a transliteration of the proper name צִידֽוֹן.

The Old Greek translation, or rather transliteration of (אֶל־)צִידוֹן) "(to)
Sidon," is (ἐπὶ) Σιδῶνα "(upon) Sidon." (Greek has no equivalent for the letter צ,
so *sigma* is used in proper names in the LXX/Old Greek complex. Greek ζ is almost always used in transliterated proper namees for Hebrew ז: the only instances
in H-R of צ becoming ζ are צֹעַר at Jer 31[48]:34[MSS ABS: Ζόγορ] and at Gen 13:
10.) There is no textual variant in Ziegler on this word, either in his first or second
apparatus.

The Armenian translation also offers a transliteration for the proper name: ի
վրայ սիդովնի "upon Sidon." The word սիդովն is a precise rendering of
the Greek. The long vowel -ով- is used to represent the long vowel - ω -.

In the margin of MS M3705 we have the variant spelling ծայդոնու
"Tsaydonu," declined now with -ու ending rather than -ի. Where could this have
come from? Could it have come from the Hebrew—which, however, does not have
the diphthong after the initial consonant? Could it have come from Greek which has
no "ts" consonant in its alphabet? What Greek spelling might underlie the Armenian, if the Armenian comes from a Greek original?

We will get closer to the origin of the marginal reading if we look at Syriac
or Arabic. The Syriac for Sidon is ܨܝܕܢ : the initial consonant ܨ is followed by a
diphthong consisting of the "a" vowel plus *yudh* and ܢ is followed by a short "o"
vowel. The Arabic is similar.

It seems to me that some copyist may have provided in the margin of MS
M3705 the contemporary pronunciation of the name of the city of Sidon. Its attribu-

tion to Symmachus is erroneous because, for one thing, the Armenian cannot have come from Greek. This conclusion is not made less certainly accurate by that fact that MS M3705 has only this one marginal reading attributed to one or all of "the Three" in Ezekiel.

These comments require little emendation—except to replace "contemporary" with the word "another"—in the light of Robert Thomson's response to my query about the marginal reading. He states:

> Sidon seems to be found in two spellings in Armenian. In the Old Testament both Tyre and Sidon begin with ծ: Ծուր և Ծայդան (note spelling with ա) [e.g. Joel 3:4]. But in medieval Armenian texts, and in the translation of Patriarch Michael's *Chronicle* , Sidon is rendered exactly that way: Sidon.
>
> Note also that in place names near the Syrian border the Greek Sophanene becomes Ծոփք, but Zabdicene is Ծաւդէք.
>
> I suspect that a marginal reading in Armenian has been affected by the older Armenian biblical text spelling.[1]

39:20

արանց] յորդիսն հիւսւսոյ կոդ մանէ Aq Sym Th

J297mg(sine ind)

The word յորդիսն appears in the MS in a shortened form, namely յրսն —with a line above it to indicate that the word is abbreviated. (The second last letter is probably an -ս- but the right side of the letter goes up and joins the upper right extremity of the -ն- so that it could conceivably be an -մ- rather than an -ս-. I take it that the scribe has simply not lifted the stylus in writing -սն.)

With v 20 Ezekiel completes his description of the gory feast that follows Gog's defeat. The fare includes "horses and charioteers [Heb *chariots*], with war-

---

[1] Personal communication 06/04/95. Because this was an electronic mail response to my query, the Armenian in the original is in transliteration. I have taken the liberty of putting these transliterations into Armenian script. I also added the reference to Joel, enclosed within square brackets.

riors and all kinds of soldiers." In Greek the phrase "and all kinds of soldiers" becomes καὶ πάντα ἄνδρα πολεμιστήν "and every fighting man." That becomes in Armenian, in turn, և յամենայն արանց պատերազմողաց "and all of the fighting men."

Though the marginal reading in MS J297 has no index sign, it stands beside v 20 and the preposition before որդիսն links it to the adjective յամենայն (արանց). The marginal reading has the signatures of Aquila, Symmachus and Theodotion with it. A marginal reading for v 21 follows immediately upon the reading being considered here, separated by a horizontal line. The two readings with signatures appear as follows:

> ___
> ակ սիմ
> թէ յրան
> հիւսւոյ
> կողմանէ
> ի մէջորէի
> ի կողմանէ

It could be that the signatures are intended for both marginal readings.

The marginal reading means "(on all the) sons of the northern region" and is derived from 38:6 and 39:2. It identifies where the soldiers of v 20 have come from. The notation is an interpretive comment of uncertain origin and it seems most likely that the ascription to Aquila, Symmachus and Theodotion is incorrect. The signatures probably gave some weight to the comment.

39:22

յորէ յայնմանէ] ի մէջորէի ի կողմանէ

J297mg(sine ind)

See the note above on 39:20.

With v 21 begins the conclusion of the oracles. The next verse says that "The house of Israel shall know that I am the LORD their God, from that day forward." The words "from that day forward" are a translation of מִן־הַיּוֹם הַהוּא וָהָלְאָה

In the Old Greek "from that day forward" becomes ἀπὸ τῆς ἡμέρας ταύτης καὶ ἐπέκεινα, which means the same thing.

In Armenian the phrase is translated յօրէ յայնմանէ և առ յապայ "from that day and for the future." The marginal reading makes the timing more precise: "from about the middle of the day." I suppose this comment makes the gory feast a mid-day meal!

The marginal reading is an exegetical comment of some kind.

XII. Conclusion

In order to assess the readings from Aquila, Symmachus and Theodotion in the margins of Armenian manuscripts it will be useful to provide a summary of such evidence as is preserved there. The chapters of this study provide a rather vast array of marginalia, which attest the diligence of Armenian scribes for the transmission of various kinds of marginal readings: corrections, comparisons among manuscripts and readings from "the Three."

Summary of the Evidence for Readings from "the Three"

I provide below a summary of the evidence that has been analyzed in the preceding chapters, in the order in which it appears there. For each book there is given the textual reference; the signature, if there is one; indication of whether it is to be found in Zohrapian's apparatus; Georgian evidence (for 4 Rgn); the signature, if that is not preserved in Armenian; the Greek witnesses that transmit the reading, if the evidence is extant in Greek — usually this is a case of Greek manuscripts; indication whether the reading is transmitted in the Syro-hexapla. Note that when the signature is present and correct in the Armenian witness it is not given for Greek and Syriac witnesses: it may be assumed that the signature is the same there. All references to Zohrapian are to the apparatus of his edition unless otherwise indicated. Signed readings in Zohrapian's apparatus were made available by Brooke-Mc-Lean-Thackeray in their second apparatus so that in the table below — almost without exception — readings found in Zohrapian can be understood to be represented in the Cambridge edition of the Greek text.

The diamond-shaped symbol (♦) preceding a text reference indicates that the reading is—as of now at least—uniquely preserved in Armenian (and in Georgian in a few instances). The three instances of uniquely Georgian preservation of readings are marked with a bullet (•).

This presentation allows one at a glance—well, relatively speaking at a glance!—to see the extent of the Armenian evidence.

Text	Sign.	Zoh	Georg	Gk/Syh sign.	Greek	Syro-hexapla

Joshua

Text	Sign.	Zoh	Georg	Gk/Syh sign.	Greek	Syro-hexapla
5:2				Aq Th	344 376 C	
13:27		Zoh		Aq Sym	Eusebius	Syh

Judges

| 15:14 | •[1]Aq | Zoh(sine nom) | | | | |

1 Reigns

Note: the Syro-hexapla is not extant for 1–2 Samuel.

Text	Sign.	Zoh	Georg	Gk/Syh sign.	Greek	Syro-hexapla
1:13				Th	108 92	
2:29		Zoh			554	
2:36		Zoh(ex Oskan)		Aq	M	
7:12	•Aq	Zoh(sine nom)				
9:12				Aq	Eusebius Onomasticon	
9:13		Zohtxt2			108 554	
10:14		Zoh		Aq	554 93(sine nom)	
13:3	Aq	Zoh(sine nom)			108(sine nom) Thdt	
20:19				Aq	707	
21:4				Aq? Sym Th	108 243 92; cf. 370	
22:9	•Aq	Zoh(sine nom)				
22:18				οἱ λ.	243	
23:7		Zoh		Sym	108 243 92 554	

---

[1]Note, however, that in the analysis of this item the possibility was raised that the Armenian reading comes from a reading attested in Greek at v 13.

[2]Zohrapian's base MS represents a witness in which the reading of text and margin have been replaced by one another.

23:15		Zoh	Aq *or* Sym Th	108(sine nom) 243 92	
30:8	Aq	Zoh(sine nom)		243	Syh

It should also be noted that at 8:3 there is an Aquila Theodotion reading in the text and the Old Greek translation in the margin; the same situation obtains at 15: 4: there is a reading from "the Three" (vid.) in the text and the translation of the Old Greek in the margin.

2 Reigns

2:13		Zoh	Aq Th	243	
2:29 2°		Zoh	Sym	243	
3:33	Sym	Zoh^txt1		M 243(sine nom)	
3:34	Sym	Zoh^txt2		243	
6:14		Zoh		243	
7:1	◆⟨Aq⟩	Zoh			
	⟨Sym⟩	Zoh^txt3		M	
8:18		Zoh		M	
12:25		Zoh	Sym	M	
17:19	◆Aq				
		Zoh	Aq Sym	M(om α′) 554	
		Zoh	Th	M	Syh-ap-Barh
20:4	◆Sym	Zoh			
20:8	⟨Sym⟩	Zoh^txt			
21:20			Sym	M 243 554	

3 Reigns

2:1			Aq Sym Th		Syh
2:4					Syh

---

[1] In this instance the Symmachus reading is in Zohrapian's text but it is in the margin in some other witnesses, indicating that it has come into the text from the margin.

[2] The reading is in the text of Zohrapian's edition, because he followed his base MS; however, he notes in his apparatus that the reading is found in the margins of some other MSS.

[3] In Zohrapian's base MS the marginal reading and reading originally in the text have been switched. There are still two marginal readings for the verse. Fortunately some other witnesses have not made the exchange.

	Aq	Zoh	Sym	243 / Syh
9:15		Zoh	Sym	Syh
9:22		Zoh	Aq	Syh
14:28	Aq	Zoh		243 119(sine nom)
		Zoh[txt1]	Sym	243
	Sym	Zoh		in txt: 19-108 158 246 243(sub o′)
				82 554 127 93 Thdt
	♦Th			
21:1	♦⟨Sym?⟩	Zoh		
♦21:21 2°		Zoh		

4 Reigns

	Aq	Zoh	Sym	243 / Syh
1:1	⟨Aq⟩			243(sine nom)
	♦⟨Sym⟩			
1:2	Aq			243
1:13	♦Aq			
2:1	Aq[2]			Syh(sine nom)
				Syh-ap-Barh
	♦Sym			
2:4	♦Sym			
2:8	♦Aq			
	Sym			Syh Syh-ap-Barh(α′ pro σ′)
2:9	♦⟨Aq⟩			
	♦Sym			
2:10	♦Aq			
2:14	Aq			243
	Sym			243 707(sine nom)
	♦Th			
3:4	Aq	Zoh(sine nom)[3]		243 Syh(vid; sine nom) Syh-ap-

---

[1] In this instance the marginal reading appears as a plus in the text, added preceding the word for which it is intended.

[2] Armenian witnesses uniquely preserve the signature.

[3] Zohrapian's base MS preserves only part of the reading attributed to Aquila in other witnesses.

					Barh-ed
	Sym[1]			243	
3:21	♦Aq				
	♦Sym				
3:27	Aq	Zoh(sine nom)			Syh Syh-ap-Barh
4:39	♦Aq[2]				
	Sym	Zoh(sine nom)	οἱ λ.	554 Thdt	
4:42	♦Aq				
	♦Sym				
	♦Th				
	♦Aq[3]				
5:3	♦Aq				
6:8		Zoh	Sym	243	
6:25	♦Aq Sym				
7:4	♦Aq				
	Sym				Syh
8:8			Sym		Syh
8:15	Aq Sym Zoh				Syh-ap-Barh
8:17	♦Aq				
	♦Sym				
9:11 1°	Aq				Syh
	♦Sym				
2°			Aq Sym		Syh
9:20	Sym	Zoh		243	
10:8	♦⟨Sym⟩[4]				
10:10	Sym	Zoh(sine nom)		243; cf. 106	
10:13	♦Aq	Zoh Georg			

---

[1]Cf. in connection with this marginal reading *caput pastorum* Syh(vid) Syh-ap-Barh(α' pro σ' codd).

[2]Note that the Armenian does not seem to preserve the same word for Aquila as do the Syriac witnesses. Both of course are translations: in Armenian the word preserved for Aquila is *malva* ; in the Syriac witnesses it is *cucurbitas* .

[3]There are two readings which bear the signature of Aquila.

[4]This reading is in the text of M2628 but it has come there from the margin.

10:19	♦Aq			
	♦Sym			
10:21	♦⟨Aq⟩			
	♦Sym			
10:24	Aq Sym			Syh
10:27	♦Aq	Zoh(sine nom)		
	Sym	Zoh(sine nom) Georg		Syh
	♦Th	Zoh(sine nom)		
11:4	Aq	Zoh Georg [α'][1]	243vid	
	Sym	Georg	243	Syh(sine nom)
11:8	Aq	Zoh Georg Aq Th	243 554[2]	Syh
11:9	Aq	Georg[3] Aq Sym		Syh
11:12	Aq	Georg	243	Syh
	Sym	Zoh(sine nom) Georg	243	Syh
11:14 1°	♦Aq			
2°	♦Aq			
	Sym	Georg		Syh
11:18	♦Aq	Zoh Georg		
11:19	♦Sym	Georg(α' mend pro σ')		
12:5 1°	♦Sym			
2°		Georg(sub α')[4]	243?[5]	
	Sym	Zoh(sine nom) Georg	243	
14:7	Sym	Zoh(sine nom) Georg		Syh
14:14	Aq(σ' mend pro α')		243(sine nom) 121(sine nom)	
				Syh Syh-ap-Barh
	Sym(θ' mend pro σ') Zoh			Syh Syh-ap-Barh
14:29		•Georg Aq		

---

[1]B-M-Thackeray place the signature within square brackets, indicating that the signature cannot be clearly read in MS 243.

[2]The reading is attributed to Aquila in MS 243; to Theodotion in 554; Syh attributes its marginal reading to Aquila.

[3]The Georgian evidence represents the switching of reading in the margin and reading in the text: the reading which should bear Aquila's signature is now in the text.

[4]This reading is not preserved in Armenian.

[5]Manuscript 243 has two readings attributed to Symmachus; Field thinks the second one should be attributed to Aquila.

		•Georg Sym			
15:5	Aq *or* Sym	Zoh(sub α′)	Georg(sub α′)	οἱ λ. 554	
15:25	♦Aq	Zoh			
16:6		Zoh	ϵβρ.		Syh
16:9	Aq			A	Syh
17:3	Sym	Zoh		243 554	Syh
17:9 1°[1]	Sym	Zoh(sine nom)	Georg		Syh(sine nom)
2°	♦Sym		Georg(sub α′)		
17:11 2°	Sym			243(sine nom)	Syh(sub α′ σ′ ϵ′)
17:24	♦⟨Sym?⟩	Georg[2]			
18:4		•Georg Sym		243(cum var)	
18:20	♦Sym	Georg(sine nom)			
19:13 1°	♦Sym				
19:28 1°	Sym				Syh
2°	♦⟨Sym⟩	Zoh			
19:37	Sym	Zoh		243(sine nom)	Syh(sine nom)
22:5	♦Sym	Zoh[3]			
22:13 1°	♦Sym	Zoh(sine nom)			
2°	♦Sym				
23:4 1°	♦Sym				
2°	Sym			243 554	
23:5 1°	Aq	Zoh			Syh
2°	Sym			56(sine nom)	
23:6	♦Sym				
23:7	Sym			243	Syh
23:9	♦Sym				
23:10				243	Syh
23:11	♦Sym	Zoh			
23:12	♦Sym				

---

[1] In this instance the Armenian and Georgian provide a signature for a reading that was already known from the Syro-hexapla; it is preserved also in the margin of Zohrapian's base MS V1508, but without signature.

[2] The Georgian also lacks the signature.

[3] Zohrapian's MS preserves part of the Symmachus reading.

23:13	♦Sym	Zoh			
23:15	♦Sym				
23:16	Sym	Zoh			Syh
23:21	♦Sym				
23:24		Zoh	Sym		Syh
23:29	♦Aq	Zoh[sine nom]			
23:35		Zoh[txt1]	οἱ λ.		Syh
24:14	♦Sym(sub α′ mend pro σ′ vid)				
25:5	Sym	Zoh		554[sine nom]	Syh
25:14	Sym(sub α′ mend pro σ′) Zoh			243	
25:16 2°	Sym				Syh
25:17 1°	Aq			243	
	Sym	Zoh		243	
2°	Sym[2]			Luc MSS[txt]	Syh[sine nom]
25:19		Zoh	σ′(?)		Syh
25:27	♦Sym	Zoh[txt3]			

Job

None of these readings is cited in Ziegler.

2:1	Aq	Zoh		*C*	
3:23	♦Aq	Zoh			
6:27		Zoh		406	
8:21	Sym			252	
9:11	♦Sym(sub α′ mend pro σ′)				
28:10 2°	Aq	Zoh	λ′	*C*	
37:18	Sym(sub α′ mend pro σ′)			252	Syh
38:32	Sym(sub α′ mend pro σ′) Zoh			248 252 *C*	Syh(mend sub α′)
39:1	Sym(sub α′ mend pro σ′) Zoh			*C* (θ′ mend pro σ′)	

---

[1] The marginal reading has replaced the reading in the text; the reading that was in the text has been moved to the margin.

[2] In this instance the Armenian evidence preserves the signature for the reading preserved in the Syro-hexapla and Lucianic MSS.

[3] The reading found in the text of Zohrapian's MS is preserved in the margins of other witnesses.

Isaiah

The Armenian version was not collated by Ziegler.

29:7	Sym	Zoh	οι γ′	Q	Syh
32:6		Zoh[1]	α′ σ′ θ′	86	
37:30	Sym	Zoh	α′ σ′ θ′	86 Eus. et Hi.(sub α′ θ′)	
				Tht.(οι γ′)	

Ezekiel

None of the following is represented in Ziegler to whom, however, only three readings were available by way of Zohrapian's apparatus.

3:13	Aq Th *or* Aq Sym			Q[txt] 86(sub α′ σ′)	
5:2	Aq Sym			86 87	
	Aq Sym			86 87	
	Aq Sym			86 87	
16:4	Aq	Zoh	δ′	Q Or.(sub ∈βρ′)	
16:33			α′	Q 87-91	
			σ′	87-91	
	♦⟨Th⟩				
17:22			α′	86	
	Sym			86	
20:43	Aq			86 87-91	
	Sym			86 87-91	
	Th			86 87-91	
21:7	Sym	Zoh(sine nom)		86	Syh
23:3	Sym			86	
23:4	♦Sym				
23:23	Aq[2]			86(sine nom)	

The information set out in the summary provided above can be reduced

---

[1]The reading in question now stands in the text of Zohrapian's base MS, having replaced the original reading which now stands in the margin. The same is true of MS J501, also an excellent source for marginal readings deriving from "the Three."

[2]In this instance the Armenian preserves the signature, not extant elsewhere.

further.

In the columns below are provided the total number of readings in Armenian for the various books; the number of those readings which have signatures (Sign.); the number of readings without signatures in the Armenian evidence which have, however, signatures where they are extant elsewhere (No. sign.); the number of marginal readings to be found in Zohrapian (Zoh); the number of those marginal readings in Zohrapian which preserve the signature (Sign.); the number of the Armenian readings from "the Three" which are uniquely preserved in Armenian (♦).

For the book of 4 Reigns three additional columns are added: the number of marginal readings preserved in Armenian and Georgian (A/G); the number of these which are uniquely shared by the Armenian and Georgian (A/G♦); the number of marginal readings which are uniquely preserved in Georgian (G•).

The abbreviations α′ σ′ θ′ are used in order to save space.

Book	Total	Sign.	No.sign.	Zoh	Sign.	♦		A/G	A/G♦	G•
Josh	2	0	1 α′ θ′ 1 α′ σ′	1	0					
Judg	1	α′		1	0	1α′				
1 Rgn	15	4α′	4α′ 1σ′ 1θ′ 1α′? σ′ θ′ 1α′ *or* σ′ θ′ 1οἱ λ.	10[1]	0	2α′				
2 Rgn	15	1α′ 3σ′	1α′ σ′ 1α′ θ′	13[2]	1	1α′ 1⟨α′⟩ 1⟨σ′⟩				

---

[1]This figure includes one instance where the reading in the margin has been switched with the one in the text, so that now what was once in the margin is now in the text and vice versa.
[2]In four instances the reading is in the text of Zohrapian.

		3σ′							
		1θ′							
3 Rgn	10	1α′	1α′	7	2	1⟨σ′⟩			
		1σ′	1α′ σ′ θ′			1θ′			
		1θ′	2σ′			1sine nom			
4 Rgn	109	22α′[1]	1α′ σ′	38	19	19α′	18	6	3
		3α′ σ′	4σ′[2]			2⟨α′⟩			
		1α′ *or* σ′ 2οἱ λ.				1α′ σ′			
		55σ′[3]	1εβρ.			27σ′			
		3θ′				3⟨σ′⟩			
						1⟨σ′?⟩			
						2θ′			
Job	9	3α′[4]		6	5	1α′			
		5σ′[5]				1σ′[6]			
Isa	3	2σ′[7]	1α′ σ′ θ′	3	2[8]				
Ezek	17	3α′[9]	2α′	2	1	1σ′			
		3α′ σ′	1σ′			1⟨θ′⟩[10]			
		1α′ σ′ *or* α′ θ′							
		5σ′							

---

[1] Includes one instance of sub σ′ mend pro α′.

[2] There is some doubt about one of these: 25:19.

[3] Includes one instance of sub θ′ mend pro σ′ and two instances of sub α′ mend pro σ′.

[4] In one case Greek witnesses preserve the signature λ.

[5] In four of these five cases the reading is sub α′ mend pro σ′.

[6] Sub α′ mend pro σ′.

[7] In the one case Greek witnesses preserve the signature οἱ γ.′; in the other α′ σ′ θ′.

[8] That is to say, Zohrapian like the MS tradition more generally preserves three readings and two of them have signatures. In one case—32:6—reading of text and margin have been switched.

[9] In one of these three cases—at 16:4—MS Q preserves the signature δ′; Or. preserves the signature εβρ.

[10] Not noted is 23:23 where the Armenian uniquely preserves the name.

The way this table should be read is as follows. For example, for Ezekiel there are 17 marginal readings. Three of these have the signature of Aquila, 3 have the signature of Aq–Sym, and so on. Aside from the signatures in the Armenian witnesses, an additional two have signatures that are extant in other witnesses: two bear the signature of Aquila, one that of Symmachus. Zohrapian has two of the 17 readings; only one of the two has a signature in his witnesses. Finally, the Armenian uniquely preserves one Symmachus reading and one Theodotion reading. In the latter case the signature is not preserved but we can attribute it to Theodotion.

The data given for the various books can now be combined in order to present the total numbers of readings for the entire corpus for which there are marginal readings in Armenian MSS — and Georgian MSS for 4 Rgn.

Total	Sign.	No. sign.	Zoh	Sign.	♦
181	45α′	7α′	81	30	24α′
	6α′ σ′	3α′ σ′			3⟨α′⟩
	1α′ *or* σ′	1α′ *or* σ′ θ′			1α′ σ′
	1α′ σ′ *or* α′ θ′	2α′ θ′			30σ′
	71σ′	11σ′			5⟨σ′⟩
	4θ′	2θ′			1⟨σ′?⟩
		2α′ σ′ θ′			3θ′
		1α′? σ′ θ′			1⟨θ′⟩
		3οἱ λ.			1sine nom
		1ἑβρ.			

The results of this entire study can now be sketched out so far as they pertain to the marginalia that belong to Aquila, Symmachus and Theodotion.

Armenian manuscripts preserve 181 marginal readings belonging to "the Three." These are found in the following books, and in a frequency as follows:

Josh   2
Judg   1
1 Rgn   15

2 Rgn	15
3 Rgn	10
4 Rgn	109
Job	9
Isa	3
Ezek	17.

The largest number of signed readings belongs to Symmachus: 71; next, Aquila: 45; finally Theodotion: 4. In addition another 6 readings are attributed to Aq Sym; one to Aq *or* Sym; one to Aq Sym *or* Aq Th. That is, of the 181 marginal readings there are 128 which are signed.

There are 48 readings from "the Three" without signature. However, in 31 of these cases the signature is preserved in either Greek manuscripts or the Syrohexapla. In 7 of these cases the signature is Aquila's; in 11 instances the reading carries the signature of Symmachus; twice the signature is that of Theodotion. That means that the Armenian witnesses offer us 82 readings attributed solely to Symmachus; 52 readings attributed solely to Aquila; 6 attributed solely to Theodotion. In addition 3 readings can be attributed to Aq Sym; one to Aq *or* Sym Th; two to Aq Th; two to Aq Sym Th; one to Aq? Sym Th; two to οἱ λοιποί; one to ὁ ἑβρ.

These combined results for signed readings can be presented in a perhaps more visual way as follows:

Aquila	52
Symmachus	82
Theodotion	6
Aq Sym	1
Aq *or* Sym Th	1
Aq Th	2
Aq Sym Th	2
Aq? Sym Th	1
οἱ λοιποί	2
ὁ ἑβρ.	1.

The largest number of marginal readings belongs to Symmachus: 82. This represents some 44% of the total. This preference for Symmachus—either by Armenian scribes or their predecessors—is true throughout the corpus with the exception of Joshua (only two unsigned readings, one Aq Th, one Aq Sym), Judges (only one signed reading, Aquila), and 1 Rgn (only four signed readings, all Aquila).

The purpose of the marginal readings drawn from "the Three"

The purpose of the marginalia likely has several dimensions. In the books of Reigns marginal readings often have the practical purpose of providing a translation for a word that is only transliterated in the text. A similar interest is at hand with the translations of the proper names in Ezekiel. Often, however, the marginalia may serve an antiquarian interest—to present the work of ancient translators who were famous, at least by reputation. The work of Aquila, Symmachus and Theodotion was added to a type of text which was given introductions to the various books, lists of chapters, section numbers—and, later, versification, variant readings noted by the comparison of manuscripts among themselves, and in some cases notes deriving from comparison with the Latin Vulgate. The addition of the translations in the margins was part of a larger phenomenon. Sometimes, I think, the work of "the Three" was added simply because it was there in Greek witnesses that were at hand.

Transliterations

So far as the translations-for-transliterations issue is concerned, we can provide a list of the transliterations. In the following list, the transliterations are in italics; to the right of the semicolon stands the translation of the marginal reading. Those who know Hebrew will recognize the underlying Hebrew—which has of course come into Armenian by way of Greek. (In some cases the Armenian word has the definite object marker *z-* : I have not removed such markers from the Armenian words.) I have taken the liberty of capitalizing proper names.

Josh 13:27   *emak* ; mg. "valley"

1 Rgn 7:12   *pagheas* ; mg. "old Bet'san"

9:12   *bama* ; mg. "the height"

20:19   *ergab* ; mg. "(by) this stone"

30:8   *geddur* ; mg. "brigand"

2 Rgn 8:18   *k'eret'in ew op'elet'in* ; mg. "archers and slingers"

12:25   *yedēdi* ; mg. "endearments"

17:19   *arabovt'* ; mg. "pomegranate"; "dried figs"; "vegetables"

21:20   *madvon* ; mg. "giant"

3 Rgn 14:28   *t'ee* cum var; mg. "room"; "place"; "corner"; *thekoue*

4 Rgn 2:14   *ap'p'ov* ; mg. "even he"; "and now"; "thus, so"

3:4   *nekat'* ; mg. "shepherd"; "shepherd"

4:39   *ariovt'* ; mg. "mallow"; "herbage of the field"

4:42   *bakeghat'aw* ; mg. "in a load"; "in a load"; "in a *bakeghat'* ; "in a piece of linen-cover"

6:8   *yeghmoni* ; mg. "in such and such"

8:8   *manna* ; mg. "gift"

8:15   *mak'man* ; mg. "bed"

10:10   *ap'p'ov* ; mg. "now therefore"

11:4   *zk'orin ew zrasim* ; mg. "leaders"; "runners"

11:8   *saderovt'n* ; mg. "the courtyards"

11:12   *zyezern* ; mg. "the consecrated things"; "what is holy"

11:18   *zmat'an* ; mg. "two hundred"

11:19   *zk'orin ew zrasim* ; mg. "the divisions and the runners"

12:5 2°   *zbedek* ; mg. "what is necessary for (re-)construction"

14:7   *mayila* ; mg. "valley of salt"

15:5   *ap'p'usovt'* ; mg. "secretly"

16:9   *Kiwrēn* ; mg. "land"

17:3   *mannay* ; mg. "something evident"

17:24   *K'ut'ay* ; mg. *Movk'ovt'ay*

[18:4[1]   *Eest'an* ; mg. *Nast'an*]

19:37   *Araraday* ; mg. "of the Armenians"

23:4 2°   *saderovt'* ; mg. "in the valley"

---

[1] This reading is unique to the Georgian.

23:5 1°   *zk'ovmarimsn* ; mg. "sacred things"

23:7   *kadēsimats'n* ; mg. "of the offerings"

23:10   *zT'op'ot'* ; mg. *zTap'et'n*

23:13   *mosat'ay* ; mg. "of Corrupting Corruption"

23:29   *Nek'awov* ; mg. "lame"

25:5   *yarabovt'* ; mg. "in the uninhabited (area)"

25:16 2° *zmek'enovt'sn* ; mg. "the base(s)"

25:17 1° *k'ovt'ar* ; mg. "capital"; "the extremity of the pillar"

25:17 2° *sabak* ; mg. "lattice-work"

Job 38:32   *zMazarovt'n* ; mg. "he will bring out Arcturus"

Isa 29:7   *Erusaghemi* ; mg. *Arieli*

Ezek 23:4   *Oogha* et *Ooghibay* ; mg. "a tent is to her" and "a tent is in her"

23:23   *zP'akud ew zSuē ew zKuē* ; "the champion and tyrant and prince"

The total number of referents in the text for which there are Armenian marginal readings is 144; the number of such referents which are transliterations is 44. That means that about one in three of the marginal readings involves a transliteration in the text. Marginal readings for 1–4 Reigns make up the majority of the number 144: there are 119 referents in the text of those four books. Here there are 40 marginal readings for transliterations in the text, i.e. the percentage is about the same as outside these books. However, one notes the large number of transliterations in these books and the large number of marginal readings for various kinds of words in the text.

Zohrapian and the marginalia from "the Three"

It is of considerable interest that Zohrapian preserves 81 of the total of 181 marginal readings, about half. Only thirty of these are signed. In 4 Reigns, which has the greatest number of marginal readings—109, Zohrapian's witnesses—which is almost always his base MS for collation, Venice 1508—have just 38 and only 19 of these are signed. On the one hand, therefore, the users of Zohrapian's edition are the heirs both of his "good luck" in using V1508 as a base MS and of his diligence in presenting such evidence as he had in his apparatus; on the other hand there is a great deal of evidence available in other Armenian MSS, indeed twice as much evidence as he was able to cite.

Brooke-McLean-Thackeray

Brooke-McLean-Thackeray as well as other editors of Old Greek texts use Zohrapian's edition. As a result, the Armenian evidence as it was known through Zohrapian has been available to textual critics for much of this century. It is really only Brooke-McLean-Thackeray who transmitted the evidence in Zohrapian: the Armenian version was not collated for Isaiah and the marginal evidence—which is not all that substantial anyway as preserved by Zohrapian—for Job, Isaiah and Ezekiel is not cited by Ziegler. This evidence, especially for Ezekiel, cannot now be overlooked.

The following readings in Zohrapian *are not* found in apparatuses of the Brooke-McLean-Thackeray edition of 1–4 Reigns. In all cases but one these are readings which lack signatures. The sole exception is 4 Rgn 17:3.

1 Rgn 2:29
   2:36
   7:12
   9:13(Zoh^{txt})
   10:14
   13:3
   23:15
   30:8
2 Rgn 2:13
   12:25
   17:19
3 Rgn 9:15
   9:22
   21:1(20:1)

       21:21(20:21)
4 Rgn 3:4
       3:27
       4:39
       6:8
       10:27
       17:3(signature!)
       17:9 1°
       19:28 2°
       22:13 1°

It appears that the editors included all the Armenian materials that included a signature; the failure to cite 4 Rgn 17:3 is probably an oversight. It must be said that it would have been difficult to work through all the unsigned marginalia that one encounters in Zohrapian's apparatus, sifting out those readings which can be attributed to "the Three."

Georgian evidence in 4 Reigns

The material published by Birdsall on the basis of an article by the Georgian scholar Janashvili is limited to 4 Reigns. The Georgian witness is dependent upon the Armenian, it appears. Nevertheless, in three cases there are readings that may be genuine, uniquely preserved in Georgian. The marginalia in Georgian manuscripts deserve a full treatment, along the lines that have been followed in this study. How extensive is the evidence for readings from "the Three" in Georgian manuscripts? How reliable is it?

For 4 Reigns there are marginal readings for some 20 passages, according to Janashvili and Birdsall.

The list of passages and readings is as follows:

8:15   sine nom: not from "the Three"
10:13 Aq
10:27 Sym

11:4   Aq
        Sym
11:8   Aq
11:9   Aq: txt in mg and mg in txt
11:12   Aq
        Sym
11:14 2° Sym
11:15   inner-Georgian gloss
11:18   Aq
11:19   Aq mend pro Sym
12:5 2° Aq: not in Arm
14:7   Sym
14:29   Aq
        Sym
15:5   Aq: sub Aq or Sym in Arm
17:9 1° Sym
     2° Aq mend pro Sym
17:24   sine nom: conj. Sym
18:4   Sym
18:20   sine nom (Sym)

One notes that these readings extend only across the middle of the book of 4 Rgn, from chapter 8 through chapter 18. These twenty-three readings include: three uniquely preserved in Georgian: 14:29 (two); 18:4, all three of them relating to proper names; eight uniquely preserved in Armenian and Georgian: 10:13; 11:4 (two), 18, 19; 17:9 2°; 17:24; 18:20; ten that the Georgian and Armenian preserve amongst other witnesses, Greek or Syriac: 10:27; 11:8, 9, 12 (two); 11:14; 12:5; 14:7; 15:5; 17:9 1°; two inner-Georgian glosses (8:15; 11:15).

This Georgian evidence will get a fuller treatment if and when a critical edition of 1–4 Reigns is undertaken by the Septuagint project in Göttingen.

Whence the Armenian marginal readings from "the Three"?

The Armenian marginalia were in all likelihood copied from Greek exemplars in the Middle Ages, namely the 13th century, in the time of the Armenian Kingdom in Cilicia. Where these Greek exemplars came from is unknown but it might be at least suggested that they came from the West. After the incorporation of this marginalia in one or a few Armenian manuscripts they were copied widely: this was a busy period for Armenian scriptoria and for the business of adding various helps to the biblical text.

Readers will have noted that the marginalia are also preserved in numbers of manuscripts of the 17th century. These manuscripts—copied in the West in Constantinople or in Poland, or in the East in Isfahan—represent copies of "old," i.e. Cilician exemplars. In manuscripts like Jerusalem 428 or 501 the marginalia are part of exquisite renditions of the Armenian Bible.

A probable exception to this mapping of the evidence is the marginalia for Ezekiel contained in manuscripts Jerusalem 297 and Venice 280. Both are 15th century manuscripts that were copied in Khlat'. Their readings for Ezekiel may well derive from a common Greek exemplar that was known at that time in that city.

So it is that Aquila, Symmachus and Theodotion travelled to Armenia by way of marginalia in Greek witnesses in the Cilician period. From there they travelled to many other places, in particular four centuries later taking up residence in Constantinople, Isfahan and places in far off Poland. In the 18th century they travelled to Venice where, fortuitously Hovhann Zohrapian selected one of the finest representatives of such an elaborated-upon text—namely MS 1508—to be the base manuscript for his important edition of the classical text of the Armenian Bible, published in 1805. From there Aquila, Symmachus and Theodotion travelled in Armenian to Cambridge, to the Cambridge edition of the Old Greek text of Samuel-Kings. It has been a long journey.

The end is not absolutely the end

There is one caveat that needs to be mentioned at the close of this study which is limited to readings from "the Three" preserved in marginalia. The Armenian version of the Old Testament is, in many of its parts, a hexaplaric type of text. That means that readings from "the Three" which Origen added to the traditional text he used in the 3rd century have passed into the text of the Armenian Bible. It would be interesting to make an examination of the materials in Armenian which represent Origen's work and are now a part of the Armenian text.

Finally, it would be presumptous to claim that every reading from "the Three" preserved in the margins of Armenian manuscripts has been caught in the net of this study. I would like to be able to claim that! It may be that in the future someone else will find some other readings. In that case it would be helpful if notice of such were sent to the *Bulletin of the International Organization for Septuagint and Cognate Studies* so that text critics of the Old Testament in Greek may be made aware of the new evidence.

Plate 1

Jerusalem Armenian Patriarchate MS 428 for 4 Reigns 23:5 (զարեզական)–33 (փարաւով ն). Shows marginal readings at 23:5 2 °, 6, 7, 9, 10, 11, 12, 13, 15, 16, (second column) 24, 29. Actual size of the MS is 23 x 17 cm; it was copied in 1620 in Constantinople.

Plate 2

J428 for 4 Reigns 25:7 ([կապա]||նաւք)–30. Marginal readings occur at vv 14, 16 1°, 16 2°, 17 1°, 17 2°, 19, (second column) 27.

Plate 3

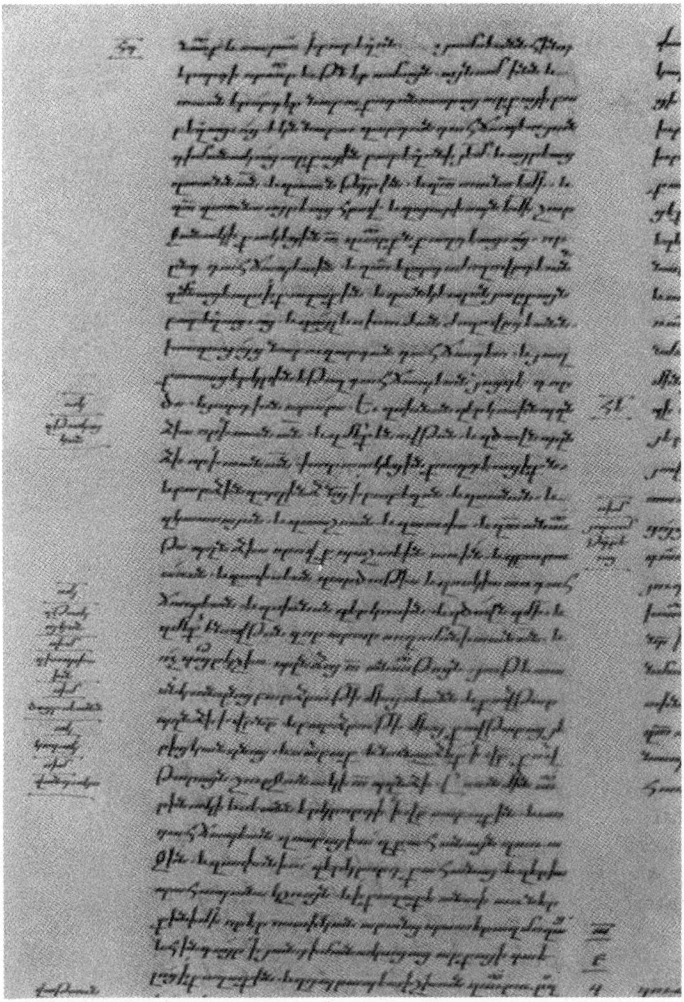

Detail of J428 for 4 Reigns 25:7–30.

Bibliography

Texts, Dictionaries, Concordances and Similar Reference Works

Adjémian [Ajamian], Shahé. *Grand Catalogue des Manuscrits Armeniens de la Bible* . Bibliothèque Arménienne de la Fondation Calouste Gulbenkian; Lisbon 19-92. [in Armenian]

Աճառյան, Հր. [Ajarian, Hr.]. Հայերեն Արմատական Բառարան [*Hayeren Armatakan Bararan* Armenian Etymological Dictionary]. Four volumes. Երեվան: Երեվան Պետական Համալսարան 1971–1979.

Arapkerts‘i, T‘adeos Astuatsaturian. Համաբարբառ Հին եւ Նոր Կտակարանաց [*Hamabarbar Hin ew Nor Ktakaranats‘* Concordance to the Old and New Testaments]. Jerusalem: St. James 1895.

Bedrossian, Matthias. *New Dictionary Armenian-English*. Venice: St. Lazarus Armenian Academy 1875–1879; repr. Beirut: Librairie du Liban 1973.

Bogharian, Norayr. Մայր Ցուցակ Ձեռագրաց Սրբոց Յակոբեանց [Grand Catalogue of St. James Manuscripts]. CGFAL; Jerusalem: St. James 1966–1991. 11 vols.

Brock, Sebastian P., C.T. Fritsch, S. Jellicoe, compilers. *A Classified Bibliography of the Septuagint* . Arbeiten zur Literatur und Geschichte des Hellenistischen Judentums VI; Leiden: Brill 1973.

Brooke, Alan E., Norman McLean and H.St.J. Thackeray, eds., *The Old Testament in Greek* . Cambridge: University Press 1906–1940.

Brown, Francis, S.R. Driver and Charles A. Briggs, eds. *A Hebrew and English Lexicon of the Old Testament* . Oxford: Clarendon 1907; repr. 1968.

Conybeare, F.C. and St. George Stock. *Grammar of Septuagint Greek, with Selected Readings from the Septuagint* . Boston: Ginn 1905; repr. Peabody: Hendrickson 1988.

Cowe, S. Peter. *The Armenian Version of Daniel* . UPATS 9; Atlanta: Scholars 19-92.

Cox, Claude E. *The Armenian Translation of Deuteronomy* . UPATS 2; Chico CA: Scholars 1981.

Elliger, K. and W. Rudolph, eds. *Biblia Hebraica Stuttgartensia* . Stuttgart: Württembergische Bibelanstalt 1967–1977. A. Jepsen prepared 1–2 Kings.

Ephrem. *Works* . Part 1: Commentary on Genesis–Chronicles. Venice: St. Lazar 1836.

Fernández Marcos, Natalio and José Ramón Busto Saiz; with the collaboration of María Victoria Spottorno, Díaz Caro and S. Peter Cowe. *El Texto Antioqueno de la Biblia Griega I: 1-2 Samuel* . Textos y Estudios «Cardenal Cisneros» de la Biblia Políglota Matritense 50; Madrid: Instituto de Filología 1989. "La versión armenia," by Peter Cowe, pp. LXXI–LXXIX, in English.

_____. *El Texto Antioqueno de la Biblia Griega II: 1-2 Reyes* . Textos y Estudios «Cardenal Cisneros» de la Biblia Políglota Matritense 53; Madrid: Instituto de Filología 1992.

Field, F. *Origenis Hexaplorum quae supersunt; sive veterum interpretum graecorum in totum vetus testamentum fragmenta* . Oxford: Clarendon 1867, 1874 (two volumes); repr. Hildesheim: Olms 1964.

Fischer, Bonifatio, I. Gribomont, H.F.D. Sparks, W. Thiele, eds. *Biblia Sacra iuxta Vulgatam versionem* . Revised, with a brief apparatus by R. Weber. Stuttgart: Württembergische Bibelanstalt 1969; 2nd ed. 1975.

Gingrich, F.W. *Shorter Lexicon of the Greek New Testament* . Chicago: University of Chicago 1965.

Hakobian, V. and A. Hovhannisian, eds. Հայերեն Ձեռագրերի ԺԷ Դարի Հիշատակարաններ (1621–1640) [*Hayeren Dzeragreri Zhē Dari Hishatakaranner* Colophons in Armenian Manuscripts (1621–1640)] vol. 2. Նյութեր Հայ ժողովրդի Պատմության 15 [Resources for the History of the Armenian People 15]; Yerevan: Academy of Sciences 1978.

Hatch, Edwin and Henry A. Redpath, eds. *A Concordance to the Septuagint and Other Greek Versions of the Old Testament (including the Apocryphal Books)* . Oxford: Clarendon 1897; repr. Graz: Academische Druck-U. Verlagsanstalt 1954.

Holladay, William L., ed. *A Concise Hebrew and Aramaic Lexicon of the Old Testament* , based on the First, Second, and Third Editions of the Koehler-Baumgartner *Lexicon in Veteris Testamenti Libros* . Grand Rapids: Eerdmans 1971.

Holmes, R. and J. Parsons, eds. *Vetus Testamentum Graecum cum variis lectioni-*

bus . Oxford 1798–1827.

Jensen, Hans. *Altarmenische Grammatik* . Indogermanische Bibliothek; Heidelberg: Carl Winter 1959.

Jepsen, A.: see Elliger.

Kh'ach'ikian, L. and A. Mnats'akanian, eds. 8ուցակ Ձեռագրաց Մաշ-տոցի Անվան Մատենադարանի [*Ts'uts'ak Dzeragrats' Mashtots'i Anvan Matenadarani* Catalogue of Manuscripts of the Mashtots' Library]. Introduction by O. Eganian; prepared by O. Eganian, A. Zeyt'unian, P'. Ant'abian; Yerevan: Academy of Sciences 1965 [vol. 1], 1970 [vol. 2].

Kittel, R., ed. *Biblia Hebraica* . Textum Masoreticum curavit P. Kahle; 3rd ed. [19-29] newly completed [1937], 7th ed. [1951] extended and corrected by A. Alt and O. Eissfeldt. Stuttgart: Württembergische Bibelanstalt 1962.

Koriwn. *Vark' Mashtots'* [Life of Mashtots]. Ed. M. Abeghyan. Yerevan: Haypethrat 1941.

Lampe, G.W.H., ed. *A Patristic Greek Lexicon* . Oxford: Clarendon 1968 [1961].

Lang, David M. *Catalogue of Georgian and Other Caucasian Printed Books in the British Museum* . London 1962.

Leverett, F.P., ed. *Lexicon of the Latin Language.* Compiled chiefly from the Magnum Totius Latinitatis Lexicon of Facciolati and Forcellini, and the German works of Scheller and Luenemann. Edited by F.P. Leverett. A New Edition, embracing the Classical Distinctions of Words, and the Etymological Index of Freund's Lexicon. Boston: Bazin & Ellsworth 1850.

Liddell, Henry George and Robert Scott, eds. *A Greek-English Lexicon* , revised and augmented by Henry Stuart Jones, with the assistance of Roderick McKenzie; with a Supplement edited by E.A. Barber. Oxford: University Press 1843; 9th ed. 1940; repr. 1968.

Lust, J., E. Eynikel, K. Hauspie, compilers; with the collaboration of G. Chamberlain. *A Greek-English Lexicon of the Septuagint* . Part I A-I. Stuttgart: Deutsche Bibelgesellschaft 1992.

Mandelkern, Solomon. *Veteris Testamenti Concordantiae Hebraicae atque Chaldaicae* . Schocken 1937; repr. Graz: Academische Druck-U. Verlagsanstalt 1955.

Marcus, Ralph, tr. *Josephus: Jewish Antiquities* . Vol. VI; Loeb Classical Library; London: Heinemann; Cambridge MA: Harvard 1937; repr. 1966.

Margolis, Max L., ed. *The Book of Joshua in Greek according to the Critically Restored Text with an Apparatus containing the Variants of the Principal Recensions and of the Individual Witnesses* . Publications of the Alexander Kohut Memorial

Foundation; Paris: Paul Geuthner 1931. Vols. 1–4. Vol. 5 was "lost" for about five decades: see next item and Tov, "The Discovery ..."

_____. *The Book of Joshua in Greek, Part V: Joshua 19:39–24:33* , ed. E. Tov. Monograph Series, Annenberg Research Institute, Philadelphia; Winona Lake IN: Eisenbrauns 1992.

Miskgian, Ionnes. *Manuale Lexicon Armeno-Latinum.* Romae: ex Typographia Polyglotta 1887; repr. Institut Orientaliste de l'Université de Louvain 1966.

Molitor, J. *Glossarium Ibericum in quattuor Evangelia et Actus Apostolorum anti-quioris versionis etiam textus Chanmeti et Haemeti complectens* . CSCO 228, 237; Subsidia 20, 21; Louvain 1962.

Moulton, W.F. and A.S. Geden. *A Concordance to the Greek Testament* . Fourth ed. rev'd by H.K. Moulton; Edinburgh: Clark 1963; repr. 1967.

Rahlfs, Alfred. *Septuaginta. Id est Vetus Testamentum graece iuxta LXX Inter-pretes* . Stuttgart: Württembergische Bibelanstalt 1965. First published in 1935.

_____. *Verzeichnis der griechischen Handschriften des Alten Testaments* . NKG-WG; Philologisch-historische Klasse, Beiheft. Berlin: Weidmannsche Buchhand-lung 1914.

Reider, Joseph. *An Index to Aquila* , completed and revised by Nigel Turner. VT Sup 12; Leiden: Brill 1966. See also Tov, "Some Corrections ..."

Sanjian, Avedis K., ed. *Colophons of Armenian Manuscripts 1301–1480. A Source for Middle Eastern History* . Cambridge MA: Harvard 1969.

Smith, J. Payne, ed. *A Compendious Syriac Dictionary* . Oxford: Clarendon 1903; repr. 1976.

Stone, Michael E. *The Testament of Levi. A First Study of the Armenian MSS of the Testaments of the XII Patriarchs in the Convent of St. James, Jerusalem* . Jeru-salem: St. James Press 1969. Includes in the Introduction a useful description of various MSS; plates of Jerusalem MSS J1925 J1927 J1933 J1934.

Tchoubinof, David. *Dictionnaire Géorgien–Russe–Français* . St. Petersburg: Im-perial Academy of Science 1840.

The New Oxford Annotated Bible with the Apocrypha , ed. Bruce M. Metzger and Roland E. Murphy. NY: Oxford 1991. Introductions and annotations for the books Samuel–Chronicles were provided by William F. Stinespring and Burke O. Long.

The Old Testament in Syriac according to the Peshitta Version, edited on behalf of the IOSOT by the Peshitta Institute, Leiden, Part II, fascicle 2: Judges–Samuel; Leiden: Brill 1978. Samuel prepared by P.A.H. de Boer.

Thomson, Robert W. *An Introduction to Classical Armenian* . Delmar NY: Caravan 1975.

Tov, Emanuel, ed. Max L. Margolis, *The Book of Joshua in Greek, Part V: Joshua 19:39–24:33* . Monograph Series, Annenberg Research Institute, Philadelphia; Winona Lake IN: Eisenbrauns 1992.

Webster's New World Dictionary of American English , ed. V. Neufeldt. 3rd College ed.; NY: Simon & Shuster 1988.

Weitenberg, J.J.S. *Parallel Aligned Text and Bilingual Concordance of the Armenian and Greek Versions of the Book of Jonah* . Dutch Studies in Armenian Language and Literature 1; Amsterdam/Atlanta: Rodopi 1992.

_____ and A. de Leeuw van Weenen. *Lemmatized Index of the Armenian Version of Deuteronomy.* Leiden Armenological Publications 1; SBLSCS 32; Atlanta: Scholars 1990.

Wevers, J.W., ed. *Septuaginta, Vetus Testamentum Graecum; Auctoritate Academiae Scientarum Gottingensis editum, I Genesis* . Vandenhoeck & Ruprecht 1974.

_____. *II, 2 Leviticus* 1986.

_____. *III, 2 Deuteronomium* 1977.

Yerevants'i, Oskan, ed. Աստուածաշունչ Հնոց եւ Նորոց Կտակարանաց [*Astuatsashunch' Hnots' ew Norots' Ktakaranats'* Bible of the Old and New Testaments]. Amsterdam: Holy Etchmiadzin and Holy Sargis Press 1666.

Zeigler, J., ed. *Septuaginta, Vetus Testamentum Graecum; Auctoritate Academiae Litterarum Gottingensis editum, XI, 4 Iob.* Göttingen: Vandenhoeck & Ruprecht 1982.

_____. *XIV Isaias* 1939; repr. 1967.

_____. *XV Ieremias, Baruch, Threni, Epistula Ieremiae* 1957.

_____. *XVI/1 Ezechiel* 1951.

Zohrapian, H., ed. Աստուածաշունչ Մատեան Հին եւ Նոր Կտակարանաց [*Astuastashunch' Matean Hin ew Nor Ktakaranats'* Scriptures of the Old and New Testaments]. Venice 1805; repr. *The Zohrab Bible* , introduction by C. Cox; Delmar, NY: Caravan 1984.

Books and Articles

Aejmelaeus, Anneli. "The Septuagint of 1 Samuel," in *On the Trail of the Septuagint Translators* . Kampen: Kok Pharos 1993.

Alexander, Philip. "The Parting of the Ways: Did the Church Steal the LXX from the Jews?" Rich Seminar on the Hexapla, Yarnton Manor, Oxford, July 25–August 4, 1994. To be published in the Proceedings, edited by Alison Salvesen.

Anasean, "Une leçon symmachienne dans les manuscrits arméniens de la Bible (pour l'histoire du texte des Hexaples d'Origène)," *REArm* N.S. 17 (1983) 201–205 (= *Handes Amsorya* 97 [1983] 1–6, col. 93–100 [in Armenian]).

Ant'abyan, P'. "Վարդան Առեւելցի," [Vardan Arevelts'i]," in B. Aghayan, Ém. A. Pivazyan, H. G. Zhamkoch'yan, ed., Հայ Մշակույթի Նշանավոր Գործիչները V–XVIII Դարեր [*Hay Mshakuyt'i Nshanavor Gortsich'nerĕ V–XVIII Darer* Significant Representatives of Armenian Culture V–XVIIIth Centuries]. Yerevan: Yerevan University 1976. Pp. 305–313.

Barr, James. "Vocalization and the Analysis of Hebrew Among the Ancient Translators," VTSup 16 (1967) 1–11. On the issue of transliterations see p. 6.

Barthélemy, Dominique. "A Reexamination of the Textual Problems in 2 Sam 11: 2–1 Kings 2:11 in the Light of Certain Criticisms of *Les Devanciers d'Aquila* ," in *1972 Proceedings IOSCS* , 16–89.

_____. *Les Devanciers d'Aquila* . VTSup 10; Leiden: Brill 1963.

_____. "Redécouverte d'un chaînon manquant de l'histoire de la LXX," *RB* 60 (1953) 18–29.

Birdsall, J. Neville. "Traces of the Jewish Greek Biblical Version in Georgian Manuscript Sources," *JSS* 17 (1972) 83–92.

Bodine, Walter R. *The Greek Text of Judges, Recensional Developments* . HSM 23; Chico, CA: Scholars 1980.

Bogharian, Arch. Norayr. "Գէորգ Սկեւռացի [George Skewrats'i]," in Հայ Գրողներ [*Hay Groghner* Armenian Writers]. Jerusalem: St. James 1971. Pp. 324–329.

Botte, B.† and P.-M. Bogaert. "Septante et Versions grecques," *Supplément au Dictionnaire de la Bible* , ed. J. Briend and É. Cothenet. Tome 12, Fasc. 68. Paris: Letouzey & Ané 1993. Cols. 536–693.

Brock, Sebastian. "A Doublet and Its Ramifications," *Biblica* 56 (1975) 550–553. Concerns 1 Sam 23:1; 14:47.

_____. "Lucian *redivivus* Some Reflections on Barthélemy's *Les Devanciers d'Aquila* ," *Studia Evangelica* 4 (1968) = TU 103, 176–181.

_____. "The Phenomenon of Biblical Translation in Antiquity," *Alta: University of Birmingham Review* 2 (1967) = *Studies in the Septuagint: Origins, Recensions, and Interpretations* , ed. S. Jellicoe. New York: Ktav 1974. Pp. 541–571.

Bundy, D. "The *Anonymous Life of Georg Skewr̄ac'i* in *Erevan 8356* . A Study in Medieval Armenian Hagiography and History," *REArm* N.S. 18 (1984) 491–502.

Burchard, Christoph. "Zur altarmenischen Übersetzung des Jakobusbriefes," *Horizonte der Christenheit (Festschrift für Friedrich Heyer zu seinem 85. Geburtstag)*, ed. Michael Kohlbacher and Markus Lesinski, *Oikonomia* 34 (1994) 195–217.

Busto Saiz, Jose Ramon. *La Traduccion de Simaco en el Libro de Los Salmos* . Textos y Estudios "Cardenal Cisneros" 22; Madrid: Instituto "Arias Montano" 19-78.

Chrysostom: see Oskeberani.

Coulie, Bernard. "Répertoire des Manuscrits arméniens/Census of Armenian Manuscripts," AIEA 1994.

Cowe, S. Peter. "An Armenian Job Fragment from Sinai and its Implications," *Oriens Christianus* 76 (1992) 123–157.

Cox, Claude E. "Concerning a Cilician Revision of the Armenian Bible," in *De Septuaginta: Studies in honour of John William Wevers on his sixty-fifth birthday* , ed. A. Pietersma and C. Cox. Mississauga ON: Benben 1984. Pp. 209–221.

_____. *Hexaplaric Materials Preserved in the Armenian Version.* SBLSCS 21. Atlanta: Scholars 1986.

_____. "The Translations of Aquila, Symmachus and Theodotion Found in the Margins of Armenian Manuscripts," in *Armenia and the Bible Papers Presented to the International Symposium Held at Heidelberg, July 16–19, 1990* , ed. Christoph Burchard. UPATS 12; Atlanta: Scholars 1993. Pp. 35–45.

_____. "The Use of the *Participium Necessitatis* in the Armenian Translation of the Pentateuch," *International Symposium on Armenian Linguistics (Yerevan, September 21–25, 1982)* , ed. G.B. Djahukian. Yerevan: Academy of Sciences 1984. Pp. 337–351.

_____. "The Vocabulary for Good and Evil in the Armenian Translation of the New Testament," *Text and Context: Studies in the Armenian New Testament* , ed. Shahé Ajamian and Michael E. Stone. UPATS 13; Atlanta: Scholars 1995. Pp. 49–57.

_____. "The Zohrab Bible," repr. of the Introduction to *The Zohrab Bible* , with bibliography updated through 1993, in *Studies in Classical Armenian Literature* , ed. John A.C. Greppin. Delmar, NY: Caravan 1994. Pp. 227–261.

Devreesse, R., ed. *Les anciens commentateurs grecs de l'Octateuque et des Rois (fragments tirés des chaînes)* . Studi e Testi/Bibliotheca apostolica vaticana 201; Vatican City: Bibliotheca vaticana 1959.

Dhorme, Édward. *A Commentary on the Book of Job* . Tr. Harold Knight; Nashville: Thomas Nelson 1984. First published in English in 1967 on the basis of the 1926 French original.

Dines, Jenny. "Jerome's View of the Hexapla," Rich Seminar on the Hexapla, Yarnton Manor, Oxford, July 25–August 4, 1994. To be published in the Proceedings, edited by Alison Salvesen.

Driver, S.R. *Notes on the Hebrew Text and the Topography of the Books of Samuel* . 2nd ed., revised and enlarged; Oxford: Clarendon 1913.

Edwards, R.W. "Settlements and Toponomy in Armenian Cilicia," *REArm* 24 (19-93) 181–249.

Evans, Helen C. "Cilician Manuscript Illumination. The Twelfth, Thirteenth, and Fourteenth Centuries," in *Treasures in Heaven. Armenian Illuminated Manuscripts,* ed. Thomas F. Mathews and Roger S. Wieck. New York: Pierpont Morgan Library 1994. Pp. 66–81.

_____ and Sylvie L. Merian, "The Final Centuries: Armenian Manuscripts of the Diaspora," in *Treasures in Heaven* . Pp. 104–123.

Fernández Marcos, Natalio. "La sigla lambda omicron (λ) en I-II Reyes-Septuaginta," *Sefarad* 38 (1978) 243–262.

_____. "Lucianic Texts and Vetus Latina. The Textual Context of the Hexapla," Rich Seminar on the Hexapla, Yarnton Manor, Oxford, July 25–August 4, 1994. To be published in the Proceedings, edited by Alison Salvesen.

_____. "Símmaco y sus predecesores judíos," in *Biblische und Judaistische Studien. Festschrift für Paolo Sacchi* , ed. Angelo Vivian. Frankfurt/Bern/New York/Paris: Peter Lang 1990. Pp. 193–202.

_____. "Some Reflections on the Antiochian Text of the Septuagint," in *Studien zur Septuaginta — Robert Hanhart zu Ehren* , ed. Detlef Fraenkel, Udo Quast, John Wm. Wevers; AAWG; MSU 20; Göttingen: Vandenhoeck & Ruprecht 1990. Pp. 219–229.

_____. "The Lucianic Text in the Books of Kingdoms: From Lagarde to the Textual Pluralism," in *De Septuaginta: Studies in honour of John William Wevers on his sixty-fifth birthday* , ed. A. Pietersma and C. Cox. Mississauga ON: Benben 19-84. Pp. 161–174.

Fohrer, Georg. *Ezechiel* . HAT, First series 13; Tübingen: Mohr [Siebeck] 1955.

Gehman, Henry S. "The Hebraic Character of Septuagint Greek," VT 1 (1951) 81–90. Repr. in *The Language of the New Testament: Classic Essays* , ed. Stanley E. Porter (JSNTSup 60; Sheffield: JSOT 1991) 163–173.

Gentry, Peter J. *The Asterisked Materials in the Greek Job* . SBLSCS 38; Atlanta: Scholars 1995.

Gooding, D.W. "Text-Sequence and Translation-Revision in 3 Reigns 9:10–10: 33," *VT* 19 (1969) 448–463.

Grabbe, Lester L. "The Translation Technique of the Greek Minor Versions: Translations or Revisions?" in George J. Brooke and Barnabas Lindars, ed., *Septuagint, Scrolls and Cognate Writings: Papers Presented to the International Symposium on the Septuagint and Its Relations to the Dead Sea Scrolls and Other Writings (Manchester 1990)* . SBLSCS 33; Atlanta: Scholars 1992. Pp. 505–556.

Gregorian, Vartan. "Minorities of Isfahan: The Armenian Community of Isfahan 1587–1722," *Studies on Isfahan: Proceedings of The Isfahan Colloquium* , Harvard University, Jan. 21–24, 1974, Part II, in *Iranian Studies* 7 (1974) 652–680.

Greenspoon, Leonard J. "Aquila's Version," "Symmachus, Symmachus's Version," "Theodotion, Theodotion's Version," *ABD* 1, 320–321; 6, 251 and 6, 447–448.

_____. "Recensions, Revision, Rabbinics: Dominique Barthélemy and Early Developments in the Greek Traditions," *Textus* 15 (1990) 152–167.

_____. *Textual Studies in the Book of Joshua* . HSM 28; Chico: Scholars 1983.

Hagedorn, Ursula and Dieter. *Nachlese zu den Fragmenten der jüngeren griechischen Übersetzer des Buches Hiob* . NAWG; I. Philologisch-Historische Klasse 10; Göttingen: Vandenhoeck & Ruprecht 1991.

Harl, Marguerite. "La « Bible d'Alexandrie» et les Études sur la Septante. Réflexions sur une première expérience," *Vigiliae Christianae* 47 (1993) 313–340.

Hovhannesian, Vahan, ed. *Eusèbe d'Émèse I. Commentaire de l'Octateuque.* Venice: St. Lazar 1980. [in Armenian]

Hyvärinen, Kyösti. *Die Übersetzung von Aquila.* CB OTS 10; Lund: CWK Gleerup, 1977.

Jellicoe, Sidney. *The Septuagint and Modern Study* . Oxford: Clarendon 1968.

Johnson, Bo. "Armenian Biblical Tradition in Comparison with the Vulgate and Septuagint," in *Medieval Armenian Culture* , ed. Thomas J. Samuelian and Michael E. Stone. UPATS 6; Chico, CA: Scholars 1984. Pp. 357–364.

_____. *Die armenische Bibelübersetzung als hexaplarischer Zeuge im 1. Samuelbuch* . CB OTS 2; Lund: CWK Gleerup 1968.

_____. "Some Remarks on the Marginal Notes in Armenian 1 Samuel," in *Armenian and Biblical Studies* , ed. Michael E. Stone. Supplementary Volume 1 to *Sion* ;

Jerusalem: St. James 1976. Pp. 18–20

Kraft, R.A. "Septuagint. B. Earliest Greek Versions ("Old Greek")," *IDB* Supplementary Volume. Nashville: Abingdon 19-76. Pp. 811–815.

de Lange, N.R.M. "Some New Fragments of Aquila on Malachi and Job?" *VT* 30 (1980) 291–294.

Long, Burke O.: see *The New Oxford Annotated Bible*.

Lust, J. "A Lexicon of Ezekiel's Hexaplaric Recensions," Rich Seminar on the Hexapla, Yarnton Manor, Oxford, July 25–August 4, 1994. To be published in the Proceedings, edited by Alison Salvesen.

McGregor, John L. *The Greek Text of Ezekiel. An Examination of Its Homogeneity*. SBLSCS 18; Atlanta: Scholars 1985.

Mistrih, Vincent. "Trois Biographies de Georges de Skevra," Extrait de Collectanea No° 14, *Studia Orientalia Christiana. Armenica*. Cairo: Editions du Centre Franciscain d'Études Orientales Chretiennes, 1970. Pp. 1–114 [250–364], plus 8 plates.

Montgomery, James A. *A Critical and Exegetical Commentary of The Books of Kings*, ed. H.S. Gehman. ICC; Edinburgh: T. & T. Clark 1951.

Munnich, Olivier. "Origène, éditeur de la *Septante* de *Daniel*," in *Studien zur Septuaginta—Robert Hanhart zu Ehren*, ed. D. Fraenkel, U. Quast, J.Wm. Wevers. AAWG; MSU 20; Göttingen: Vandenhoeck & Ruprecht 1990. Pp. 187–218.

Oskeberani, Hovhannu. *Meknut'iwn Esayeay Margareї* [Commentary on Isaiah the Prophet]. *Matenagrut'iwnk' Nakhneats' —Oskeberan*; Venice: St. Lazar 1880.

Peters, M.K.H. "Septuagint," *ADB*, 5, 1093–1104. Bibliography: 1102–1104.

Salvesen, Alison. *Symmachus in the Pentateuch*. JSS Monograph 15; Manchester: University of Manchester 1991. Review: M.K.H. Peters for *JBL* 112, 4 (Winter 1993) 699–700.

Schiftman, Lawrence H. Review of *The Greek Minor Prophets Scroll from Naḥal Ḥever (8ḤevXIIGr) (The Seiyal Collection I)* by E. Tov, with R. A. Kraft and P. J. Parsons; DJD 8; Oxford: Clarendon 1990: in *JBL* 111/3 (Fall 1992) 532–535.

Shenkel, J.D. *Chronology and Recensional Development in the Greek Text of Kings*. HSM 1; Cambridge, MA: Harvard 1968.

Soisalon-Soininen, Ilmari. "Einige Merkmale der Übersetzungsweise von Aquila," in *Wort, Lied und Gottesspruch. Beiträge zur Septuaginta. Festschrift für Joseph Ziegler*, ed. J. Schreiner. Forschung zur Bibel 1; Wurzburg: Echter 1972. Vol. 1, 177–184.

Stinespring, William F.: see *The New Oxford Annotated Bible*.

Stone, M. E. "Additional Note on the Marginalia in 4 Kingdoms," in *Armenian and Biblical Studies,* ed. Michael E. Stone. Jerusalem: St. James Press, 1976. Pp. 21–22.

Swete, Henry Barclay. *An Introduction to the Old Testament in Greek* ; revised by R.R. Ottley; with an Appendix containing the *Letter of Aristeas* . Cambridge: University Press 1902; repr. New York: Ktav 1968.

Taylor, Bernard A. *The Lucianic Manuscripts of 1 Reigns* . HSM 50, 51; Atlanta: Scholars 1992, 1993.

Terian, Abraham. "Had the Works of Philo Been Newly Discovered," *Biblical Archeologist* 57:2 (1994) 86–97.

Ter-Movsessian, Mesrop. *Istoriia Perevoda Biblii na Armianskii Yazyk* [History of the Translation of the Bible into the Armenian Language]. St. Petersburg: Pyshkinskaia Skoropechatnia 1902.

Thackeray, H.St.J. "The Greek Translators of the Four Books of Kings," *JTS* 8 (1906/7) 262–278.

Thierry, J.M. *Réportoire des monasteres arméniens* . Turnhout: Brepols 1993.

Thomson, Robert W., ed. *Moses Khorenats'i: History of the Armenians* . HATS 4; Cambridge, MA/London: Harvard 1978.

Tov, Emanuel. "Some Corrections to Reider-Turner's *Index to Aquila* ," *Textus* 8 (1973) 164–174.

_____. *Textual Criticism of the Hebrew Bible* . Minneapolis MN: Fortress/Assen-Maastricht: Van Gorcum 1992.

_____. "The Discovery of the Missing Part of Margolis' Edition of Joshua," *BIOSCS* 14 (1981) 17–21.

_____. *The Text-Critical Use of the Septuagint in Biblical Research* . JBS 3; Jerusalem: Simor 1981.

_____. "Transliterations of Hebrew Words in the Greek Versions of the Old Testament: A Further Characteristic of the *kaige* -Th. Revision?" *Textus* 8 (1972) 78–92.

Trebolle-Barrera, Julio C. *Jehú y Joás. Texto y composición literaria de 2 Reyes 9–11* . Universidad Pontificia de Salamanca; Valencia: Artes Gráficas Soler 1984.

Veltri, Giuseppe. "Der griechische Targum Aquilas. Ein Beitrag zum rabbinischen Übersetzungsverständnis," in *Die Septuaginta zwischen Judentum und Christentum* , ed. Martin Hengel and Anna Maria Schwemer. Wissenschaftliche Untersuchungen zum Neuen Testament 72; Tübingen: Mohr [Siebeck] 1994. Pp. 92–115. Bibliography: 113–115.

Wevers, J.W. "An Apologia for Septuagint Studies," *BIOSCS* 18 (1985) 16–38.

_____. "Pre-Origen Recensional Activity in the Greek Exodus," *Studien zur Septuaginta—Robert Hanhart zu Ehren* , ed. D. Fraenkel, U. Quast, J.Wm. Wevers. AAWG; MSU 20; Göttingen: Vandenhoeck & Ruprecht 1990. Pp. 121–139.

_____. "Septuaginta Forschungen seit 1954," *ThR* n.F. 33 (1968) 18–76.

_____. "The Lucianic Problem," in *Text History of the Greek Genesis* . AAWG; MSU 11; Göttingen: Vandenhoeck & Ruprecht 1974. Pp. 158–175.

Zanolli, Almo. "Lezioni marginali ai quattro libri dei Re. In un codice armeno dell' anno 1328," *Atti del Reale Istituto Veneto di scienze, lettere ed arti* 87 (1927–1928) second part, 1217–1235. Examination of marginal readings from Aquila, Symmachus and Theodotion in Venice MS 280 (10).

Indexes

Armenian Words

Georgian Words

Greek Words

Hebrew Words

Latin Words

Syriac Words

Biblical References

Genesis

1:9 216
1:10 216
1:11 107
1:12 107
2:5 107
6:4 116
12:3 46
13:10 386
13:17 104
14:5 116
18:7 193
19:14 47
19:28 150
27:9 175
28:3 216
31:19 292
31:46 199
38:13 374
49:10 274
49:19(Arm 18) 80–81
49:26 198
49:6 128
50:21 108

Exodus

4:25 29
8:14(10) 199
12:11 291
14:5 104
16:21 207
18:21 267
26:13 134
27:4 189
35:16 189
35:22 267
38:30 189
38:4f. 189
39:17 34
39:39 189
40:21 321

Leviticus

2:14 174, 177
18:17 62
19:31 262
19:33 262
19:34 262
22:18 262
23:14 174–175
25:9 329
25:29 253
26:5 176–177
26:19 266

Numbers

9:2 291
9:14 262
12:8 206
13:33(Arm 34) 116
15:13(LXX 14) 262
15:15 262
15:30 267
20:19 162
23:28 87
24:6 77
36:7 262

Deuteronomy

1:36 262
2:27 165

Manuscripts

Some manuscripts are referred to so very frequently that this index is limited to a selection of references.

Personal Names

Place Names

Other Titles in the Septuagint and Cognate Studies Series

ROBERT A. KRAFT (editor)
Septuagintal Lexicography (1975)
Code: 06 04 01
Not Available

ROBERT A KRAFT (editor)
1972 Proceedings: Septuagint and Pseudepigrapha Seminars (1973)
Code: 06 04 02
Not Available

RAYMOND A. MARTIN
Syntactical Evidence of Semitic Studies in Greek Documents (1974)
Code: 06 04 03
Not Available

GEORGE W. E. NICKELSBURG, JR. (editor)
Studies on the *Testament of Moses* (1973)
Code: 06 04 04
Not Available

GEORGE W.E. NICKELSBURG, JR. (editor)
Studies on the *Testament of Joseph* (1975)
Code: 06 04 05
Not Available

GEORGE W.E. NICKELSBURG, JR. (editor)
Studies on the *Testament of Abraham* (1976)
Code: 06 04 06
Not Available

JAMES H. CHARLESWORTH
Pseudepigrapha and Modern Research (1976)
Code: 06 04 07
Not Available

JAMES H. CHARLESWORTH
Pseudepigrapha and Modern Research with a Supplement (1981)
Code: 06 04 07 S

JOHN W. OLLEY
"Righteousness" in the Septuagint of Isaiah: A Contextual Study (1979)
Code: 06 04 08

MELVIN K. H. PETERS
An Analysis of the Textual Character of the Bohairic of Deuteronomy (1980)
Code: 06 04 09
Not Available

DAVID G. BURKE
The Poetry of Baruch (1982)
Code: 06 04 10

JOSEPH L. TRAFTON
Syriac Version of the Psalms of Solomon (1985)
Code: 06 04 11

JOHN COLLINS, GEORGE NICKELSBURG
Ideal Figures in Ancient Judaism: Profiles and Paradigms (1980)
Code: 06 04 12

ROBERT HANN
The Manuscript History of the Psalms of Solomon (1982)
Code: 06 04 13

J.A.L. LEE
A Lexical Study of the Septuagint Version of the Pentateuch (1983)
Code: 06 04 14

MELVIN K. H. PETERS
A Critical Edition of the Coptic (Bohairic) Pentateuch Vol. 5: Deuteronomy (1983)
Code: 06 04 15

T. MURAOKA
A Greek-Hebrew/Aramaic Index to I Esdras (1984)
Code: 06 04 16

JOHN RUSSIANO MILES
Retroversion and Text Criticism:
The Predictability of Syntax in An Ancient Translation
from Greek to Ethiopic (1985)
Code: 06 04 17

LESLIE J. MCGREGOR
The Greek Text of Ezekiel (1985)
Code: 06 04 18

MELVIN K.H. PETERS
A Critical Edition of the Coptic (Bohairic) Pentateuch,
Vol. 1: Genesis (1985)
Code: 06 04 19

ROBERT A. KRAFT AND EMANUEL TOV (project directors)
Computer Assisted Tools for Septuagint Studies
Vol 1: Ruth (1986)
Code: 06 04 20

CLAUDE E. COX
Hexaplaric Materials Preserved in the Armenian Version (1986)
Code: 06 04 21

MELVIN K.H. PETERS
A Critical Edition of the Coptic (Bohairic) Pentateuch
Vol. 2: Exodus (1986)
Code: 06 04 22

CLAUDE E. COX (editor)
VI Congress of the International Organization for Septuagint
and Cognate Studies: Jerusalem 1986
Code: 06 04 23

JOHN KAMPEN
The Hasideans and the Origin of Pharisaism: A Study of 1 and 2 Maccabees
Code: 06 04 24

THEODORE BERGREN
Fifth Ezra: The Text, Origin, and Early History
Code: 06 04 25

BENJAMIN WRIGHT
No Small Difference: Sirach's Relationship to Its Hebrew Parent Text
Code: 06 04 26

TAKAMITSU MURAOKA (editor)
Melbourne Symposium on Septuagint Lexicography
Code: 06 04 28

JOHN JARICK
Gregory Thaumaturgos' Paraphrase of Ecclesiastes
Code: 06 04 29

JOHN WILLIAM WEVERS
Notes on the Greek Text of Exodus
Code: 06 04 30

CLAUDE E. COX (editor)
VII Congress of the International Organization for Septuagint and Cognate Studies
Code: 06 04 31

J. J. S. WEITENBERG and A. DE LEEUW VAN WEENEN
Lemmatized Index of the Armenian Version of Deuteronomy
Code: 06 04 32

GEORGE J. BROOKE AND BARNABAS LINDARS, S.S.F. (editors)
Septuagint, Scrolls and Cognate Writings: Papers Presented to the International Symposium on the Septuagint and Its Relations to the Dead Sea Scrolls and Other Writings

MICHAEL E. STONE
A Textual Commentary on the Armenian Version of IV Ezra
Code: 06 04 34

JOHN WILLIAM WEVERS
Notes on the Greek Text of Genesis
Code: 06 04 35

JOHN JARICK
A Comprehensive Bilingual Concordance of the Hebrew and Greek Texts of Ecclesiastes
Code: 06 04 36

Order from:
Scholars Press Customer Services
P.O. Box 6996
Alpharetta, GA 30239-6996
1-800-437-6692 or 770-442-8633